Fifth Edition

AMERICAN ISSUES: VOLUME 2: SINCE 1865

A Primary Source Reader in United States History

Fifth Edition

AMERICAN ISSUES: VOLUME 2: SINCE 1865

A Primary Source Reader in United States History

Edited by

Irwin Unger
New York University

Robert R. Tomes
St. John's University

Prentice Hall

Boston   Columbus   Indianapolis   New York   San Francisco   Upper Saddle River   Amsterdam
Cape Town   Dubai   London   Madrid   Milan   Munich   Paris   Montreal   Toronto   Delhi
Mexico City   Sao Paulo   Sydney   Hong Kong   Seoul   Singapore   Taipei   Tokyo

Publisher: Charlyce Jones-Owen
Editorial Assistant: Maureen Diana
Senior Marketing Manager: Maureen Prado-Roberts
Marketing Assistant: Marissa O'Brien
Production Manager: Meghan DeMaio
Creative Director: Jayne Conte
Cover Designer: Suzanne Behnke

Cover Art: Byron Takashi Tsuzuki/Masako Nakagawa
Full-Service Project Management and Composition: Joseph Malcolm/PreMediaGlobal
Printer/Binder/Cover Printer: R. R. Donnelley & Sons
Text Font: Palatino

Credits and acknowledgments borrowed from other sources and reproduced, with permission, in this textbook appear on appropriate page within text.

NC 07 05 2023 1119

Library of Congress Cataloging-in-Publication Data
American issues : a primary source reader in United States history, volume 1 to 1877 / edited by Irwin Unger, Robert R. Tomes.
    p. cm.
  ISBN-13: 978-0-205-80345-3
  ISBN-10: 0-205-80345-8
 1. United States—History—Sources. I. Unger, Irwin. II. Tomes, Robert R.
  E173.A745 2011
  973.1—dc22

2010026142

Prentice Hall
is an imprint of

www.pearsonhighered.com

ISBN 10:   0-205-80344-X
ISBN 13: 978-0-205-80344-6

BRIEF CONTENTS

CONTENTS

PREFACE

Americans worry about the state of education in the United States today. Recently Americans have been told how little students know about science, geography, mathematics, and history; we fear that the United States will be unprepared to compete against the other advanced industrial societies in years to come. We are also concerned that the new generation will lack the shared civic knowledge essential for a functioning democratic system. Study after study reveals that participation in the political process, knowledge and understanding of newsworthy events, and interest in public life are declining, particularly among younger Americans. Stated simply, the younger you are, the less likely you are to vote, read a newspaper, or be aware of current political issues. A growing body of research bemoans a deterioration in the quality and quantity of community life as unchecked individualism and a new, unchecked privatism characterize the American experience. What will the future hold for American political, social, economic, and cultural institutions if these trends continue?

There is indeed reason to be dismayed by how small a stock of historical information young Americans possess. But it is also important to realize that education is not just transmission of data. It is also the fostering of critical thinking. The most encyclopedic knowledge does students little good if they cannot use it to reach valid and useful conclusions. It is this belief that has inspired *American Issues*. This two-volume work will stimulate critical thinking and active learning about U.S. history—leading students to reject received ideas when appropriate, relate the past to their own experience, and reach conclusions on the basis of evidence. At times, no doubt, students will have to do additional reading beyond this textbook; that, of course, is all to the good.

American Issues is not a compendium of scholars' views. It is constructed out of *primary documents*, the raw material of history. In its pages participants and contemporary observers express their opinions, make their observations, and reach their conclusions about events and issues of their own day that affected the United States and American society. The selections do not point in one direction on any given issue. On the contrary, they were chosen to raise questions and force the student to confront disparity, complexity, and apparent contradiction. *American Issues* avoids giving students the "simple bottom line." Rather, it compels them to grapple with the same ambiguous raw materials that historians process to reach their conclusions. To further the engagement process, each selection asks specific questions of the student. That approach, we believe, is an incomparable way to enlighten students about the rich complexity and fullness of historical reality.

The selections in Volume 1 and Volume 2 range widely in subject matter across the American past. Besides the key political questions, they deal with the social, cultural, economic, and gender problems our predecessors faced. *American Issues* is guided by the sense that America has always been a heterogeneous society whose inhabitants led their lives in many ways. Yet it does not abandon the view that all of our forebears were also part of the same American experience and shared many concerns of their era.

What can we expect from conscientious use of *American Issues*? No single text can turn a passive human sponge into an active seeker and a thinker. But *American Issues* can, we believe, engage college students' natural curiosity and tendency to differ and encourage the habit of critical appraisal. Instructors and students alike will find *American Issues* a stimulating and challenging introduction to informed and discriminating thinking about the American past.

WHAT'S NEW IN THIS EDITION?

The fifth edition includes twenty-two new primary source documents.

Chapter 1 Reconstruction

An Appeal for Protection from the KKK (1871)

Chapter 2 Industrial Growth and the Last Frontier

Andrew Carnegie, *Wealth* (1889)
Report on Illinois Sweatshops (1893)
Emma Lazarus, *The New Colossus* (1886)
Charles Loring Brace, *The Dangerous Classes of New York* (1872)
Songs of New York
The Bowery
Sidewalks of New York

Chapter 3 The Final Frontier

Washington Gladden, *Embattled Farmers* (1890)

Chapter 4 Outward Thrust

Charles Eliot Norton on American Ideals (1899)
Morrison I. Swift Views Imperialism as a Threat to Liberty (1899)

Chapter 8 Women's Issues, 1900–1940

Let Us All Speak Our Minds (c. 1926)

Chapter 9 The New Deal

Franklin D. Roosevelt, *The Only Thing We Have to Fear Is Fear Itself* (1933)
Harry Hopkins and the Federal Emergency Relief Administration (1934)
John Maynard Keyes Makes Public Recommendations (1934)

Chapter 10 World War II

Universal Declaration of Human Rights (1948)

Chapter 11 The Cold War

Winston Churchill, *The Iron Curtain* (1946)

Chapter 13 The Great Society

Pamphlet of Columbia University Students (1968)

ACKNOWLEDGMENTS

We would like to acknowledge the following reviewers of this text: Carolyn F. Hoffman, Prince George's Community College; Christine Flood, University of North Carolina, Greensboro; David Welky, University of Central Arkansas; Jeffrey G. Strickland, Montclair State University; and Anthony O. Edmonds, Ball State University. We express our deep and sincere appreciation to the staff of St. John's University Libraries, particularly Joan Daly, Mark Meng, Anthony Todman, and, most of all, Benjamin Turner, for their generous, patient, and knowledgeable assistance.

At Pearson/Prentice Hall, we are also grateful to Charlyce Jones-Owen, Publisher; Maureen Diana, Editorial Assistant; Meghan DeMaio, Production Manager; and Cheryl Keenan, Production Editor for their expertise in producing this new edition.

Irwin Unger

Robert R. Tomes

CHAPTER 1

Reconstruction

In April 1865 the nation faced colossal problems of readjustment and repair. The South was a devastated region, its railroads, its banking system, and many of its towns and cities reduced to ruins. The human cost in the former Confederacy had been enormous. Thousands of young Southern men had died or been maimed. Most difficult of all, in some ways, 4 million former slaves had been wrenched from their accustomed place within the South's social and labor systems and left without clear roles and firm moorings.

The new circumstances also raised urgent constitutional problems for the nation as a whole. Having fought to leave the Union, the South was now out of constitutional alignment with the rest of the states. Should the North accept the logic of its own position—that secession was illegal—and simply allow the former Confederate states to return to full constitutional status without conditions? That response would go easy on the ex-rebels and at the same time allow the Southern states a free hand in dealing with the newly freed men and women. Could white Southerners be trusted to be fair to the former slaves? Should erstwhile Confederates be allowed to resume their place in the Union without punishment for committing atrocities against Union prisoners, for violating federal oaths of office, for creating the mountain of dead and wounded the American people had suffered?

For over a decade following Confederate defeat, the nation's politics would be roiled by the debate over how to manage the Reconstruction process. Americans would be deeply divided. Congress would battle the president, Southerners would battle Northerners, whites would battle blacks, Democrats would battle Republicans. On each issue there would often be a bewildering array of positions not easily categorized as pro or con.

The following selections express a range of views on important Reconstruction problems. They do not exhaust the full spectrum of either opinions or issues on this complex event in our history; they are only a sample of how Americans thought. As you read the selections that follow, try to determine the gist of each argument and try to understand why particular individuals felt the way they did.

1.1 HARSH VERSUS LENIENT VICTORS (1865)

Besides being influenced by differing ideologies or philosophies, Northern leaders were swayed in their approaches to Reconstruction by differences of temperament and personality. Abraham Lincoln, a pragmatist and a compassionate man, was inclined to make the return of the Southern states to full constitutional equality a relatively easy process. In several states that had been occupied by Union forces before the final Confederate surrender, he was able to put his lenient policies in effect.

The first selection is an excerpt from Lincoln's last recorded address, remarks he made from the White House balcony to a group of citizens who had come to "serenade" him just four days before his death by an assassin's bullet. Lincoln discusses the issue of the constitutional status of the seceded states, a legalistic issue that had important implications for policy. If it was held that the Southern states had never actually left the Union, then they remained sovereign entities like the other states, and Washington had only limited powers over them. But if it was decided that they had left the Union and reverted to territorial status, as some believed, then Congress could constitutionally impose a wide range of conditions on them.

What does Lincoln say about this issue? What is his overall tone? Was his estimate of the best thing for the nation to do valid in light of all that followed? How would you characterize Lincoln's views of the rights of the former slaves?

The second selection is a May 1865 proclamation by President Andrew Johnson establishing a provisional government for South Carolina. In the next two months Johnson issued six other proclamations establishing governments for other former Confederate states.

Johnson was himself a Southerner (from Tennessee), but a strong unionist who had refused to disavow his government when his state seceded. Like Lincoln, he believed the Southern states should be readmitted to the Union with as few preconditions as possible. What preconditions are imposed by the president's proclamation? Are they severe? What obvious conditions that might have been imposed are omitted? Is there any mention of a role for Congress in the Reconstruction process? Should Johnson have assumed sole leadership in this all-important matter?

The third selection is from a speech by Representative Thaddeus Stevens of Pennsylvania. Stevens was a "Radical Republican." During the war he had, as other Radicals, pushed for the early emancipation of the slaves and aggressive policies against the Confederacy and its leaders. After the war he and his fellow Radicals would demand that the South be compelled to repudiate its prewar planter leadership and guarantee equal social and political rights for the freedmen.[1] Southerners and conservative Northerners, mostly Democrats, would call Stevens and his colleagues mean-spirited "vindictives," who lacked Christian compassion toward their former enemies and were moved primarily by partisan political ends.

After Lincoln's assassination, Stevens rallied the congressional opposition to President Johnson's lenient Reconstruction policy. He and his supporters would seize from the president the management of the Reconstruction process. Ultimately they would break completely with

---

[1] Though the term might seem sexist today it was used to refer to *all* the freed slaves after 1865, and it is still so used—ED.

Johnson, and in 1868 the Radical-controlled Congress would impeach the president—although not convict him—for defying the will and the laws of Congress.

From the following excerpt, would you say that Stevens deserves to be considered vindictive? Do his sympathies for the freed slaves seem sincere? Does his reference to "perpetual ascendency to the party of the Union" seem like a blatant grab for power by Republicans? Putting yourself in Stevens's shoes, how can such a partisan position be justified?

RECONSTRUCTION MUST BE GRADUAL AND CAREFUL

Abraham Lincoln

I have been shown a letter . . . in which the writer expresses regret that my mind has not seemed to be definitely fixed upon the question whether the seceded States, so called, are in the Union or out of it. I would perhaps add astonishment to his regret were he to learn that since I have found professed Union men endeavoring to answer that question, I have purposely forborne any public expression upon it. As appears to me, that question has not been nor yet is a practically material one, and that any discussion of it, while it thus remains practically immaterial, could have no effect other than the mischievous one of dividing our friends. As yet, whatever it may become, that question is bad as the basis of a controversy, and good for nothing at all—a merely pernicious abstraction. We all agree that the seceded States, so called, are out of their proper practical relation with the Union, and that the sole object of the Government, civil and military, in regard to these States, is to again get them into their proper practical relation. I believe that is not only possible, but in fact [it is] easier to do this without deciding or even considering whether these States have ever been out of the Union, than with it. Finding themselves safely at home, it would be utterly immaterial whether they have been abroad. Let us all join in doing the act necessary to restore the proper practical relations between these States and the Union, and each forever after innocently indulge his own opinion whether, in doing the acts, he brought the States from without the Union, or only gave them proper assistance, they never having been out of it. The amount of constituency, so to speak, on which the Louisiana government rests, would be more satisfactory to all if it contained fifty thousand, or thirty thousand, or even twenty thousand, instead of twelve thousand, as it does. It is also unsatisfactory to some that the elective franchise is not given to the colored man. I would myself prefer that it were now conferred on the very intelligent, and on those who serve our cause as soldiers. Still, the question is not whether the Louisiana government, as it stands, is quite all that is desirable. The question is, Will it be wiser to take it as it is and help to improve it, or to reject and disperse [*sic*]? Can Louisiana be brought into proper practical relation with the Union sooner by sustaining or by discarding her new State government? Some twelve thousand voters in the heretofore Slave State of Louisiana have sworn allegiance to the Union, assumed to be the rightful political power of the State, held elections, organized a State government, adopted a Free State constitution, giving the benefit of public schools equally to black and white, and empowering the Legislature to confer the elective franchise upon the colored man. This Legislature has

Arthur B. Lapsley, *Writings of Abraham Lincoln* (New York: G. P. Putnam's Sons, 1906), vol. 7, pp. 362–68.

already voted to ratify the Constitutional Amendment recently passed by Congress, abolishing slavery throughout the nation. These twelve thousand persons are thus fully committed to the Union, and to perpetuate freedom in the State—committed to the very things, and nearly all things, the nation wants—and they ask the nation's recognition and its assistance to make good this committal. Now, if we reject and spurn them, we do our utmost to disorganize and disperse them. We, in fact, say to the white man: You are worthless or worse; we will neither help you nor be helped by you. To the blacks we say: This cup of liberty which these, your old masters, held to your lips, we will dash from you, and leave you to the chances of gathering the spilled and scattered contents in some vague and undefined when, where, and how. If this course, discouraging and paralyzing both white and black, has any tendency to bring Louisiana into proper practical relations with the Union, I have so far been unable to perceive it. If, on the contrary, we recognize and sustain the new government of Louisiana, the converse of all this is made true. We encourage the hearts and nerve the arms of twelve thousand to adhere to their work, and argue for it, and proselyte for it, and fight for it, and feed it, and grow it, and ripen it to a complete success. The colored man, too, in seeing all united for him, is inspired with vigilance, and energy, and daring to the same end. Grant that he desires the elective franchise, will he not attain it sooner by saving the already advanced steps towards it, than by running backward over them? Concede that the new government of Louisiana is only to what it should be as the egg is to the fowl, we shall sooner have the fowl by hatching the egg than by smashing it. Again, if we reject Louisiana, we also reject one vote in favor of the proposed amendment to the National Constitution. To meet this proposition, it has been argued that no more than three fourths of those States which have not attempted secession are necessary to validly ratify the amendment. I do not commit myself against this, further than to say that such a ratification would be questionable, and sure to be persistently questioned, while a ratification by three fourths of all the States would be unquestioned and unquestionable. I repeat the question, Can Louisiana be brought into proper practical relation with the Union sooner by sustaining or by discarding her new State government? What has been said of Louisiana will apply to other States. And yet so great peculiarities pertain to each State, and such important and sudden changes occur in the same State, and withal so new and unprecedented is the whole case, that no exclusive and inflexible plan can safely be prescribed as to details and collaterals. Such exclusive and inflexible plan would surely become a new entanglement. Important principles may and must be inflexible. In the present situation as the phrase goes, it may be my duty to make some new announcement to the people of the South. I am considering, and shall not fail to act, when satisfied that action will be proper.

AMNESTY PROCLAMATION

Andrew Johnson

By the President of the United States of America. A Proclamation.

Whereas the fourth section of the fourth article of the Constitution of the United States declares that the United States shall guarantee to every State in the Union a

James D. Richardson, ed., *A Compilation of the Messages and Papers of the Presidents* (New York: Bureau of National Literature, 1897), vol. 8, pp. 3508–10.

republican form of government and shall protect each of them against invasion and domestic violence; and

Whereas the President of the United States is by the Constitution made Commander in Chief of the Army and Navy, as well as chief civil executive officer of the United States, and is bound by solemn oath faithfully to execute the office of President of the United States and to take care that the laws be faithfully executed; and

Whereas the rebellion which has been waged by a portion of the people of the United States against the properly constituted authorities of the Government thereof in the most violent and revolting form, but whose organized and armed forces have now been almost entirely overcome, has in its revolutionary progress deprived the people of the State of South Carolina of all civil government; and

Whereas it becomes necessary and proper to carry out and enforce the obligations of the United States to the people of South Carolina in securing them in the enjoyment of a republican form of government:

Now, therefore, in obedience to the high and solemn duties imposed upon me by the Constitution of the United States and for the purpose of enabling the loyal people of said State to organize a State government whereby justice may be established, domestic tranquillity insured, and loyal citizens protected in all their rights of life, liberty, and property, I, Andrew Johnson, President of the United States and Commander in Chief of the Army and Navy of the United States, do hereby appoint Benjamin F. Perry, of South Carolina, provisional governor of the State of South Carolina, whose duty it shall be, at the earliest practicable period, to prescribe such rules and regulations as may be necessary and proper for convening a convention composed of delegates to be chosen by that portion of the people of said State who are loyal to the United States, and no others, for the purpose of altering or amending the constitution thereof, and with authority to exercise within the limits of said State all the powers necessary and proper to enable such loyal people of the State of South Carolina to restore said State to its constitutional relations to the Federal Government and to present such a republican form of State government as will entitle the State to the guaranty of the United States therefor and its people to protection by the United States against invasion, insurrection, and domestic violence: *Provided*, That in any election that may be hereafter held for choosing delegates to any State convention as aforesaid no person shall be qualified as an elector or shall be eligible as a member of such convention unless he shall have previously taken and subscribed the oath of amnesty as set forth in the President's proclamation of May 29, A.D. 1865, and is a voter qualified as prescribed by the constitution and laws of the State of South Carolina in force immediately before the 17th day of November, A.D. 1860, the date of the so-called ordinance of secession; and the said convention, when convened, or the legislature that may be thereafter assembled, will prescribe the qualification of electors and the eligibility of persons to hold office under the constitution and laws of the State—a power the people of the several States composing the Federal Union have rightfully exercised from the origin of the Government to the present time.

And I do hereby direct—

First. That the military commander of the department and all officers and persons in the military and naval service aid and assist the said provisional governor in carrying into effect this proclamation; and they are enjoined to abstain from in any way hindering, impeding, or discouraging the loyal people from the organization of a State government as herein authorized.

Second. That the Secretary of State proceed to put in force all laws of the United States the administration whereof belongs to the State Department applicable to the geographical limits aforesaid.

Third. That the Secretary of the Treasury proceed to nominate for appointment assessors of taxes and collectors of customs and internal revenue and such other officers of the Treasury Department as are authorized by law and put in execution the revenue laws of the United States within the geographical limits aforesaid. In making appointments the preference shall be given to qualified loyal persons residing within the districts where their respective duties are to be performed; but if suitable residents of the districts shall not be found, then persons residing in other States or districts shall be appointed.

Fourth. That the Postmaster-General proceed to establish post-offices and post routes and put into execution the postal laws of the United States within the said State, giving to loyal residents the preference of appointment; but if suitable residents are not found, then to appoint agents, etc., from other States.

Fifth. That the district judge for the judicial district in which South Carolina is included proceed to hold courts within said State in accordance with the provisions of the act of Congress. The Attorney-General will instruct the proper officers to libel and bring to judgment, confiscation, and sale property subject to confiscation and enforce the administration of justice within said State in all matters within the cognizance and jurisdiction of the Federal courts.

Sixth. That the Secretary of the Navy take possession of all public property belonging to the Navy Department within said geographical limits and put in operation all acts of Congress in relation to naval affairs having application to the said State.

Seventh. That the Secretary of the Interior put in force the laws relating to the Interior Department applicable to the geographical limits aforesaid.

WE MUST HAVE A RADICAL RECONSTRUCTION

Thaddeus Stevens

It is obvious . . . that the first duty of Congress is to pass a law declaring the condition of these outside or defunct States, and providing proper civil governments for them. Since the conquest they have been governed by martial law. Military rule is necessarily despotic, and ought not to exist longer than is absolutely necessary. As there are no symptoms that the people of these provinces will be prepared to participate in constitutional government for some years, I know of no arrangement so proper for them as territorial governments. There they can learn the principles of freedom and eat the fruit of foul rebellion. Under such governments, while electing members to the Territorial Legislatures, they will necessarily mingle with those to whom Congress shall extend the right of suffrage. In Territories Congress fixes the qualifications of electors; and I know of no better place nor better occasion for the conquered rebels and the conqueror to practice justice to all men, and accustom themselves to make and to obey equal laws.

Congressional Globe, 39th Cong., 1st sess., December 18, 1865, pp. 72–75.

As these fallen rebels cannot at their option reënter the heaven which they have disturbed, the garden of Eden which they have deserted, and flaming swords are set at the gates to secure their exclusion, it becomes important to the welfare of the nation to inquire when the doors shall be reopened for their admission.

According to my judgment they ought never to be recognized as capable of acting in the Union, or of being counted as valid States, until the Constitution shall have been so amended as to make it what its framers intended; and so as to secure perpetual ascendency to the party of the Union; and so as to render our republican Government firm and stable forever. The first of those amendments is to change the basis of representation among the States from Federal numbers to actual voters. Now all the colored freemen in the slave States, and three fifths of the slaves, are represented, though none of them have votes. The States have nineteen representatives of colored slaves. If the slaves are now free then they can add, for the other two fifths, thirteen more, making the slave representation thirty-two. I suppose the free blacks in those States will give at least five more, making the representation of non-voting people of color about thirty-seven. The whole number of representatives now from the slave States is seventy. Add the other two fifths and it will be eighty-three.

If the amendment prevails, and those States withhold the right of suffrage from persons of color, it will deduct about thirty-seven, leaving them but forty-six. With the basis unchanged, the eighty-three southern members, with the Democrats that will in the best times be elected from the North, will always give them a majority in Congress and in the Electoral College. They will at the very first election take possession of the White House and the halls of Congress. I need not depict the ruin that would follow. Assumption of the rebel debt or repudiation of the Federal debt would be sure to follow. The oppression of the freedmen; the reamendment of their State constitutions, and the reëstablishment of slavery would be the inevitable result. That they would scorn and disregard their present constitutions, forced upon them in the midst of martial law, would be both natural and just. No one who has any regard for freedom of elections can look upon those governments, forced upon them in duress, with any favor. If they should grant the right of suffrage to persons of color, I think there would always be Union white men enough in the South, aided by the blacks, to divide the representation, and thus continue the Republican ascendency. If they should refuse to thus alter their election laws it would reduce the representatives of the late slave States to about forty-five and render them powerless for evil.

It is plain that this amendment must be consummated before the defunct States are admitted to be capable of State action, or it never can be. . . .

But this is not all that we ought to do before these inveterate rebels are invited to participate in our legislation. We have turned, or are about to turn, loose four million slaves without a hut to shelter them or a cent in their pockets. The infernal laws of slavery have prevented them from acquiring an education, understanding the commonest laws of contract, or of managing the ordinary business of life. This Congress is bound to provide for them until they can take care of themselves. If we do not furnish them with homesteads, and hedge them around with protective laws; if we leave them to the legislation of their late masters, we had better have left them in bondage. Their condition would be worse than that of our prisoners at Andersonville. If we fail in this great duty now, when we have the power, we shall deserve and receive the execration of history and of all future ages. . . .

This Congress owes it to its own character to set the seal of reprobation upon a doctrine which is becoming too fashionable, and unless rebuked will be the recognized principle of our Government. Governor Perry[2] and other provisional governors and orators proclaim that "this is the white man's Government." The whole copperhead party, pandering to the lowest prejudices of the ignorant, repeat the cuckoo cry, "This is the white man's Government." Demagogues of all parties, even some high in authority, gravely shout, "This is the white man's Government." What is implied by this? That one race of men are to have the exclusive right forever to rule this nation, and to exercise all acts of sovereignty, while all other races and nations and colors are to be their subjects, and have no voice in making the laws and choosing the rulers by whom they are to be governed. Wherein does this differ from slavery except in degree? Does not this contradict all the distinctive principles of the Declaration of Independence? When the great and good men promulgated that instrument, and pledged their lives and sacred honors to defend it, it was supposed to form an epoch in civil government. Before that time it was held that the right to rule was vested in families, dynasties, or races, not because of superior intelligence or virtue, but because of a divine right to enjoy exclusive privileges.

Our fathers repudiated the whole doctrine of the legal superiority of families or races, and proclaimed the equality of men before the law. Upon that they created a revolution and built the Republic. They were prevented by slavery from perfecting the superstructure whose foundation they had thus broadly laid. For the sake of the Union they consented to wait, but never relinquished the idea of its final completion. The time to which they looked forward with anxiety has come. It is our duty to complete their work. If this Republic is not now made to stand on their great principles, it has no honest foundation, and the Father of all men will still shake it to its center. If we have not yet been sufficiently scourged for our national sin to teach us to do justice to all God's creatures, without distinction of race or color, we must expect the still more heavy vengeance of an offended Father, still increasing his inflictions as he increased the severity of the plagues of Egypt until the tyrant consented to do justice. And when that tyrant repented of his reluctant consent, and attempted to re-enslave the people, as our southern tyrants are attempting to do now, he filled the Red sea with broken chariots and drowned horses, and strewed the shores with dead carcasses.

Mr. Chairman, I trust the Republican party will not be alarmed at what I am saying. I do not profess to speak their sentiments, nor must they be held responsible for them. I speak for myself, and take the responsibility, and will settle with my intelligent constituents.

This is not a "white man's Government," in the exclusive sense in which it is used. To say so is political blasphemy, for it violates the fundamental principles of our gospel of liberty. This is man's Government; the Government of all men alike; not that all men will have equal power and sway within it. Accidental circumstances, natural and acquired endowment and ability, will vary their fortunes. But equal rights to all the privileges of the Government is innate in every immortal being, no matter what the shape or color of the tabernacle which it inhabits.

---

[2] Benjamin F. Perry of South Carolina, a Unionist rewarded by Johnson with an appointment as provisional governor of the state—ED.

If equal privileges were granted to all, I should not expect any but white men to be elected to office for long ages to come. The prejudice engendered by slavery would not soon permit merit to be preferred to color. But it would still be beneficial to the weaker races. In a country where political divisions will always exist, their power, joined with just white men, would greatly modify, if it did not entirely prevent, the injustice of majorities. Without the right of suffrage in the late slave States, (I do not speak of the free States.) I believe the slaves had far better been left in bondage. I see it stated that very distinguished advocates of the right of suffrage lately declared in this city that they do not expect to obtain it by congressional legislation, but only by administrative action, because, as one gallant gentleman said, the States had not been out of the Union. Then they will never get it. The President is far sounder than they. He sees that administrative action has nothing to do with it. If it ever is to come, it must be constitutional amendments or congressional action in the Territories, and in enabling acts.

How shameful that men of influence should mislead and miseducate the public mind! They proclaim, "This is the white man's Government," and the whole coil of copperheads echo the same sentiment, and upstart, jealous Republicans join the cry. Is it any wonder ignorant foreigners and illiterate natives should learn this doctrine, and be led to despise and maltreat a whole race of their fellow-men?

Sir, this doctrine of a white man's Government is as atrocious as the infamous sentiment that damned the late Chief Justice [Roger Taney] to everlasting fame; and, I fear, to everlasting fire.

1.2   THE WHITE SOUTH RESPONDS (1865, 1866, 1868)

White Southerners were themselves divided over Reconstruction. In the immediate aftermath of Confederate surrender, many were too stunned to resist the North's dictation. But that mood did not last very long. In a matter of months many Southern leaders, including former Confederate officials, had regained their composure and were preparing to salvage what they could from the shambles of defeat. The state governments reestablished under President Johnson's auspices saw these leaders resisting major changes in relations between the races and refused to express contrition at their section's secessionist past. When Thaddeus Stevens and his Radical allies in Congress imposed more stringent conditions, they fought back even harder.

The first selection is an example of the Black Codes passed by the conservative Southern state governments established under Johnson's 1865 proclamations. These state laws were designed to regularize legal relations between blacks and the dominant white society now that slavery was gone. They accepted the end of slavery, but in most cases they cast blacks as inferior beings, not full citizens, and even placed them in jeopardy of quasi-reenslavement.

Among the harshest of the state Black Codes was that of Mississippi, a state, like South Carolina, with a black majority in its population. What elements of this code implied recognition of the end of the slave system? What provisions suggest that white Mississippians were not willing to accord the freed men and women full equality? Can you see from this selection why black leaders and Radical Republicans considered Johnson's Reconstruction policy too lenient?

A substantial minority of native-born white Southerners for a time came to terms with the Radical state administrations imposed by Congress when it seized control of Reconstruction policy. Called "scalawags," these Republican voters were particularly numerous in the former nonslaveholding parts of the South and among businessmen of Whig antecedents. To scalawags, the enemy was often the former planter elite that had pulled the South into a disastrous war, not the Republican politicians in Washington. Joining with blacks, newly enfranchised under the Fourteenth and Fifteenth Amendments to the Constitution, and with "carpetbaggers"— Northern whites who came South to make their fortunes after 1865—they won control for a time over the state governments established under the Reconstruction Acts.

The second selection is by a scalawag. James W. Hunnicutt was a South Carolina Baptist minister who had originally supported secession and then changed his mind. The selection is his testimony before the congressional Joint Committee on Reconstruction in early 1866. Why does Hunnicutt emphasize the treatment of white unionists in the South? Do you feel that the questioner, Radical Republican Senator Jacob Howard of Michigan, is leading the witness?

The third item in this section represents the position of the "redeemers," the ardent white conservatives who fought to wrest political supremacy from the Radical Republicans who controlled the state Reconstruction governments. An editorial from the Atlanta News of September 10, 1874, it charges the Republicans and blacks with barbarism. Were the charges valid? Do you know if the Radical regimes in the South were more corrupt, wasteful, and incompetent than state governments elsewhere during this era? Were the charges based more on race prejudice than on reality? How do you explain the vitriol of the conservative Southern attack on the Radical regimes?

MISSISSIPPI BLACK CODE

Mississippi Legislature

1. Civil Rights of Freedmen in Mississippi

Sec. 1. *Be it enacted,* . . . That all freedmen, free negroes, and mulattoes may sue and be sued, implead and be impleaded, in all the courts of law and equity of this State, and may acquire personal property, and choses [*sic*] in action, by descent or purchase, and may dispose of the same in the same manner and to the same extent that white persons may: *Provided,* That the provisions of this section shall not be so construed as to allow any freedman, free negro, or mulatto to rent or lease any lands or tenements except in incorporated cities or towns, in which places the corporate authorities shall control the same. . . .

Sec. 3. . . . All freedmen, free negroes, or mulattoes who do now and have heretofore lived and cohabited together as husband and wife shall be taken and held in law as legally married, and the issue shall be taken and held as legitimate for all purposes; that it shall not be lawful for any freedman, free negro, or mulatto to intermarry with any white person; nor for any white person to intermarry with any freedman, free negro, or mulatto; and any person who shall so intermarry, shall be deemed guilty of felony, and on conviction thereof shall be confined in the State penitentiary for life; and those shall be deemed freedmen, free negroes, and mulattoes who are of pure negro blood, and those descended from a negro to the third generation, inclusive, though one ancestor in each generation may have been a white person.

Laws of the State of Mississippi Passed at the Regular Session of the Mississippi Legislature, Held in the City of Jackson, October–December, 1865 (Jackson: J. J. Shannon and Company, 1866), pp. 82–93.

Sec. 4. . . . In addition to cases in which freedmen, free negroes, and mulattoes are now by law competent witnesses, freedmen, free negroes, or mulattoes shall be competent in civil cases, when a party or parties to the suit, either plaintiff or plaintiffs, defendant or defendants, and a white person or white persons, is or are the opposing party or parties, plaintiff or plaintiffs, defendant or defendants. They shall also be competent witnesses in all criminal prosecutions where the crime charged is alleged to have been committed by a white person upon or against the person or property of a freedman, free negro, or mulatto: *Provided*, that in all cases said witnesses shall be examined in open court, on the stand; except, however, they may be examined before the grand jury, and shall in all cases be subject to the rules and tests of the common law as to competency and credibility. . . .

Sec. 6. . . . All contracts for labor made with freedmen, free negroes, and mulattoes for a longer period than one month shall be in writing, and in duplicate, attested and read to said freedman, free negro, or mulatto by a beat, city or county officer, or two disinterested white persons of the county in which the labor is to be performed, of which each party shall have one; and said contracts shall be taken and held as entire contracts, and if the laborer shall quit the service of the employer before the expiration of his term of service, without good cause, he shall forfeit his wages for that year up to the time of quitting.

Sec. 7. . . . Every civil officer shall, and every person may, arrest and carry back to his or her legal employer any freedman, free negro, or mulatto who shall have quit the service of his or her employer before the expiration of his or her term of service without good cause; and said officer and person shall be entitled to receive for arresting and carrying back every deserting employe aforesaid the sum of five dollars, and ten cents per mile from the place of arrest to the place of delivery; and the same shall be paid by the employer, and held as a set-off for so much against the wages of said deserting employe: *Provided*, that said arrested party, after being so returned, may appeal to the justice of the peace or member of the board of police of the county, who, on notice to the alleged employer, shall try summarily whether said appellant is legally employed by the alleged employer, and has good cause to quit said employer; either party shall have the right of appeal to the county court, pending which the alleged deserter shall be remanded to the alleged employer or otherwise disposed of, as shall be right and just; and the decision of the county court shall be final. . . .

Sec. 9. . . . If any person shall persuade or attempt to persuade, entice, or cause any freedman, free negro, or mulatto to desert from the legal employment of any person before the expiration of his or her term of service, or shall knowingly employ any such deserting freedman, free negro, or mulatto, or shall knowingly give or sell to any such deserting freedman, free negro, or mulatto, any food, raiment, or other thing, he or she shall be guilty of a misdemeanor, and, upon conviction, shall be fined not less than twenty-five dollars and not more than two hundred dollars and the costs; and if said fine and costs shall not be immediately paid, the court shall sentence said convict to not exceeding two months' imprisonment in the county jail, and he or she shall moreover be liable to the party injured in damages: *Provided*, if any person shall, or shall attempt to, persuade, entice, or cause any freedman, free negro, or mulatto to desert from any legal employment of any person, with the view to employ said freedman, free negro, or mulatto without the limits of this State, such person, on conviction, shall be fined not less than fifty dollars, and not more than five hundred dollars and costs; and if said fine and costs shall not be immediately paid, the court shall sentence said convict to not exceeding six months imprisonment in the county jail. . . .

2. Mississippi Apprentice Law

Sec. 1. . . . It shall be the duty of all sheriffs, justices of the peace, and other civil officers of the several counties in this State, to report to the probate courts of their respective counties semi-annually, at the January and July terms of said courts, all freedmen, free negroes, and mulattoes, under the age of eighteen, in their respective counties, beats or districts, who are orphans, or whose parent or parents have not the means or who refuse to provide for and support said minors; and thereupon it shall be the duty of said probate court to order the clerk of said court to apprentice said minors to some competent and suitable person, on such terms as the court may direct, having a particular care to the interest of said minor: *Provided*, that the former owner of said minors shall have the preference when, in the opinion of the court, he or she shall be a suitable person for that purpose.

Sec. 2. . . . The said court shall be fully satisfied that the person or persons to whom said minor shall be apprenticed shall be a suitable person to have the charge and care of said minor, and fully to protect the interest of said minor. The said court shall require the said master or mistress to execute bond and security, payable to the State of Mississippi, conditioned that he or she shall furnish said minor with sufficient food and clothing; to treat said minor humanely; furnish medical attention in case of sickness; teach, or cause to be taught, him or her to read and write, if under fifteen years old, and will conform to any law that may be hereafter passed for the regulation of the duties and relation of master and apprentice. . . .

Sec. 3. . . . In the management and control of said apprentice, said master or mistress shall have the power to inflict such moderate corporal chastisement as a father or guardian is allowed to inflict on his or her child or ward at common law: *Provided*, that in no case shall cruel or inhuman punishment be inflicted.

Sec. 4. . . . If any apprentice shall leave the employment of his or her master or mistress, without his or her consent, said master or mistress may pursue and recapture said apprentice, and bring him or her before any justice of the peace of the county, whose duty it shall be to remand said apprentice to the service of his or her master or mistress; and in the event of a refusal on the part of said apprentice so to return, then said justice shall commit said apprentice to the jail of said county, on failure to give bond, to the next term of the county court; and it shall be the duty of said court at the first term thereafter to investigate said case, and if the court shall be of opinion that said apprentice left the employment of his or her master or mistress without good cause, to order him or her to be punished, as provided for the punishment of hired freedmen, as may be from time to time provided for by law for desertion, until he or she shall agree to return to the service of his or her master or mistress: . . . if the court shall believe that said apprentice had good cause to quit his said master or mistress, the court shall discharge said apprentice from said indenture, and also enter a judgment against the master or mistress for not more than one hundred dollars, for the use and benefit of said apprentice. . . .

3. Mississippi Vagrant Law

Sec. 1. *Be it enacted*, etc., . . . That all rogues and vagabonds, idle and dissipated persons, beggars, jugglers, or persons practicing unlawful games or plays, runaways, common drunkards, common night-walkers, pilferers, lewd, wanton, or lascivious persons, in speech or behavior, common railers and brawlers, persons who neglect their calling or employment, misspend what they earn, or do not provide for the support of themselves or their families, or dependents, and all other idle and disorderly persons, including all who neglect all lawful business, habitually misspend their time by frequenting houses of ill-fame, gaming-houses, or tippling shops, shall be deemed and considered vagrants, under the provisions of this act, and upon conviction thereof shall be fined not exceeding one hundred dollars, with all accruing costs, and be imprisoned at the discretion of the court, not exceeding ten days.

Sec. 2. . . . All freedmen, free negroes and mulattoes in this State, over the age of eighteen years, found on the second Monday in January, 1866, or thereafter, with no lawful employment or business, or found unlawfully assembling themselves together, either in the day or night time, and all white persons so assembling themselves with freedmen, free negroes or mulattoes, or usually associating with freedmen, free negroes or mulattoes, on terms of equality, or living in adultery or fornication with a freed woman, free negro or mulatto, shall be deemed vagrants, and on conviction thereof shall be fined in a sum not exceeding, in the case of a freedman, free negro or mulatto, fifty dollars, and a white man two hundred dollars, and imprisoned at the discretion of the court, the free negro not exceeding ten days, and the white man not exceeding six months. . . .

Sec. 7. . . . If any freedman, free negro, or mulatto shall fail or refuse to pay any tax levied according to the provisions of the sixth section of this act, it shall be *prima facie* evidence of vagrancy, and it shall be the duty of the sheriff to arrest such freedman, free negro, or mulatto or such person refusing or neglecting to pay such tax, and proceed at once to hire for the shortest time such delinquent tax-payer to any one who will pay the said tax, with accruing costs, giving preference to the employer, if there be one. . . .

4. Penal Laws of Mississippi

Sec. 1. *Be it enacted*, . . . That no freedman, free negro or mulatto, not in the military service of the United States government, and not licensed so to do by the board of police of his or her county, shall keep or carry fire-arms of any kind, or any ammunition, dirk or bowie knife, and on conviction thereof in the county court shall be punished by fine, not exceeding ten dollars, and pay the costs of such proceedings, and all such arms or ammunition shall be forfeited to the informer; and it shall be the duty of every civil and military officer to arrest any freedman, free negro, or mulatto found with any such arms or ammunition, and cause him or her to be committed to trial in default of bail.

Sec. 2. . . . Any freedman, free negro, or mulatto committing riots, routs, affrays, trespasses, malicious mischief, cruel treatment to animals, seditious speeches, insulting gestures, language, or acts, or assaults on any person, disturbance of the peace, exercising the function of a minister of the Gospel without a license from some regularly organized church, vending spirituous or intoxicating liquors, or committing any other misdemeanor, the punishment of which is not specifically provided for by law, shall, upon conviction thereof in the county court, be fined not less than ten dollars, and not more than one hundred dollars, and may be imprisoned at the discretion of the court, not exceeding thirty days.

Sec. 3. . . . If any white person shall sell, lend, or give to any freedman, free negro, or mulatto any fire-arms, dirk or bowie knife, or ammunition, or any spirituous or intoxicating liquors, such person or persons so offending, upon conviction thereof in the county court of his or her county, shall be fined not exceeding fifty dollars, and may be imprisoned, at the discretion of the court, not exceeding thirty days. . . .

Sec. 5. . . . If any freedman, free negro, or mulatto, convicted of any of the misdemeanors provided against in this act, shall fail or refuse for the space of five days, after conviction, to pay the fine and costs imposed, such person shall be hired out by the sheriff or other officer, at public outcry, to any white person who will pay said fine and all costs, and take said convict for the shortest time.

JOHNSON'S POLICIES CRITICIZED

James W. Hunnicutt

MR. [JACOB] HOWARD: What is the effect of President Johnson's policy of reconstruction there?

[SOUTH CAROLINA]—A.:   . . . They are all in favor of President Johnson's policy of reconstruction. As soon as they get their ends served by him they would not touch him, but he is their man now. They say that in 1868 the South will be a unit, and that with the help of the copperhead party of the North they will elect a President. They do not care to have slavery back, but they will try and make the federal government pay them for their slaves. A man from Virginia told me today that they would be paid for their Negroes. This gentleman lost forty Negroes. This is their idea; they do not want slavery back, but they want to be paid for their slaves. They say that unless you accept their debt they will repudiate yours. They say they are not interested in this government.

Q.:   They would be glad to have Uncle Sam assume the payment of the Confederate debt?—

A.:   Yes, sir, and to pay them for their Negroes and to indemnify them for their loss of property in the war. It is an impression of most of them, men, women, and children, that they are going to be paid for every rail burned, for every stick of timber destroyed, and for every Negro lost. One man told me in my house that as soon as they could get the reins of government in their hands they would undo everything that this administration has done, with an awful adjective prefixed to the word "administration." He said, "We have as much right to undo what the administration has done as they have to destroy the government of the Constitution"—as they claim the administration has done.

Q.:   They propose to get back into the Union for the purpose of restoring the Constitution?—

Report of the Joint Committee on Reconstruction (Washington, DC: United States Government Printing Office, 1866), pt. 2, pp. 150–51.

A.:   Yes, sir; and the testimony of the Negroes will not be worth a snap of your finger, and all this is done for policy. A Negro can come and give his testimony, and it passes for what it is worth with the courts. They can do what they please with it; there are the judges, the lawyers, and the jury against the Negro, and perhaps every one of them is sniggering and laughing while the Negro is giving his testimony.

Q.:   Has not the liberal policy of President Johnson in granting pardons and amnesties rather tended to soothe and allay their feelings towards the government of the United States?—A.: No, sir, not towards the government of the United States nor towards the Union men.

Q.:   What effect has it had in that respect?—

A.:   It has made them more impudent. They were once humble and felt that they had done wrong, but this policy has emboldened them, and they are more impudent today, more intolerant, and more proscriptive than they were in 1864. They say that we are the traitors and went over to the damned Yankees. Our present mayor [of Fredericksburg] Slaughter, had sixty men of Grant's army, who were wounded in the wilderness and sent to Fredericksburg, forwarded to General [Robert E.] Lee as prisoners-of-war. When Fredericksburg fell into our hands Slaughter made his escape. The federals arrested sixty citizens of Fredericksburg to be held as hostages for these sixty soldiers whom Slaughter had sent to the enemy, and among them was my wife's brother, who was living in Fredericksburg, and yet that same Slaughter was reelected mayor of Fredericksburg last summer after the collapse of the rebellion. Old Tom Barton, the commonwealth's attorney, said in 1861 (and I suppose his feelings are the same still) that all these Union shriekers ought to be hung as high as Haman, and this old man was reelected commonwealth attorney by the people of the county. Every member of the rebel common council was reelected. One of the men who were elected members of the common council from that district stated that none of the Union men who went over to the Yankees during the war should be allowed to return to Fredericksburg; he was also appointed director of a bank there. These are the men we have got over us, and what kind of justice can we expect in the courts?

Q.:   You will probably get pretty summary justice?—

A.:   I think so; these are facts.

Q.:   Where is Slaughter now?—

A.:   He is now mayor of Fredericksburg and will be reelected next month; we need not run a Union man there; we are disfranchised.

Q.:   Is not Slaughter a good Union man?—

A.:   Oh! He has been notoriously Union all the time, as the papers say—notoriously Union! I saw that stated in a Fredericksburg paper; it stated that they had been persecuting Mayor Slaughter, who had been notoriously Union all the time.

Q.:   You have not a great deal of confidence in the truthfulness of secession?—

A.:   No, sir; I have not.

Q.:   Where their political standing is concerned?—

A.:   I used to have some confidence, not in secession, but in the people; but it seems to me that their whole nature and character has been changed, and that when treason enters a man's heart, every virtue he has departs.

Q.:   Could Jefferson Davis be convicted of treason in that part of Virginia?—

A.:   As I went home last Sunday week in the boat, I was in company with a delegation from the Virginia legislature which waited upon President Johnson, and I heard one of them say that there could not be a jury obtained south of the Potomac who would convict Jeff Davis, and that the man who would write down there that Jeff Davis should be punished would be in danger. Jeff Davis cannot be punished down there, and they would elect Lee tomorrow, if there were no difficulty in the way, governor of Virginia. There is no question about that in my mind.

Q.:   Do you think of anything that you wish to relate?—

A.:   No, sir; I simply wish to state that I make these remarks conscientiously. I was born and raised in the South; my interests of every kind, social, financial, religious and political, are in the South; my church is in the South, and I am going soon to Richmond to edit a paper. Nothing but the good of the country, my own safety, and the safety of my children, and of Union men and of freedmen, could have induced me to come before you and make this statement. I am a friend of the South. I have written for the South, and I shall write in behalf of the South, but the South is one thing, and traitors and treason in the South are different things.

WHITE PEOPLE MUST REGAIN CONTROL OF THEIR STATES

Editor, Atlanta News

Let there be White Leagues formed in every town, village and hamlet of the South, and let us organize for the great struggle which seems inevitable. If the October elections which are to be held at the North are favorable to the radicals, the time will have arrived for us to prepare for the very worst. The radicalism of the republican party must be met by the radicalism of white men. We have no war to make against the United States Government, but against the republican party our hate must be unquenchable, our war interminable and merciless. Fast fleeting away is the day of wordy protests and idle appeals to the magnanimity of the republican party. By brute force they are endeavoring to force us into acquiescence to their hideous programme. We have submitted long enough to indignities, and it is time to meet brute-force with brute-force. Every Southern State should swarm with White Leagues, and we should stand ready to act the moment [President Ulysses S.] Grant signs the civil-rights bill.

Walter L. Fleming, ed., *Documentary History of Reconstruction: Political, Military, and Industrial, 1865 to the Present Time* (Cleveland: The Arthur H. Clark Company, 1907), vol. 2, pp. 387–88.

[1]It will not do to wait till radicalism has fettered us to the car of social equality before we make an effort to resist it. The signing of the bill will be a declaration of war against the southern whites. It is our duty to ourselves, it is our duty to our children, it is our duty to the white race whose prowess subdued the wilderness of this continent, whose civilization filled it with cities and towns and villages, whose mind gave it power and grandeur, and whose labor imparted to it prosperity, and whose love made peace and happiness dwell within its homes, to take the gage of battle the moment it is thrown down. If the white democrats of the North are men, they will not stand idly by and see us borne down by northern radicals and half-barbarous negroes. But no matter what they may do, it is time for us to organize. We have been temporizing long enough. Let northern radicals understand that military supervision of southern elections and the civil-rights bill mean war, that war means bloodshed, and that we are terribly in earnest, and even they, fanatical as they are, may retrace their steps before it is too late.

ORGANIZATION AND PRINCIPLES OF THE KU KLUX KLAN (1868)

Organization and Principles of the Ku Klux Klan

U.S. 42nd Congress, 2nd Session, Senate Report, No. 41 on the Ku Klux Klan, Washington, DC, 1871.

Appellation

This Organization shall be styled and denominated, the Order of the * * *

Creed

We, the Order of the * * * , reverentially acknowledge the majesty and supremacy of the Divine Being, and recognize the goodness and providence of the same. And we recognize our relation to the United States Government, the supremacy of the Constitution, the Constitutional Laws thereof, and the Union of States thereunder.

Character and Objects of the Order

This is an institution of Chivalry, Humanity, Mercy, and Patriotism; embodying in its genius and its principles all that is chivalric in conduct, noble in sentiment, generous in manhood, and patriotic in purpose; its peculiar objects being

First: To protect the weak, the innocent, and the defenseless, from the indignities, wrongs, and outrages of the lawless, the violent, and the brutal; to relieve the injured and oppressed; to succor the suffering and unfortunate, and especially the widows and orphans of Confederate soldiers.

Second: To protect and defend the Constitution of the United States, and all laws passed in conformity thereto, and to protect the States and the people thereof from all invasion from any source whatever.

Third: To aid and assist in the execution of all constitutional laws, and to protect the people from unlawful seizure, and from trial except by their peers in conformity to the laws of the land.

---

[1]A bill proposed by Charles Sumner in 1870–1871 that sought to guarantee blacks nonsegregated, equal access to all public accommodations—ED.

Titles

Sec. 1. The officers of this Order shall consist of a Grand Wizard of the Empire, and his ten Genii; a Grand Dragon of the Realm, and his eight Hydras; a Grand Titan of the Dominion, and his six Furies; a Grand Giant of the Province, and his four Goblins; a Grand Cyclops of the Den, and his two Night Hawks; a Grand Magi, a Grand Monk, a Grand Scribe, a Grand Exchequer, a Grand Turk, and a Grand Sentinel.

Sec. 2. The body politic of this Order shall be known and designated as "Ghouls."

Territory and Its Divisions

Sec. 1. The territory embraced within the jurisdiction of this Order shall be coterminous with the States of Maryland, Virginia, North Carolina, South Carolina, Georgia, Florida, Alabama, Mississippi, Louisiana, Texas, Arkansas, Missouri, Kentucky, and Tennessee; all combined constituting the Empire.

Sec. 2. The Empire shall be divided into four departments, the first to be styled the Realm, and coterminous with the boundaries of the several States; the second to be styled the Dominion and to be coterminous with such counties as the Grand Dragons of the several Realms may assign to the charge of the Grand Titan. The third to be styled the Province, and to be coterminous with the several counties: *provided* the Grand Titan may, when he deems it necessary, assign two Grand Giants to one Province, prescribing, at the same time, the jurisdiction of each. The fourth department to be styled the Den, and shall embrace such part of a Province as the Grand Giant shall assign to the charge of a Grand Cyclops. . . .

Interrogations to Be Asked

1st. Have you ever been rejected, upon application for membership in the * * * , or have you ever been expelled from the same?

2d. Are you now, or have you ever been, a member of the Radical Republican party, or either of the organizations known as the "Loyal League" and the "Grand Army of the Republic?"

3d. Are you opposed to the principles and policy of the Radical party, and to the Loyal League, and the Grand Army of the Republic, so far as you are informed of the character and purposes of those organizations?

4th. Did you belong to the Federal army during the late war, and fight against the South during the existence of the same?

5th. Are you opposed to negro equality, both social and political?

6th. Are you in favor of a white man's government in this country?

7th. Are you in favor of Constitutional liberty, and a Government of equitable laws instead of a Government of violence and oppression?

8th. Are you in favor of maintaining the Constitutional rights of the South?

9th. Are you in favor of the re-enfranchisement and emancipation of the white men of the South, and the restitution of the Southern people to all their rights, alike proprietary, civil, and political?

10th. Do you believe in the inalienable right of self-preservation of the people against the exercise of arbitrary and unlicensed power? . . .

. . . 9. The most profound and rigid secrecy concerning any and everything that relates to the Order, shall at all times be maintained.

10. Any member who shall reveal or betray the secrets of this Order, shall suffer the extreme penalty of the law.

1.3   THE BLACK RESPONSE (1865, 1868, 1866)

Emancipation and Union victory liberated almost 4 million black Americans from bondage. What role would they now play in the life of their region? Would they be citizens and voters? How would they earn a living? What claim did they have on their communities for education and other services? These and other questions confronted Northern policy makers and voters after Confederate defeat.

To educated blacks, many of them former "free people of color," the most important right that the government could confer was that of suffrage, the right to vote. In the first selection, Frederick Douglass, the prominent black abolitionist, argues for the necessity of giving the vote to the newly freed slaves. What are Douglass's arguments? This address was greeted with applause by his audience, but he was speaking to a Boston abolitionist convention. How do you think white Southerners felt about suffrage for blacks? Do you know how most white Northerners felt about giving black men the vote at this time—Douglass's Boston audience notwithstanding? Note Douglass's reference to woman suffrage. Why does he believe black males should be given the vote before white women?

The second selection is an excerpt from a debate at the 1868 South Carolina constitutional convention, which was called after Congress refused to accept the state's "Johnson government" and established stricter rules for Southern readmission to the Union.

One of the many topics the convention delegates debated was land ownership. If conservative Southern whites sought to reestablish a system of near slavery, blacks and some of their Radical defenders wanted what seemed to many contemporaries to be the other extreme: to create a black farm-owner class by redistributing white-owned land. The participants in the following selection are Richard H. Cain, a black minister originally from New York; Francis L. Cardozo, a South Carolinian of mixed race, also a minister; and N. G. Parker and C. P. Leslie, white carpetbaggers. Their debate focuses on a resolution asking the federal Congress to appropriate $1 million to be used to buy small homesteads for South Carolina freed men and women. What are the arguments pro and con? What is the reference to "confiscation"? Congress never made the appropriation.

Can you guess why from the evidence in this debate? What would have been the advantage to the nation at large if ideas such as Cardozo's and Cain's had been enacted?

The third selection adds education to the "wish list" of Southern blacks during Reconstruction. Why were they so eager for education? Did they have access to education in slave days? Was their faith in education as salvation part of the American tradition? Was it misguided or exaggerated?

The fourth selection is a petition from freedmen for Federal protection from local Ku Klux Klan violence and political corruption. Do the conditions described in this petition suggest a long history of racial tension and oppression to come?

WHAT THE BLACK MAN WANTS

Frederick Douglass

MR. PRESIDENT,—I came here [to the annual meeting of the Massachusetts Anti-Slavery Society at Boston], as I come always to the meetings in New England, as a

---

William D. Kelley, Wendell Phillips, and Frederick Douglass, *The Equality of Men Before the Law Claimed and Defended* (Boston: n.p., 1865), pp. 36–39.

listener, and not as a speaker; and one of the reasons why I have not been more frequently to the meetings of this society, has been because of the disposition on the part of some of my friends to call me out upon the platform, even when they knew that there was some difference of opinion and of feeling between those who rightfully belong to this platform and myself; and for fear of being misconstrued, as desiring to interrupt or disturb the proceedings of these meetings, I have usually kept away, and have thus been deprived of that educating influence, which I am always free to confess is of the highest order, descending from this platform. I have felt, since I have lived out West, that in going there I parted from a great deal that was valuable; and I feel, every time I come to these meetings, that I have lost a great deal by making my home west of Boston, west of Massachusetts; for, if anywhere in the country there is to be found the highest sense of justice, or the truest demands for my race, I look for it in the East, I look for it here. The ablest discussions of the whole question of our rights occur here, and to be deprived of the privilege of listening to those discussions is a great deprivation.

I do not know, from what has been said, that there is any difference of opinion as to the duty of abolitionists, at the present moment. How can we get up any difference at this point, or at any point, where we are so united, so agreed? I went especially, however, with that word of Mr. [Wendell] Phillips, which is the criticism of Gen. Banks and Gen. Banks's policy. I hold that that policy is our chief danger at the present moment; that it practically enslaves the negro, and makes the [Emancipation] Proclamation of 1863 a mockery and delusion. What is freedom? It is the right to choose one's own employment. Certainly it means that, if it means any thing; and when any individual or combination of individuals, undertakes to decide for any man when he shall work, where he shall work, at what he shall work, and for what he shall work, he or they practically reduce him to slavery. (Applause.) He is a slave. That I understand Gen. Banks to do—to determine for the so-called freedman, when, and where, and at what, and for how much he shall work, when he shall be punished, and by whom punished. It is absolute slavery. It defeats the beneficent intentions of the Government, if it has beneficent intentions, in regard to the freedom of our people.

I have had but one idea for the last three years, to present to the American people, and the phraseology in which I clothe it is the old abolition phraseology. I am for the "immediate, unconditional, and universal" enfranchisement of the black man, in every State in the Union. (Loud applause.) Without this, his liberty is a mockery; without this, you might as well almost retain the old name of slavery for his condition; for, in fact, if he is not the slave of the individual master, he is the slave of society, and holds his liberty as a privilege, not as a right. He is at the mercy of the mob, and has no means of protecting himself.

It may be objected, however, that this pressing of the negro's right to suffrage is premature. Let us have slavery abolished, it may be said, let us have labor organized, and then, in the natural course of events, the right of suffrage will be extended to the negro. I do not agree with this. The constitution of the human mind is such, that if it once disregards the conviction forced upon it by a revelation of truth, it requires the exercise of a higher power to produce the same conviction afterwards. The American people are now in tears. The Shenandoah has run blood—the best blood of the North. All around Richmond, the blood of New England and of the North has been shed—of your sons, your brothers and your fathers. We all feel, in the existence of this Rebellion, that judgments terrible, wide-spread, far-reaching, overwhelming, are abroad in the land; and we feel, in view of these judgments, just now, a disposition to learn righteous-ness. This is the hour. Our streets are in mourning, tears are falling at every fireside, and under the chastisement of this Rebellion we have almost come up to the point of conceding this great, this all-important right of suffrage. I fear that if we fail to do it now, if abolitionists fail to press it now, we may not see, for centuries to come, the same disposition that exists at this moment. (Applause.) Hence, I say, now is the time to press this right.

It may be asked, "Why do you want it? Some men have got along very well without it. Women have not this right." Shall we justify one wrong by another? That is a sufficient answer. Shall we at this moment justify the deprivation of the negro of the right to vote, because some one else is deprived of that privilege? I hold that women, as well as men, have the right to vote (applause), and my heart and my voice go with the movement to extend suffrage to woman; but that question rests upon another basis than that on which our right rests. We may be asked, I say, why we want it. I will tell you why we want it. We want it because it is our *right*, first of all. (Applause.) No class of men can, without insulting their own nature, be content with any deprivation of their rights. We want it, again, as a means for educating our race. Men are so constituted that they derive their conviction of their own possibilities largely from the estimate formed of them by others. If nothing is expected of a people, that people will find it difficult to contradict that expectation. By depriving us of suffrage, you affirm our incapacity to form an intelligent judgment respecting public men and public measures; you declare before the world that we are unfit to exercise the elective franchise, and by this means lead us to undervalue ourselves, to put a low estimate upon ourselves, and to feel that we have no possibilities like other men. Again, I want the elective franchise, for one, as a colored man, because ours is a peculiar government, based upon a peculiar idea, and that idea is universal suffrage. If I were in a monarchical government, or an autocratic or aristocratic government, where the few bore rule and the many were subject, there would be no special stigma resting upon me, because I did not exercise the elective fran-chise. It would do me no great violence. Mingling with the mass, I should partake of the strength of the mass; I should be supported by the mass, and I should have the same in-centives to endeavor with the mass of my fellow-men; it would be no particular burden, no particular deprivation; but here, where universal suffrage is the rule, where that is the fundamental idea of the Government, to rule us out is to make us an exception, to brand us with the stigma of inferiority, and to invite to our heads the missiles of those about us; therefore, I want the franchise for the black man.

There are, however, other reasons, not derived from any consideration merely of our rights, but arising out of the condition of the South, and of the country—considerations which have already been referred to by Mr. Phillips—considerations which must arrest the attention of statesmen. I believe that when the tall heads of this Rebellion shall have been swept down, as they will be swept down, when the [Jefferson] Davises and [Robert] Toombses and [Alexander] Stephenses, and others who are leading in this Rebellion shall have been blotted out, there will be this rank undergrowth of treason, to which reference has been made, growing up there, and interfering with, and thwarting the quiet operation of the Federal Government in those States. You will see those trai-tors handing down, from sire to son, the same malignant spirit which they have mani-fested, and which they are now exhibiting, with malicious hearts, broad blades, and bloody hands in the field, against our sons and brothers. That spirit will still remain;

and whoever sees the Federal Government extended over those Southern States will see that Government in a strange land, and not only in a strange land, but in an enemy's land. A post-master of the United States in the South will find himself surrounded by a hostile spirit; a collector in a Southern port will find himself surrounded by a hostile spirit; a United States marshal or United States judge will be surrounded there by a hostile element. That enmity will not die out in a year, will not die out in an age. The Federal Government will be looked upon in those States precisely as the Governments of Austria and France are looked upon in Italy at the present moment. They will endeavor to circumvent, they will endeavor to destroy, the peaceful operation of this Government. Now, where will you find the strength to counterbalance this spirit, if you do not find it in the negroes of the South? They are your friends, and have always been your friends. They were your friends even when the Government did not regard them as such. They comprehended the genius of this war before you did. It is a significant fact, it is a marvellous fact, it seems almost to imply a direct interposition of Providence, that this war, which began in the interest of slavery on both sides, bids fair to end in the interest of liberty on both sides. (Applause.) It was begun, I say, in the interest of slavery on both sides. The South was fighting to take slavery out of the Union, and the North fighting to keep it in the Union; the South fighting to get it beyond the limits of the United-States Constitution, and the North fighting to retain it within those limits; the South fighting for new guarantees, and the North fighting for the old guarantees;—both despising the negro, both insulting the negro. Yet, the negro, apparently endowed with wisdom from on high, saw more clearly the end from the beginning than we did. When [William] Seward said the status of no man in the country would be changed by the war, the negro did not believe him. (Applause.) When our generals sent their underlings in shoulder-straps to hunt the flying negro back from our lines into the jaws of slavery, from which he had escaped, the negroes thought that a mistake had been made, and that the intentions of the Government had not been rightly understood by our officers in shoulder-straps, and they continued to come into our lines, threading their way through bogs and fens, over briers and thorns, fording streams, swimming rivers, bringing us tidings as to the safe path to march, and pointing out the dangers that threatened us. They are our only friends in the South, and we should be true to them in this their trial hour, and see to it that they have the elective franchise.

I know that we are inferior to you in some things—virtually inferior. We walk about among you like dwarfs among giants. Our heads are scarcely seen above the great sea of humanity. The Germans are superior to us; the Irish are superior to us; the Yankees are superior to us (laughter); they can do what we cannot, that is, what we have not hitherto been allowed to do. But while I make this admission, I utterly deny that we are originally, or naturally, or practically, or in any way, or in any important sense, inferior to anybody on this globe. (Loud applause.) This charge of inferiority is an old dodge. It has been made available for oppression on many occasions. It is only about six centuries since the blue-eyed and fair-haired Anglo-Saxons were considered inferior by the haughty Normans, who once trampled upon them. If you read the history of the Norman Conquest, you will find that this proud Anglo-Saxon was once looked upon as of coarser clay than his Norman master, and might be found in the highways and byways of old England laboring with a brass collar on his neck, and the name of his master marked upon it. *You* were down then! (Laughter and applause.) You are up now. I am glad you are up, and I want you to be glad to help us up also. (Applause.)

The story of our inferiority is an old dodge, as I have said; for wherever men oppress their fellows, wherever they enslave them, they will endeavor to find the needed apology for such enslavement and oppression in the character of the people oppressed and enslaved. When we wanted, a few years ago, a slice of Mexico, it was hinted that the Mexicans were an inferior race, that the old Castilian blood had become so weak that it would scarcely run down hill, and that Mexico needed the long, strong and beneficent arm of the Anglo-Saxon care extended over it. We said that it was necessary to its salvation, and a part of the "manifest destiny" of this Republic, to extend our arm over that dilapidated government. So, too, when Russia wanted to take possession of a part of the Ottoman Empire, the Turks were "an inferior race." So, too, when England wants to set the heel of her power more firmly in the quivering heart of old Ireland, the Celts are an "inferior race." So, too, the negro, when he is to be robbed of any right which is justly his, is an "inferior man." It is said that we are ignorant; I admit it. But if we know enough to be hung, we know enough to vote. If the negro knows enough to pay taxes to support the government, he knows enough to vote; taxation and representation should go together. If he knows enough to shoulder a musket and fight for the flag, fight for the government, he knows enough to vote. If he knows as much when he is sober as an Irishman knows when drunk, he knows enough to vote, on good American principles. (Laughter and applause.)

But I was saying that you needed a counterpoise in the persons of the slaves to the enmity that would exist at the South after the Rebellion is put down. I hold that the American people are bound, not only in self-defence, to extend this right to the freedmen of the South, but they are bound by their love of country, and by all their regard for the future safety of those Southern States, to do this—to do it as a measure essential to the preservation of peace there. But I will not dwell upon this. I put it to the American sense of honor. The honor of a nation is an important thing. It is said in the Scriptures, "What doth it profit a man if he gain the whole world and lose his own soul?" It may be said, also, What doth it profit a nation if it gain the whole world, but lose its honor? I hold that the American government has taken upon itself a solemn obligation of honor, to see that this war—let it be long or let it be short, let it cost much or let it cost little—that this war shall not cease until every freedman at the South has the right to vote. (Applause.) It has bound itself to it. What have you asked the black men of the South, the black men of the whole country, to do? Why, you have asked them to incur the deadly enmity of their masters, in order to befriend you and to befriend this Government. You have asked us to call down, not only upon ourselves, but upon our children's children, the deadly hate of the entire Southern people. You have called upon us to turn our backs upon our masters, to abandon their cause and espouse yours; to turn against the South and in favor of the North; to shoot down the Confederacy and uphold the flag—the American flag. You have called upon us to expose ourselves to all the subtle machinations of their malignity for all time. And now, what do you propose to do when you come to make peace? To reward your enemies, and trample in the dust your friends? Do you intend to sacrifice the very men who have come to the rescue of your banner in the South, and incurred the lasting displeasure of their masters thereby? Do you intend to sacrifice them and reward your enemies? Do you mean to give your enemies the right to vote, and take it away from your friends? Is that wise policy? Is that honorable? Could American honor withstand such a blow? I do not believe you will do it. I think you will see to it that we have the right to vote. There is something too mean in looking upon the negro, when you are in trouble, as a citizen, and when you are free from trouble, as an alien. When this nation was in trouble, in its early struggles, it looked upon the negro as a citizen. In 1776 he was a citizen. At the time of the formation of the Constitution the negro had the right to vote in eleven States out of the old thirteen. In your trouble you have made us citizens. In 1812 Gen. [Andrew] Jackson addressed us as citizens—"fellow-citizens." He wanted us to fight. We were citizens then! And now, when you come to frame a conscription bill, the negro is a citizen again. He has been a citizen just three times in the history of this government, and it has always been in time of trouble. In time of trouble we are citizens. Shall we be citizens in war, and aliens in peace? Would that be just?

I ask my friends who are apologizing for not insisting upon this right, where can the black man look, in this country, for the assertion of this right, if he may not look to the Massachusetts Anti-Slavery Society? Where under the whole heavens can he look for sympathy, in asserting this right, if he may not look to this platform? Have you lifted us up to a certain height to see that we are men, and then are any disposed to leave us there, without seeing that we are put in possession of all our rights? We look naturally to this platform for the assertion of all our rights, and for this one especially. I understand the anti-slavery societies of this country to be based on two principles,— first, the freedom of the blacks of this country; and, second, the elevation of them. Let me not be misunderstood here. I am not asking for sympathy at the hands of abolitionists, sympathy at the hands of any. I think the American people are disposed often to be generous rather than just. I look over this country at the present time, and I see Educational Societies, Sanitary Commissions, Freedmen's Associations, and the like,— all very good: but in regard to the colored people there is always more that is benevolent, I perceive, than just, manifested towards us. What I ask for the negro is not benevolence, not pity, not sympathy, but simply *justice*. (Applause.) The American people have always been anxious to know what they shall do with us. Gen. Banks was distressed with solicitude as to what he should do with the negro. Everybody has asked the question, and they learned to ask it early of the abolitionists, "What shall we do with the negro?" I have had but one answer from the beginning. Do nothing with us! Your doing with us has already played the mischief with us. Do nothing with us! If the apples will not remain on the tree of their own strength, if they are worm-eaten at the core, if they are early ripe and disposed to fall, let them fall! I am not for tying or fastening them on the tree in any way, except by nature's plan, and if they will not stay there, let them fall. And if the negro cannot stand on his own legs, let him fall also. All I ask is, give him a chance to stand on his own legs! Let him alone! If you see him on his way to school, let him alone,—don't disturb him! If you see him going to the dinner-table at a hotel, let him go! If you see him going to the ballot-box, let him alone,—don't disturb him! (Applause.) If you see him going into a work-shop, just let him alone,— your interference is doing him a positive injury. Gen. Banks's "preparation" is of a piece with this attempt to prop up the negro. Let him fall if he cannot stand alone! If the negro cannot live by the line of eternal justice, so beautifully pictured to you in the illustration used by Mr. Phillips, the fault will not be yours, it will be his who made the negro, and established that line for his government. (Applause.) Let him live or die by that. If you will only untie his hands, and give him a chance, I think he will live. He will work as readily for himself as the white man. A great many delusions have been swept away by this war. One was, that the negro would not work; he has proved his ability to work. Another was, that the negro would not fight; that he possessed only the most sheepish attributes of humanity; was a perfect lamb, or an "Uncle Tom"; disposed to take off his coat whenever required, fold his hands, and be whipped by anybody who wanted to whip him. But the war has proved that there is a great deal of human nature in the negro, and that "he will fight," as Mr. Quincy, our President, said, in earlier days than these, "when there is a reasonable probability of his whipping anybody." (Laughter and applause.)

The Ex-Slaves Should Have Land

MR. [RICHARD H.] CAIN: I offer this resolution with good intentions. I believe that there is need for immediate relief to the poor people of the State. I know from my experience among the people, there is a pressing need of some measures to meet the wants of the utterly destitute. The gentleman [C. P. Leslie] says that it will only take money out of the Treasury. Well, that is the intention. I do not expect to get it anywhere else. I expect to get the money, if at all, through the Treasury of the United States, or some other department. It certainly must come out of the Government. I believe such an appropriation would remove a great many of the difficulties now in the State and do a vast amount of good to poor people. It may be that we will not get it, but that will not debar us from asking. It is our privilege and right. Other Conventions have asked from Congress appropriations. Georgia and other States have sent in their petitions. One has asked for $30,000,000 to be appropriated to the Southern States. I do not see any inconsistency in the proposition presented by myself.

MR. C. P. LESLIE: Suppose I should button up my coat and march up to your house and ask you for money or provisions, when you had none to give, what would you think of me.

MR. CAIN: You would do perfectly right to run the chance of getting something to eat. This is a measure of relief to those thousands of freed people who now have no lands of their own. I believe the possession of lands and homesteads is one of the best means by which a people is made industrious, honest and advantageous to the State. I believe it is a fact well known, that over three hundred thousand men, women and children are homeless, landless. The abolition of slavery has thrown these people upon their own resources. How are they to live? I know the philosopher of the *New York Tribune* says, "root hog or die"; but in the meantime we ought to have some place to root. My proposition is simply to give the hog some place to root. I believe if the proposition is sent to Congress, it will certainly receive the attention of our friends. I believe the whole country is desirous to see that this State shall return to the Union in peace and quiet, and that every inhabitant of the State shall be made industrious and profitable to the State.

Proceedings of the Constitutional Convention of South Carolina, 1868 (New York: Arno Press, 1968), pp. 378–424.

I am opposed to this Bureau system.[2] I want a system adopted that will do away with the Bureau, but I cannot see how it can be done unless the people have homes. As long as people are working on shares and contracts, and at the end of every year are in debt, so long will they and the country suffer. But give them a chance to buy lands, and they become steady, industrious men. That is the reason I desire to bring this money here and to assist them to buy lands. . . .

I do not desire to have a foot of land in this State confiscated. I want every man to stand upon his own character. I want these lands purchased by the government, and the people afforded an opportunity to buy from the government. I believe every man ought to carve out for himself a character and position in this life. I believe every man ought to be made to work by some means or other, and if he does not, he must go down. . . . I want to have the satisfaction of showing that the freedmen are as capable and willing to work as any men on the face of the earth. This measure will save the State untold expenses. I believe there are hundreds of persons in the jail and penitentiary cracking rock to-day who have all the instincts of honesty, and who, had they an opportunity of making a living, would never have been found in such a place. I think if Congress will accede to our request, we shall be benefited beyond measure, and save the State from taking charge of paupers, made such by not having the means to earn a living for themselves. . . .

MR. C. P. LESLIE: . . . I assert that time will prove that the petition offered, and the addresses made here to-day, were most inopportune. These addresses have been listened to by a large concourse of spectators, and have held out to them that within a very short time they are to get land. We all know that the colored people want land. Night and day they think and dream of it. It is their all in all. As these men retire from the hall and go home, the first thing they do is to announce to the people "joy on earth, and good will to all mankind." We are all going to have a home. . . . And when I know as they know, that without land a race of people, four millions in number, travelling up and down the earth without a home are suffering, I cannot but denounce those who would, for political purposes, add to their misery by raising expectations that could never be realized. . . .

Let us have a little more light upon the subject. Parson French, who, it is well known, has the welfare of the colored people at heart, did go to Washington and portrayed to leading Senators and members of Congress the terrible predicament of the colored people in the State. He said that cotton had sold so low that all the people were poverty stricken. The white people, he told them, were not able to plant, and there being no necessity to employ laborers, the colored people were turned out of house and home, and he begged them to loan the people, or the State, a million of

---

[2] Cain probably means the work of the Freedmen's Bureau in negotiating labor contracts for the ex-slaves, contracts that were difficult to enforce—ED.

dollars. Their answer was, "Mr. French, for God's sake, send up no petitions for money, for we cannot give one dollar." . . .

MR. F[RANCIS] L. CARDOZO: . . . The poor freedmen were induced, by many Congressmen even, to expect confiscation. They held out the hope of confiscation. [Union] General [William Tecumseh] Sherman did confiscate, gave the lands to the freedmen; and if it were not for President Johnson, they would have them now. The hopes of the freedmen have not been realized, and I do not think that asking for a loan of one million, to be paid by a mortgage upon the land, will be half as bad as has been supposed. I have been told by the Assistant Commissioner that he has been doing on a private scale what this petition proposes to do. I say every opportunity for helping the colored man should be seized upon. I think the adoption of this measure will do honor to the Convention. We should certainly vote for some measure of relief for the colored men, as we have to the white men, who mortgaged their property to perpetuate slavery, and whom they have liberated from their bonds.

MR. N. G. PARKER: I am glad that the gentleman who has just taken his seat has distinctly laid down the proposition that any member who votes against this petition votes against the colored man. I am a friend to the colored man, and he knows it. I have a record extending back for twenty years that shows it. . . .

I tell you, Mr. President, that the destitution that prevails this winter in those snow clad [Northern and Western] States is greater than it has ever been before. Thousands, yes millions, are out of employment, and what is the cause of it. I cannot stop now to elaborate the causes, but I will only briefly allude to them. War and its results are directly the cause of it. One of the results of the war, and the principal one, was the overthrow of slavery and tyranny in the Southern States; this was the good result of it; but the expense it caused the nation to do this, and the debt it incurred, and the overthrow of the labor system and consequent disturbance of trade and commerce, was the immediate evil. The burdensome taxation which followed is another principle cause of distress which now prevails in the Northern and Western States. The fact is patent that all the manufacturing States need aid; and let me tell you if the Congress of the United States grants additional aid to any of the unreconstructed States, for anything further than to perfect the reconstruction already half consummated, and the support of the Military and the Freedmen's Bureau, that in my opinion such a howl will go up as never was heard before, and I for one, would despair of success.

Our friends are trembling at Washington to-day, and all over the country, lest New Hampshire should cast a Democratic vote at her approaching election. I am of the opinion that if Congress should pass the appropriation called for just at this particular time, that every State from Maine to California would roll up such a Democrat vote in the coming election that was never heard of, or dreamt of, by the most ardent Democrat in this country. The result of the elections for the last year should not be unheeded.

Where would be our reconstruction if Andrew Johnson and the Democratic party had the handling of us? . . .

The Treasury of the United States has already as many drafts upon it as it can well bear. They have no money to purchase lands in South Carolina to sell on a credit—it is asking too much. Look at the almost overwhelming debt of the nation, and would you colored men, or white men, seek to increase it? For what was it contracted? and what keeps the expenses of Government today so large? It was contracted to make you free, and it is continually increased to preserve, protect and defend your freedom.

There never was a more liberal and humane government, nor never one that made such herculian [sic] efforts to retrieve the past as she has made and is making. We cannot ask her to do more than she is doing. There is such a thing as disgusting our friends. Do not let us weary them. If she will continue to afford us the protection she has afforded us in the past three years, if she will continue to the end in sustaining the reconstruction she commenced, if she will sustain the Freedmen's Bureau as long as it is a necessity, and give us the military necessary to protect and defend us, in God's name let us be satisfied. . . .

MR. R. H. CAIN: This measure, if carried out, therefore, will meet a want which the Bureau never can meet. A man may have rations today and not tomorrow, but when he gets land and a homestead, and is once fixed on that land, he never will want to go to the Commissary again. It is said that I depicted little farms by the roadside, chickens roosting on the fence, and all those poetical beauties. . . . I prefer this to seeing strong men working for the paltry sum of five or ten dollars a month, and some for even three dollars a month. How can a man live at that rate. I hate the contract system as I hate the being of whom my friend from Orangeburg (Mr. [Benjamin F.] Randolph) spoke last week (the devil). It has ruined the people. After fifty men have gone on a plantation, worked the whole year at raising twenty thousand bushels of rice, and then go to get their one-third, by the time they get through the division, after being charged by the landlord twenty-five or thirty cents a pound for bacon, two or three dollars for a pair of brogans that costs sixty cents, for living that costs a mere song, two dollars a bushel for corn that can be bought for one dollar; after I say, these people have worked the whole season, and at the end make up their accounts, they find themselves in debt. . . . I want to see a change in this country. Instead of the colored people being always penniless, I want to see them coming in with their mule teams and ox teams. I want to see them come with their corn and potatoes and exchange for silks and satins. I want to see school houses and churches in every parish and township. I want to see children coming forth to enjoy life as it ought to be enjoyed. This people know nothing of what is good and best for mankind until they get homesteads and enjoy them.

With these remarks, I close. I hope the Convention will vote for the proposition. Let us send up our petition. The right to petition is a jealous right. It was a right guaranteed to the Barons of England. The American people have always been jealous of that right, and regarded it as sacred and inviolate. That right we propose to maintain. It is said here that some high officers are opposed to it. I do not care who is opposed to it. It is none of their business. I do not care whether General [Robert K.] Scott, General [Ulysses S.] Grant or General anybody else is opposed to it, we will petition in spite of them. I appeal to the delegates to pass this resolution. It will do no harm if it does no good, and I am equally confident that some gentleman will catch what paddy gave the drum when they go back to their constituents.

THE EX-SLAVES CRAVE EDUCATION

The Desire of the Blacks for Education

Senate Ex. Doc. no. 27, 39 Cong., 1 Sess. Report of J. W. Alvord, Superintendent of Schools for the Freedmen's Bureau

January 1, 1866

A general desire for education is everywhere manifested. In some instances, as in Halifax county [Virginia], very good schools were found taught and paid for by the colored people themselves. Said a gentleman to me, "I constantly see in the streets and on the door-steps opposite my dwelling groups of little negroes studying their spelling-books." . . .

Not only are individuals seen at study, and under the most untoward circumstances, but in very many places I have found what I will call "native schools," often rude and very imperfect, but there they are, a group, perhaps, of all ages, trying to learn. Some young man, some woman, or old preacher, in cellar, or shed, or corner of a negro meeting-house, with the alphabet in hand, or a torn spelling-book, is their teacher. All are full of enthusiasm with the new knowledge the book is imparting to them.

Freedmen's Bureau Schools in North Carolina

Senate Ex. Doc. no. 6, 39 Cong., 2 Sess., p. 104. Report of Gen[eral] John C. Robinson of the Freedmen's Bureau

1866

It is no unfrequent occurrence to witness in the same rooms, and pursuing the same studies, the child and parent—youth and gray hairs—all eagerly grasping for that by which, obtained, they are intellectually regenerated. . . .

As an evidence of the great interest manifested for acquiring knowledge, an instance, probably never before equalled in the history of education, is to be found in one of the schools of this State, where side by side sat representatives of four generations in a direct line, viz.: a child six years old, her mother, grandmother, and great-grandmother, the latter over 75 years of age. All commenced their alphabet together, and each one can read the Bible fluently.

Walter L. Fleming, ed., *Documentary History of Reconstruction: Political, Military, and Industrial, 1865 to the Present Time* (Cleveland: The Arthur H. Clark Company, 1907), vol. 2, pp. 182–83.

Night schools have met with gratifying success, and are eagerly sought for by those whose labors are of such a character as to prevent their attendance during the day. . . .

Sunday schools have been established at many points where teachers reside. . . . It is evident much good has been accomplished by their establishment, and no estimate can be made of the beneficial results of their full development.

An Appeal for Protection from the KKK (1871)*

To the Senate and House of Representative in Congress assembled:

We the colored citizens of Frankfort and vicinity do this day memorialize your honorable bodies upon the condition of affairs now existing in this the state of Kentucky.

We would respectfully state that life, liberty, and property are unprotected among the colored race of this state. Organized bands of desperate and lawless men, mainly composed of soldiers of the late Rebel armies, armed, disciplined, and disguised, and bound by oath and secret obligations, have by force, terror, and violence subverted all civil society among colored people, thus utterly rendering insecure the safety of persons and property, overthrowing all those rights which are the primary basis and objects of the government which are expressly guaranteed to us by the Constitution of the United States as amended.

We believe you are not familiar with the description of the Ku Klux Klan's riding nightly over the county, going from county to county, and in the county towns spreading terror wherever they go by robbing, whipping, ravishing, and killing our people without provocation, compelling colored people to break the ice and bathe in the chilly waters of the Kentucky River.

The legislature has adjourned; they refused to enact any laws to suppress Ku Klux disorder. We regard them as now being licensed to continue their dark and bloody deeds under cover of the dark night. They refuse to allow us to testify in the state courts where a white man is concerned. We find their deeds are perpetrated only upon colored men and white Republicans. We also find that for our services to the government and our race we have become the special object of hatred and persecution at the hands of the Democratic Party.

Our people are driven from their homes in the great numbers, having no redress, only the U.S. courts, which is in many cases unable to reach them. We would state that we have been law-abiding citizens, pay our tax, and, in many parts of the state, our people have been driven from the polls—refused the right to vote. Many have been slaughtered while attempting to vote; we ask how long is this state of things to last.

We appeal to you as law-abiding citizens to enact some laws that will protect us and that will enable us to exercise the rights of citizens. We see that the senator from this state denies there being organized bands of desperadoes in the state; for information we

*National Archives, Record Group 46, Records of the U.S. Senate Memorial. . . .April 11, 1871 (42 Congress).

lay before you a number of violent acts [that] occurred during his administration. Although he, Stevenson, says half-dozen instances of violence did occur, these are not more than one-half the acts that have occurred.

The Democratic Party has here a political organization composed only of Democrats not a single Republican can join them. Where many of these acts have been committed, it has been proven that they were the men, done with arms from the state arsenal. We pray you will take some steps to remedy these evils.

Done by a committee of grievances appointed at a meeting of all the colored citizens of Frankfort and vicinity.

CHAPTER 2

Industrial Growth

During the thirty-five years following the Civil War, the United States became the world's richest and most productive industrial nation. The drive to industrial supremacy was not effortless or untroubled, however. It was accompanied by greed, corruption, and exploitation; it also threatened older patterns of living, degraded the physical environment, and weakened traditional political values.

Yet most Americans of the day probably thought of the sweeping economic and social changes of that era as progress. Today, although the beneficiaries of our predecessors' sacrifices, we are perhaps more skeptical. Do our greater doubts derive from our ability to see further and clearer than our forebears? Or have we, without knowing what it was really like, romanticized preindustrial rural life?

There was a vast churning of American population after 1865. As some Americans moved west, others moved to the cities. Urban growth during the half-century following the Civil War was spectacular. In 1870 a little over a quarter of all Americans lived in cities; in 1920 over half. In sheer numbers this meant an increase from 10 million to over 54 million city dwellers.

These people came from several sources. City folk begat city folk; many urbanites were the children of urbanites. Most, however, were newcomers, people born in rural communities who moved to the cities. They came from many parts of the world. One giant contingent consisted of native-born citizens from America's own farms and villages. Most of the remainder came from Europe's farms and villages and, after about 1890, predominantly from the rural areas of southern and eastern Europe.

The mass migration to the cities was part of the great shift in the Atlantic world's economy from agriculture to commerce and industry. Most of the newcomers were drawn by the economic advantages of the cities over their rural homes. Since the movement continued over many decades, we must assume that the urban edge in jobs and living standards persisted year after year.

Yet this is not to say that the newcomers found their new urban environment ideal. The cities of America were less-than-perfect places to live. To use a modern phrase, they had a "deficient infrastructure," especially early in this period. Housing, sanitation, health, and transportation facilities could not meet the surging demand. The cities' institutions also were imperfect. City governments were feeble and corrupt. They lacked the power to do what was needed, and what they did do was often accomplished at high cost. The cities were also deficient in civility. Anonymity, diversity, and poverty generated crime, disorder, and social breakdown. Urban law authorities were often unable to ensure safety for life and property. Churches and philanthropic organizations tried to help but were often pushed beyond their capacities.

Yet at worst Americans had mixed feelings about their cities, for despite their drawbacks, they also had advantages. What follows is an assortment of contemporary views, pro and con, of cities and city life in the period 1870–1920.

In the following selections, Americans who lived through the late nineteenth-century surge of growth describe their experiences or evaluate the processes that swept them along. In considering what these people said, remember that no one individual could see more than a tiny part of what was a truly massive event. Where some workers may have experienced hardship, for example, others may have found the good life. (In this connection, see if you can determine from the work of economic historians whether income per person in America was growing or declining in this period. You may also want to know what was happening to "real" annual wages, that is, the total buying power of wage earners' yearly wages.)

2.1 CONCENTRATED WEALTH (1889, 1886)

American educated and middle classes tended to support the economic changes occurring in the late nineteenth century. Optimistic acceptances of drastic economic inequality could easily be rationalized through the highly popular, conventional faith in "social Darwinism." In the following selection, Andrew Carnegie, a self-made man who rose from humble origins to become the wealthiest individual in the world, explains why he supports the system. His reasoning reflects the main tenets of this prevalent ideology. What are they? How do they connect to other themes of American individualism and freedom? Do they foreshadow present-day ideologies on economics? Yet not all agreed. Former President Rutherford B. Hayes and a small number of social activists feared the concentration of wealth in the hands of a few. They also expressed concerns that conditions for the poor were growing worse. Some even argued that it was morally unacceptable for a society containing so much wealth to allow so many to live in destitution and severe poverty.

WEALTH

Andrew Carnegie

Objections to the foundations upon which society is based are not in order, because the condition of the race is better with these than with any others which have been tried. Of the effect of any new substitutes proposed we cannot be sure. The Socialist or

Andrew Carnegie, "Wealth," *North American Review*, June, 1889.

Anarchist who seeks to overturn present conditions is to be regarded as attacking the foundation upon which civilization itself rests, for civilization took its start from the day when the capable, industrious workman said to his incompetent and lazy fellow, "If thou dost not sow, thou shalt not reap," and thus ended primitive Communism by separating the drones from the bees. One who studies this subject will soon be brought face to face with the conclusion that upon the sacredness of property civilization itself depends—the right of the laborer to his hundred dollars in the savings bank, and equally the legal right of the millionaire to his millions. To those who propose to substitute Communism for this intense Individualism, the answer therefore is: The race has tried that. All progress from that barbarous day to the present time has resulted from its displacement. Not evil, but good, has come to the race from the accumulation of wealth by those who have had the ability and energy to produce it. . . .

We start, then, with a condition of affairs under which the best interests of the race are promoted, but which inevitably gives wealth to the few. Thus far, accepting conditions as they exist, the situation can be surveyed and pronounced good. The question then arises, . . . What is the proper mode of administering wealth after the laws upon which civilization is founded have thrown it into the hands of the few?

There are but three modes in which surplus wealth can be disposed of. It can be left to the families of the decedents or it can be bequeathed for public purposes; or finally, it can be administered during their lives by its possessors. Under the first and second modes most of the wealth of the world that has reached the few has hitherto been applied. Let us in turn consider each of these modes. The first is the most injudicious. . . . Why should men leave great fortunes to their children? If this is done from affection, is it not misguided affection? Observation teaches that, generally speaking, it is not well for the children that they should be so burdened. Neither is it well for the state. Beyond providing for the wife and daughters moderate sources of income, and very moderate allowances indeed, if any, for the sons, men may well hesitate, for it is no longer questionable that great sums bequeathed often work more for the injury than for the good of the recipients. . . .

It is not suggested that men who have failed to educate their sons to earn a livelihood shall cast them adrift in poverty. If any man has seen fit to rear his sons with a view to their living idle lives, or, what is highly commendable, has instilled in them the sentiment that they are in a position to labor for public ends without reference to pecuniary considerations, then, of course, the duty of the parent is to see that such are provided for *in moderation*. There are instances of millionaires' sons unspoiled by wealth, who, being rich, still perform great services in the community. Such are the very salt of the earth, as valuable as, unfortunately, they are rare. It is not the exception, however, but the rule, that men must regard; and, looking at the usual result of enormous sums conferred upon legatees, the thoughtful man must shortly say, "I would as soon leave my son a curse as the almighty dollar," and admit to himself that it is not the welfare of the children, but family pride, which inspires these enormous legacies.

As to the second mode, that of leaving wealth at death for public uses, it may be said that this is only a means for the disposal of wealth, provided a man is content to wait until he is dead before he becomes of much good in the world. . . .

There remains, then, only one mode of using great fortunes; but in this we have the true antidote for the temporary unequal distribution of wealth, the reconciliation of the rich and the poor—a reign of harmony. . . . Under its sway we shall have an ideal state, in which the surplus wealth of the few will become, in the best sense, the property of the many, because administered for the common good; and this wealth, passing through the hands of the few, can be made a much more potent force for the elevation of our race than if it had been distributed in small sums to the people themselves. Even the poorest can be made to see this, and to agree that great sums gathered by some of their fellow-citizens and spent for public purposes, from which the masses reap the principal benefit, are more valuable to them than if scattered among them through the course of many years.

ON CONCENTRATED WEALTH (1886)

Rutherford B. Hayes

January 22, 1886. Friday. How to distribute more equally the property of our country is a question we (Theodore Clapp and I) considered yesterday. We ought not to allow a permanent aristocracy of inherited wealth to grow up in our country. How would it answer to limit the amount that could be left to any one person by will or otherwise? What should be the limit? Let no one receive from another more than the law gives to the chief justice, to the general of the Army, or to the president of the Senate. Let the income of the property transmitted equal this, say $10,000 to $20,000. If after distributing on this principle there remains undistributed part of the estate, let it go to the public. The object is to secure a distribution of great estates to prevent accumulation.

January 24. Sunday. The question for the country now is how to secure a more equal distribution of property among the people. There can be no republican institutions with vast masses of property permanently in a few hands, and large masses of voters without property. To begin the work, as a first step, prevent large estates from passing, by wills or by inheritance or by corporations, into the hands of a single man. Let no man get by inheritance or by will more than will produce at 4 percent interest an income equal to the salary paid to the chief justice, to the general of the Army, or to the highest officer of the Navy—say an income of $15,000 per year or an estate of $500,000. . . .

March 17. Wednesday. I go to Toledo to attend the celebration of St. Patrick's Day by Father Hannan's people. I shall talk to the text, "America, the Land of the Free and the Home of the Brave," with special reference to Father Hannan's motto "Religion, Education, Temperance, Industry"; and this again in behalf of such measures and laws as will give to every workingman a reasonable hope that by industry, temperance, and frugality he can secure a home for himself and his family, education for his children, and a comfortable support for old age.

March 18. Thursday. At Toledo yesterday and until 1 P.M. today. At Father Hannan's St. patrick's Institute last evening. I spoke of the danger from riches *in* a few hands, and the poverty of the masses. The capital and labor question. General Comly regards the speech as important. My point is that free government cannot long endure if property is largely in a few hands and large masses of the people are unable to earn homes, education, and a support in old age. . . .

March 19. Friday.   No man, however benevolent, liberal, and wise, can use a large fortune so that it will do half as much good in the world as it would if it were divided into moderate sums and in the hands of workmen who had earned it by industry and frugality. The piling up of estates often does great and conspicuous good. Such men as Benjamin Franklin and Peter Cooper knew how to use wealth. But no man does with accumulated wealth so much good as the same amount would do in many hands.

March 20. Saturday.   The funeral of General Devereux (at Cleveland today) was largely attended. With General Leggett, General Barnett, and General Elwell, and many others of the Loyal Legion—those named as honorary pallbearers—saw and heard all that belonged to the impressive funeral. The leading traits of General Devereux were unusual tact in dealing with all sorts of men and all sorts of difficult questions, courage, and integrity. The president of the New York Central, Mr. (Chauncey M.) Depew, introduced me to Cornelius Vanderbilt. I could not help regarding him with sympathy. One of our Republican kings—one of our railroad kings. Think of the inconsistency of allowing such vast and irresponsible power as he possesses to be vested by law in the hands of one man!

March 26. Friday.   Am I mistaken in thinking that we are drawing near the time when we must decide to limit and control great wealth, corporations, and the like, or resort to a strong military government? Is this the urgent question? I read in the (Cleveland) *Leader* of this morning that Rev. Dr. Washington Gladden lectured in Cleveland last night on "Capital and Labor." Many good things were said. The general drift and spirit were good. But he leaves out our railroad system. Shall the railroads govern the country, or shall the people govern the railroads? Shall the interest of railroad kings be chiefly regarded, or shall the interest of the people be paramount?

May 12.   On the labor question, my position is: 1. The previous question always must be in any popular excitement *the supremacy of law.* All lawless violence must be suppressed *instantly, with overwhelming force and at all hazards.* To hesitate or tamper with it is a fatal mistake. *Justice, humanity, and safety* all require this. 2. I agree that labor does not get its fair share of the wealth it creates. The Sermon on the Mount, the Golden Rule, the Declaration of Independence all require extensive reforms to the end that labor may be so rewarded that the workingman can, with temperance, industry, and thrift, *own a home, educate his children, and lay up a support for old age.* 3. The United States must begin to deal with the whole subject. I approve heartily of President Cleveland's message and so said at the great soldiers' meeting at Cleveland.

February 25, 1887. Friday.   As to pensions I would say our Union soldiers fought in the divinest war that was ever waged. Our war did more for our country than any other war ever achieved for any other country. It did more for the world, more for mankind, than any other war in all history. It gave to those who remained at home and to those who come after it in our country opportunities, prosperity, wealth, a future, such as no war ever before conferred on any part of the human race.

No soldier who fought in that war on the right side nor his widow nor his orphans ought ever to be forced to choose between starvation and the poorhouse. Lincoln in his last inaugural address—just before the war closed, when the last enlistments were going on—pledged the nation "to care for him who hath borne the battle and for his widow and orphans." Let that sacred pledge be sacredly kept.

December 4. Sunday.   In church it occurred to me that it is time for the public to hear that the giant evil and danger in this country, the danger which transcends all others, is the vast wealth owned or controlled by a few persons. Money is power. In Congress, in state legislatures, in city councils, in the courts, in the political conventions, in the press, in the pulpit, in the circles of the educated and the talented its influence is growing greater and greater. Excessive wealth in the hands of the few means extreme poverty, ignorance, vice, and wretchedness as the lot of the many. It is not yet time to debate about the remedy.

The previous question is as to the danger—the evil. Let the people be fully informed and convinced as to the evil. Let them earnestly seek the remedy and it will be found. Fully to know the evil is the first step toward reaching its eradication. Henry George is strong when he portrays the rottenness of the present system. We are, to say the least, not yet ready for his remedy. We may reach and remove the difficulty by changes in the laws regulating corporations, descents of property, wills, trusts, taxation, and a host of other important interests, not omitting lands and other property.

2.2   THE INDUSTRIAL WORKER (1885)

Although real wages had been rising for American wage earners in the half-century following the Civil War, they remained low compared to the incomes of the professional and business classes. That gap in itself would undoubtedly have produced social resentment, but there were other aspects of wage earners' lives that also created discontent. The workday was long and mind-deadening, on-the-job health conditions were poor, industrial accidents were frequent, and unemployment was common. Laboring people at times responded to these conditions with strikes and riots. Some also turned to trade unionism to solve their difficulties. A small but significant minority even questioned the validity of private property rights and the basic assumptions of capitalism.

"Report on Illinois Sweatshops" reveals that many industrial workers lived in difficult and dangerous circumstances. The workplace was often hazardous, the workers were exploited, and life beyond the sweatshop was filled with social ills. Nonetheless, they kept coming, often because things were even worse from where they came. In stark contrast to the dire conditions described in the sweatshop report, the last five lines of Emma Lazarus's poem, "The New Colossus," was inscribed on the pedestal of the Statue of Liberty when it opened in 1886. Which of these views presents the most accurate depiction of reality? How do they both tell different components of the same American story?

"REPORT ON ILLINOIS SWEATSHOPS" (1893)

Seventh Biennial Report of the Bureau of Labor Statistics of Illinois

Any inquiry into the occupations of working women in Chicago, or in any other of the larger cities, must lead the inquirer, sooner or later, to the so-called sweating system, under which the manufacture of ready-made clothing is chiefly conducted. The peculiarities of this phase of industrial life are, however, so marked, and have

---

Springfield, 1893, pp. 357–402: "The Sweating System."

recently attracted so much attention, that it has been deemed proper to extend the observations of the bureau in this matter beyond the women employed under this system and to gather whatever facts or figures were available concerning all the shops of this kind, and all the people, both men and women, employed in them in Chicago. This has involved the collection of some memoranda as to the distinctive features of the system as well as the statistics of its present development in this state.

The "sweating system" is one of respectable antiquity and is a surviving remnant of the industrial system which preceded the factory system, when industry was chiefly conducted on the piece-price plan in small shops or the homes of the workers. Machinery developed the modern factory and concerned labor, but in the tailoring trades, the practice of sending out garments, ready-cut, to be made by journeymen at their homes and at a price-per-garment, has survived and is still maintained in custom work, in which the journeyman is still a skilled tailor who makes the whole garment. The modern demand for ready-made clothing in great quantities and of the cheaper grades has, however, led to much subdivision of the labor on garments and, with it, to the substitution of the contractor, or sweater, with groups of employees in separate processes for the individual tailor skilled in all of them.

The odious but expressive name "sweating" has been attached to the business because of its evil nature and consequences. In its worst form, and there are doubtless degrees in its development, it is simply extortion practiced upon people whose environment prevents their escape from it; in other words, it is a deliberate preying upon the month, necessities of the poor. In its economical aspect it is the culmination and final fruit of the competitive system in industry.

In practice, sweating consists of the farming out by competing manufacturers to competing contractors the material for garments, which, in turn, is distributed among competing men and women to be made up. The middleman, or contractor, is the sweater (though he also may be himself subjected to pressure from above) and his employees are the sweated or oppressed. He contracts to make up certain garments, at a given price per piece, and then hires other people to do the work at a less price. His profit lies in the difference between the two prices. In the process he will furnish shop room and machines to some, and allow others, usually the finishers, to take the work to their living and lodging rooms in tenements.

The sweater may be compelled to underbid his fellow contractor in order to get work, but he can count with a degree of certainty on the eagerness of the people who work for him to also underbid each other, so as to leave his margin of profit but little impaired. The system thrives upon the increasing demand for cheap, ready-made clothing, cheap cloaks, and cheap suits for children, which demand springs in turn from the rivalry of competing dealers and producers. Thus each class preys upon the other, and all of them upon the last and weakest.

Such is the logic and the operation of the process called sweating; it is practiced somewhat in other industries, but finds its fullest scope in the garment trade, because the articles can readily, and with comparative safety, be distributed to the shops and abodes of the workers. But the system is not new, except in new countries and new cities, and it is now hardly new in Chicago. . . .

In this country the whole ready-made clothing trade rests upon the sweating system in some of its various forms. From Boston, for many years, garments have been sent throughout New England to be made by the wives and daughters of the country people, but the more recent migration of Poles and Italians to that city has introduced a new form of cheap labor, and much clothing of the poorer grades goes to their shops and is finished in their homes. Recent legislation and tenement inspection has, however, done much to improve sanitary conditions among them and remove much of the danger from infectious diseases.

From Philadelphia, garments are sent into New Jersey and Delaware, as well as throughout the farming districts of Pennsylvania, to be stitched by women. Vast quantities of clothing, such as cotton and woolen shirts and women's underwear, are farmed out under contract to charitable and other institutions, while clothing for the Army and Navy and for the postal service is largely made under the sweating system, both in Philadelphia and Baltimore.

The great center of the clothing trade is, however, in New York City. There, whole streets are reported as having shops or home finishers in every house. It is particularly difficult to ascertain the number of persons thus employed in that city because it is augmented by every shipload of emigrants from Russia, Bohemia, Scandinavia, and Italy, and again reduced by deportations to the West. Sweaters' shops are now scattered even among those villages of Long Island and New Jersey which are easily accessible by ferryboat from New York. No successful check upon the system has yet been accomplished by legislation in that state. A measure recently passed embraces somewhat trenchant provisions, but its results remain as yet to be seen. The reports of the factory inspector reveal a state of things not surpassed by the English reports.

In Chicago, where it dates back scarcely a generation, the sweating system seems to be a direct outgrowth of the factory system; that is, the sweatshops have gradually superseded the manufacturers' shops. It increases, with the demand for cheap clothing, the influx of cheap labor and the consequent subdivision of the processes of manufacture. In the clothing trades in Chicago, three different sorts of shops have been developed, known among the employees as the "inside shops," or those conducted on the factory system by the manufacturers themselves; the "outside shops," or those conducted by the contractors; and the "home shops," or family groups.

In the inside shops the manufacturer deals with his employees through foremen and forewomen instead of contractors. These shops are in large buildings, steam is provided for motive power, the sanitary ordinances are, in a measure, observed, and the establishments, being large and permanent, are known to the municipal authorities and are subject to inspection. Even these shops, in which there is, strictly, no subletting, are pervaded and dominated by the influence of the sweating system. There is but little uniformity of hours, wages, rules, length of season, or proportion of men to women and children. The competition of the outside contractors renders the position of employees constantly more precarious, and the inside shops which thrive are those which approximate most closely to the organization of the sweaters' shops, substituting many subdivisions of labor for the skilled workman.

Formerly, these shops employed cutters, buttonholers and tailors or cloakmakers who did the whole work, taking the garment from the cutter and completing it, doing both machine and handwork. To increase their speed, these skilled hands now have "hand girls" who do the simple sewing put on buttons, draw basting threads, etc.

Formerly, the skilled tailors or cloakmakers constituted a large majority of the employees, but with the growth of the sweating system the cutters alone increase in number and their speed is multiplied by the use of steam machinery. All goods not needed to fill urgent orders are now given direct from the cutters to the sweaters' shops. Some manufacturers have modified their own shops to mere cutters' shops and send all their garments to the contractors; others have found it unprofitable to manufacture for themselves and have resorted to the sweaters entirely. Thus the sweating system strengthens itself and eliminates the clothing factory proper. Very few of these remain, and those which were found are not enumerated as sweating shops.

Substantially all manufacturers employ a number of sweaters who conduct small shops on their own account. These underbid each other to obtain work. They do not make common cause against the manufacturers, either by combining among themselves or by uniting with their employees. On the contrary, they exploit their employees to the utmost to compensate themselves for the exactions of the manufacturers and the competition among themselves.

The economic position of the sweater is anomalous. He has no commercial risks; he gives the manufacturer no considerable security for the goods entrusted to his care, and rarely has more than a wagonload of them in his possession; he pays one week's rent in advance for his shop (which may also be his dwelling) and buys his sewing machines on the installment plan, paying for them 75 cents a week each; or, he may still further reduce his investment by requiring his operators to furnish their own machines. Finally, he does not pay his employees until he receives his money for the finished lot.

In the small shops the characteristics of the sweating system are accentuated, and the most marked of these are disorder and instability. The latter results from the irresponsibility of the sweater and the facility with which he may either establish himself or change his location. This has very much embarrassed the process of enumeration. A man may work in his bedroom today, in another man's shop tomorrow, in his own shop in a month, and, before the end of the season, abandon that for a place in a factory. If an inspector orders sanitary changes to be made within a week the sweater may prefer to disappear before the close of the week and open another shop in another place. Such easy evasion of the authorities places the sweater almost beyond official control, and many of them overcrowd their shops, overwork their employees, hire small children, keep their shops unclean, and their sanitary arrangements foul and inadequate.

The provisional nature of the small shops also accounts largely for the absence of steam motive power for the sewing machines, though it is also explained by the statement that "leg power is cheaper than steam." The increasing employment of girls aged from twelve to sixteen years as machine operators is making this motive power still cheaper and at the same time more destructive of health and life.

The minute subdivision of the work in the sweaters' shops reduces the skill required to the lowest point. The whole number of employees, therefore, in all the outside shops includes, besides a few of the skilled, who would, under the old system, be employed in the inside shops, a majority of unskilled hands of both sexes, earning low wages, easily replaced, and wholly at the mercy of the sweater. Subdivision thus reaches its highest development; operators stitch, pressers press, basters baste, button girls sew on buttons, others draw basting threads, and finishers finish. Sometimes one girl, with a buttonhole machine, makes a specialty of the inside bands of knee pants, making buttonholes by the thousand gross. On the other hand, coats requiring buttonholes made in cloth, and with more skill, are sent by the contractor to a buttonhole shop, where two or three young men work machines, and where small boys or girls smear the holes in preparation for them.

In nearly every small shop there are some finishers, but in the case of knee pants trousers, cloaks, and vests, the garments, after being cut, basted, stitched and button-holed, are given out to have all that remains, the felling and handstitching, done at home before the garment is pressed and sent to factory.

These tenement workers are known as "finishers." They are generally associated with someone of the shops, but will take work from any of them. Hundreds of women and girls compete among themselves, keeping their names on the contractors' lists, as the contractors compete among themselves for work from the manufacturers.

These women sew in the intervals of their housework and the garments lie about the living rooms, across greasy chairs and tables, upon filthy floors and vermin-infested beds. Soils upon garments are so common that the presser in the shops is also a cleaner, provided with benzene, alcohol, etc., for the removal of grease and stains. The competition of the home finishers constantly presses upon the wages of the shop hands. In some localities nearly every house contains some of these home finishers; our enumerators have located a total of 1,836 of them in the several districts; and they increase as the shops increase and as immigration increases.

Many of the Bohemians and Scandinavians have acquired their own homes and their own shops, which are usually built upon the same premises, and are properly lighted and ventilated. Very few of the Scandinavians have shop in their dwellings. They prefer to combine, in groups of from three to eight, and rent a large building, which is then partitioned off according to their needs. There are of course exceptions even among these people, and some of them set up shops in places wholly unfit for such uses; but the baser localities and shops are usually occupied by Russian Jews, Poles, and Italians. In the regions occupied by these, unclean and offensive conditions are not confined to the shops; they are equally features of the dwellings and persons and habits of the people. In these districts the worst of the shops are found located often in basements, and on alleys, or in wholly inadequate and unsanitary rooms in the dilapidated structures of these neighborhoods.

A few examples may be cited illustrating what some of these places are like. In one case, several men were found at work pressing knee pants in a low basement room, poorly lighted and ventilated by two small windows. There was no floor in this room, and the people were living on the bare earth, which was damp and littered with every sort of rubbish. In another case, seven persons were at work in a room 12 by 15 feet in dimensions and with but two windows. These people, with the sewing machines of operators and the tables used by the pressers, so filled this meager space that it was impossible to move about. Charcoal was used for heating the pressers' irons, and the air was offensive and prostrating to a degree. Separated from this shop room by a trail partition which did not reach to the ceiling was a bedroom about 7 by 15 feet in size, containing two beds, for the use of the family of the sweater. In another instance, in a small basement room which measured only 7 feet 10 inches by 6 feet 6 inches, and without door or window opening to the outer air, a man was at work pressing knee pants by the light of a very poor gasoline lamp and using a gasoline stove for heating his irons.

One of the principal aims of the sweater is the avoidance of rent; hence the only requirement for a sweaters' shop is that the structure must be strong enough to sustain the jar of the machines. This condition being filled, any tenement room is available, whether in lot, or basement, or stable. Fire escapes in such buildings are unknown; water for flushing closets is rarely found, and the employees are equally at the mercy of fire and disease. Frequently the sweater's home is his shop, with a bed among the machines; or, the family sleeps on cots, which are removed during the day to make room for employees. Sometimes two or three employees are also boarders or lodgers, and the tenement dwelling is the shop; and cooking, sleeping, sewing, and the nursing of the sick are going on simultaneously.

A shop was found in which twelve persons lived in six rooms, of which two were used as a shop. Knee pants in all stages of completion filled the shop, the bedrooms, and kitchen. Nine men were employed at machines in a room 12 by 14, and there knee pants were being manufactured by the thousand gross. This is in the rear of a swarming tenement in a wretched street. Sometimes the landlord is the sweater, using his own basement or outhouse for a shop and renting his rooms to his employees for dwellings. Only one case was found in which a tailor, not a sweater, had acquired a house. He is a skilled tailor, still doing "the whole work" at home assisted by his wife. For nineteen years he has lived and worked in two wretched rear tenement rooms, paying by installments for his house, which is still encumbered. All others in the trade who owned houses were found to be either sweaters or women finishers, whose able-bodied husbands follow other occupations, such as teaming, peddling, ditching, street cleaning, etc.

But the worst conditions of all prevail among the families who finish garments at home. Here the greatest squalor and filth abounds and the garments are of necessity exposed to it and a part of it during the process of finishing. A single room frequently serves as kitchen, bedroom, living room, and working room. In the Italian quarter, four families were found occupying one four-room flat, using one cook stove, and all the women and children sewing in the bedrooms. For this flat they pay $10 a month, each family contributing $2.50 a month. Another group was found consisting of thirteen persons, of whom four were fathers of families and five were women and girls sewing on cloaks at home. These thirteen people pay $8 per month rent, each family contributing $2.

A house-to-house canvass in this district establishes the fact that it is only the poorest of the poor who finish garments at home, only the worst tenements being occupied by them, or the worst rooms of the better houses. A widow, who is a finisher, and two children were found in a rear shanty, in the one room, below the street grade, and with only a narrow slit in the wall for a window. For this she pays $3 a month. Another was finishing knee pants in a room so dark it required some time to discern her. This room was lighted by a single window obscured by an adjacent four-story building. She also pays $3 a month rent. One of the vilest tenements in Chicago is owned by a woman whose husband is an Italian street sweeper. She lives on the premises and sews cloaks at 8 cents apiece, collects rent from thirty families under one roof, and tolerates a wretched sweatshop on her top floor. Eight of her tenants sew cloaks or knee pants in their living rooms. They pay $3 a month for the worst apartments and $10 for the best. . . .

Wages are paid by the piece and by the week; by the piece to skilled hands and to the home finishers; by the week uniformly to beginners and usually to shop hands; but all employees, whether paid by the piece or by the week, are subject to the "task" system; that is, they must accomplish a certain amount of work in a given time or forfeit their places. The best rates of wages are naturally found in the manufactures' "inside" shops and in the better contractors shop, in both of which the employees are usually of the more skilled class who speak some English and have some trade organization. . . .

The people who are found in sweatshops are rarely illiterate in their own languages, with perhaps the exception of the Italian peasants. Every Hebrew is taught to read his own literature in childhood, though very few of them can write and still fewer can keep books of account. Almost none of them can read or write in the English language. The Scandinavians and Germans are all educated in excellent schools in their own countries, and read, write and keep accounts in their own language. Wholly illiterate are the Italians. Women finishers are found by scores who cannot count the pennies due them. None of them can read or write in any language.

The ability and desire to learn English varies with the nationality. Bohemians and many Poles send their children to parochial schools, but they learn neither to speak nor read English. Hebrew children go to the public schools, but, like many others, get only half-time instruction for want of school accommodations. Italian parents gladly avail themselves of this excuse and do not attempt to send their children to school at all. Italians do not learn English in the first generation, and in the second their children learn only what can be picked up in the streets. The boys are newsboys, ragpickers, and shoe blacks; the girls are ragpickers or button girls, and even begin to sew on cloaks at a very early age.

In the matter of religion, the sweaters' employees are either Catholics, Hebrews, or Lutherans, the latter both Scandinavian and German, and principally women. The Hebrews are usually strictly Orthodox and are held together in swarming colonies by the need of having their own butchers. Sweaters' victims all keep the church holidays, except during the busy season, when work is frequently continued through seven days in the week. At other times the Italians, particularly, are punctilious about the observance of their *festas*, and the Hebrews in the observance of their holy days. To many of them amusement is almost unknown. They sleep late on Sundays and holidays, and sit listlessly about the rest of the day, except when in church. Young men and girls are disposed to attend night schools or other free or cheap classes, when out of work or the opportunity is afforded.

There are a number or organizations among the more intelligent and self-helpful in the garment trades, among which are unions of the cutters, the custom tailors, the ladies'-garment tailors, the cloakmakers, the women cloakmakers, cloak cutters, and cloak pressers. The differences of race, language, and religion prove an obstacle to the growth or organization.

The food and clothing of these communities is necessarily simple and meager. Among the Italians, bread and macaroni, with stale fruit and vegetables, constitute the diet, almost to the exclusion of meat. Among the Hebrews, the Mosaic prescription is some protection against the sale and use of improper meats, but in general the groceries and meat shops in these districts deal only in goods of defective and, consequently, cheap quality. There is nothing fresh and good offered for sale. Milk is conspicuously absent even from the diet of little children, and every winter there are long periods of rye bread and water in hundreds of families where the father is an operator without work in the shop or credit at the store.

In the matter of clothing, all sorts of makeshifts are resorted to, except the appropriation of the garments they make. Italian women wear the peasant costumes with which they come to this country as long as possible, which is usually very long, and buy secondhand clothing for their children. Shoes are a very heavy item of expense among these people, especially if they have far to walk to their work, or run sewing machines after they get there. In many small shops, men dispense with all clothing except trousers and short-sleeved gauze undershirts, even in the presence of women, and work in their bare feet. Girls who are thrown upon their own resources were found still wearing the clothing brought from the Old Country, and with small prospect of buying any other as the earnings of the busy season are otherwise absorbed during the dull season.

Very few sweaters' victims accumulate any savings. When they do they become sweaters themselves. So far as observation extended, no disposition was discovered among them to return to the countries whence they became able to do so. On the other hand, they manifest great desire to see their children attain some degree of prosperity greater than their own. Unfortunately, their eagerness in this particular frequently defeats itself, for they send their young children to the shop instead of to the school. Here their health is undermined; their presence in the shop reduces the wages of adults, and both parents and children become involved in a common struggle for existence. The result is that discontent is universal. The sweater complains of increased competition and reduced prices and profits; the victims complain of low wages, of poor pay, of the long dull season, of the heat and overcrowding in the busy season, and of the poverty and toil from which they cannot escape.

"THE NEW COLOSSUS" (1886)

Emma Lazarus

THE NEW COLOSSUS
Not like the brazen giant of Greek fame,
With conquering limbs astride from land to land,
Here at our sea-washed sunset gates shall stand
A mighty woman with a torch, whose flame
Is the imprisoned lighting, and her name
Mother of exiles, from her beacon-hand
Glows world-wide welcome; her mild eyes command
The air-bridged harbor that twin cities frame.
"Keep, ancient lands, your storied pomps!" cries she
With silent lips. "Give me your tired, your poor,
Your hurdled masses yearning to breathe free,
The wretched refuse of your teeming shore,
Send these, the homeless, tempest-tossed to me:
I lift my lamp beside the golden door!"

2.3 LABOR UNREST (1889, 1881)

Gilded Age America had its share of militant labor unions and dramatic strikes. The Knights of Labor were the most radical labor movement to challenge capital and management. Repeatedly police force and scab labor broke strikes but not before major turbulence resulted. The Railroad Strike of 1877 was one of the largest and most traumatic in American history.

Poems, Boston, Vol. II.

PREAMBLE TO THE CONSTITUTION OF THE KNIGHTS OF LABOR[1]

The recent alarming development and aggression of aggregated wealth, which, unless checked, will invariably lead to the pauperization and hopeless degradation of the toiling masses, render it imperative, if we desire to enjoy the blessings of life, that a check should be placed upon its power and upon unjust accumulation, and a system adopted which will secure to the laborer the fruits of his toil; and as this much-desired object can only be accomplished by the thorough unification of labor, and the united efforts of those who obey the divine injunction that "In the sweat of thy brow shalt thou eat bread," we have formed the [association] with a view of securing the organization and direction, by co-operative effort, of the power of the industrial classes; and we submit to the world the objects sought to be accomplished by our organization, calling upon all who believe in securing "the greatest good to the greatest number" to aid and assist us:

    I. To bring within the folds of organization every department of productive industry, making knowledge a stand-point for action, and industrial and moral worth, not wealth, the true standard of individual and national greatness.

    II. To secure to the toilers a proper share of the wealth that they create; more of the leisure that rightfully belongs to them; more societary advantages; more of the benefits, privileges, and emoluments of the world; in a word, all those rights and privileges necessary to make them capable of enjoying, appreciating, defending, and perpetuating the blessing of good government.

    III. To arrive at the true condition of the producing masses in their educational, moral, and financial condition, by demanding from the various governments the establishment of bureaus of Labor and Statistics.

    IV. The establishment of co-operative institutions, productive and distributive.

    V. The reserving of the public lands—the heritage of the people—for the actual settler; not another acre for railroads or speculators.

    VI. The abrogation of all laws that do not bear equally upon capital and labor, the removal of unjust technicalities, delays, and discriminations in the administration of justice, and the adopting of measures providing for the health and safety of those engaged in mining, manufacturing, or building pursuits.

    VII. The enactment of laws to compel chartered corporations to pay their employes weekly, in full, for labor performed during the preceding week, in the lawful money of the country.

    VIII. The enactment of laws giving mechanics and laborers first lien on their work for their full wages.

    IX. The abolishment of the contract system on national, State, and municipal work.

    X. The substitution of arbitration for strikes, whenever and wherever employers and employes are willing to meet on equitable grounds.

    XI. The prohibition of the employment of children in workshops, mines and factories before attaining their fourteenth year.

Terence V. Powderly, *Thirty Years of Labor* (Columbus, OH: Excelsior Publishing House, 1889), pp. 243–45.

[1] Footnotes deleted.

XII. To abolish the system of letting out by contract the labor of convicts in our prisons and reformatory institutions.

XIII. To secure for both sexes equal pay for equal work.

XIV. The reduction of the hours of labor to eight per day, so that the laborers may have more time for social enjoyment and intellectual improvement, and be enabled to reap the advantages conferred by the labor-saving machinery which their brains have created.

XV. To prevail upon governments to establish a purely national circulating medium, based upon the faith and resources of the nation, and issued directly to the people, without the intervention of any system of banking corporations, which money shall be legal tender in payment of all debts, public or private.

THE RAILROAD STRIKE OF 1877

Henry Demarest Lloyd

The remarkable series of eight railroad strikes, which began during the Centennial Exposition of the prosperity of our first century and the perfection of our institutions, culminated on July 16, 1877, in the strike on the Baltimore and Ohio Railroad at Martinsburg, West Virginia. This spread into the greatest labor disturbance on record. For a fortnight there was an American Reign of Terror. We have forgotten it,—that is, it has taught us nothing; but if Freeman outlives us to finish his History of Federal Government from the Achaian League to the Disruption of the United States, he will give more than one chapter to the labor rising of 1877. The strike at Martinsburg was instantly felt at Chicago and Baltimore in the stoppage of shipments. In a few hours the Baltimore and Ohio, one of the chief commercial arteries of Maryland, Virginia, West Virginia, Ohio, Indiana, and Illinois, was shut up. The strike spread to the Pennsylvania, the Erie and the New York Central railroads, and to the Great Western lines, with their countless branches, as far west as Omaha and Topeka, and as far south as the Ohio River and the Texas Pacific. The feeling of the railroad employés all over the country was expressed by the address of those of the Pennsylvania Railroad to its stock-holders. The stockholders were reminded that "many of the railroad's men did not average wages of more than seventy-five cents a day"; that "the influence of the road had been used to destroy the business of its best customers, the oil producers, for the purpose of building up individual interests." "What is the result? The traffic has almost disappeared from the Pennsylvania Railroad, and in place of $7,000,000 revenue this year, although shipments are in excess of last year, your road will receive scarcely half the amount. This alone would have enabled your company to pay us enough for a living." The address also refers pointedly to the abuses of fast freight lines, rolling-stock companies, and other railroad inventions for switching business into private pockets. Other workingmen followed the example of the railroad employés. At Zanesville, Ohio, fifty manufactories stopped work. Baltimore ceased to export petroleum. The rolling mills, foundaries, and refineries of Cleveland were closed. Chicago, St. Louis, Cincinnati, all the cities large and small, had the same experience. At Indianapolis, next

---

Henry Demarest Lloyd, "The Story of a Great Monopoly," *Atlantic Monthly*, March, 1881.

to Chicago the largest point for the eastward shipment of produce, all traffic was stopped except on the two roads that were in the hands of the national government. At Erie, Pa., the railroad struck, and notwithstanding the remonstrance of the employés refused to forward passengers or the United States mails. The grain and cattle of the farmer ceased to move to market, and the large centres of population began to calculate the chances of famine. New York's supply of Western cattle and grain was cut off. Meat rose three cents a pound in one day, while Cleveland telegraphed that hogs, sheep, beeves, and poultry billed for New York were dying on the side-tracks there. Merchants could not sell, manufacturers could not work, banks could not lend. The country went to the verge of panic, for the banks, in the absence of remittances, had resolved to close if the blockade lasted a few days longer. President Garrett, of the Baltimore and Ohio Railroad, wrote that his "great national highway could be restored to public use only by the interposition of the United States army." President Scott, of the Pennsylvania Railroad, telegraphed the authorities at Washington, "I fear that unless the general government will assume the responsibility of order throughout the land, the anarchy which is now present will become more terrible than has ever been known in the history of the world." The governors of ten States—West Virginia, Maryland, New Jersey, New York, Pennsylvania, Ohio, Illinois, Wisconsin, Missouri, and Kentucky—issued dispersing proclamations which did not disperse. The governors of four of them—West Virginia, Maryland, Pennsylvania, and Illinois—appealed to the national government for help against domestic insurrection, which the State could not suppress. The president of the United States issued two national proclamations to the insurgents. The state troops were almost useless, as in nearly all cases they fraternized with the strikers. All the national troops that could be spared from the Indian frontier and the South were ordered back to the centres of civilization. The regulars were welcomed by the frightened people of Chicago with cheers which those who heard will never forget. Armed guards were placed at all the public buildings of Washington, and ironclads were ordered up for the protection of the national capital. Cabinet meetings were continuous. General Winfield S. Hancock was sent to Baltimore to take command, General Sherman was called back from the West, and General Schofield was ordered from West Point into active services. Barricades, in the French style, were thrown up by the voters of Baltimore. New York and Philadelphia were heavily garrisoned. In Philadelphia every avenue of approach to the Pennsylvania Railroad was patrolled, and the city was under a guard of six thousand armed men, with eight batteries of artillery. There were encounters between troops and voters, with loss of life, at Martinsburg, Baltimore, Pittsburgh, Chicago, Reading, Buffalo, Scranton, and San Francisco. In the scene at Pittsburgh, there was every horror of revolution. Citizens and soldiers were killed, the soldiers were put to flight, and the town left at the mercy of the mob. Railroad cars, depots, hotels, stores, elevators, private houses, were gutted and burned. The city has just compromised for $1,810,000 claims for damages to the amount of $2,938,460, and has still heavy claims to settle. The situation was described at this point by a leading newspaper as one of "civil war with the accompanying horrors of murder, conflagration, rapine, and pillage." These were days of greater bloodshed, more actual suffering, and wider alarm in the North than that part of the country experienced at any time during the civil war, except when Lee invaded Pennsylvania. As late as August 3d, the beautiful valley of the Wyoming, in Pennsylvania, was a military camp, traversed by trains loaded with Gatling guns and bayonets, and was guarded by Governor Hartranft in person with five thousand soldiers. These strikes, penetrating twelve States and causing insurrections in ten of them, paralyzed the operation of twenty thousand miles of railroad, and directly and indirectly threw one million men temporarily out of employment. While they lasted they caused greater losses than any blockade which has been made by sea or land in the history of war. Nonsensational observers, like the Massachusetts Board of Railroad Commissioners, look to see the outburst repeated, possibly to secure a rise of wages. The movement of the railroad trains of this country is literally the circulation of its blood. Evidently, from the facts we have recited, the States cannot prevent its arrest by the struggle between these giant forces within society, outside the law.

2.4 THE CITIES ACCLAIMED (1905)

Cities have always been problematical to country folk. Americans, moreover, even more than most other Western peoples, have long prized the Arcadian ideal of a happy, virtuous, prosperous society set in the unspoiled countryside.

Frederic C. Howe was a widely published journalist-reformer who flourished during the Progressive Era early in this century. The Progressives were preponderantly urban dwellers, and they did much of their work as reformers within the urban setting. It was thus natural for them to regard cities as showcases for the virtues and values of the new, reformed society. In the following selection, what does Howe foresee for the city in the near future? Has much of what he anticipated come to pass? Have the changes he describes produced the results he expected?

THE HOPE OF DEMOCRACY

Frederic C. Howe

The city is not only the problem of our civilization, it is the hope of the future. In the city democracy is awakening, it is beginning to assert itself. Here life is free and eager and countless agencies coöperate to create a warmer sympathy, a broader sense of responsibility, and a more intelligent political sense. Already the city has attained a higher degree of political responsiveness than has the commonwealth which gave it being and which jealously resents its growing independence. In many instances it is better governed than is the state or the nation at large. It is freer from the more subtle forms of corruption. For the open bribe, the loan, or even the game of poker in which the ignorant councilman is permitted to win a handsome stake are not the only means employed. Self-interest, a class-conscious feeling, the fancied advantage of party may be as powerful a motive for evil as the more vulgar methods with which we are familiar. The sinister influences bent on maintaining the *status quo*, on the prevention of necessary legislation, the control of the party, the caucus, or the convention; methods which are in vogue in national and state affairs, may be even more dangerous to democracy than the acts which violate the criminal code and which are becoming intolerable to public opinion. Moreover, in national affairs, the public is less alert, much less able to act collectively or to concentrate

Frederic C. Howe, *The City: The Hope of Democracy* (New York: Charles Scribner's Sons, 1905), pp. 280–87, 292–93, 298–99.

attention upon a given issue. The same is true in state affairs, where the divergent interests of the country and the city render united action well-nigh impossible.

The city is also being aroused to social and economic issues as well as to political ones. It is constantly taking on new activities and assuming new burdens. Everything tends to encourage this, while many things render it imperative. By necessity we are forced to meet the burdens of a complex life. We cannot live in close association without common activities, without abandoning some of our liberties to regulation. Not only do health, comfort, and happiness demand this, self-protection necessitates it.

Some of the activities which the city has assumed, or will assume, have been suggested. Through them many of the losses which the city has created will be made good. By these means the city will become fuller of opportunity than the scattered rural life which it has displaced. A conscious housing policy will be adopted. The tenement will become habitable, comfortable, and safe. Cheap and rapid transit will lure the population from the crowded slum into smaller suburban centres. For the city of the future will cover a wide area.

The same motives that have opened up breathing spots in the form of parks, as well as public baths and gymnasiums, in the crowded quarters will, in time, lead to the establishment of city clubhouses, winter recreation centres, where such advantages as are now found in the social settlement will be offered. About these centres the life of the community will focus for study, play, recreation, and political activity. Here concerts, lectures, and human intercourse will be offered. A sense of the city as a home, as a common authority, a thing to be loved and cared for, will be developed. In the city club the saloon will find a rival. From such centres charity work will be carried on. Here neglected children will be cared for, here the boys and girls will find an opportunity of escape from the street, and the mother and father a common meeting ground which is now denied them. For city life not only destroys the home of the poor, it promotes divorce. The tenement drives its dwellers to the streets and to the saloon. Private philanthropy has done much to relieve this condition through the settlement, but the service it renders is as much a public one as are the parks, the hospitals, or the schools. For the settlement is the equivalent of the outdoor park. Even from a pecuniary point of view it is a good investment to the city. The settlement promotes order, it lessens crime, it reduces petty misdemeanors, and organizes the life and energy of the slum and turns it into good channels. The uniform testimony of police officials is to the effect that a settlement or a playground is as good as a half-dozen policemen.

When the city becomes its own factory inspector, the problem of school attendance will be simplified. Then the city will be able to coördinate its administration and enforce its own ordinances. With reduced cost of transportation, through the public ownership of the means of transit, with free books and possibly free luncheons to school children, compulsory education will become a possibility. For the problem of education is largely economic or industrial. Our cities are now in the illogical position of enforcing school attendance upon those who cannot afford even the insignificant cost of the same.

These reforms will be possible through home rule, through the city-republic. With the city free in these regards it will be able to raise the educational age, adopt manual-training and trades' schools, fit its instruction to local needs, and ultimately elevate the standard of life of all classes. With the city free, the administration of our correctional institutions may be fitted to the crime. Probation courts and city farm schools may then be established and provision made for those of tender years who, in many cities, are still imprisoned with criminals, branded with the mark of crime, a brand which they can never outlive, a memory which they can never forget, an influence that can never be eradicated. Then the city will be able to discriminate between the offences of ignorance and poverty and those of instinct. Today they are all classed together. The poor who have unwittingly violated some local ordinance, such as blocking a sidewalk, driving a garbage cart without a license, failing to remove rubbish, or the like, when arrested, if unable to find bail, are cast into jail to await trial or to serve their time. An examination of the police-court blotter of the average city leads one to wonder if the offences of society against its own do not equal those of the individual against his fellows. Justice, as administered in these courts, probably hurts quite as much as it helps, and society, by its thoughtlessness, creates as much crime as it prevents. The solicitude of the common law for the occasional innocent has not been extended to the thousands of real innocents, to the children, the unfortunate, the ignorant, whom indifference punishes and, in punishing, destroys. Thousands of men and women are sent to the jails, workhouses, and penitentiary every year who should have been sent to the hospital, to an inebriate asylum, to the country, or, much better, given work. Their offence is of a negative sort. It is not wilful. It is industrial or economic; they could not catch on.

By natural processes inability to maintain life in store, factory, or sweat-shop produces the outcast woman, just as sickness, irregular employment, hard times yield their unvarying harvest of vagrants, with the sequence of the lodging house, the street, and ultimately a life of petty crime. Such a career is not often taken from choice, but by misfortune. And society often arrests, sentences, and punishes, when it should help and endeavor to reclaim by work, kindness, and assistance.

We have had our public schools for so long that we accept them as a commonplace. But we do not appreciate that the high schools are raising millions of citizens to an educated estate which was known to but a limited number a few years ago. The effect of this infusion of culture into our life is beginning to make itself felt. And in the years to come, when education has, in fact, become compulsory, and the school age has been raised to a higher standard, the effect will be tremendous. Along with the schools go the public libraries. Branches and distributing agencies are extending their influence into every part of the city. Through them opportunity is offered for a continuation of study, even after the door of the school has closed.

Provision for public concerts in summer as well as in winter has already found a place in many municipal budgets. With the development of the city club there will come public orchestras, art exhibitions, and the like that will brighten the life of the community. Something like this is already being done through the libraries which are being constructed with assembly halls and meeting rooms for this purpose. Here and there the idea is taking form of utilizing the public-school buildings as local clubs. The basement, gymnasiums, and assembly rooms are being opened in the evening and during the summer months. In time there will be a modification in their architecture, equipment, and facilities, so that they will be available for a multitude of purposes instead of the limited one of education. In New York City the school buildings are already being erected with roof-gardens, where music, recreation, and a common centre for the life of the locality are offered.

These are some of the things the new city will do. It will also care for the sick, as it now does in many cities, through district physicians or visiting nurses attached to the school departments. It will find work and maintain employment agencies. It will supervise factories, mills, and work-shops. The latter function is now inadequately performed by the state at large, and the inefficiency of its performance is largely attributable to the fact that the state is attempting to supervise a matter of local concern. The regulation of the conditions of employment is as much a city function as is the preservation of the health and well-being of the community. It is also a necessary part of school administration. . . .

It is along these lines that the advance of society is to be made. It is to come about through the city. For here life is more active, while the government is close to the people. It is already manifest on every hand. Through the divorce of the city from state control this progress will be stimulated. The city will become a centre of pride and patriotism. Here art and culture will flourish. The citizen will be attached to his community just as were the burghers of the mediaeval towns. Through direct legislation the city will be democratized. Public opinion will be free to act. Then the official will be holden to a real responsibility, while national politics will no longer dominate local affairs, for the test of the candidate for office will be his citizenship in the community which he serves. . . .

. . . The city will cease to be a necessary abyss of poverty. It is our institutions and our laws, not a divine ordinance or the inherent viciousness of humankind, that are at fault. Our evils are economic, not personal. Relief is possible through a change in our laws, in an increase in the positive agencies of the government, and the taxing for the common weal of those values which are now responsible for much of the common woe. It is not personal goodness that is demanded so much as public intelligence. For the worst of the evils under which America suffers are traceable to laws creating privileges. The evils can be largely corrected through their abolition. This is most easily obtainable in the city, for it is in the city that democracy is organizing and the power of privilege most rampant.

2.5   THE CITIES DEPLORED (1903)

Post–Civil War American cities were rife with problems.

The Danish-born journalist Jacob Riis focuses on the housing problems of America's growing urban centers. The cities by and large were able to meet the housing needs of the middle class. Builders constructed numerous brick, stone, and wooden homes on shady streets for the cities' professional and business families. They also began to put up large apartment buildings with spacious "flats" for those prosperous urbanites who liked to live close to the center of town.

The housing needs of wage earners were less successfully met, however. Most working-class people were unable to pay more than modest rents, and many blue-collar families and individuals were forced to live with others for financial reasons. Some had to live in cellars and the cast-off, minimally reworked former homes of the middle class who left for better neighborhoods. There was a supply of new apartments for the working class, but these were usually shoddily constructed tenements, thrown up by speculative builders, that often lacked heat and full interior plumbing. They quickly deteriorated into slums.

Charles Loring Brace depicted the dark side of life in the poor neighborhoods of New York City. He called attention to numerous social ills and vices. Brace identified some of the subcultures that groups living in the tenements belonged to. Some were "working class," others were gangs. Two popular "working class" songs of the period, "The Bowery" and "Sidewalks of New York," introduce a new element to this discussion: the theme of the slum as a place of entertainment and excitement where new cultural trends are born amidst depravity. What is your impression of life in the slums? How did it combine with life in the "sweatshops"? Do you feel that reformers like Brace were justified in expressing fear of these conditions?

THE DANGEROUS CLASSES OF NEW YORK (1872)

Charles Loring Brace

The Prolétaires of New York

New York is a much younger city than its European rivals, and with perhaps one-third the population of London; yet it presents varieties of life among the "masses" quite as picturesque and elements of population even more dangerous. The throng of different nationalities in the American city gives a peculiarly variegated air to the life beneath the surface, and the enormous overcrowding in portions of the poor quarters intensifies the evils, peculiar to large towns, to a degree seen only in a few districts in such cities as London and Liverpool.

The *mass* of poverty and wretchedness is, of course, far greater in the English capital. There are classes with inherited pauperism and crime more deeply stamped in them in London or Glasgow than we ever behold in New York; but certain small districts can be found in our metropolis with the unhappy fame of containing more human beings packed to the square yard and stained with more acts of blood and riot, within a given period, than is true of any other equal space of earth in the civilized world.

There are houses, well known to sanitary boards and the police, where fever has taken a perennial lease and will obey no legal summons to quit; where cholera—if a single germ seed of it float anywhere in American atmosphere—at once ripens a black harvest; where murder has stained every floor of its gloomy stories, and vice skulks or riots from one year's end to the other. Such houses are never reformed. The only hope for them is in the march of street improvements, which will utterly sweep them away.

It is often urged that the breaking-up of these "dens" and "fever nests" only scatters the pestilence and moral disease but does not put an end to them.

The objection is more apparent than real. The abolishing of one of these centers of crime and poverty is somewhat like withdrawing the virus from one diseased limb and diffusing it through an otherwise healthy body. It seems to lose its intensity. The diffusion weakens. Above all, it is less likely to become hereditary.

One of the remarkable and hopeful things about New York, to a close observer of its "dangerous classes," is . . . that they do not tend to become fixed and inherited as in European cities. But, though the crime and pauperism of New York are not so deeply stamped in the blood of the population, they are even more dangerous.

The intensity of the American temperament is felt in every fiber of these children of poverty and vice. Their crimes have the unrestrained and sanguinary character of a race accustomed to overcome all obstacles. They rifle a bank, when English thieves pick a pocket; they murder, where European *prolétaires* cudgel or fight with fists; in a riot, they begin what seems about to be the sacking of a city, where English rioters would merely batter policemen or smash lamps. The "dangerous classes" of New York are mainly American-born but the children of Irish and German immigrants. They are as ignorant as London flashmen or costermongers. They are far more brutal than the peasantry from whom they descend, and they are much banded together in associations, such as "Dead Rabbit," "Plug-ugly," and various target companies.

Charles Loring Brace, *The Dangerous Classes of New York, and Twenty Years Among Them*, 3rd edition, New York, 1980: "The Prolétaires of New York."

They are our *enfants perdus*, grown up to young manhood.

The murder of an unoffending old man, like Mr. Rogers, is nothing to them. They are ready for any offense or crime, however degraded or bloody. New York has never experienced the full effect of the nurture of these youthful ruffians as she will one day. They showed their hand only slightly in the riots during the war. At present, they are like the athletes and gladiators of the Roman demagogues. They are the "roughs" who sustain the ward politicians and frighten honest voters. They can "repeat" to an unlimited extent and serve their employers. They live on *"Panem et circenses,"* or city hall places and pothouses, where they have full credit . . .

We may say in brief that the young ruffians of New York are the products of accident, ignorance, and vice. Among a million people such as compose the population of this city and its suburbs, there will always be a great number of misfortunes; fathers die and leave their children unprovided for; parents drink and abuse their little ones, and they float away on the currents of the street; stepmothers or stepfathers drive out, by neglect and ill-treatment, their sons from home. Thousands are the children of poor foreigners who have permitted them to grow up without school, education, or religion.

All the neglect and bad education and evil example of a poor class tend to form others, who, as they mature, swell the ranks of ruffians and criminals. So, at length, a great multitude of ignorant, untrained, passionate, irreligious boys and young men are formed, who become the "dangerous class" of our city. They form the "19th Street Gangs," the young burglars and murderers, the garroters and rioters, the thieves and flashmen, the "repeaters" and ruffians. So well known to all who know this metropolis.

The Dangers

IT HAS BEEN COMMON, since the recent terrible Communistic outbreak in Paris, to assume that France alone is exposed to such horrors; but, in the judgment of one who has been familiar with our "dangerous classes" for twenty years, there are just the same explosive social elements beneath the surface of New York as of Paris.

There are thousands of thousands in New York who have no assignable home and "flit" from attic to attic and cellar to cellar; there are other thousands more or less connected with criminal enterprises; and still other tens of thousands, poor, hard-pressed, and depending for daily bread on the day's earnings, swarming in tenement houses, who behold the gilded rewards of toil all about them but are never permitted to touch them.

All these great masses of destitute, miserable, and criminal persons believe that for ages the rich have had all the good things of life, while to them have been left the evil things. Capital to them is the tyrant. Let but law lift its hand from them for a season, or let the civilizing influences of American life fail to reach them, and, if the opportunity offered, we should see an explosion from this class which might leave this city in ashes and blood.

To those incredulous of this, we would recall the scenes in our streets during the riots in 1863, when, for a short period, the guardians of good order, the local militia, had been withdrawn for national purposes and when the ignorant masses were excited by dread of the draft.

Who will ever forget the marvelous rapidity with which the better streets were filled with a ruffianly and desperate multitude, such as in ordinary times we seldom see—creatures who seemed to have crept from their burrows and dens to join in the plunder of the city—how quickly certain houses were marked out for sacking and ruin, and what wild and brutal crimes were committed on the unoffending Negroes? It will be recalled, too, how much women figured in these horrible scenes, as they did in the Communistic outbreak in Paris. It was evident to all careful observers then that had another day of license been given the crowd, the attack would have been directed at the apparent wealth of the city—the banks, jewelers' shops, and rich private houses.

No one doubted then, or during the Orange Riot of 1871, the existence of "dangerous classes" in New York. And yet the separate members of these riotous and ruffianly masses are simply neglected and street-wandering children who have come to early manhood.

The true preventives of social catastrophes like these are . . . Christian reformatory and educational movements. . . .

Of the number of the distinctively homeless and vagrant youth in New York, it is difficult to speak with precision. We should be inclined to estimate it, after long observation, as fluctuating each year between 20,000 and 30,000. But to these, as they mature, must be added, in the composition of the dangerous classes, all those who are professionally criminal, and who have homes and lodging places. And again to these, portions of that vast and ignorant multitude, who, in prosperous times, just keep their heads above water, who are pressed down by poverty or misfortune, and who look with envy and greed at the signs of wealth and luxury all around them, while they themselves have nothing but hardship, penury, and unceasing drudgery.

THE BOWERY

Oh! the night that I struck New York,
I went out for a quiet walk.
Folks who are on to the city say,
Better by far that I took Broadway.
But I was out to enjoy the sights.
There was the Bowery ablaze with lights.
I had one of the devil's own nights!
I'll never go there any more!

Chorus:
The Bowery, the Bowery!
They say such things, and they do such things
On the Bowery! the Bowery!
I'll nerve go there any more!
I had walked but a block or two,
When up came a fellow and me he knew.
Then a policeman came walking by,
Chased him away, and I asked him why.
"Wasn't he pulling your leg?" said he.
Said I, "He never laid hands on me!"
"Get off the Bowery, you fool!" said he.

I'll never go there any more!
Struck a place that they called a "dive,"
I was in luck to get out alive.
When the policeman heard my woes,
Saw my black eyes and my battered nose,
"You've been held up!" said the "copper" fly!
"No sir! but I've been knocked down!" said I.
Then he laughed, though I couldn't see why!
I'll never go there any more!

CHARLES H. HOYT

SIDEWALKS OF NEW YORK

Down in front of Casey's old brown wooden stoop,
On a summer's evening we formed a merry group.
Boys and girls together we would sing and waltz,
While Tony played the organ on the sidewalks of New York.

Chorus:
East Side, West Side, all around the town,
The tots sang "Ring-a-ros-ie," "London Bridge is falling down."
Boys and girls together—me and Mamie O'Rourke—
Tripped the light fantastic on the sidewalks of New York.
That's where Johnny Casey, little Jimmy Crowe,
Jakey Krause, the baker, who always had the dough,
Pretty Nellie Shannon, with shoes as light as cork,
She first picked up the waltz step on the sidewalks of New York.
Things have changed since those times, some are up in "G";
Others they are wand'rers, but they all feel just like me.
They'd part with all they've got, could they once more walk
With their best girl and have a twirl on the sidewalks of New York.

JAMES BLAKE

2.6 CITY GOVERNMENT (1905)

Historians have been of two minds about city government in the late nineteenth and early twentieth centuries. On the one hand, it was corrupt and inefficient, providing poor services at high cost. On the other hand, in the absence of formal welfare agencies, these corrupt governments, ruled by political machines, were more generous, more compassionate, and more effective than the reform administrations that periodically, and temporarily, replaced them.

The following selection is an account of how a precinct captain ("ward heeler"), early in this century, helped build and retain voter loyalty for Tammany Hall, the venal machine of the Democratic Party in New York City. Some of it comes from the diary of George Washington Plunkitt, a Tammany leader, but most is comment by the journalist William L. Riordan, who interviewed Plunkitt extensively.

How would you characterize the way Plunkitt goes about his job? Judging from this description, could the Tammany machine, with a little stretching, be characterized as a social welfare organization? Were there other agencies at this time that performed these same functions? Does Plunkitt's account suggest anything significant about the relations of immigrants to the city machines? Did city dwellers pay an excessively high price for the machine's help?

STRENUOUS LIFE OF THE TAMMANY DISTRICT LEADER[2]

William L. Riordan

The life of the Tammany district leader is strenuous. To his work is due the wonderful recuperative power of the organization.

One year it goes down to defeat and the prediction is made that it will never again raise its head. The district leader undaunted by defeat, collects his scattered forces, organizes them as only Tammany knows how to organize, and in a little while the organization is as strong as ever.

No other politician in New York or elsewhere is exactly like the Tammany district leader or works as he does. As a rule, he has no business or occupation other than politics. He plays politics every day and night in the year, and his headquarters bears the inscription, "Never closed."

Everybody in the district knows him. Everybody knows where to find him, and nearly everybody goes to him for assistance of one sort or another, especially the poor of the tenements.

He is always obliging. He will go to the police courts to put in a good word for the "drunks and disorderlies" or pay their fines, if a good word is not effective. He will attend christenings, weddings, and funerals. He will feed the hungry and help bury the dead.

A philanthropist? Not at all. He is playing politics all the time.

Brought up in Tammany Hall, he has learned how to reach the heart of the great mass of voters. He does not bother about reaching their heads. It is his belief that arguments and campaign literature have never gained votes.

He seeks direct contact with the people, does them good turns when he can, and relies on their not forgetting him on election day. His heart is always in his work, too, for his subsistence depends on its results.

If he holds his district and Tammany is in power, he is amply rewarded by a good office and the opportunities that go with it. What these opportunities are has been shown by the quick rise to wealth of so many Tammany district leaders. With the examples before him of Richard Croker, once leader of the Twentieth District; John F. Carroll, formerly leader of the Twenty-ninth; Timothy ("Dry Dollar") Sullivan, late leader of the

William L. Riordan, *Plunkitt of Tammany Hall: Plain Talks and Practical Politics* (New York: McClure Phillips and Company, 1905), pp. 167–83, *passim*.

[2] This chapter is based on extracts from [George Washington] Plunkitt's Diary and on my daily observation of the work of the district leader.—W.L.R.

Sixth, and many others, he can always look forward to riches and ease while he is going through the drudgery of his daily routine.

This is a record of a day's work by Plunkitt:

2 A.M.: Aroused from sleep by the ringing of his door bell; went to the door and found a bartender, who asked him to go to the police station and bail out a saloon-keeper who had been arrested for violating the excise law. Furnished bail and returned to bed at three o'clock.

6 A.M.: Awakened by fire engines passing his house. Hastened to the scene of the fire, according to the custom of the Tammany district leaders, to give assistance to the fire sufferers, if needed. Met several of his election district captains who are always under orders to look out for fires, which are considered great vote-getters. Found several tenants who had been burned out, took them to a hotel, supplied them with clothes, fed them, and arranged temporary quarters for them until they could rent and furnish new apartments.

8:30 A.M.: Went to the police court to look after his constituents. Found six "drunks." Secured the discharge of four by a timely word with the judge, and paid the fines of two.

9 A.M.: Appeared in the Municipal District Court. Directed one of his district captains to act as counsel for a widow against whom dispossess proceedings had been instituted and obtained an extension of time. Paid the rent of a poor family about to be dispossessed and gave them a dollar for food.

11 A.M.: At home again. Found four men waiting for him. One had been discharged by the Metropolitan Railway Company for neglect of duty, and wanted the district leader to fix things. Another wanted a job on the road. The third sought a place on the Subway and the fourth, a plumber, was looking for work with the Consolidated Gas Company. The district leader spent nearly three hours fixing things for the four men, and succeeded in each case.

3 P.M.: Attended the funeral of an Italian as far as the ferry. Hurried back to make his appearance at the funeral of a Hebrew constituent. Went conspicuously to the front booth in the Catholic church and the synagogue, and later attended the Hebrew confirmation ceremonies in the synagogue.

7 P.M.: Went to district headquarters and presided over a meeting of election district captains. Each captain submitted a list of all the voters in his district, reported on their attitude toward Tammany, suggested who might be won over and how they could be won, told who were in need, and who were in trouble of any kind and the best way to reach them. District leader took notes and gave orders.

8 P.M.: Went to a church fair. Took chances on everything, bought ice-cream for the young girls and the children. Kissed the little ones, flattered their mothers and took their fathers out for something down at the corner.

9 P.M.: At the club-house again. Spent $10 on tickets for a church excursion and promised a subscription for a new church-bell. Bought tickets for a base-ball game to be played by two nines from his district. Listened to the complaints of a dozen push-cart peddlers who said they were persecuted by the police and assured them he would go to Police Headquarters in the morning and see about it.

10:30 P.M.: Attended a Hebrew wedding reception and dance. Had previously sent a handsome wedding present to the bride.

12 P.M.: In bed.

That is the actual record of one day in the life of Plunkitt. He does some of the same things every day, but his life is not so monotonous as to be wearisome.

Sometimes the work of a district leader is exciting, especially if he happens to have a rival who intends to make a contest for the leadership at the primaries. In that case, he is even more alert, tries to reach the fires before his rival, sends our runners to look for "drunks and disorderlies" at the police stations, and keeps a very close watch on the obituary columns of the newspapers.

A few years ago there was a bitter contest for the Tammany leadership of the Ninth District between John C. Sheehan and Frank J. Goodwin. Both have had long experience in Tammany politics and both understood every move of the game.

Every morning their agents went to their respective headquarters before seven o'clock and read through the death notices in all the morning papers. If they found that anybody in the district had died, they rushed to the homes of their principals with information and then there was a race to the house of the deceased to offer condolences, and, if the family were poor, something more substantial.

On the day of the funeral there was another contest. Each faction tried to surpass the other in the number and appearance of the carriages it sent to the funeral, and more than once they almost came to blows at the church or in the cemetery.

On one occasion the Goodwinites played a trick on their adversaries which has since been imitated in other districts. A well-known liquor dealer who had a considerable following died, and both Sheehan and Goodwin were eager to become his political heir by making a big showing at the funeral.

Goodwin managed to catch the enemy napping. He went to all the livery stables in the district, hired all the carriages for the day, and gave orders to two hundred of his men to be on hand as mourners.

Sheehan had never had any trouble about getting all the carriages that he wanted, so he let the matter go until the night before the funeral. Then he found that he could not hire a carriage in the district.

He called his district committee together in a hurry and explained the situation to them. He could get all the vehicles he needed in the adjoining district, he said, but if he did that, Goodwin would rouse the voters of the Ninth by declaring that he (Sheehan) had patronized foreign industries.

Finally, it was decided that there was nothing to do but go over to Sixth and Broadway for carriages. Sheehan made a fine turnout at the funeral, but the deceased was hardly in his grave before Goodwin raised the cry of "Protection to home industries," and denounced his rival for patronizing livery-stable keepers outside of his district. The cry had its effect in the primary campaign. At all events, Goodwin was elected leader.

A recent contest for the leadership of the Second District illustrated further the strenuous work of the Tammany district leaders. The contestants were Patrick Divver, who had managed the district for years, and Thomas F. Foley.

Both were particularly anxious to secure the large Italian vote. They not only attended all the Italian christenings and funerals, but also kept a close lookout for the marriages in order to be on hand with wedding presents.

At first, each had his own reporter in the Italian quarter to keep track of the marriages. Later, Foley conceived a better plan. He hired a man to stay all day at the City Hall marriage bureau, where most Italian couples go through the civil ceremony, and telephone to him at his saloon when anything was doing at the bureau.

Foley had a number of presents ready for use and, whenever he received a telephone message from his man, he hastened to the City Hall with a ring or a watch or a piece of silver and handed it to the bride with his congratulations. As a consequence, when Divver got the news and went to the home of the couple with the present, he always found that Foley had been ahead of him. Toward the end of that campaign, Divver also stationed a man at the marriage bureau and then there were daily foot races and fights between the two leaders.

Sometimes the rivals come into conflict at the death-bed. One night a poor Italian peddler died in Roosevelt Street. The news reached Divver and Foley about the same time, and as they knew the family of the man was destitute, each went to an undertaker and brought him to the Roosevelt tenement.

The rivals and the undertakers met at the house and an altercation ensued. After much discussion the Divver undertaker was selected. Foley had more carriages at the funeral, however, and he further impressed the Italian voters by paying the widow's rent for a month, and sending her half a ton of coal and a barrel of flour.

The rivals were put on their mettle toward the end of the campaign by the wedding of a daughter of one of the original Cohens of the Baxter Street region. The Hebrew vote in the district is nearly as large as the Italian vote, and Divver and Foley set out to capture the Cohens and their friends.

They stayed up nights thinking what they would give the bride. Neither knew how much the other was prepared to spend on a wedding present, or what form it would take; so spies were employed by both sides to keep watch on the jewelry stores, and the jewelers of the district were bribed by each side to impart the desired information.

At last Foley heard that Divver had purchased a set of silver knives, forks, and spoons. He at once bought a duplicate set and added a silver tea service. When the presents were displayed at the home of the bride Divver was not in a pleasant mood and he charged his jeweler with treachery. It may be added that Foley won at the primaries.

One of the fixed duties of a Tammany district leader is to give two outings every summer, one for the men of his district and the other for the women and children, and a beefsteak dinner and a ball every winter. The scene of the outings is, usually, one of the groves along the [Long Island] Sound.

The ambition of the district leader on these occasions is to demonstrate that his men have broken all records in the matter of eating and drinking. He gives out the exact number of pounds of beef, poultry, butter, etc., that they have consumed and professes to know how many potatoes and ears of corn have been served.

According to his figures, the average eating record of each man at the outing is about ten pounds of beef, two or three chickens, a pound of butter, a half peck of potatoes, and two dozen ears of corn. The drinking records, as given out, are still more phenomenal. For some reason, not yet explained, the district leader thinks that his popularity will be greatly increased if he can show that his followers can eat and drink more than the followers of any district leader.

The same idea governs the beefsteak dinners in the winter. It matters not what sort of steak is served or how it is cooked; the district leader considers only the question of quantity, and when he excels all others in this particular, he feels, somehow, that he is a bigger man, and deserves more patronage than his associates in the Tammany Executive Committee.

As to the balls, they are events of the winter in the extreme East Side and West Side society. Mamie and Maggie and Jennie prepare for them months in advance, and their young men save up for the occasion just as they save for the summer trips to Coney Island.

The district leader is in his glory at the opening of the ball. He leads the cotillion with the prettiest woman present—his wife, if he has one, permitting—and spends almost the whole night shaking hands with his constituents. The ball costs him a pretty penny, but he has found that the investment pays.

By these means the Tammany district leader reaches out into the homes of his district, keeps watch not only on the men, but also on the women and children; knows their needs, their likes and dislikes, their troubles and their hopes, and places himself in a position to use his knowledge for the benefit of his organization and himself. Is it any wonder that scandals do not permanently disable Tammany and that it speedily recovers from what seems to be crushing defeat?

CHAPTER 3

The Final Frontier

The United States continued to grow in strength as an agriculture power, producing an ever-expanding share of the world's food from the end of the Civil War to the middle decades of the twentieth century. Farm exports remained a crucial aspect of America's overall economy, despite its ever-expanding industrial sector. One measure of the importance of America's farms is that the urban population did not equal the rural population until the Census of 1930. But another census, the Census of 1890, announced a significant development: the closing of the American Frontier. The expansion of the agrarian economy was not without pain and controversy. Life for the American farmer was filled with economic hardship, and one agrarian political movement after another attempted to address the woes of the American farmer from 1865 through 1932. Relentless exploitation of new natural resources led to additional problems of overproduction, waste, and eco-catastrophe.

3.1 SETTLING THE FINAL FRONTIER (1889)

During the half-century following the Civil War, the huge expanse of territory between the Missouri River and the Pacific slope was absorbed into the national economy. This was a region of wide deserts and rugged mountains, fertile plains and valleys, dense timber stands, and rich mineral deposits. In 1865 it was thinly peopled by scores of Native American tribes living primarily as nomadic hunters and foragers who relied on the teeming herds of bison (buffalo) for the food and materiel of their lives.

White Americans regarded the "last West," as previous "Wests," as a land of opportunity to be conquered and exploited by the plow, the cow, the spade, and the ax. The Native Americans seemed an impediment to be swept aside or forced to yield to "civilization."

Agriculture also made an important contribution to the economic surge of the post–Civil War years. From the nation's farms, plantations, and ranches poured an ever-widening flood of wheat, corn, cotton, fruit, vegetables, beef, pork, and dairy products. Many Americans—and people around the world—benefited from this torrent of food and fiber. Yet the farmers were not happy. As production rose, farm prices fell, farm debt soared, and land values stagnated. Many farmers and farm leaders denounced the economic and political arrangements they believed had contributed to their plight.

THE GREAT RACE FOR LAND

Hamilton S. Wicks

As our train slowly moved through the Cherokee strip, a vast procession of "boomers" was seen moving across the plains to the Oklahoma lines, forming picturesque groups on the otherwise unbroken landscape. The wagon road through the "strip," extemporized by the boomers, ran for long distances parallel with the railway, and the procession that extended the whole distance illustrated the characteristic of western American life. Here, for instance, would be a party consisting of a "prairie schooner" drawn by four scrawny, raw-boned horses, and filled with a tatterdemalion group, consisting of a shaggy-bearded man, a slatternly-looking woman, and several girls and boys, faithful images of their parents, in shabby attire, usually with a dog and a coop of chickens. In striking contrast to this frontier picture, perhaps a couple of flash real-estate men from Wichita would come jogging on a short distance behind, driving a spanking span of bays, with an equipage looking for all the world as though it had just come from a fashionable livery stable. Our train, whirling rapidly over the prairie, overtook many such contrasted pictures. There were single rigs and double rigs innumerable; there were six-mule team and four-in-hands, with here and there parties on horseback, and not a few on foot, trudging along the wayside. The whole procession marched, rode, or drove, as on some gala occasion, with smiling faces and waving hands. Every one imagined that Eldorado was just ahead, and I dare say the possibility of failure or disappointment did not enter into the consideration of a single individual on that cool and delightful April day. For many, alas, the anticipations were "April hopes, the fools of chance."

As our train neared the Oklahoma border the "procession" became more dense, and in some instances clogged the approaches to the fords of the small streams that crossed its pathway. When we finally slowed up at the dividing line the camps of the "boomers" could be seen extending in every direction, and a vast amount of stock was strewn over the green prairie.

And now the hour of twelve was at hand, and every one on the *qui vive* for the bugle blast that would dissolve the chain of enchantment hitherto girding about this coveted land. Many of the "boomers" were mounted on high-spirited and fleet-footed horses, and had ranged themselves along the territorial line, scarcely restrained even by the presence of the troop of cavalry from taking summary possession. The better class of wagons and carriages ranged themselves in line with the horsemen, and even here and there mule teams attached to canvas-covered vehicles stood in the front ranks, with the reins and whip grasped by the "boomers' " wives. All was excitement and expectation. Every nerve was on tension and every muscle strained. The great event for which these

Hamilton S. Wicks, "The Opening of Oklahoma," *The Cosmopolitan*, VII, Sept. 1889.

brawny noblemen of the West have been waiting for years was on the point of transpiring. Suddenly the air was pierced with the blast of a bugle. Hundreds of throats echoed the sound with shouts of exultation. The quivering limbs of saddled steeds, no longer restrained by the hands that held their bridles, bounded forward simultaneously into the "beautiful land" of Oklahoma; and wagons and carriages and buggies and prairie schooners and a whole congregation of curious equipages joined in the unparalleled race, where every starter was bound to win a prize—the "Realization Stakes" of home and prosperity.

Here was a unique contest in which thousands participated and which was to occur but once for all time. Truly an historical event! We, the spectators, witnessed the spectacle with most intense interest. Away dashed the thoroughbreds, the broncos, the pintos, and the mustangs at a breakneck pace across the uneven surface of the prairie. It was amazing to witness the recklessness of those cow-boy riders: they jumped obstacles; they leaped ditches; they cantered with no diminution of speed through water-pools; and when they came to a ravine too wide to leap, down they would go with a rush, and up the other side with a spurt of energy, to scurry once more like mad over the level plain. This reckless riding was all very well at the fore part of the race, but it could not prevail against the more discreet maneuvering of several elderly "boomers" who rode more powerful and speedy horses. One old white-bearded fellow especially commanded attention. He was mounted on a coal-black thoroughbred, and avoided any disaster by checking the pace of his animal when ravines had to be crossed. But his splendid bursts of speed when no obstructions barred the way soon placed him far in advance of all his competitors. It took but a short time to solve this question of speed among the riders, and after a neck-and-neck race for half a mile or more they spread like a fan over the prairie, and were eventually lost to our vision. . . .

The occupants of our train now became absorbed in their own fate. Indeed our train was one of the participants in this unexampled race, and, while watching the scurrying horsemen, we ourselves had been gliding through the picturesque landscape. It was rather hard pulling for our engine until we reached the apex of the heavy grade that commanded a view of the Cimarron Valley, spread out in picturesque beauty at our very feet. Our train now rushed along down grade with the speed of a limited express—crossing the fine bridge that spans the Cimarron with a roar, and swinging around the hills that intervened between the river and the Guthrie town-site with the rapidity of a swallow's flight. All that there was of Guthrie, the now famous "magic city" on April 22d, at 1.30 P.M., when the first train from the north drew up at the station and unloaded its first instalment of settlers, was a water-tank, a small station-house, a shanty for the Wells, Fargo Express, and a Government Land Office—a building twenty by forty feet, hastily constructed five hundred feet from the depot, on the brow of the gently-sloping acclivity that stretches eastward from the railway track. It is true that a handful of enterprising United States deputy marshals, a few railroad boys, and one or two newspaper correspondents had already surveyed and staked out several hundred acres of town site, and had, by way of maintaining their claims to this extensive property, erected a few tents here and there in the neighborhood of the Land Office building. The imbecile policy of the government in the manner of opening the new Territory for settlement invited just this sort of enterprise. But when the hundreds of people from our train and the thousands from following trains arrived, they "coppered the situation," to speak in Western parlance, with very little consideration for the privileges, interest, or rights of the deputies and their friends.

I remember throwing my blankets out of the car window the instant the train stopped at the station. I remember tumbling after them through the self-same window. Then I joined the wild scramble for a town lot up the sloping hillside at a pace discounting any "go-as-you-please" race. There were several thousand people converging on the same plot of ground, each eager for a town lot which was to be acquired without cost or without price, each solely dependent on his own efforts, and animated by a spirit of fair play and good humor.

The race was not over; when you reached the particular lot you were content to select for your possession. The contest was still who should drive their stakes first, who would erect their little tents soonest, and then, who would quickest build a little wooden shanty.

The situation was so peculiar that it is difficult to convey correct impressions of the situation. It reminded me of playing blindman's-bluff. One did not know how far to go before stopping; it was hard to tell when it was best to stop, and it was a puzzle whether to turn to the right or the left. Every one appeared dazed, and all for the most acted like a flock of stray sheep. Where the boldest led, many others followed. I found myself, without exactly knowing how, about midway between the government building and depot. It occurred to me that a street would probably run past the depot. I accosted a man who looked like a deputy, and asked him if this was to be a street along here.

"Yes," he replied. "We are laying off four corner lots right here for a lumber yard."

"Is this the corner where I stand?" I inquired.

"Yes," he responded, approaching me.

"Then I claim this corner lot!" I said with decision, as I jammed my location stick in the ground and hammered it securely home with my heel. "I propose to have one lot at all hazards on this town site, and you will have to limit yourself to three, in this location at least."

An angry altercation ensued, but I stoutly maintained my position, and my rights. I proceeded at once to unstrap a small folding cot I brought with me, and by standing it on its end it made a tolerable center-pole for a tent. I then threw a couple of my blankets over the cot, and staked them securely into the ground on either side. Thus I had a claim that was unjumpable because of substantial improvements, and I felt safe and breathed more freely until my brother arrived on the third train, with our tent and equipments. Not long after his arrival, an enterprising individual came driving by with a plow, and we hired him for a dollar to plow around the lot I had stepped off, twenty-five feet in front and one hundred and forty feet in depth. Before dusk we had a large wall tent erected on our newly-acquired premises, with a couple of cots inside and a liberal amount of blankets for bedding. Now we felt doubly secure in our possession, and as night approached I strolled up on the eminence near the land office, and surveyed the wonderful cyclorama spread out before me on all sides. Ten thousand people had "squatted" upon a square mile of virgin prairie that first afternoon, and as the myriad of white tents suddenly appeared upon the face of the country, it was as though a vast flock of huge white-winged birds had just settled down upon the hillsides and in the valleys. Here indeed was *a city laid out and populated in half a day*. Thousands of camp-fires sparkled upon the dark bosom of the prairie as far as the eye could reach, and there arose from this huge camp a subdued hum declaring that this almost innumerable multitude of the brave and self-reliant men had come to stay and work, and build in that distant Western wilderness a city that should forever be a trophy to American enterprise and daring.

3.2   AGRARIAN HARDSHIP

American farmers faced a relentless series of problems in the decades following the Civil War. Overproduction led to plummeting prices, but improved technologies led to mounting debt. This led to a series of radical political demands. Farmers called for "soft money" and "easy credit" policies; they demanded improvements in transportation networks and begged for government relief from exorbitant railroad rates. In the first selection, Washington Gladden identifies many of the financial pressures facing farmers. The second selection presents the People's Party or "Populist" political response. Do you think that their concerns over financial issues were similar? What additional dimensions of human suffering emerge from the platform.

Meeting at Omaha in July 1892, the People's Party adopted a platform that went beyond the demands of the dirt farmers' leaders to express the concerns of social critics and reformers who foresaw imminent social catastrophe for America if something were not done soon. The preamble of this platform was written by Ignatius Donnelly, novelist, journalist, intellectual, and former Republican congressman from Minnesota.

How do you explain the platform's apocalyptic tone? In what ways does it seek to create a farmer-labor alliance? It has been said that Populism foreshadowed twentieth-century liberalism. Is there anything in the platform that reminds you of later Progressive and New Deal policies and programs?

"EMBATTLED FARMERS" (1890)

Washington Gladden

The farmers of the United States are up in arms. They are the bone and sinew of the nation; they produce the largest share of its wealth; but they are getting, they say, the smallest share for themselves. The American farmer is steadily losing ground. His burdens are heavier every year and his gains are more meager; he is beginning to fear that he may be sinking into servile condition. He has waited long for the redress of his grievances; he purposes to wait no longer. Whatever he can do by social combinations or by united political action to remove the disabilities under which he is suffering, he intends to do at once and with all his might.

There is no doubt at all that the farmers of this country are tremendously in earnest just now, and they have reason to be. Beyond question they are suffering sorely. The business of farming has become, for some reasons, extremely unprofitable. With the hardest work and with the sharpest economy, the average farmer is unable to make both ends meet; every year closes with debt, and the mortgage grows till it devours the land. The Labor Bureau of Connecticut has shown, by an investigation of 693 representative farms, that the average annual reward of the farm proprietor of that state for his expenditure of muscle and brain is $181.31. While the average annual

Forum, November 1890.

wages of the ordinary hired man is $386.36. Even if the price of board must come out of the hired man's stipend, it still leaves him a long way ahead of his employer. In Massachusetts the case is a little better; the average farmer makes $326.49, while his hired man gets $345.

In a fertile district in the state of New York, a few weeks ago, an absentee land lord advertised for a man to manage his farm. The remuneration offered was not princely. The farm manager was to have his rent, his garden, pasturage for one cow, and a salary of $250 a year for his services and those of his wife. There was a rush of applicants for the place. Who were they? Many of them were capable and intelligent farmers who had lost their own farms in the hopeless struggle with adverse conditions and who were now well content to exchange their labor and their experience against a yearly reward of $250. The instance is typical. Throughout the Eastern states, with the home market which protection is supposed to have built up at their very doors, the farmers are falling behind. Says Professor C. S. Walker:

> A careful study of New England farming in the light of all points of view, car-
> ried on for the past ten years by means of statistical investigation, personal
> observation during carriage drives from Canada to Long Island Sound and
> intimate association with all classes of farmers assures one that the man who
> cultivates an average farm and depends upon its profits alone for the support
> of himself and family, if he pay his taxes and debts, cannot compete with his
> brothers or attain to their standard of living, who, with equal powers, employ
> them in other walks of life.

The same story is heard in the Central states. In Ohio, farms are offered for beggarly rents, and even on these favorable terms farming does not pay. Tenant farmers are throwing up their leases and moving into the cities, well content to receive as common laborers $1.25 a day, and to pay such rents and to run such risks of enforced idleness as the change involves. At the South the case is even worse. Under a heavy burden of debt the farmer struggles on from year to year, the phenomenal growth of the manufacturing interests in his section seeming to bring him but slight relief. And even in the West we find the same state of things. A large share of recent corn crops has been consumed for fuel; and over vast areas, Mr. C. Wood Davis tells us, "wheat sells at from 40 to 50 cents, oats at from 9 to 12 cents, and corn at from 10 to 13 cents a bushel, and fat cattle at from 1½ to 3 cents a pound." Under such conditions the life of the Western farmer cannot be prosperous. From Kansas and Nebraska and Dakota the cry is no less loud and bitter than from Connecticut and New York and North Carolina.

The causes of this lamentable state of things are many. Who shall estimate them? Mr. Davis gives this list: "Monometallism, deficient or defective circulating medium, protective tariffs, trusts, dressed-beef combinations, speculation in farm products, overgreedy middleman, and exorbitant transportation rates." These are a few of the disadvantages of which the farmers now complain. Doubtless several of these causes are working against them. Whether, in their diagnosis of the disease, they always put their finger on the right spot may be doubted. People cannot always be trusted to tell what ails them. The patient knows that he is suffering, but he does not always discover the nature of his malady. Mr. Davis gives strong reasons for the belief that the root of the difficulty is overproduction; that there are too many farms, and that more corn, wheat, oats, beef, and pork have been raised than the country can use.

There is the foreign market, to be sure; but in that the farmer of the West must compete with the low-priced labor of India and Russia. If his product is very greatly in excess of the wants of his own country, he will be forced to sell at very low prices. The fact seems to be that the less of these staples the farmers raise, the more they get for them. The short crops of this year may, very likely, bring them more money than enormous crops of 1889. The comforting assurance of Mr. Davis that the acreage of farms cannot increase so rapidly in the future, and that the population will soon grow up to the food supply and will redress the balance in the farmer's favor is one that may well be cherished.

But granting that this is the chief cause of the depression of agriculture, other causes of considerable importance should not be overlooked. The enormous tribute which the farmers of the West are paying to the moneylenders of the East is one source of their poverty. Scarcely a week passes that does not bring to me circulars from banking firms and investment agencies all over. The West begging for money to be loaned on farms at 8 or 9 percent net. The cost of negotiation and collection, which the farmer must pay, considerably increases these rates. The descriptive lists of farms which accompany these circulars show that the mortgages are not all given for purchase money.

I find in one of the agricultural papers the following figures indicating the increase in farm mortgages in Dane Country, Wisconsin, during the year 1889. The number of mortgages filed was 467; the average amount of each, $1,252; the total amount, $584,727.80; the number of mortgages given for purchase money, only 9. But whether the mortgages represent debts incurred in the purchase of the land or those incurred for other purposes, it is evident that when they bear such rates of interest they constitute a burden under which no kind of business can be profitably carried on. The farmer who voluntarily pays such tribute as this to the moneylenders is quite too sanguine. Other businessmen will not handicap themselves in this way. But probably the larger proportion of these mortgages are extorted from the farmers by hard necessity. Not their hope of increased prosperity makes them incur these debts so often as the pressure of obligations which have been incurred and which must be met.

The steady and increasing migration from the farms to the cities is in part an effect of the depression of agriculture and in part a cause of that depression. If a large part of the most vigorous and enterprising members of the farmer's families leave the farms, it is evident that the farms will not be carried on with the enterprise and vigor which are necessary to the success of any business. Is it not true that less ingenuity and less invention have been developed in this business than in most other occupations? There is plenty of money in the country; might not the farmer, by the application of brains to his calling, get a little more of it? Of the great staples, the country can consume only a limited quantity; but the country is ready to take all sorts of fancy food products—delicacies, luxuries, gastronomic novelties—and to pay good prices for them. . . .

Along some such lines as these the farmers will most surely draw to themselves a larger share of the surplus wealth of the country. That surplus is abundant, but all sorts of people with keen wits and strenuous energies are competing for it. Those who have it are ready to exchange it for gratifications of various sorts. The problem is to please them. Within the bounds of innocent and wholesome delectation, there is a wide range for the exercise of invention by the food producers of the nation. If they confine them-selves to the business of raising corn and wheat and pork and beef, their market will be narrow. They can widen it almost indefinitely if they will devote to their business the same kind of ingenuity that manufacturers of all classes are constantly exercising in their efforts to attract to their own coffers the abundance of the land.

Such methods, however, are not those by which the farmers now hope to better their condition. They are organized mainly for other purposes. They believe that the miseries under which they are suffering are largely due to political causes and can be cured by legislation. They have found out that of the 20 million breadwinners they comprise 8 or 9 million, and they think that if they stand together they can get such legislations as they desire. The old Grange kept pretty well out of politics; the new Farmer's Alliance and its affiliated organizations intend to work the political placer for all that it can be made to yield. Hear them:

> The prime object of this association is to better the condition of the farmers of America, mentally, morally, and financially; to suppress personal, sectional, and national prejudices, all unhealthful rivalry and selfish ambition; to return to the principles on which the government was founded by adhering to the doctrine of equal right and equal chances to all and special privileges to none; to educate and commingle with those of the same calling to the end that country life may become less lonely and more social; to assist the weak with the strength of the strong, thereby rendering the whole body more able to resist; and to bequeath to posterity conditions that will enable them, as honest, intelligent, industrious producers, to cope successfully with the exploiting class of middlemen.

For the promotion of these objects three methods are named—"social, business, and political." The social feature is easily understood; the business methods involve various forms of cooperative buying and selling; and the political methods are defined only by saying that they are strictly nonpartisan, and that they must ever remain so. This seems to mean that the farmers decline to attach themselves to either political party, but that they will try to make both parties serve them.

> All questions in political economy will be thoroughly discussed, and when the order can agree on a reform as necessary, they will demand it of the government and of every political party; and if the demand goes unheeded, they will find ways to enforce it. The most essential reforms must come from legislation, but that does not necessarily compel the necessity of choosing candidates and of filling the offices. Such a course may become necessary, but it will not be resorted to under any other circumstances.

This is pretty explicit, and it is beginning to exert a solemnizing influence in the coun-cils of the politicians. The Farmers' Alliance is not unconscious of its power. The movement is running like wildfire over all our hills and prairies, and it is claimed that forty members of the next Congress will be pledged to support its demands. What will be its demands?

Cheap money, to begin with. The farmers are generally debtors; they want cheap money wherewith to pay their debts. Of course the cheaper the money, the less groceries and clothing and machinery can be bought with it; but the farmers think of their debts more than of their necessities, and the longing of their souls is for cheap money. They are therefore in favor of the free coinage of silver; but they insist that even this would be an ineffectual remedy, since only about $45 million a year, at the utmost, could thus be added to the currency of the country, and this amount, they think, would be ridiculously inadequate.

1. The subtreasury plan, so called, by which warehouses are to be built in every country where they are demanded, wherein the farmers may deposit cotton, wheat, corn oats, or tobacco, receiving in return a Treasury note for 80 percent of the value of the product so deposited, at the current market price. These Treasury notes are to be legal tender for debts and receivable for customs. A warehouse receipt, also, is to be given to the depositor, designating the amount and grade of the product deposited and the amount of money advanced upon it, and indicating that interest upon the money thus advanced is to be paid by the depositor at the rate of 1 percent per annum. These receipts are to be negotiable by endorsement.

2. The holder of a receipt, by presenting it at the warehouse, returning the money advanced, and paying interest and charges, may obtain the product deposited; and the money thus returned is to be destroyed by the secretary of the Treasury. This scheme for getting an ample supply of money directly into the hands of the farmers, at a nominal rate of interest, appears to have the endorsement of the Alliance. The journals of the organization are discussing it freely and are adducing various historical instances to show that the principle involved in it has been tested and economists and financiers is strongly against the measure.

3. The ownership by the government of all the railroads, telegraphs, and telephones is another plank in the platform of the Alliance. Here is a measure which is certainly debatable; let us hope that the farmers will secure for it a thorough discussion.

4. The prohibition of gambling in stocks and that of alien ownership of land are propositions which will also receive considerable support outside the Alliance.

5. The abolition of national banks and the substitution of legal-tender Treasury notes for national-bank notes, will not, probably, command universal assent.

6. The adoption of a constitutional amendment requiring the choice of United States senators by the people seems to be a popular measure among the members of the Alliance. To this they will be able to rally a strong support.

7. With these and other demands inscribed upon their banners, the farmers are in the field. They will make lively work for the politicians in the West and in the South during the pending campaign. No small amount of dodging and ducking on the part of these worthies may be looked for. Several of the strong agricultural districts will return to Congress men pledged to advocate the measures of the Alliance. Already they have picked out the place which they wish their contingent to occupy on either side of the center aisle in the House of Representatives, where they expect to hold the balance of power and to take the place of the Center in the French Assembly.

8. How long they will hold together is difficult to predict. It may be that the discussions in which they must take part will show them that some of the measures of direct relief on which they are chiefly depending are impracticable; and it is conceivable

that this discovery will tend to demoralize them. That they can become a permanent political force is not likely, for parties which represent only classes cannot live in a republic. But several results, by no means undesirable, may be looked for as the outcome of this farmers' uprising.

1. They will secure thorough discussion of some important economical questions. They will force the people to consider carefully the problem of the state ownership of the great public highways. It is not absurd to demand that the state should own and control, even if it does not operate, the railroads; and that it should own and operate the telegraphs. The conclusion to which such an experienced railway manager as the president of the Chicago and railway has already come is one to which many other people are likely to come in the course of this debate. If the farmers can stick together and can stick to their text long enough to get this business thoroughly ventilated, they will do a good service.

2. They are loosening the bands of partisanship and are opening the way for a rational cooperation of citizens for all desirable purposes. "The most hopeful feature of this whole uprising," writes a shrewd observer, "is the smashing of the old party shackles that goes along with it." That it may lead to a reconstruction of parties is not improbable.

3. They are helping to make an end of the sectionalism which has been a larger part of the capital of a certain class of politicians. Their manifestoes point to this as the one striking result of their work thus far. "Scarcely a vestige," they say, "of the old sectional prejudice of a few years ago is now visible within our ranks." The South and the West are coming into fraternal relations. Mr. Lodge has already discovered that the West is not supporting his Force Bill. "The demagogue politician who now attempts to array sectional prejudice in order that he may keep farmers equally divided on important questions" is admonished that he is about to confront "a superior intelligence that will soon convince him that his occupation is gone."

4. The farmers' movement is not, probably, the deluge; but it will prove to be something of a shower—in some quarters, a cyclone—and it will clear the atmosphere.

THE PREAMBLE OF THE PLATFORM OF THE PEOPLE'S PARTY

Assembled upon the 166th anniversary of the Declaration of Independence, the People's Party of America, in their first national convention, invoking upon their action the blessing of Almighty God, puts forth, in the name and on behalf of the people of this country, the following preamble and declaration of principles:—The conditions which surround us best justify our cooperation: we meet in the midst of a nation brought to the verge of moral, political, and material ruin. Corruption dominates the ballot-box,

Edward McPherson, *A Handbook of Politics for 1892* (Washington, DC: James J. Chapman, 1892), pp. 269–71.

the legislatures, the Congress, and even touches the ermine of the bench. The people are demoralized; most of the states have been compelled to isolate the voters at the polling-places to prevent universal intimidation or bribery. The newspapers are largely subsidized or muzzled; public opinion silenced; business prostrated; our homes covered with mortgages; labor impoverished; and the land concentrating in the hands of the capitalists. The urban workmen are denied the right of organization for self-protection; imported pauperized labor beats down their wages; a hireling standing army, unrecognized by our laws, is established to shoot them down, and they are rapidly degenerating into European conditions. The fruits of the toil of millions are boldly stolen to build up colossal fortunes for a few, unprecedented in the history of mankind; and the possessors of these, in turn, despise the Republic and endanger liberty. From the same prolific womb of governmental injustice we breed two great classes—tramps and millionaires.

The national power to create money is appropriated to enrich bondholders; a vast public debt, payable in legal tender currency, has been funded into gold bearing bonds, thereby adding millions to the burdens of the people. Silver, which has been accepted as coin since the dawn of history, has been demonetized to add to the purchasing power of gold by decreasing the value of all forms of property as well as human labor; and the supply of currency is purposely abridged to fatten usurers, bankrupt enterprise, and enslave industry. A vast conspiracy against mankind has been organized on two continents, and it is rapidly taking possession of the world. If not met and overthrown at once, it forebodes [sic] terrible convulsions, the destruction of civilization, or the establishment of an absolute despotism.

We have witnessed for more than a quarter of a century the struggles of the two great political parties for power and plunder, while grievous wrongs have been inflicted upon the suffering people. We charge that the controlling influences dominating both these parties have permitted the existing dreadful conditions to develop without serious effort to prevent or restrain them. Neither do they now promise us any substantial reform. They have agreed together to ignore in the coming campaign every issue but one. They propose to drown the outcries of a plundered people with the uproar of a sham battle over the tariff, so that capitalists, corporations, national banks, rings, trusts, watered stock, the demonetization of silver, and the oppressions of the usurers may all be lost sight of. They propose to sacrifice our homes, lives and children on the altar of mammon; to destroy the multitude in order to secure corruption funds from the millionaires.

Assembled on the anniversary of the birthday of the nation, and filled with the spirit of the grand general and chieftain who established our independence, we seek to restore the government of the Republic to the hands of "the plain people," with whose class it originated. We assert our purposes to be identical with the purposes of the National Constitution, "to form a more perfect union and establish justice, insure domestic tranquility, provide for the common defence, promote the general welfare, and secure the blessings of liberty for ourselves and our posterity." We declare that this republic can only endure as a free government while built upon the love of the whole people for each other and for the nation; that it cannot be pinned together by bayonets; that the civil war is over, and that every passion and resentment which grew out of it must die with it; and that we must be in fact, as we are in name, one united brotherhood of freemen.

Our country finds itself confronted by conditions for which there is no precedent in the history of the world; our annual agricultural productions amount to billions of dollars in value, which must in a few weeks or months, be exchanged for billions of dollars of commodities consumed in their production; the existing currency supply is wholly inadequate to make this exchange; the results are falling prices, the formation of combines and rings, the impoverishment of the producing class. We pledge ourselves, if given power, we will labor to correct these evils by wise and reasonable legislation, in accordance with the terms of our platform. We believe that the powers of government—in other words, of the people—should be expanded (as in the case of the postal service) as rapidly and as far as the good sense of an intelligent people and the teachings of experience shall justify, to the end that oppression, injustice, and poverty shall eventually cease in the land.

While our sympathies as a party of reform are naturally upon the side of every proposition which will tend to make men intelligent, virtuous, and temperate, we nevertheless regard these questions—important as they are—as secondary to the great issues now pressing for solution, and upon which not only our individual prosperity but the very existence of free institutions depends; and we ask all men to first help us to determine whether we are to have a republic to administer before we differ as to the conditions upon which it is to be administered; believing that the forces of reform this day organized will never cease to move forward until every wrong is remedied, and equal rights, and equal privileges securely established for all the men and women of this country.

We declare therefore,—

First—That the union of the labor forces of the United States this day consummated shall be permanent and perpetual; may its spirit enter all hearts for the salvation of the republic and the uplifting of mankind!

Second—Wealth belongs to him who creates it, and every dollar taken from industry without an equivalent is robbery. "If any will not work, neither shall he eat." The interests of rural and civic labor are the same; their enemies are identical.

Third—We believe that the time has come when the railroad corporations will either own the people or the people must own the railroads; and, should the government enter upon the work of owning and managing all railroads, we should favor an amendment to the Constitution by which all persons engaged in the government service shall be placed under a civil service regulation of the most rigid character, so as to prevent the increase of the power of the national administration by the use of such additional government employees.

First. *Money*—We demand a national currency, safe, sound, and flexible, issued by the general government only, a full legal tender for all debts, public and private, and that, without the use of banking corporations, a just, equitable, and efficient means of distribution direct to the people, at a tax not to exceed two per cent per annum, to be provided as set forth in the sub-treasury plan of the Farmers' Alliance, or a better system; also, by payments in discharge of its obligation for public improvements.

   a. We demand free and unlimited coinage of silver and gold at the present legal ratio of sixteen to one.
   b. We demand that the amount of circulating medium be speedily increased to not less than fifty dollars per capita.
   c. We demand a graduated income tax.
   d. We believe that the money of the country should be kept as much as possible in the hands of the people, and hence we demand that all state and national

revenues shall be limited to the necessary expenses of the government economically and honestly administered.

e. We demand that postal savings banks be established by the government for the safe deposit of the earnings of the people and to facilitate exchange.

Second, *Transportation*—Transportation being a means of exchange and a public necessity, the government should own and operate the railroads in the interest of the people.

Third, *Land*—The land, including all the natural sources of wealth, is the heritage of the people, and should not be monopolized for speculative purposes, and alien ownership of land should be prohibited. All land now held by railroads and other corporations in excess of their actual needs, and all lands now owned by aliens, should be reclaimed by the government and held for actual setttlers only.

The year 1892 was the high-water mark of the People's Party; thereafter its support declined, but not its influence. The Populists gave voice to a widespread mood of the day that economic inequality and the dominance of wealth had progressed too far and should be reversed. Following the Panic of 1893, Populist ideas invaded the Democratic Party, especially in the West and South, where it expressed in part festering sectional resentment against the power centers of the East.

In some of the following selections you will encounter the views of Populists and Populist-influenced Democrats as well as their opponents. Consider, as previously, the spirit as well as the logic behind the arguments advanced.

3.3   THE BUFFALO DESTROYED (1876–1877)

Much of the trans-Missouri region was too rugged or too dry for conventional agriculture, but in many places it produced an annual crop of short grass that provided forage for grazing animals. Before the arrival of white people the eastern half of the region, the high Plains, supported enormous herds of buffalo, and these in turn provided the Native American tribes with food (their flesh), clothing (their hides), rope (their sinews), and fuel (their droppings). By the late 1870s most of the buffalo were gone, leaving the land for domestic cattle and depriving the Indians of a basic necessity.

The destruction of the buffalo is not a pretty page in American history. In the following selection, a professional buffalo hunter describes his occupation during the late 1870s. What were the hunter's motives? What part might the transcontinental railroads have played in the destruction of the buffalo herds? Some scholars believe that the slaughter of the buffalo was part of a deliberate policy designed to "tame" the nomadic Plains Indians. Was it?

THE DESTRUCTION OF THE PLAINS BUFFALO

W. Skelton Glenn

There were several methods to kill [buffalos] and each [hunter] adopted his own course and plan. They would get together and while one gained a point from another, he, in turn, would gain a point from him. One method was to run beside them, shooting them as they ran. Another was to shoot from the rear, what was termed tail shooting: [always

Rex W. Stickland, ed., "The Recollections of W. S. Glenn, Buffalo Hunter," *Panhandle Plains Historical Review*, vol. 22 (1949), pp. 20–26.

shooting] the hindmost buffalo and when a day's hunt was done, they would be strung on the ground for a mile or more, from ten to fifteen yards apart.

We first noticed that the buffaloes always went around a ravine or gulch, unless going for water straight down a bluff; and as the buffalo always followed these trails a man on foot by a mere cut-off of a hundred yards could cut him off. That is why they were so far apart in tail-hunting, as it was called.

Another method of hunting was to leave your horse out of sight after you had determined the direction and course of the wind, and then get as near as possible. If the herd was lying at rest, he would pick out some buffalo that was standing up on watch and shot his ball in the side of him so that it would not go through, but would lodge in the flesh; as on many times it had been proven by men [who were] well hid and the wind taking the sound of the gun and the whizz of the bullet off, [that] if a ball passed through a buffalo the herd would stampede and run for miles. A buffalo shot in this manner would merely hump up his back as if he had the colic and commence to mill round and round in a slow walk. The other buffalo sniffing the blood and following would not be watching the hunter, and he would continue to shoot the outside cow buffalo; if there were old cows they would take them as there would be some two or three offsprings following her. If she would hump up, he would know that he had the range, and in this way hold the herd as long as they acted in this way as well as the well trained cowpuncher would hold his herd, only the hunter would use his gun. This was termed mesmerising the buffalo so that we could hold them on what we termed a stand, which afterwards proved to be the most successful way of killing the buffalo.

It was not always the best shot but the best hunger that succeeded, that is, the man who piled his buffalo in a pile so as to be more convenient for the skinner to get at and not have to run all over the country.

The hunger was hired by the piece: if robe hides were worth $3.00, [he was] given twenty-five cents for every one that he killed and was brought in by the skinners—was tallied up at camp. It was the camp rustler's business to keep tally of the number of hides killed each day. If the hides were worth $2.50, he [the hunter] got 20 cents; $2.00, he got 15 cents; $1.50, he got 10 cents; and $1.00, he got 5 cents.

I have seen their bodies so thick after being skinned, that they would look like logs where a hurricane had passed through a forest [sic]. If they were lying on a hillside, the rays of the sun would make it look like a hundred glass windows. These buffalo would lie in this way until warm weather, drying up, and I have seen them piled fifty or sixty in a pile where the hunter had made a stand. As the skinner commenced on the edge, he would have to roll it out of the way to have room to skin the next, and when finished they would be rolled up as thick as saw logs around a mill. In this way a man could ride over a field and pick out the camps that were making the most money out of the hunt.

These hides, like all other commodities, would rise and fall in price and we had to be governed by the prices [in the] East. This man, J. R. Loganstein, that run the hunt, has known them to be shipped to New York, then to Liverpool and back again in order to raise the price or corner the market. . . .

We will now describe a camp outfit. They would range from six to a dozen men, there being one hunter who killed the buffalo and took out the tongues, also the tallow. As the tallow was of an oil nature, it was equal to butter; [it was used] for lubricating our guns and we loaded our own shells, each shell had to be lubricated and [it] was used also for greasing wagons and also for lights in camp. Often chunks as large as an ear of corn were thrown on the first to make heat. This [i.e., the removal of the tallow] had to be done while the meat was fresh, the hunter throwing it into a tree to wind dry; if the skinner forgot it, it would often stay there all winter and still be good to eat in the spring and better to eat after hanging there in the wind a few days.

We will return to the wagon man. [There were] generally two men to the wagon and their business was to follow up the hunter, if they were not in sight after the hunter had made a killing, he would proceed in their direction until he had met them, and when they would see him, he would signal with his hat where the killing was. If they got to the buffalo when they were fresh, their duty was to take out all the humps, tongues and tallow from the best buffalo. The hunter would then hunt more if they did not have hides enough to make a load or finish their day's work.

A remarkable good hunter would kill seventy-five to a hundred in a day, an average hunter about fifty, and a common one twenty-five, some hardly enough to run a camp. It was just like in any other business. A good skinner would skin from sixty to seventy-five, an average man from thirty to forty, and a common one from fifteen to twenty-five. These skinners were also paid by the hide[,] about five cents less than the hunter was getting for killing, being furnished with a grind stone, knives and steel and a team and wagon. The men were furnished with some kind of a gun, not as valuable as Sharp's rifle, to kill cripples with, also kips and calves that were standing around. In several incidents [instances?] it has been known to happen while the skinner was busy, they would slip up and knock him over. Toward the latter part of the hunt, when all the big ones were killed, I have seen as many as five hundred up to a thousand in a bunch, nothing but calves and have ridden right up to them, if the wind was right.

3.4 NATIVE AMERICANS (1877, 1881)

The most resistant barriers to white exploitation of the "last West" were the Native American peoples who, until the 1850s, occupied the Great Plains as "One Big Reservation." These were formidable mounted warriors capable of firing a shower of deadly arrows at a target while riding their ponies at full gallop. Yet in the end, they could not stand up to the superior organization and numbers of the whites who coveted their lands.

Beginning in the 1850s the federal government, responding to the demands of western farmers, miners, and railroad promoters, began to force the Plains tribes into smaller and smaller reservations. Using bribery, deception, and threats, the federal government strong-armed the Indians into treaties that reduced their lands to ever more limited tracts, often arid and rugged terrain that no one else wanted. The Indians resisted, and between 1866 and 1890 the Plains tribes and the U.S. Army fought a series of wars in which the Indians often gave as good as they got. In 1866, the Sioux killed eighty-two soldiers under the command of Captain W. J. Fetterman; in 1876, commanded by Chiefs Sitting Bull and Crazy Horse, they were again victorious, killing all 265 men under the command of the foolhardy army general George Custer, at the Little Big Horn River.

The first selection that follows is Sitting Bull's account of the battle on the Little Big Horn as given to a New York newspaper reporter. Why, according to Sitting Bull, were the Indians able to destroy Custer's force? What does the chief's description reveal of Indian values? Do you know if Custer and his men were badly outnumbered? Why, do you think, past generations romanticized Custer? Is he still considered a tragic hero?

The second selection is a portion of President Chester A. Arthur's 1881 State of the Union Address in which Arthur, an easterner, says that the government must cease to treat the Indians as collective members of separate, autonomous nations, and deal with them instead as individuals to be absorbed into mainstream American life. In what way can Arthur's approach be considered generous and enlightened for the day? Is there any significance in the fact that Arthur was an easterner? (The "severalty" proposal for land ownership by individual families, as contrasted with the former communal ownership by tribes, was finally enacted by Congress in 1887 as the Dawes Act.)

Do you know if the Indians benefited or lost under the new policy? What is the significance of Arthur's suggestion concerning education for the Indians? What sort of education, do you suppose, he had in mind?

SITTING BULL TELLS HOW HE DEFEATED CUSTER

Sitting Bull

"When the fight commenced here," I asked, pointing to the spot where Custer advanced beyond the Little Big Horn, "what happened?"

"Hell!"

"You mean, I suppose, a fierce battle?"

"I mean a thousand devils."

"The village was by this time thoroughly aroused?"

"The squaws were like flying birds; the bullets were like humming bees."

"You say that when the first attack was made up here on the right of the map, the old men and the squaws and children ran down the valley toward the left. What did they do when this second attack came from up here toward the left?"

"They ran back again to the right, here and here," answered Sitting Bull, placing his swarthy finger on the place where the words "Abandoned Lodges" are.

"And where did the warriors run?"

"They ran to the fight—the big fight."

"So that, in the afternoon, after the fight, on the right hand side of the map was over, and after the big fight toward the left hand side began, you say that the squaws and children all returned to the right hand side, and that the warriors, the fighting men of all the Indian camps, ran to the place where the big fight was going on?"

"Yes."

"Why was that? Were not some of the warriors left in front of these intrenchments on the bluffs, near the right side of the map? Did not you think it necessary—did not your war chiefs think it necessary—to keep some of your young men there to fight the troops who had retreated to those intrenchments?"

"No."

"Why?"

"You have forgotten."

"How?"

New York Herald, November 16, 1877.

"You forget that only a few soldiers were left by the Long Hair[1] on those bluffs. He took the main body of his soldiers with him to make the big fight down here on the left."

"So there were no soldiers to make a fight left in the intrenchments on the right hand bluffs?"

"I have spoken. It is enough. The squaws could deal with them. There were none but squaws and pappooses in front of them that afternoon."

"Well then," I inquired of Sitting Bull, "Did the cavalry, who came down and made the big fight, fight?"

Again Sitting Bull smiled.

"They fought. Many young men are missing from our lodges. But is there an American squaw who has her husband left? Were there any Americans left to tell the story of that day? No."

"How did they come on to the attack?"

"I have heard that there are trees which tremble."

"Do you mean the trees with trembling leaves?"

"Yes."

"They call them in some parts of the western country Quaking Asps; in the eastern part of the country they call them Silver Aspens."

"Hah! A great white chief, whom I met once, spoke these words 'Silver Aspens,' trees that shake; there were the Long Hair's soldiers."

"You do not mean that they trembled before your people because they were afraid?"

"They were brave men. They were tired. They were too tired."

"How did they act? How did they behave themselves?"

At this Sitting Bull again arose. I also arose from my seat, as did the other persons in the room, except the stenographer.

"Your people," said Sitting Bull, extending his right hand, "were killed. I tell no lies about deadmen. These men who came with the Long Hair were as good men as ever fought. When they rode up their horses were tired and they were tired. When they got off from their horses they could not stand firmly on their feet. They swayed to and fro—so my young men have told me—like the limbs of cypresses in a great wind. Some of them staggered under the weight of their guns. But they began to fight at once; but by this time, as I have said, our camps were aroused, and there were plenty of warriors to meet them. They fired with needle guns. We replied with magazine guns—repeating rifles. It was so (and here Sitting Bull illustrated by patting his palms together with the rapidity of a fusilade). Our young men rained lead across the river and drove the white braves back."

"And then?"

"And then, they rushed across themselves."

"And then?"

"And then they found that they had a good deal to do."

"Was there at that time some doubt about the issue of the battle, whether you would whip the Long Hair or not?"

"Where was so much doubt about it that I started down there (here again pointing to the map) to tell the squaws to pack up the lodges and get ready to move away."

---

[1] Custer, who wore his hair down his back—ED.

"You were on that expedition, then, after the big fight had fairly begun?"

"Yes."

"You did not personally witness the rest of the big fight? You were not engaged in it?"

"No. I have heard of it from the warriors."

"When the great crowds of your young men crossed the river in front of the Long Hair what did they do? Did they attempt to assault him directly in his front?"

"At first they did, but afterward they found it better to try and get around him. They formed themselves on all sides of him except just at his back."

"How long did it take them to put themselves around his flanks?"

"As long as it takes the sun to travel from here to here" (indicating some marks upon his arm with which apparently he is used to gauge the progress of the shadow of his lodge across his arm, and probably meaning half an hour. An Indian has no more definite way than this to express the lapse of time.)

"The trouble was with the soldiers," he continued; "they were so exhausted and their horses bothered them so much that they could not take good aim. Some of their horses broke away from them and left them to stand and drop and die. When the Long Hair, the General, found that he was so outnumbered and threatened on his flanks, he took the best course he could have taken. The bugle blew. It was an order to fall back. All the men fell back fighting and dropping. They could not fire fast enough, though. But from our side it was so," said Sitting Bull, and here he clapped his hands rapidly twice a second to express with what quickness and continuance the balls flew from the Henry and Winchester rifles wielded by the Indians. "They could not stand up under such a fire," he added.

"Were any military tactics shown? Did the Long Haired Chief make any disposition of his soldiers, or did it seem as though they retreated all together, helter skelter, fighting for their lives?"

"They kept in pretty good order. Some great chief must have commanded them all the while. They would fall back across a *coulee* and make a fresh stand beyond on higher ground. The map is pretty nearly right. It shows where the white men stopped and fought before they were all killed. I think that is right—down there to the left, just above the Little Big Horn. There was one part driven out there, away from the rest, and there a great many men were killed. The places marked on the map are pretty nearly the places where all were killed."

"Did the whole command keep on fighting until the last?"

"Every man, so far as my people could see. There were no cowards on either side."

THE INDIANS MUST BE ASSIMILATED

Chester A. Arthur

Prominent among the matters which challenge the attention of Congress at its present session is the management of our Indian affairs. While this question has been a cause of trouble and embarrassment from the infancy of the Government, it is but recently that

---

James D. Richardson, ed., *A Compilation of the Message and Papers of the Presidents* (New York: Bureau of National Literature, 1897), vol. 10, pp. 4641–43.

any effort has been made for its solution at once serious, determined, consistent, and promising success.

It has been easier to resort to convenient makeshifts for tiding over temporary difficulties than to grapple with the great permanent problem, and accordingly the easier course has almost invariably been pursued.

It was natural, at a time when the national territory seemed almost illimitable and contained many millions of acres far outside the bounds of civilized settlements, that a policy should have been initiated which more than aught else has been the fruitful source of our Indian complications.

I refer, of course, to the policy of dealing with the various Indian tribes as separate nationalities, of relegating them by treaty stipulations to the occupancy of immense reservations in the West, and of encouraging them to live a savage life, undisturbed by any earnest and well-directed efforts to bring them under the influences of civilization.

The unsatisfactory results which have sprung from this policy are becoming apparent to all.

As the white settlements have crowded the borders of the reservations, the Indians, sometimes contentedly and sometimes against their will, have been transferred to other hunting grounds, from which they have again been dislodged whenever their new-found homes have been desired by the adventurous settlers.

These removals and the frontier collisions by which they have often been preceded have led to frequent and disastrous conflicts between the races.

It is profitless to discuss here which of them has been chiefly responsible for the disturbances whose recital occupies so large a space upon the pages of our history.

We have to deal with the appalling fact that though thousands of lives have been sacrificed and hundreds of millions of dollars expended in the attempt to solve the Indian problem, it has until within the past few years seemed scarcely nearer a solution than it was half a century ago. But the Government has of late been cautiously but steadily feeling its way to the adoption of a policy which has already produced gratifying results, and which, in my judgment, is likely, if Congress and the Executive accord in its support, to relieve us ere long from the difficulties which have hitherto beset us.

For the success of the efforts now making to introduce among the Indians the customs and pursuits of civilized life and gradually to absorb them into the mass of our citizens, sharing their rights and holden to their responsibilities, there is imperative need for legislative action.

My suggestions is that regard will be chiefly such as have been already called to the attention of Congress and have received to some extent its consideration.

First, I recommend the passage of an act making the laws of the various States and Territories applicable to the Indian reservations within their borders and extending the laws of the State of Arkansas to the portion of the Indian Territory not occupied by the Five Civilized Tribes.

The Indian should receive the protection of the law. He should be allowed to maintain in court his rights of person and property. He has repeatedly begged for this privilege. Its exercise would be very valuable to him in his progress toward civilization.

Second. Of even greater importance is a measure which has been frequently recommended by my predecessors in office, and in furtherance of which several bills have been from time to time introduced in both Houses of Congress. The enactment of a general law permitting the allotment in severalty, to such Indians, at least, as desire it, of a reasonable quantity of land secured to them by patent, and for their own protection made inalienable for twenty or twenty-five years, is demanded for their present welfare and their permanent advancement.

In return for such considerate action on the part of the Government, there is reason to believe that the Indians in large numbers would be persuaded to sever their tribal relations and to engage at once in agricultural pursuits. Many of them realize the fact that their hunting days are over and that it is now for their best interests to conform their manner of life to the new order of things. By no greater inducement than the assurance of permanent title to the soil can they be led to engage in the occupation of tilling it.

The well-attested reports of their increasing interest in husbandry justify the hope and belief that the enactment of such a statute as I recommend would be at once attended with gratifying results. A resort to the allotment system would have a direct and powerful influence in dissolving the tribal bond, which is so prominent a feature of savage life, and which tends so strongly to perpetuate it.

Third. I advise a liberal appropriation for the support of Indian schools, because of my confident belief that such a course is consistent with the wisest economy.

CHAPTER 4

Outward Thrust

For a time during the closing years of the nineteenth century, the United States joined the big power race for overseas markets and colonies. Although the country had acquired Alaska and several small islands soon after the Civil War, until the 1890s most of its expansionist energies had been expended on settling and exploiting the broad expanse within its own national boundaries. Numerous, rich, and aggressive, Americans had not been averse to bullying weaker neighbors and forcibly dispossessing Native Americans. Still, they had avoided acquiring territory detached from the North American continent. Nor had they been particularly interested in overseas investment or, with the notable exception of the South's cotton, in overseas markets. All told, as the nation entered the post-Reconstruction era, the inward-looking United States was a relatively minor player on world economic and political stages.

These attitudes soon changed. The selections that follow address the issues of why this occurred. They suggest why the self-satisfied and prosperous republic abandoned its inward focus and, at least for a time, dreamed of an empire. In the following selections, you will encounter a range of opinion on America's outward thrust of the 1890s that culminated in the Spanish-American War and the acquisition of the Philippines, Puerto Rico, Hawaii, and other lands beyond the nation's continental borders.

4.1 RACIAL DESTINY (1885)

Darwinian survival-of-the-fittest ideas not only sanctioned laissez-faire (free market) economics but also encouraged American expansionism. Nations and races, like individuals, differed in natural talent and abilities, many Darwinists believed. Some nations and races were superior and, like superior individuals, deserved to rule the rest. Writing in 1885, the Congregational minister Josiah Strong depicted in Darwinian terms the triumph of the American branch of the Anglo-Saxon race over all its competitors and its ultimate dominion over much of the world.

Historians note that in his book Our Country, which is excerpted here, Strong put into words what many educated Americans implicitly believed during this period.

Is it surprising that a Protestant minister should announce views such as those Strong expressed? Are they Christian beliefs? Would it be fair to liken the notion of Anglo-Saxon superiority that Strong asserts to the views of Aryan supremacy that the Nazis disseminated during the 1930s and 1940s? What do you suppose foreigners thought of Strong's vision of an American-dominated world? It is interesting that Strong was a part of the reformist Social Gospel trend in organized Protestantism, which sought to improve social conditions for the poor and for labor. Do his statements seem compatible with this position? How could he maintain the two perspectives simultaneously?

WHY THE ANGLO-SAXONS WILL TRIUMPH

Josiah Strong

It is not necessary to argue to those for whom I write that the two great needs of mankind, that all men may be lifted up into the light of the highest Christian civilization, are, first, a pure, spiritual Christianity, and, second, civil liberty. Without controversy, these are the forces which, in the past, have contributed most to the elevation of the human race, and they must continue to be, in the future, the most efficient ministers to its progress. It follows, then, that the Anglo-Saxon, as the great representatives of these two ideas, the depositary of these two greatest blessings, sustains peculiar relations to the world's future, is divinely commissioned to be, in a peculiar sense, his brother's keeper. Add to this the fact of his rapidly increasing strength in modern times, and we have well nigh a demonstration of his destiny. . . .

There can be no reasonable doubt that North America is to be the great home of the Anglo-Saxon, the principal seat of his power, the center of his life and influence. Not only does it constitute seven-elevenths of his possessions, but his empire is unsevered, while the remaining four-elevenths are fragmentary and scattered over the earth. . . .

But we are to have not only the larger portion of the Anglo-Saxon race for generations to come, we may reasonably expect to develop the highest type of Anglo-Saxon civilization. If human progress follows a law of development, if

"Time's noblest offspring is the last,"

our civilization should be the noblest; for we are

"The heirs of all the ages in the foremost files of time,"

and not only do we occupy the latitude of power, but *our land is the last to be occupied in that latitude.* There is no other virgin soil in the North Temperate Zone. If the consummation of human progress is not to be looked for here, if there is yet to flower a higher civilization, where is the soil that is to produce it? . . .

Josiah Strong, *Our Country* (New York: Baker and Taylor, for the Home Missionary Society, 1885), pp. 161, 165, 168, 170–171, 172–175.

Mr. Darwin is not only disposed to see, in the superior vigor of our people, an illustration of his favorite theory of natural selection, but even intimates that the world's history thus far has been simply preparatory for our future, and tributary to it. He says: "There is apparently much truth in the belief that the wonderful progress of the United States, as well as the character of the people, are the results of natural selection; for the more energetic, restless and courageous men from all parts of Europe have emigrated during the last ten or twelve generations to that great country, and have there succeeded best. Looking at the distant future, I do not think that the Rev. Mr. Zincke takes an exaggerated view when he says: 'All other series of events— as that which resulted in the culture of mind in Greece, and that which resulted in the Empire of Rome—only appear to have purpose and value when viewed in connection with, or rather as subsidiary to, the great stream of Anglo-Saxon emigration to the West.' "

There is abundant reason to believe that the Anglo-Saxon race is to be, is, indeed, already becoming, more effective here than in the mother country. . . .

It may be easily shown, and is of no small significance, that the two great ideas of which the Anglo-Saxon is the exponent are having a fuller development in the United States than in Great Britain. There the union of Church and State tends strongly to paralyze some of the members of the body of Christ. Here there is no such influence to destroy spiritual life and power. Here, also, has been evolved the form of government consistent with the largest possible civil liberty. Furthermore, it is significant that the marked characteristics of this race are being here emphasized most. Among the most striking features of the Anglo-Saxon is his money-making power—a power of increasing importance in the widening commerce of the world's future. . . . [A]lthough England is by far the richest nation of Europe we have already outstripped her in the race after wealth, and we have only begun the development of our vast resources.

Again, another marked characteristic of the Anglo-Saxon is what may be called an instinct of genius for colonizing. His unequaled energy, his indomitable perseverance, and his personal independence, made him a pioneer. He excels all others in pushing his way into new countries. It was those in whom this tendency was strongest that came to America, and this inherited tendency has been further developed by the westward sweep of successive generations across the continent. So noticeable has this characteristic become that English visitors remark it. Charles Dickens once said that the typical American would hesitate to enter heaven unless assured that he could go further west.

Again, nothing more manifestly distinguishes the Anglo-Saxon than his intense and persistent energy; and he is developing in the United States an energy which, in eager activity and effectiveness, is peculiarly American. This is due partly to the fact that Americans are much better fed than Europeans, and partly to the undeveloped resources of a new country, but more largely to our climate, which acts as a constant stimulus. Ten years after the landing of the Pilgrims, the Rev. Francis Higginson, a good observer, wrote: "A sup of New England air is better than a whole flagon of English ale." Thus early had the stimulating effect of our climate been noted. Moreover, our social institutions are stimulating. In Europe the various ranks of society are, like the strata of the earth, fixed and fossilized. There can be no great change without a terrible upheaval, a social earthquake. Here society is like the waters of the sea, mobile; as General [James] Garfield said, and so signally illustrated in his own experience, that which is at the bottom today may one day flash on the crest of the highest wave. Every one is free to become whatever he can make of himself; free to transform himself from a rail-splitter or a tanner or a canal-boy, into the nation's President. Our aristocracy, unlike that of Europe, is open to all comers. Wealth, position, influence, are prizes offered for energy; and every farmer's boy, every apprentice and clerk, every friendless and penniless immigrant, is free to enter the lists. Thus many causes co-operate to produce here the most forceful and tremendous energy in the world.

What is the significance of such facts? These tendencies infold the future; they are the mighty alphabet with which God writes his prophecies. May we not, by a careful laying together of the letters, spell out something of his meaning? It seems to me that God, with infinite wisdom and skill, is training the Anglo-Saxon race for an hour sure to come in the world's future. Heretofore there has always been in the history of the world a comparatively unoccupied land westward, into which the crowded countries of the East have poured their surplus populations. But the widening waves of migration, which millenniums ago rolled east and west from the valley of the Euphrates, meet today on our Pacific coast. There are no more new worlds. The unoccupied arable lands of the earth are limited, and will soon be taken. The time is coming when the pressure of population on the means of subsistence will be felt here as it is now felt in Europe and Asia. Then will the world enter upon a new stage of its history—*the final competition of races, for which the Anglo-Saxon is being schooled.* Long before the thousand millions are here, the mighty *centrifugal* tendency, inherent in this stock and strengthened in the United States, will assert itself. Then this race of unequaled energy, with all the majesty of numbers and the might of wealth behind it—the representative, let us hope, of the largest liberty, the purest Christianity, the highest civilization—having developed peculiarly aggressive traits calculated to impress its institutions upon mankind, will spread itself over the earth. If I read not amiss, this powerful race will move down upon Mexico, down upon Central and South America, out upon the islands of the sea, over upon Africa and beyond. And can any one doubt that the result of this competition of races will be the "survival of the fittest"?

4.2 RACE AND POWER (1903)

American and European imperialists and expansionists usually assumed, and then attempted to assert, the cultural and racial supremacy of their own stock. Not all agreed. Dissent, however exceptional to the norm, did challenge the conventional pseudoscientific theories advocated by many social scientists. The root of these "racialist" or "genetic" theories often stemmed from incorrect or distorted applications of the evolutionary theories of Charles Darwin. Jingoism also played a role in mobilizing the masses. W.E.B. Du Bois, the first African American to earn a doctoral degree at Harvard University (his discipline was history), challenged these assumptions. The following passage is taken from his classic study The Souls of Black Folk, which pioneered methods championed in the social sciences to this day.

What are the fundamental differences between Du Bois' philosophical and theoretical assumptions and those of other selections in this chapter? How does he view progress? Culture? Morality? Most of all, in his view, how did European powers achieve their status of global power? Do inherent qualities or intrinsic characteristics influence outcomes? Does his view have much in common with ours today?

THE SOULS OF BLACK FOLK

W.E.B. Du Bois

The world-old phenomenon of the contact of diverse races of men is to have new exemplification during the new century. Indeed, the characteristic of our age is the contact of European civilization with the world's undeveloped peoples. Whatever we may say of the results of such contact in the past, it certainly forms a chapter in human action not pleasant to look back upon. War, murder, slavery, extermination, and debauchery,—this has again and again been the result of carrying civilization and the blessed gospel to the isles of the sea and the heathen without the law. Nor does it altogether satisfy the conscience of the modern world to be told complacently that all this has been right and proper, the fated triumph of strength over weakness, of righteousness over evil, of superiors over inferiors. It would certainly be soothing if one could readily believe all this; and yet there are too many ugly facts for everything to be thus easily explained away. We feel and know that there are many delicate differences in race psychology, numberless changes that our crude social measurements are not yet able to follow minutely, which explain much of history and social development. At the same time, too, we know that these considerations have never adequately explained or excused the triumph of brute force and cunning over weakness and innocence.

It is, then, the strife of all honorable men of the twentieth century to see that in the future competition of races the survival of the fittest shall mean the triumph of the good, the beautiful, and the true; that we may be able to preserve for future civilization all that is really fine and noble and strong, and not continue to put a premium on greed and impudence and cruelty. To bring this hope to fruition, we are compelled daily to turn more and more to a conscientious study of the phenomena of race-contact,—to a study frank and fair, and not falsified and colored by our wishes or our fears. And we have in the South as fine a field for such a study as the world affords,— a field, to be sure, which the average American scientist deems somewhat beneath his dignity, and which the average man who is not a scientist knows all about, but nevertheless a line of study which by reason of the enormous race complications with which God seems about to punish this nation must increasingly claim our sober attention, study, and thought, we must ask, what are the actual relations of whites and blacks in the South? and we must be answered, not by apology or fault-finding, but by a plain, unvarnished tale.

4.3 MANHOOD AND IMPERIALISM (1899)

One of the most vigorous proponents of American expansion was the young politician Theodore Roosevelt. During the early 1880s he had tried his hand at ranching in the Dakotas. In 1897, he became assistant secretary of the navy under President William McKinley and in that capacity in 1898 dispatched the American Pacific fleet to the Philippines to prepare for war with Spain. During

---

W.E.B. Du Bois. *The Souls of Black Folk* (Boston: A.C. McClurg and Company, 1903), Preamble to Chapter ix.

the Spanish-American War, Roosevelt quit his navy post to organize a cavalry regiment, known as the Rough Riders, for service in Cuba. TR returned from Cuba a war hero and in 1899 ran successfully for governor of New York. Eventually, of course, he became president of the United States.

In the following selection, written before he was elected to high office, Roosevelt expresses views that would influence how many Americans regarded the rest of the world. How would you characterize these attitudes? Can you see any connection between these opinions and Roosevelt's interest in ranching? Can you guess what a modern feminist might say about the source of Roosevelt's views? Why does TR believe that unpatriotic attitudes were especially widespread among the educated? Can Roosevelt's opinions be found among Americans today?

MANHOOD AND FOREIGN POLICY

Theodore Roosevelt

It is a matter of serious concern to every college man, and, indeed, to every man who believes in the good effects of a liberal education, to see the false views which seem to obtain among so many of the leaders of educated thought, not only upon the Monroe Doctrine, but upon every question which involves the existence of a feeling of robust Americanism. Every educated man who puts himself out of touch with the current of American thought, and who on conspicuous occasions assumes an attitude hostile to the interest of America, is doing what he can to weaken the influence of educated men in American life. The crude, ill-conditioned jealousy of education, which is so often and so lamentably shown by large bodies of our people, is immensely stimulated by the action of those prominent educated men in whom education seems to have destroyed the strong, virile virtues and especially the spirit of Americanism.

. . . .

There are many upright and honorable men who take the wrong side, that is, the anti-American side, of the Monroe Doctrine because they are too short-sighted or too unimaginative to realize the hurt to the nation that would be caused by the adoption of their views. There are other men who take the wrong view simply because they have not thought much of the matter, or are in unfortunate surroundings, by which they have been influenced to their own moral hurt. There are yet other men in whom the mainspring of the opposition to that branch of American policy known as the Monroe Doctrine is sheer timidity. This is sometimes the ordinary timidity of wealth. Sometimes, however, it is peculiarly developed among educated men whose education has tended to make them over-cultivated and over-sensitive to foreign opinion. They are generally men who undervalue the great fighting qualities, without which no nation can ever rise to the first rank.

The timidity of wealth is proverbial, and it was well illustrated by the attitude taken by too many people of means at the time of the Venezuela trouble.[1] Many of them, including bankers, merchants, and railway magnates, criticized the action of the

---

Theodore Roosevelt, *American Ideals* (New York: G. P. Putnam's Sons, 1897), pp. 240–45.

[1] A confrontation between the U.S. and Britain in 1895 over the Venezuela-British Guiana boundary—ED.

President and the Senate, on the ground that it had caused business disturbance. Such a position is essentially ignoble. When a question of national honor or of national right or wrong is at stake, no question of financial interest should be considered for a moment. Those wealthy men who wish the abandonment of the Monroe Doctrine because its assertion may damage their business, bring discredit to themselves, and, so far as they are able, discredit to the nation of which they are a part.

It is an evil thing for any man of education to forget that education should intensify patriotism, and that patriotism must not only be shown by striving to do good to the country from within, but by readiness to uphold its interests and honor, at any cost, when menaced from without. Educated men owe to the community the serious per-formance of this duty. We need not concern ourselves with the *emigré* educated man, the American who deliberately takes up his permanent abode abroad, whether in London or Paris; he is usually a man of weak character, unfitted to do good work either abroad or at home, who does what he can for his country by relieving it of his presence. But the case is otherwise with the American who stays at home and tries to teach the youth of his country to disbelieve in the country's rights, as against other countries, and to regard it as the sign of an enlightened spirit to decry the assertion of those rights by force of arms. This man may be inefficient for good; but he is capable at times of doing harm, because he tends to make other people inefficient likewise. . . . Similarly the anæmic man of refinement and cultivation, whose intellect has been educated at the expense of his character, and who shrinks from all these struggles through which alone the world moves on to greatness, is inclined to consider any expression of the Monroe Doctrine as truculent and ill advised.

. . . .
. . . No triumph of peace is quite so great as the supreme triumphs of war. The courage of the soldier, the courage of the statesman who has to meet storms which can be quelled only by soldierly qualities—this stands higher than any quality called out merely in time of peace. . . .

. . . .
. . . It is through strife, or the readiness for strife, that a nation must win greatness. We ask for a great navy, partly because we think that the possession of such a navy is the surest guaranty of peace, and partly because we feel that no national life is worth having if the nation is not willing, when the need shall arise, to stake everything on the supreme arbitrament of war, and to pour out its blood, its treasure, and its tears like water, rather than submit to the loss of honor and renown.

4.4 TRADE AND MARKETS (1897, 1900)

If most Americans in 1898 felt Spain's brutality against the Cuban people and its apparent sabotage of the American battleship Maine[1] in Havana harbor were ample justifications for war, the American business community, just pulling out of the mid-1890s depression, felt otherwise. War, many business leaders feared, would create further economic uncertainty. Yet America's

[1] An American naval commission investigated the *Maine* disaster and concluded that the explo-sion came from outside the vessel's hull. Although the commission could not fix blame for the tragedy, most Americans assumed that a deliberately set Spanish mine was responsible.

quick victory over Spain changed the minds of many industrialists and bankers. Perhaps, they now felt, an emerging American empire would create new trade opportunities, especially in East Asia, and save the nation from market saturation at home. Particularly intriguing were the possibilities of the formerly Spanish-ruled Philippines, just a few hundred miles off the East Asian coast, which had fallen into American hands soon after the declaration of war.

Even before this, hawks and jingoists called for the expansion of American military power.

Albert Beveridge, a young Republican Senator from Indiana, was not a businessman, but he believed that the Philippines were a potentially valuable economic asset for America. In the following selection, Beveridge argues for retaining the islands rather than surrendering them or permitting them to become an independent country. What were the supposed economic advantages of retaining the Philippines? Has history shown Beveridge to be correct regarding the important commercial role of the Philippines? What other arguments for keeping the islands in American hands does he marshal? The senator seems uneasy about fitting colonies into the American constitutional system. Why would new colonies challenge American constitutional precedents?

WHY WE MUST KEEP THE PHILIPPINES

Albert Beveridge

Mr. President, I address the Senate at this time because Senators and Members of the House on both sides have asked that I give to Congress and the country my observations in the Philippines and the far East, and the conclusions which those observations compel. . . .

Mr. President, the times call for candor. The Philippines are ours forever, "territory belonging to the United States," as the Constitution calls them. And just beyond the Philippines are China's illimitable markets. We will not retreat from either. We will not repudiate our duty in the archipelago. We will not abandon our opportunity in the Orient. We will not renounce our part in the mission of our race, trustee, under God, of the civilization of the world. And we will move forward to our work, not howling out regrets like slaves whipped to their burdens, but with gratitude for a task worthy of our strength, and thanksgiving to Almighty God that He has marked us as His chosen people, henceforth to lead in the regeneration of the world.

This island empire is the last land left in all the oceans. If it should prove a mistake to abandon it, the blunder once made would be irretrievable. If it proves a mistake to hold it, the error can be corrected when we will. Every other progressive nation stands ready to relieve us.

But to hold it will be no mistake. Our largest trade henceforth must be with Asia. The Pacific is our ocean. More and more Europe will manufacture the most it needs, secure from its colonies the most it consumes. Where shall we turn for consumers of our surplus? Geography answers the question. China is our natural customer. She is nearer to us than to England, Germany, or Russia, the commercial powers of the present and the future. They have moved nearer to China by securing permanent bases on her borders. The Philippines give us a base at the door of all the East.

Congressional Globe, 56th Cong., 1st sess., 1900, 33, pt. O: 704–12.

Lines of navigation from our ports to the Orient and Australia; from the Isthmian Canal to Asia; from all Oriental ports to Australia, converge at and separate from the Philippines. They are a self-supporting, dividend-paying fleet, permanently anchored at a spot selected by the strategy of Providence, commanding the Pacific. And the Pacific is the ocean of the commerce of the future. Most future wars will be conflicts for commerce. The power that rules the Pacific, therefore, is the power that rules the world. And, with the Philippines, that power is and will forever be the American Republic. . . .

Nothing is so natural as trade with one's neighbors. The Philippines make us the nearest neighbors of all the East. Nothing is more natural than to trade with those you know. This is the philosophy of all advertising. The Philippines bring us permanently face to face with the most sought-for customers of the world. National prestige, national propinquity, these and commercial activity are the elements of commercial success. The Philippines give the first; the character of the American people supply the last. It is a providential conjunction of all the elements of trade, of duty, and of power. If we are willing to go to war rather than let England have a few feet of frozen Alaska, which affords no market and commands none, what should we not do rather than let England, Germany, Russia, or Japan have all the Philippines? And no man on the spot can fail to see that this would be their fate if we retired. . . .

Here, then, Senators, is the situation. Two years ago there was no land in all the world which we could occupy for any purpose. Our commerce was daily turning toward the Orient, and geography and trade developments made necessary our commercial empire over the Pacific. And in that ocean we had no commercial, naval, or military base. We have one of the three great ocean possessions of the globe, located at the most commanding commercial, naval, and military points in the eastern seas, within hail of India, shoulder to shoulder with China, richer in its own resources than any equal body of land on the entire globe, and peopled by a race which civilization demands shall be improved. Shall we abandon it? That man little knows the common people of the Republic, little understands the instincts of our race, who thinks we will not hold it fast and hold it forever, administering just government by simplest methods. We may trick up devices to shift our burden and lessen our opportunity; they will avail us nothing but delay. We may tangle conditions by applying academic arrangements of self-government to a crude situation; their failure will drive us to our duty in the end. . . .

But, Senators, it would be better to abandon this combined garden and Gibraltar of the Pacific, and count our blood and treasure already spent a profitable loss, than to apply any academic arrangement of self-government to these children. They are not capable of self-government. How could they be? They are not of a self-governing race. They are Orientals, Malays, instructed by Spaniards in the latter's worst estate.

They know nothing of practical government except as they have witnessed the weak, corrupt, cruel, and capricious rule of Spain. What magic will anyone employ to dissolve in their minds and characters those impressions of governors and governed which three centuries of misrule has created? What alchemy will change the oriental quality of their blood and set the self-governing currents of the American pouring through their Malay veins? How shall they, in the twinkling of an eye, be exalted to the heights of self-governing peoples which required a thousand years for us to reach, Anglo-Saxon though we are? . . .

Blind indeed is he who sees not the hand of God in events so vast, so harmonious, so benign. Reactionary indeed is the mind that perceives not that this vital people is the strongest of the saving forces of the world; that our place, therefore, is at the head of the constructing and redeeming nations of the earth; and that to stand aside while events march on is a surrender of our interests, a betrayal of our duty as blind as it is base. Craven indeed is the heart that fears to perform a work so golden and so noble; that dares not win a glory so immortal. . . .

Mr. President and Senators, adopt the resolution offered, that peace may quickly come and that we may begin our saving, regenerating, and uplifting work. . . . Reject it, and the world, history, and the American people will know where to forever fix the awful responsibility for the consequences that will surely follow such failure to do our manifest duty. How dare we delay when our soldiers' blood is flowing? [Applause in the galleries]

4.5   THE ANTI-IMPERIALISTS (1899)

Most Americans undoubtedly supported the decision to go to war with Spain in 1898. But what transpired in the Philippines after the American occupation did not seem very different from Spanish rule in Cuba. The Filipinos quickly came to resent the American presence and rose up against the new oppressor. For two years Americans and Filipinos fought a nasty and brutal guerrilla war to determine the islands' fate. In the end American troops put down the Filipino fighters and imposed U.S. rule on the archipelago. But the Philippine Insurrection made a mockery of benevolent American claims.

Many Americans strongly opposed their nation's role in the Philippines, and in November 1898 a group of reformers, journalists, academics, clergy, business leaders, and maverick politicians formed the Anti-Imperialist League to resist the colonialist drift. The League initially campaigned to defeat the annexation of the Philippines. Once the annexation treaty was ratified, however, it turned its efforts against the cruel war to subdue the Filipinos. Some Americans did in fact oppose expansionist and imperialistic tendencies in general and the Spanish American War in particular. Two eloquent examples, Charles Eliot Norton and Morrison Swift, are included. Do these minority views bear any similarity to the views of Americans who opposed other wars in our history, including the War on Terror in our own day?

CHARLES ELIOT NORTON ON AMERICAN IDEALS (1899)

I have read your little volume on the *Expansion of Westerns Ideals and the World's Peace* with great interest. As you are aware, your position and my own differ widely on the fundamental question which underlies your essays. But I read with genuine sympathy your very able statement of your own views. I do not think that you do quite justice to the opinions of the men who regard the present policy of America as a misfortune. It is not that we would hold America back from playing her full part in the world's affairs, but that we believe that her part could be better accomplished by close adherence to those high principles which are ideally embodied in her institutions—by the establishment of her own democracy in such wise as to make it a symbol of noble self-government and by exercising the influence of a great, unarmed, and peaceful power on the affairs and the moral temper of the world.

We believe that America had something better to offer to mankind than those aims she is now pursuing, and we mourn her desertion of ideals which were not selfish or limited in their application, but which are of universal worth and validity. She has lost her unique position as a potential leader in the progress of civilization and has taken up her place simply as one of the grasping and selfish nations of the present day. We all know how far she has fallen short in the past of exhibiting in her conduct a fidelity to those ideals which she professed, but some of us, at least, had not lost the hope that she would ultimately succeed in becoming more faithful to them.

There are many points in your two papers which, were you here, I should be glad to talk over with you. But it is hardly worthwhile to write of them. Your presentation of the imperialistic position has this great value at least, that it shows that men who hold it are cherishing ideals which, if they can be fulfilled, will make the course on which America has entered Less disastrous than we who do not hold them now fear.

"MORRISON I, SWIFT VIEWS IMPERIALISM AS A THREAT TO LIBERTY" (1899)

Our Crime in the Philippine Islands

1. The New Policy of Corruption.

We now propose to show that the new American Imperialism is a strict reproduction of the British Imperialism that has been described. If that is lovely and desirable, so is its American imitation. But let us permit American Imperialists to speak for themselves and to disclose their own character as we have allowed the English to do. This will show whether the Anglo-Saxonism that would be carried to the Philippines and elsewhere is worth carrying, or should be watchfully kept at home and extinguished.

Charles Denby, our one time minister to China and now a member of McKinely's commission to study the Philippines, has published a brief paper in answer to the question "Shall We Keep the Philippines?" Being a man of prominence and authority among the expansionist we give his words their due weight. They express the change in American morality toward the world which expansionists are inculcating and practising. This man is the type of those who surround and influence the president. He defines a hard and selfish national policy towards the weak. Every important thing that has happened, everything that is happening, goes to establish this proposition:

That hard and selfish men, and hard and selfish policies, will control our imperialist relations; that the kind and well-meaning will be overruled. There is no intention of mildness, humanity and justice, in the forces that are now gaining ascendancy in American life.

Here is Mr. Denby, the type of the hard and selfish imperialist politician of the new school, openly impressing the country this crass and vulgar European doctrine. Thus Mr. Denby:

. . .We have become a great people. We have a great commerce to take care of. We have to compete with the commercial nations of the world in far-distant markets. Commerce, not politics, is king. The manufacturer and the merchant dictate to diplomacy,

Imperialism and Liberty, Los Angeles, 1899, pp. 34–43, 87–99, 150–154, 171.

and control elections. The art of arts is the extension of commercial relations,—in plain language, the selling of native products and manufactured goods.

"I learned what I know of diplomacy in a severe school. *I found among my colleagues not the least hesitation in proposing to their respective Governments to do anything which was supposed to be conducive to their interests. There can be no other rule for the government of all persons who are charged with the conduct of affairs than the promotion of the welfare of their respective countries.*"

This then is what expansion and that noble 'world diplomacy' with which our ears are being daily tickled, bring, us to! Here is Mr. Denby, corrupt and confessedly corrupted by this high diplomacy which is to make us a sainted and respected nation before mankind, glorying in the corruption and trying to corrupt his countrymen. If there was ever needed proof that we should keep ourselves unspotted from the filth and foulness of those European and Asiatic complications that territory stealing will assuredly bring, here is that proof. For contact with European codes inflicts those codes upon us. Denby continues his exposure of Imperialism, and applies its Chris like morality to the Philippines:

"We have the right as conquerors to hold the Philippines. We have the right to hold them as part payment of a war indemnity. This policy may be characterized as unjust to Spain; but is the result of the fortunes of war. All nations recognize that the conqueror may dictate the terms of peace."

I am the favor of holding the Philippines because I cannot conceive of any alternative to our doing so, *except the seisure of territory in China;* and I prefer to hold them rather than to oppress further the helpless Government and people of China. I want China to preserve her autonomy, to become great and prosperous; and *I want these results not for the interests of China, but for our interests. I am not the agent or attorney of China; and, as an American, I do not look to the promotion of China's interest, or Spain's, or any other country's—but simply of our own.*

"The whole world sees in China a splendid market for our native products,—our timber, our locomotives, our rails, our coal oil, our sheetings, our mining-plants and numberless other articles."

"Dewey's victory is an epoch in the affairs of the Far Fast. We hold our heads higher. We are coming to our own. We are stretching out our hands for what nature meant should be ours. We are taking our proper rank among the nations of the world. *We are after markets, the greatest markets now existing in the world. Along with these markets will go our beneficent institutions, and humanity will bless us.*"

This is an exquisite example of the British cant and bathos which is exhibiting itself serenely in the new Imperial America. Wherever the basest of international principles of pilfering and freebooting are applied to gain markets, "along with these markets will go our beneficent institutions." The halo of our blessed institutions will pervade and rectify rapacity and wrong! But it will not. We shall not build beneficent institutions on ruffianism and rapacity. 'We are after markets, the greatest markets in the world,' we do not care what we do to get them; we will cheerfully rob and kill, we will wrench their fatherland from the weak and call it ours, we admit it in cold blood, but like the praying professional murderer, we piously declare that God and humanity will bless us in it. How did our war of humanity to rescue Cuba establish the irrelevant and unheard-of conclusion that unless we take the Philippines there is 'no alternative except the seizure of territory in China?' There is no bridge between these two irreconcilable opposites excepting the beneficent institutions of American rapacity. The Philippines have done us no wrong, China has done us no wrong, but because Spain wronged Cuba and we had compassion, we do no wrong in wronging either the Philippines or China. This is the imperialists' creed.

Now we do not expect to reach such men as Mr. Denby or Mr. Denby's type—the president, the advisers of the president, the whole tribe of commercial, political and newspaper Imperialists, who are hounding the nation to crime. "Commerce, not politics, is king. The manufacturer and the merchant dictate to diplomacy, *and control elections.*" We realize this. But we turn away from these classes to *the people.* We think that when they realize the brazen fraud being practised on them, *they* will decide to control elections, not only to put an end to the dishonest and ruffianly policy of Imperialism, but to put an end to the supremacy of commerce over man.

But Mr. Denby has not even yet conveyed to us all the light he has in him. In a more recent article he presents Imperialistic principles in their engaging nakedness without the usual shreds of moral clothing.

"If," he says, "the argument made herein has any force, the legal and constitutional difficulties which were quoted against expansion have disappeared, and the cold, hard, practical question alone remains. Will the possession of these islands benefit us as a nation? *If it will not, set them free tomorrow, and let their people, if they please, cut each other's throats, or play what pranks they please. To this complexion we must come at last, that, unless it is beneficial for us to hold these islands, we should turn them loose,*"

We ask this question: Why, this being the mind and purpose of our imperialist politicians and commercialists, are they allowed to grimace and pose before the nation as philanthropists and moralists? Why do we not enforce upon them silence about the good they intend to do the conquered savages, when it is an acknowledged lie? 'Let the Filipinos cut each other's throats unless the appropriation of their country will help our trade. Damn the good we might do them. We are not in this expansion business for their good.' It is true we are not, but we command you to stop telling us that we are. We propose to hold this argument on your basis, that of hard brutal selfishness, and to decide whether it is best for us to put ourselves and the peoples absorbed into your selfish hands by adopting your Imperialist policy. And is it too solemn a question to press upon the *moral* expansionists, whether they think in their own unselfish minds that they will be able to overcome and rule these selfish commercial Imperialists and keep them in the paths of righteousness after the deed is done? If they are so moonstruck let them study the forces that now rule this country, and compare them with the paths of righteousness.

Mr. Denby, who is willing the Filipinos shall cut each other's throats if preventing them will not fill our pockets, has one more word which makes an easy transition from Imperialist theory to Imperialist practice. He writes as an inspired commercial prophet and a poet:

"In other lands and other wars the condition of the conquered people has been hard and deplorable. In our case we march bearing gifts, the choicest gifts— liberty and hope and happiness. We carry with us all that gives to the flower of life its perfume. The dusky East rises at our coming; and the Filipino springs to his feet and becomes a free man. This is not poetry, but reality wrought out by a people to whom freedom is the breath of life, and who would scorn to enslave a country or a race."

2. McKinley's Proclamation of War.

When our Congress passed the resolutions which involved us in war with Spain it pledged the following:

Fourth: That the United States hereby disclaims any disposition or intention to exercise *sovereignty, jurisdiction, or control over said island [Cuba]*, except for the pacification thereof, *and asserts its determination, when that is accomplished, to leave the government and control of the island to its people.*

In his message to Congress of December, 1897, McKinley recorded and pledged himself in now famous and memorable language. Said he:

"I speak not of forcible annexations because that is not to be thought of, and under our code of morality that would be criminal aggression."

But one year later, on December 21, 1898, this man on his own initiative, without the authority of Congress or the people, more than a month before the Treaty of Peace was ratified by the Senate. . . .

This proclamation drove the Filipinos into war against the United States. There was nothing left for them to do unless they consented to national enslavement. It was not only natural but right that they should go to war against us. Our Chief Man had notified them by arbitrary decree that if they did not submit to the usurped authority of the United States—"the absolute domain of military authority," he called it—they would be forced into submission by shell and grapeshot. "Honest submission," or death: they had their choice. "Honest submission," or "forcible annexation." All who did not honestly submit to the proclamation of the tyrant were to be "brought within the lawful rule we have assumed, with firmness if need be." On the 5th of February that firmness began to be applied and 4000 heroic Filipinos who could not honestly submit to the self-made despot were killed. The man who killed them was William McKinley. The death of each one of them was groundless manslaughter, McKinley was their murderer. He was their self-condemned murderer, convicted by his own words of one year before. "I speak not of forcible annexation, because that is not to be thought of, and *under our code of morality that would be criminal aggression."*

Under the light of this solemn promise and its bloody repudiation McKinley reveals himself to be the crowning fraud and hypocrite of the age, who has no right to respect from any honest man in the United States. He originally declared a true American principle, that we cannot take any form of authority over a people that is opposed to that authority without criminal aggression and breaking our code of morality; this code holds of Cuba, of the Philippines, and of every foot of ground not our own under the sun that our cupidity might be disposed to seize. The breaking of this code, consciously held and publicly announced, was therefore an act of detestable piracy, bringing shame and dishonor upon the whole nation.

The administration and the imperialist press have striven to convince our people that the Filipinos are responsible for the war. This is one of the lies that we must tell each other to save a last remnant of our self-respect. But it is nevertheless a lie with no mitigation. McKinley declared war in his Proclamation, and the Filipinos began hostilities. The feeble McKinley doubtless honestly hoped that they would honestly submit to his declaration that they were to be as a conquered and subject people to the United States, without the sad necessity of being obliged to forcibly conquer them. The subterfuge did not work. They had never acknowledged the sovereignty of the United States: for the United States to declare sovereignty was therefore for the United States to declare war.

After the "criminal aggression" of McKinley's proclamation that a state of virtual war already existed, that they must submit or be killed, there was nothing for them to do but to fight. And every true American who resents this dastardly aggression by the president upon a harmless race of barbarians should be deeply thankful that they did fight, and must hope that our arms will not be able to subdue them. No honorable American can uphold the criminal attempt of American potentates to deprive a weak race of its liberty in the name of liberty. As liberty-loving American citizens it is our duty to uphold the Filipinos in their righteous and patriotic attempt to keep our yoke from falling on them.

3. **All Our Rights Forfeited.**

For those who hesitate at this let us examine the president's rights when he proclaimed honest submission or kind but firm death to the Filipinos. 1. There was no technical, formal, legal, or constitutional sanction for his proclamation. 2. There would have been no right or sanction for it if the peace treaty had been ratified when he issued it.

Let us first consider what rights we had in the Philippines *before* the treaty was approved, remembering that its subsequent approval was not retroactive, and could not lend legality to anything that was done before. Now whether we had any after its ratification, we certainly had no status of authority in the Philippines before that act. We were there purely as opponents of Spain. We were not there as conquerors of the Filipinos, but as conquerors of Spain; the Filipinos had helped us drive Spain out. When hostilities ceased the islands were not ours except by temporary occupation. They were not ours either legally or morally. Spain had not ceded them and we had not decided to accept or even ask for them. The only power in America that could make our request for them legal and binding, or accept them if offered, was the Senate, and that had not done so. The propositions drawn up by the Peace Commissioners at Paris were merely an arrangement by which the United States, acting through the Senate as ordered in the Constitution, could request or demand the islands of Spain if it saw fit. The Senate had not acted on the treaty and had consequently not even decided to ask for the Philippines.

Our rights even technically were therefore *nil*.

A proclamation of sovereignty from the president when the whole question whether we should take or claim the islands was pending was justified by nothing but the arbitrary will of that ruler. It was no less an outrage than if he should proclaim our sovereignty over Canada, Ireland or the British Indies. The act was an insult to Spain and a profligate attack upon the Filipinos.

Having issued this unlawful proclamation and so declared war on the Philippine Islanders, we forfeited all further claims over them excepting such as we might win by force if our challenge to war were taken up. After that proclamation the ratification of the treaty was a dead letter, for by our unlawful action all possibility of obtaining the Philippines legally or morally was lost. The question was now between us and them and was one of force. Of course if they chose to accept the position of a people conquered by us without being conquered, that was their business; but legally and morally they ought not to have accepted that humiliation, and they did not do so. The president's impudent aggression also deserved anything but success.

To recapitulate: as we now stand we have no rights in the Philippines and can obtain none except by brute force. We ruled ourselves out by McKinley's act of usurpation. Spain would have been justified in resenting that act had she been able, and Spain being unable the natives were justified. Until the acceptance of the treaty by both nations our policy in the islands could be only provisional. If Spain finally approved the treaty she transferred to us such rights of sovereignty the Philippines as she possessed. . . .

Business Enterprise of Generals

The words of our fighting classes at home in favor of imperialism likewise lose all their force when we consider who these people are and the motives of selfishness which move them to seek for this country a military future. It is almost enough to name these classes over to understand why they wish expansion. Have we not lately had some deep experiences what a precious set of self-seekers our military officers of all grades and sorts are? Is there anything in the daily conduct of our fire—eating professional politicians to make us think they care for the world, their country, or for aught beyond their own skins and interests? What of our eruptive press? What of great makers of trusts, so disinterested that they are taking all America as their own and damning the people to a hell of poverty and hardship? We charge these classes with seeking their own despicable private ends in painting the glories and profits of expansion.

Let us study them one by one. The trade of officers of war is war. Through schemes of war they promote themselves in the great objects of their lives, salaries, renown, affluence and influence. All their aspirations and hopes center on military magnification. And it is their trade art to make others see things as they do. They are a species of commercial drummer, whose business success hangs upon their convincing others that wars and rumors and preparations for wars are the most important affairs of human society. They must do this or remain always little people. They have the galling example of foreign countries. There a general is a truly great man; he is really a god with his clanking sword, his glittering uniform, his awful majesty of mien, his towering disdainment of the common carcasses of mere citizens which creep on the low earth below him. It is a thing to be a general in Europe. Life has character if you can feel yourself reposing on the clouds of power, master of instruments to blow the groveling herd of men to dust if they run amuck the doctrines that you patron. How different in America! How abominable, how degrading! A general is only a mortal here adored and deified by none—until recently. He swallows wind into his stomach and swells himself out in vain. He has been kept down in his proper place.

But times have changed and he thinks that if he throws a little more business enterprise into his trade he may win the privilege to expand and swagger and become a tinselled deity. Will he miss such a chance? Will he stint his arguments to convince his darling countrymen how good for them will be the owning of islands and invading of Asia? He looks forward to the time when he will not have to beg and argue to these countrymen, the time when with docile battalions behind his ramrod back he can stride haughty and ferocious across our part of earth and not demean himself by knowing that he has countrymen. Oh people Of America, watch this fellow argue now! Because the army is still small, see how small and humble he is. With the deferential modesty of impassioned concern for us, he tells us of the danger of our coasts, talks soulfully of universal love, of duty, and of civilization!—this professional murderer, this smasher and preventer of civilization, verily talks of duty! But give him his army and what will you hear him talk of then? Go to Russia and listen to the generals; are they talking of love? To civilized Germany, free France, liberal England: are their generals talking as we would wish to give ours liberty to talk?

1. The New Treason.

Beware. Can you not already note a change of tone, a growing insolence, since we took to war and yielded to the importunities of our war lords for a greater body of fighters? When have we before heard such language as this?

The army and the navy are the sword and the shield which this nation must carry, if she is to do her duty among the nations of the earth—if she is not to stand merely as the China of the Western Hemisphere.

When before now has anyone dared to use such raw twaddle to us? But the author of this febrile slush says more:

To no body of men in the United States is the country so much indebted as to the splendid officers and enlisted men of the regular army and navy; there is no body from which the country has less to fear; and none of which it should be prouder, none which it should be more anxious to upbuild.

Is not this something wholly new and thunderingly preposterous? Is not the officer that can ooze this foul offense from his self-seeking mind already far on in his dreams toward a European America, where the military swashbuckler will eclipse and terrorize the toiling snail of peace? And yet even this is a lullaby beside the rabid impudence which the same nascent bully already ventures to express.

As for those in our country who encourage the foe, we can afford contemptuously to disregard them; but it must be remembered that their utterances are saved from being treasonable merely from the fact that they are despicable.

So then with an army of only 60,000 men our semi-military gentry dare apply these abusive words to a number of American people so great that it may turn out when counted to be the majority. What will be said and done as time goes on and the army grows according to the rampant military determination which now neither slumbers nor sleeps? Then those who differ in opinion from our military sheiks will be attended to for treason as they do it in Germany. Treason is something for which men are jailed, hanged and shot. Treason is any thing. That displeases those in power, and the number of things that are treasonable increases in proportion to the increase of military force. Treason is merely a political label which those who want to establish their private opinions by force, and rule arbitrarily, apply to those with different opinions. The man who says a thing is treason is a tyrant in embryo; he is a person with the blood of the inquisitors in him; he has not learned the smallest lessons of human appreciation, toleration and progress; he is of that beastly fiber which burned men at the stake in earlier days for thinking as nature ordained them to think. Civilization has been one long and fearful struggle against this cruel beastliness, always betraying itself in new forms. The religious brute has been conquered, but the political brute and the military brute are here still, with the same old mighty will to destroy liberty, the same depraved frenzy to make mankind grovel to them in thought and act, the same aboriginal club with a new name to beat their brains out who resist. Heresy was the ancient name of the club, the recent name is treason. If you do not believe in God as I do, I will kill you: If you do not believe in my politics, I will kill you. The same foulness in the human mind brings out ever fresh the same hideous deformity of conduct under later conditions, as they say that small-pox is a disease which arose out of syphilis, caused by the lives of abominable nastiness and abandonment of those who lived before us, and which now lives on to, infect and injure a cleaner age with its horrid syphilitic substance. So is the cry of treason a recrudescence of the mental syphilis of heresy. . . .

The Bandit Press

1. As General Hell-Maker.

The press of the United States vaunts itself the possessor of great power. It has a power similar in many respects to that of the politician. The politician is a representative personage, whose force lies in the fact that after the people have performed the single self-governing act of his election he does as he pleases. The press is a representative personage for whose erection to influence not even one democratic act is needed or performed. The owner of the press must have money; that answers for the periodic election of the politician. With money the newspaper becomes a representative voice of the people, not because the people chose or established it but because few people have vast sums of money to put into a newspaper and make it stand. The people accept what is given them and it passes for representative because they are unable to put anything really representative in its place.

But the people are thoroughly conscious that the press does not represent them and chafe increasingly under its pretensions to do so. With the concentration of wealth the press becomes less and less representative, less and less truly popular, for it ceases to depend on popular support for existence and depends on bodies of concentrated wealth, its great advertisers. The people recognize this change of the press center of gravity and feel it distinctly in newspaper treatment of popular issues.

The difference that has taken place is this. Formerly the newspapers sought to discover and vocalize the sentiments of the people, because if they had not done so it would have wrecked their prosperity; now they coolly give out as popular opinion whatever it suits them to have pass for public opinion; and as they are entirely independent of the will of the people and do not subsist by the people's support, it does not affect them or their interests if what they publish as popular will is the strict reverse of it. It was formerly the boast of the press to mould public opinion by educating it, but now it is able to produce at a moment's notice, over night, any public opinion that is required without asking or needing the public concurrence. In this sense public opinion is absolutely controlled by the press. Whatever popular sentiment it desires it manufactures, publishes, announces to be the will of everybody, hears no dissenting voice, and accepts the matter as settled—and so do the people.

The single fault of this process is that the opinion published has no element of the public in it. The popular sentiment which the press thus creates and sends out labeled, 'By the people,' is always that sentiment which is agreeable not to the masses of people but to the masses of press capital and the other volumes of concentrated riches from which the press draws its current sustenance. But it is as if these utterances were the public mind, for the press holds the avenues of popular speech and the people are obliged to be mute.

It is a circumstance of no slight meaning, this total detachment of the press from the people. Its significance is that public opinion is never really expressed and therefore never really even formed—in short, that public opinion has ceased to be a force or to exist. This is certainly startling when we reflect on the decay of the pulpit and platform, the other leading modes of public expression. Whether the press was the main cause, it was a great cause in the decadence of these institutions, for the audiences reached by the press grew so large that in contrast the number addressed by a pulpit or platform orator seemed hardly worth the labor and machinery of gathering them together. The press has even taken to preaching as a business investment, having a corner in its Sunday edition for compact little sermonlets from the pens of divines, for five cents—much less than the rental of a pew—furnishing the public with religion and rescuing it from the Sabbath labor of walking to church.

Rather the greater cause for the decline of the sacred and secular platforms has been the moral shrinkage of those who occupy them. The pastor has declined into an advocate and retainer of the wealthy class, the platform reasoner into a party politician and monger of prejudice, in each instance forfeiting popular confidence and leaving the field in possession of the press which at least makes thin moral pretensions.

The people are left without a voice. The effect upon them of this loss of speaking power is a paralysis of both thinking and action, while those who command the avenues of expression are able to palm off ready-made, self-interested opinions on the people, making the impression upon each reader that although he does not believe this way others do and leading him to act or acquiesce with what he believes to be the majority view. The main influence of the press comes through this deception. It brazenly proclaims what it calls public sentiment, in which perhaps not a single unit of the public agrees, but all are silent because each dimly fancies that there must be such a sentiment somewhere, not crediting the press with the lying effrontery to declare an absolute fiction so shamelessly. Each asks himself, too, what will be the use if I protest, since the papers will not spread a dissenting note? The people's mouths are closed with the rivets of necessity for they have no journals of any magnitude through which they are free to speak, the journals that profess to side with the people being conducted by just the same rules and just the same motives as the others and differing only in the opinions which they publish as public opinion.

The will of the people never governs these publications of a millionaire capitalist, the will of his capital governs, the prosperity of the capital invested in the plant is the pole star of his newspaper policy, and that is never identical with the prosperity of the people, even if the most skillfully educated brains are employed to prove the identity in daily editorials. By them also something which the people are said to want is daily published in lieu of that which they do want, and success, what can succeed, what they think will succeed, not what ought to succeed, is the dominant criterion of everything that is done.

It ought to be made a proverb that the proprietors of none of the great dailies are in the business for principle any more than for their health; they are in it to prosper and they follow the laws of prosperity: so that a great privately owned sheet which stands out for popular reform is certain to be unsound at the core because of the conditions that govern all private millionaire things. They live by advertisement and sensation. They increase advertisements by increasing sensations. If reform is a prolific sensation some of them seize upon that as their province, not for the reform itself but for the money that is in it, and their advocacy mutilates it because instead of using it as a grand end they are abusing and degrading it as a means to increase sensation, circulation, and advertisement. . . .

. . .The millionaires fill the papers full of their views daily, the people utter nothing, for not an inch of the papers belongs to them. Is this freedom of speech? It passes for it, yet in fact the people are as much gagged and suppressed as if the heaviest laws and penalties locked their lips.

The millionaires tailor our thoughts for us, as in Russia the Government cuts out the thinking of the Czar's subjects. There press autocrats censor what goes in, here the editors employed by the millionaire owners are the censors; our way is much better for it causes no ill-feeling; through the marvelous magic of monopoly the people do not feel the hand of censorship, though it works as implacably as if in Russia the Czar owned and edited, as he now censors, all the papers of influence. . .

Without Consent of The American Governed

The most momentous fact of the century is the *manner* of foisting imperialism upon us. To do it with our consent would have been one thing, to do it *without our consent,* as it has been done, is the greatest fourth-dimensional marvel of time. The guy of humanity which laid Spain at our feet opened the problem to the Millionaire Administration how to rob Spain and disarm popular suspicion. The act of confiscating instead of liberating Spain's territory had to be painted as an act of humanity. It was easy enough to say that all the Spanish islands should be liberated from Spain, but the pinch came in showing the humanity of our keeping them, particularly on top of our biblical asseverations not to do so. Our rulers got over that by inventing that the islanders are not fit to govern themselves. It is an invention, because it certainly had not and has not been proved. The hardest tussle came when the unselfish Trust Administration was called on to establish the humanity of exterminating a race to give it liberty. This intention was flatly stated by our war bosses. During that long bright period when we had the rebels 'well in hand,' "Secretary Alger said that the situation was most encouraging, and that it was apparent that the Filipinos realized the strength of the United States and saw that resistance would mean extermination for them if they persisted in defying authority."* The invention used to clothe this deformity in virtuous humanity was the happiness of unborn future generations to spring from the exterminated. This guy also was soberly perpetrated and soberly received by a people proud of its susceptibility to humor.

Finally the evolution of imperialism reached a stage where the pretense of acting for humanity was an impediment. It prevented steps which were necessary if the juggernaut of progress was to murder on. It was an impediment, yet so tasteful a bait to the pious that it could not be done without. A very daring experiment was tried, that of disclosing the true purpose, territorial conquest for wealth, and painting the stars and stripes humanity upon it. This plan included the full confession that trade had become the A and Z of the whole matter, but asserting that Yankee trade never went anywhere without carrying a superior article of humanity and civilization in its pack. If this atrocious humbug found lodgment in the American spleen, every conceivable thing necessary for the world-spread of American monopolies would be tolerated by the people, even down to the vivisection of whole savage races for trade experiments. This might be called a dull joke; it is still too early to say whether Americans, renowned among themselves for their biting perception of humor, will be able to see it. Our rulers have conducted their game very artfully, and the work now is to unravel the mesh in which that art has tangled us. How, from the essence of humanity, did the president extract the right to steal? His accomplices in this highwayman's synthesis in commercial chemistry were his politicians and editors. In their passage from God to Greed the steps are as follows. The president began this Fagin performance as soon as Spain was whipped, his instrument was our Peace Commission at Paris.

Step 1. It would be unhumanitarian to leave the Philippines and Porto Rico with Spain. Step 2. It is our duty to take them away. Step 3. We shall not know what to do with them, but duty will always disclose a way. Step 4. We have a perfect right to take them. If humanity does not give the right war does. Step 5. Although we fought purely for humanity we have a right to consider our own good in the settlement incidentally, only incidentally. Step 6. Considering our own good is in this instance identical with pure humanity because, as the most generous people on earth, we can do nothing ungenerous. Step 7. It may be our duty to appropriate Spain's possessions to save Europe from an unnecessary quarrel. If we do so it will be against our will and for purely humanitarian reasons. Step 8. It may be that these possessions would be a great advantage to our trade, but that is not certain, and their climate is bad. Step 9. If it should be thrust upon us to take these lands for humanitarian and commercial reasons it will be the best thing that could happen to them. Our use of them for trade purposes would be identical with civilizing them, for this great enlightened nation can do nothing selfishly. We should teach them self-government and liberty, under us. Step 10. These semi-savage peoples have all shown themselves worthless and unthankful. Even the Cubans are low and ungrateful. They do not deserve the blood we shed for their liberty, nor much consideration of their wishes. We know better than they do what is best for them. *We must save them from themselves.* Step 11. Our trade in the East depends on the Philippines. There is no disguising it. We must have the Philippines. It is our right and duty to look after our own interests in the world. That is the only way that we can preserve and spread the light of our enlightenment to others who need it. The dark places of the earth call upon us to trade with them that they may be enlightened. Step 12. All human prosperity rests on trade. The powers of Europe will take away our trade if we do not make ourselves a great world-power in army and navy to protect and extend it. It would be a crime to permit less civilized and humane races than ourselves to capture and people the untilled place of the earth.

By these step God is hammered into Greed and yet retains the image of God. The transition from God to Trade is accomplished, but all the trade language remains divine and biblical. The most miraculous part of this miracle is that the people of America had no part in it anywhere. . . .

CHAPTER 5

The Progressive Impulse

During the first two decades of the twentieth century, as the United States shifted from rural to urban, its political structure also altered. More prosperous than ever, many Americans nevertheless felt uneasy over the rapid economic and social changes taking place. Their discomfort with the unfamiliar spawned a many-sided reform movement we call Progressivism.

Progressivism has long been a puzzle to scholars. Its shape seems fuzzy and changing, including within its boundaries a wide range of views, programs, and personnel. Its origins too seem unclear. Who favored reform during the early twentieth century? Were they the same people who had supported Populist political insurgency during the 1890s? And why did the movement appear when it did?

The following selections represent different and often competing aspects of Progressive thought. As you read these, you might consider whether there is a single thread connecting all of them, or whether Progressivism is just a convenient name for a grab bag of reformist demands that fortuitously surfaced together in the decade preceding World War I.

5.1 THE DANGER OF CONCENTRATED WEALTH (1912, 1913, 1899)

The wave of business combinations formed between 1898 and 1903 was a response to the single national market that emerged following the completion of the transportation and communications network. Deprived of local monopoly power and forced into cutthroat competition with aggressive distant firms, business leaders sought to consolidate their operations. In the six-year period straddling the turn of the century, there were 234 industrial mergers representing some $6 billion in capital.

The merger movement dismayed the public. How could small producers survive in an era of huge trusts? How severely would consumers be hurt by price fixing when competition waned? How could representative government fend off giant business firms when they sought favors?

The four selections reflect various views of business consolidation. The first two, by Theodore Roosevelt and Woodrow Wilson, represent different Progressive responses.

The third and fourth selections reflect the complexity of new financial institutions made possible by the development of vast new amounts of capital. John Rockefeller's oil company required huge amounts of capital to reach its monopolistic size. J. P. Morgan, America's leading investment banker, addressed charges of centralization before the Pujo Committee in 1913. In both cases, we need to evaluate these remarks in light of self-interest.

As you read the Roosevelt and Wilson pieces, consider the differences in approach of the two political leaders, who were both within the Progressive orbit. Do they have identical attitudes toward concentrated business power? How are their prescriptions for cure related to their long-term party allegiances? Has the passage of eighty years since the speeches were delivered demonstrated which of the formulas for dealing with concentrated economic power is more effective in protecting the public interest?

REPUBLICAN ANTI-TRUST

Theodore Roosevelt

An important volume entitled "Concentration and Control" has just been issued by President Charles R. Van Hise of the University of Wisconsin. The University of Wisconsin has been more influential than any other agency in making Wisconsin what it has become, a laboratory for wise social and industrial experiment in the betterment of conditions. President Van Hise is one of those thoroughgoing but sane and intelligent radicals from whom much of leadership is to be expected in such a matter. The sub-title of his book shows that his endeavor is to turn the attention of his countrymen toward practically solving the trust problem of the United States.

In his preface he states that his aim is to suggest a way to gain the economic advantages of the concentration of industry and at the same time to guard the interests of the public and to assist in the rule of enlightenment, reason, fair play, mutual consideration, and toleration. In sum, he shows that unrestrained competition as an economic principle has become too destructive to be permitted to exist, and that the small men must be allowed to co-operate under penalty of succumbing before their big competitors; and yet such co-operation, vitally necessary to the small man, is criminal under the present law. He says:

> With the alternative before the business men of co-operation or failure, we may be sure that they will co-operate. Since the law is violated by practically every group of men engaged in trade from one end of the country to the other, they do not feel that in combining they are doing a moral wrong. The selection of the individual or corporation for prosecution depends upon the arbitrary choice of the Attorney General, perhaps somewhat influenced by the odium which attaches to some of the violators of the law. They all take their chance, hoping that the blow will fall elsewhere. With general violation and sporadic enforcement of an impracticable law, we cannot hope that our people will gain respect for it.

New York Times, August 7, 1912.

In conclusion, there is presented as the solution of the difficulties of the present industrial situation, concentration, co-operation, and control. Through concentration we may have the economic advantages coming from magnitude of operations. Through co-operation we may limit the wastes of the competitive system. Through control by commission we may secure freedom for fair competition, elimination of unfair practices, conservation of our natural resources, fair wages, good social conditions, and reasonable prices.

Concentration and co-operation in industry in order to secure efficiency are a world-wide movement. The United States cannot resist it. If we isolate ourselves and insist upon the subdivision of industry below the highest economic efficiency, and do not allow co-operation, we shall be defeated in the world's markets. We cannot adopt an economic system less efficient than our great competitors, Germany, England, France, and Austria. Either we must modify our present obsolete laws regarding concentration and co-operation so as to conform with the world movement, or else fall behind in the race for the world's markets. Concentration and co-operation are conditions imperatively essential for industrial advance; but if we allow concentration and co-operation there must be control in order to protect the people, and adequate control is only possible through the administrative commission. Hence concentration, co-operation, and control are the keywords for a scientific solution of the mighty industrial problem which now confronts this Nation. . . .

We Progressives stand for the rights of the people. When these rights can best be secured by insistence upon States' rights, then we are for States' rights; when they can best be secured by insistence upon National rights, then we are for National rights. Inter-State commerce can be effectively controlled only by the Nation. The States cannot control it under the Constitution, and to amend the Constitution by giving them control of it would amount to a dissolution of the Government. The worst of the big trusts have always endeavored to keep alive the feeling in favor of having the States themselves, and not the Nation, attempt to do this work, because they know that in the long run such effort would be ineffective. There is no surer way to prevent all successful effort to deal with the trusts than to insist that they be dealt with by the States rather than by the Nation, or to create a conflict between the States and the Nation on the subject. The well-meaning ignorant man who advances such a proposition does as much damage as if he were hired by the trusts themselves, for he is playing the game of every big crooked corporation in the country. The only effective way in which to regulate the trusts is through the exercise of the collective power of our people as a whole through the Governmental agencies established by the Constitution for this very purpose.

Grave injustice is done by the Congress when it fails to give the National Government complete power in this matter; and still graver injustice by the Federal courts when they endeavor in any way to pare down the right of the people collectively to act in this matter as they deem wise; such conduct does itself tend to cause the creation of a twilight zone in which neither the Nation nor the States have power. Fortunately, the Federal courts have more and more of recent years tended to adopt the true doctrine, which is that all these matters are to be settled by the people themselves, and that the conscience of the people, and not the preferences of any servants of the people, is to be the standard in deciding what action shall be taken by the people.

As Lincoln phrased it: "The [question] of National power and State rights as a principle is no other than the principle of generality and locality. Whatever concerns the whole should be confided to the whole—to the General Government; while whatever concerns only the State should be left exclusively to the State."

It is utterly hopeless to attempt to control the trusts merely by the antitrust law, or by any law the same in principle, no matter what the modifications may be in detail. In the first place, these great corporations cannot possibly be controlled merely by a succession of lawsuits. The administrative branch of the Government must exercise such control. The preposterous failure of the Commerce Court has shown that only damage comes from the effort to substitute judicial for administrative control of great corporations. In the next place, a loosely drawn law which promises to do everything would reduce business to complete ruin if it were not also so drawn as to accomplish almost nothing. . . .

Contrast what has actually been accomplished under the inter-State commerce law with what has actually been accomplished under the anti-trust law. The first has, on the whole, worked in a highly efficient manner and achieved real and great results; and it promises to achieve even greater results, (although I firmly believe that if the power of the Commissioners grows greater it will be necessary to make them and their superior, the President, even more completely responsible to the people for their acts). The second has occasionally done good, has usually accomplished nothing, but generally left the worst conditions wholly unchanged, and has been responsible for a considerable amount of downright and positive evil.

What is needed is the application to all industrial concerns and all cooperating interests engaged in inter-State commerce in which there is either monopoly or control of the market of the principles on which we have gone in regulating transportation concerns engaged in such commerce. The anti-trust law should be kept on the statute books and strengthened so as to make it genuinely and thoroughly effective against every big concern tending to monopoly or guilty of anti-social practices.

At the same time, a National industrial commission should be created which should have complete power to regulate and control all the great industrial concerns engaged in inter-State business—which practically means all of them in this country. This commission should exercise over these industrial concerns like powers to those exercised over the railways by the Inter-State Commerce Commission, and over the National banks by the Controller of the Currency, and additional powers if found necessary. The establishment of such a commission would enable us to punish the individual rather than merely the corporation, just as we now do with banks, where the aim of the Government is not to close the bank but to bring to justice personally any bank official who has gone wrong.

This commission should deal with all the abuses of the trusts—all the abuses such as those developed by the Government suit against the Standard Oil and Tobacco Trusts—as the Inter-State Commerce Commission now deals with rebates. It should have complete power to make the capitalization absolutely honest and put a stop to all stock watering. Such supervision over the issuance of corporate securities would put a stop to exploitation of the people by dishonest capitalists desiring to declare dividends on watered securities, and would open this kind of industrial property to ownership by the people at large. It should have free access to the books of each corporation and power to find out exactly how it treats its employees, its rivals, and the general public. It should have power to compel the unsparing publicity of all the acts of any corporation which goes wrong.

The regulation should be primarily under the administrative branch of the Government and not by lawsuit. It should prohibit and effectually punish monopoly achieved through wrong, and also actual wrongs done by industrial corporations which are not monopolies, such as the artificial raising of prices, the artificial restriction on productivity, the elimination of competition by unfair or predatory practices, and the like; leaving industrial organizations free within the limits of fair and honest dealing to promote through the inherent efficiency of organization the power of the United States as a competitive Nation among Nations, and the greater abundance at home that will come to our people from that power wisely exercised.

DEMOCRATIC ANTI-TRUST

Woodrow Wilson

I take my stand absolutely, where every Progressive ought to take his stand, on the proposition that private monopoly is indefensible and intolerable. And there I will fight my battle. And I know how to fight it. Everybody who has even read the newspapers knows the means by which these men built up their power and created these monopolies. Any decently equipped lawyer can suggest to you statutes by which the whole business can be stopped. What these gentlemen do not want is this: they do not want to be compelled to meet all comers on equal terms. I am perfectly willing that they should beat any competitor by fair means; but I know the foul means they have adopted, and I know that they can be stopped by law. If they think that coming into the market upon the basis of mere efficiency, upon the mere basis of knowing how to manufacture goods better than anybody else and to sell them cheaper than anybody else, they can carry the immense amount of water that they have put into their enterprises in order to buy up rivals, then they are perfectly welcome to try it. But there must be no squeezing out of the beginner, no crippling his credit; no discrimination against retailers who buy from a rival; no threats against concerns who sell supplies to a rival; no holding back of raw material from him; no secret arrangements against him. All the fair competition you choose, but no unfair competition of any kind. And then when unfair competition is eliminated, let us see these gentlemen carry their tanks of water on their backs. All that I ask and all I shall fight for is that they shall come into the field against merit and brains everywhere. If they can beat other American brains, then they have got the best brains.

But if you want to know how far brains go, as things now are, suppose you try to match your better wares against these gentlemen, and see them undersell you before your market is any bigger than the locality and make it absolutely impossible for you to get a fast foothold. If you want to know how brains count, originate some invention which will improve the kind of machinery they are using, and then see if you can borrow enough money to manufacture it. You may be offered something for your patent by the corporation,—which will perhaps lock it up in a safe and go on using the old machinery; but you will not be allowed to manufacture. I know men who have tried it, and they could not get the money, because the great money lenders of this country are in the arrangement with the great manufacturers of this country, and they do not propose to see their control of the market interfered with by outsiders. And who are outsiders? Why, all the rest of the people of the United States are outsiders.

Woodrow Wilson, *The New Freedom* (New York: Doubleday, Page and Company, 1913), pp. 167–75, 176–77, 179–81.

They are rapidly making us outsiders with respect even of the things that come from the bosom of the earth, and which belong to us in a peculiar sense. Certain monopolies in this country have gained almost complete control of the raw material, chiefly in the mines, out of which the great body of manufactures are carried on, and they now discriminate, when they will, in the sale of that raw material between those who are rivals of the monopoly and those who submit to the monopoly. We must soon come to the point where we shall say to the men who own these essentials of industry that they have got to part with these essentials by sale to all citizens of the United States with the same readiness and upon the same terms. Or else we shall tie up the resources of this country under private control in such fashion as will make our independent development absolutely impossible.

There is another injustice that monopoly engages in. The trust that deals in the cruder products which are to be transformed into the more elaborate manufactures often will not sell these crude products except upon the terms of monopoly—that is to say, the people that deal with them must buy exclusively from them. And so again you have the lines of development tied up and the connections of development knotted and fastened so that you cannot wrench them apart.

Again, the manufacturing monopolies are so interlaced in their personal relationships with the great shipping interests of this country, and with the great railroads, that they can often largely determine the rates of shipment. . . .

And when you reflect that the twenty-four men who control the United States Steel Corporation, for example, are either presidents or vice-presidents or directors in 55 percent of the railways of the United States, reckoning by the valuation of those railroads and the amount of their stock and bonds, you know just how close the whole thing is knitted together in our industrial system, and how great the temptation is. These twenty-four gentlemen administer that corporation as if it belonged to them. The amazing thing to me is that the people of the United States have not seen that the administration of a great business like that is not a private affair; it is a public affair. . . .

The big trusts, the big combinations, are the most wasteful, the most uneconomical, and, after they pass a certain size, the most inefficient way of conducting the industries of this country.

A notable example is the way in which Mr. Carnegie was bought out of the steel business. Mr. Carnegie could build better mills and make better steel rails and make them cheaper than anybody else connected with what afterward became the United States Steel Corporation. They didn't dare leave him outside. He had so much more brains in finding out the best processes; he had so much more shrewdness in surrounding himself with the most successful assistants; he knew so well when a young man who came into his employ was fit for promotion and was ripe to put at the head of some branch of his business and was sure to make good, that he could undersell every mother's son of them in the market for steel rails. And they bought him out at a price that amounted to three or four times,—I believe actually five times,—the estimated value of his properties and of his business, because they couldn't beat him in competition. And then in what they charged afterward for their product,—the product of his mills included,—they made us pay the interest on the four or five times the difference.

That is the difference between a big business and a trust. A trust is an arrangement to get rid of competition, and a big business is a business that has survived competition by conquering in the field of intelligence and economy. A trust does not bring efficiency to the aid of business; it *buys efficiency out of business.* I am for big business, and I am against the trusts. Any man who can survive by his brains, any man who can put the others out of the business by making the thing cheaper to the consumer at the same time that he is increasing its intrinsic value and quality, I take off my hat to, and I say: "You are the man who can build up the United States, and I wish there were more of you." . . .

We have restricted credit, we have restricted opportunity, we have controlled development, and we have come to be one of the worst ruled, one of the most completely controlled and dominated, governments in the civilized world—no longer a government by free opinion, no longer a government by conviction and the vote of the majority, but a government by the opinion and the duress of small groups of dominant men.

If the government is to tell big business men how to run their business, then don't you see that big business men have to get closer to the government even than they are now? Don't you see that they must capture the government, in order not to be restrained too much by it? Must capture the government? They have already captured it. Are you going to invite those inside to stay inside? They don't have to get there. They are there. Are you going to own your own premises, or are you not? That is your choice. Are you going to say: "You didn't get into the house the right way, but you are in there, God bless you; we will stand out here in the cold and you can hand us out something once in a while"?

At the least, under the plan I am opposing, there will be an avowed partnership between the government and the trusts. I take it that the firm will be ostensibly controlled by the senior member. For I take it that the government of the United States is at least the senior member, though the younger member has all along been running the business. But when all the momentum, when all the energy, when a great deal of the genius, as so often happens in partnerships the world over, is with the junior partner, I don't think that the superintendence of the senior partner is going to amount to very much. And I don't believe that benevolence can be read into the hearts of the trusts by the superintendence and suggestions of the federal government; because the government has never within my recollection had its suggestions accepted by the trusts. On the contrary, the suggestions of the trusts have been accepted by the government.

There is no hope to be seen for the people of the United States until the partnership is dissolved. And the business of the party now entrusted with power is going to be to dissolve it.

The "Monopolists" Respond

John D. Rockefeller Defends Standard Oil

Q. What was the first combination in which you were interested of different establishments in the oil industry?—.A. The first combination of different establishments in the oil industry in which I was interested was the union of William Rockefeller & Co., Rockefeller & Andrews, Rockefeller & Co., S. V. Harkness, and H. M. Flagler, about the year 1867.

U.S. Industrial Commission, *Preliminary Report on Trusts and Industrial Combinations,*
56th Congress, First Session, December 30, 1899, Document No. 476, Part 1.

2. Q. What were the causes leading to its formation?—A. The causes leading to its formation were the desire to unite our skill and capital in order to carry on a business of some magnitude and importance in place of the small business that each separately had theretofore carried on. As time elapsed and the possibilities of the business became apparent, we found further capital to be necessary, obtained the required persons and capital, and organized the Standard Oil Company with a capital of $1,000,000. Later we found more capital could be utilized and found persons with capital to interest themselves with us, and increased our capital to $3,500,000. As the business grew, and markets were obtained at home and abroad, more persons and capital were added to the business, and new corporate agencies were obtained or organized, the object being always the same, to extend our business by furnishing the best and cheapest products.

3. Q. Did the Standard Oil Company or other affiliated interests at any time before 1887 receive from the railroads rebates on freight shipped, or other special advantages?—A. The Standard Oil Company of Ohio, of which I was president, did receive rebates from the railroads prior to 1880, but received no special advantages for which it did not give full compensation. The reason for rebates was that such was the railroad's method of business. A public rate was made and collected by the railway companies, but so far as my knowledge extends, was never really retained in full, a portion of it was repaid to the shippers as a rebate. By this method the real rate of freight which any shipper paid was not known by his competitors nor by other railway companies, the amount being in all cases a matter of bargain with the carrying company. Each shipper made the best bargain he could, but whether he was doing better than his competitor was only a matter of conjecture.

5. Q. About what percentage of the profits of the Standard Oil Company came from special advantages given by the railroads when these were greatest?—A. No percentage of the profits of the Standard Oil Company came from advantages given by railroads at any time. Whatever advantage it received in its constant efforts to reduce rates of freight was deducted from the price of oil. The advantages to the Standard from low freight rates consisted solely in the increased volume of its business arising from the low price of its products. . . .

9. Q. To what advantages, or favors, or methods of management do you ascribe chiefly the success of the Standard Oil Company?—A. I ascribe the success of the Standard to its consistent policy to make the volume of its business large through the merits and cheapness of its products. It has spared no expense in finding, securing, and utilizing the best and cheapest methods of manufacture. It has sought for the best superintendents and workmen and paid the best wages. It has not hesitated to sacrifice old machinery and old plants for new and better ones. It has placed its manufactories at the points where they could supply markets at the least expense. It has not only sought markets for its principal products, but for all possible by-products, sparing no expense in introducing them to the public. It has not hesitated to invest millions of dollars in methods for cheapening the gathering and distribution of oils by pipe lines, special cars, tank steamers, and tank wagons. It has erected tank stations at every important railroad station to cheapen the storage and delivery of its products. It has spared no expense in forcing its products into the markets of the world among people civilized and uncivilized. . . .

10. Q. What are, in your judgment, the chief advantages from industrial combinations—(*a*) financially to stockholders; (*b*) to the public?—A. All the advantages which can be derived from a cooperation of persons and aggregation of capital. Much that one man can not do alone two can do together, and once admit the fact that cooperation, or, what is the same thing, combination, is necessary on a small scale, the limit depends solely upon the necessities of business. Two persons in partnership may be a sufficiently large combination for a small business, but if the business grows or can be made to grow, more persons and more capital must be taken in. The business may grow so large that a partnership ceases to be a proper instrumentality for its purposes, and then a corporation becomes a necessity. In most countries, as in England, this form of industrial combination is sufficient for a business coextensive with the parent country, but it is not so in this country. Our Federal form of government, making every corporation created by a State foreign to every other State, renders it necessary for persons doing business through corporate agency to organize corporations in some or many of the different States in which their business is located. Instead of doing business through the agency of one corporation they must do business through the agencies of several corporations. If the business is extended to foreign countries, and Americans are not to-day satisfied with home markets alone, it will be found helpful and possibly necessary to organize corporations in such countries, . . .

It is too late to argue about advantages of industrial combinations. They are a necessity. . . .

I speak from my experience in the business with which I have been intimately connected for about 40 years. Our first combination was a partnership and afterwards a corporation in Ohio. That was sufficient for a local refining business. But dependent solely upon local business we should have failed years ago. We were forced to extend our markets and to seek for export trade. This latter made the seaboard cities a necessary place of business, and we soon discovered that manufacturing for export could be economically carried on at the seaboard, hence refineries at Brooklyn, at Bayonne, at Philadelphia, and necessary corporations in New York, New Jersey, and Pennsylvania.

We soon discovered as the business grew that the primary method of transporting oil in barrels could not last. The package often cost more than the contents and the forests of the country were not sufficient to supply the necessary material for an extended length of time. Hence we devoted attention to other methods of transportation, adopted the pipe-line system, and found capital for pipe-line construction. . . .

To operate pipe lines required franchises from the States in which they were located, and consequently corporations in those States, just as railroads running through different States, are forced to operate under separate State charters. . . .

11. Q. What are the chief disadvantages or dangers to the public arising from them?—A. The dangers are that the power conferred by combination may be abused; that combinations may be formed for speculation in stocks rather than for conducting business, and that for this purpose prices may be temporarily raised instead of being lowered. These abuses are possible to a greater or less extent in all combinations, large or small, but this fact is no more of an argument against combinations than the fact that steam may explode is an argument against steam. Steam is necessary and can be made comparatively safe. Combination is necessary and its abuses can be minimized; . . .

J. P. Morgan and Company

To Honorable A. P. Pujo, Chairman,

Committee on Banking and Currency

House of Representatives,

Washington, D.C.

Dear Sir:

You have invited us to supplement the recent inquiry of your committee by presenting "such considerations as may occur to you (us) bearing upon the question of concentration and control of money and credit." . . .

    We would suggest, . . . with the utmost respect, that a large part of the valuable time of your Committee, in our belief, has been consumed in an endeavor to piece out a certain theory as to money and credit, which theory it will be impossible ever to demonstrate; for its establishment is, and always will be, prevented by economic laws which have operated ever since the beginnings of barter and trade.

    We suggest to you that such ills—and they are neither few nor trifling—as are existent in this country's financial affairs are the outcome of a clumsy and outworn banking system rather than of the schemes of men; and that to eradicate such ills at their source, there is needed not legislation upon some one or more isolated symptoms, but rather a careful diagnosis of our whole banking system; a study of the successful system of other countries which for decades have been free from periodic panics which have distressed this country; and finally cooperation among all committees in Congress which consider this subject to the one end of wise and comprehensive—as contrasted with piecemeal—legislation . . . such "concentration" as has taken place in New York and other financial centres has been due, not to the purposes and activities of men, but primarily to the operation of our antiquated banking system which automatically compels interior banks to concentrate in New York City hundreds of millions of reserve funds; and next, to economic laws which in every country create some one city as the great financial centre, and which draw to it, in enormous volume, investment funds for the development of industrial enterprises throughout the country. . . .

    We lay especial stress upon this point of economic rule, for the reason that not only the Resolution (H. Res. 504) under which your Committee acts, but many questions to witnesses, indicated a belief that for their own selfish ends certain men,

---

Letter from Messrs. J. P. Morgan and Company (New York: privately printed, February 25, 1913), pp. 1–13 *passim.*

or a group of them, have succeeded in transcending the laws of supply and demand (which operate all over the world) and in establishing new economic laws....

If any one man, or group of men had the ability and resources—which they do not—to withhold credits in any one market like New York, the situation would ordinarily be promptly relieved by the automatic inflow of credits from some altogether foreign source....

For the maintenance of such an impossible economic theory there have been spread before your Committee elaborate tables of so-called interlocking directorates from which exceedingly mistaken inferences have been publicly drawn. In these tables it is shown that 180 bankers and bank directors serve upon the boards of corporations having resources aggregating twenty-five billion dollars, and it is implied that this vast aggregate of the country's wealth is at the disposal of these 180 men. But such an implication rests solely upon the untenable theory that these men, living in different parts of the country, in many cases personally unacquainted with each other, and in most cases associated only in occasional transactions, vote always for the same policies and control with united purpose the directorates of the 132 corporations on which they serve. The testimony failed to establish any concerted policy or harmony of action binding these 180 men together, and as a matter of fact no such policy exists. The absurdity of the assumption of such control becomes more apparent when one considers that on the average these directors represent only one quarter of the memberships of their boards. It is preposterous to suppose that every "interlocking" director has full control in every organization with which he is connected, and that the majority of directors who are not "interlocking" are mere figureheads, subject to the will of a small minority of their boards....

Such growth in the size of banks in New York and Chicago has frequently been erroneously designated before your Committee as "concentration," whereas we have hitherto pointed out the growth of banking resources in New York City has been less rapid than that of the rest of the country. But increase of capital and merger of two or more banks into one institution (with the same resources as the aggregate of the banks merging into it) has [sic] been frequent, especially since January 1, 1908.

These mergers, however, are a development due simply to the demand for larger banking facilities to care for the growth of the country's business. As our cities double and treble in size and importance, as railroads extend and industrial plants expand, not only is it natural, but it is necessary that our banking institutions should grow in order to care for the increased demands put upon them. Perhaps it is not known as well as it should be that in New York City the largest banks are far inferior in size to banks in the commercial capitals of other and much smaller countries.... [The letter then points out that it takes either large banks to finance large enterprises or cooperation between several smaller ones.]

For a private banker to sit upon ... a directorate is in most instances a duty, not a privilege. Inquiry will readily develop the fact that the members of the leading banking houses in this country—and it was the leading houses only against which animadversions were directed—are besought continually to act as directors in various corporations, whose securities they handle, and that in general they enter only those boards which the opinion of the investing public requires them to enter, as an evidence of good faith that they are willing to have their names publicly associated with the management.

Yet, before your Committee, this natural and eminently desirable relationship was made to appear almost sinister and no testimony whatever was adduced to show the actual working of such relationships. . . . [The letter concludes with an explanation as to why banks felt it necessary to sell securities, appoint fiscal agents, and maintain such close scrutiny over corporations, and a comment that unlimited liability and the force of public opinion prevented most banks from malpractice.]

Respectfully submitted,
(Signed) J. P. MORGAN & CO.
New York City
February 25, 1913.

5.2   CONSERVATION AND EFFICIENCY (1908, 1912)

A recent school of historians has emphasized the importance of "efficiency" in the Progressive agenda. Progressives were not so much defenders of the weak against the strong, they say, as missionaries for applying expert knowledge to administration—even if the weak suffered.

This aspect of Progressivism can, in fact, be detected in several realms—business regulation, scientific management, and municipal government, for example. But it appeared most clearly in the conservation movement, where the mainstream, led by Roosevelt and his friend and ally Gifford Pinchot, emphasized the use of America's natural endowment in a prudent and effective manner to maximize its commercial returns and extend its life.

These "utilitarian" conservationists competed with a wing of the natural resources movement moved by a different rationale and set of goals. "Preservationists" cherished unspoiled nature for its aesthetic and "spiritual" values and wished to keep it inviolate for future generations, even if this meant forgoing economic advantage. The most prominent preservationist was John Muir, a Scottish-born naturalist whose experiences in California in the late 1860s stimulated his love of nature. The differences between the preservationists and utilitarians did not prevent Muir and Roosevelt from being friends.

The two selections that follow bracket the utilitarian-preservationist controversy. The first is a statement composed by a conference of governors in 1908. The second, by Muir, is an attack on the plans of San Francisco officials to dam the Tuolumne River in the Sierras in order to supply water to the fast-growing Bay City. (The city won.)

What are the differences in tone and emphasis between the two statements? In what ways does the first selection express the utilitarian conservationist viewpoint? How does the battle over the Tuolumne dam reveal the strain between the two positions on America's natural *endowment? In what ways do the selections reveal a tension between the "efficiency" and the moral dimensions of Progressivism? Which of the two positions comes closest to the philosophy of the ecology movement of today?*

CONSERVATION STATEMENT

Governors of the States

Declaration

We the Governors of the States and Territories of the United States of America, in Conference assembled, do hereby declare the conviction that the great prosperity of our country rests upon the abundant resources of the land chosen by our forefathers for their homes and where they laid the foundation of this great Nation.

We look upon these resources as a heritage to be made use of in establishing and promoting the comfort, prosperity, and happiness of the American People, but not to be wasted, deteriorated, or needlessly destroyed.

We agree that our country's future is involved in this; that the great natural resources supply the material basis on which our civilization must continue to depend, and on which the perpetuity of the Nation itself rests.

We agree, in the light of facts brought to our knowledge and from information received from sources which we can not doubt, that this material basis is threatened with exhaustion. Even as each succeeding generation from the birth of the Nation has performed its part in promoting the progress and development of the Republic, so do we in this generation recognize it as a high duty to perform our part; and this duty in large degree lies in the adoption of measures for the conservation of the natural wealth of the country.

We declare our firm conviction that this conservation of our natural resources is a subject of transcendent importance, which should engage unremittingly the attention of the Nation, the States, and the People in earnest cooperation. These natural resources include the land on which we live and which yields our food; the living waters which fertilize the soil, supply power, and form great avenues of commerce; the forests which yield the materials for our homes, prevent erosion of the soil, and conserve the navigation and other uses of our streams; and the minerals which form the basis of our industrial life, and supply us with heat, light, and power.

We agree that the land should be so used that erosion and soil-wash shall cease; that there should be reclamation of arid and semi-arid regions by means of irrigation, and of swamp and overflowed regions by means of drainage; that the waters should be so conserved and used as to promote navigation, to enable the arid regions to be reclaimed by irrigation, and to develop power in the interests of the People; that the forests which regulate our rivers, support our industries, and promote the fertility and

Proceedings of a Conference of Governors in The White House May 13–15, 1908 (Washington, DC: Government Printing Office, 1909), pp. 192–93.

productiveness of the soil should be preserved and perpetuated; that the minerals found so abundantly beneath the surface should be so used as to prolong their utility; that the beauty, healthfulness, and habitability of our country should be preserved and increased; that the sources of national wealth exist for the benefit of the People, and that monopoly thereof should not be tolerated.

We commend the wise forethought of the President in sounding the note of warning as to the waste and exhaustion of the natural resources of the country, and signify our high appreciation of his action in calling this Conference to consider the same and to seek remedies therefore through cooperation of the Nation and the States.

We agree that this cooperation should find expression in suitable action by the Congress within the limits of and coextensive with the national jurisdiction of the subject, and, complementary thereto, by the legislatures of the several States within the limits of and coextensive with their jurisdiction.

We declare the conviction that in the use of the natural resources our independent States are interdependent and bound together by ties of mutual benefits, responsibilities and duties.

We agree in the wisdom of future conferences between the President, Members of Congress, and the Governors of States on the conservation of our natural resources with a view of continued cooperation and action on the lines suggested; and to this end we advise that from time to time, as in his judgment may seem wise, the President call the Governors of the States and Members of Congress and others into conference.

We agree that further action is advisable to ascertain the present condition of our natural resources and to promote the conservation of the same; and to that end we recommend the appointment by each State of a Commission on the Conservation of Natural Resources, to cooperate with each other and with any similar commission of the Federal Government.

We urge the continuation and extension of forest policies adapted to secure the husbanding and renewal of our diminishing timber supply, the prevention of soil erosion, the protection of headwaters, and the maintenance of the purity and navigability of our streams. We recognize that the private ownership of forest lands entails responsibilities in the interests of all the People, and we favor the enactment of laws looking to the protection and replacement of privately owned forests.

We recognize in our waters a most valuable asset of the People of the United States, and we recommend the enactment of laws looking to the conservation of water resources for irrigation, water supply, power, and navigation, to the end that navigable and source streams may be brought under complete control and fully utilized for every purpose. We especially urge on the Federal Congress the immediate adoption of a wise, active, and thorough waterway policy, providing for the prompt improvement of our streams and the conservation of their watersheds required for the uses of commerce and the protection of the interests of our People.

We recommend the enactment of laws looking to the prevention of waste in the mining and extraction of coal, oil, gas, and other minerals with a view to their wise conservation for the use of the People, and to the protection of human life in the mines.

Let us conserve the foundations of our prosperity.

Respectfully submitted,

[Signatures]

Hetch Hetchy

John Muir

Yosemite[1] is so wonderful that we are apt to regard it as an exceptional creation, the only valley of its kind in the world; but Nature is not so poor as to have only one of anything. Several other yosemites have been discovered in the Sierra that occupy the same relative positions on the Range and were formed by the same forces in the same kind of granite. One of these, the Hetch Hetchy Valley, is in the Yosemite National Park about twenty miles from Yosemite and is easily accessible to all sorts of travelers by road and trail. . . .

I have always called it the "Tuolumne Yosemite," for it is a wonderfully exact counterpart of the Merced Yosemite not only in its sublime rocks and waterfalls but in the gardens, groves and meadows of its flowery park-like floor. . . .

Imagine yourself in Hetch Hetchy on a sunny day in June, standing waist-deep in grass and flowers . . . while the great pines sway dreamily with scarcely perceptible motion. Looking northward across the Valley you see a plain, gray granite cliff arising abruptly out of the gardens and groves to a height of 1800 feet, and in front of it Tueeulala's silvery scarf burning with irised sun-fire. In the first white outburst at the head there is an abundance of visible energy, but it is speedily hushed and concealed in divine repose, and its tranquil progress to the base of the cliff is like that of a downy feather in a still room. Now observe the fineness and marvelous distinctiveness of the various sun-illumined fabrics into which the water is woven; they sift and float from form to form down the face of that grand gray rock in so leisurely and unconfused a manner that you can examine their texture, and patterns of and tones of color as you would a piece of embroidery held in the hand. Toward the top of the fall you see groups of booming, comet-like masses, their solid white heads separate, their tails like combed silk interlacing among delicate gray and purple shadows, ever forming and dissolving, worn out by friction in their rush through the air. . . . Near the bottom the width of the fall has increased from about twenty-five feet to a hundred feet. Here it is composed of even finer tissues, and is still without a trace of disorder—air, water and sunlight woven into stuff that spirits might wear. . . .

It appears, therefore, that Hetch Hetchy Valley, far from being a plain, common, rock-bound meadow, as many who have not seen it seem to suppose, is a grand landscape garden, one of Nature's rarest and most precious mountain temples. As in Yosemite, the sublime rocks of its walls seem to glow with life, whether leaning back in repose or standing erect in thoughtful attitudes, giving welcome to storms and calms alike, their brows in the sky, their feet set in the groves and gay flowery meadows, while birds, bees and butterflies help the river and waterfalls to stir all the air into music—things frail and fleeting and types of permanence meeting here and blending, just as they do at Yosemite, to draw her lovers into close and confiding communion with her.

John Muir, *The Yosemite* (New York: The Century Company, 1912), pp. 249–62.

[1] The Yosemite is the beautiful Sierra Valley in California set aside as a national park in 1890 through the efforts of Muir and others—ED.

Sad to say, this most precious and sublime feature of the Yosemite National Park, one of the greatest of all our natural resources for the uplifting joy and peace and health of the people, is in danger of being dammed and made into a reservoir to help supply San Francisco with water and light, thus flooding it from wall to wall and burying its gardens and groves one or two hundred feet deep. This grossly destructive commercial scheme has long been planned and urged (though water as pure and abundant can be got from sources outside of the people's park, in a dozen different places), because of the comparative cheapness of the dam and of the territory which it is sought to divert from the great uses to which it was dedicated in the Act of 1890 establishing the Yosemite National Park.

The making of gardens and parks goes on with civilization all over the world, and they increase both in size and number as their value is recognized. Everybody needs beauty as well as bread, places to play in and pray in, where Nature may heal and cheer and give strength to body and soul alike. This natural beauty-hunger is made manifest in the little window-sill gardens of the poor, though perhaps only a geranium slip in a broken cup, as well as in the carefully tended rose and lily gardens of the rich, the thousands of spacious city parks and botanical gardens, and in our magnificent National parks—the Yellowstone, Yosemite, Sequoia, etc.—Nature's sublime wonderlands, the admiration and joy of the world. Nevertheless, like anything else worth while, from the very beginning, however well guarded, they have always been subject to attack by despoiling gain-seekers and mischief-makers of every degree from Satan to Senators, eagerly trying to make everything immediately and selfishly commercial, with schemes disguised in smug-smiling philanthropy, industriously, shampiously crying, "Conservation, conservation, panutilization," that man and beast may be fed and the dear Nation made great. Thus long ago a few enterprising merchants utilized the Jerusalem temple as a place of business instead of a place of prayer, changing money, buying and selling cattle and sheep and doves; and earlier still, the first forest reservation, including only one tree, was likewise despoiled. Ever since the establishment of the Yosemite National Park, strife has been going on around its borders and I suppose this will go on as part of the universal battle between right and wrong, however much its boundaries may be shorn, or its wild beauty destroyed.

The first application to the Government by the San Francisco Supervisors for the commercial use of Lake Eleanor and the Hetch Hetchy Valley was made in 1903, and on December 22nd of that year it was denied by the Secretary of the Interior, Mr. Hitchcock, who truthfully said:

> Presumably the Yosemite National Park was created such by law because of the natural objects of varying degrees of scenic importance located within its boundaries, inclusive alike of its beautiful small lakes, like Eleanor, and its majestic wonders, like Hetch Hetchy and Yosemite Valley. It is the aggregation of such natural scenic features that makes the Yosemite Park a wonderland which the Congress of the United States sought by law to reserve for all coming time as nearly as practicable in the condition fashioned by the hand of the Creator—a worthy object of National pride and a source of healthful pleasure and rest for the thousands of people who may annually sojourn there during the heated months.

In 1907 when Mr. Garfield became Secretary of the Interior the application was renewed and granted; but under his successor, Mr. Fisher, the matter has been referred to a Commission, which as this volume goes to press still has it under consideration. . . .

That any one would try to destroy such a place seems incredible; but sad experience shows that there are people good enough and bad enough for anything. The proponents of the dam scheme bring forward a lot of bad arguments to prove that the only righteous thing to do with the people's parks is to destroy them bit by bit as they are able. Their arguments are curiously like those of the devil, devised for the destruction of the first garden—so much of the very best Eden fruit going to waste; so much of the best Tuolumne water and Tuolumne scenery going to waste. Few of their statements are even partly true, and all are misleading.

Thus, Hetch Hetchy, they say, is a "low-lying meadow." On the contrary, it is a high-lying natural landscape garden, as the photographic illustrations show.

"It is a common minor feature, like thousands of others." On the contrary it is a very uncommon feature; after Yosemite, the rarest and in many ways the most important in the National Park.

"Damming and submerging it 175 feet deep would enhance its beauty by forming a crystal-clear lake." Landscape gardens, places of recreation and worship, are never made beautiful by destroying and burying them. The beautiful sham lake, forsooth, would be only an eyesore, a dismal blot on the landscape, like many others to be seen in the Sierra. For, instead of keeping it at the same level all the year, allowing Nature centuries of time to make new shores, it would, of course, be full only a month or two in the spring, when the snow is melting fast; then it would be gradually drained, exposing the slimy sides of the basin and shallower parts of the bottom, with the gathered drift and waste, death and decay of the upper basins, caught here instead of being swept on to decent natural burial along the banks of the river or in the sea. Thus the Hetch Hetchy dam-lake would be only a rough imitation of a natural lake for a few of the spring months, an open sepulcher for the others.

"Hetch Hetchy water is the purest of all to be found in the Sierra, unpolluted, and forever unpollutable." On the contrary, excepting that of the Merced below Yosemite, it is less pure than that of most of the other Sierra streams, because of the sewerage of camp grounds draining into it, especially of the Big Tuolumne Meadows camp ground, occupied by hundreds of tourists and mountaineers, with their animals, for months every summer, soon to be followed by thousands from all the world.

These temple destroyers, devotees of ravaging commercialism, seem to have a perfect contempt for Nature, and, instead of lifting their eyes to the God of the mountains, lift them to the Almighty Dollar.

Dam Hetch Hetchy! As well dam for water-tanks the people's cathedrals and churches, for no holier temple has ever been consecrated by the heart of man.

5.3 SOCIAL JUSTICE PROGRESSIVISM (1892, 1906, 1908)

Although efficient administration may have been the core issue for some Progressives, others were moved by broader social sympathies. These social justice reformers were particularly numerous among the settlement house workers—middle-class men and women who established community centers in the urban slums where the poor, many of them foreign born, could learn skills, absorb American ways, and find refuge from the harsh city environment. The settlements were actually precursors of Progressivism. Many were established in the 1890s, but their impact on the larger society awaited the stirring of the urban middle class in the new century.

The social justice Progressives did not confine their labors to the settlement houses. Many were active in city-wide good-government movements and efforts on the state and national levels to shelter women and child workers from exploitation, reduce the hazards of dangerous occupations, improve protection for consumers, and make government machinery more responsive to voter majorities than to special interests.

The first selection, by Jane Addams, describes the activities of Hull House, the settlement she founded in the Chicago slums in 1889. It has been said that the white middle-class settlement workers patronized the people they sought to help and failed to respect their values and traditions. Does this attitude come through in Addams's description? Or does she seem alert to this danger and seek to avoid it? Did most slum dwellers in early twentieth-century America themselves want to assimilate middle-class "American" values?

Finally, not only political reformers called for change. A rising interest in what became known as the "Social Gospel" swept through many of the established churches. Stated briefly, these religious reformers hoped to apply the principles of Christianity to the world around them. They sought to organize and institutionalize charitable and humanitarian efforts. The "Social Creed of the Churches" reflects this concern. Would you label this selection idealistic or practical? In addition to economic woes, what other problems did industrialization unleash that these clergymen attempted to address?

HULL HOUSE, CHICAGO: AN EFFORT TOWARD SOCIAL DEMOCRACY[1]

Jane Addams

Hull House, Chicago's first Social Settlement, was established in September, 1889. It . . . was opened by two women, supported by many friends, in the belief that the mere foothold of a house, easily accessible, ample in space, hospitable and tolerant in spirit, situated in the midst of the large foreign colonies which so easily isolate themselves in American cities, would be in itself a serviceable thing for Chicago. . . . It was opened on the theory that the dependence of classes on each other is reciprocal; and that as "the social relation is essentially a reciprocal relation, it gave a form of expression that has peculiar value." . . .

Hull House is an ample old residence, well built and somewhat ornately decorated after the manner of its time, 1856. . . . It once stood in the suburbs, but the city has steadily grown up around it and its site now has corners on three or four distinct foreign colonies. Between Halsted Street and the river live about ten thousand Italians. . . . To the south on Twelfth Street are many Germans, and side streets are given over almost entirely to Polish and Russian Jews. Further south, these Jewish colonies merge into a huge Bohemian colony, so vast that Chicago ranks as the third Bohemian city in the

Jane Addams, "Hull House, Chicago: An Effort toward Social Democracy," *Forum*, vol. 14 (October 1892), pp. 226–41.

[1] Footnotes deleted.

world. To the northwest are many Canadian-French, . . . and to the north are many Irish and first-generation Americans. . . .

The streets are inexpressibly dirty, the number of schools inadequate, factory legislation unenforced, the street-lighting bad, and paving miserable, . . . and the stables defy all laws of sanitation. . . . The Hebrews and Italians do the finishing for the great clothing-manufacturers. . . . As the design of the sweating system is the elimination of rent from the manufacture of clothing, the "outside work" is begun after the clothing leaves the cutter. For this work no basement is too dark, no stable loft too foul, no rear shanty too provisional, no tenement room too small, as these conditions imply low rental. Hence these shops abound in the worst of the foreign districts, where the sweater easily finds his cheap basement and his home finishers. . . .

This site for a Settlement was selected . . . because of its diversity and the variety of activity for which it presented an opportunity. It has been the aim of the residents to respond to all sides of the neighborhood life . . . One thing seemed clear in regard to entertaining these foreigners: to preserve and keep for them whatever of value their past life contained and to bring them into contact with a better type of Americans. For two years, every Saturday evening, our Italian neighbors were our guests; entire families came . . . and the house became known as a place where Italians were welcome and where national holidays were observed. They came to us with their petty law-suits, sad relics of the *vendetta*, with their incorrigible boys, with their hospital cases, with their aspirations for American clothes, and with their needs for an interpreter. . . .

But our social evenings are by no means confined to foreigners. Our most successful clubs are entirely composed of English speaking and American-born young people. . . . The boys who are known as the Young Citizens' Club are supposed to inform themselves on municipal affairs. . . . The gymnasium is a somewhat pretentious name for a building next door which was formerly a saloon, but which we rented last fall, repaired, and fitted up with simple apparatus. . . . The more definite humanitarian effect of Hull House has taken shape in a day nursery. . . . During two months of this summer the reports sent in from Hull House to the Municipal Order League and through it to the Health Department were one thousand and thirty-seven, . . . and a marked improvement has taken place in the scavenger service and in the regulation of the small stables of the ward. . . .

Last May twenty girls from a knitting factory who struck because they were docked for loss of time when they were working by the piece, came directly from the factory to Hull House. . . . They had heard that we "stood by working people." We were able to have the strike arbitrated . . . and we had the satisfaction of putting on record one more case of arbitration in the slowly growing list. . . . It is difficult to classify the Working Peoples' Social Science Club, which meets weekly at Hull House. It is social, educational, and civic in character, the latter because it strongly connects the house with the labor problems in their political and social aspects. . . .

I am always sorry to have Hull House regarded as philanthropy, although it doubtless has strong philanthropic tendencies. . . . Working people live in the same streets with those in need of charity, but they themselves require and want none of it. As one of their number has said, they require only that their aspirations be recognized and stimulated and the means of attaining them put at their disposal. Hull House makes a constant effort to secure these means, but to call that effort philanthropy is to use the word unfairly and to underestimate the duties of good citizenship.

THE SOCIAL CREED OF THE CHURCHES STATEMENT ADOPTED BY THE GENERAL CONFERENCE OF THE METHODIST EPISCOPAL CHURCH, MAY 1908

The Methodist Episcopal Church stands:

For equal rights and complete justice for all men in all stations of life.

For the principle of conciliation and arbitration in industrial dissensions.

For the protection of the worker from dangerous machinery, occupational disease, injuries and mortality.

For the abolition of child labor.

For such regulation of the conditions of labor for women as shall safeguard the physical and moral health of the community.

For the suppression of the "sweating system."

For the gradual and reasonable reduction of the hours of labor to the lowest practical point, with work for all; and for that degree of leisure for all which is the condition of the highest human life.

For a release from employment one day in seven.

For a living wage in every industry.

For the highest wage that each industry can afford, and for the most equitable division of the products in industry that can ultimately be devised.

For the recognition of the Golden Rule, and the mind of Christ as the supreme law of society and the sure remedy for all social ills.

General Conference of the Methodist Episcopal Church. The Social Creed of the Churches adopted May 1908. Quoted from *A Year Book of the Church and Social Service in the United States*, ed. by H. F. Ward, 1916, pp. 197–98.

CHAPTER **6**

Race and Ethnicity

The two decades on either side of 1900 witnessed a vast turnover of nationalities and races in the United States. As noted, sometime in the 1890s the source of immigrants to America shifted decisively from western and northern Europe to eastern and southern Europe. Particularly after 1900, far fewer proportionately of the newcomers came from Britain, Germany, Ireland, and Scandinavia and far more from Poland, Russia, Austria-Hungary, Greece, and Italy. Meanwhile, in the years just preceding World War I, there began a migration to northern cities of African American people, until then tied overwhelmingly, as during slavery days, to the rural South.

There were important differences between these two human streams. The people from the Southern countryside who came to New York, Chicago, Philadelphia, and Cleveland were English-speaking, Protestant, American citizens. The transatlantic arrivals were, of course, foreigners, who spoke alien tongues, and were predominantly Catholic, Greek Orthodox, or Jewish. The migrants from the rural South were black; the newcomers from Europe were white. Race would make a difference.

But there were also significant overlaps between the two groups. Both were rural peoples, new to city life and city ways. Both were predominantly unskilled workers who found their economic niches in the mines, factories, and construction sites doing the hard, dirty, menial labor the industrial society of the day required. Both met prejudice and bigotry from old-stock white Americans already on the scene, although African Americans undoubtedly suffered more than immigrants.

The selections that follow depict how the post-1890 newcomers to northern cities were perceived and received. The new arrivals were not uniformly scorned. There remained among old-stock white Americans a residue of goodwill toward immigrants and black people based on the nation's democratic, egalitarian traditions. Many business leaders welcomed the newcomers, especially the white immigrants, as a source of cheap labor. Still, the balance was clearly tipped against a generous toleration, as the following selections suggest.

6.1 THE GREAT MIGRATION: THE DARK SIDE (1905, 1919)

Southern black people began to move north in substantial numbers in the earliest years of the twentieth century. The trickle became a torrent after 1915, when World War I blocked the normal flow of European immigrants and created major labor shortages in northern industry.

Jobs, however, were not the only magnet drawing rural African Americans northward. The North also promised to be freer and less repressive than Dixie, where segregation by race, known as "Jim Crow," remained entrenched, and violence against blacks had accelerated.

Ray Stannard Baker's article in McClure's describes a lynching in Springfield, Ohio. Are you surprised by this account? Was white racial supremacy and mob violence confined to the South?

One of the black newcomers' favorite destinations was booming Chicago, where the stockyards and the city's many industrial plants provided employment. By 1920 the Windy City had almost 110,000 African American residents, almost four times the number in 1900.

One of the following selections describes the Chicago "Black Belt" shortly after the turn of the century. Even in this early period some of the major problems that continued to plague black urban dwellers in the North had surfaced. What are some of these? What does the reference to "strike-breakers" suggest? What are some of the hopeful aspects of life in the "Black Belt" as described here? What are some of the sources of racial tension?

Another selection depicts the savage Chicago race riot of 1919, fourteen years after the scene described in the previous selection. This was one of a dozen shameful racial disorders that erupted in the first two decades of the twentieth century. Can you deduce from the account the causes of the barbaric behavior described? Group antagonisms have been very widespread in the United States, but they were seldom so brutal and destructive as those between whites and blacks in the cities, especially in the early part of this century. What explains this ferocity? Did race riots continue long past this period? Have recent racial disorders been similar to the Chicago riot of 1919?

WHAT IS A LYNCHING? A STUDY OF MOB JUSTICE, SOUTH AND NORTH

Ray Stannard Baker

I cite these facts to show the underlying conditions in Springfield[1]; a soil richly prepared for an outbreak of mob law—with corrupt politics, vile saloons, the law paralysed by non-enforcement against vice, a large venal Negro vote, lax courts of justice.

Gathering of the Lynching Mob

Well, on Monday afternoon the mob began to gather. At first it was an absurd, ineffectual crowd, made up largely of lawless boys of sixteen to twenty—a pronounced feature of every mob—with a wide fringe of more respectable citizens, their hands in their pockets and no convictions in their souls, looking on curiously, helplessly. They gathered hooting around the jail, cowardly, at first, as all mobs are, but growing bolder as

---

Ray Stannard Baker, "What Is a Lynching? A Study of Mob Justice, North and South," *McClure's*, February, 1905.

[1] Springfield, Ohio.

darkness came on and no move was made to check them. The murder of Collis was not a horrible, soul-rending crime like that at Statesboro, Georgia; these men in the mob were not personal friends of the murdered man; it was a mob from the back rooms of the swarming saloons of Springfield; and it included also the sort of idle boys "who hang around cigar stores," as one observer told me. The newspaper reports are fond of describing lynching mobs as "made up of the foremost citizens of the town." In no cases that I know of, either South or North, . . . has a mob been made up of what may be called the best citizens; but the best citizens have often stood afar off "decrying the mob"—as a Springfield man told me piously—and letting it go on. A mob is the method by which good citizens turn over the law and the government to the criminal or irresponsible classes.

And no official in direct authority in Springfield that evening, apparently, had so much as an ounce of grit within him. The sheriff came out and made a weak speech in which he said he "didn't want to hurt anybody." They threw stones at him and broke his windows. The chief of police sent eighteen men to the jail but did not go near himself. All of these policemen undoubtedly sympathised with the mob in its efforts to get at the slayer of their brother officer; at least, they did nothing effective to prevent the lynching. An appeal was made to the Mayor to order out the engine companies that water might be turned on the mob. He said he didn't like to; *the hose might be cut!* The local militia company was called to its barracks, but the officer in charge hesitated, vacillated, doubted his authority, and objected finally because he had no ammunition *except* Krag-Jorgenson cartridges, which, if fired into a mob, would kill too many people! The soldiers did not stir that night from the safe and comfortable precincts of their armory.

A sort of dry rot, a moral paralysis, seems to strike the administrators of law in a town like Springfield. What can be expected of officers who are not accustomed to enforce the law, or of a people not accustomed to obey it—or who make reservations and exceptions when they do enforce it or obey it?

Threats to Lynch the Judges

When the sheriff made his speech to the mob, urging them to let the law take its course they jeered him. The law! When, in the past, had the law taken its proper course in Clark County? Someone shouted, referring to Dixon:

"He'll only get fined for shooting in the city limits."

"He'll get ten days in jail and suspended sentence."

Then there were voices:

"Let's go hang Mower and Miller"—the two judges.

This threat, indeed, was frequently repeated both on the night of the lynching and on the day following.

So the mob came finally, and cracked the door of the jail with a railroad rail. This jail is said to be the strongest in Ohio, and having seen it, I can well believe that the report is true. But steel bars have never yet kept out a mob; it takes something a good deal stronger: human courage backed up by the consciousness of being right.

They murdered the Negro in cold blood in the jail doorway; then they dragged him to the principal business street and hung him to a telegraph-pole, afterward riddling his lifeless body with revolver shots.

Lesson of a Hanging Negro

That was the end of that! Mob justice administered! And there the Negro hung until day-light the next morning—an unspeakably grisly, dangling horror, advertising the shame of the town. His head was shockingly crooked to one side, his ragged clothing, cut for souvenirs, exposed in places his bare body: he dripped blood. And, with the crowds of men both here and at the morgue where the body was publicly exhibited, came young boys in knickerbockers, and little girls and women by scores, horrified but curious. They came even with baby carriages! Men made jokes: "A dead nigger is a good nigger." And the purblind, dollars-and-cents man, most despicable of all, was congratulating the public:

"It'll save the county a lot of money!"

Significant lessons, these, for the young!

But the mob wasn't through with its work. Easy people imagine that, having hanged a Negro, the mob goes quietly about its business; but that is never the way of the mob. Once released, the spirit of anarchy spreads and spreads, not subsiding until it has accomplished its full measure of evil.

Mob Burning of Negro Saloons

All the following day a rumbling, angry crowd filled the streets of Springfield, threaten-ing to burn out the notorious Levee, threatening Judges Mower and Miller, threatening the "niggers." The local troops—to say nothing of the police force—which might easily have broken up the mob, remained sedulously in their armories, vacillating, doubtful of authority, knowing that there were threats to burn and destroy, and making not one move toward the protection of the public. One of the captains was even permitted to go to a neighboring city to a dance! At the very same time the panic-stricken officials were summoning troops from other towns. So night came on, the mob gathered around the notorious dives, someone touched a match, and the places of crime suddenly disgorged their foul inhabitants. Black and white, they came pouring out and vanished into the darkness where they belonged and whence they have not yet returned. Eight buildings went up in smoke, the fire department deliberating—intentionally, it is said—until the flames could not be controlled. The troops, almost driven out by the county prosecutor, McGrew, appeared after the mob had completed its work.

Good work, badly done, a living demonstration of the inevitability of law—if not orderly, decent law, then of mob-law.

For days following the troops filled Springfield, costing the state large sums of money, costing the county large sums of money. They chiefly guarded the public foun-tain; the mob had gone home—until next time.

Efforts to Punish the Mob

What happened after that? A perfunctory court-martial that did absolutely nothing. A grand jury of really good citizens that sat for weeks, off and on; and like the moun-tain that was in travail and brought forth a mouse, they indicted two boys and two men out of all that mob, not for murder but for "breaking into jail." And, curiously enough, it developed—how do such things develop?—that every man on the grand jury was a Republican, chosen by Republican county officers, and in their report they severely censored police force (Democratic), and the mayor (Democratic), and had not one word of disapproval for the sheriff (Republican). Curiously enough, also, the public did not become enthusiastic over the report of that grand jury. . . .

But the worst feature of all in this Springfield lynching was the apathy of the public. No one really seemed to care. A "nigger" had been hanged: what of it? But the law itself had been lynched. What of that? I had just come from the South, where I had found the people of several lynching towns in a state of deep excitement—moral excitement if you like, thinking about this problem, quarrelling about it, expelling men from the church, impeaching sheriffs, dishonourably discharging whole militia companies. Here in Springfield, I found cold apathy, except for a few fine citizens, one of whom City Solicitor Stewart L. Tatum, promptly offered his services to the sheriff and assisted in a vain effort to remove the Negro in a closed carriage and afterward at the risk of personal assault earnestly attempted to defeat the purposes of the mob. Another of these citizens, the Rev. Father Cogan, pleaded with the mob on the second night of the rioting at risk to himself; another withdrew from the militia company because it had not done its duty. And afterward the city officials were stirred by the faintest of faint spasms of righteousness; some of the Negro saloons were closed up, but within a month, the most notorious of all the dive-keepers, Hurley, the Negro political boss, was permitted to open an establishment—through the medium of a brother-in-law!

If there ever was an example of good citizenship lying flat on its back with political corruption squatting on its neck, Springfield furnished an example of that condition.

SOCIAL BONDS IN THE "BLACK BELT" OF CHICAGO: NEGRO ORGANIZATIONS AND THE NEW SPIRIT PERVADING THEM[1]

Fannie Barrier Williams

The last federal census [1900] showed the Negro population of Chicago to be about 35,000. The present population is estimated to be over 50,000, an increase of about forty per cent in five years. The colored people who are thus crowding into Chicago come mostly from the states of Kentucky, Tennessee, Alabama, Mississippi, Louisiana, Arkansas, and Missouri. . . . [The] many industrial strikes . . . in the last ten years have brought thousands of colored people to Chicago, either for immediate work as strikebreakers, or with the prospect of employment for both skilled and unskilled workers; . . . thousands of Negro men and women are now employed in the stockyards and other large industrial plants where ten years ago this would not have been thought of.

This increase of Negro population has brought with it problems that directly affect the social and economic life of the newcomers. Prevented from mingling easily and generally with the rest of the city's population, according to their needs and deservings, but with no preparation made for segregation . . . they have been subject to more social ills than any other nationality among us. . . . The real problem of the social life of the colored

---

Fannie Barrier Williams, "Social Bonds in the 'Black Belt' of Chicago: Negro Organizations and the New Spirit Pervading Them," *Charities*, October 7, 1905, pp. 40–44.

[1] Footnotes deleted.

people in Chicago, as in all northern cities, lies in the fact of their segregation. While they do not occupy all the worst streets and live in all the unsanitary houses in Chicago, what is known as the "Black Belt" is altogether forbidding and demoralizing. . . .

The organizations created and maintained by them in Chicago are numerous and touch almost every phase of our social life. . . . First in importance is the Negro church. There are 25 regularly organized colored churches. This number includes 9 Methodist, 8 Baptist, 1 Catholic, 1 Episcopal, 1 Christian and 1 Presbyterian. In addition to these there are numerous missions in various parts of the "Black Belt." . . . Most of these churches are burdened with oppressive indebtedness, and because of this their usefulness as agents of moral up-lift is seriously handicapped. . . . Thousands of Negroes know and care for no other entertainment than that furnished by the church. . . .

Next to the Negro church, in importance, as affecting the social life of the people are the secret orders, embracing such organizations as the Masons, Odd Fellows, Knights of Pythias, True Reformers, the United Brotherhood, . . . the Ancient Order of Foresters, and the Elks. Nearly all of these secret orders have auxiliary associations composed of women. . . .

In the matter of employment, the colored people of Chicago have lost in the last ten years nearly every occupation of which they once had almost a monopoly. There is now scarcely a Negro barber left in the business district. Nearly all the janitor work in the large buildings has been taken away from them by the Swedes. White men and women as waiters have supplanted colored men in nearly all the first-class hotels and restaurants. Practically all the shoe polishing is now done by Greeks. Negro coachmen and expressmen and teamsters are seldom seen in the business districts. It scarcely need be stated that colored young men and women are almost never employed as clerks and bookkeepers in business establishments. . . .

The increase of the Negro population in Chicago . . . has not tended to liberalize public sentiment; in fact hostile sentiment has been considerably intensified by the importation from time to time of colored men as strikebreakers. Then again a marked increase of crime among the Negro population has been noted in recent years. All these things have tended to put us in a bad light, resulting in an appreciable loss of friends and well-wishers.

CHICAGO COMMISSION ON RACE RELATIONS: CAUSES OF THE RACE RIOT

Sunday afternoon, July 27, 1919, hundreds of white and Negro bathers crowded the lake-front beaches at Twenty-sixth and Twenty-ninth streets. This is the eastern boundary of the thickest Negro residence area. At Twenty-sixth Street Negroes were in great majority; at Twenty-ninth Street there were more whites. An imaginary line in the water separating the two beaches had been generally observed by the two races. Under the prevailing relations, aided by wild rumors and reports, this line served virtually as a challenge to either side to cross it. Four Negroes who attempted to enter the water from the "white" side were driven away by the whites. They returned with more Negroes,

---

Chicago Commission on Race Relations: The Negro in Chicago (Chicago: University of Chicago Press, 1927), pp. 596–98. © University of Chicago Press.

and there followed a series of attacks with stones, first one side gaining the advantage, then the other.

Eugene Williams, a Negro boy of seventeen, entered the water from the side used by Negroes and drifted across the line supported by a railroad tie. He was observed by the crowd on the beach and promptly became a target for stones. He suddenly released the tie, went down and was drowned. Guilt was immediately placed on Stauber, a young white man, by Negro witnesses who declared that he threw the fatal stone.[1]

White and Negro men dived for the boy without result. Negroes demanded that the policeman present arrest Stauber. He refused; and at this crucial moment arrested a Negro on a white man's complaint. Negroes then attacked the officer. These two facts, the drowning and the refusal of the policeman to arrest Stauber, together marked the beginning of the riot.

Two hours after the drowning, a Negro, James Crawford, fired into a group of officers summoned by the policeman at the beach and was killed by a Negro policeman. Reports and rumors circulated rapidly, and new crowds began to gather. Five white men were injured in clashes near the beach. As darkness came Negroes in white districts to the west suffered severely. Between 9:00 P.M. and 3:00 A.M. twenty-seven Negroes were beaten, seven stabbed, and four shot. Monday morning was quiet, and Negroes went to work as usual.

Returning from work in the afternoon many Negroes were attacked by white ruffians. Street-car routes, especially at transfer points, were the centers of lawlessness. Trolleys were pulled from the wires, and Negro passengers were dragged into the street, beaten, stabbed, and shot. The police were powerless to cope with these numerous assaults. During Monday, four Negro men and one white assailant were killed, and thirty Negroes were severely beaten in street-car clashes. Four white men were killed, six stabbed, five shot, and nine severely beaten. It was rumored that the white occupants of the Angelus Building at Thirty-fifth Street and Wabash Avenue had shot a Negro. Negroes gathered about the building. The white tenants sought police protection, and one hundred policemen, mounted and on foot, responded. In a clash with the mob the police killed four Negroes and injured many.

Raids into the Negro residence area then began. Automobiles sped through the streets, the occupants shooting at random. Negroes retaliated by "sniping" from ambush. At midnight surface and elevated car service was discontinued because of a strike for wage increases, and thousands of employees were cut off from work.

On Tuesday, July 29, Negro men en route on foot to their jobs through hostile territory were killed. White soldiers and sailors in uniform, aided by civilians, raided the "Loop" business section, killing two Negroes and beating and robbing several others. Negroes living among white neighbors in Englewood, far to the south, were driven from their homes, their household goods were stolen, and their houses were burned or wrecked. On the West Side an Italian mob, excited by a false rumor that an Italian girl had been shot by a Negro, killed Joseph Lovings, a Negro.

Wednesday night at 10:30 Mayor [William] Thompson yielded to pressure and asked the help of the three regiments of militia which had been stationed in nearby

---

[1] A jury later determined that Williams had drowned because he was kept from coming ashore by the white stone-throwers—ED.

armories during the most severe rioting, awaiting the call. They immediately took up positions throughout the South Side. A rainfall Wednesday night and Thursday kept many people in their homes, and by Friday the rioting had abated. On Saturday incendiary fires burned forty-nine houses in the immigrant neighborhood west of the Stock Yards. Nine hundred and forty-eight people, mostly Lithuanians, were made homeless, and the property loss was about $250,000. Responsibility for the fires was never fixed.

The total casualties of this reign of terror were thirty-eight deaths—fifteen white, twenty-three Negro—and 537 people injured. Forty-one per cent of the reported clashes occurred in the white neighborhood near the Stock Yards between the south branch of the Chicago River and Fifty-fifth Street, Wentworth Avenue and the city limits, and 34 per cent in the "Black Belt" between Twenty-second and Thirty-ninth streets, Wentworth Avenue and Lake Michigan. Others were scattered.

Responsibility for many attacks was definitely placed by many witnesses upon the [white] "athletic clubs," including "Ragen's Colts," the "Hamburgers," "Aylwards," "Our Flag," the "Standard," the "Sparklers," and several others. The mobs were made up for the most part of boys between fifteen and twenty-two. Older persons participated, but the youth of the rioters was conspicuous in every clash. Little children witnessed the brutalities and frequently pointed out the injured when the police arrived.

6.2   THE KU KLUX KLAN (1924)

The most extreme expression of traditional America's hostility to "alien" trends and "alien" groups was the Ku Klux Klan. The Klan of the 1920s aped the Klan of the Reconstruction period, but it had both a broader agenda and a wider geographical range than its predecessor. With its program of racial and religious intolerance, cultural conformity, and superpatriotism, the Klan in the twenties spread beyond the South and for a time threatened to become a decisive force in U.S. politics on a national level.

The first selection that follows includes statements from two local Klan organizations, the first from New Jersey, the second from Louisiana. What are the essential ingredients of the Klan philosophy as expressed in these selections? Although they do not mention blacks and do not deal with political viewpoints, what do you suppose, judging from these selections, the Klan felt about black Americans and political dissenters?

STATEMENTS FROM THE KU KLUX KLAN

The New Jersey Klan Speaks Out

The Rising of the Ku Klux Klan—The New Reformation

On account of the abuses of religion by the Roman Catholic hierarchy, civilization had reached a universal crisis in the sixteenth century; and Martin Luther, the chosen instrument of God, was placed in the breach to prevent the wheels of progress from being reversed and the world from being plunged into greater darkness than that of the Dark Ages.

The thousand years preceding the Reformation, known by religions historians as Satan's Millennium, was brought on by the Romish Church with her paganistic worship and practices, during which time millions of men and women poured out their blood as martyrs of the Christian religion. . . .

The White-Robed Army

Now come the Knights of the Ku Klux Klan in this crucial hour of our American history to contend for the faith of our fathers who suffered and died in behalf of freedom. At the psychological moment they have arrived to encourage the hearts of those who have been battling heroically for the rights and privileges granted them under the Constitution of the United States.

How our hearts have been thrilled at the sight of this army! Words fail to express the emotions of the soul at the appearance of this mighty throng upon the battle-field, where a few faithful followers of the lowly Nazarene have been contending for the faith once delivered to the Saints, against Papal mobs who have torn down gospel tabernacles, wrecked buildings and imprisoned Protestant worshipers.

Our National Peril

The World War was the signal for greater alarm than the average American has been willing to admit. Notwithstanding the sacrifices that had to be made at home and the thousands of our young men who crossed the sea and laid down their lives on the battlefields of the Old World, it has taken the Ku Klux Klan to awaken even a portion of the population of the United States to our national peril. Our religious and political foes are not only within our gates, but are coming by the hundreds of thousands, bringing the chaos and ruin of old European and Asiatic countries to un-Americanize and destroy our nation, and to make it subserve the purposes of the Pope in his aspirations for world supremacy.

Rome Would Overthrow Public Schools

One of the great efforts of the Roman hierarchy toward this end is to get control of our public schools by placing Roman Catholics on school boards and in the schoolrooms and taking the Bible out of the schools. In the event of their success in their efforts to overthrow our present school system there would be a string of beads around every Protestant child's neck and a Roman Catholic catechism in his hand. 'Hail Mary, Mother of God,' would be on every child's lips, and the idolatrous worship of dead saints a part of the daily programme.

The Jewish and Catholic Alliance

The money-grasping Jew, who has no use for the Christ of Calvary, does all in his power to bring discredit on Christianity, and would be pleased to see the whole structure broken down, and in this way get rid of his responsibility for crucifying the Christ on Calvary and bringing the curse on his race, which they have had to suffer since the beginning of the Christian era. The sons of Abraham have therefore become a strong ally to the Papacy, not because they have anything in common with it in religion, but in their political propaganda against American institutions and principles.

"While no true Christian has anything against the Jew, it must be admitted that this alliance with the Papacy is a dangerous menace to our flag and country. The Jew is insoluble and indigestible; and when he grows in numbers and power till he becomes a menace to Christianity and the whole moral fabric, drastic measures will have to be taken to counteract his destructive work, and more especially when he is in alliance with the old Papal religio-political machine."

The Louisiana Klan's Manifesto

Awake! Americans, Awake!

Awake, Americans! You descendants of the patriots of the Revolution! You sons of the Pilgrim Fathers who fought back the hordes of the Tyrant! Gird on the armor of God who led you out of bondage and chased slavery from out of our land! There is an enemy without our gates ten thousand times more dangerous than the redcoats ever were!

Catholic politicians are filling the air with propaganda which would lead you to believe that old Ship of State has broken loose from her moorings and is drifting far to sea. They cry out in tones of agony that people are growing intolerant and Protestants are seeking to abridge religious liberty. Catholics will prescribe our religion and forbid a Protestant funeral in a Catholic Church. Forbid Catholics attendance at Masonic funerals and then lay claim to a corner on tolerance. Now when Rome is caught red handed in her designs to make American Catholics and Protestants interfere, she cries intolerance and would have you believe that liberty is crushed and bleeding.

When Protestants exercise a right guaranteed to all under the Constitution, when Americans meet in peaceable assembly, Catholics arm themselves with bludgeons and blunderbusses and try to beat down honest men and murder American citizens. Only fools resort to force to settle a dispute and bricks and rocks are only used by savages. Rome not having any grounds on which to fight in the realm of reason seeks to unite State and Church by the use of sandbags and billies. Reason and enlightenment with them are taboo. Blind passion is appealed to and ignorance is made a virtue. Intellectual darkness for the masses is sought by Rome as surely as a robber seeks the shadows. For when the bright light of reason shines upon her, priests lose their power, and her influence crumbles as hastily as would a snowbank in the nether regions.

Catholic politicians, if intrusted with power, would pass laws to force American organizations out of existence and shackle liberty, as they have done in every clime wherein they have reigned supreme.

There are men seeking high office in Louisiana to-day who if elected in numbers sufficient would jail Americans for assembling in peaceful meetings and give to Rome the revenue of our State. Take the Eagle from off the dollar and in its stead place a likeness of the unholy face of [Pope] Pius. Strip the stripes from the American Flag and rend the Stars asunder, and make for us a National banner with background dark and gloomy, and mount upon it a cluster of garlic to commemorate the odor that permeates the Vatican. Turn back the march of civilization and chain the Bible to a box. Tether the intellects of man and enslave reason. Place a statue of a priest where now stands the Goddess of Liberty and place in his hand the torch of intolerance. Demolish our free institutions of learning and imprison those bold enough to preach freedom of the masses. Have black-robed nuns who know only slavery teach our children and drown our art in miasmic ignorance.

"Not all Catholics are of this stripe, but those who seek high office are tainted woefully with Catholic teachings and some have been so bold as to proclaim no Protestant is fit for office and Catholics are the only hope of liberty."

6.3 BLACK AMERICANS RESPOND (1905, 1923)

People of goodwill, black and white, were appalled by what one Progressive called "the race war in the North." In 1909, soon after a shocking race riot in Springfield, Illinois, a group of reformers established the National Association for the Advancement of Colored People (NAACP) to work for better black-white relations and for improved economic conditions for black workers.

The NAACP represented a union of two elements: white Progressives and a new African American leadership, northern-born and northern-educated. Many of the latter were members of the Niagara Movement, a black defense group established in 1905 that rejected the acquiescence in segregation and second-class citizenship associated with Booker T. Washington, head of Tuskegee Institute in Alabama.[1] The leading figure in the Niagara Movement was W.E.B. Du Bois, a brilliant black scholar who had earned a doctorate in history at Harvard and gone on to a successful academic career. Du Bois became the head of publicity and research for the NAACP and remained with it as a leading militant voice for over twenty years.

The first selection that follows is a statement composed by Du Bois for the Niagara Movement. What changes in the treatment of black Americans does it demand? How does Du Bois seek to awaken the support of the white majority? Why would contemporaries have considered a statement like this a bold departure from the past? Why does it end with a pledge that blacks themselves will seek to fulfill certain obligations?

The second selection is by Marcus Garvey, a black West Indian who came to the United States in 1916 with his plan for a Universal Negro Improvement Association. Garvey was a nationalist who sought to awaken black racial pride, establish ties between blacks of the Americas and Africa, and encourage the independence of black Africa, then almost totally under European colonial dominion. He too opposed Booker T. Washington's timid approach to race improvement, but his alternative was different from Du Bois's.

In the United States, Garvey proved an effective voice of black pride, and thousands of urban blacks joined the Universal Negro Improvement Association and contributed to several of Garvey's black run commercial and political ventures. Eventually, opposition from established black leaders, including Du Bois, and from the federal government led to Garvey's conviction for mail fraud. He died in obscurity in London in 1940.

How would you characterize the essential differences between the Du Bois and the Garvey responses to racial oppression? Whose recent views do Garvey's foreshadow? Were Garvey's plans practical ones? Why did they appeal to black city dwellers in the 1920s?

---

[1] Washington was author of the so-called *Atlanta Compromise* that pledged black Americans to abandon claims to suffrage rights and social equality in exchange for economic opportunity. Its pronouncement at the 1895 Cotton States Exposition in Atlanta won wide applause from the white community and made Washington a "leader" of his race in the eyes of whites.

WHAT BLACK AMERICANS WANT

W.E.B. Du Bois

We believe that [Negro-American] citizens should protest emphatically and continually against the curtailment of their political rights. We believe in manhood suffrage: we believe that no man is so good, intelligent or wealthy as to be entrusted wholly with the welfare of his neighbor.

We believe also in protest against the curtailment of our civil rights. All American citizens have the right to equal treatment in places of public entertainment according to their behavior and deserts.

We especially complain against the denial of equal opportunities to us in economic life; in the rural districts of the south this amounts to peonage and virtual slavery; all over the south it tends to crush labor and small business enterprises: and everywhere American prejudice, helped often by iniquitous laws, is making it more difficult for Negro-Americans to earn a decent living.

Common school education should be free to all American children and compulsory. High school training should be adequately provided for all, and college training should be the monopoly of no class or race in any section of our common country. We believe that in defense of its own institutions, the United States should aid common school education, particularly in the south, and we especially recommend concerted agitation to this end. We urge an increase in public high school facilities in the south, where the Negro-Americans are almost wholly without such provisions. We favor well-equipped trade and technical schools for the training of artisans, and the need of adequate and liberal endowment for a few institutions of higher education must be patent to sincere well-wishers of the race.

We demand upright judges in courts, juries selected without discrimination on account of color and the same measure of punishment, and the same efforts at reformation for black as for white offenders. We need orphanages and farm schools for dependent children, juvenile reformatories for delinquents, and the abolition of the dehumanizing convict-lease system. . . .

We hold up for public execration the conduct of two opposite classes of men; the practice among employers of importing ignorant Negro-American laborers in emergencies, and then affording them neither protection nor permanent employment; and the practice of labor unions of proscribing and boycotting and oppressing thousands of their fellow-toilers, simply because they are black. These methods have accentuated and will accentuate the war of labor and capital, and they are disgraceful to both sides. . . .

We regret that this nation has never seen fit adequately to reward the black soldiers who in its five wars, have defended their country with their blood, and yet have been systematically denied the promotions which their abilities deserve. And we regard as unjust, the exclusion of black boys from the military and navy training schools. . . .

The Negro race in America, stolen, ravished and degraded, struggling up through difficulties and oppression, needs sympathy and receives criticism, needs help and is given hindrance, needs protection and is given mob-violence, needs justice and is given

The Cleveland Gazette, July 22, 1905.

charity, needs leadership and is given cowardice and apology, needs bread and is given a stone. This nation will never stand justified before God until these things are changed.

Especially are we surprised and astonished at the recent attitude of the church of Christ—on the increase of a desire to bow to racial prejudice, to narrow the bounds of human brotherhood, and to segregate black men in some outer sanctuary. This is wrong, unchristian and disgraceful to twentieth century civilization. . . .

And while we are demanding, and ought to demand, and will continue to demand the rights enumerated above, God forbid that we should ever forget to urge corresponding duties upon our people.

The duty to vote.

The duty to respect the rights of others.

The duty to work.

The duty to obey the laws.

The duty to be clean and orderly.

The duty to send our children to school.

The duty to respect ourselves, even as we respect others.

BLACK PRIDE

Marcus Garvey

I saw the injustice done my race because it was black, and I became dissatisfied on that account. I went traveling to South and Central America and parts of the West Indies to find out if it was so elsewhere, and I found the same situation. I set sail for Europe to find out if it was different there, and again I found the same stumbling block—"You are black." I read of the conditions in America. I read "Up From Slavery," by Booker T. Washington, and then my doom—if I may call it—of being a race leader dawned upon me in London after I had traveled through almost half of Europe.

I asked, "Where is the black man's Government?" "Where is his King and his king-dom?" "Where is his President, his country, and his ambassador, his army, his navy, his men of big affairs?" I could not find them, and then I declared, "I will help to make them."

Becoming naturally restless for the opportunity of doing something for the advancement of my race, I was determined that the black man would not continue to be kicked about by all the other races and nations of the world, as I saw in the West Indies, South and Central America and Europe and as I read of it in America. My young and ambitious mind led me into flights of great imagination. I saw before me, even as I do now, a new world of black men, not peons, serfs, dogs and slaves, but a nation of sturdy men making their impress upon civilization and causing a new light to dawn upon the human race. My brain was afire. There was a world of thought to conquer. I had to start ere it became too late and the work be not done. Immediately I boarded a ship at Southampton [England] for Jamaica, where I arrived on July 15, 1914. The Universal

---

Marcus Garvey, "The Negro's Greatest Enemy." Reprinted with permission from *Current History* magazine (18, September 1923), pp. 951–57. © 1923, Current History, Inc.

Negro Improvement Association and African Communities (Imperial) League was founded and organized five days after my arrival with the program of uniting all the negro peoples of the world into one great body to establish a country and Government absolutely their own. . . .

Being black, I have committed an unpardonable offense against the very light colored negroes in America and the West Indies by making myself famous as a negro leader of millions. In their view no black man must rise above them, but I still forge ahead determined to give to the world the truth about the new negro who is determined to make and hold for himself a place in the affairs of men. The Universal Negro Improvement Association has been misrepresented by my enemies. They have tried to make it appear that we are hostile to other races. This is absolutely false. We love all humanity. We are working for the peace of the world which we believe can only come about when all races are given their due.

We feel that there is absolutely no reason why there should be any differences between the black and white races, if each stops to adjust and steady itself. We believe in the purity of both races. We do not believe the black man should be encouraged in the idea that his highest purpose in life is to marry a white woman, but we do believe that the white man should be taught to respect the black woman in the same way as he wants the black man to respect the white woman. It is a vicious and dangerous doctrine of social equality to urge, as certain colored leaders do, that black and white should get together, for that would destroy the racial purity of both.

We believe that the black people should have a country of their own where they should be given the fullest opportunity to develop politically, socially and industrially. The black people should not be encouraged to remain in white people's countries and expect to be Presidents, Governors, Mayors, Senators, Congressmen, Judges and social and industrial leaders. We believe that with the rising ambition of the negro, if a country is not provided for him in another 50 or 100 years, there will be a terrible clash that will end disastrously to him and disgrace our civilization. We desire to prevent such a clash by pointing the negro to a home of his own. We feel that all well disposed and broad minded white men will aid in this direction. It is because of this belief no doubt that my negro enemies, so as to prejudice me further in the opinion of the public, wickedly state that I am a member of the Ku Klux Klan, even though I am a black man.[1]

I have been deprived of the opportunity of properly explaining my work to the white people of America through the prejudice worked up against me by jealous and wicked members of my own race. My success as an organizer was much more than rival negro leaders could tolerate. They, regardless of consequences, either to me or to the race, had to destroy me by fair means or foul. The thousands of anonymous and other hostile letters written to the editors and publishers of the white press by negro rivals to prejudice me in the eyes of public opinion are sufficient evidence of the wicked and vicious opposition I have had to meet from among my own people, especially among the very lightly colored. But they went further than the press in their attempts to discredit me. They organized clubs all over the United States and the West Indies, and wrote both open and anonymous letters to city, State and Federal officials of this and

---

[1] Garvey was accused of cooperating with the Klan because he favored separation of the races, a position the Klan endorsed, though for different purposes from Garvey's—ED.

other Governments to induce them to use their influence to hamper and destroy me. No wonder, therefore, that several Judges, District Attorneys and other high officials have been against me without knowing me. No wonder, therefore, that the great white population of this country and of the world has a wrong impression of the aims and objects of the Universal Negro Improvement Association and of the work of Marcus Garvey.

The Struggle of the Future

Having had the wrong education as a start in his racial career, the negro has become his own greatest enemy. Most of the trouble I have had in advancing the cause of the race has come from negroes. Booker Washington aptly described the race in one of his lectures by stating that we were like crabs in a barrel, that none would allow the other to climb over, but on any such attempt all would continue to pull back into the barrel the one crab that would make the effort to climb out. Yet, those of us with vision cannot desert the race, leaving it to suffer and die.

Looking forward a century or two, we can see an economic and political death struggle for the survival of the different race groups. Many of our present-day national centres will have become over-crowded with vast surplus populations. The fight for bread and position will be keen and severe. The weaker and unprepared group is bound to go under. That is why, visionaries as we are in the Universal Negro Improvement Association, we are fighting for the founding of a negro nation in Africa, so that there will be no clash between black and white and that each race will have a separate existence and civilization all its own without courting suspicion and hatred or eyeing each other with jealousy and rivalry within the borders of the same country.

White men who have struggled for and built up their countries and their own civilizations are not disposed to hand them over to the negro or any other race without let or hindrance. It would be unreasonable to expect this. Hence any vain assumption on the part of the negro to imagine that he will one day become President of the Nation, Governor of the State, or Mayor of the city in the countries of white men, is like waiting on the devil and his angels to take up their residence in the Realm on High and direct there the affairs of Paradise.

6.4 THE NEW IMMIGRATION AND AMERICAN TOLERATION (1916, 1912)

Although individual immigrants sometimes endured physical attack and intimidation, intolerance toward European immigrants in the early twentieth century primarily took verbal, economic, and legislative forms. Groups such as the Immigration Restriction League agitated for laws excluding immigrants unable to read and write (in any language) in the expectation that many from the newer regions of immigration would be disqualified. Other anti-immigrant organizations demanded laws capping the total admitted each year and setting quotas on specific nationality groups.

Americans had always worried that foreign newcomers would be difficult to assimilate culturally. But by the 1890s there were racial fears as well. The latest wave of foreigners, said many immigration restrictionists, derived from inferior human stock and so could never become a desirable element of U.S. society, no matter how many classes they took in U.S. civics or in the English language.

The following selections touch on several issues that concerned native-born Americans—and the immigrants as well—during the years 1890–1930.

Few U.S. writers were more outspoken against immigration than Madison Grant. Educated at Yale and Columbia, he combined conventional scientific theories with social and legal concerns to formulate his belief that ethnic and social diversity would threaten American democracy. This selection, taken from his anti-immigration tract, The Passing of the Great Race, is not only racist propaganda, but raises dangerous misconceptions about science and genetics that seem alarmingly relevant to our own time. What does Grant claim is the relationship between race and heredity? What does he mean by racial regression, and how is culture affected by it? What is obviously wrong with what he argues, and why would we consider such writing intolerable today?

The final selection is from the autobiography of Mary Antin, a young Jewish woman born in Polotzk, Poland, who came to the United States with her family in 1894 at the age of thirteen and became a writer and social worker. In what way does she challenge the views of the Dillingham Commission? Do you think her experience was typical of that of the new immigrants in general? What role was the school system expected to play in the process of assimilating the immigrants? Is there any indication that her teacher encouraged Antin to retain any of her family heritage? Was her experience in school different from that of immigrants of our own day? Does the role of Antin's teacher tell us anything about the attitudes of some native-born Americans toward newcomers?

THE PASSING OF THE GREAT RACE

Madison Grant

Failure to recognize the clear distinction between race and nationality and the still greater distinction between race and language, the easy assumption that the one is indicative of the other, has been in the past a serious impediment to an understanding of racial values. Historians and philologists have approached the subject from the viewpoint of linguistics, and as a result we have been burdened with a group of mythical races, such as the Latin, the Aryan, the Caucasian, and, perhaps, most inconsistent of all, the "Celtic" race.

Man is an animal differing from his fellow inhabitants of the globe, not in kind but only in degree of development, and an intelligent study of the human species must be preceded by an extended knowledge of other mammals, especially the primates. Instead of such essential training, anthropologists often seek to qualify by research in linguistics, religion, or marriage customs, or in designs of pottery or blanket weaving, all of which relate to ethnology alone.

The question of race has been further complicated by the effort of old-fashioned theologians to cramp all mankind into the scant six thousand years of Hebrew chronology, as expounded by Archbishop Ussher. Religious teachers have also maintained the proposition not only that man is something fundamentally distinct from other living creatures, but that there are no inherited differences in humanity that cannot be obliterated by education and environment.

Madison Grant, *The Passing of the Great Race* (New York: C. Scribner's Sons, 1916), selected from the introduction pp. 1–16.

It is, therefore, necessary at the outset for the reader to thoroughly appreciate that race, language, and nationality are three separate and distinct things, and that in Europe these three elements are only occasionally found persisting in combination, as in the Scandinavian nations.

To realize the transitory nature of political boundaries, one has only to consider the changes of the past century, to say nothing of those which may occur at the end of the present war. As to language, here in America we daily hear the English language spoken by many men who possess not one drop of English blood, and who, a few years since, knew not one word of Saxon speech.

As a result of certain religious and social doctrines, now happily becoming obsolete, race consciousness has been greatly impaired among civilized nations, but in the beginning all differences of class, of caste, and of color marked actual lines of racial cleavage.

In many countries the existing classes represent races that were once distinct. In the city of New York, and elsewhere in the United States, there is a native American aristocracy resting upon layer after layer of immigrants of lower races, and the native American, while, of course, disclaiming the distinction of a patrician class, nevertheless has, up to this time, supplied the leaders of thought and the control of capital, of education, and of the religious ideals and altruistic bias of the community.

In the democratic forms of government the operation of universal suffrage tends toward the selection of the average man for public office rather than the man qualified by birth, education, and integrity. How this scheme of administration will ultimately work out remains to be seen, but from a racial point of view, it will inevitably increase the preponderance of the lower types and cause a corresponding loss of efficiency in the community as a whole.

The tendency in a democracy is toward a standardization of type and a diminution of the influence of genius. A majority must of necessity be inferior to a picked minority, and it always resents specializations in which it cannot share. In the French Revolution the majority, calling itself "the people," deliberately endeavored to destroy the higher type, and something of the same sort was, in a measure, done after the American Revolution by the expulsion of the Loyalists and the confiscation of their lands.

In America we have nearly succeeded in destroying the privilege of birth; that is, the intellectual and moral advantage a man of good stock brings into the world with him. We are now engaged in destroying the privilege of wealth; that is, the reward of successful intelligence and industry, and in some quarters there is developing a tendency to attack the privilege of intellect and to deprive a man of the advantages of an early and thorough education. Simplified spelling is a step in this direction. Ignorance of English grammar or classic learning must not be held up as a reproach to the political and social aspirant.

Mankind emerged from savagery and barbarism under the leadership of selected individuals whose personal prowess, capacity, or wisdom gave them the right to lead and the power to compel obedience. Such leaders have always been a minute fraction of the whole, but as long as the tradition of their predominance persisted they were able to use the brute strength of the unthinking herd as part of their own force, and were able to direct at will the blind dynamic impulse of the slaves, peasants, or lower classes. Such a despot had an enormous power at this disposal which, if he were benevolent or even intelligent, could be used, and most frequently was used, for the general uplift of the race. Even those rulers who most abused this power put down with merciless rigor the antisocial elements, such as pirates, brigands, or anarchists, which impair the progress of a community, as disease or wounds cripple an individual.

True aristocracy is government by the wisest and best, always a small minority in any population. Human society is like a serpent dragging its long body on the ground, but with the head always thrust a little in advance and a little elevated above the earth. The serpent's tail, in human society represented by the antisocial forces, was in the past dragged by sheer force along the path of progress. Such has been the organization of mankind from the beginning, and such it still is in older communities than ours. What progress humanity can make under the control of universal suffrage, or the rule of the average, may find a further analogy in the habits of certain snakes which wiggle sideways and disregard the head with its brains and eyes. Such serpents, however, are not noted for their ability to make rapid progress.

To use another simile, in an aristocratic as distinguished from a plutocratic, or democratic organization, the intellectual and talented classes form the point of the lance, while the massive shaft represents the body of the population and adds by its bulk and weight to the penetrative impact of the tip. In a democratic system this concentrated force at the top is dispersed throughout the mass, supplying, to be sure, a certain amount of leaven, but in the long run the force and genius of the small minority is dissipated, if not wholly lost. *Vox populi*, so far from being *Vox Dei*, thus becomes an unending wail for rights, and never a chant of duty.

Where a conquering race is imposed on another race the institution of slavery often arises to compel the servient race to work, and to introduce it forcibly to a higher form of civilization. As soon as men can be induced to labor to supply their own needs slavery becomes wasteful and tends to vanish. Slaves are often more fortunate than freemen when treated with reasonable humanity, and when their elemental wants of food, clothing, and shelter are supplied. . . .

The continuity of physical traits and the limitation of the effects of environment to the individual only are now so thoroughly recognized by scientists that it is at most a question of time when the social consequences which result from such crossings will be generally understood by the public at large. As soon as the true bearing and import of the facts are appreciated by lawmakers, a complete change in our political structure will inevitably occur, and our present reliance on the influences of education will be superseded by a readjustment based on racial values.

Bearing in mind the extreme antiquity of physical and spiritual characters and the persistency with which they outlive those elements of environment termed language, nationality, and forms of government, we must consider the relation of these facts to the development of the race in America. We may be certain that the progress of evolution is in full operation to-day under those laws of nature which control it, and that the only sure guide to the future lies in the study of the operation of these laws in the past.

We Americans must realize that the altruistic ideals which have controlled our social development during the past century, and the maudlin sentimentalism that has made America "an asylum for the oppressed," are sweeping the nation toward a racial abyss. If the Melting Pot is allowed to boil without control, and we continue to follow our national motto and deliberately blind ourselves to all "distinctions of race, creed, or color," the type of native American of Colonial descent will become as extinct as the Athenian of the age of Pericles, and the Viking of the days of Rollo.

THE PROMISED LAND

Mary Antin

The public school has done its best for us foreigners, and for the country, when it has made us into good Americans. I am glad it is mine to tell how the miracle was wrought in one case. You should be glad to hear of it, you born Americans; for it is the story of the growth of your country; of the flocking of your brothers and sisters from the far ends of the earth to the flag you love; of the recruiting of your armies of workers, thinkers, and leaders. And you will be glad to hear of it, my comrades in adoption; for it is a rehearsal of your own experience, the thrill and wonder of which your own hearts have felt.

How long would you say, wise reader, it takes to make an American? By the middle of my second year in school I had reached the sixth grade. When, after the Christmas holidays, we began to study the life of Washington, running through a summary of the Revolution, and the early days of the Republic, it seemed to me that all my reading and study had been idle until then. The reader, the arithmetic, the song book, that had so fascinated me until now, became suddenly sober exercise books, tools wherewith to hew a way to the source of inspiration. When the teacher read to us out of a big book with many bookmarks in it, I sat rigid with attention in my little chair, my hands tightly clasped on the edge of my desk; and I painfully held my breath, to prevent sighs of disappointment escaping, as I saw the teacher skip the parts between bookmarks. When the class read, and it came my turn, my voice shook and the book trembled in my hands. I could not pronounce the name of George Washington without a pause. Never had I prayed, never had I chanted the songs of David, never had I called upon the Most Holy, in such utter reverence and worship as I repeated the simple sentences of my child's story of the patriot. I gazed with adoration at the portraits of George and Martha Washington, till I could see them with my eyes shut. And whereas formerly my self-consciousness had bordered on conceit, and I thought myself an uncommon person, parading my schoolbooks through the streets, and swelling with pride when a teacher detained me in conversation, now I grew humble all at once, seeing how insignificant I was beside the Great.

As I read about the noble boy who would not tell a lie to save himself from punishment, I was for the first time truly repentant of my sins. Formerly I had fasted and prayed and made sacrifice on the Day of Atonement, but it was more than half play, in mimicry of my elders. I had no real horror of sin, and I knew so many ways of escaping punishment. I am sure my family, my neighbors, my teachers in Polotzk—all my world, in fact—strove together, by example and precept, to teach me goodness. Saintliness had a new incarnation in about every third person I knew. I did respect the saints, but I could not help seeing that most of them were a little bit stupid, and that mischief was much more fun than piety. Goodness, as I had known it, was respectable, but not necessarily admirable. The people I really admired, like my Uncle Solomon, and Cousin Rachel, were those who preached the least and laughed the most. My sister Frieda was perfectly good, but she did not think the less of me because I played tricks.

Mary Antin, *The Promised Land* (Boston: Houghton Mifflin Company, 1912), pp. 222–28.

What is loved in my friends was not inimitable. One could be downright good if one really wanted to. One could be learned if one had books and teachers. One could sing funny songs and tell anecdotes if one travelled about and picked up such things, like one's uncles and cousins. But a human being strictly good, perfectly wise, and unfailingly valiant, all at the same time, I had never heard or dreamed of. This wonderful George Washington was as inimitable as he was irreproachable. Even if I had never, never told a lie, I could not compare myself to George Washington; for I was not brave—I was afraid to go out when snowballs whizzed—and I could never be the First President of the United States.

So I was forced to revise my own estimate of myself. But the twin of my new-born humility, paradoxical as it may seem, was a sense of dignity I had never known before. For if I found that I was a person of small consequence, I discovered at the same time that I was more nobly related than I had ever supposed. I had relatives and friends who were notable people by the old standards,—I had never been ashamed of my family,—but this George Washington, who died long before I was born, was like a king in greatness, and he and I were Fellow Citizens. There was a great deal about Fellow Citizens in the patriotic literature we read at this time; and I knew from my father how he was a Citizen, through the process of naturalization, and how I also was a citizen, by virtue of my relation to him. Undoubtedly I was a Fellow Citizen, and George Washington was another. It thrilled me to realize what sudden greatness had fallen on me; and at the same time it sobered me, as with a sense of responsibility. I strove to conduct myself as befitted a Fellow Citizen.

Before books came into my life, I was given to stargazing and daydreaming. When books were given me, I fell upon them as a glutton pounces on his meat after a period of enforced starvation. I lived with my nose in a book, and took no notice of the alternations of the sun and stars. But now, after the advent of George Washington and the American Revolution, I began to dream again. I strayed on the common after school instead of hurrying home to read. I hung on fence rails, my pet book forgotten under my arm, and gazed off to the yellow-streaked February sunset, and beyond, and beyond. I was no longer the central figure of my dreams; the dry weeds in the lane crackled beneath the tread of Heroes.

What more could America give a child? Ah, much more! As I read how the patriots planned the Revolution, and the women gave their sons to die in battle, and the heroes led to victory, and the rejoicing people set up the Republic, it dawned on me gradually what was meant by *my country*. The people all desiring noble things, and striving for them together, defying their oppressors, giving their lives for each other— all this it was that made *my country*. It was not a thing that I *understood*; I could not go home and tell Frieda about it, as I told her other things I learned at school. But I knew one could say "my country" and *feel* it, as one felt "God" or "myself." My teacher, my schoolmates, Miss Dillingham, George Washington himself could not mean more than I when they said "my country," after I had once felt it. For the Country was for all the Citizens, and *I was a Citizen*. And when we stood up to sing "America," I shouted the words with all my might. I was in very earnest proclaiming to the world my love for my new-found country.

I love thy rocks and rills,
Thy woods and templed hills.

Boston Harbor, Crescent Beach, Chelsea Square—all was hallowed ground to me. As the day approached when the school was to hold exercises in honor of Washington's Birthday, the halls resounded at all hours with the strains of patriotic songs; and I, who was a model of the attentive pupil, more than once lost my place in the lesson as I strained to hear, through closed doors, some neighboring class rehearsing "The Star-Spangled Banner." If the doors happened to open, and the chorus broke out unveiled—

O! say, does that Star-Spangled Banner yet wave
O'er the land of the free, and the home of the brave?—

delicious tremors ran up and down my spine, and I was faint with suppressed enthusiasm.

Where had been my country until now? What flag had I loved? What heroes had I worshipped? The very names of these things had been unknown to me. Well I knew that Polotzk was not my country. It was *goluth*—exile. On many occasions in the year we prayed to God to lead us out of exile. The beautiful Passover service closed with the words, "Next year, may we be in Jerusalem." On childish lips, indeed, those words were no conscious aspiration; we repeated the Hebrew syllables after our elders, but without their hope and longing. Still not a child among us was too young to feel in his own flesh the lash of the oppressor. We knew what it was to be Jews in exile, from the spiteful treatment we suffered at the hands of the smallest urchin who crossed himself; and thence we knew that Israel had good reason to pray for deliverance. But the story of the Exodus was not history to me in the sense that the story of the American Revolution was. It was more like a glorious myth, a belief in which had the effect of cutting me off from the actual world, by linking me with a world of phantoms. Those moments of exaltation which the contemplation of the Biblical past afforded us, allowing us to call ourselves the children of princes, served but to tinge with a more poignant sense of disinheritance the long humdrum stretches of our life. In very truth we were a people without a country. Surrounded by mocking foes and detractors, it was difficult for me to realize the persons of my people's heroes or the events in which they moved. Except in moments of abstraction from the world around me, I scarcely understood that Jerusalem was an actual spot on the earth, where once the Kings of the Bible, real people, like my neighbors in Polotzk, ruled in puissant majesty. For the conditions of our civil life did not permit us to cultivate a spirit of nationalism. The freedom of worship that was grudgingly granted within the narrow limits of the Pale by no means included the right to set up openly any ideal of a Hebrew State, any hero other than the Czar. What we children picked up of our ancient political history was confused with the miraculous story of the Creation, with the supernatural legends and hazy associations of Bible lore. As to our future, we Jews in Polotzk had no national expectations; only a lifeworn dreamer here and there hoped to die in Palestine. If Fetchke and I sang, with my father, first making sure of our audience, "Zion, Zion, Holy Zion, not forever is it lost," we did not really picture to ourselves Judæa restored.

So it came to pass that we did not know what *my country* could mean to a man. And as we had no country, so we had no flag to love. It was by no farfetched symbolism that the banner of the House of Romanoff became the emblem of our latter-day bondage in our eyes. Even a child would know how to hate the flag that we were forced, on pain of severe penalties, to hoist above our housetops, in celebration of the advent of one of our oppressors. And as it was with country and flag, so it was with heroes of war. We hated the uniform of the soldier, to the last brass button. On the person of a Gentile, it was the symbol of tyranny; on the person of a Jew, it was the emblem of shame.

So a little Jewish girl in Polotzk was apt to grow up hungry-minded and empty-hearted; and if, still in her outreaching youth, she was set down in a land of outspoken patriotism, she was likely to love her new country with a great love, and to embrace its heroes in a great worship. Naturalization, with us Russian Jews, may mean more than the adoption of the immigrant by America. It may mean the adoption of America by the immigrant.

CHAPTER 7

World War I

In the summer of 1914, the great powers of Europe went to war. In a matter of weeks the armies and navies of two great coalitions, the Central Powers (Germany, Austria-Hungary, and later Turkey) and the Entente, or Allies (France, Great Britain, Russia, and later Italy), were locked in murderous combat in Europe and around the world.

For two and a half years, the United States remained on the sidelines, the largest and most powerful neutral in a world at war. President Woodrow Wilson initially urged his compatriots to remain "impartial in thought as well as in action," but from the outset this proved impossible. Too many Americans were tied by sentiment or culture to one side or the other. Moreover, the United States, with its great industrial and financial resources, could not easily detach itself economically from Europe's confrontation.

Both sides sought to mold U.S. policy for their own ends. The Allies saw the United States as a source of credit, supplies, and munitions and tried to insure free access to these resources. Beyond this, some Allied leaders hoped to draw the great American republic into the war as an actual military partner. The Central Powers also could not ignore the United States. Unable themselves to procure U.S. goods through the Allied blockade and with no expectation of U.S. alliance, they limited their goals to keeping the United States neutral and preventing the Allies from taking full advantage of America's financial, industrial, and military might.

Inevitably, America's relations with the belligerents were colored by disagreements over neutral rights in time of war. The Wilson administration defended the right of Americans under international law to trade a wide range of goods with whomever they wished, and to travel wherever and however they wished.

Neither the Allies nor Central Powers accepted America's broad definition of neutral rights, but the British and French benefited more from free trade with the United States than did the Germans and Austro-Hungarians, and so clashed with America less. Indeed, the Germans soon sought to block U.S. trade with the Allies in the only way they could: by use of the U-boat, a torpedo-armed submarine that could sink without warning any merchant vessel suspected of carrying war material to the enemy. The tactic was often brutal. Crews and passengers could not be saved by the small, vulnerable U-boats and so often perished. To charges of inhumanity, the Germans responded that the Allied blockade of food to German civilians was as barbarous as submarine warfare.

Americans disagreed over which policies to pursue toward the warring powers during 1914–1917. Their views were affected by ethnicity, ideology, patriotism, politics, culture, material interest, and other considerations. These differing attitudes and the motives behind them are suggested in the selections that follow.

Eventually, intervention unleashed internationalist and idealistic feelings, much encouraged by Wilson's leadership. Wilson proposed that the nation assume a much larger role in world affairs, increasing its interest, commitments, and responsibilities. Patriotic sentiment supported the president while U.S. soldiers fought in Europe during the last year of the war, but during the tense peace negotiations that followed, disillusionment and political impasse dashed the hopes of a new world order. Wilson's presidency ended in bitter stalemate over the Treaty of Versailles, which the United States never signed, and the nation once again returned to isolationism in the 1920s.

7.1 THE SUBMARINE DIMENSION (1915)

No belligerent action during World War I set off as explosive a response in the United States as did the German submarine campaign against Allied and neutral shipping. In February 1915, the German government announced that all merchant vessels, whether neutral or enemy, found in a broad zone surrounding the British Isles would be sunk on sight, even if this meant injury or death to crews and passengers. This "unrestricted" U-boat warfare violated the traditional usages of war, and the U.S. government threatened to hold the Imperial German government "to a strict accountability" for any loss of U.S. lives and property under the order. The first selection that follows is the note sent by Secretary of State William Jennings Bryan to the German government conveying the U.S. position. In fact, Bryan correctly stated the normal practices of war, but the Germans felt they had no choice.

The second selection is the response of the German foreign minister, Gottlieb von Jagow, to the U.S. protest against the sinking in May 1915 of the British passenger liner the Lusitania, with the loss of 1,200 civilian lives, including 128 Americans. American opinion was outraged, and the attack had been almost universally condemned. But is it fair to see the Germans as barbarians, indifferent to human life? Does the German foreign minister make a convincing case for his country's use of the submarine weapon in the instances he describes? Why was the U.S. government, do you suppose, so unsympathetic to German arguments? Was the U.S. government even willing, in later years, to limit the travel of its citizens in dangerous war zones?

PROTESTING UNRESTRICTED U-BOAT WARFARE

William Jennings Bryan
Washington, February 10, 1915

Please address a note immediately to the Imperial German Government to the following effect:

The Government of the United States, having had its attention directed to the proclamation of the German Admiralty issued on the 4th of February, . . . feels it to be its duty to call the attention of the Imperial German Government, with sincere respect and the most friendly sentiments but very candidly and earnestly, to the very serious possibilities of the course of action apparently contemplated under that proclamation.

The Government of the United States views those possibilities with such grave concern that it feels it to be its privilege, and indeed its duty in the circumstances, to request the Imperial German Government to consider before action is taken the critical situation in respect of the relations between this country and Germany which might arise were the German naval forces, in carrying out the policy foreshadowed in the Admiralty' proclamation, to destroy any merchant vessel of the United States or cause the death of American citizens.

It is of course not necessary to remind the German Government that the sole right of a belligerent in dealing with neutral vessels on the high seas is limited to visit and search, unless a blockade is proclaimed and effectively maintained, which this Government does not understand to be proposed in this case. To declare or exercise a right to attack and destroy any vessel entering a prescribed area of the high seas without first certainly determining its belligerent nationality and the contraband character of its cargo would be an act so unprecedented in naval warfare that this Government is reluctant to believe that the Imperial Government of Germany in this case contemplates it as possible. The suspicion that enemy ships are using neutral flags improperly can create no just presumption that all ships traversing a prescribed area are subject to the same suspicion. It is to determine exactly such questions that this Government understands the right of visit and search to have been recognized.

This Government has carefully noted the explanatory statement issued by the Imperial German Government at the same time with the proclamation of the German Admiralty, and takes this occasion to remind the Imperial German Government very respectfully that the Government of the United States is open to none of the criticisms for unneutral action to which the German Government believe the governments of certain other neutral nations have laid themselves open; that the Government of the United States has not consented to or acquiesced in any measures which may have been taken by the other belligerent nations in the present war which operate to restrain neutral trade, but has, on the contrary, taken in all such matters a position which warrants it in holding those governments responsible in the proper way for any untoward effects upon American shipping which the accepted principles of international law do not justify; and that it, therefore, regards itself as free in the present instance to take with a clear conscience and upon accepted principles the position indicated in this note.

[U.S. Department of State], *Papers Relating to the Foreign Relations of the United States, 1915. Supplement: The World War* (Washington, DC: Government Printing Office, 1928), pp. 98–100.

If the commanders of German vessels of war should act upon the presumption that the flag of the United States was not being used in good faith and should destroy on the high seas an American vessel or the lives of American citizens, it would be difficult for the Government of the United States to view the act in any other light than as an indefensible violation of neutral rights which it would be very hard indeed to reconcile with the friendly relations now so happily subsisting between the two Governments.

If such a deplorable situation should arise, the Imperial German Government can readily appreciate that the Government of the United States would be constrained to hold the Imperial German Government to a strict accountability for such acts of their naval authorities and to take any steps it might be necessary to take to safeguard American lives and property and to secure to American citizens the full enjoyment of their acknowledged rights on the high seas.

The Government of the United States, in view of these considerations, which it urges with the greatest respect and with the sincere purpose of making sure that no misunderstanding may arise and no circumstance occur that might even cloud the intercourse of the two Governments, expresses the confident hope and expectation that the Imperial German Government can and will give assurance that American citizens and their vessels will not be molested by the naval forces of Germany otherwise than by visit and search, though their vessels may be traversing the sea area delimited in the proclamation of the German Admiralty.

It is added for the information of the Imperial Government that representations have been made to His Britannic Majesty's Government in respect to the unwarranted use of the American flag for the protection of British ships.

[Secretary of State William Jennings] Bryan

THE GERMANS DEFEND THEIR SUBMARINE POLICY

Gottlieb Von Jagow
Berlin, May 28, 1915

The Imperial Government has subjected the statements of the Government of the United States to a careful examination and has the lively wish on its part also to contribute in a convincing and friendly manner to clear up any misunderstandings which may have entered into the relations of the two Governments through the events mentioned by the American Government. . . .

With regard to the loss of life when the British passenger steamer *Lusitania* was sunk, the German Government has already expressed its deep regret to the neutral Governments concerned that nationals of those countries lost their lives on that occasion. The Imperial Government must state for the rest the impression that certain important facts most directly connected with the sinking of the *Lusitania* may have escaped the attention of the Government of the United States. It therefore considers it necessary in the interest of the clear and full understanding aimed at by either Government primarily to convince itself that the reports of the facts which are before the two Governments are complete and in agreement.

[U.S. Department of State]. *Papers Relating to the Foreign Relations of the United States, 1915. Supplement: The World War* (Washington, DC: Government Printing Office, 1928), pp. 419–21.

The Government of the United States proceeds on the assumption that the *Lusitania* is to be considered as an ordinary unarmed merchant vessel. The Imperial Government begs in this connection to point out that the *Lusitania* was one of the largest and fastest English commerce steamers, constructed with Government funds as auxiliary cruisers, and is expressly included in the navy list published by British Admiralty. It is moreover known to the Imperial Government from reliable information furnished by its officials and neutral passengers that for some time practically all the more valuable English merchant vessels have been provided with guns, ammunition, and other weapons, and reinforced with a crew specially practiced in manning guns. According to reports at hand here, the *Lusitania* when she left New York undoubtedly had guns on board which were mounted under decks and masked.

The Imperial Government furthermore has the honor to direct the particular attention of the American Government to the fact that the British Admiralty by a secret instruction of February of this year advised the British merchant marine not only to seek protection behind neutral flags and markings, but even when so disguised to attack German submarines by ramming them. High rewards have been offered by the British Government as a special incentive for the destruction of the submarines by merchant vessels, and such rewards have already been paid out. In view of these facts, which are satisfactorily known to it, the Imperial Government is unable to consider English merchant vessels any longer as "undefended territory" in the zone of maritime war designated by the Admiralty Staff of the Imperial German Navy, the German commanders are consequently no longer in a position to observe the rules of capture otherwise usual and with which they invariably complied before this. Lastly, the Imperial Government must specially point out that on her last trip the *Lusitania*, as on earlier occasions, had Canadian troops and munitions on board, including no less than 5,400 cases of ammunition destined for the destruction of brave German soldiers who are fulfilling with self-sacrifice and devotion their duty in the service of the Fatherland. The German Government believes that it acts in just self-defense when it seeks to protect the lives of its soldiers by destroying ammunition destined for the enemy with the means of war at its command. The English steamship company must have been aware of the dangers to which passengers on board the *Lusitania* were exposed under the circumstances. In taking them on board in spite of this the company quite deliberately tried to use the lives of American citizens as protection for the ammunition carried, and violated the clear provisions of American laws which expressly prohibit, and provide punishment for, the carrying of passengers on ships which have explosives on board. The company thereby wantonly caused the death of so many passengers. According to the express report of the submarine commander concerned, which is further confirmed by all other reports, there can be no doubt that the rapid sinking of the *Lusitania* was primarily due to the explosion of the cargo of ammunition caused by the torpedo. Otherwise, in all human probability, the passengers of the *Lusitania* would have been saved.

The Imperial Government holds the facts recited above to be of sufficient importance to recommend them to a careful examination by the American Government. The Imperial Government begs to reserve a final statement of its position with regard to the demand made in connection with the sinking of the *Lusitania* until a reply is received from the American Government.

[Foreign Minister Gottlieb] von Jagow

7.2 VOICES FOR INTERVENTION (1915)

There was never any serious support in the United States for entering the war on the side of the Central Powers. But from the beginning some Americans sought to align the United States militarily with Britain and France. There have been many explanations for this tilt to the Allies. The following are three contemporary selections that suggest reasons for U.S. sympathy for the Allied side and for the military support for Britain and France America finally provided.

The first is an excerpt from the Bryce Report of 1915, a British indictment of German behavior toward civilians in the German-occupied regions of France and Belgium. James Bryce, chief author of the report, was the former British ambassador to the United States, a respected figure who had written a famous book about America a generation before.

The Bryce Report was part of a concerted Allied propaganda campaign to influence U.S. public opinion. Do the statements of the report ring true? Is it clear that the brutality against civilians described was deliberate German policy? How do Bryce and his colleagues link the Belgian and French atrocities to German, or "Prussian," militarism?

The second selection is a memo from the private papers of Robert Lansing, the man who succeeded William Jennings Bryan as secretary of state in 1915. Although he represented an officially neutral nation, clearly Lansing himself was not neutral. What were the bases for his pro-Allies feelings? Were they shared by other influential Americans? Were his views of German policies and goals valid?

The third selection is a letter by Lansing to President Wilson on the issue of extending financial credits to the Allies to allow them to continue to buy U.S. munitions and other war supplies. Earlier, in 1914, the U.S. government had sought to discourage U.S. loans to any of the belligerents as an unneutral act. Lansing's proposal represents a retreat from that policy. By April 1917 U.S. investors had bought $2.3 billion of Allied bonds.

Critics of U.S. intervention in World War I have said that the liberal loan policy of the Wilson administration created an economic stake in Allied victory that powerfully influenced U.S. policy. What were Lansing's reasons for wanting to liberalize U.S. loan policies? Are his arguments convincing? Did America have an economic stake in the Allied cause, and was this a significant factor in drawing the United States into the war in 1917?

BRITISH REPORT ON GERMAN ATROCITIES IN BELGIUM

Ambassador James Bryce

In the minds of Prussian officers War seems to have become a sort of sacred mission, one of the highest functions of the omnipotent State, which is itself as much an Army as a State. Ordinary morality and the ordinary sentiment of pity vanish in its presence, superseded by a new standard which justifies to the soldier every means that can conduce to success, however shocking to a natural sense of justice and humanity, however revolting to his own feelings. The Spirit of War is deified. Obedience to the State and its War Lord leaves no room for any other duty or feeling. Cruelty becomes legitimate when it promises victory. Proclaimed by the heads of the army, this doctrine would

Report of the Committee on Alleged German Outrages (London: His Majesty's Stationery Office, 1915), pp. 44–61.

seem to have permeated the officers and affected even the private soldiers, leading them to justify the killing of non-combatants as an act of war, and so accustoming them to slaughter that even women and children become at last the victims. It cannot be supposed to be a national doctrine, for it neither springs from nor reflects the mind and feelings of the German people as they have heretofore been known to other nations. It is a specifically military doctrine, the outcome of a theory held by a ruling caste who have brooded and thought, written and talked and dreamed about War until they have fallen under its obsession and been hypnotised by its spirit. . . .

a. **Killing of Non-Combatants**

The killing of civilians in Belgium has been already described sufficiently. Outrages on the civilian population of the invaded districts, the burning of villages, the shooting of innocent inhabitants and the taking of hostages, pillage and destruction continued as the German armies passed into France. . . .

b. **The Treatment of Women and Children**

The evidence shows that the German authorities, when carrying out a policy of systematic arson and plunder in selected districts, usually drew some distinction between the adult male population on the one hand and the women and children on the other. It was a frequent practice to set apart the adult males of the condemned district with a view to the execution of a suitable number—preferably of the younger and more vigorous—and to reserve the women and children. . . .

We find many well-established cases of the slaughter (often accompanied by mutilation) of whole families, including not infrequently that of quite small children. In two cases it seems to be clear that preparations were made to burn a family alive. These crimes were committed over a period of many weeks and simultaneously in many places, and the authorities must have known or ought to have known that cruelties of this character were being perpetrated, nor can anyone doubt that they could have been stopped by swift and decisive action on the part of the heads of the German army. . . .

Whatever excuse may be offered by the Germans for the killing of grown-up women, there can be no possible defence for the murder of children, and if it can be shown that infants and small children were not infrequently bayoneted and shot it is a fair inference that many of the offences against women require no explanation more recondite than the unbridled violence of brutal or drunken criminals. . . .

Conclusions

i. That there were in many parts of Belgium deliberate and systematically organised massacres of civil population, accompanied by many isolated murders and other outrages.

ii. That in the conduct of the war generally innocent civilians, both men and women, were murdered in large numbers, women violated, and children murdered.

iii. That looting, house burning, and the wanton destruction of property were ordered and countenanced by the officers of the German Army, that elaborate provision had been made for systematic incendiarism at the very outbreak of the war, and that the burnings and destruction were frequent where no military necessity could be alleged, being indeed part of a system of general terrorization.

iv. That the rules and usages of war were frequently broken, particularly by the using of civilians, including women and children, as a shield for advancing forces exposed to fire, to a less degree by killing the wounded and prisoners, and in the frequent abuse of the Red Cross and the White Flag.

GERMANY MUST NOT BE ALLOWED TO WIN THE WAR

Robert Lansing
July 11, 1915

I have come to the conclusion that the German Government is utterly hostile to all nations with democratic institutions because those who compose it see in democracy a menace to absolutism and the defeat of the German ambition for world domination. Everywhere German agents are plotting and intriguing to accomplish the supreme purpose of their Government.

Only recently has the conviction come that democracy throughout the world is threatened. Suspicions of the vaguest sort only a few months [ago] have been more and more confirmed. From many sources evidence has been coming until it would be folly to close one's eyes to it.

German agents have undoubtedly been at work in Mexico arousing anti-American feeling and holding out false hopes of support. The proof is not conclusive but is sufficient to compel belief. Germans also appear to be operating in Haiti and San Domingo and are probably doing so in other Latin American republics.

I think that this is being done so that this nation will have troubles in America and be unable to take part in the European War if a repetition of such outrages as the LUSI-TANIA sinking should require us to act. It may even go further and have in mind the possibility of a future war with this Republic in case the Allies should be defeated.

In these circumstances the policies we adopt are vital to the future of the United States and, I firmly believe to the welfare of mankind, for I see in the perpetuation of democracy the one hope of universal peace and progress for the world. Today German absolutism is the great menace to democracy.

I think that we should, therefore, adopt the following for the present and pursue these policies until conditions materially change:

1. The settlement for the time being at least of present submarine controversy because the American people are still much divided on the merits of the war. As it progresses, I believe, that the real objects of the German Government will be disclosed and there will be united opposition. Meanwhile we should get ready to meet the worst.

2. A rigorous and continuing prosecution of all plots in this country and a vigilant watch on Germans and their activities here.

Private Memoranda Books, The Papers of Robert Lansing, Manuscripts Division, Library of Congress, Washington, DC.

3. Secret investigations of German activities in Latin America, particularly Mexico, and the adoption of means to frustrate them.
4. The cultivations of a Pan American doctrine with the object of alienating the American republics from European influence, especially the German influence. . . .
5. The actual participation of this country in the war in case it becomes evident that Germany will be the victor. A triumph for Germany imperialism *must not be*. We ought to look forward to this possibility and make ready to meet it. . . .

My judgment is that the German Government, cherishing the same ambition of world empire which now possesses it, would with its usual vigor and thoroughness prepare to renew its attack on democracy. I think, however, that it would not pursue the course taken in this war which had failed because it would realize that the democratic nations would be more watchful and less trustful and better prepared to resist. It would probably endeavor to sow dissentions [sic] among the nations with liberal institutions and seek an alliance with other governments based to a more or less degree on the principle of absolutism.

The two powers, which would probably be approached by Germany, would be Russia and Japan, which are almost as hostile to democracy as Germany and which have similar ambitions of territorial expansion.

These three great empires would constitute an almost irresistible [sic] coalition against the nations with republican and liberal monarchical institutions. It would be the old struggle of absolutism against democracy, an even greater struggle than the one now in progress. The outcome would be doubtful, with, as it seems to me, the chances in favor of the autocratic allies.

The success of these three empires would mean a division for the time being at least of the world among them. I imagine that Germany would be master of Western Europe, of Africa and probably of the Americas; that Russia would dominate Scandinavia, and Western and Southern Asia; and Japan would control the Far East, the Pacific and possibly the West Coast of North America.

Their success would mean the overthrow of democracy in the world, the suppression of individual liberty, the setting up of evil ambitions, the subordination of the principles of right and justice to physical might directed by arbitrary will, and the turning back of the hands of human progress two centuries.

These, I believe, would be the consequences of the triumph of this triple alliance of autocratic empires, a triumph which even the most optimistic cannot deny to be a reasonable expectation.

The remedy seems to me to be plain. It is that Germany must not be permitted to win this war and to break even, though to prevent it this country is forced to take an active part. This ultimate necessity must be constantly in our minds in all our controversies with the belligerents. American public opinion must be prepared for the time, which may come, when we will have to cast aside our neutrality and become one of the champions of democracy.

We must in fact risk everything rather than leave the way open for a new combination of powers, stronger and more dangerous to liberty than the Central Allies are today.

LENDING THE ALLIES MONEY

Robert Lansing

Washington, September 6, 1915

My dear Mr. President:

Doubtless Secretary [William] McAdoo has discussed with you the necessity of floating government loans for the belligerent nations, which are purchasing such great quantities of goods in this country, in order to avoid a serious financial situation which will not only affect them but this country as well.

Briefly, the situation, as I understand it, is this: Since December 1st, 1914, to June 30, 1915, our exports have exceeded our imports by nearly a billion dollars, and it is estimated that the excess will be from July 1st to December 31, 1915, a billion and three quarters. Thus for the year 1915 the excess will be approximately two and [a] half billions of dollars.

It is estimated that the European banks have about three and [a] half billions of dollars in gold in their vaults. To withdraw any considerable amount would disastrously affect the credit of the European nations, and the consequence would be a general state of bankruptcy.

If the European countries cannot find means to pay for the excess of goods sold to them over those purchased from them, they will have to stop buying and our present export trade will shrink proportionately. The result would be restriction of outputs, industrial depression, idle capital and idle labor, numerous failures, financial demoralization, and general unrest and suffering among the laboring classes.

Probably a billion and three quarters of the excess of European purchases can be taken care of by the sale of American securities held in Europe and by the transfer of trade balances of oriental countries, but that will leave three quarters of a billion to be met in some other way. Furthermore, even if that is arranged, we will have to face a more serious situation in January, 1916, as the American securities held abroad will have been exhausted.

I believe that Secretary McAdoo is convinced and I agree with him that there is only one means of avoiding this situation which would so seriously affect economic conditions in the country, and that is the flotation of large bond issues by the belligerent governments. Our financial institutions have the money to loan and wish to do so. On account of the great balance of trade in our favor the proceeds of these loans would be expended here. The result would be a maintenance of the credit of the borrowing nations based on their gold reserve, a continuance of our commerce at its present volume and industrial activity with the consequent employment of capital and labor and national prosperity....

Manifestly the Government has committed itself to the policy of discouraging general loans to belligerent governments. The practical reasons for the policy at the time we adopted it were sound, but basing it on the ground that loans are "inconsistent with the true spirit of neutrality" is now a source of embarrassment. This latter ground is as strong today as it was a year ago, while the practical reasons for discouraging loans have largely disappeared. We have more money than we can use. Popular sympathy has become crystallized in favor of one or another of the belligerents to such an extent that the purchase of bonds would in no way increase the bitterness of partisanship or cause a possibly serious situation.

Now, on the other hand, we are face to face with what appears to be a critical economic situation, which can only be relieved apparently by the investment of American capital in foreign loans to be used in liquidating the enormous balance of trade in favor of the United States.

Can we afford to let a declaration as to our conception of "the true spirit of neutrality" made in the first days of the war stand in the way of our national interests which seem to be seriously threatened?

If we cannot afford to do this, how are we to explain away the declaration and maintain a semblance of consistency?

My opinion is that we ought to allow the loans to be made for our own good, and I have been seeking some means of harmonizing our policy, so unconditionally announced, with the flotation of general loans. As yet I have found no solution to the problem.

Secretary McAdoo considers that the situation is becoming acute and that something should be done at once to avoid the disastrous results which will follow a continuance of the present policy.

Faithfully yours,
Robert Lansing

7.3   OPPONENTS OF INTERVENTION (1917)

From the outset several groups opposed U.S. intervention in the European war. First there were the pacifists, whether members of "peace churches," like the Quakers and Mennonites, or adherents of various secular pacifist groups. Many Socialists also opposed U.S. intervention, although on political, not moral, grounds. Ethnic considerations also played a role in opposing going to war. Many German Americans and Irish Americans either favored the Central Powers or disliked the Allies. Finally, some midwestern Progressives were "isolationists" who denied that the United States had any vital interest in European affairs and urged their fellow citizens to steer clear of overseas entanglements.

The antiwar forces were unable to keep the United States neutral, however. Soon after the German government announced resumption of unrestricted U-boat warfare in early 1917, the United States declared war on the Central Powers. The first selection that follows is a statement issued by the Socialist Party of America in early April, several days after the U.S. war declaration, expressing their opposition to the war. What were the bases of the Socialist position? Were they consistent with Socialist analyses of the nature of contemporary society? From this statement, can you deduce the Socialist attitude toward national loyalty and traditional patriotism?

The second selection is an excerpt from Wisconsin Senator Robert La Follette's remarks during the war-declaration debate in Congress. It is representative of the views of many midwestern Progressives. What is La Follette's analysis of the origins of the war? How does it differ from that of the Socialists? How does his analysis influence his view of the war's justice? Do his remarks betray national biases and prejudices? La Follette's own state, Wisconsin, was home to a very large German American population. Could the senator's views have been colored by that fact?

SOCIALIST PARTY CONVENTION: THE SOCIALISTS PROTEST THE WAR

The Socialist Party and the War[1]

The Socialist Party of the United States in the present grave crisis, solemnly reaffirms its allegiance to the principle of internationalism and working class solidarity the world over, and proclaims its unalterable opposition to the war just declared by the government of the United States.

Modern wars as a rule have been caused by the commercial and financial rivalry and intrigues of the capitalist interests in the different countries. Whether they have been frankly waged as wars of aggression or have been hypocritically represented as wars of "defense," they have always been made by the classes and fought by the masses. Wars bring wealth and power to the ruling classes, and suffering, death and demoralization to the workers.

They breed a sinister spirit of passion, unreason, race hatred and false patriotism. They obscure the struggles of the workers for life, liberty and social justice. They tend to sever the vital bonds of solidarity between them and their brothers in other countries, to destroy their organizations and to curtail their civic and political rights and liberties.

The Socialist Party of the United States is unalterably opposed to the system of exploitation and class rule which is upheld and strengthened by military power and sham national patriotism. We, therefore, call upon the workers of all countries to refuse support to their governments in their wars. The wars of the contending national groups of capitalists are not the concern of the workers. The only struggle which would justify the workers in taking up arms is the great struggle of the working class of the world to free itself from economic exploitation and political oppression, and we particularly warn the workers against the snare and delusion of so-called defensive warfare. As against the false doctrine of national patriotism we uphold the ideal of international working-class

---

The American Labor Yearbook, vol. 2 (1917–18), pp. 50–52.

[1]Majority report adopted at the St. Louis Convention of the Socialist Party, April 7–14, 1917, and ratified by referendum.

solidarity. In support of capitalism, we will not willingly give a single life or a single dollar; in support of the struggle of the workers for freedom we pledge our all.

The mad orgy of death and destruction which is now convulsing unfortunate Europe was caused by the conflict of capitalist interests in the European countries.

In each of these countries, the workers were oppressed and exploited. They produced enormous wealth but the bulk of it was withheld from them by the owners of the industries. The workers were thus deprived of the means to repurchase the wealth which they themselves had created.

The capitalist class of each country was forced to look for foreign markets to dispose of the accumulated "surplus" wealth. The huge profits made by the capitalists could no longer be profitably reinvested in their own countries, hence, they were driven to look for foreign fields of investment. The geographical boundaries of each modern capitalist country thus became too narrow for the industrial and commercial operations of its capitalist class.

The efforts of the capitalists of all leading nations were therefore centered upon the domination of the world markets. Imperialism became the dominant note in the politics of Europe. The acquisition of colonial possessions and the extension of spheres of commercial and political influence became the object of diplomatic intrigues and the cause of constant clashes between nations.

The acute competition between the capitalist powers of the earth, their jealousies and distrusts of one another and the fear of the rising power of the working class forced each of them to arm to the teeth. This led to the mad rivalry of armament, which, years before the outbreak of the present war, had turned the leading countries of Europe into armed camps with standing armies of many millions, drilled and equipped for war in times of "peace."

Capitalism, imperialism and militarism had thus laid the foundation of an inevitable general conflict in Europe. The ghastly war in Europe was not caused by an accidental event, nor by the policy or institutions of any single nation. It was the logical outcome of the competitive capitalist system.

The six million men of all countries and races who have been ruthlessly slain in the first thirty months of this war, the millions of others who have been crippled and maimed, the vast treasures of wealth that have been destroyed, the untold misery and sufferings of Europe, have not been sacrifices exacted in a struggle for principles or ideals, but wanton offerings upon the altar of private profit.

The forces of capitalism which have led to the war in Europe are even more hideously transparent in the war recently provoked by the ruling class of this country.

When Belgium was invaded, the government enjoined upon the people of this country the duty of remaining neutral, thus clearly demonstrating that the "dictates of humanity," and the fate of small nations and of democratic institutions were matters that did not concern it. But when our enormous war traffic was seriously threatened, our government calls upon us to rally to the "defense of democracy and civilization."

Our entrance into the European war was instigated by the predatory capitalists in the United States who boast of the enormous profit of seven billion dollars from the manufacture and sale of munitions and war supplies and from the exportation of American food stuffs and other necessaries. They are also deeply interested in the continuance of war and the success of the allied arms through their huge loans to the governments of the allied powers and through other commercial ties. It is the same interests which strive for imperialistic domination of the Western Hemisphere.

The war of the United States against Germany cannot be justified even on the plea that it is a war in defense of American rights or American "honor." Ruthless as the unrestricted submarine war policy of the German government was and is, it is not an invasion of the rights of the American people, as such, but only an interference with the opportunity of certain groups of American capitalists to coin cold profits out of the blood and sufferings of our fellow men in the warring countries of Europe.

It is not a war against the militarist regime of the Central Powers. Militarism can never be abolished by militarism.

It is not a war to advance the cause of democracy in Europe. Democracy can never be imposed upon any country by a foreign power by force of arms.

It is cant and hypocrisy to say that the war is not directed against the German people, but against the Imperial Government of Germany. If we send an armed force to the battlefields of Europe, its cannons will mow down the masses of the German people and not the Imperial German Government.

Our entrance into the European conflict at this time will serve only to multiply the horrors of the war, to increase the toll of death and destruction and to prolong the fiendish slaughter. It will bring death, suffering and destitution to the people of the United States and particularly to the working class. It will give the powers of reaction in this country the pretext for an attempt to throttle our rights and to crush our democratic institutions, and to fasten upon this country a permanent militarism.

The working class of the United States has no quarrel with the working class of Germany or of any other country. The people of the United States have no quarrel with the people of Germany or any other country. The American people did not want and do not want this war. They have not been consulted about the war and have had no part in declaring war. They have been plunged into this war by the trickery and treachery of the ruling class of the country through its representatives in the National Administration and National Congress, its demagogic agitators, its subsidized press, and other servile instruments of public expression.

We brand the declaration of war by our government as a crime against the people of the United States and against the nations of the world.

In all modern history there has been no war more unjustifiable than the war in which we are about to engage.

No greater dishonor has ever been forced upon a people than that which the capitalist class is forcing upon this nation against its will.

A PROGRESSIVE OPPOSES THE DECLARATION OF WAR

Robert La Follette

MR. LA FOLLETTE. Mr. Chairman, when history records the truth about this awful act we are about to commit here, which means the maiming and dismembering of thousands of our noble boys and the deaths of thousands more, it will record that the Congress of the United States made this declaration of war under a misapprehension of the facts inexcusable in itself and that the people at large acquiesced in it on the theory that the

Congressional Record, 65th Cong., 1st sess. (1917), pp. 371–72.

Congress should have the facts, and would not make a declaration of war not justified by every rule of equity and fair dealing between nations, impartially applied by this country to all belligerents, and that after our following that course one of these contesting nations, despite our impartial action, had wantonly destroyed our legitimate commerce and destroyed the lives of some of our people.

I say the people acquiesce in our actions here to-day on exactly that false assumption of the facts. We have not treated, as a Government, these belligerents with any degree of impartiality; but, on the contrary, have demanded of one of them absolute obedience to our ideas and interpretations of international law, and have allowed at least one of the other belligerents to override at will the established rules and practice of all the civilized nations of the world for a hundred years with but feeble protest, and, in many cases, with no protest at all.

We surrendered to Great Britain practically all we contested for in the War of 1812. It is true, as far as we know, that she has not impressed our seamen, but she has seized and appropriated to her own use entire cargoes and the ships that carried them. Not carriers in European trade, but carriers to South America.

One of the underlying causes of the awful holocaust in Europe was because Germany had by her systematized reductions in cost of manufacturing, by subsidization of transportation lines and methods of credits made such serious inroads on Great Britain's trade in South America as to seriously disturb her equanimity and threaten her prestige as well as attendant profits.

Mr. Chairman, this war now devastating Europe so ruthlessly is not a war of humanity, but a war of commercialism, and there is not a student of economic conditions within the sound of my voice but knows that to be the fundamental cause of that war, although there are many primary and intermediate questions entering into it. . . .

The President of the United States in his message of the 2d of April [1917] said that the European war was brought on by Germany's rulers without the sanction or will of the people. For God's sake, what are we doing now? Does the President of the United States feel that the will of the American people is being consulted in regard to this declaration of war? The people of Germany surely had as much consideration as he has given the people of the United States. He has heard the cry of the Shylocks calling for their pound of flesh; later on he will hear the cry of Rachel weeping for her children and mourning because they are not, sacrificed to make good the pound of flesh in the name of liberty. The exclamation "O Liberty! Liberty! how many crimes are committed in thy name!" was well made.

Ours is the greatest Nation on the face of the globe. We have had a chance, if we had maintained a strict neutrality, to have bound up the wounds of the oppressed and to have upheld the tenets of the highest civilization throughout the world. But, no; we are asked to go into partnership with the country that has never allowed justice and right to have any weight with her when conquest and gold were placed in the balance. In India, which she held by right of conquest, as a punishment to those natives of that country who desired to be free of England's yoke and rebelled, even as did we in our Revolutionary period, she mercifully tied many of the rebels to the mouths of her cannon and humanely blew them to atoms as a sample of English Christianity. She destroyed the Boer Republic by intrigue and force of arms; she forced, for love of gold, the opium trade on China. Christian England, our would-be partner! In the Napoleonic wars she, by force of arms, confiscated the entire shipping of small but neutral nations to her own use, just as she has in a smaller degree appropriated ships of our citizens to her own use within the past two years. During the Civil War she fell over herself to recognize the Confederacy, and gave it every encouragement possible. Now we are asked to become her faithful ally against a country that, whatever her faults, surely has no blacker record than that of Christian England; to contribute our money and our people in the holy name of liberty to destroy one belligerent, which the President designates as Prussian militarism, a menace of the world; but English navalism, which is surely as great a menace, we enter into partnership with. George Washington said, "Avoid European entanglements," but we are recklessly entering a path to the end of which no man can foresee or comprehend, at the behest of, in many cases, a venal press and of a pacifist President.

God pity our country, gentlemen of the House of Representatives, if you desire that this cup be placed to our country's lips to quaff for crimes committed by a country for unneutral actions and that we enter into an alliance with another country which has been much less neutral. You may do so; I can not so vote at this time. . . .

Mr. Chairman, throughout the country patriotic meetings are being held to encourage enlistments of our young men and boys into the Army to engage in this war in advance of our declaration.

Mr. Chairman, I suggest a resolution, which should be passed and adhered to by the young men of our country and by our soldiers who are asked to enter the trenches of Europe:

"I hereby pledge myself to the service of my country and will guarantee to go and uphold its honor and its flag as soon as the sons of all the newspaper editors who have stood out for our entering the war, and who are of age for enlistment, have enlisted for the cause and the proprietors and editors themselves have patriotically enlisted, on the theory that they should feel it their duty to do so as instigators of the act."

Likewise, Mr. Chairman, the sons of manufacturers of ammunition and war supplies, and all stockholders making profits from such trade. They should freely offer their sons on the altar of their country and, in case of their being under military age, go themselves. Likewise, Mr. Chairman, the J. Pierpont Morgans and their associates, who have floated war loans running into millions which they now want the United States to guarantee by entering the European war; after they and all the holders of such securities have offered their sons and themselves, when of military age, on the altar of their country, and, Mr. Chairman, when the above-mentioned persons have no sons and are too old themselves to accept military service, then they shall, to make good their desire for the upholding of American honor and American rights, donate in lieu of such service of selves or sons one-half of all their worldly goods to make good their patriotic desire for our entering the European war in the name of liberty and patriotism.

Mr. Chairman, it will be fitting for those who have really nothing at stake in this war but death to enter into it and give their lives in the name of liberty and patriotism, after the persons covered by the above resolution have done their part as above suggested and many thousands of our citizens will see it that way ere long.

7.4 MAKING THE WORLD SAFE FOR DEMOCRACY (1917, 1925)

In asking Congress to declare war on Germany in 1917, Woodrow Wilson employed lofty rhetoric and invoked idealism to an unprecedented degree in the making of American foreign policy. Wilson informed Congress that the war was not merely over specific grievances, like the violation of neutral rights and the use of unrestricted submarine warfare, but universal principles as well. Wilson claimed that the war presented clear choices between differing visions of world order. Most of all, he believed that America's role in the war entailed a mission to "make the world safe for democracy."

Wilson's democratic visions quickly yielded to curtailment and restriction of civil liberties at home. Significantly, American citizens of German origin were interned in detention centers. Ethnic hysteria and intolerance were by-products of the war effort at home. Frederick Howe, Ellis Island's immigration officer, describes the anti-immigrant activities that occurred. Do either of these selections raise themes related to the current War on Terror?

WILSON'S WAR ADDRESS (1917)

I have called the Congress into extraordinary session because there are serious, very serious, choices of policy to be made, and made immediately, which it was neither right nor constitutionally permissible that I should assume the responsibility of making. . . .

With a profound sense of the solemn and even tragical character of the step I am taking and of the grave responsibilities which it involves, but in unhesitating obedience to what I deem my constitutional duty, I advise that the Congress declare the recent course of the imperial German government to be in fact nothing less than war against the government and people of the United States, that it formally accept the status of belligerent which has thus been thrust upon it, and that it take immediate steps not only to put the country in a more thorough state of defense but also to exert all its power and employ all its resources to bring the government of the German Empire to terms and end the war.

We have no quarrel with the German people. We have no feeling toward them but one of sympathy and friendship. It was not upon their impulse that their government acted in entering this war. It was not with their previous knowledge or approval. It was a war determined upon as wars used to be determined upon in the old, unhappy days when peoples were nowhere consulted by their rulers and wars were provoked and waged in the interest of dynasties or of little groups of ambitious men who were accustomed to use their fellow men as pawns and tools. . . .

We are accepting this challenge of hostile purpose because we know that in such a government, following such methods, we can never have a friend, and that in the presence of its organized power, always lying in wait to accomplish we know not what purpose, there can be no assured security for the democratic governments of the world. We are now about to accept gauge of battle with this natural foe to liberty and shall, if necessary, spend the whole force of the nation to check and nullify its pretensions and its power. We are glad, now that we see the facts with no veil of false pretense about them, to fight thus for the ultimate peace of the world and for the liberation of its peoples, the German peoples included: for the rights of nations great and small and the privilege of men everywhere to choose their way of life and of obedience. The world must be made safe for democracy. Its peace must be planted upon the tested foundations of political liberty. We have no selfish ends to serve. We desire no conquest, no dominion. We seek

---

Woodrow Wilson, Address to Congress, April 2, 1917.

no indemnities for ourselves, no material compensation for the sacrifices we shall freely make. We are but one of the champions of the rights of mankind. We shall be satisfied when those rights have been made as secure as the faith and the freedom of nations can make them. . . .

It is a distressing and oppressive duty, gentlemen of the Congress, which I have performed in thus addressing you. There are, it may be, many months of fiery trial and sacrifice ahead of us. It is a fearful thing to lead this great peaceful people into war, into the most terrible and disastrous of all wars, civilization itself seeming to be in the balance. But the right is more precious than peace, and we shall fight for the things which we have always carried nearest our hearts—for democracy, for the right of those submit to authority to have a voice in their own governments, for the rights and liberties of small nations, for a universal dominion of right by such a concert of free peoples as shall bring peace and safety to all nations and make the world itself at last free. To such a task we can dedicate our lives and our fortunes, everything that we are and everything that we have, with the pride of those who know that the day has come when America is privileged to spend her blood and her might for the principles that gave her birth and happiness and the peace which she has treasured. God helping her, she can do no other.

NATIVIST HYSTERIA CHALLENGES DEMOCRACY AT HOME

Frederic C. Howe, Confessions of a Reformer (Charles Scribner's Sons, 1925)

Hysteria over the immoral alien was followed by a two-year panic over the "Hun." Again inspectors, particularly civilian secret-service agents, were given carte blanche to make arrests on suspicion. Again Ellis Island was turned into a prison, and I had to protect men and women from a hue and cry that was but little concerned over guilt or innocence. During these years thousands of Germans, Austrians, and Hungarians were taken without trial from their homes and brought to Ellis Island. Nearly two thousand officers and seamen from sequestered German ships were placed in my care. Many of them had married American wives. They conducted themselves decently and well. They were obedient to discipline. They accepted the situation and they gave practically no trouble. They were typical of the alien enemies the country over that were arrested under the hysteria that was organized and developed into a hate that lingers on to this day.

Again I had either to drift with the tide or assume the burden of seeing that as little injustice as possible was done. I realized that under war conditions convincing evidence could not be demanded. I accepted that fact, but not the assumption that "the Hun should be put against the wall and shot." From our entrance into the war until after the armistice my life was a nightmare. My telephone rang constantly with inquiries from persons seeking news of husbands and fathers who had been arrested. On my return home in the evening I would often find awaiting me women in a state of nervous collapse whose husbands had mysteriously disappeared, and who feared that they had been done away with. I furnished them with such information as was possible.

Frederic C. Howe, Commissioner of Immigration at the port of New York, 1914–1919.

On the island I had to stand between the official insistence that the German should be treated as a criminal and the admitted fact that the great majority of them had been arrested by persons with little concern about their innocence or guilt and with but little if any evidence to support the detention.

Within a short time I was branded as pro-German. I had to war with the local staff to secure decent treatment for the aliens, and with the army of secret-service agents to prevent the island from being filled with persons against whom someone or other had filed a suspicious inquiry. . . .

The final outbreak of hysteria was directed against the "Reds" the winter of 1918–19. It started in the State of Washington in the lumber camps, and was directed against members of the I. W. W. organizations which had superseded the more conservative craft unions affiliated with the American Federation of Labor. There was a concerted determination on the part of employers to bring wages back to pre-war conditions and to break the power of organized labor. The movement against alien labor leaders had the support of the Department of Justice. Private detective agencies and strike-breakers acted with assurance that in any outrages they would be supported by the government itself. The press joined in the cry of "Red revolution," and frightened the country with scare head-lines of an army of organized terrorists who were determined to usher in revolution by force. The government borrowed the agent provocateur from old Russia; it turned loose innumerable private spies. For two years we were in a panic of fear over the Red Revolutionists, anarchists, and enemies of the Republic who were said to be ready to overthrow the government.

For a third time I had to stand against the current. Men and women were herded into Ellis Island. They were brought under guards and in special trains with instructions to get them away from the country with as little delay as possible. Most of the aliens had been picked up in raids on labor headquarters; they had been given a drum-head trial by an inspector with no chance for the defense; they were held incommunicado and often were not permitted to see either friends or attorneys, before being shipped to Ellis Island. In these proceedings the inspector who made the arrest was prosecutor, witness, judge, jailer, and executioner. He was clerk and interpreter as well. This was all the trial the alien could demand under the law. In many instances the inspector hoped that he would be put in charge of his victim for a trip to New York and possibly to Europe at the expense of the government. Backed by the press of his city and by the hue and cry of the pack, he had every inducement to find the alien guilty. . . .

I was advised by the Commissioner-General to mind my own business and carry out orders, no matter what they might be. Yet such obvious injustice was being done that I could not sit quiet. Moreover, I was an appointee of the President, and felt that I owed responsibility to him whose words at least I was exemplifying in my actions. My words carried no weight with my superior officials, who were intoxicated with the prominence they enjoyed and the publicity which they received from the press. The bureaucratic organization at the island was happy in the punishing powers which all jailers enjoy, and resented any interference on behalf of its victims. Members of Congress were swept from their moorings by an organized business propaganda, and demanded that I be dismissed because I refused to railroad aliens to boats made ready for their deportation. I took the position from which I would not be driven, that the alien should not be held incommunicado and should enjoy the right of a writ of habeas corpus in the United States courts, . . .

In maintaining this position I had to quarrel with my superiors and the official force at the island. I faced a continuous barrage from members of Congress, from the press, from business organizations, and prosecuting attorneys. Yet day by day aliens, many of whom had been held in prison for months, came before the court; and the judge, after examining the testimony, unwillingly informed the immigration authorities that there was not a scintilla of evidence to support the arrest. For in deportation cases it is not necessary to provide a preponderance of testimony, or to convince the court of the justice of the charge; all that the government needs to support its case is a "scintilla" of evidence, which may be any kind of evidence at all. If there is a bit of evidence, no matter how negligible it may be, the order of deportation must be affirmed.

Again the pack was unleashed. No one took the trouble to ascertain the facts. The press carried stories to the effect that I had released hundreds of persons ordered deported. I had released aliens, but in each case I had been ordered to do so by the courts or the bureau. I had observed the law when organized hysteria demanded that it be swept aside. I had seen to it that men and women enjoyed their legal rights, but evidently this was the worse offense I could have committed. . . .

As I look back over these years, my outstanding memories are not of the immigrants. They are rather of my own people. Things that were done forced one almost to despair of the mind, to distrust the political state. Shreds were left of our courage, our reverence. . . .

I had fondly imagined that we prized individual liberty; I had believed that to Anglo-Saxons human rights were sacred and they would be protected at any cost.

Latin peoples might be temperamental, given to hysteria; but we were hard-headed, we stood for individuality. But I found that we were lawless, emotional, given to mob action. We cared little for freedom of conscience, for the rights of men to their opinions. Government was a convenience of business. Discussion of war profiteers was not to be permitted. The Department of Justice lent itself to the suppression of those who felt that war should involve equal sacrifice. Civil liberties were under the ban. Their subversion was not, however, an isolated thing; it was an incident in the ascendancy of business privileges and profits acquired during the war—an ascendancy that did not bear scrutiny or brook the free discussion which is the only safe basis of orderly popular government.

7.5   IDEALISM AND DISILLUSIONMENT (1918, 1920)

Once the war ended, Woodrow Wilson quickly became preoccupied with the establishment of a new world order. America's military role at the end of the war had been small but significant, and it soon became apparent that America's economic role in the postwar world would be great. Wilson, like most Americans, held the institutions of Europe as largely responsible for the tragedy of World War I—monarchies that rarely extended political power to the masses and economic imperialism that ensured hostility and rivalry among nations. If corrupt diplomatic practices like secret treaties could be replaced by international law that would guarantee such rights as freedom of the seas, peace might have a chance. If the great autocratic and imperial political machines of the world loosened their grip, and individual peoples were each allowed national self-determination, then peace might have a chance. To replace Europe's sagging imperial structures and their inevitable rivalries, Wilson proposed a new scheme of international law to be called the League of Nations.

Wilson's philosophy was concisely defined in "The Fourteen Points" and permeated his thinking and diplomatic activity throughout the last three years of his presidency. "The Fourteen Points" have often been assailed as too idealistic to have been successful and full of basically unresolvable, inherent contradictions. Although the U.S. Senate never ratified the peace treaty that ended World War I, and the United States never joined the League of Nations that Wilson had worked so hard to establish, many of the main principles of "The Fourteen Points" found their way into the mainstream of U.S. thinking on foreign policy years later.

Are "The Fourteen Points" an idealistic proclamation that should have been dismissed as mere rhetoric or propaganda? Did they have an economic component? Did Wilson have a legitimate point in saying that a war would remain inevitable if the institutions of Europe did not change? Most of all, how do "The Fourteen Points" reflect America's emerging role as a global economic and political force, and how, if implemented, would U.S. interests have been served by them? Finally, although the United States retreated into isolationism in the 1920s and 1930s, how did the principles of Wilsonian idealism prove prophetic?

Finally, in evaluating the Senate's refusal to ratify the treaty unamended, yet another controversy was created. Did Wilson overstep the bounds of presidential authority by negotiating such a treaty without Congressional approval? Or did Wilson behave irrationally by refusing to sign an amended version that was acceptable to the Senate? Compare the Senate Resolution ratifying the treaty to "The Fourteen Points" and ask if the differences between the two are substantive or cosmetic.

THE FOURTEEN POINTS: WILSON'S ADDRESS TO CONGRESS, JANUARY 8, 1918

Gentlemen of the Congress:

. . . It will be our wish and purpose that the processes of peace, when they are begun, shall be absolutely open and that they shall involve and permit henceforth no secret understandings of any kind. The day of conquest and aggrandizement is gone by; so is also the day of secret covenants entered into in the interest of particular governments and likely at some unlooked-for moment to upset the peace of the world. It is this happy fact, now clear to the view of every public man whose thoughts do not still linger in an age that is dead and gone, which makes it possible for every nation whose purposes are consistent with justice and the peace of the world to avow now or at any other time the objects it has in view.

We entered this war because violations of right had occurred which touched us to the quick and made the life of our own people impossible unless they were corrected and the world secured once for all against their recurrence. What we demand in this war, therefore, is nothing peculiar to ourselves. It is that the world be made fit and safe to live in; and particularly that it be made safe for every peace-loving nation which, like our own, wishes to live its own life, determine its own institutions, be assured of justice and fair dealing by the other peoples of the world as against force and selfish aggression. All the peoples of the world are in effect partners in this interest, and for our own

---

Wilson's Address to Congress, January 8, 1918. Quoted from *Supplement to the Messages and Papers of the Presidents Covering the Second Administration of Woodrow Wilson* (Washington, DC: United States Government Printing Office), p. 8421 ff.

part we see very clearly that unless justice be done to others it will not be done to us. The program of the world's peace, therefore, is our program; and that program, the only possible program, as we see it, is this:

I. Open covenants of peace, openly arrived at, after which there shall be no private international understandings of any kind but diplomacy shall proceed always frankly and in the public view.

II. Absolute freedom of navigation upon the seas, outside territorial waters, alike in peace and in war, except as the seas may be closed in whole or in part by international action of the enforcement of international covenants.

III. The removal, so far as possible, of all economic barriers and the establishment of an equality of trade conditions among all the nations consenting to the peace and associating themselves for its maintenance.

IV. Adequate guarantees given and taken that national armaments will be reduced to the lowest point consistent with domestic safety.

V. A free, open-minded, and absolutely impartial adjustment of all colonial claims, based upon a strict observance of the principle that in determining all such questions of sovereignty the interests of the populations concerned must have equal weight with the equitable claims of the government whose title is to be determined.

VI. The evacuation of all Russian territory and such a settlement of all questions affecting Russia as will secure the best and freest coöperation of the other nations of the world in obtaining for her an unhampered and unembarrassed opportunity for the independent determination of her own political development and national policy and assure her of a sincere welcome into the society of free nations under institutions of her own choosing; and, more than a welcome, assistance also of every kind that she may need and may herself desire. The treatment accorded Russia by her sister nations in the months to come will be the acid test of their good will, of their comprehension of her needs as distinguished from their own interests, and of their intelligent and unselfish sympathy.

VII. Belgium, the whole world will agree, must be evacuated and restored, without any attempt to limit the sovereignty which she enjoys in common with all other free nations. No other single act will serve as this will serve to restore confidence among the nations in the laws which they have themselves set and determined for the government of their relations with one another. Without this healing act the whole structure and validity of international law is forever impaired.

VIII. All French territory should be freed and the invaded portions restored, and the wrong done to France by Prussia in 1871 in the matter of Alsace-Lorraine, which has unsettled the peace of the world for nearly fifty years, should be righted, in order that peace may once more be made secure in the interest of all.

IX. A readjustment of the frontiers of Italy should be effected along clearly recognizable lines of nationality.

X. The peoples of Austria-Hungary, whose place among the nations we wish to see safe-guarded and assured, should be accorded the freest opportunity of autonomous development.

XI. Rumania, Serbia, and Montenegro should be evacuated; occupied territories restored; Serbia accorded free and secure access to the sea; and the relations of the several Balkan states to one another determined by friendly counsel along historically established lines of allegiance and nationality; and international guarantees of the political and economic independence and territorial integrity of the several Balkan states should be entered into.

XII. The Turkish portions of the present Ottoman Empire should be assured a secure sovereignty, but the other nationalities which are now under Turkish rule should be assured an undoubted security of life and an absolutely unmolested opportunity of autonomous development, and the Dardanelles should be permanently opened as a free passage to the ships and commerce of all nations under international guarantees.

XIII. An independent Polish state should be erected which should include the territories inhabited by indisputably Polish populations, which should be assured a free and secure access to the sea, and whose political and economic independence and territorial integrity should be guaranteed by international covenant.

XIV. A general association of nations must be formed under specific covenants for the purpose of affording mutual guarantees of political independence and territorial integrity to great and small states alike.

In regard to these essential rectifications of wrong and assertions of right we feel ourselves to be intimate partners of all the governments and peoples associated together against the Imperialists. We cannot be separated in interest or divided in purpose. We stand together until the end.

For such arrangements and covenants we are willing to fight and to continue to fight until they are achieved; but only because we wish the right to prevail and desire a just and stable peace such as can be secured only by removing the chief provocations to war, which this program does not remove. We have no jealousy of German greatness, and there is nothing in this program that impairs it. We grudge her no achievement or distinction of learning or of pacific enterprise such as have made her record very bright and very enviable. We do not wish to injure her or to block in any way her legitimate influence or power. We do not wish to fight her either with arms or with hostile arrangements of trade if she is willing to associate herself with us and the other peace-loving nations of the world in covenants of justice and law and fair dealing. We wish her only to accept a place of equality among the peoples of the world,—the new world in which we now live,—instead of a place of mastery.

Neither do we presume to suggest to her any alteration or modification of her institutions. But it is necessary, we must frankly say, and necessary as a preliminary to any intelligent dealings with her on our part, that we should know whom her spokesmen speak for when they speak to us, whether for the Reichstag majority or for the military party and the men whose creed is imperial domination.

We have spoken now, surely, in terms too concrete to admit of any further doubt or question. An evident principle runs through the whole program I have outlined. It is the principle of justice to all peoples and nationalities, and their right to live on equal terms of liberty and safety with one another, whether they be strong or weak. Unless this principle be made its foundation no part of the structure of international justice can stand.

The people of the United States could act upon no other principle; and to the vindication of this principle they are ready to devote their lives, their honor, and everything that they possess. The moral climax of this the culminating and final war for human liberty has come, and they are ready to put their own strength, their own highest purpose, their own integrity and devotion to the test.

THE DEFEAT OF THE LEAGUE OF NATIONS

Resolution of Ratification of Treaty of Peace with Germany and the League of Nations, March 19, 1920

Resolution of ratification

Resolved (two-thirds of the Senators present concurring therein), That the Senate advise and consent to the ratification of the treaty of peace with Germany concluded at Versailles on the 28th day of June, 1919, subject to the following reservations and understandings, which are hereby made a part and condition of this resolution of ratification, which ratification is not to take effect or bind the United States until the said reservations and understandings adopted by the Senate have been accepted as a part and a condition of this resolution of ratification by the allied and associated powers and a failure on the part of the allied and associated powers to make objection to said reservations and understandings prior to the deposit of ratification by the United States shall be taken as a full and final acceptance of such reservations and understandings by said powers:

1. The United States so understands and construes article 1 that in case of notice of withdrawal from the League of Nations, as provided in said article, the United States shall be the sole judge as to whether all its international obligations and all its obligations under the said covenant have been fulfilled, and notice of withdrawal by the United States may be given by a concurrent resolution of the Congress of the United States.

2. The United States assumes no obligation to preserve the territorial integrity or political independence of any other country by the employment of its military or naval forces, its resources, or any form of economic discrimination, or to interfere in any way in controversies between nations, including all controversies relating to territorial integrity or political independence, whether members of the league or not, under the provisions of article 10, or to employ the military or naval forces of the United States, under any article of the treaty for any purpose, unless in any particular case the Congress, which, under the Constitution, has the sole power to declare war or authorize the employment of the military or naval forces of the United States, shall, in the exercise of full liberty of action, by act or joint resolution so provide.

Resolution of Ratification of Treaty of Peace with Germany and the League of Nations, March 19, 1920. *Congressional Record*, vol. LIX, p. 4599.

3. No mandate shall be accepted by the United States under article 22, part 1, or any other provision of the treaty of peace with Germany, except by action of the Congress of the United States.

4. The United States reserves to itself exclusively the right to decide what questions are within its domestic jurisdiction and declares that all domestic and political questions relating wholly or in part to its internal affairs, including immigration, labor, coast-wise traffic, the tariff, commerce, the suppression of traffic in women and children and in opium and other dangerous drugs, and all other domestic questions, are solely within the jurisdiction of the United States and are not under this treaty to be submitted in any way either to arbitration or to the consideration of the council or of the assembly of the League of Nations, or any agency thereof, or to the decision or recommendation of any other power.

5. The United States will not submit to arbitration or to inquiry by the assembly or by the council of the League of Nations, provided for in said treaty of peace, any questions which in the judgment of the United States depend upon or relate to its long-established policy, commonly known as the Monroe doctrine; said doctrine is to be interpreted by the United States alone and is hereby declared to be wholly outside the jurisdiction of said League of Nations and entirely unaffected by any provision contained in the said treaty of peace with Germany.

6. The United States withholds its assent to articles 156, 157, and 158, and reserves full liberty of action with respect to any controversy which may arise under said articles.

7. No person is or shall be authorized to represent the United States, nor shall any citizen of the United States be eligible, as a member of any body or agency established or authorized by said treaty of peace with Germany, except pursuant to an act of the Congress of the United States providing for his appointment and defining his powers and duties.

8. The United States understands that the reparation commission will regulate or interfere with exports from the United States to Germany, or from Germany to the United States, only when the United States by act or joint resolution of Congress approves such regulation or interference.

9. The United States shall not be obligated to contribute to any expenses of the League of Nations, or of the secretariat, or of any commission, or committee, or conference, or other agency, organized under the League of Nations or under the treaty or for the purpose of carrying out the treaty provisions, unless and until an appropriation of funds available for such expenses shall have been made by the Congress of the United States: *Provided.* That the foregoing limitation shall not apply to the United States' proportionate share of the expense of the office force and salary of the secretary general.

10. No plan for the limitation of armaments proposed by the council of the League of Nations under the provisions of article 8 shall be held as binding the United States until the same shall have been accepted by Congress, and the United States reserves the right to increase its armament without the consent of the council whenever the United States is threatened with invasion or engaged in war.

11. The United States reserves the right to permit, in its discretion, the nationals of a covenant-breaking State, as defined in article 16 of the covenant of the League of Nations, residing within the United States or in countries other than such

covenant-breaking State, to continue their commercial, financial, and personal relations with the nationals of the United States.

12. Nothing in articles 296, 297, or in any of the annexes thereto or in any other article, section, or annex of the treaty of peace with Germany shall, as against citizens of the United States, be taken to mean any confirmation, ratification, or approval of any act otherwise illegal or in contravention of the rights of citizens of the United States.

13. The United States withholds its assent to Part XIII (articles 387 to 427, inclusive) unless Congress by act or joint resolution shall hereafter make provision for representation in the organization established by said Part XIII, and in such event the participation of the United States will be governed and conditioned by the provisions of such act or joint resolution.

14. Until Part I, being the covenant of the League of Nations, shall be so amended as to provide that the United States shall be entitled to cast a number of votes equal to that which any member of the league and its self-governing dominions, colonies, or parts of empire, in the aggregate shall be entitled to cast, the United States assumes no obligation to be bound, except in cases where Congress has previously given its consent, by any election, decision, report, or finding of the council or assembly in which any member of the league and its self-governing dominions, colonies, or parts of empire, in the aggregate have cast more than one vote.

    The United States assumes no obligation to be bound by any decision, report, or finding of the council or assembly arising out of any dispute between the United States and any member of the league if such member, or any self-governing dominion, colony, empire, or part of empire united with it politically has voted.

15. In consenting to the ratification of the treaty with Germany the United States adheres to the principle of self-determination and to the resolution of sympathy with the aspirations of the Irish people for a government of their own choice adopted by the Senate June 6, 1919, and declares that when such government is attained by Ireland, a consummation it is hoped is at hand, it should promptly be admitted as a member of the League of Nations.

CHAPTER 8

Women's Issues, 1900–1940

Leaders of the Women's Movement introduced a new set of goals as the twentieth century began. The early decades of the century were preoccupied with politics; women forged ahead toward a common goal: the right to vote. Women achieved many victories in their long struggle for voting rights on the state and local levels during these years, but it was not until 1920 that a constitutional amendment would guarantee universal voting rights in all states and in all elections. The suffragist movement raised many issues: Would the new contingent of female voters transform American politics by tipping the scales in current voting blocs or altering the agenda of issues considered by governments? How would women's lives change, now that they had political equality with men? What percentage of American women would take advantage of the right to vote, and what backlash could be expected from male society? Voting rights proved less controversial than two other important issues to come to attention during these years: the right to work and reproductive rights, better known as the birth control movement. Male resistance in these areas would prove to be even more pronounced than in previous struggles for female equality.

8.1 VOTING RIGHTS (1902)

The movement by women to gain the right to vote made enormous headway during the Progressive Era scoring many victories on the local level, then on the national level, first drafting and then winning ratification of a constitutional amendment. The Progressive Movement was a complex and diverse phenomenon, but it galvanized women because so many women were personally involved in the politics of individual reformist measures. Many of these areas had long been in the domain of what many in the nineteenth century considered women's charitable role in society, being that females, not males, were the "moral sex." The frenzy of women in politics as a result of new legislation and organizations, therefore, had a role in mobilizing the suffrage campaign. The achievements of British women working toward the same goal in their country during these years also provided a source of inspiration.

Address to National American Women Suffrage Association

Carrie Chapman Catt

The question of woman suffrage is a very simple one. The plea is dignified, calm and logical. Yet, great as is the victory over conservatism which is represented in the accomplishment of man suffrage, infinitely greater will be the attainment of woman suffrage. Man suffrage exists through the surrender of many a stronghold of ancient thought, deemed impregnable, yet these obstacles were the veriest Don Quixote windmills compared with the opposition which has stood arrayed against woman suffrage.

Woman suffrage must meet precisely the same objections which have been urged against man suffrage, but in addition, it must combat sex-prejudice, the oldest, the most unreasoning, the most stubborn of all human idiosyncrasies. What *is* prejudice? An opinion, which is not based upon reason; a judgment, without having heard the argument; a feeling, without being able to trace from whence it came. And sex-prejudice is a pre-judgment against the rights, liberties and opportunities of women. A belief, without proof, in the incapacity of women to do that which they have never done. Sex-prejudice has been the chief hindrance in the rapid advance of the woman's rights movement to its present status, and it is still a stupendous obstacle to be overcome.

In the United States, at least, we need no longer argue woman's intellectual, moral and physical qualification for the ballot with the intelligent. The Reason of the best of our citizens has long been convinced. The justice of the argument has been admitted, but sex-prejudice is far from conquered.

When a great church official exclaims petulantly, that if women are no more modest in their demands men may be obliged to take to drowning female infants again; when a renowned United States Senator declares no human being can find an answer to the arguments for woman suffrage, but with all the force of his position and influence he will oppose it; when a popular woman novelist speaks of the advocates of the movement as the "shrieking sisterhood," when a prominent politician says "to argue against woman suffrage is to repudiate the Declaration of Independence," yet he hopes it may never come, the question flies entirely outside the domain of reason, and retreats within the realm of sex-prejudice, where neither logic nor common sense can dislodge it. . . .

Four chief causes led to the subjection of women, each the logical deduction from the theory that men were the units of the race—obedience, ignorance, the denial of personal liberty, and the denial of right to property and wages. These forces united in cultivating a spirit of egotism and tyranny in men and weak dependence in women. . . . In fastening these disabilities upon women, the world acted logically when reasoning from the premise that man is the race and woman his dependent. The perpetual tutelage and subjection robbed women of all freedom of thought and action, and all incentive for growth, and they logically became the inane weaklings the world would have them, and their condition strengthened the universal belief in their incapacity. This

---

Carrie Chapman Catt, "An Address to National American Woman Suffrage Association," 1902.

world taught woman nothing skillful and then said her work was valueless. It permitted her no opinions and said she did not know how to think. It forbade her to speak in public, and said the sex had no orators. It denied her the schools, and said the sex had no genius. It robbed her of every vestige of responsibility, and then called her weak. It taught her that every pleasure must come as a favor from men, and when to gain it she decked herself in paint and fine feathers, as she had been taught to do, it called her vain.

This was the woman enshrined in literature. She was immortalized in song and story. Chivalry paid her fantastic compliments. Surrounded by a halo of mysticism woman was encouraged to believe herself adored. This woman who was pretty, coquettish, affectionate, obedient, now gentle and meek, now furious and emotional, always ignorant, weak and silly, became the ideal woman of the world.

When at last the New Woman came, bearing the torch of truth, and with calm dignity asked a share in the world's education, opportunities and duties, it is no wonder these untrained weaklings should have shrunk away in horror. . . . Nor was it any wonder that man should arise to defend the woman of the past, whom he had learned to love and cherish. Her very weakness and dependence were dear to him and he loved to think of her as the tender clinging vine, while he was the strong and sturdy oak. He had worshiped her ideal through the age of chivalry as though she were a goddess, but he had governed her as though she were an idiot. Without the slightest comprehension of the inconsistency of his position, he believed this relation to be in accordance with God's command. . . .

The whole aim of the woman movement has been to destroy the idea that obedience is necessary to women: to train women to such self-respect that they would not grant obedience and to train men to such comprehension of equity they would not exact it. . . . As John Stuart Mill said in speaking of the conditions which preceded the enfranchisement of men: "The noble has been gradually going down on the social ladder and the commoner has been gradually going up. Every half century has brought them nearer to each other": so we may say, for the past hundred years, man as the dominant power in the world has been going down the ladder and woman has been climbing up. Every decade has brought them nearer together. The opposition to the enfranchisement of women is the last defense of the old theory that obedience is necessary for women, because man alone is the creator of the race.

The whole effort of the movement has been to destroy obedience of woman in the home. That end has been very generally attained, and the average civilized woman enjoys the right of individual liberty in the home of her father, her husband, and her son. The individual woman no longer obeys the individual man. She enjoys self-government in the home and in society. The question now is, shall all women as a body obey all men as a body? Shall the woman who enjoys the right of self-government in every other department of life be permitted the right of self-government in the State? It is no more right for all men to govern all women than it was for one man to govern one woman. It is no more right for men to govern women that it was for one man to govern other men.

8.2 THE RIGHT TO WORK (1898)

Working patterns of American women remained unchanged until World War II. Most work done by women was difficult and provided low wages. Typically, women worked as domestic workers or in certain lines of factory work, such as the textile industry. Working conditions for women were at least as undesirable as those under which men performed. Wages, sadly, were considerably lower. Most women left the workforce when they bore children or, in many cases, as soon as they married. Poor women, women of color, widows, or women with children who had been deserted by their husbands did often find work, but usually under difficult circumstances. Class played a role in who worked and at what jobs. Middle-class women were discouraged from working and few educational or professional opportunities existed for them. Some professions, such as nursing or teaching, did allow opportunities for women, but most sectors of the economy did not. For the most part, only women of privilege had limited access to higher education and professional training. In the following selection, Charlotte Perkins Gilman challenges sexual discrimination and prejudice in employment. She draws important connections between economics and power. By restricting the role of women in the workforce, men could continue to assert further domination and perpetuate dependency. Gilman also discusses the key problem of wage inequality, a problem that still persists in many occupations or professions to this day.

WOMEN AND ECONOMICS

Charlotte Perkins Gilman

We are the only animal species in which the female depends on the male for food, the only animal species in which the sex-relation is also an economic relation. With us an entire sex lives in a relation of economic dependence upon the other sex, and the economic relation is combined with the sex-relation. The economic status of the human female is relative to the sex-relation. . . .

In the human species the condition is permanent and general, though there are exceptions, and though the present century is witnessing the beginnings of a great change in this respect. We have not been accustomed to face this fact beyond our loose generalization that it was "natural," and that other animals did so, too.

To many this view will not seem clear at first; and the case of working peasant women or females of savage tribes, and the general household industry of women, will be instanced against it. Some careful and honest discrimination is needed to make plain to ourselves the essential facts of the relation, even in these cases. The horse, in his free natural condition, is economically independent. He gets his living by his own exertions, irrespective of any other creature. The horse, in his present condition of slavery, is economically dependent. He gets his living at the hands of his master; and his exertions, though strenuous, bear no direct relation to his living. In fact, the horses who are the best fed and cared for and the horses who are the hardest worked are quite different animals. The horse works, it is true; but what he gets to eat depends on the power and will of his master. His living comes through another. He is economically dependent. So with the hard-worked savage or peasant women. Their labor is the property of another; they work under another will; and what they receive depends not their labor, but on the power and will of another. They are economically dependent. This is true of the human female both individually and collectively.

In studying the economic position of the sexes collectively, the difference is most marked. As a social animal, the economic status of man rests on the combined

Charlotte Perkins Gilman, *Women and Economics* (Boston, 1898).

and exchanged services of vast numbers of progressively specialized individuals. The economic progress of the race, its maintenance at any period, its continued advance, involve the collective activities of all the trades, crafts, arts, manufactures, inventions, discoveries, and all the civil and military institutions that go to maintain them. The economic status of any race at any time, with its involved effect on all the constituent individuals, depends on their world-wide labors and their free exchange. Economic progress, however, is almost exclusively masculine. Such economic processes as women have been allowed to exercise are of the earliest and most primitive kind. Were men to perform no economic services save such as are still performed by women, our racial status in economics would be reduced to most painful limitations.

To take from any community its male workers would paralyze it economically to a far greater degree than to remove its female workers. The labor now performed by the women could be performed by the men, requiring only the setting back of many advanced workers into earlier forms of industry; but the labor now performed by the men could not be performed by the women without generations of effort and adaptation. Men can cook, clean, and sew as well as women; but the making and managing of the great engines of modern industry, the threading of earth and sea in our vast systems of transportation, the handling of our elaborate machinery of trade, commerce, government—these things could not be done so well by women in their present degree of economic development.

This is not owing to lack of the essential human faculties necessary to such achievements, nor to any inherent disability of sex, but to the present condition of woman, forbidding the development of this degree of economic ability. The male human being is thousands of years in advance of the female in economic status. . . .

Studied individually, the facts are even more plainly visible, more open and familiar. From the day laborer to the millionaire, the wife's worn dress or flashing jewels, her low roof or her lordly one, her weary feet or her rich equipage—these speak of the economic ability of the husband. The comfort, the luxury, the necessities of life itself, which the woman receives, are obtained by the husband, and given her by him. And, when the woman, left alone with no man to "support" her, tries to meet her own economic necessities, the difficulties which confront her prove conclusively what the general economic status of the woman is. None can deny these patent facts—that the economic status of women generally depends upon that of men generally, and that the economic status of women individually depends upon that of men individually, those men to whom they are related. But we are instantly confronted by the commonly received opinion that, although it must be admitted that men make and distribute the wealth of the world, yet women earn their share of it as wives. This assumes either that the husband is in the position of employer and the wife as employee, or that marriage is a "partnership," and the wife an equal factor with the husband in producing wealth. . . .

Women consume economic goods. What economic product do they give in exchange for what they consume? The claim that marriage is a partnership, in which the two persons married produce wealth which neither of them, separately, could produce, will not bear examination. A man happy and comfortable can produce more than one unhappy and uncomfortable, but this is as true of a father or son as of a husband. To take from a man any of the conditions which make him happy and strong is to cripple his industry, generally speaking. But those relatives who make him happy are not therefore his business partners, and entitled to share his income.

Grateful return for happiness conferred is not the method of exchange in a partnership. The comfort a man takes with his wife is not in the nature of a business partnership, nor are her frugality and industry. A housekeeper, in her place, might be as frugal, as industrious, but would not therefore be a partner. Man and wife are partners truly in their mutual obligation to their children—their common love, duty, and service. But a manufacturer who marries, or a doctor, or a lawyer, does not take a partner in his business, when he takes a partner in parenthood, unless his wife is also a manufacturer, a doctor, or a lawyer. In his business, she cannot even advise wisely without training and experience. To love her husband, the composer, does not enable her to compose; and the loss of a man's wife, though it may break his heart, does not cripple his business, unless his mind is affected by grief. She is in no sense a business partner, unless she contributes capital or experience or labor, as a man would in like relation. Most men would hesitate very seriously before entering a business partnership with any woman, wife or not.

If the wife is not, then, truly a business partner, in what way does she earn from her husband the food, clothing, and shelter she receives at his hands? By house service, it will be instantly replied. This is the general misty idea upon the subject—that women earn all they get, and more, by house service. Here we come to a very practical and definite economic ground. Although not producers of wealth, women serve in the final processes of preparation and distribution. Their labor in the household has a genuine economic value.

For a certain percentage of persons to serve another persons, in order that the ones so served may produce more, is a contribution not to be overlooked. The labor of women in the house, certainly, enables men to produce more wealth than they otherwise could; and in this way women are economic factors in society. But so are horses. The labor of horses enables men to produce more wealth than they otherwise could. The horse is an economic factor in society. But the horse is not economically independent, nor is the woman. If a man plus a valet can perform more useful service than he could minus a valet, then the valet is performing useful service. But, if the valet is the property of the man, is obliged to perform this service, and is not paid for it, he is not economically independent.

The labor which the wife performs in the household is given as part of her functional duty, not as employment. The wife of the poor man, who works hard in a small house, doing all the work for the family, or the wife of the rich man, who wisely and gracefully manages a large house and administers its function, each is entitled to fair pay for services rendered.

To take this ground and hold it honestly, wives, as earners through domestic service, are entitled to the wages of cooks, housemaids, nursemaids, seamstresses, or housekeepers, and to no more. This would of course reduce the spending money of the wives of the rich, and put it out of the power of the poor man to "support" a wife at all. . . .

But the salient fact in this discussion is that, whatever the economic value of the domestic industry of women is, they do not get it. The women who do the most work get the least money, and the women who have the most money do the least work. Their labor is neither given nor taken as a factor in economic exchange. . . . We are told that the duties and services of the mother entitle her to support.

If this is so, if motherhood is an exchangeable commodity given by women in payment for clothes and food, then we must of course find some relation between the quantity or quality of the motherhood and the quantity and quality of the pay. This being true, then the women who are not mothers have no economic status at all; and the economic status of those who are must be shown to be relative to their motherhood. This is obviously absurd. The childless wife has as much money as the mother of many—more; for the children of the latter consume what would otherwise be hers; and the inefficient mother is no less provided for than the efficient one. Visibly, and upon the face of it, women are not maintained in economic prosperity proportioned to their motherhood. Motherhood bears no relation to their economic status. . . . Are we willing to consider motherhood as a business, a form of commercial exchange? Are the cares and duties of the mother, her travail and her love, commodities to be exchanged for bread?

It is revolting so to consider them; and, if we dare face our own thoughts, and force them to their logical conclusion, we shall see that nothing could be more repugnant to human feeling, or more socially and individually injurious, than to make motherhood a trade. Driven off these alleged grounds of women's economic independence; shown that women, as a class, neither produce nor distribute wealth; that women, as individuals, labor mainly as house servants, are not paid as such, and would not be satisfied with such an economic status if they were so paid; that wives are not business partners or co-producers of wealth with their husbands, unless they actually practise the same profession; that they are not salaried as mothers, and that it would be unspeakably degrading if they were—what remains to those who deny that women are supported by men? This (and a most amusing position it is)—that the function of maternity unfits a woman for economic production. . . .

. . . Because of her maternal duties, the human female is said to be unable to get her own living. As the maternal duties of other females do not unfit them for getting their own living and also the livings of their young, it would seem that the human maternal duties require the segregation of the entire energies of the mother to the service of the child during her entire adult life, or so large a proportion of them that not enough remains to devote to the individual interests of the mother.

Such a condition, did it exist, would of course excuse and justify the pitiful dependence of the human female, and her support by the male. As the queen bee, modified entirely to maternity, is supported, not by the male, to be sure, but by her co-workers, the "old maids," the barren working bees, who labor so patiently and lovingly in their branch of the maternal duties of the hive, so would the human female, modified entirely to maternity, become unfit for any other exertion, and a helpless dependant.

Is this the condition of human motherhood? Does the human mother, by her motherhood, thereby lose control of brain and body, lose power and skill and desire for any other work? Do we see before us the human race, with all its females segregated entirely to the uses of motherhood, consecrated, set apart, specially developed, spending every power of their nature on the service of their children?

We do not. We see the human mother worked far harder than a mare, laboring her life long in the service, not of her children only, but of men; husbands, brothers, fathers, whatever male relatives she has; for mother and sister also; for the church a little, if she is allowed; for society, if she is able; for charity and education and reform—working in many ways that are not the ways of motherhood.

It is not motherhood that keeps the housewife on her feet from dawn till dark; it is house service, not child service. Women work longer and harder than most men, and not solely in maternal duties. . . .

In spite of her supposed segregation to maternal duties, the human female, the world over, works at extra-maternal duties for hours enough to provide her with an independent living, and then is denied independence on the ground that motherhood prevents her working! . . .

. . . A human female, healthy, sound, has twenty-five years of life before she is a mother, and should have twenty-five years more after the period of such maternal service as is expected of her has been given. . . .

. . . The women whose splendid extravagance dazzles the world, whose economic goods are the greatest, are often neither houseworkers nor mothers, but simply the women who hold most power over the men who have the most money. The female of genus homo is economically dependent on the male. He is her food supply.

8.3   REPRODUCTIVE RIGHTS (1931)

Today's battles over abortion are mild compared to the first decades of the battle over women's right to use contraceptives. Margaret Sanger, a heroic nurse and mother, first used the term "birth control" and launched the first crusade to secure reproductive rights for American women shortly before World War I. Sanger's initial concern was with poverty-stricken immigrant women who had large families and numerous problems. But almost immediately, Sanger's work attracted the interest and support of many American women, particularly those who were members of the middle class or fortunate enough to have access to higher education. Traditional America struck back with a vengeance. Sanger was arrested; her writings and publications were censored and suppressed; her clinic was closed by local authorities and, at one point, she was even forced to leave the United States. Despite these difficulties, she nonetheless fought on, founding the American Birth Control League (1921), Birth Control Clinical Research Bureau (1923), and Planned Parenthood (1942). Throughout all, she remained a gifted public speaker and writer who conveyed her message relentlessly. This selection is taken from her autobiography written in 1931, My Fight for Birth Control. Can you observe a new attitude or assertiveness in this selection? Has a new day dawned as the final selection suggests?

Margaret Sanger

Early in the year 1912 I came to a sudden realization that my work as a nurse and my activities in social service were entirely palliative and consequently futile and useless to relieve the misery I saw all about me. . . .

It is among the mothers here that the most difficult problems arise—the outcasts of society with theft, filth, perjury, cruelty, brutality oozing from beneath.

Ignorance and neglect go on day by day; children born to breathe but a few hours and pass out of life; pregnant women toiling early and late to give food to four or five children, always hungry; boarders taken into homes where there is not sufficient room for the family; little girls eight and ten years of age sleeping in the same room with dirty, foul smelling, loathsome men; women whose weary, pregnant, shapeless bodies refuse to accommodate themselves to the husbands' desires find husbands looking with lustful eyes upon other women, sometimes upon their own little daughters, six and seven years of age.

In this atmosphere abortions and birth become the main theme of conversation. On Saturday nights I have seen groups of fifty to one hundred women going into questionable offices well known in the community for cheap abortions. I asked several women what

Margaret Sanger, *My Fight for Birth Control* (New York, 1931), chap. 3.

took place there, and they all gave the same reply: a quick examination, a probe inserted into the uterus and turned a few times to disturb the fertilized ovum, and then the woman was sent home. Usually the flow began the next day and often continued four or five weeks. Sometimes an ambulance carried the victim to the hospital for a curettage, and if she returned home at all she was looked upon as a lucky woman.

This state of things became a nightmare with me. There seemed no sense to it all, no reason for such waste of mother life, no right to exhaust women's vitality and to throw them on the scrap-heap before the age of thirty-five.

Everywhere I looked, misery and fear stalked—men fearful of losing their jobs, women fearful that even worse conditions might come upon them. The menace of another pregnancy hung like a sword over the head of every poor woman I came in contact with that year. The question which met me was always the same: What can I do to keep from it? or, What can I do to get out of this? Sometimes they talked among themselves bitterly.

"It's the rich that know the tricks," they'd say, "while we have all the kids." Then, if the women were Roman Catholics, they talked about "Yankee tricks," and asked me if I knew what the Protestants did to keep their families down. When I said that I didn't believe that the rich knew much more than they did I was laughed at and suspected of holding back information for money. . . .

I heard over and over again of their desperate efforts at bringing themselves "around"—drinking various herb-teas, taking drops of turpentine on sugar, steaming over a chamber of boiling coffee or of turpentine water, rolling down stairs, and finally inserting slippery-elm sticks, or knitting needles, or shoe hooks into the uterus. I used to shudder with horror as I heard the details and, worse yet, learned of the conditions *behind the reason* for such desperate actions.

. . . Each time I returned it was to hear that Mrs. Cohen had been carried to a hospital but had never come back, that Mrs. Kelly had sent the children to a neighbor's and had put her head into the gas oven to end her misery. Many of the women had consulted mid-wives, social workers and doctors at the dispensary and asked a way to limit their families, but they were denied this help, sometimes indignantly or gruffly, sometimes jokingly; but always knowledge was denied them. Life for them had but one choice: either to abandon themselves to incessant childbearing, or to terminate their pregnancies through abortions. Is it any wonder they resigned themselves hopelessly, as the Jewish and Italian mothers, or fell into drunkenness, as the Irish and Scotch? The latter were often beaten by husbands, as well as by their sons and daughters. . . .

One by one these women, with their worried, sad, pensive and ageing faces would marshal themselves before me in my dreams, sometimes appealingly, sometimes accusingly. I could not escape from the facts of their misery, neither was I able to see the way out of their problems and their troubles. . . .

Finally the thing began to shape itself, to become accumulative during the three weeks I spent in the home of a desperately sick woman living on Grand Street, a lower section of New York's East Side.

Mrs. Sacks was only twenty-eight years old; her husband, an unskilled worker, thirty-two. Three children, aged five, three and one, were none too strong nor sturdy, and it took all the earnings of the father and the ingenuity of the mother to keep them clean, provide them with air and proper food, and give them a chance to grow into decent manhood and womanhood.

Both parents were devoted to these children and to each other. The woman had become pregnant and had taken various drugs and purgatives, as advised by her neighbors. Then, in desperation, she had used some instrument lent to her by a friend. She was found prostrate on the floor amidst the crying children when her husband returned from work. Neighbors advised against the ambulance, and a friendly doctor was called. The husband would not hear of her going to a hospital, and as a little money had been saved in the bank a nurse was called and the battle for that precious life began.

. . . The three-room apartment was turned into a hospital for the dying patient. Never had I worked so fast, so concentratedly as I did to keep alive that little mother. . . .

. . . July's sultry days and nights were melted into a torpid inferno. Day after day, night after night, I slept only in brief snatches, ever too anxious about the condition of that feeble heart bravely carrying on, to stay long from the bedside of the patient. With but one toilet for the building and that on the floor below, everything had to be carried down for disposal, while ice, food and other necessities had to be carried three flights up. It was one of those old airshaft buildings of which there were several thousands then standing in New York City.

At the end of two weeks recovery was in sight, and at the end of three weeks I was preparing to leave the fragile patient to take up the ordinary duties of her life, including those of wifehood and motherhood. . . .

But as the hour for my departure came nearer, her anxiety increased, and finally with trembling voice she said: "Another baby will finish me, I suppose."

"It's too early to talk about that," I said, and resolved that I would turn the question over to the doctor for his advice. When he came I said: "Mrs. Sacks is worried about having another baby."

"She well might be," replied the doctor, and then he stood before her and said: "Any more such capers, young woman, and there will be no need to call me."

"Yes, yes—I know, Doctor," said the patient with trembling voice, "but," and she hesitated as if it took all of her courage to say it, "*what* can I do to prevent getting that way again?"

"Oh ho!" laughed the doctor good naturedly. "You want your cake while you eat it too, do you? Well, it can't be done." Then, familiarly slapping her on the back and picking up his hat and bag to depart, he said: "I'll tell you the only sure thing to do. Tell Jake to sleep on the roof."

With those words he closed the door and went down the stairs, leaving us both petrified and stunned.

Tears sprang to my eyes, and a lump came in my throat as I looked at that face before me. It was stamped with sheer horror. I thought for a moment she might have gone insane, but she conquered her feelings, whatever they may have been, and turning to me in desperation said: "He can't understand, can he?—he's a man after all—but you do, don't you? You're a woman and you'll tell me the secret and I'll never tell it to a soul."

She clasped her hands as if in prayer, she leaned over and looked straight into my eyes and beseechingly implored me to tell her something—something *I really did not know*. . . .

I had to turn away from that imploring face. I could not answer her then. I quieted her as best I could. She saw that I was moved by the tears in my eyes. I promised that I would come back in a few days and tell her what she wanted to know. The few simple means of limiting the family like *coitus interruptus* or the condom were laughed at by the neighboring women when told these were the means used by men in the well-to-do families. That was not believed, and I knew such an answer would be swept aside as useless were I to tell her this at such a time. . . .

The intelligent reasoning of the young mother—how to *prevent* getting that way again—how sensible, how just she had been—yes, I promised myself I'd go back and have a long talk with her and tell her more, and perhaps she would not laugh but would believe that those methods were all that were really known.

But time flew past, and weeks rolled into months. . . . I was about to retire one night three months later when the telephone rang and an agitated man's voice begged me to come at once to help his wife who was sick again. It was the husband of Mrs. Sacks, and I intuitively knew before I left the telephone that it was almost useless to go.

. . . I arrived a few minutes after the doctor, the same one who had given her such noble advice. The woman was dying. She was unconscious. She died within ten minutes after my arrival. It was the same result, the same story told a thousand times before—death from abortion. She had become pregnant, had used drugs, had then consulted a five-dollar professional abortionist, and death followed.

The doctor shook his head as he rose from listening for the heart beat. . . . The gentle woman, the devoted mother, the loving wife had passed on leaving behind her a frantic husband, helpless in his loneliness, bewildered in his helplessness as he paced up and down the room, hands clenching his head, moaning "My God! My God! My God!"

The Revolution came—but not as it has been pictured nor as history relates that revolutions have come. . . .

After I left that desolate house I walked and walked and walked; for hours and hours I kept on, bag in hand, thinking, regretting, dreading to stop; fearful of my conscience, dreading to face my own accusing soul. At three in the morning I arrived home still clutching a heavy load the weight of which I was quite unconscious.

. . . As I stood at the window and looked out, the miseries and problems of that sleeping city arose before me in a clear vision like a panorama: crowded homes, too many children; babies dying in infancy; mothers overworked; baby nurseries; children neglected and hungry—mothers so nervously wrought they could not give the little things the comfort nor care they needed; mothers half sick most of their lives—"always ailing, never failing"; women made into drudges; children working in cellars; children aged six and seven pushed into the labor market to help earn a living; another baby on the way; still another; yet another; a baby born dead—great relief; an older child dies—sorrow, but nevertheless relief—insurance helps; a mother's death—children scattered into institutions; the father, desperate, drunken; he slinks away to become an outcast in a society which has trapped him.

. . . There was only one thing to be done: call out, start the alarm, set the heather on fire! Awaken the womanhood of America to free the motherhood of the world! I released from my almost paralyzed hand the nursing bag which unconsciously I had clutched, threw it across the room, tore the uniform from the body, flung it into a corner, and renounced all palliative work forever.

I would never go back again to nurse women's ailing bodies while their miseries were as vast as the stars. I was now finished with superficial cures, with doctors and nurses and social workers who were brought face to face with this overwhelming truth of women's needs and yet turned to pass on the other side. They must be made to see these facts. I resolved that women should have knowledge of contraception. They have every right to know about their own bodies. I would strike out—I would scream from the housetops. I would tell the world what was going on in the lives of these poor women. I *would* be heard. No matter what it should cost. *I would be heard.*

"SONG FROM THE WOMEN'S MOVEMENT: LET US ALL SPEAK OUR MINDS" (C. 1920)

Men tell us 'tis fit that wives should submit
To their husbands submissively, weakly;
That whatever they say, their wives should obey,
Unquestioning, stupidly, meekly.
Our husbands would make us their own dictum take
Without ever a wherefore or why for it;
But I don't and I can't and I won't and I shan't;
No, I will speak my mind if I die for it.
For we know it's all fudge to say man's the best judge
Of what should be and shouldn't, and so on,
That woman should bow, nor attempt to say how
She considers that matters should go on.
I never yet gave up myself thus a slave,
However my husband might try for it;
For I can't and I won't and I shan't and I don't;
But I will speak my mind if I die for it!
And all ladies I hope who've with husbands to cope,
With the rights of the sex will not trifle.
We all, if we choose our tongues but to use,
Can all opposition soon stifle.
Let man, if he will, then bid us be still
And silent, a price he'll pay high for it;
For we won't and we can't and we don't and we shan't—
Let us all speak our minds if we die for it!

CHAPTER 9

The New Deal

In October 1929, the stock market boom collapsed, triggering the longest and steepest economic slide in U.S. history. At the Depression's worst, in the winter of 1932–1933, America's total output was 31 percent below its 1929 peak; unemployment reached 25 percent of the labor force. During that appalling period millions of citizens wondered whether the existing social order could long survive the economic collapse.

In their desperation Americans might have turned for salvation to extremist leaders outside the liberal tradition, as many did in Europe under similar pressures. Instead they chose as their president Franklin Roosevelt, the standard-bearer of the party out of power at the time of the crash. What followed was the New Deal, a legislative program more sweeping and comprehensive than any in our history.

The New Deal was many things simultaneously. It was a relief program to provide jobs and income to millions of unemployed men and women. It was a drive to stimulate the stalled economy and get private production moving again. It was a bid to reform the nation's financial institutions, provide insurance against social hazards, encourage trade union organization, and revitalize natural resource management. It was inconsistent and changeable. Roosevelt and his advisers had no clear idea of exactly what was wrong with the economy and no certain formula for fixing it. Their policies and programs were often improvised, although their reform agenda drew heavily on early twentieth-century Progressivism for inspiration.

Frightened by the devastating economic and financial breakdown, at first most Americans were willing to give Roosevelt and the Democrats a blank check for change. By 1934, however, many old conservatives had regained their confidence and were beginning to take aim at the president and his policies. The left rallied, too, and Marxists and various neo-Populists were soon attacking FDR as a friend of big business and even a covert fascist.

In the following selections, you will encounter both defenders and opponents of the New Deal. But the voices are not simply pro and con. In their support or opposition, the authors have individual perspectives that reward analysis.

9.1 ROOSEVELT EXPLAINS HIS POLICIES (1934)

Franklin Delano Roosevelt was one of the most effective political leaders in U.S. history. Himself a patrician from old, pre-Revolutionary stock, he communicated effectively with working-class and middle-class Americans of all origins through the new electronic medium, the radio, and won their support for his policies. FDR was not a systematic thinker. He was a pragmatist and an improviser. His first Inaugural Address created one of the most dramatic public moments in American political history. Contained herein was FDR's famous statement, "the only thing we have to fear is fear itself." FDR roused the nation but gave few specific details of how the New Deal would solve the economic ills of the Great Depression. Why then do you think this moment is so often noted as a highlight in the history of leadership? The next two selections are from key New Dealers. Harry Hopkins would be one of FDR's closest advisors, charged with administering numerous public works projects. In this radio address, Hopkins has just taken charge of the newly created Federal Emergency Relief Administration and explains his goal of getting people back to work. In the long run, no economist would prove more important to the New Deal than John Maynard Keynes. In 1934, Keynes received an honorary degree from Columbia University and publicly made these recommendations to FDR. Although FDR did not embrace all of them immediately, they provide a profound insight into the economic philosophy which would come to dominate American politics for five decades.

"THE ONLY THING WE HAVE TO FEAR IS FEAR ITSELF"

Franklin D. Roosevelt

I am certain that my fellow Americans expect that on my induction into the presidency I will address them with a candor and a decision which the present situation of our nation impels. This is preeminently the time to speak the truth, the whole truth, frankly and boldly. Nor need we shrink from honestly facing conditions in our country today. This great nation will endure as it has endured, will revive and will prosper.

So, first of all, let me assert my firm belief that the only thing we have to fear is fear itself—nameless, unreasoning, unjustified terror which paralyzes needed efforts to convert retreat into advance. In every dark hour of our national life a leadership of frankness and vigor has met with that understanding and support of the people themselves which is essential to victory. I am convinced that you will again give that support to leadership in these critical days.

In such a spirit on my part and on yours we face our common difficulties. They concern, thank God, only material things. Values have shrunken to fantastic levels; taxes have risen; our ability to pay has fallen; government of all kinds is faced by serious curtailment of income; the means of exchange are frozen in the currents of trade; the withered leaves of industrial enterprise lie on every side; farmers find no markets for their produce; the savings of many years in thousands of families are gone.

Inaugural Address, March 4, 1933, *Record*, 73 Cong., Special Sess. of the Senate, pp. 5–6.

More important, a host of unemployed citizens face the grim problem of existence, and an equally great number toil with little return. Only a foolish optimist can deny the dark realities of the moment.

Yet our distress comes from no failure of substance. We are stricken by no plague of locusts. Compared with the perils which our forefathers conquered because they believed and were not afraid, we have still much to be thankful for. Nature still offers her bounty, and human efforts have multiplied it. Plenty is at our doorstep, but a generous use of it languishes in the very sight of the supply. Primarily this is because the rulers of the exchange of mankind's goods have failed, through their own stubbornness and their own incompetence, have admitted their failure, and abdicated. Practices of the unscrupulous money changers stand indicted in the court of public opinion, rejected by the hearts and minds of men.

True they have tried, but their efforts have been cast in the pattern of an outworn tradition. Faced by failure of credit, they have proposed only the lending of more money. Stripped of the lure of profit by which to induce our people to follow their false leadership, they have resorted to exhortations, pleading tearfully for restored confidence. They know only the rules of a generation of self-seekers. They have no vision, and when there is no vision the people perish.

The money changers have fled from their high seats in the temple of our civilization. We may now restore that temple to the ancient truths. The measure of the restoration lies in the extent to which we apply social values more noble than mere monetary profit.

Happiness lies not in the mere possession of money; it lies in the joy of achievement, in the thrill of creative effort. The joy and moral stimulation of work no longer must be forgotten in the mad chase of evanescent profits. These dark days will be worth all they cost us if they teach us that our true destiny is not to be ministered unto but to minister to ourselves and to our fellowmen.

Recognition of the falsity of material wealth as the standard of success goes hand in hand with the abandonment of the false belief that public office and high political position are to be valued only by the standards of pride of place and personal profit; and there must be an end to a conduct in banking and in business which too often has given to a sacred trust the likeness of callous and selfish wrongdoing. Small wonder that confidence languishes, for it thrives only on honesty, on honor, on the sacredness of obligations, on faithful protection, on unselfish performance; without them it cannot live.

Restoration calls, however, not for changes in ethics alone. This nation asks for action, and action now.

Our greatest primary task is to put people to work. This is no unsolvable problem if we face it wisely and courageously. It can be accomplished in part by direct recruiting by the government itself, treating the task as we would treat the emergency of a war, but, at the same time, through this employment, accomplishing greatly needed projects to stimulate and reorganize the use of our natural resources. . . .

If I read the temper of our people correctly, we now realize as we have never realized before our interdependence on each other; that we cannot merely take but we must give as well; that if we are to go forward, we must move as a trained and loyal army willing to sacrifice for the good of a common discipline, because without such discipline no progress is made, no leadership becomes effective. We are, I know, ready and willing to submit our lives and property to such discipline, because it makes possible a leadership which aims at a larger good. This I propose to offer, pledging that the larger purposes will bind upon us all as a sacred obligation, with a unity of duty hitherto evoked only in time of armed strife.

With this pledge taken, I assume unhesitatingly the leadership of this great army of our people dedicated to a disciplined attack upon our common problems.

Action in this image and to this end is feasible under the form of government which we have inherited from our ancestors. Our Constitution is so simple and practical that it is possible always to meet extraordinary needs by changes in emphasis and arrangement without loss of essential form. That is why our constitutional system has proved itself the most superbly enduring political mechanism the modern world has produced. It has met every stress of vast expansion of territory, of foreign wars, of bitter internal strife, of world relations.

It is to be hoped that the normal balance of executive and legislative authority may be wholly adequate to meet the unprecedented task before us. But it may be that an unprecedented demand and need for undelayed action may call for temporary departure from that normal balance of public procedure.

I am prepared under my constitutional duty to recommend the measures that a stricken nation in the midst of a stricken world may require. These measures, or such other measures as the Congress may build out of its experience and wisdom, I shall seek, within my constitutional authority, to bring to speedy adoption.

But in the event that the Congress shall fail to take one of these two courses, and in the event that the national emergency is still critical, I shall not evade the clear course of duty that will then confront me. I shall ask the Congress for the one remaining instrument to meet the crisis—broad executive power to wage a war against the emergency, as great as the power that would be given to me if we were in fact invaded by a foreign foe.

For the trust reposed in me I will return the courage and the devotion that befit the time, I can do no less.

We face the arduous days that lie before us in the warm courage of national unity; with the dear consciousness of seeking old and precious moral values; with the clean satisfaction that comes from the stern performance of duty by old and young alike. We aim at the assurance of a rounded and permanent national life.

We do not distrust the future of essential democracy. The people of the United States have not failed. In their need they have registered a mandate that they want direct, vigorous action. They have asked for discipline and direction under leadership. They have made me the present instrument of their wishes. In the spirit of the gift I take it.

In this dedication of a nation we humbly ask the blessing of God. May He protect each and every one of us. May He guide me in the days to come.

Happy Hopkins and the Federal Emergency Relief Administration

It is a curious thing what a quantity of sickness, coldness, hunger, and barefootedness we are willing to let other men suffer. It literally has no limit. You can hear it in the cautious tone of voice of a man who says, "We'd better be careful or we will have a major disaster." What, might we ask him, would he consider to be a major disaster? Obviously it has nothing to do with numbers. For 18 million persons is a large enough number used in any

RADR ADDRESS VSD, December 31, 1934, pp. 210–212.

connection to satisfy most men. Eighteen million men in an army is a large army. Eighteen million sick men is an epidemic larger than any we have ever recorded. Eighteen million criminals would turn the country into a jail. Eighteen million madmen would keep us locked in our rooms in a state of dithering terror. It is a figure large enough so that even in dollars we have to count carefully to know their full purchasing power. For most people large figures are as unusable to their reasoning processes as the astronomer's light-years are to a man with a piece of smoked glass. Yet we can easily roll across our tongues, without a reaction setting up in the heart or mind, the simple statement that 18 million Americans are so poor of this world's goods that they are on relief. . ..

Many of you will say to me that these people like being on relief and that they are better off on relief than they have ever been before. We have heard that one very often. We are told they will not work any more. May I ask you one thing? When you know that a relief budget, for lack of funds, is placed at the very minimum of a family's needs and that in very few places it can take care of rent and that it can hope to do little more than keep body and soul together; and when you realize that this is a nominal budget only, and because we lack funds sometimes families are permitted to receive less than 50 percent of that so-called ideal budget, which is in itself inadequate to life, may I ask you if this is an indictment of relief, that it is said to offer more than life offered before, or is it an indictment of something else?

For myself, I do not call it an indictment of relief. I grant you that examples which you cite of chiseling, racketeering, politics, and laziness may be true, but I also say that we are in a position to know the proportions of these evils, and that it is a fact beyond contradiction that most men do not give up without a struggle that intangible thing they call their independence.

We have lately had a new kind of complaint from a very astute and humorous economist. He asks: "Why are you people in federal relief always apologizing for straight relief, always talking about its being so demoralizing, and such a shameful thing, why are you always saying that as soon as you can, you are going to have work relief for all these people?" (For you know that we harp upon that a good deal in the Relief Administration. We are aware that it costs more in the beginning so we have to fight pretty hard for it.) This economist says: "Of course, you should be apologetic for the amount you give out. The whole matter would be righted and men could hold up their heads again if you gave them $130 a week and called it independent income."

The only trouble with this is that the unemployed themselves want work. We do not have to tell them that not having a job spoils a man for work. They go soft, they lose skill, they lose work habits. But they know it before you and I know it and it is their lives that are being wrecked, not ours. . . .

There are those who tell us that we should not have work relief. They say that straight relief is cheaper. No one will deny this contention. It costs money to put a man to work. Apparently, to the advocates of direct relief, the primary object of relief is to save the government money. The ultimate humane cost to the government never occurs to them of a continued situation through which its citizens lose their sense of independence and strength and their sense of individual destiny. Work for the unemployed is something we have fought for since the beginning of the administration and we shall continue to insist upon it. It preserves a man's morale. It saves his skill. It gives him a chance to do something socially useful.

Let me say again that we should allow ourselves no smug feelings of charity at this holiday season to know that the federal government is attempting to take care of the actual physical wants of 18 million people. We are merely paying damages for not having had a thought about these things many years ago. We will have to do a great deal of thinking from here out.

I should like to say a word right here about the housing which we have been allowing to stand as the shelter of American citizens. It is evil. It is unnecessary. No civilized nation needs to stand for it. Something has got to be done about housing and something is going to be done. . . .

It is safe to say that poverty in any city is as old as that city and that it has grown in every city from little to big. It is part of its economic nature that poverty is infectious. It is like the old proverb of the shoemaker's children. The children of thousands of unemployed workers in the shoe district of New England are unshod. It would seem that the more you make the more you can't have. It is true that while we have thousands of unemployed cotton textile workers, there are literally hundreds of thousands of beds in the United Stares that have no sheets and that people sleep on pieces of old carpet placed upon bare springs, or stretch burlap out upon sawdust and lay their babies to sleep on gunny sacks filled with old rags.

I have painted you a very bleak picture. There are the facts with which we have to contend but even though we do not attempt to gloss them over, and it would be idle and even cruel to do so, there is in some ways a more hopeful color in it than any American Christmas has known before. In this country, for the first time, we have a President in the White House whose mind and heart are consecrated to the ending forever of such conditions. It has been one of the outstanding virtues of this administration that it has been willing to uncover the extent of the problem with which it has to deal. It is the motivating force behind the President and his aides to bring about a day when these men and women who have endured so much will come again, or even come, some of them, for the first time, into the inheritance which rightfully belongs to every citizen of the richest country in the world.

And this is not all still in the stage of hope. Much has been accomplished. It lacks some months of being two years since the President undertook a task which was years in preparing. Remember that already at least 3.5 million of unemployed persons have gone back to work. Remember that in spite of the natural seasonal rise of unemployment in winter, and the additional physical needs that people experience in cold weather, and in spite of the fact that depleted family resources have forced newcomers to list themselves upon the relief rolls, there are fewer families on relief at this moment than there were in March 1933. Besides this, new social movements have been begun that will protect and enrich our common life. These good effects are even now at the beginning of a longtime program, substantial enough to be felt. Not only have pledges been made but pledges have been fulfilled.

JOHN MAYNARD KEYNES PUBLIC RECOMMENDATIONS (1934)

These are a few notes on the New Deal by one who has come here on a brief visit of pure inquisitiveness—made under the limitations of imperfect knowledge, but gaining, perhaps, from the detachment of a bird's-eye view.

New York Times, June 10, 1934.

My purpose is to consider the prospects rather than the past—taking the legislation of this Congress for granted and examining what might be done on the basis thus given. I am in sympathy with most of the social and reforming aims of this legislation; and the principal subject of these notes is the problem of consolidating economic and business recovery.

For this reason, I have not much to say about NRA. I doubt if this measure is either such an advantage to recovery or such a handicap as its advocates and its critics suppose. It embodies some important improvements in labor conditions and for obtaining fair-trade practices. But I agree with the widespread opinion that much of it is objectionable because of its restrictionist philosophy which has a proper place in agricultural adjustment today but not in American industry, and because of its excessive complexity and regimentation.

In particular, it would be advisable to discard most of the provisions to fix prices and to forbid sales below an alleged, but undefinable, cost basis. Nevertheless, its net effect on recovery can easily be overestimated either way.

I find most Americans divided between those who believe that higher wages are good because they increase purchasing power and those who believe that they are bad because they raise costs. But both are right, and the net result of the two opposing influences is to cancel out. The important question is the proper adjustment of relative wage rates. Absolute wage rates are not of primary importance in a country where their effect on foreign trade has been offset by exchange devaluation.

The case for AAA, on the other hand, is much stronger. For the farmer has had to shoulder more than his share of the trouble and also has more lasting difficulties ahead of him than industry has. AAA is organizing for the farmer the advisable measure of restriction which industry long ago organized for it self. Thus the task which AAA is attempting is necessary though difficult; whereas some part of what NRA seems to be aiming at is not only impracticable but unnecessary.

I see the problem of recovery, accordingly, in the following light: How soon will normal business enterprise come to the rescue? What measures can be taken to hasten the return of normal enterprise? On what scale, by which expedients, and for how long is abnormal government expenditure advisable in the meantime? For this, I think, is how the administration should view its task.

I see no likelihood that business, of its own initiative, will invest in durable goods on a sufficient scale for many months to come. There are several reasons for this.

In the first place, the important but intangible state of mind, which we call business confidence, is signally lacking. It would be easy to mention specific causes of this, for some of which the administration may be to blame. Probably the most important is the menace of possible labor troubles. But the real explanation, in my judgment, lies deeper than the specific causes. It is to be found in the perplexity and discomfort which the business world feels from being driven so far from its accustomed moorings into unknown and uncharted waters. The businessman, who may be adaptable and quick on his feet in his own particular field, is usually conservative and conventional in the larger aspects of social and economic policy. At the start he was carried away, like other people, by the prevailing enthusiasm—without being converted at bottom or suffering a sea-change. Thus, he has easily reverted to where he was. He is sulky and bothered; and, with the short memory characteristic of contemporary man, even begins to look back with longing to the good old days of 1932.

This atmosphere of disappointment, disillusion, and perplexity is nothing to wonder at. I doubt if it could have been avoided without undue concession to conventional ideas. But it is not incurable. The mere passage of time for business to work out its new bearings and recover its equanimity should do much. If the President could convince businessmen that they know the worst, so to speak, and can settle down to adjust themselves to a known situation, that might hasten matters. Above all, the actual experience of gradually improving conditions might work wonders.

In the second place, there are still serious obstacles in the way of reopening the capital market to large-scale borrowing for new investment; particularly, the high cost of borrowing to those who need loans most and the attitude of the finance houses to the Securities Act, though I consider that they should accept the amended act as workable.

Moreover, many types of durable goods are already in sufficient supply, so that business will not be inclined to repair or modernize plant until a stronger demand is being experienced than can be met with existing plant; to which should be added the excessively high cost of building relatively to rents and incomes.

None of these obstacles can be overcome in a day or by a stroke of the pen. The notion that, if the government would retire altogether from the economic field, business, and left to itself, would soon work out its own salvation, is, to my mind, foolish; and, even if it were not, it is certain that public opinion would allow no such thing. This does not mean that the administration should not be assiduously preparing the way for the return of normal investment enterprise. But this will unavoidably take time. When it comes, it will intensify and maintain a recovery initiated by other means. But it belongs to the second chapter of the story and not to the first.

I conclude, therefore, that, for six months at least, and probably a year, the measure of recovery to be achieved will mainly depend on the degree of the direct stimulus to production deliberately applied by the administration. Since I have no belief in the efficacy for this purpose of the price and wage raising activities of NRA, this must chiefly mean the pace and volume of the government's emergency expenditure.

Up to last November, such expenditure, excluding refinancing and advances to banks, was relatively small—about $90 million a month. From November onward, the figure rose sharply and, for the first four months of this year, the monthly average exceeded $300 million. The effect on business was excellent. But then came what seems to me to have been an unfortunate decision. The expenditure of the Civil Works Administration was checked before the expenditure of the Public Works Administration was ready to take its place.

Thus, the aggregate emergency expenditure is now declining. If it is going to decline to $200 million monthly, much of the ground already gained will probably be lost. If it were to rise to $400 million monthly, I should be quite confident that a strong business revival would set in by the autumn.

So little divides a retreat from an advance. Most people greatly underestimate the effect of a given emergency expenditure, because they overlook the multiplier—the cumulative effect of increased individual incomes, because the expenditure of these incomes improves the incomes of a further set of recipients and so on. Four hundred million dollars monthly is not much more than 11 percent of the national income; yet. it may, directly and indirectly, increase the national income by at least three or four times this amount. Thus the difference between a monthly emergency expenditure of $400 million, financed out of loans and not out of taxation, which would represent a mere redistribution of incomes, and a $100 million expenditure, may be, other things being equal, to increase the national money income by 25 to 30 percent. . . .

This brings me to my agenda for the President:

1. Sufficient appropriations should be obtained before Congress adjourns to provide the necessary ammunition. I believe that this has been obtained.
2. A small office should be set up to collate the spending programs, both realized and prospective, of the various emergency organizations, to compare estimates with results and to report to the President weekly.
3. If the volume or pace of prospective estimates appear to be deficient, the emergency organization should be instructed to report urgently on further available projects. Housing and the railroads appear to offer the outstanding opportunities. The new housing bill is brilliantly conceived, and, if it is operated vigorously, may prove to be a measure of the first importance. Drought relief may be an unexpectedly large factor in the coming months.
4. Meanwhile, active preparations should be on foot to make sure that normal enterprise will take the place of the emergency programs as soon as possible. Much progress has already been made with the problem of remedying the widespread and paralyzing loss of liquidity. But that task must still be carried on.
5. With the Securities Act and the Stock Exchange Act carried into law, the battle is over and the time has come for sincere efforts on both sides to establish cooperative and friendly relations between the commission which will work the acts and the leading financial interests, for it is vital to reopen the capital market.
6. Continuous pressure should be exerted by the Treasury and the Federal Reserve System to bring down the long-term rate of interest. For it assuredly lies in their power, and it is a mistake to suppose that, because the government will be a large borrower, interest rates will rise—inasmuch as the Treasury's resources in gold and the Reserve System's excess reserves put the market wholly in their hands. . .
7. To an Englishman the high level of building costs in this country appears to be scandalous, both of building materials and of direct labor. They must be more than 50 percent above, and perhaps double, what they are in England. So long as the volume of work remains as low as it is now, these high costs do not mean high incomes to producers. Thus, no one benefits. It is of the first importance for the administration to take whatever steps are in its power to reduce unit costs in these industries against an undertaking to increase the volume of business sufficiently to maintain and probably to increase actual earnings. This might involve a national program of building working-class houses to rent, which would be, in itself, a great benefit. The measure of recovery now enjoyed in England is largely due to the activity of house building.
8. Either by skill or by good fortune the United States has arrived at what seems to me an excellent currency policy. It was right to devalue. It is right to have a value for the dollar currently fixed in terms of gold. It is prudent to keep a discretionary

margin to allow future changes in the gold value of the dollar, if a change in circumstances makes this advisable. But all these measures have been carried fully far enough. Thus there would be no risk, in my judgment, if the President were to make it plain that he has now successfully attained his objects, so far as they can be attained by monetary policy, and that, henceforth, a wise spending policy and a gradual but obstinate attack on high interest rates through the agency of the Federal Reserve System and otherwise will occupy the foreground of the economic program.

9. A word as to the budget. Expenditures fall into three classes: the normal expenditure of administration, relief expenditures, and capital expenditures represented by valuable assets and obligations. The first two classes should, probably, be balanced by revenue by 1936. But it would be a disastrous error, and an instrument of strong deflation, to attempt to cover capital expenditure out of current revenue. At present, the public mind is apt to be confused, because relief and capital expenditure are linked together indiscriminately as emergency expenditure. . . .

If, in conclusion, I may give for what they are worth the impressions of a brief visit to Washington, I believe that there is much devoted and intelligent work in progress there, and that the fittest ideas and the fittest men are tending to survive. In many parts of the world the old order has passed away. But, of all the experiments to evolve a new order, it is the experiment of young America which most attracts my own deepest sympathy. For they are occupied with the task of trying to make the economic order work tolerably well, while preserving freedom of individual initiative and liberty of thought and criticism.

The older generation of living Americans accomplished the great task of solving the technical problem of how to produce economic goods on a scale adequate to human needs. It is the task of the younger generation to bring to actual realization the potential blessings of having solved the technical side of the problem of poverty. The central control which the latter requires involves an essentially changed method and outlook. The minds and energies which have found their fulfillment in the achievements of American business are not likely to be equally well adapted to the further task. That must be, as it should be, the fulfillment of the next generation.

The new men will often appear to be at war with the ideas and convictions of their seniors. This cannot be helped. But I hope that these seniors will look as sympathetically as they can at a sincere attempt—I cannot view it otherwise—to complete, and not to destroy, what they themselves have created.

9.2   THE NEW DEAL AND THE "COMMON MAN" (1934, 1936)

Roosevelt and the New Deal proved immensely popular with middle- and lower-income Americans. In 1936, FDR won in an extraordinary popular landslide when he ran for reelection.

In the following selections—letters written by working-class Americans to New Deal politicians, to FDR's wife, Eleanor, and to the president himself—we learn why the "common man" supported the administration's programs. How would you characterize the sources of this support? What New Deal programs particularly seemed to awaken the gratitude of ordinary Americans?

"SAINT ROOSEVELT"

Cedarburg, Wis.
10:45 A.M. Mar. 5, 1934

Mrs. F. D. Roosevelt
Washington, D.C.

My dear Friend:

Just listened to the address given by your dear husband, our wonderful President. During the presidential campaign of 1932 we had in our home a darling little girl, three years old. My husband & I were great admirers of the Dem. candidate and so Dolores had to listen to much talk about the great man who we hoped and prayed would be our next Pres. We are Lutherans and she is Catholic so you'll get quite a thrill out of what I'm to tell you now. That fall Judge Karel of Mil. sent me a fine picture of our beloved President, which I placed in our Public Library. When I received this fine picture my dear mother (who has since been called Home) said to Dolores "Who is this man?" and Dolores answered without any hesitation "Why who else, but Saint Roosevelt!" The old saying goes fools and children often tell the truth and indeed we all feel if there ever was a Saint. He is one. As long as Pres. Roosevelt will be our leader under Jesus Christ we feel no fear. His speech this morning showed he feels for the "least of these" I am enclosing a snap shot of the dear little girl who acclaimed our President a Saint and rightly so.

I'm sure Pres. Roosevelt had a great day on Feb. 16, the world day of prayer, when many hearts were lifted in prayer for him all over this great land of ours.

We shall continue to ask our heavenly Father to guide and guard him in his great task as leader of the great American people.

With all good wishes for you and your fine family I am your most sincerely

Mrs. L.K.S.

Nov 25, 1934
Arkansas City, Kansas

Mrs. Eleanor Roosevelt
White House
Washington, D.C.

Dear Madam:

I beg to inform you that I have been reading your writings in the Wichita Beacon and I must say that the whole nation should be enthused over them. I especially

Reprinted from *Down and Out in the Great Depression: Letter from the Forgotten Man*, by Robert S. McElvaine, ed. Copyright © 1983 by The University of North Carolina Press. Used by permission of the publisher.

was carried away with the one on Old Age Pensions. It brought my mind back to the day of the Chicago Convention, when Mr. Roosevelt was nominated for the presidency.

In our little home in Arkansas City, my family and I were sitting around the radio, to hear and we heard you when you flew over from N.Y. and entered the great hall and when he spoke it seems as though some Moses had come to alleviated us of our sufferings. Strange to say when he was speaking to see the moisten eyes and the deep feeling of emotions that gave vent to his every word and when you spoke then we knew that the white house would be filled with a real mother to the nation.

I am . . . glad to say . . . you have not failed us, you have visited the slums, the farms and homes of your people, and formed first handed ideas for their benefits. Oh what a blessing while you have always had a silver spoon in your own mouth you have not failed to try and place one in every mouth in the land and when I read in the Beacon your brilliant ideas of the Old Age Pensions. You said the only thing laking [sic] was the way to do it. So I said the first lady is seeking a way to help us and so let us help her to find it. . . .

Dear Madam, I am afraid to write more to you at this time as this is my first letter to the lady of the land as the others did not seem to be interested in the welfare of the people. Wife and I pray continually to God for your success. Every time the news boy hollers Extra our hearts are filled with fear that something has happened to the president, but as we go marching on to higher hills of prosperity through the new deal we are hoping and working to that point that all will be well. But one thing I was just about to forget I think that the home building program should be furnished means for back taxes included for repairs and etc. As many places are handicapped to get loans from government on account of being back taxes. Our heart in hand is ever with you and the Pres. to carry on.

Respectfuly Yours,
P.F.A. [male]

[Columbus, Ga.
October 24, 1934]

[Dear President Roosevelt:][1]

I hope you can spare the time for a few words from a cotton mill family, out of work and almost out of heart and in just a short while out of a house in which to live. you know of course that the realators are putting the people out when they cannot pay the rent promptly. and how are we to pay the rent so long as the mills refuse us work, merely because we had the nerve to ask or "demand," better working conditions.[2]

---

[1] Misspellings are part of the original letter—ED.

[2] This is a reference to the unsuccessful 1934 textile workers' strike—ED.

I realize and appreciate the aid and food which the government is giving to the poor people out of work Thanks to you.

but is it even partly right for us to be thrown out of our homes, when we have no chance whatever of paying, so long as the big corporations refuse of work. I for one am very disheartened and disappointed guess my notice to move will come next.

what are we to do. wont you try to help us wont you appeal, "for us all," to the real estate people and the factories

hoping you'll excuse this, but I've always thought of F.D.R. as my personal friend.

C.L.F. [male]

[Akron, Ohio
February 1936]

My Dear Mrs Roosevelt.[3]

I thought I would write a letter hoping you would find time to read it, and if you thought it was worth while answering it, I would be glad of any advise you would care to give me. A few weeks ago, I heard your talk over the air, on the subject of the Old age pension, and I got to thinking what a blessing it would be to my mother, if it was possible for her to receive that pension, if the bill should pass. My mother has been in this country since April 1914 but she has never made herself a American Citizen, as she was sixty years old when she came here, and now she is eighty.

Mother come out to this country nineteen years ago [from Scotland][4] *. . . .*

I thought as long as I lived there was no need to worry about her being taken care of, but I never dreamed of a depression like we have had well it has changed the whole course of our lives we have suffered, and no one knowes but our own family, I have two children one nineteen, graduated from high school last June, and the girl graduates this coming June, and we have had the awfullest time trying to get the bare necessary things in life.

I am in no position to do the right thing for mother, I cant give her anything but her living but I thought if it was possible for her to get that pension it would be like a gift from heaven, as in all the years she has been in this country she has never had a dollar of her own.

I wish she could get it her days may not be long on this earth, and if she just had a little money coming once in a while, to make her feel independent of her family, I at least would know that if anything happened to me she could get a living, and not have to go back to the rest of her family, because she says she would rather go to a poor house, than live with any of the others.

---

[3] Misspellings are part of the original letter—ED.

[4] Eighteen years ago—ED.

Mrs Roosevelt you might think I have lots of nerve writing to you when you have so much to attend to but I could not help admiring you for the splended way you talked about the old people of this nation I feel sorry for all of them, they seem to be forgotten, and most young people think they have had there day and should be glad to die. but this is not my idea, I think that their last few years should be made as plesent for them as it is possible, I know that if it was in my power to make my mother happy by giving her what she justly deservs, I would gladly do so. Well whither my mother ever gets anything or not, I hope all the other old people that is intilted to it gets it soon, because there is nothing sadder than old people who have struggled hard all there lives to give there family a start in life, then to be forgotten, when they them self need it most.

I will finish now but befor I do I want to thank you Mrs Roosevelt and also Mr Roosevelt for the good both of you are doing for this country you have gave people new hope and every real American has faith in you and may you both be spared to carry on the good work and lead this nation on to victory.

Yours Respectfully,
Mrs J. S.
Akron, Ohio.

9.3   ATTACK FROM THE RIGHT (1928)

Herbert Hoover agreed with conventional views that government involvement in economic matters should be kept at a minimal level. Despite experimenting with some innovative measures like McNary-Haugenism in agriculture, Hoover for the most part adhered to laissez-faire economic policies. After being defeated in the election of 1932, he remained an outspoken critic of the New Deal and staunchly defended his own policies while president. The following selection echoes themes that Hoover referred to repeatedly in his condemnation of government "socialism."

GOVERNMENT MUST NOT LIMIT FREE ENTERPRISE

Herbert Hoover

. . . The first responsibility of the Republican administration was to renew the march of progress from its collapse by the war. That task involved the restoration of confidence in the future and the liberation and stimulation of the constructive energies of our people. It discharged that task. There is not a person within the sound of my voice who does not know the profound progress which our country has made in this period. Every man and woman knows that American comfort, hope, and confidence for the future are immeasurably higher this day than they were seven and one-half years ago.

Herbert Hoover, Speech in New York City, October 31, 1928. Adapted from *The State Papers and Other Public Writings of Herbert Hoover* (New York: Doubleday, Doran, 1934).

It is not my purpose to enter upon a detailed recital of the great constructive measures of the past seven and one-half years by which this has been brought about. It is sufficient to remind you of the restoration of employment to the millions who walked your streets in idleness; to remind you of the creation of the budget system; the reduction of six billions of national debt which gave the powerful impulse of that vast sum returned to industry and commerce; the four sequent reductions of taxes and thereby the lift to the living of every family; the enactment of adequate protective tariff and immigration laws which have safeguarded our workers and farmers from floods of goods and labor from foreign countries; the creation of credit facilities and many other aids to agriculture; the building up of foreign trade; the care of veterans; the development of aviation, of radio, of our inland waterways, of our highways; the expansion of scientific research, of welfare activities; the making of safer highways; safer mines, better homes; the spread of outdoor recreation; the improvement in public health and the care of children; and a score of other progressive actions. . . .

But in addition to this great record of contributions of the Republican Party to progress, there has been a further fundamental contribution—a contribution underlying and sustaining all the others—and that is the resistance of the Republican Party to every attempt to inject the government into business in competition with its citizens. . . .

There has been revived in this campaign, however, a series of proposals which, if adopted, would be a long step toward the abandonment of our American system and a surrender to the destructive operation of governmental conduct of commercial business. Because the country is faced with difficulty and doubt over certain national problems—that is, prohibition, farm relief, and electrical power—our opponents propose that we must thrust government a long way into the businesses which give rise to these problems. In effect, they abandon the tenets of their own party and turn to state socialism as a solution for the difficulties presented by all three. It is proposed that we shall change from prohibition to the state purchase and sale of liquor. If their agricultural relief program means anything, it means that the government shall directly or indirectly buy and sell and fix prices of agricultural products. And we are to go into the hydro-electric power business. In other words, we are confronted with a huge program of government in business.

There is, therefore, submitted to the American people a question of fundamental principle. That is: shall we depart from the principles of our American political and economic system, upon which we have advanced beyond all the rest of the world, in order to adopt methods based on principles destructive of its very foundations? And I wish to emphasize the seriousness of these proposals. I wish to make my position clear; for this goes to the very roots of American life and progress.

I should like to state to you the effect that this projection of government in business would have upon our system of self-government and our economic system. That effect would reach to the daily life of every man and woman. It would impair the very basis of liberty and freedom not only for those left outside the fold of expanded bureaucracy but for those embraced within it.

Let us first see the effect upon self-government. When the Federal Government undertakes to go into commercial business it must at once set up the organization and administration of that business, and it immediately finds itself in a labyrinth, every alley of which leads to the destruction of self-government.

Commercial business requires a concentration of responsibility. Self-government requires decentralization and many checks and balances to safeguard liberty. Our government to succeed in business would need become in effect a despotism. There at once begins the destruction of self-government.

The first problem of the government about to adventure in commercial business is to determine a method of administration. It must secure leadership and direction. Shall this leadership be chosen by political agencies or shall we make it elective? The hard practical fact is that leadership in business must come through the sheer rise in ability and character. That rise can only take place in the free atmosphere of competition. . . .

9.4 THUNDER FROM THE LEFT (1934)

The New Deal not only offended political conservatives; it also angered many radicals. During the opening years of the Roosevelt administration, no organized group was as hostile to it as the Communist Party of the United States. The following selection is from a 1934 Communist Party pamphlet presenting "a program for U.S. labor" that interprets the New Deal as the enemy of the U.S. working class.

Why did the American Communists compare the New Deal with contemporary fascism? What aspects of the New Deal did they have in mind? What did they mean by fascism? Within a year or two the Communist Party of the United States would do a complete reversal on the Roosevelt administration. Can you guess why? What was the ultimate source of Communist attitudes toward American politics and politicians in these years?

THE COMMUNIST PARTY: THE NEW DEAL MEANS FASCISM AND WAR

Mass Starvation and Misery

. . . Sixteen million workers stand idle outside closed factories, mines, suffering from the lack of the very things they could produce in these industries. The total income of the working class is less than 40 per cent of what it was four years ago. The oppressed Negro masses are suffering new economic attacks, and a rising wave of lynch terror. Large sections of poor and middle farmers are being crushed and driven off their land or reduced to the position of tenants and peons for the bankers and monopolists. Great numbers of the middle class intellectuals, professionals, teachers, and white collar workers have likewise been cast into poverty. Especially hard hit as a result of the crisis is the youth of the working class, farmer and middle class. Millions of working class children are suffering from undernourishment and actual starvation, unable to go to school because of lack of food, clothing and even school facilities, which are everywhere reduced.

New Deal—Program of Fascism and War

. . . The "New Deal" of Roosevelt is the aggressive effort of the bankers and trusts to find a way out of the crisis at the expense of the millions of toilers. Under cover of the most shameless demagogy, Roosevelt and the capitalists carry through drastic attacks upon

---

The Way Out: A Program for American Labor (New York: Workers' Library Publishers, 1934), pp. 33–35.

the living standards of the masses, increased terrorism against the Negro masses, increased political oppression and systematic denial of existing civil rights, and are strengthening the control of the big monopolists over the economic and political life of the country. The "New Deal" is a program of fascization and the most intense preparations for imperialist war. Its class character is especially seen in the policy of the subsidies to the railroads, banks, and insurance companies, accompanied by increased parasitism, corruption, and bureaucratism. The devaluation of the dollar has resulted in a rapid rise of prices of commodities, and the lowering of . . . real wages. The N.R.A. machinery, with its labor boards on the one hand, and the most brutal police and military force on the other, has been used for the purpose of breaking up the workers' struggles and their organizations. Strike struggles, not only those of the independent class unions, against whom the attack has been most vicious, but also the struggles of the workers in the A. F. of L.,[1] have been violently suppressed. Its farm policy has helped to enrich the big farmers and capitalists at the expense of the agricultural workers, the poor and middle farmers.

. . . The right of organization which was so loudly hailed by the social-fascists, which was to be guaranteed by section 7a of the N.R.A., has been used as a new instrument in the hands of the employers for the development of company unions, to block the desire of the workers to organize into real trade unions, independent of the bosses and government. It is an instrument to prop up the boss-controlled A. F. of L. bureaucracy, where the workers cannot be forced into company unions, and a means to divert the fight and organization of the working class away from militant trade unions. The system of codes has been a step in the direction of government control and fascization of the trade unions. The codes fixed minimum wages in the face of inflation and rising prices. The so-called Public Works Program has been used for the building up of the army and navy—an additional important weapon for the whole program of Roosevelt, which is one of preparation for war. All of this proves that the Roosevelt regime is not, as the liberals and Socialist Party leaders claim, a progressive regime, but is a government serving the interests of finance capital and moving toward the fascist suppression of the workers' movement.

Threatening War Danger

. . . The capitalist class is feverishly preparing for war as a way out of the crisis. It has embarked on a naval race with its main imperialist rivals, Great Britain and Japan. The army has been further mechanized, and the world's largest air fleet has been provided for, coast defense has been strengthened, army cantonments throughout the country have been provided; and the C.C.C.[2] has served as a trial mobilization and training ground for a great army, both for imperialist war and for civil war against the workers at home, as openly admitted by Roosevelt's assistant secretary of war, Woodring.

In all the markets of the world, the struggle between Great Britain and the United States grows more acute. The Roosevelt regime, through its inflation, is engaged in a war on British goods and on British currency, in an effort to win world hegemony. The struggle for

---

[1] The American Federation of Labor, a conservative labor group—ED.

[2] The Civilian Conservation Corps, a New Deal program to employ city youths in National Parks and forests under semimilitary control—ED.

hegemony in the Pacific between the United States and Japan daily becomes more marked, with both nations building up their naval armaments in anticipation of war. All the chief imperialist powers are clashing for the lion's share in the dismemberment of China. The imperialist aggressiveness of Roosevelt's policies is shown most clearly in Cuba, in Latin America (Bolivia-Paraguay war), and in the Philippines. Roosevelt's policies are interlocked with the policies of world capitalism, characterized everywhere by the desperate attempt to get out of the crisis at the expense of the masses by means of fascism, war and intervention.

. . . The preparations for war are being carried through especially by Roosevelt under the cover of pacifist and "democratic" demagogy. In this trickery of the masses, Roosevelt has the utmost support of the A. F. of L. bureaucrats, Socialists and liberals. The A. F. of L. bureaucrats carry on the most violent attacks against the Socialist fatherland. They support the preparations for an army and navy on the plea that it gives employment. The Socialists have invested the "New Deal" war and fascist program with the halo of Socialism. Now openly and now covertly, they continue their attacks against the Soviet Union. . . .

The Fascization of the American Government

. . . American capitalism is more and more fascizing its rule. This is particularly being performed by the Roosevelt administration under the cover of the "New Deal." Under the mask of saving the "democratic institutions of the United States, the Roosevelt government and the bourgeoisie are: (a) increasing the violence against the workers, particularly revolutionary workers and Negro masses, against whom they have unleashed a wave of lynch terror; (b) increasing tendencies to suppress and deny the right to strike; (c) establishing labor Arbitration Boards with direct participation of the employers and the bureaucrats, with the object of preventing, suppressing, and disorganizing the struggles of the workers; (d) directly concentrating into the hands of the President almost dictatorial powers, and vesting power, formerly executed by Congress, in direct appointees of the President over matters of most vital concern to millions of toilers; (e) developing a wave of chauvinism and carrying through the whole N.R.A. campaign with the greatest emphasis upon nationalism.

CHAPTER 10

World War II

By 1938, the attention of the Roosevelt administration was shifting rapidly from domestic to foreign concerns. Some scholars claim that this change of focus derived from the impasse over America's economic problems. Unemployment would simply not go away, and FDR and his colleagues, they say, found foreign affairs more congenial and politically rewarding than the intractable Depression. Other scholars feel there is no need to look beyond the growing menace abroad: the rise of the "dictators," especially the leader of Nazi Germany, Adolf Hitler, which truly threatened the world balance of power and the survival of the liberal democracies, including the United States.

In 1938, as tensions grew in Europe, the administration steeled itself for an eventual confrontation with the "aggressors." But the public's attitudes failed to keep in step. Through the 1920s and well into the 1930s, most Americans felt that their country's World War I intervention had been a mistake and rejected any commitment to collective international action to preserve peace. Europe's—and Asia's—concerns were not ours.

The U.S. isolationism of the period between the wars was compounded of many elements: traditional U.S. xenophobia, pacifism, mid-Western Progessivism, and an emotional backlash among ethnic groups humiliated during World War I by repressive superpatriotism. It was reinforced by a seductive intellectual construct. During the 1930s, a rash of scholarly books and a burst of congressional hearings held by the Nye Committee in 1934–1936 blamed U.S. involvement in World War I on the connivance of bankers and munitions manufacturers. The United States, it was argued, had been duped into the war to benefit the "merchants of death." Profits, rather than patriotism, had driven U.S. foreign policy from 1914 to 1917.

Whatever the source of this distancing from foreign concerns, beginning in 1935 Congress enacted a number of Neutrality Acts designed to prevent U.S. entanglement in another great European conflict. These measures prohibited

U.S. loans to belligerents, restricted Americans' travel on belligerent ships, and forbade the export of U.S. arms and munitions to belligerents. In effect, Congress sought to keep the United States from becoming enmeshed in Europe's problems, even if it meant surrendering some of its traditional rights.

But Congress had failed to take account of the deteriorating international environment. In 1932, Japan had seized Manchuria from China and, five years later, began a war to reduce all of the Chinese Republic to colonial status. In Africa, the Italian fascist dictator, Benito Mussolini, attacked Ethiopia, virtually the last of Africa's free nations, and in 1936 annexed it as a colony. Most ominous of all was the aggressive posture of Germany under its brutal dictator, Adolf Hitler.

Hitler had risen to power pledged to undo the Versailles Treaty, rearm Germany, and restore it to its former level of influence. In 1936 he remilitarized the Rhineland border with France; in 1938 he annexed Austria to Germany. He was soon demanding Czech surrender of the Sudeten area, a part of the Czechoslovak Republic inhabited mainly by Germans. Meanwhile, in Germany itself he had destroyed the liberal Weimar Republic and imposed a viciously racist totalitarian regime that reversed a century of democratic progress in Europe.

It was against this background of Japanese, Italian, and German militarism and tyranny that Americans debated their country's role in international affairs. Isolationists remained unconvinced of the need for the United States to intrude into these conflicts. Interventionists believed that America's own vital interests, and indeed its very safety, were involved. In the following selections, you will encounter samples of both the isolationist and interventionist arguments that shaped the intense debate over peace or war during the 1930s and in the months preceding the Japanese attack on Pearl Harbor in December 1941.

U.S. foreign policy and public opinion were transformed by World War II. Intervention led to a bold new internationalism that would reveal itself in global war aims and major global commitments once the Allies began discussing the terms of the peace settlement and postwar order that would follow. The end of the war left the United States the world's undisputed economic, military, and diplomatic leader. In the thought of Franklin Roosevelt during the war years, it is easy to trace America's rise to globalism.

10.1   ISOLATIONISM (1935, 1939)

One of the most prominent of the isolationist spokespersons during the 1930s was the Democratic senator from Missouri, Bennett Champ Clark. A member of the Nye Committee, Clark was an ardent isolationist and opponent of the New Deal. In the following selection, taken from an address he delivered in May 1935, Clark defends the views and policies incorporated into the mid-thirties neutrality legislation.

Clark's attitudes are based on an analysis of how the United States became involved in World War I. Is the analysis valid? Could the United States have avoided war in 1917 if it had not insisted on its rights as a neutral nation? Had the Neutrality Acts passed in the 1930s been retained, would they have kept the United States out of the great new war emerging on the horizon?

Another prominent isolationist leader was the Republican senator from Ohio, Robert Taft, son of the twenty-seventh president of the United States. By early 1939, when Taft delivered the talk excerpted here, the world was already on the verge of war, and Roosevelt had begun to question the wisdom of the neutrality legislation, which, he believed, helped aggressors and penalized their victims. Roosevelt was particularly concerned that applying the U.S. arms embargo would benefit the rebellion of the far right against the Spanish Loyalists then underway, led by General Francisco Franco and supported by fascist Italy and Nazi Germany.

Taft professes not to oppose collective action to stop aggressors, but he rejects unilateral U.S. action. Is his position sincere, or was it a dodge? Did many isolationists favor U.S. cooperation with other nations to prevent international aggression?

THE EXPERIENCE OF THE LAST WAR SHOULD GUIDE US TODAY

Bennett Champ Clark

In the light of experience it is high time that we gave some thought to the hard, practical question of just how we propose to avoid war if it comes again. No one who has made an honest attempt to face the issue will assert that there is any easy answer. No one who has studied the history of our participation in the World War will tell you that there is a simple way out. There is none—no simple panacea, no magic formula. But if we have learned anything at all we know the inevitable and tragic end to a policy of drifting and trusting to luck. We know that however strong is the will of the American people to refrain from mixing in other peoples' quarrels, that will can only be made effective if we have a sound, definite policy from the beginning. No lesson of the last war is more clear than that such a policy cannot be improvised after war breaks out. It must be worked out in advance, before it is too late to apply reason. I say with all possible earnestness that if we want to avoid another war we must begin at once to formulate a policy based upon an understanding of the problem confronting us. . . .

The best way . . . is to examine the forces which are likely to involve us in war. In 1914 we knew very little about those forces. President Wilson issued his proclamation of neutrality and we went on with business as usual, in the happy belief that 3,000 miles of ocean would keep us out of the mess. Our professional diplomats were not much more astute. They assumed that all we had to do to keep out was to observe the rules of international law and insist upon our neutral rights. About 2 weeks after the outbreak of hostilities our State Department issued a public circular on the rights and duties of a neutral in war time. They took the position that "the existence of war between foreign governments does not suspend trade or commerce between this country and those at war." They told American merchants that there was nothing in international law to prevent them from trading with the warring nations. They told munitions makers that they were free to sell their war materials to either or both sides. They took no steps to warn American citizens of the dangers of travel on vessels of the warring nations, even after passenger ships had been sunk without warning. This attitude, strange as it may seem today, was in full accord with the rules of international law as generally understood at that time.

We are wiser today. We know more about war and much more about neutrality. And yet it is remarkable how much we seem to have forgotten. In the course of the Senate investigation of the munitions industry this winter Senator Nye and I have had

28 May 1935, *Congressional Record*, 74th Cong., 1st sess., 8335–38.

occasion to go rather deeply into the activities of our arms merchants and other traders in war material during the early years of the conflict. We have examined again the tortuous record of our diplomatic correspondence. From this survey four broad conclusions stand out:

1. That a policy based on defense of our so-called "neutral rights" led us into serious diplomatic controversy with both the Allies and the Central Powers, and in the end brought us to a point where we were compelled to choose between surrendering those rights or fighting to defend them. In 1917 we chose to fight.
2. The "national honor" and "prestige" of the nation are inevitably involved when American ships are sunk on the high seas—even though the owners of these ships and their cargoes are private citizens seeking to profit from other nations' wars. Passions are quickly aroused when American lives are lost—even though the citizens who took passage on belligerent ships knew in advance the risks they ran.
3. That the economic forces, set in motion by our huge war trade with the Allies, made it impossible to maintain that "true spirit of neutrality" which President Wilson urged upon his fellow citizens at the outbreak of the conflict.
4. That among these economic forces, those which involved us most deeply were the huge trade in arms and ammunition and other war materials with the Allies.

LET US RETAIN THE NEUTRALITY ACTS

Robert Taft

On January fourth [1939] the President of the United States devoted his annual message to Congress to an appeal for increased armament. He pictured a world about to be enveloped in the flames of war, and he pictured the United States as surrounded by deadly armaments and threats of new aggression. He appealed for increased appropriations for adequate defense. His message was followed several days later by a program calling for approximately $525,000,000, of which only $200,000,000 is to be spent in the fiscal year which ends July 1, 1940.

There can be no difference of opinion among Americans on the principle of providing for this country a completely adequate defense against attack by foreign nations. . . .

But the message of the President suggests that he favors a foreign policy very different from mere defense of the United States, and one which in the end would require much greater armament. A year ago, in Chicago, he declared his belief that we should "quarantine the aggressor nations." Now he says that "The defense of religion, of democracy and of good faith among nations is all the same fight. To save one, we must make up our minds to save all." It is somewhat difficult to see how we can save democracy and good faith among nations by any policy of mere defense of the United States. The President says that we cannot safely be indifferent to international lawlessness anywhere in the world, and cannot let pass, without effective protest, acts of

Robert Taft, *Vital Speeches* (February 1, 1939). (Mt. Pleasant, SC: South Carolina City News Publishing), vol. 5, pp. 254–56.

aggression against sister nations. It is true that he assumes that the American people are not willing to go to war in other parts of the world, but he says, "There are many methods short of war, but stronger and more effective than mere words, of bringing home to aggressor government the aggregate sentiments of our own people." He declares against neutrality legislation and implies that he favors the repeal of the neutrality law. All this cannot mean anything except that the President wishes power granted to him by Congress to favor one nation or another in any dispute that arises, and to employ economic sanction or embargoes against a nation that he does not like at the same time that he assists those he does like. . . .

In my opinion, such a policy leads inevitably to foreign war. It is contrary to the traditional policy of the United States from the days of George Washington. The position of this country has always been that it would remain neutral in any foreign war, no matter how much its sympathies might be on one side, as long as its own rights or those of its citizens were not infringed upon. This is a policy which was emphatically reaffirmed by the American people in 1920 when it was proposed that we join the League of Nations.

There is something to be said in favor of a general agreement for collective security by which a number of nations, sufficiently strong to dominate the world, undertake to prevent aggression even though it leads to war. There is a reasonable chance that such a policy must succeed. Our people, however, refused in 1920 to adopt it, and the efforts made under the League of Nations, without our cooperation, have now completely broken down. But the policy of the President . . . is not the policy of a League of Nations; it is completely original. No one has ever suggested before that a single nation should range over the world like a knight-errant, protecting democracy and ideals of good faith, and tilting, like Don Quixote, against the windmills of Fascism. . . .

Of course, such a policy is not only vain, but almost inevitably leads to war. If we enforce an effective embargo against Japan, driving its people to starvation . . . it would be only natural for Japan to attack the Philippines, and our whole standing and prestige would become involved in an Asiatic war. If the Spanish embargo is lifted and an American ship carrying munitions is sunk by an Italian cruiser as it approaches Barcelona, it is hard to see how we could avoid controversy with Italy, which might flame into a general war. We apparently are asked to line up with England and France, and probably Communist Russia, without even knowing what their policies may be or whether they will back up the stand that we may take. . . .

Congress was wise in adopting the neutrality bill, which prohibits the shipment of arms, ammunition, and implements of war to belligerent states, and to states where civil strife exists. I believe the President should long ago have found a state of war to exist between China and Japan, which he had full power to do, so that munitions might not be shipped to Japan. The neutrality bill intends that we shall not manufacture munitions for foreign wars. It provides further that in case of war, nations must come to this country and pay for all articles, other than munitions, to be shipped abroad before they are shipped. Its purpose is to reduce the chances of our becoming involved, and I believe it will assist very much the accomplishment of that purpose. It is in accord in spirit with the whole policy of American neutrality for 150 years.

But now it is suggested that the whole world is different. It is said that distances are so short we cannot possibly avoid being involved in a general war. I don't believe it. I think if we are sufficiently determined not to become involved, we can stay out. We learned our lesson in 1917. We learned that modern war defeats its own purposes.

A war to preserve democracy resulted in the destruction of more democracies than it preserved. We may go in on the side of France and England because they are democracies, and find before we are through that they are Communist or Fascist.

Not only that, a war whether to preserve democracy or otherwise would almost certainly destroy democracy in the United States. We have moved far towards totalitarian government already. The additional powers sought by the President in case of war, the nationalization of all industry and all capital and all labor, already proposed in a bill before Congress, would create a socialist dictatorship which it would be impossible to dissolve when the war ended. . . .

There is a general illusion that we see in Germany and Italy forces which threaten to overwhelm England and France, and march on to attack the United States. But this is surely an imaginary fear at the present time. There is no reason to believe that Germany and Italy could defeat England and France in any protracted war. It is hard to see what they would gain even after a successful war by an attack on the United States. Certainly the strength of our position would make any nation hesitate, no matter how strong it might be.

It is natural that the sympathy of the people should be strongly aroused on one side when they see what is going on under the totalitarian governments. Perhaps the President should tell them what we think of them, especially as the day seems to have passed when nations go to war because others call them unpleasant names. But the great majority of the people are determined that those sympathies do not lead us into overt acts of embargo, blockade, or economic sanctions.

Considering the attitude which the President has taken, it seems essential that Congress shall strengthen the neutrality bill rather than repeal it. It seems essential that the President shall not have discretion to take sides in foreign wars, or impose sanctions against those nations which he might find to be aggressor nations. It seems wise not to repeal the Johnson Act, as it is now being suggested, and to maintain a policy of lending as little money as possible abroad. Congress is the body upon whom is conferred by the Constitution power to declare war. It should not permit the executive to go too far towards war, without consulting Congress, that Congress no longer has the power to prevent war.

I do not say that some special situation may not arise in the future, under which it may seem desirable to go to war as the first step in an effective defense. But if such a situation ever arises, it should be undertaken deliberately, after a public discussion by Congress as the representatives chosen by the people.

Many justifiable criticisms can be made of the neutrality act, and of any special type of neutrality. But the horrors of modern war are so great, its futility is so evident, its effect on democracy itself so destructive, that almost any alternative is more to be desired.

10.2 INTERVENTIONISTS (1936)

Not every American endorsed the prevailing isolationist mood of the 1930s. One dissenter was Henry L. Stimson, secretary of state under Herbert Hoover and later, following a long absence from public life, secretary of war under Roosevelt.

Stimson was the quintessential "eastern establishment" figure, a man from an affluent old family with an elite education. As secretary of state he had condemned Japanese aggression against China and, as the 1930s advanced, foresaw increasing danger for the United States in a chaotic world. Stimson delivered the following radio talk in October 1935, after the Italian attack on Ethiopia.

What is the basis for Stimson's desire that the United States cooperate with the League of Nations to stop Mussolini? Did the United States accept League of Nations sanctions against Italy? Did the sanctions work?

REPEAL THE ARMS EMBARGO

Henry L. Stimson

In discussing the dangers and problems which confront us arising out of the war in Ethiopia, we start from the common ground that we all wish to keep our country out of war. The only differences of opinion between us are as to the methods which will serve to accomplish this common end and will avoid the danger to America of being ultimately embroiled in what is taking place on the other side of the world. The basic difficulty lies in the fact that the modern world has become interconnected and economically interdependent.

A great war anywhere in the world today will seriously affect all the nations, whether they go into that war or not. We have already been given a terrific lesson on this in the great war, but unfortunately in this country we have not all of us learned that lesson. Many of us are accustomed to say that in this great depression we are now suffering from the results of having gone into that war. This is not entirely true. We are really suffering principally from things which happened in that war long before we joined it. For three years we kept out. It was during those three years that the principal economic dislocations took place which have resulted in America's sufferings now.

When in 1914 the European farmers stopped farming and the European manufacturers, traders and laborers left manufacturing and commerce, and all of them concentrated on fighting, the dislocation was begun which has since resulted in the great depression. Our farmers began to plow up new marginal lands in Kansas and other places to take advantage of the high wheat prices which were thus offered; and our manufacturers and traders similarly enlarged their factories and facilities to seek the rich rewards in commerce which were thus thrown at their feet. Out of these dislocations came the foundation for our present trouble. We would have been suffering from them even if we had never entered the war.

From these patent facts we should have learned thoroughly that a war anywhere is dangerous and that a great war will ultimately make us suffer whether we go in or not. We should have learned that the chief problem of the world today is war prevention, not isolation; and that isolation in the modern world is a fantastic impossibility, so far as keeping out of economic trouble is concerned. Most of the other nations of the world have learned this lesson. They have learned that the only method of saving us from war's consequences is for all the nations of the world to cooperate to prevent war from starting. If it starts it must be at once stamped out before it spreads.

Congressional Digest, vol. 15 (January 1936), pp. 25–27.

The League of Nations is the machinery which these other nations have adopted to secure such cooperation. No one questions the great difficulty of successfully securing cooperative action among the nations of the world, and the work of the League during the last fifteen years has met with much discouragement and opposition. Nevertheless, during those years they have been making progress and have achieved successes which we in this country have never fully appreciated. This autumn the League in its treatment of the war crisis between Italy and Ethiopia has taken more vigorous action and accomplished more signal results than ever before in its history. . . .

These nations of the League are now working upon the steps which shall be taken to stamp out this dangerous conflagration. They have pointed out to Premier [Benito] Mussolini the covenants of the League which he is breaking and have called upon him to stop, and he has thus far defied them and is pushing ahead. Without resorting to arms, they are seeking to hold him back by cutting off their trade with him and thus gradually depriving him of the necessary supplies for his expensive adventure. This is a most delicate undertaking, for it involves the stoppage of normal channels of trade between Italy and many other countries. The process may last a long time and lead to complications which no one can now foresee. Over fifty nations, however, have determined that it must be done. They feel that it is the last recourse left them for preventing a war which may spread to all the rest of the world.

In the face of this situation the conduct of our own government is prescribed by the terms of the joint resolution adopted by our Congress on the 31st of August last [1930], which directs the imposition of an embargo upon the export of "arms, ammunition or implements of war" from this country to either Italy or Ethiopia. Under this law the President on October 5 issued a proclamation containing a list of the commodities which are thus prohibited from export. This list covers only the actually completed articles which constitute arms, ammunition and other engines of warfare. It does not cover the raw materials out of which such arms are manufactured, nor does it cover food and other supplies which are just as necessary as arms to an army in the field. It does not cover copper which goes into shells, or cotton or nitrates which go into powder, or oil which goes into transport.

The evident purpose of our Congress in enacting this resolution was similar to that of the fifty nations who are now taking action against Italy at Geneva—namely, to check the progress of the war by cutting off supplies. But the joint resolution as interpreted in the President's proclamation is likely to do more harm than good. It will have very little deterrent effect upon Italy, who is the aggressor and who is able to manufacture her own arms and ammunition, and it is already threatening to be a serious obstacle to the peace efforts of the other nations. If they take no further action than we have taken, the prospect of stamping out the war by holding back the aggressor, Italy, is much diminished. On the other hand, if they put embargoes on these other supplies which are not on our list, the only effect may be to leave the field entirely open for American traders to rush in and take advantage of the enticing market which is thus presented for selling supplies to Italy. That would produce a very serious danger of ultimate trouble between us and the nations which are doing their best to stamp out this war. . . .

On the same day when [President Roosevelt] proclaimed his embargo on arms, ammunition and implements of war, he took a further step. He uttered a further warning in these words:

"In these specific circumstances I desire to be understood that any of our people who voluntarily engage in transactions *of any character* with either of the belligerents do so at their own risk."

By these words he virtually urged our people to cut off all relations with Italy and Ethiopia and to impose a voluntary boycott upon all transactions with them. If this was rendered necessary on account of the limitations of his Congressional authority, I think it was an act of wise leadership on the part of Mr. Roosevelt, taken to avoid future serious complications, and should be commended.

But in order to make this step effective I think eventually he will have to say more. The American President is the natural leader of the public opinion of his people in all matters of foreign relations, particularly in time of war. They look to him for their information and for their guidance. In this pending crisis not a word has yet been said by our government to indicate to our people the impelling moral reason why they should voluntarily make the sacrifices involved in this warning of the President. Not a word has been said to indicate that there is any moral difference between Italy, which has begun this war, and the other nations which are trying to stop it. Not a word has been uttered to point out that Italy has violated solemn covenants and treaties and that those other nations are endeavoring to uphold these treaties; not a word to recall to our people the promises which Italy made to us in the Pact of Paris in respect to renouncing war, promises which, according to the President's own proclamation of October 5, must have been violated.

In short, nothing has yet been said to rouse in our people any feeling that a moral issue is involved in the present crisis which should impel all patriotic men and women to follow the President's advice and to refrain from embarking on the tempting trade with Italy which the Congressional embargo has left open to them. They have not even been advised of the tremendous moral implications represented by the fact that over fifty nations of the world, with all their national differences and interests have been able to unite in a verdict against the nation which is now seeking our assistance to get supplies for an aggressive war. . . .

The public opinion of America is not indifferent to moral issues. The great masses of our countrymen do not wish to drift into a position of blocking the efforts of other nations to stamp out war. The only person who can effectively rouse and marshal moral opinion is the President of the United States, and when he tries to do so I have no doubt of his eventual success.

10.3   AMERICA FIRST VERSUS AID TO BRITAIN (1940, 1941)

America's sense of security plummeted dramatically in September 1939, when Hitler invaded Germany's neighbor, Poland. Within hours Britain and France, pledged to defend Poland, declared war on Germany. Poland quickly collapsed under the awesome blows of the Nazi Wehrmacht, and then, in the spring and summer of 1940, the powerful German army attacked Denmark, Norway, Belgium, Holland, and France. In a few weeks of blitzkrieg, the Nazi war machine had smashed all the Western armies arrayed against it.

By the end of 1940 Britain alone of Hitler's enemies held out, protected for the moment by its island position. But few believed Britain could stop the Nazi juggernaut. Meanwhile, in Nazi-occupied Europe a regime of unexampled savagery was being imposed on the helpless conquered people. At the same time, in the Far East militaristic Japan was taking advantage of the European colonial powers' preoccupation with Hitler to expand its empire in China and Southeast Asia.

The startling success of the aggressors, loosely organized as the Rome-Berlin-Tokyo Axis, dismayed most Americans. But public opinion split over how best to confront the international danger. Isolationists believed that the United States should continue to stay aloof from the Old World's wars while arming itself against any possible attack. In September 1940 they organized America First, headed by a prominent group of businesspeople, politicians, and civic leaders. The interventionists had their own organization, the Committee to Defend America by Aiding the Allies. Led by William Allen White, the Progressive Republican editor from Kansas, the committee sought to rally Americans to support the cause of faltering Britain and the surviving enemies of the Axis powers.

Many of the interventionists were, at heart, convinced that nothing short of full military involvement on Britain's side could protect America's vital interests. But the committee's public focus was on the repeal of the neutrality measures so that the United States could freely supply the anti-Axis forces with the guns, ships, tanks, and planes they needed to survive. The interventionists also sought, even more aggressively than their opponents, to build up America's own military power.

In the first selection that follows, interventionist James B. Conant, president of Harvard University, expresses his views in a radio address in late May 1940. Conant's words were delivered just as Belgium surrendered to the Germans and as the defeated British forces in France gathered at the French port of Dunkirk for escape across the English Channel from the advancing Nazi army.

How does Conant seek to arouse U.S. support for Britain? Is he trying to disguise the risk that the United States might be compelled to go to war? Are his arguments about the Nazis' designs on the United States correct? Was Hitler interested in conquering the United States? Could he have done so given the breadth of the Atlantic Ocean? Would a Nazi-dominated Europe have threatened the United States in any way?

The second selection is from a speech made by isolationist Senator Burton K. Wheeler of Montana in 1941. Like a number of other isolationists, Wheeler was a liberal from the American heartland who disliked Europe and its age-old quarrels. Here he is speaking in opposition to Roosevelt's recent proposal that Congress enact a measure allowing the president to lease vital arms and supplies to Britain for future repayment.

"Lend-lease," as this policy was known, was a late step in the dismantling of the neutrality legislation of the 1930s. At the end of 1939 Congress had repealed the arms embargo provision of the Neutrality Acts and replaced it with "cash and carry." But that was before the fall of France and the Dunkirk evacuation. Now Britain was running out of cash to pay for vital U.S. supplies, and loans seemed the only way to guarantee it could fight on. In mid-December 1940, the president proposed that the United States "lend" or "lease" military equipment to Hitler's only remaining enemy with payment for the portion not returned after use to be postponed until after the war.[1]

Wheeler attacks the president's proposal on several grounds. What are these? To what American emotions and views is Wheeler playing?

---

[1] The proposal was specious: The United States could not conceivably be interested in any used guns, tanks, and airplanes that might be returned after the war. Roosevelt was actually proposing nothing less than that the United States supply Britain with arms for free.

WE MUST AID THE ALLIES

James B. Conant

There is no need for me to dwell on the agonizing news of the last few days. Tonight the Germans stand on the shores of the English Channel and along the Somme. Tomorrow looms before us like a menacing question-mark. A total victory for German arms is now well within the range of possibility. . . .

Let me ask you to visualize our future as a democratic free people in a world dominated by ruthless totalitarian states. There are those who argue that Hitler's war machine, when its task is done in Europe, will be converted to an instrument of peaceful industrial activity. I do not think so. There are those who imagine that a government which has broken promise after promise, which has scorned the democratic countries and all they stand for, which mocks and laughs at free institutions as a basis for civilization,—that such a government can live in a peaceful relationship with the United States. I do not think so.

To my mind a complete Nazi victory over France and England would be, by necessity, but a prelude to Hitler's attempt to dominate the world. If Germany were triumphant, at best there would result an armed truce. This country would be feverishly endeavoring to put itself into an impregnable position based on a highly militarized society. Our way of life would be endangered for years to come. If this be so, what should we do in these desperate, tragic hours?

We must rearm at once, that much is clear. The vision rises before us of the United States suddenly left alone and unprotected in a totalitarian and destructive world. It is obvious we are unprepared to meet an emergency of this nature. It is also obvious that our first aim must be to prepare with all rapidity. England's failure to listen to Winston Churchill, warning of approaching danger, is responsible for her plight. We must not make the same mistake. We are all agreed on that. . . .

My purpose tonight is to urge another course of action equally important. I am advocating immediate aid to the Allies. I shall mince no words. *I believe the United States should take every action possible to insure the defeat of Hitler.* And let us face honestly the possible implications of such a policy. The actions we propose might eventuate in war. But fear of war is no basis for a national policy. In a free state public opinion must guide the Government, and a wise public opinion on matters of foreign policy can result only if there is a continuous, clear-headed, realistic discussion of all eventualities, including war.

At this moment, the entry of the United States into the war certainly does not seem necessary or wise. . . .

What are then the actions that can be taken at once?

Let us state a few of them: first, the release to France and England of army and navy airplanes and other implements of war, without impairing our own security; second, repeal of the laws which prevent United States citizens from volunteering to serve in foreign armies; third, control of exports with the purpose of aiding the Allies by avoiding leaks to Germany and giving priority to France and England; four, the cooperation of our Maritime Commission with the Allies in every way possible under our present laws to expedite the sending of supplies and munitions. These steps, if

Congressional Record, 76th Cong., 3rd sess., Appendix, 3669–70.

promptly taken by our Government, would render effective aid which some experts believe might tip the scales in favor of an Allied victory. Furthermore, they would be of infinite value in strengthening the morale of the Allied nations and would serve notice to the world that our resources were now enlisted in the democratic cause.

I have purposely avoided the use of the words "moral issues." The younger generation in particular is highly suspicious of this phrase. Their feeling is chiefly due to a widespread misinterpretation of the reasons for America's participation in the war in 1914–1918. I have avoided this issue, not because I sympathize with those who proclaim that there is no fundamental difference between the actions and aims of the democracies on the one hand and the totalitarian powers on the other. Far from it. There is to my mind all the difference between piracy and peaceful trade, all the difference between ruthless tyranny and enlightened intercourse among free men.

But I am endeavoring to confine my argument this evening to a realistic appraisal of our foreign policy. Let me make this clear. I advocate no moral crusade to distant lands. If crusading were a proper policy, we should have had more than one provocation for war in the last dozen years. I am arguing that the changed military situation in Europe actually threatens our way of life.

At this moment, today, the war is in effect veering towards our shores. The issue before the United States is, I repeat, can we live as a free, peaceful, relatively unarmed people in a world dominated by the totalitarian states? Specifically, can we look with indifference as a nation (as a nation, mind you, not as individuals) on the possible subjugation of England by a Nazi State? If your answer is yes, then my words are in vain. If your answer is no, I urge you as a citizen to act.

Write or telegraph to the President of the United States, to your Congressman and your Senators, stating your belief that this nation must give immediate, effective aid to the Allies. Let your elected agents of Government have your thoughts. Urge that Congress stay in session to consider emergency legislation as may be necessary, and speed the process of rearmament.

Above all else, let us consider the situation boldly. This is no time for defeatism or despair. The Allies may be expected to hold out if they have help from us and the promise of further help to come. The wrath of moral indignation is impotent in days like these. A struggle to the death is once again in progress on the fields of western Europe. The British Isles are making ready to stand a siege. . . . It is not too late but it is long past time to act. I urge you, let your voice be heard!

LEND-LEASE WILL LEAD TO WAR

Burton K. Wheeler

The lend-lease policy, translated into legislative form, stunned a Congress and a nation wholly sympathetic to the cause of Great Britain. The Kaiser's blank check to Austria-Hungary in the first World War[1] was a piker compared to the Roosevelt blank

---

Congressional Record, 77th Cong., 1st sess., Appendix, 178–79.

[1] Supposedly the German kaiser had promised to aid Austria-Hungary if war ensued from its 1914 ultimatum to Serbia—ED.

check of World War II. It warranted my worst fears for the future of America, and it definitely stamps the President as war-minded.

The lend-lease-give program is the New Deal's triple A foreign policy; it will plow under every fourth American boy.[2]

Never before have the American people been asked or compelled to give so bounteously and so completely of their tax dollars to any foreign nation. Never before has the Congress of the United States been asked by any President to violate international law. Never before has this Nation resorted to duplicity in the conduct of its foreign affairs. Never before has the United States given to one man the power to strip this Nation of its defenses. Never before has a Congress coldly and flatly been asked to abdicate.

If the American people want a dictatorship—if they want a totalitarian form of government and if they want war—this bill should be steam-rollered through Congress, as is the wont of President Roosevelt.

Approval of this legislation means war, open and complete warfare. I, therefore, ask the American people before they supinely accept it, Was the last World War worth while?

If it were, then we should lend and lease war materials. If it were, then we should lend and lease American boys. President Roosevelt has said we would be repaid by England. We will be. We will be repaid, just as England repaid her war debts of the first World War—repaid those dollars wrung from the sweat of labor and the toil of farmers with cries of "Uncle Shylock." Our boys will be returned—returned in caskets, maybe; returned with bodies maimed; returned with minds warped and twisted by sights of horrors and the scream and shriek of high-powered shells.

Considered on its merits and stripped of its emotional appeal to our sympathies, the lend-lease-give bill is both ruinous and ridiculous. Why should we Americans pay for war materials for Great Britain who still has $7,000,000,000 in credit or collateral in the United States? Thus far England has fully maintained rather than depleted her credits in the United States. The cost of the lend-lease-give program is high in terms of American tax dollars, but it is even higher in terms of our national defense. Now it gives to the President the unlimited power to completely strip our air forces of its every bomber, of its every fighting plane.

It gives to one man—responsible to no one—the power to denude our shores of every warship. It gives to one individual the dictatorial power to strip the American Army of our every tank, cannon, rifle, or antiaircraft gun. No one would deny that the lend-lease-give bill contains provisions that would enable one man to render the United States defenseless, but they will tell you, "The President would never do it." To this I say, "Why does he ask the power if he does not intend to use it?" Why not, I say, place some check on American donations to a foreign nation?

Is it possible that the farmers of America are willing to sell their birthright for a mess of pottage?

---

[2] A reference to the policy set by the Agricultural Adjustment Administration (AAA) in 1933 of destroying crops to raise farm prices—ED.

Is it possible that American labor is to be sold down the river in return for a place upon the Defense Commission, or because your labor leaders are entertained at pink teas?

Is it possible that the American people are so gullible that they will permit their representatives in Congress to sit supinely by while an American President demands totalitarian powers—in the name of saving democracy?

I say in the kind of language used by the President—shame on those who ask the powers—and shame on those who would grant them.

You people who oppose war and dictatorship, do not be dismayed because the war-mongers and interventionists control most of the avenues of propaganda, including the motion-picture industry.

Do not be dismayed because Mr. Willkie,[3] of the Commonwealth & Southern, agrees with Mr. Roosevelt. This merely puts all the economic and foreign "royalists" on the side of war.

Remember, the interventionists control the money bags, but you control the votes.

10.4 UNDECLARED WAR (1941)

By mid-1941 Roosevelt was convinced that the United States could not avoid intervening militarily to stop the Axis powers. By defeating the German attempt to destroy the Royal Air Force, Britain had thwarted a cross-Channel Nazi invasion from occupied France, but it was losing the battle of supply against Axis U-boats on the Atlantic and was incapable of striking back effectively against the Germans on the continent. Meanwhile, by this time Japan was reeling in much of Southeast Asia like a large fish. Then, in June, Hitler attacked the Soviet Union, and in a few weeks Nazi columns had plunged deep into the Russian heartland, in the process destroying much of the Soviet army and air force.

In the fall of 1941, with the submarine menace growing more serious by the day, Roosevelt ordered the U.S. navy to help escort lend-lease supplies to Britain and the Soviet Union. U.S. Navy ships and Nazi submarines were soon exchanging fire on the North Atlantic.

In the following selection from a speech of late October 1941, FDR reveals a new tone. Some historians believe that he was preparing the U.S. public for an actual shooting war on the Atlantic as a back door to full U.S. military participation in the anti-Axis struggle. Does Roosevelt seem to be setting things up for war? (It has been said that he also goaded the Japanese into attacking Pearl Harbor by freezing their financial assets in the United States and embargoing scrap iron and petroleum, both vital to Japan.) How convincing are Roosevelt's remarks about a secret map showing Nazi plans for conquest in the Western Hemisphere and his statement about Hitler's scheme to abolish all religion? Are they demagogic claims, playing on the ill-informed fears of the U.S. people? Given the gravity of the Nazi menace, can the president be forgiven some exaggeration? Did the ends justify the means in this instance?

---

[3] Wendell Willkie, the Republican presidential nominee in 1940. He had been president of the Commonwealth and Southern Utility Company—ED.

THE GERMAN MENACE

Franklin Delano Roosevelt

Five months ago tonight I proclaimed to the American people the existence of a state of unlimited emergency. Since then much has happened. Our Army and Navy are temporarily in Iceland in the defense of the Western Hemisphere.

Hitler has attacked shipping in areas close to the Americas in the North and South Atlantic.

Many American-owned ships have been sunk on the high seas. One American destroyer was attacked on September 4. Another destroyer was attacked and hit on October 17. Eleven brave and loyal men of our Navy were killed by the Nazis.

We have wished to avoid shooting. But the shooting has started. And history has recorded who fired the first shot. In the long run, however, all that will matter is who fired the last shot.

America has been attacked. . . .

The purpose of Hitler's attacks was to frighten, frighten the American people off the high seas—to force us to make a trembling retreat. This is not the first time that he has misjudged the American spirit. And today that spirit is . . . aroused.

If our national policy were to be dominated by the fear of shooting, then all of our ships and those of our sister republics would have to be tied up in home harbors. Our Navy would have to remain respectfully, abjectedly, behind any line which Hitler might decree on any ocean as his own dictated version of his own war zone.

Naturally we reject that absurd and insulting suggestion. We reject it because of our own self-interest, because of our own self-respect and because, most of all, of our own good faith. Freedom of the seas is now, as it always has been, the fundamental policy of your government and mine.

Hitler has often protested that his plans for conquest do not extend across the Atlantic Ocean. But his submarines and raiders prove otherwise. And so does the entire design of his new world order.

For example, I have in my possession a secret map made in Germany by Hitler's government, by the planners of the new world order. It is a map of South America and a part of Central America, as Hitler proposes to reorganize it. Today in this area there are fourteen separate countries. But the geographical experts of Berlin have ruthlessly obliterated all existing boundary lines. They have divided South America into five vassal States, bringing the whole continent under their domination. And they have also so arranged it that the territory of one of these new puppet States includes the Republic of Panama and our great life line, the Panama Canal.

That is his plan. It will never go into effect.

And that map, my friends, makes clear the Nazi design, not only against South America but against the United States as well.

And your government has in its possession another document, a document made in Germany by Hitler's government. It is a detailed plan, which, for obvious reasons, the Nazis do not wish to publicize just yet, but which they are ready to impose a little later on a dominated world, if Hitler wins.

New York Times, October 28, 1941.

It is a plan to abolish all existing religions, Catholic, Protestant, Mohammedan, Hindu, Buddhist and Jewish alike. The property of all churches will be seized by the Reich and its puppets. The cross and all other symbols of religion are to be forbidden. The clergy are to be ever liquidated, silenced under penalty of the concentration camps, where even now so many fearless men are being tortured because they have placed God above Hitler.

In the place of the churches of our civilization there is to be set up an international Nazi church, a church which will be served by orators sent out by the Nazi government. And in the place of the Bible, the words of "Mein Kampf"[1] will be imposed and enforced as Holy Writ. And in the place of the cross of Christ will be put two symbols, the swastika and the naked sword.

A god, the god of blood and iron, will take the place of the God of love and mercy. Let us well ponder that statement which I have made tonight.

These grim truths which I have told you of the present and future plans of Hitlerism will of course be hotly denied tonight and tomorrow in the controlled press and radio of the Axis powers. And some Americans, not many, will continue to insist that Hitler's plans need not worry us—that we should not concern ourselves with anything that goes on beyond rifle shot of our own shores.

The protestations of these few American citizens will, as usual, be paraded with applause through the Axis press and radio during the next few days in an effort to convince the world that the majority of Americans are opposed to their duly chosen government, and in reality are only waiting to jump on Hitler's band wagon when it comes this way.

The motive of such Americans is not the point at issue. The fact is that Nazi propaganda continues in desperation to seize upon such isolated statements as proof of American disunity.

The Nazis have made up their own list of modern American heroes. It is, fortunately, a short list and I am glad that it does not contain my name.

And so all of us Americans, of all opinions, in the last analysis are faced with the choice between the kind of world we want to live in and the kind of world which Hitler and his hordes would impose upon us.

None of us wants to burrow under the ground and live in total darkness like a comfortable mole.

The forward march of Hitler and of Hitlerism can be stopped, and it will be stopped.

Very simply and very bluntly—we are pledged to pull our own oar in the destruction of Hitlerism.

And when we have helped to end the curse of Hitlerism, we shall help to establish a new peace which will give to decent people everywhere a better chance to live and prosper in security and in freedom and in faith.

Every day that passes we are producing and providing more and more arms for the men who are fighting on actual battlefronts. That is our primary task.

And it is the nation's will that these vital arms and supplies of all kinds shall neither be locked up in American harbors nor sent to the bottom of the sea. It is the nation's will that America shall deliver the goods. In open defiance of that will, our ships have been sunk and our sailors have been killed.

---

[1] *Mein Kampf* was the title of Hitler's memoirs, an account of his life and ideology and a blueprint for his future career as Germany's ruler—ED.

And I say that we do not propose to take this lying down.

That determination of ours not to take it lying down has been expressed in the orders to the American Navy to shoot on sight. And those orders stand.

Furthermore, the House of Representatives has already voted to amend a part of the Neutrality Act of 1937, today outmoded by force of violent circumstances. And the Senate Committee on Foreign Relations has also recommended the elimination of other hamstringing provisions in that act. That is the course of honesty and of realism.

Our American merchant ships must be armed to defend themselves against the rattlesnakes of the sea.

Our American merchant ships must be free to carry our American goods into the harbors of our friends.

And our American merchant ships must be protected by our American Navy.

In the light of a good many years of personal experience I think that it can be said that it can never be doubted that the goods will be delivered by this nation, whose Navy believes in the tradition of "damn the torpedoes; full steam ahead!"

Yes, our nation will and must speak from every assembly line—yes, from every coal mine, the all-inclusive whole of our vast industrial machine. Our factories and our shipyards are constantly expanding. Our output must be multiplied. . . .

The lines of our essential defense now cover all the seas; and to meet the extraordinary demands of today and tomorrow our Navy grows to unprecedented size. Our Navy is ready for action. . . . Its officers and men need no praise from me.

Our new Army is steadily developing the strength needed to withstand the aggressors. Our soldiers of today are worthy of the proudest traditions of the United States Army. But tradition cannot shoot down dive-bombers or destroy tanks. That is why we must and shall provide for every one of our soldiers equipment and weapons, not merely as good but better than that of any other army on earth. And we are doing that right now.

For this, and all of this, is what we mean by total national defense.

The first objective of that defense is to stop Hitler. He can be stopped and can be compelled to dig in. And that will be the beginning of the end of his downfall, because dictatorship of the Hitler type can live only through continuing victories and increasing conquests.

The facts of 1918 are proof that a mighty German Army and a tired German people can crumble rapidly and go to pieces when they are faced with successful resistance.

Nobody who admires qualities of courage and endurance can fail to be stirred by the full-fledged resistance of the Russian people. The Russians are fighting for their own soil and their own homes. Russia needs a help—planes and tanks, guns and medical supplies and other aids—toward the successful defense against the invaders. From the United States and from Britain she is getting great quantities of these essential supplies. But the needs of her huge army will continue, and our help and British help will also continue.

The other day the Secretary of State of the United States was asked by a Senator to justify our giving aid to Russia. His reply was:

"The answer to that, Senator, depends on how anxious a person is to stop, to destroy the march of Hitler in his conquest of the world. If he were anxious enough to defeat Hitler, he would not worry about who was helping to defeat him."

Upon our American production falls the colossal task of equipping our own armed forces, and helping to supply the British and the Russians and the Chinese. In the performance of that task we dare not fail. And we will not fail.

10.5 A NEW AMERICAN INTERNATIONALISM (1941)

Franklin Roosevelt did not simply believe that the United States could or should play a greater role in world affairs; he believed that the world was changing rapidly, and that if Americans wished to preserve their way of life, they had no choice but to do so. Roosevelt was appalled by the forces of dictatorship and totalitarianism that swept the world into war, and he believed that the United States had a moral responsibility to do what it could to oppose these forces. But he also saw the economic and political consequences of these forces and realized their potential threat to American interests. Roosevelt's outlook became increasingly global as time went on. In his famous "Four Freedoms" speech, what is more apparent, idealism or realpolitik? Can you discern an element of each? Why was the Atlantic Charter so well received? Roosevelt's thinking also set the stage for far grander expectations on the part of the American people regarding foreign affairs. Americans would soon come to see their role and mission in world affairs in a new light. The final selection asserts that many of the rights that Americans cherish at home should be universal in the world of nations.

ROOSEVELT'S "FOUR FREEDOMS" SPEECH, JANUARY 6, 1941

. . . Every realist knows that the democratic way of life is at this moment being directly assailed in every part of the world—assailed either by arms, or by secret spreading of poisonous propaganda by those who seek to destroy unity and promote discord in nations still at peace. During sixteen months this assault has blotted out the whole pattern of democratic life in an appalling number of independent nations, great and small. The assailants are still on the march, threatening other nations, great and small. . . .

As men do not live by bread alone, they do not fight by armaments alone. Those who man our defenses, and those behind them who build our defenses, must have the stamina and courage which come from an unshakable belief in the manner of life which they are defending. The mighty action which they are calling for cannot be based on a disregard of all things worth fighting for.

The Nation takes great satisfaction and much strength from the things which have been done to make its people conscious of their individual stake in the preservation of democratic life in America. Those things have toughened the fibre of our people, have renewed their faith and strengthened their devotion to the institutions we make ready to protect. Certainly this is no time to stop thinking about the social and economic problems which are the root cause of the social revolution which is today a supreme fact in the world.

There is nothing mysterious about the foundations of a healthy and strong democracy. The basic things expected by our people of their political and economic system are simple. They are: equality of opportunity for youth and for others: jobs for those who can work; security for those who need it; the ending of special privilege for the few, the preservation of civil liberties for all; the enjoyment of the fruits of scientific progress in a wider and constantly rising standard of living.

These are the simple and basic things that must never be lost sight of in the turmoil and unbelievable complexity of our modern world. The inner and abiding strength of our economic and political systems is dependent upon the degree to which they fulfill these expectations.

Franklin D. Roosevelt, Annual Message to Congress, January 6, 1941. Quoted from *The Public Papers of F. D. Roosevelt* (Washington, DC: United States Government Printing Office), vol. 9, p. 663.

Many subjects connected with our social economy call for immediate improvement. As examples: We should bring more citizens under the coverage of old age pensions and unemployment insurance. We should widen the opportunities for adequate medical care. We should plan a better system by which persons deserving or needing gainful employment may obtain it.

I have called for personal sacrifice. I am assured of the willingness of almost all Americans to respond to that call. . . .

In the future days, which we seek to make secure, we look forward to a world founded upon four essential human freedoms.

The first is freedom of speech and expression—everywhere in the world.

The second is freedom of every person to worship God in his own way—everywhere in the world.

The third is freedom from want—which, translated into world terms, means economic understandings which will secure to every nation a healthy peace time life for its inhabitants—everywhere in the world.

The fourth is freedom from fear—which, translated into world terms, means a worldwide reduction of armaments to such a point and in such a thorough fashion that no nation will be in a position to commit an act of physical aggression against any neighbor—anywhere in the world.

That is no vision of a distant millennium. It is a definite basis for a kind of world attainable in our own time and generation. That kind of world is the very antithesis of the so-called new order of tyranny which the dictators seek to create with the crash of a bomb.

To that new order we oppose the greater conception—the moral order. A good society is able to face schemes of world domination and foreign revolutions alike without fear.

Since the beginning of our American history we have been engaged in change—in a perpetual peaceful revolution—a revolution which goes on steadily, quietly adjusting itself to changing conditions—without the concentration camp or the quick-lime in the ditch. The world order which we seek is the cooperation of free countries, working together in a friendly, civilized society.

This nation has placed its destiny in the hands and heads and hearts of its millions of free men and women; and its faith in freedom under the guidance of God. Freedom means the supremacy of human rights everywhere. Our support goes to those who struggle to gain those rights or keep them. Our strength is in our unity of purpose.

THE ATLANTIC CHARTER, AUGUST 14, 1941

The President of the United States of America and the Prime Minister, Mr. Churchill, representing His Majesty's Government in the United Kingdom, being met together, deem it right to make known certain common principles in the national policies of their respective countries on which they base their hopes for a better future for the world.

First, their countries seek no aggrandizement, territorial or other;

Second, they desire to see no territorial changes that do not accord with the freely expressed wishes of the peoples concerned;

The Public Papers of F. D. Roosevelt (Washington, DC: United States Government Printing Office), vol. 10, p. 314.

Third, they respect the right of all peoples to choose the form of government under which they will live; and they wish to see sovereign rights and self government restored to those who have been forcibly deprived of them;

Fourth, they will endeavor, with due respect for their existing obligations, to further the enjoyment by all States, great or small, victor or vanquished, of access, on equal terms, to the trade and to the raw materials of the world which are needed for their economic prosperity;

Fifth, they desire to bring about the fullest collaboration between all nations in the economic field with the object of securing, for all, improved labor standards, economic advancement and social security;

Sixth, after the final destruction of the Nazi tyranny, they hope to see established a peace which will afford to all nations the means of dwelling in safety within their own boundaries, and which will afford assurance that all the men in all the lands may live out their lives in freedom from fear and want;

Seventh, such a peace should enable all men to traverse the high seas and oceans without hindrance:

Eighth, they believe that all of the nations of the world, for realistic as well as spiritual reasons must come to the abandonment of the use of force. Since no future peace can be maintained if land, sea or air armaments continue to be employed by nations which threaten, or may threaten, aggression outside of their frontiers, they believe, pending the establishment of a wider and permanent system of general security, that the disarmament of such nations is essential. They will likewise aid and encourage all other practicable measures which will lighten for peace-loving peoples the crushing burden of armaments.

Franklin D. Roosevelt
Winston S. Churchill

UNIVERSAL DECLARATION OF HUMAN RIGHTS

Preamble

Whereas recognition of the inherent dignity and of the equal and inalienable rights of all members of the human family is the foundation of freedom, justice and peace in the world,

Whereas disregard and contempt for human rights have resulted in barbarous acts which have outraged the conscience of mankind, and the advent of a world in which human beings shall enjoy freedom of speech and belief and freedom from fear and want has been proclaimed as the highest aspiration of the common people,

Whereas it is essential, if man is not to be compelled to have recourse, as a last resort, to rebellion against tyranny and oppression, that human rights should be protected by the rule of law,

Whereas it is essential to promote the development of friendly relations between nations,

---

Adopted by the United Nations General Assembly, December 10, 1948.

Whereas the people of the United Nations have in the Charter reaffirmed their faith fundamental human rights, in the dignity and worth of the human person and in the equal rights of men and women and have determined to promote social progress and better standards of life in larger freedom,

Whereas Member States have pledged themselves to achieve, in cooperation with the United Nations, the promotion of universal respect for and observance of human rights and fundamental freedoms,

Whereas a common understanding of these rights and freedoms is of the greatest importance for the full realization of this pledge,

Now, therefore,

The General Assembly,

Proclaims this Universal Declaration of Human Rights as a common standard of achievements for all people and all nations, to the end that every individual and every organ of society, keeping this Declaration constantly in mind, shall strive by teaching and education to promote respect for these rights and freedoms and by progressive measure, national and international, to secure their universal and effective recognition and observance, both among the peoples of Member States themselves and among the peoples of territories under their jurisdiction.

Article 1

All human being are born free and equal in dignity and rights. They are endowed with reason and conscience and should act towards one another in a sprit of brotherhood.

Article 2

Every is entitled to all the rights and freedom set fourth in this Declaration, without distinction of any kind, such as race, color, sex, language, religion, political or other opinion, national or social origin, property, birth or status. Furthermore, no distinction shall be made on the basis of the political, jurisdictional or international status of the country or territory to which a person belongs, whether it be independent, trust, non-self-governing or under any other limitation of sovereignty.

Article 3

Everyone has the right to life, liberty and security of person.

Article 4

No one shall be held in slavery or servitude; slavery and the slave trade shall be prohibited in all their forms.

Article 5

No one shall be subjected to torture or to cruel, in human or degrading treatment or punishment.

Article 6

Everyone has the right to recognition everywhere as a person before the law.

Article 7

All are equal before the law and are entitled without any discrimination to equal protection of the law. All are entitled to equal protection against any discrimination in violation of this Declaration and against any incitement to such discrimination.

Article 8
Everyone has the right to an effective remedy by the competent national tribunals for acts violating the fundamental rights granted him by the constitution or by law.

Article 9
No one shall be subjected to arbitrary arrest, detention or exile.

Article 10
Everyone is entitled in full equality to a fair and public hearing by an independent and impartial tribunal, in determination of his rights and obligations and of any criminal charge against him.

Article 11

1. Everyone charged with a penal offence has the right to be presumed innocent until proved guilty according to law in a public trial at which he has had all the guarantees necessary for his defence.
2. No one shall be held guilty of any penal offence on account of any act or omission which did not constitute a penal offence, under national or international law, at the time when it was committed. Nor shall a heavier penalty be imposed than the one that was applicable at the time the penal offence was committed.

Article 12
No one shall be subjected to arbitrary interference with his privacy, family, home or correspondence, not to attacks upon his honors and reputation. Everyone has the right to the protection of law against such interference or attacks.

Article 13

1. Everyone has the right to freedom of movement and residence within the borders of each State.
2. Everyone has the right to leave any country, including his own, and to return to his country.

Article 14

1. Everyone has the right to seek and to enjoy in other countries asylum from persecution.
2. This right may not be invoked in the case of prosecutions genuinely arising from non-political crimes or from acts contrary to the purpose and principles of the United Nations.

Article 15

1. Everyone has the right to a nationality.
2. No one shall be arbitrarily deprived of his nationality nor denied the right to change his nationality.

Article 16

1. Men and women of full age, without any limitation due to race, nationality or religion, have the right to marry and to found a family. They are entitled to equal rights as to marriage, during marriage and at its dissolution.
2. Marriage shall be entered into only with the free and full consent of the intending spouses.

3. The family is the natural and fundamental group unit of society and is entitled to protection by society and the State.

Article 17

1. Everyone has the right to own property alone as well as in association with others.
2. No one shall be arbitrarily deprived of his property.

Article 18

Everyone has the right to freedom of thought, conscience and religion; this right includes freedom to change his religion or belief, and freedom, either alone or in community with others and in public or private, to manifest his religion or belief in teaching, practice, worship and observance.

Article 19

Everyone has the right to freedom of opinion and expression; this right includes freedom to hold opinions without interference and to seek, receive and impart information and ideas through any media and regardless of frontiers.

Article 20

1. Everyone has the right to freedom of peaceful assembly and association.
2. No one may be compelled to belong to an association.

Article 21

1. Everyone has the right to take part in the government of his country, directly or through freely chosen representatives.
2. Everyone has the right to equal access to public service in his country.
3. The will of the people shall be the basis of the authority of government; this will shall be expressed in periodic and genuine elections which shall be by universal and equal suffrage and shall be held by secret vote or by equivalent free voting procedures.

Article 22

Everyone, as a member of society, has the right to social security and is entitled to realization, through national effort and international co-operation and in accordance with the organization and resources of each State, of the economic, social and cultural right indispensable for his dignity and the free development of his personality.

Article 23

1. Everyone has the right to work, to free choice of employment, to just and favourable conditions of work and to protection against unemployment.
2. Everyone, without any discrimination, has the right to equal pay for equal work.
3. Everyone who works has the right to just and favourable remuneration ensuring for himself and his family an existence worthy of human dignity, and supplemented, if necessary, by other means of social protection.
4. Everyone has the right to form and to join trade unions for the protection of interests.

Article 24

Everyone has the right to rest and leisure, including reasonable limitation of working hours and periodic holidays with pay.

Article 25

1. Everyone has the right to a standard of living adequate for the health and well-being of himself and of his family, including food, clothing, housing and medical care and necessary social services, and the right to security in the event of unemployment, sickness, disability, widowhood, old age or other lack of livelihood in circumstances beyond his control.
2. Motherhood and childhood are entitled to special care and assistance. All children, whether born in or out of wedlock, shall enjoy the same social protection.

Article 26

1. Everyone has the right to education. Education shall be free, at least in the elementary and fundamental stages. Elementary education shall be compulsory. Technical and professional education shall be made generally available and higher education shall be equally accessible to all on the basis of merit.
2. Education shall be directed to the full development of the human personality and to the strengthening of respect for human rights and fundamental freedoms. It shall promote understanding, tolerance and friendship among all nations, racial or religious groups, and shall further the activities of the United Nations for the maintenance of peace.
3. Parents have a prior right to choose the kind of education that shall be given to their children.

Article 27

1. Everyone has the right freely to participate in the cultural life of the community, to enjoy the arts and to share in scientific advancement and its benefits.
2. Everyone has the right to the protection of the moral and materials interests resulting from any scientific, literacy or artistic production of which he is the author.

Article 28
Everyone is entitled to a social and international order in which the rights and freedoms set forth in this Declaration can be fully realized.

Article 29

1. Everyone has duties to the community in which alone the free and full development of his personality is possible.
2. In the exercise of his rights and freedoms. everyone shall be subject only to such limitations as are determined by law solely for the purpose of securing due recognition and respect for the rights and freedoms of others and of meeting the just requirements of morality, public order and the general welfare in a democratic society.
3. These rights and freedoms may in no case be exercised contrary to the purposes and principles of the United Nations.

Article 30
Nothing in this Declaration may be interpreted as implying for any State, group or person any right to engage in any activity or to perform any act aimed at the destruction of any of the rights and freedoms set forth herein.

CHAPTER **11**

The Cold War

The international rivalry of the United States and the Soviet Union was, of course, the ultimate source of McCarthyism. Wartime allies against the Axis powers, America and the USSR became global antagonists after 1945 and remained so for almost half a century. During this period of Cold War, they battled ferociously for ideological, diplomatic, technological, and economic supremacy. Meanwhile, both the superpowers and their allies and satellites engaged in an immense, draining arms race that piled up mountains of weapons of mass destruction. At several points of crisis the world would cower under the threat of nuclear holocaust and the possible extinction of the human race. This disaster never happened, of course, but a number of times, through allies and stand-ins, superpower differences boiled over into costly conventional military confrontations.

Americans have disagreed over the origins of the Cold War. A majority have undoubtedly blamed it on Soviet aggression and the need to check it. A smaller group has seen the United States as primarily at fault: to protect capitalism, they say, America pursued unnecessarily provocative policies. And some have assigned responsibility more evenly than either of these two positions.

Following are documents that focus on early U.S. moves to contain what most Washington policy makers perceived as dangerous and illegitimate Soviet expansionism. These actions set the stage, on the U.S. side, for the long and menacing struggle that has finally subsided only since the end of the 1980s.

11.1 THE SOVIET MENACE, THE TRUMAN DOCTRINE, THE MARSHALL PLAN, AND MASSIVE RETALIATION (1947, 1954)

Wartime British and U.S. suspicions of the Soviet Union did not surface officially until the post-war peace-making process began. Then, after Germany's defeat, the Soviet Union imposed its will and system on the nations along its western borders and began to fish for political advantage

225

in the waters of a troubled and impoverished Western Europe. Whether propelled by legitimate concern for its national security, Stalinist paranoia, or inherent Marxist imperatives, the USSR's actions set off alarm bells in Western capitals.

One man who detected aggressive Soviet designs early on was George Kennan, a scholarly U.S. career diplomat familiar with the USSR from his service at the U.S. embassy in Moscow and from his long study of Russian history. In late 1945, Kennan sent a riveting telegraphic dispatch to the U.S. State Department from Moscow predicting serious difficulties with the Soviet Union in the emerging postwar period. In it he clearly outlined the sources of Soviet foreign policy and recommended an approach—known as containment—for checking Soviet expansion. Containment soon became the guiding principle of U.S. foreign policy and continued to govern America's relations with the Soviet Union until the 1990s.

Intellectual formulations such as George Kennan's were important in shaping U.S. Cold War policy, but actual events were even more compelling. In 1946–1947, the Soviet Union provoked a Western response by a series of moves in the Middle East and the Mediterranean designed to extend Soviet power. It refused at first to remove occupation troops that had been stationed in Iran during World War II. It next put pressure on Turkey to surrender control of the strategic Dardanelles Straits and to allow the USSR to base troops and ships on Turkish soil. It fed arms and money to a Communist-led guerrilla war in Greece against the existing pro-Western government.

Concerned with preserving its communications with India, Britain had been the traditional guarantor of autonomy for Greece and Turkey, but in January 1947 the war-exhausted British told the Americans that they could no longer afford to help them. The signal to the United States was clear: Either the Americans stepped in or the eastern Mediterranean would fall under Soviet domination.

Meanwhile, a more diffuse crisis was developing in Western Europe. There, following Axis defeat, chaos threatened. On the continent war devastation, social disruption, and moral exhaustion, aggravated by the severe winter of 1946–1947, played into the hands of radical political forces that looked to the Soviet Union for leadership. During this grim period millions of Western Europeans lost their faith in capitalism and liberal democratic institutions and joined pro-Soviet Communist parties. If something were not done soon, said democratic leaders in Europe and the United States, the Communists might achieve power through legal parliamentary processes. They would then destroy democracy and impose pro-Soviet authoritarian regimes.

The U.S. response to these crises took the form of the Truman Doctrine and the Marshall Plan. The first was announced on March 12, 1947, when President Harry Truman appeared before a joint session of Congress to request U.S. aid to Greece and Turkey. Truman had come to agree with Winston Churchill that the Soviet Union should be considered a hostile power and a new policy to keep Soviet expansionist tendencies in check needed to be created.

What were the bases for Truman's request for U.S. money for the Greek and Turkish governments? His reasons are couched in idealistic terms. Was it idealism alone that moved Truman? Many scholars consider the speech one of the most important ever made by a president. Why was it so important? What long-established precedents in U.S. foreign policy might Truman be brushing aside?

The Marshall Plan, first announced by Secretary of State George Marshall at the Harvard University commencement in June 1947, sought to check Communist advance by restoring the prosperity of the whole European continent, East as well as West.[1] Eventually

---

[1] In the end the Soviet Union and its satellites refused to accept Marshall Plan aid, considering it an American plot—ED.

Congress appropriated billions of dollars to implement the plan, and, before long, food, equip-
ment, coal, and steel were flowing to Europe in enormous volume.

What are Marshall's avowed motives for American aid? Why does he say that "our policy
is directed not against any country or doctrine"? Was the Soviet Union excluded from Marshall
Plan aid? Do you know what the results of the Marshall Plan were?

"THE IRON CURTAIN"

Winston Churchill

Speech delivered at Western College, Fulton, Missouri, March 5, 1946.

Neither the sure prevention of war nor the continuous rise of world organization
will be gained without what I have called the fraternal association of the English-speaking
peoples. This means a special relationship between the British Commonwealth and
Empire and the United States.

This is no time for generalities. I will venture to be precise. Fraternal association
requires not only the growing friendship and mutual understanding between our two
vast but kindred systems of society but the continuance of the intimate relationships
between our military advisors, leading to common study of potential dangers, similarity of weapons and manuals of instruction, and interchange of officers and cadets at
colleges. It should carry with it the continuance of the present facilities for mutual
security by the joint use of all naval and air force bases in the possession of either country all over the world. This would perhaps double the mobility of the American Navy
and Air Force. It would greatly expand that of the British Empire forces, and it might
well lead, if and as the world calms down, to important financial savings. Already we
use together a large number of islands; many more will be entrusted to our joint care in
the near future.

The United States already has a permanent defense agreement with the Dominion
of Canada, which is so devotedly attached to the British Commonwealth and Empire.
This agreement is more effective than many of those which have often been made under
formal alliances. This principle should be extended to all the British commonwealths
with full reciprocity. Thus, whatever happens, and thus only we shall be secure ourselves and able to work together for the high and simple causes that are dear to us and
bode no ill to any. Eventually these may come the principle of common citizenship, but
that we may be content to leave to destiny, whose outstretched arm so many of us can
clearly see.

There is, however, an important question we must ask ourselves. Would a special
relationship between the United States and the British Commonwealth be inconsistent
with our overriding loyalties to the world organizations? I reply that, on the contrary, it
is probably the only means by which that organization will achieve its full stature and
strength. There are already the special United States relations with Canada and between
the United States and South American republics. We also have our twenty-year treaty of
collaboration and mutual assistance with soviet Russia. I agree with Mr. Bevin that it
might well be a fifty-year treaty. We have an alliance with Portugal unbroken since
1384. None of these clash with the general interest of a world agreement. "In my
father's house are many mansions." Special associations between members of the

United Nations which have no aggressive point against any other country, which harbor no design incompatible with the Charter of the United Nations, far from being harmful, are beneficial and, as I believe, indispensable.

I spoke earlier of the temple of peace. Workmen from all countries must build that temple. If two of the workmen know each other particularly well and are old friends, if their families are intermingled and if they have faith in each other's purpose, hope in each other's future and charity toward each other's shortcomings, to quote some good words I read here the other day, why cannot they work together at common task as friends and partners? Why cannot they share their tools and thus increase each other's working powers? Indeed, they must do so or else the temple may not be built, or, being built, it may collapse, and we shall all be proved unreachable and have to go and try to learn again for a third time, in a school of war, incomparably more rigorous than that from which we have just been released. The Dark Ages may return, the Stone Age may return on the gleaming wings of science, and what might now shower immeasurable material blessings upon mankind may even bring about its total destruction.

Beware, I say; time may be short. Do not let us take the course of letting events drift along till it is too late. If there is to be a fraternal association of the kind I have described, with all the extra strength and security which both our countries can derive from it, let us make sure that that great fact is known to the world, and that it plays its part in steadying and stabilizing the foundations of peace. Prevention is better than cure.

A shadow has fallen upon the scenes so lately lighted by the Allied victory. Nobody knows what Soviet Russia and its Communist international organization intends to do in the immediate future, or what are the limits, if any, to their expansive and proselytizing tendencies, I have a strong admiration and regard for the valiant Russian people and for my wartime comrade Marshal Stalin. There is sympathy and goodwill in Britain—and I doubt not here also—toward the peoples of all the Russias and a resolve to persevere through many differences and rebuffs in establishing lasting friendships.

We understand the Russians need to be secure on her western frontiers from all renewal of German aggression. We welcome her to her rightful place among the leading nations of the world. Above all we welcome constant, frequent, and growing contacts between the Russian people and our own people on both sides of the Atlantic. It is my duty, however, to place before you certain facts about the present position in Europe—I am sure I do not wish to, but it is my duty, I feel, to present them to you.

From Stettin in the Baltic to Trieste in the Adriatic, an iron curtain has descended across the Continent. Behind that line lie all the capitals of the ancient states of central and eastern Europe. Warsaw, Berlin, Prague, Vienna, Budapest, Belgrade, Bucharest, and Sofia, all these famous cities and the populations around them lie in the Soviet sphere and all are subject in one form or another , not only to Soviet influence but to a very high and increasing measure of control from Moscow. Athens alone, with its immortal glories, is free to decide its future at an election under British, American, and French observation. The Russian-dominated Polish government has been encouraged to make enormous and wrongful inroads upon Germany, and mass expulsions of millions of Germans on a scale grievous and undreamed of are now taking place.

The Communist parties, which were very small in all these Eastern states of Europe, have been raised to preeminence and power far beyond their numbers and are seeking everywhere to obtain totalitarian control. Police governments are prevailing in nearly every case, and so far, except in Czechoslovakia, there is no true democracy.

Turkey and Persia are both profoundly alarmed and disturbed at the claims which are made upon them and at the pressure being exerted by the Moscow government. An attempt is being made by the Russians in Berlin to build up a quasi-Communist Party in their zone of occupied Germany by showing special favors to groups of left-wing German leaders.

At the end of the fighting last June, the American and British armies withdrew westward in accordance with an earlier agreement to a depth, at some points, 150 miles on a front of nearly 400 miles to allow the Russians to occupy this vast expanse of territory which the Western democracies had conquered. If now the Soviet government tries, by separate action, to build up a pro-Communist Germany in their areas, this will cause new serious difficulties in the British and American zones and will give the defeated Germans the power of putting themselves up to auction between the Soviets and Western democracies. Whatever conclusions may be drawn from these facts—and facts they are—this is certainly not the liberated Europe we fought to build up. Nor is it one which contains the essentials of permanent peace.

The safety of the world, ladies and gentlemen, requires a new unity in Europe from which no nation should be permanently outcast.

It is impossible not to comprehend—twice we have seen them drawn by irresistible forces in time to secure the victory but only after frightful slaughter and devastation have occurred. Twice the United States has had to send millions of its young men to fight a war, but now war can find any nation between dusk and drawn. Surely we should work within the structure of the United Nations and in accordance with our Charter. That is an open course of policy.

In front of the iron curtain which lies across Europe are other causes for anxiety.

In Italy the Communist Party is seriously hampered by having to support the Communist-trained Marshal Tito's claims to former Italian territory at the head of the Adriatic. Nevertheless, the future of Italy hangs in the balance. Again one cannot imagine a regenerated Europe without a strong France. All my public life I have worked for a strong France and I never lost faith in her destiny, even in the darkest hours. I will not lose faith now.

However, in a great number of countries, far from the Russian frontiers, and throughout the world, Communist fifth columns are established and work in complete unity and absolute obedience to the directions they receive from the Communist center. Except in the British Commonwealth and in this United States, where Communism is in its infancy, the Communist parties or fifth columns constitute a growing challenge and peril to Christian civilization. These are somber facts for anyone to have to recite on the morrow of a victory gained by so much splendid comradeship-in-arms and in the cause of freedom and democracy, and we should be most unwise not to face them squarely while time remains.

The outlook is also anxious in the Far East, and especially in Manchuria. The agreement which was made at Yalta, to which I was a party, was extremely favorable to Soviet Russia, but it was made at a time when no one could say that the German war might not extend all through the summer and autumn of 1945 and when the Japanese war was expected to last for a further eighteen months from the end of the German war. In this country you are all so well informed about the Far East, and such devoted friends of china, that I do not need to experience on the situation there.

I have felt bound to portray the shadow which, alike in the West and in the East, falls upon the world. I was a minister at the time of the Versailles Treaty and a close friend of Mr. Lloyd George. I did not myself agree with many things that were done, but I have a very vague impression in my mind of that situation, and I find it painful to contrast it with that which prevails now. In those days there were high hopes and unbounded confidence that the wars were over and that the League of Nations would become all-powerful. I do not see or feel the same confidence or even the same hopes in the haggard world at this time.

On the other hand I repulse the idea that a new war is inevitable; still more that it is imminent. It is because I am so sure that our fortunes are in our own hands and that we hold the power to save the future that I feel the duty to speak out now that I have an occasion to do so. I do not believe that Soviet Russia desires war. What they desire is the fruits of war and the indefinite expansion of their power and doctrines. But what we have to consider here today, while time remains, is the permanent prevention of war and the establishment of conditions of freedom and democracy as rapidly as possible in all countries.

Our difficulties and dangers will not be removed by closing our eyes to them. They will not be removed by mere waiting to see what happens; nor will they be relieved by a policy of appeasement. What is needed is a settlement, and the longer this is delayed the more difficult it will be and the greater our dangers will become. From what I have seen of our Russian friends and allies during the war, I am convinced that there is nothing they admire so much as strength, and there is nothing for which they have less respect than for military weakness. For that reason the old doctrine of a balance of power is unsound. We cannot afford, if we can help it, to work on narrow margins, offering temptations to a trial of strength.

If the Western democracies stand together in strict adherence to the principles of the United Nations Charter, their influence for furthering these principles will be immense and no one is likely to molest them. If, however, they become divided and falter in their duty, and if these all-important years are allowed to slip away, then indeed catastrophe may overwhelm us all.

Last time I saw it all coming and cried aloud to my fellow countrymen and to the world, but no one paid any attention. Up till the year 1933, or even 1935, Germany might have been saved from the awful fate which has overtaken her and we might all have been spared the miseries Hitler let loose upon mankind. There never was a war in all history easier to prevent by timely action than the one which has just desolated such great areas of the globe. It could have been prevented without the firing of a single shot, and Germany might be powerful, prosperous, and honored today, but no one would listen, and one by one we were all sucked into the awful whirlpool.

We surely must not let that happen again. This can only be achieved by reaching now, in 1946, a good understanding on all points with Russia under the general authority of the United Nations Organization and by the maintenance of that good understanding through many peaceful years, by the world instrument, supported by the whole strength of the English-speaking world and all its connections.

Let no man underrate the abiding power of the British Empire and Commonwealth. Because you see the 46 million in our island harassed about their food supply, of which they grew only one-half, even in wartime, or because we have difficulty in restarting our industries and export trade after six years of passionate war effort, do not suppose that we shall not come through these dark years of privation as we have come through the glorious years of agony, or that half a century from now you will not see 70 or 80 million Britons spread about the world and united in defense of our traditions, our way of life, and of the world cause we and you espouse.

If population of the English-speaking Commonwealth be added to that of the United States, with all that such cooperation implies in the air, on the sea, and in science and industry, there will be no quivering, precarious balance of power to offer its temptation to ambition or adventure. On the contrary, there will be an overwhelming assurance of security. If we adhere faithfully to the Charter of the United Nations and walk forward in sedate and sober strength, seeking no one's land or treasure, or seeking to lay no arbitrary control on the thoughts of men, if all British moral and material forces and convictions are joined with your own in fraternal association, the highroads of the future will be clear, not only for us but for all, not only for our time but for a century to come.

THE SOURCES OF SOVIET CONDUCT

"X" [George Kennan]

The political personality of Soviet power as we know it today is the product of ideology and circumstances: Ideology inherited by the present Soviet leaders from the movement in which they had their political origin, and circumstances of the power which they have now exercised for nearly three decades in Russia. . . .

It is difficult to summarize the set of ideological concepts with which the Soviet leaders came into power. Marxian ideology . . . has always been in process of subtle evolution. . . . But the outstanding features of Communist thought as it existed in 1916 may perhaps be summarized as follows: (a) that the central factor in the life of man, the fact which determines the character of public life and the "physiognomy of society," is the system by which material goods are produced and exchanged; (b) that the capitalist system of production is a nefarious one which inevitably leads to the exploitation of the working class by the capital-owning class and is incapable of developing adequately the economic resources of society or of distributing fairly the material goods produced by human labor; (c) that capitalism contains the seeds of its own destruction and must, in view of the inability of the capital-owning class to adjust itself to economic change, result eventually and inescapably in a revolutionary transfer of power to the working class; and (d) that imperialism, the final phase of capitalism, leads directly to war and revolution. . . .

AID TO GREECE AND TURKEY

Harry S Truman

Mr. President, Mr. Speaker, Members of the Congress of the United States:

The gravity of the situation which confronts the world today necessitates my appearance before a joint session of the Congress.

The foreign policy and the national security of this country are involved.

One aspect of the present situation, which I wish to present to you at this time for your consideration and decision, concerns Greece and Turkey.

"X" [George Kennan], "The Sources of Soviet Conduct," *Foreign Affairs,* July 1947, pp. 566–82.

The Public Papers of the Presidents . . . Harry S Truman . . . 1947 (Washington, DC: Government Printing Office, 1963), pp. 176–80.

The United States has received from the Greek Government an urgent appeal for financial and economic assistance. Preliminary reports from the American Economic Mission now in Greece and reports from the American Ambassador in Greece corroborate the statement of the Greek Government that assistance is imperative if Greece is to survive as a free nation.

I do not believe that the American people and the Congress wish to turn a deaf ear to the appeal of the Greek Government.

Greece is not a rich country. Lack of sufficient natural resources has always forced the Greek people to work hard to make both ends meet. Since 1940 this industrious and peace-loving country has suffered invasion, four years of cruel enemy occupation, and bitter internal strife. . . .

The very existence of the Greek state is today threatened by the terrorist activities of several thousand armed men, led by Communists, who defy the Government's authority at a number of points, particularly along the northern boundaries. A commission appointed by the United Nations Security Council is at present investigating disturbed conditions in northern Greece and alleged border violations along the frontier between Greece on the one hand and Albania, Bulgaria, and Yugoslavia on the other.

Meanwhile, the Greek Government is unable to cope with the situation. The Greek Army is small and poorly equipped. It needs supplies and equipment if it is to restore authority to the Government throughout Greek territory.

Greece must have assistance if it is to become a self-supporting and self-respecting democracy.

The United States must supply that assistance. We have already extended to Greece certain types of relief and economic aid, but these are inadequate.

There is no other country to which democratic Greece can turn.

No other nation is willing and able to provide the necessary support for a democratic Greek Government.

The British Government, which has been helping Greece, can give no further financial or economic aid after March 31. Great Britain finds itself under the necessity of reducing or liquidating its commitments in several parts of the world, including Greece.

We have considered how the United Nations might assist in this crisis. But the situation is an urgent one requiring immediate action, and the United Nations and its related organizations are not in a position to extend help of the kind that is required.

It is important to note that the Greek Government has asked for our aid in utilizing effectively the financial and other assistance we may give to Greece, and in improving its public administration. It is of the utmost importance that we supervise the use of any funds made available to Greece, in such a manner that each dollar spent will count toward making Greece self-supporting, and will help to build an economy in which a healthy democracy can flourish.

No government is perfect. One of the chief virtues of a democracy, however, is that its defects are always visible and under democratic processes can be pointed out and corrected. The Government of Greece is not perfect. Nevertheless it represents 85 percent of the members of the Greek Parliament who were chosen in an election last year. Foreign observers, including 692 Americans, considered this election to be a fair expression of the views of the Greek people.

The Greek Government has been operating in an atmosphere of chaos and extremism. It has made mistakes. The extension of aid by this country does not mean that the

United States condones everything that the Greek Government has done or will do. We have condemned in the past, and we condemn now, extremist measures of the right or the left. We have in the past advised tolerance, and we advise tolerance now.

Greece's neighbor, Turkey, also deserves our attention.

The future of Turkey as an independent and economically sound state is clearly no less important to the freedom-loving peoples of the world than the future of Greece. The circumstances in which Turkey finds itself today are considerably different from those of Greece. Turkey has been spared the disasters that have beset Greece. And during the war the United States and Great Britain furnished Turkey with material aid.

Nevertheless, Turkey now needs our support.

Since the war Turkey has sought additional financial assistance from Great Britain and the United States for the purpose of effecting that modernization necessary for the maintenance of its national integrity.

That integrity is essential to the preservation of order in the Middle East.

The British Government has informed us that, owing to its own difficulties, it can no longer extend financial or economic aid to Turkey.

As in the case of Greece, if Turkey is to have the assistance it needs, the United States must supply it. We are the only country able to provide that help.

I am fully aware of the broad implications involved if the United States is the creation of conditions in which we and other nations will be able to work out a way of life free from coercion. This was a fundamental issue in the war with Germany and Japan. Our victory was won over countries which sought to impose their will, and their way of life upon other nations.

To insure the peaceful development of nations, free from coercion, the United States has taken a leading part in establishing the United Nations. The United Nations is designed to make possible lasting freedom and independence for all its members. We shall not realize our objectives, however, unless we are willing to help free peoples to maintain their free institutions and their national integrity against aggressive movements that seek to impose upon them totalitarian regimes. This is no more than a frank recognition that totalitarian regimes imposed upon free peoples, by direct or indirect aggression, undermine the foundations of international peace and hence the security of the United States.

The peoples of a number of countries of the world have recently had totalitarian regimes forced upon them against their will. The Government of the United States has made frequent protests against coercion and intimidation, in violation of the Yalta agreement, in Poland, Rumania, and Bulgaria. I must also state that in a number of other countries there have been similar developments.

At the present moment in world history nearly every nation must choose between alternative ways of life. The choice is too often not a free one.

One way of life is based upon the will of the majority, and is distinguished by free institutions, representative government, free elections, guaranties of individual liberty, freedom of speech and religion, and freedom from political oppression.

The second way of life is based upon the will of a minority forcibly imposed upon the majority. It relies upon terror and oppression, a controlled press and radio, fixed elections, and the suppression of personal freedoms.

I believe that it must be the policy of the United States to support free peoples who are resisting attempted subjugation by armed minorities or by outside pressures.

I believe that we must assist free peoples to work out their own destinies in their own way.

I believe that our help should be primarily through economic and financial aid which is essential to economic stability and orderly political processes.

The world is not static, and the *status quo* is not sacred. But we cannot allow changes in the *status quo* in violation of the Charter of the United Nations by such methods as coercion, or by such subterfuges as political infiltration. In helping free and independent nations to maintain their freedom, the United States will be giving effect to the principles of the Charter of the United Nations.

It is necessary only to glance at a map to realize that the survival and integrity of the Greek nation are of grave importance in a much wider situation. If Greece should fall under the control of an armed minority, the effect upon its neighbor, Turkey, would be immediate and serious. Confusion and disorder might well spread throughout the entire Middle East.

Moreover, the disappearance of Greece as an independent state would have a profound effect upon those countries in Europe whose peoples are struggling against great difficulties to maintain their freedoms and their independence while they repair the damages of war.

It would be an unspeakable tragedy if these countries, which have struggled so long against overwhelming odds, should lose that victory for which they sacrificed so much. Collapse of free institutions and loss of independence would be disastrous not only for them but for the world. Discouragement and possibly failure would quickly be the lot of neighboring peoples striving to maintain their freedom and independence.

Should we fail to aid Greece and Turkey in this fateful hour, the effect will be far-reaching to the West as well as to the East.

We must take immediate and resolute action.

I therefore ask the Congress to provide authority for assistance to Greece and Turkey in the amount of $400,000,000 for the period ending June 30, 1948. In requesting these funds, I have taken into consideration the maximum amount of relief assistance which would be furnished to Greece out of the $350,000,000 which I recently requested that the Congress authorize for the prevention of starvation and suffering in countries devastated by the war.

In addition to funds, I ask the Congress to authorize the detail of American civilian and military personnel to Greece and Turkey, at the request of those countries, to assist in the tasks of reconstruction, and for the purpose of supervising the use of such financial and material assistance as may be furnished. I recommend that authority also be provided for the instruction and training of selected Greek and Turkish personnel.

Finally, I ask that the Congress provide authority which will permit the speediest and most effective use, in terms of needed commodities, supplies, and equipment, of such funds as may be authorized.

If further funds, or further authority, should be needed for purposes indicated in this message, I shall not hesitate to bring the situation before the Congress. On this subject the Executive and Legislative branches of the Government must work together.

This is a serious course upon which we embark.

I would not recommend it except that the alternative is much more serious.

The United States contributed $341,000,000,000 toward winning World War II. This is an investment in world freedom and world peace.

The assistance that I am recommending for Greece and Turkey amounts to little more than one-tenth of one percent of this investment. It is only common sense that we should safeguard this investment and make sure that it was not in vain.

The seeds of totalitarian regimes are nurtured by misery and want. They spread and grow in the evil soil of poverty and strife. They reach their full growth when the hope of a people for a better life has died.

We must keep that hope alive.

The free peoples of the world look to us for support in maintaining their freedoms.

If we falter in our leadership, we may endanger the peace of the world—and we shall surely endanger the welfare of our own Nation.

Great responsibilities have been placed upon us by the swift movement of events.

I am confident that the Congress will face these responsibilities squarely.

WE MUST HELP EUROPE RECOVER

George Marshall

I need not tell you gentlemen that the world situation is very serious. That must be apparent to all intelligent people. I think one difficulty is that the problem is one of such enormous complexity that the very mass of facts presented to the public by press and radio make it exceedingly difficult for the man in the street to reach a clear appraisement of the situation. Furthermore, the people of this country are distant from the troubled areas of the earth and it is hard for them to comprehend the plight and consequent reactions of the longsuffering peoples, and the effect of those reactions on their governments in connection with our efforts to promote peace in the world.

In considering the requirements for the rehabilitation of Europe, the physical loss of life, the visible destruction of cities, factories, mines, and railroads was correctly estimated, but it has become obvious during recent months that this visible destruction was probably less serious than the dislocation of the entire fabric of European economy. For the past ten years conditions have been highly abnormal. The feverish preparation for war and the more feverish maintenance of the war effort engulfed all aspects of national economies. Machinery has fallen into disrepair or is entirely obsolete. Under the arbitrary and destructive Nazi rule, virtually every possible enterprise was geared into the German war machine. Long-standing commercial ties, private institutions, banks, insurance companies, and shipping companies disappeared, through loss of capital, absorption through nationalization, or by simple destruction. In many countries, confidence in the local currency has been severely shaken. The breakdown of the business structure of Europe during the war was complete. Recovery has been seriously retarded by the fact that two years after the close of hostilities a peace settlement with Germany and Austria has not been agreed upon. But even given a more prompt solution of these difficult problems, the rehabilitation of the economic structure of Europe quite evidently will require a much longer time and greater effort than had been foreseen.

There is a phase of this matter which is both interesting and serious. The farmer has always produced the foodstuffs to exchange with the city dweller for the other

The Department of State Bulletin, vol. 16 (June 15, 1947), pp. 1159–60.

necessities of life. This division of labor is the basis of modern civilization. At the present time it is threatened with breakdown. The town and city industries are not producing adequate goods to exchange with the food-producing farmer. Raw materials and fuel are in short supply. Machinery is lacking or worn out. The farmer or the peasant cannot find the goods for sale which he desires to purchase. So the sale of his farm produce for money which he cannot use seems to him an unprofitable transaction. He, therefore, has withdrawn many fields from crop cultivation and is using them for grazing. He feeds more grain to stock and finds for himself and his family an ample supply of food, however short he may be on clothing and the other ordinary gadgets of civilization. Meanwhile people in the cities are short of food and fuel. So the governments are forced to use their foreign money and credits to procure these necessities abroad. This process exhausts funds which are urgently needed for reconstruction. Thus a very serious situation is rapidly developing which bodes no good for the world. The modern system of the division of labor upon which the exchange of products is based is in danger of breaking down.

The truth of the matter is that Europe's requirements for the next three or four years of foreign food and other essential products—principally from America—are so much greater than her present ability to pay that she must have substantial additional help or face economic, social, and political deterioration of a very grave character.

The remedy lies in breaking the vicious circle and restoring the confidence of the European people in the economic future of their own countries and of Europe as a whole. The manufacturer and the farmer throughout wide areas must be able and willing to exchange their products for currencies the continuing value of which is not open to question.

Aside from the demoralizing effect on the world at large and the possibilities of disturbances arising as a result of the desperation of the people concerned, the consequences to the economy of the United States should be apparent to all. It is logical that the United States should do whatever it is able to do to assist in the return of normal economic health in the world, without which there can be no political stability and no assured peace. Our policy is directed not against any country or doctrine but against hunger, poverty, desperation, and chaos. Its purpose should be the revival of a working economy in the world so as to permit the emergence of political and social conditions in which the free institutions can exist. Such assistance, I am convinced, must not be on a piecemeal basis as various crises develop. Any assistance that this Government may render in the future should provide a cure rather than a mere palliative. Any government that is willing to assist in the task of recovery will find full cooperation, I am sure, on the part of the United States Government. Any government which maneuvers to block the recovery of other countries cannot expect help from us. Furthermore, governments, political parties, or groups which seek to perpetuate human misery in order to profit therefrom politically or otherwise will encounter the opposition of the United States.

It is already evident that, before the United States Government can proceed much further in its efforts to alleviate the situation and help start the European world on its way to recovery, there must be some agreement among the countries of Europe as to the requirements of the situation and the part of those countries themselves will take in order to give proper effect to whatever action might be undertaken by this Government. It would be neither fitting nor efficacious for this Government to undertake to draw up unilaterally a program designed to place Europe on its feet economically. This is the business of the Europeans. The initiative, I think, must come from Europe. The role of this country should consist of friendly aid in the drafting of a European program and of later support of such a program so far as it may be practical for us to do so. The program should be a joint one, agreed to by a number, if not all, European nations.

An essential part of any successful action on the part of the United States is an understanding on the part of the people of America of the character of the problem and the remedies to be applied. Political passion and prejudice should have no part. With foresight, and a willingness on the part of our people to face up to the vast responsibility which history has clearly placed upon our country, the difficulties I have outlined can and will be overcome.

. . . This program will cost our country billions of dollars. It will impose a burden on the American taxpayer. It will require sacrifices today in order that we may enjoy security and peace tomorrow. Should the Congress approve the program for European recovery, as I urgently recommend, we Americans will have made an historic decision of our peacetime history.

A nation in which the voice of its people directs the conduct of its affairs cannot embark on an undertaking of such magnitude and significance for light or purely sentimental reasons. Decisions of this importance are dictated by the highest considerations of national interest. There are none higher, I am sure, than the establishment of enduring peace and the maintenance of true freedom for the individual. In the deliberations of the coming weeks I ask that the European Recovery Program be judged in these terms and on this basis. . . .

The program is *not* one of a series of piecemeal relief measures. I ask that you note this difference, and keep it in mind throughout our explanations. The difference is absolutely vital.

SECRETARY DULLES' STRATEGY OF MASSIVE RETALIATION

January 12, 1954

We live in a world where emergencies are always possible, and our survival may depend upon our capacity to meet emergencies. Let us pray that we shall always have that capacity. But, having said that, it is necessary also to say that emergency measures—however good for the emergency—do not necessarily make good permanent policies. Emergency measures are costly; they are superficial; and they imply that the enemy has the initiative. They cannot be depended on to serve our long-time interests.

This "long time" factor is of critical importance. The Soviet Communists are planning for what they call "an entire historical era," and we should do the same. They seek, through many types of maneuvers, gradually to divide and weaken the free nations by overextending them in efforts which, as Lenin put it, are "beyond their strength, so that they come to practical bankruptcy." Then, said Lenin, "our victory is assured." Then, said Stalin, will be "the moment for the decisive blow."

In the face of this strategy, measures cannot be judged adequate merely because they ward off an immediate danger. It is essential to do this, but it is also essential to do so without exhausting ourselves.

Department of State Bulletin, Vol. 30, pp. 107–10.

When the Eisenhower administration applied this test, we felt that some transformations were needed. It is not sound military strategy permanently to commit U.S. land forces to Asia to a degree that leaves us no strategic reserves. It is not sound economics, or good foreign policy, to support permanently other countries; for in the long run, that creates as much ill will as good will. Also, it is not sound to become permanently committed to military expenditures so vast they lead to "practical bankruptcy."

Change was imperative to assure the stamina needed for permanent security. But it was equally imperative that change should be accompanied by understanding of our true purposes. Sudden and spectacular change had to be avoided. Otherwise, there might have been a panic among our friends and miscalculated aggression by our enemies. We can, I believe, make a good report in these respects.

We need allies and collective security. Our purpose is to make these relations more effective, less costly. This can be done by placing more reliance on deterrent power and less dependence on local defensive power.

This is accepted practice so far as local communities are concerned. We keep locks on our doors, but we do not have an armed guard in every home. We rely principally on a community security system so well equipped to punish any who break in and steal that, in fact, would-be aggressors are generally deterred. That is the modern way of getting maximum protection at a bearable cost. What the Eisenhower administration seeks is a similar international security system. We want, for ourselves and the other free nations, a maximum deterrent at a bearable cost.

Local defense will always be important. But there is no local defense which alone will contain the mighty land power of the Communist world. Local defenses must be reinforced by the further deterrent of massive retaliatory power. A potential aggressor must know that he cannot always prescribe battle conditions that suit him. Otherwise, for example, a potential aggressor, who is glutted with manpower, might be tempted to attack in confidence that resistance would be confined to manpower. He might be tempted to attack in places where his superiority was decisive.

The way to deter aggression is for the free community to be willing and able to respond vigorously at places and with means of its own choosing.

So long as our basic policy concepts were unclear, our military leaders could not be selective in building our military power. If an enemy could pick his time and place and method of warfare—and if our policy was to remain the traditional one of meeting aggression by direct and local opposition—then we needed to be ready to fight in the Arctic and in the Tropics; in Asia, the Near East, and in Europe; by sea, by land, and by air; with old weapons and with new weapons. . . .

Before military planning could be changed, the President and his advisers, as represented by the National Security Council, had to make some basic policy decisions. This has been done. The basic decision was to depend primarily upon a great capacity to retaliate, instantly, by means and at places of our choosing. Now the Department of Defense and the Joint Chiefs of Staff can shape our military establishment to fit what is *our* policy, instead of having to try to be ready to meet the enemy's many choices. That permits of a selection of military means instead of a multiplication of means. As a result, it is now possible to get, and share, more basic security at less cost.

Let us now see how this concept has been applied to foreign policy, taking first the Far East.

In Korea this administration effected a major transformation. The fighting has been stopped on honorable terms. That was possible because the aggressor, already thrown back to and behind his place of beginning, was faced with the possibility that the fighting might, to his now great peril, soon spread beyond the limits and methods which he had selected.

The cruel toll of American youth and the nonproductive expenditure of many billions have been stopped. Also our armed forces are no longer largely committed to the Asian mainland. We can begin to create a strategic reserve which greatly improves our defensive posture.

This change gives added authority to the warning of the members of the United Nations which fought in Korea that, if the Communists renewed the aggression, the United Nations response would not necessarily be confined to Korea.

I have said in relation to Indochina that, if there were open Red Chinese army aggression there, that would have "grave consequences which might not be confined to Indochina." . . .

In the ways I outlined we gather strength for the long-term defense of freedom. We do not, of course, claim to have found some magic formula that insures against all forms of Communist successes. It is normal that at some times and at some places there may be setbacks to the cause of freedom. What we do expect to insure is that any setbacks will have only temporary and local significance, because they will leave unimpaired those free world assets which in the long run will prevail.

If we can deter such aggression as would mean general war, and that is our confident resolve, then we can let time and fundamentals work for us. . . .

11.2   A MILITARY-INDUSTRIAL COMPLEX? ECONOMIC ASPECTS OF THE COLD WAR (1949, 1959, 1981)

The Cold War's impact on the U.S. and global economies was profound. Cold warriors and critics alike obsessed about the emergence of a "military-industrial complex" as the U.S. national security state took shape. Wherever diplomatic and military issues emerged around the world, economic factors also seemed relevant.

In the first selection, Paul M. Sweezy, a Marxist economist, criticizes the Marshall Plan. His views, published in 1949, shortly after the policy was launched, provide a rather interesting economic interpretation of U.S. behavior. What are Sweezy's contentions about peace and prosperity? In what ways do his views reflect traditional Marxist methodology? Has time been kind to his predictions?

The second selection comes from the opposite end of the political spectrum—Richard Nixon, an ardent cold warrior during the 1950s, visited the Soviet Union to engage in the famed "kitchen debates" of 1959. Reflecting an entirely different philosophical perspective, Nixon too arrived at the importance of economics in defining Cold War differences. In many ways, his views are less intellectually consistent than Sweezy's, but far more prophetic. How and why?

Finally, the final reading is a speech by Barry Goldwater supporting Ronald Reagan's revitalization of Cold War policies in the 1980s. It displays both the persistence of old ideas and their undeniable economic ramifications. Do you think that ideological or economic forces were more important in propelling the Cold War?

THE MARSHALL PLAN, AN INSTRUMENT OF PEACE?

Paul M. Sweezy

The annual question of how much money should be appropriated to carry out the purposes of the Marshall Plan is again before the Congress. It is a good time to recall what those purposes were supposed to be and to examine the extent to which they are being realized in practice.

The Marshall Plan was sold to the American people as a program of aid to the countries of western Europe which would enable them to achieve, within the space of about five years, full economic independence. That is certainly a praiseworthy aim. Economically independent countries can also afford to be politically independent. A politically independent western Europe, tied to no blocs and defending its own interests in the arena of international politics, would be a powerful force for peace. If the Marshall Plan were really calculated to create an independent Western Europe, it should receive support.

It is for precisely this reason that by far the most important fact about the Marshall Plan is that it is not creating an economically independent western Europe. There is not the slightest prospect that it will create an economically independent western Europe.

Official analyses of the Marshall Plan reveal this fact even though they dare not admit it. Honest evaluations of the Marshall Plan say it frankly and unequivocally.

Here, for example, is what Walter Lippman[1] had to say in his column in the *Herald-Tribune* of June 13:

> There is current a good deal of pretense and propaganda about how well in hand everything is. Yet ever since the report of the Marshall Plan countries which was made available at the end of 1948 it has been known to the relatively few who studied it that the goal of European recovery, in the official and popular sense of the words, was unattainable by 1952—during the period set by Congress and agreed to by the Marshall Plan countries. It was certain that even with almost unlimited wishful thinking the leading industrial countries of Europe could not become self-supporting and still achieve and maintain a tolerable standard of life by 1952, or in fact at any foreseeable date.

I believe this is a sober statement of the truth—the bedrock from which any rational evaluation of the Marshall Plan must start.

Why is the Marshall Plan failing to achieve its announced goals? Many theories are currently being put forward to explain this. Some say that it is because the United States is perverting the Marshall Plan into an instrument of American imperialism. Some say that it is because the British are selfishly looking out for their own recovery and neglecting the interests of western Europe as a whole. Some say that it is because of

---

Paul M. Sweezy, "The Marshall Plan, An Instrument of Peace?" *Monthly Review*, vol. 1, no. 3 (July 1949), pp. 80–84. Copyright © 1949 by Monthly Review, Inc. Reprinted by permission of Monthly Review Foundation.

[1]Lippman was a famous columnist and political pundit—ED.

the maze of regulations and restrictions which are choking trade among the Marshall Plan countries themselves.

There is, of course, something to each one of these theories. But they are all essentially superficial, and even if the conditions to which they call attention were remedied the situation as a whole would not be decisively altered. The Marshall Plan might be administered without a thought for the interests of American business. The British might be as altruistic as they are alleged to be selfish. Trade restrictions among the Marshall Plan countries might be completely eliminated. There would still be no economically independent western Europe by the end of 1952.

The truth is that the Marshall Plan does not touch the real problem of western Europe. The Marshall Plan is based on the tacit assumption that western Europe was temporarily knocked out by the war and that what it needs is help in getting back on its feet again. This is a totally inadequate diagnosis. In fact the war was merely the climax of a long-term trend. The *status quo ante* in western Europe is dead; no amount of outside assistance can bring it to life again. To quote Thomas Balogh, an eminent Oxford economist: "Western Europe's crisis is not a temporary or short lived departure from an 'equilibrium position' to which it is easy to return. It is a historically unique, harsh break with all that has gone before, a fundamental crisis."

In broad outline the nature of this crisis is clear and simple. Western Europe was the original home of capitalism. During the 18th and 19th centuries it was economically by far the most advanced region in the world. It used its wealth and power to establish relations with the rest of the world which were enormously advantageous to western Europe. On the strength of these advantageous relations with the rest of the world, western Europe developed a very numerous population and provided it with a relatively high standard of living.

It is easy to see now, looking back, that the foundation of western Europe's extraordinary prosperity was temporary. The rest of the world was bound to catch up and to demand a redefinition of its relations with western Europe. When that happened western Europe could no longer go on living in the old way. It would have to face up to the problem of reconstructing and reorienting its economy to meet the requirements of a changed world.

The two world wars greatly accelerated this inevitable historical development. Already in the inter-war period, the day of reckoning was clearly approaching. By the end of World War II it was obvious that it had at last arrived.

What were the practical alternatives?

First, outside aid which would permit western Europe to evade the real problem but would in no sense contribute to its solution.

Or, second, a thorough-going economic revolution which would cut through centuries-old vested interests, drastically redirect and reorganize the utilization of human and material resources, and open the way for a planned coordination of the western European economy with the economies of other regions which would be both willing and able to enter into firm long-term commitments of a mutually beneficial nature. The watchword of such a revolution would have to be planning and still more planning—vigorous, disciplined, comprehensive.

Only a political imbecile could believe that the traditional ruling classes of western Europe would or could carry through such a revolution. It would have to be done by the working class which has few privileges to lose and is capable of toil and sacrifice for a communal goal. And in the very process of carrying out this great revolution, the workers of western Europe would inevitably be forced to scrap the old capitalist system of production for profit and to substitute a new socialist system of production for use.

In the actual circumstances which prevailed after World War II such a revolution was a very real possibility. On the continent the Resistance movements, under the leadership of Socialists and Communists, were everywhere spearheading the drive for radical economic reform. In England the Labor Party was swept into power on a wave of popular enthusiasm for its stated socialist aims. A firm Socialist-Communist front could have led the way forward despite all obstacles.

But the leaders of the United States, and especially those who have their offices in the skyscrapers of New York rather than in the government buildings of Washington, feared nothing so much as a real revolution in western Europe. They had one, and only one, weapon with which to fight it—economic subsidies which would give the old order a new lease on life and permit western Europe, for the time being at any rate, to evade rather than tackle the basic problem which confronted it. They used their weapon skillfully and ruthlessly; and they found valuable allies among the social democratic leaders of western Europe.

At first the subsidies took the form of a variety of loans and grants. Later they were systematized in the more effective form of the Marshall Plan with its centralized administrative apparatus, its network of bilateral treaties, and its agents in each of the countries affected.

Thus we see that while the Marshall Plan was sold to the American people as a *solution* to the crisis of western Europe, in reality it is just the opposite. It is the means by which American capitalism seeks to prevent western Europe from solving its own crisis in the only possible way it can solve the crisis, by the adoption of socialism.

It is only against this background that we can properly evaluate the relation of the Marshall Plan to peace and war. The relation is not a simple one and nothing is gained by pretending that it is.

If the ruling elements in the United States were prepared to continue the Marshall Plan indefinitely, if the support of the American people for such a policy could be secured, and if the economy of the United States could be stabilized by a continuing export surplus of this magnitude, then the Marshall Plan would have a tendency to reduce international tensions, at least for a considerable period. Western Europe would become the passive dumping ground for an economic system which is always in danger of choking on its own surplus product.

But none of these conditions is likely to be fulfilled. Subsidizing western Europe is not a directly profitable form of investment for American capitalists; the people of the United States are not sufficiently initiated into the mysteries of capitalist economics to understand the need for giving away 5 or 6 billion dollars a year forever; and in any case 5 or 6 billion dollars is not enough to keep American capitalism from choking.

Hence the Marshall Plan must be looked upon as a stopgap expedient which solves neither the problems of western Europe nor the problems of the United States. Being essentially temporary and inadequate by any standards, it cannot but play a disturbing role in international relations.

And yet it is hardly accurate to say that the Marshall Plan as such is a threat to peace.

The real threat to peace comes from the utter and complete inability of the rulers of the United States to devise a non-warlike program for dealing with the overwhelming problems which are pressing in on them from all sides.

When the Marshall Plan runs out, the crisis of western Europe will be no nearer solution than it was two years ago—and it may be added that the obvious and continued success of socialist planning in eastern Europe will by that time have shown the western Europeans how they can solve their crisis if they but have the will and the resolve. American capitalism is already giving signs of sliding into the inevitable depression which all the world expects and which our rulers know will deal a body-blow to their prestige and authority. Worst of all from their point of view, if something isn't done, even the American people may wake up from their propaganda-created nightmare of Soviet aggression and Communist plots to discover that the real world is one in which those nations and peoples who manage their affairs in their own interests go forward in spite of all obstacles, while those who put their trust in the gods of free enterprise find themselves hopelessly stuck in the mire of economic insecurity and political reaction.

These are the problems which stare the rulers of America in the face. They do not know how to overcome them. In truth there is no way to overcome them within the framework of the self-contradictory system to which they are wedded. In the long run the replacement of capitalism by a rational socialist order is as certain in the United States as elsewhere. But in the meantime, the greatest danger to world peace, and indeed to much that is best in human civilization itself, is that the rulers of America will seek to put off the day of reckoning by embarking on a career of unlimited militarism and imperialism.

They are already moving in this direction—whether consciously or not is beside the point. If they continue, war may not come soon; but it is hard to see how it can be avoided indefinitely. Militarism and imperialism have their own logic, and its final term is war.

Is it too late to call a halt? That will depend on how quickly the people everywhere, but especially the people of western Europe and America, can be brought to understand that the only possibly guarantee of lasting peace is a new social order which puts the interests of producers and consumers above the interests of private capital.

WHAT FREEDOM MEANS TO US: AMERICAN PEOPLE ARE PEACE-LOVING PEOPLE

Richard M. Nixon

Delivered on the occasion of the opening of The American National Exhibition in Moscow, Sokolniki Park, Moscow, U.S.S.R., July 24, 1959

I am honored on behalf of President Eisenhower to open this American Exhibition in Moscow. Mrs. Nixon and I were among the many thousands of Americans who were privileged to visit the splendid Soviet Exhibition in New York, and we want to take this opportunity to congratulate the people of the U.S.S.R. for the great achievements and progress so magnificently portrayed by your Exhibition.

Vital Speeches, August 1959, pp. 677–79.

We, in turn, hope that many thousands of Soviet citizens will take advantage of this opportunity to learn about life in the United States by visiting our Exhibition.

Of course, we both realize that no exhibition can portray a complete picture of all aspects of life in great nations like the U.S.S.R. and the United States.

Among the questions which some might raise with regard to our Exhibition are these: To what extent does this Exhibition accurately present life in the United States as it really is? Can only the wealthy people afford the things exhibited here? What about the inequality, the injustice, the other weaknesses which are supposed to be inevitable in a Capitalist society?

As Mr. Khrushchev often says: "You can't leave a word out of a song." Consequently, in the limited time I have, I would like to try to answer some of these questions so that you may get an accurate picture of what America is really like.

Let us start with some of the things in this Exhibit. You will see a house, a car, a television set—each the newest and most modern of its type we can produce. But can only the rich in the United States afford such things? If this were the case we would have to include in our definition of rich the millions of America's wage earners.

Let us take, for example, our 16 million factory workers. The average weekly wage of a factory worker in America is $90.54. With this income he can buy and afford to own a house, a television set, and a car in the price range of those you will see in this Exhibit. What is more, the great majority of American wage earners have done exactly that.

Putting it another way, there are 44 million families in the United States. Twenty-five million of these families live in houses or apartments that have as much or more floor space than the one you see in this Exhibit. Thirty-one million families own their own homes and the land on which they are built. America's 44 million families own a total of 56 million cars, 50 million television sets and 143 million radio sets. And they buy an average of 9 dresses and suits and 14 pairs of shoes per family per year.

Why do I cite these figures? Not because they indicate that the American people have more automobiles, TV sets, or houses than the people of the U.S.S.R.

In fairness we must recognize that our country industrialized sooner than the Soviet Union. And Americans are happy to note that Mr. Khrushchev has set a goal for the Soviet economy of catching up in the production of consumer goods.

We welcome this kind of competition because when we engage in it, no one loses—everyone wins as the living standards of people throughout the world are raised to higher levels. It also should be pointed out that while we may be ahead of you as far as these items are concerned, you are ahead of us in other fields—for example, in the size of the rockets you have developed for the exploration of outer space.

But what these statistics do dramatically demonstrate is this: That the United States, the world's largest capitalist country, has from the standpoint of distribution of wealth come closest to the ideal of prosperity for all in a classless society.

As our revered Abraham Lincoln said ". . . We do not propose any war upon capital; we do wish to allow the humblest man an equal chance to get rich with everybody else."

The 67 million American wage earners are not the downtrodden masses depicted by the critics of capitalism in the latter part of the 19th and early part of the 20th Centuries. They hold their heads high as they proudly enjoy the highest standard of living of any people in the world's history.

The caricature of capitalism as a predatory, monopolist dominated society is as hopelessly out of date, as far as the United States is concerned, as a wooden plow.

This does not mean that we have solved all of our problems. Many of you have heard about the problem of unemployment in the United States. What is not so well known is that the average period that these unemployed were out of work even during our recent recession was less than three months. And during that period the unemployed had an average income from unemployment insurance funds of $131.49 per month. The day has passed in the United States when the unemployed were left to shift for themselves.

The same can be said for the aged, the sick, and others who are unable to earn enough to provide an adequate standard of living. An expanded program of Social Security combined with other government and private programs provides aid and assistance for those who are unable to care for themselves. For example, the average retired couple on Social Security in the United States receives an income of $116 per month apart from the additional amounts they receive from private pensions and savings accounts.

What about the strikes which take place in our economy, the latest example of which is the steel strike which is going on? The answer is that here we have a firsthand example of how a free economy works. The workers right to join with other workers in a union and to bargain collectively with management is recognized and protected by law. No man or woman in the United States can be forced to work for wages he considers to be inadequate or under conditions he believes are unsatisfactory.

Another problem which causes us concern is that of racial discrimination in our country. We are making great progress in solving this problem but we shall never be satisfied until we make the American ideal of equality of opportunity a reality for every citizen regardless of his race, creed or color.

We have other problems in our society but we are confident that for us our system of government provides the best means for solving them. But the primary reason we believe this is not because we have an economy which builds more than one million houses, produces six million cars and six million television sets per year.

Material progress is important but the very heart of the American ideal is that "man does not live by bread alone." To us, progress without freedom to use a common expression is like "potatoes without fat."

Let me give you some examples of what freedom means to us.

President Eisenhower is one of the most popular men ever to hold that high office in our country. Yet never an hour or a day goes by in which criticism of him and his policies cannot be read in our newspapers, heard on our radio and television, or in the Halls of Congress.

And he would not have it any other way. The fact that our people can and do say anything they want about a government official, the fact that in our elections, as this voting machine in our exhibit illustrates, every voter has a free choice between those who hold public office and those who oppose them makes ours a true peoples' government.

We trust the people. We constantly submit big decisions to the people. Our history convinces us that over the years the people have been right much more often than they have been wrong.

As an indication of the extent of this freedom and of our faith in our own system, forty hours of radio broadcasts from the Soviet Union can be heard without jamming in the United States each day, and over a million and a half copies of Soviet publications are purchased in our country each year.

Let us turn now to freedom of religion. Under our Constitution no church or religion can be supported by the State. An American can either worship in the church of his choice or choose to go to no church at all if he wishes. Acting with this complete freedom of choice, 103 million of our citizens are members of 308 thousand American churches.

We also cherish the freedom to travel, both within our country and outside the United States. Within our country we live and travel where we please without travel permits, internal passports or police registration. We also travel freely abroad. For example, 11 million Americans will travel to other countries during this year, including 10,000 to the Soviet Union. We look forward to the day when millions of Soviet citizens will travel to ours and other countries in this way.

Time will not permit me to tell you of all of the features of American life, but in summary I think these conclusions can objectively be stated.

The great majority of Americans like our system of government. Much as we like it, however, we would not impose it on anyone else. We believe that people everywhere should have a right to choose the form of government they want.

There is another characteristic of the American people which I know impresses itself on any visitor to our country. As Mr. Mikoyan and Mr. Kozlov both pointed out after their visits to the United States, the American people are a peace-loving people. There are a number of reasons for this attitude: As this Exhibition so eloquently demonstrates, we Americans enjoy an extraordinarily high standard of living.

There is nothing we want from any other people except the right to live in peace and friendship with them.

After fighting two World Wars we did not ask for or receive an acre of land from any other people. We have no desire to impose our rule on other lands today.

Our hearts go out to Mr. Khrushchev who lost a son, to Mr. Kozlov who lost two brothers, and to the millions of other Soviet mothers and fathers, brothers and sisters, sons and daughters who mourn for their loved ones lost in defending their homeland.

But while it is generally recognized that the American people want peace, I realize that it has sometimes been charged that our government does not share the attitude of our people. Nothing could be further from the truth.

For seven years I have sat in the high councils of our government and I can tell you that the primary aim of our discussions has been to find ways that we could use our strength in behalf of peace throughout the world.

Let me tell you of the background of some of those who participate in our policy discussions. The Secretary of State lost his brother in World War I. I saw boys as close to me as brothers die on barren islands four thousand miles from home in World War II. No man in the world today has more knowledge of war and is more dedicated to peace than President Eisenhower.

Those who claim that the policies of the American government do not represent and are not supported by the American people are engaging in a completely inaccurate and dangerous form of self-deception. Any administration which follows policies which do not reflect the views of our people on major issues runs the risk of defeat at the next election. When our elected officials cease to represent the people, the people have the power to replace them with others who do. The reason the leaders of both our major political parties are united in supporting President Eisenhower's foreign policy is that they are reflecting the views of a people who are united behind these policies.

The government and people of the United States are as one in their devotion to the cause of peace.

But dedication to peace, good will and human brotherhood should never be mistaken for weakness, softness and fear.

Much as we want peace we will fight to defend our country and our way of life just as you have fought so courageously to defend your homeland throughout your history.

The peace we want and the peace the world needs is not the peace of surrender but the peace of justice, not peace by ultimatum but peace by negotiation.

The leaders of our two great nations have such tremendous responsibilities if peace is to be maintained in our time.

We cannot and should not gloss over the fact that we have some great and basic differences between us. What we must constantly strive to do is to see that those differences are discussed and settled at the conference table and not on the battlefield.

And until such settlements are agreed to, our leaders must exercise the greatest restraint, patience and understanding in their actions and their statements. They must do nothing which might provoke a war no one wants.

The fact that one of us may have a bigger bomb, a faster plane, or a more powerful rocket than the other at any particular time no longer adds up to an advantage. Because we have reached the point in world history where the biblical injunction "they that take the sword shall perish with the sword" is literally true today.

The nation which starts a war today will destroy itself. Completely apart from any retaliatory action which might be taken by a nation which is attacked, the deadly dust from radioactive bombs used in an attack will be carried by the winds back to the homeland of the aggressor.

With both of our great nations holding this terrible power in our hands neither must ever put the other in a position where he has no choice but to fight or surrender. No nation in the world today is strong enough to issue an ultimatum to another without running the risk of self-destruction.

The Soviet Exhibition in New York and the American Exhibition which we open tonight are dramatic examples of what a great future lies in store for all of us if we can devote the tremendous energies of our peoples and the resources of our countries to the ways of peace rather than the ways of war.

The last half of the 20th Century can be the darkest or the brightest page in the history of civilization. The decision is in our hands to make. The genius of the men who produced the magnificent achievements represented by these two Exhibitions can be directed either to the destruction of civilization or to the creation of the best life that men have ever enjoyed on this earth.

As I have said on previous occasions, let us expand the idea of peaceful competition which Mr. Khrushchev has often enunciated. Let us extend this competition to include the spiritual as well as the material aspects of our civilization. Let us compete not in how to take lives but in how to save them. Let us work for victory not in war but for the victory of plenty over poverty, of health over disease, of understanding over ignorance wherever they exist in the world.

Above all, let us find more and more areas where we can substitute cooperation for competition in achieving our goal of a fuller, freer, richer life for every man, woman and child on this earth.

11.3   THE RED SCARE (1950)

One serious blot on the comfort and complacency of the 1950s was the era's anxiety over "disloy-alty" and the "Communist menace." Whether the danger of subversion was real or a case of hyste-ria, the issue of domestic Communism roiled the placid surface of the decade as did few other issues.

At the center of the storm, although not its instigator, was the junior senator from Wisconsin, Joseph R. McCarthy. McCarthy came to the Senate in 1946, a banner year for con-servative Republicans, and served much of his first term as an undistinguished backbench parti-san. By 1950, without the record of achievement that an incumbent could normally show the voters, he faced the prospect of a hazardous reelection campaign two years down the road.

But there was an issue at hand that might bail him out—anti-Communism. This was a time of the emerging Cold War, when Americans perceived a remorseless spread of Communist influence over ever larger portions of the globe. This advance, many felt, did not derive solely from Communist aggression abroad; it must also stem from subversion within.

Out of this suspicion McCarthy would forge a potent political weapon. Day after day his charges of hidden Communists in the government, the media, the clergy, and other influential portions of U.S. society made headlines and cast the Wisconsin senator in the role of champion of true Americanism. McCarthy won reelection in 1952 and, in tandem with other obsessive anti-Communists, helped make the remainder of the 1950s a decade of fear and repression.

The following selections represent opening shots in the battles that would swirl around McCarthyism. The first is a speech by McCarthy himself before a women's Republican group in Wheeling, West Virginia, on Lincoln's Birthday in 1950.[2] Is McCarthy's indictment of Communism valid? Was his claim that Communism had made great gains since the end of World War II correct? What is McCarthy's explanation for these gains? Does his explanation hold up to examination? Are there qualities of his attack that might be disturbing to a prudent thinker and policy maker? McCarthy's sentiments were so deeply shared by Congress and the U.S. public that the McCarran Internal Security Act was passed over President Truman's veto and general warning of its unconstitutionality.

The third selection is from a report by a Senate subcommittee, headed by Senator Millard Tydings of Maryland, that was empowered to investigate McCarthy's charges against the State Department. The subcommittee, clearly critical of the Wisconsin senator, held hearings and examined official files. It called the Wisconsin senator to testify in defense of his charges. McCarthy and his supporters fought back with angry attacks on Tydings and the investigating committee.

It is difficult for students to tell, without more information than it is possible to provide here, whether the charges of Communists in the State Department were correct. But you can evaluate Tydings' claims regarding the effects of charges like McCarthy's on public attitudes, the morale of government employees, and the climate of tolerance in the United States.

In evaluating the McCarthy controversy, you should consider matters like the differences between subversion and espionage, the valid limits of political and ideological dissent in a democ-racy, and the connection between the Cold War and demands for internal intellectual and ideolog-ical conformity. You also should consider whether there was a political motive at work in the anti-Communist campaign. McCarthy was a Republican; Tydings a Democrat. Was the party dif-ference significant?

---

[2]Actually, this text is a later reconstruction of the speech. The original seems lost forever.

WHY COMMUNISM IS GAINING

Joseph R. McCarthy

Ladies and gentlemen, tonight as we celebrate the one hundred and forty-first birthday of one of the greatest men in American history, I would like to be able to talk about what a glorious day today is in the history of the world. As we celebrate the birth of this man who with his whole heart and soul hated war, I would like to be able to speak of peace in our time, of war being outlawed, and of worldwide disarmament. These would be truly appropriate things to be able to mention as we celebrate the birthday of Abraham Lincoln.

Five years after a world war has been won, men's hearts should anticipate a long peace, and men's minds should be free from the heavy weight that comes with war. But this is not such a period—for this is not a period of peace. This is a time of the "cold war." This is a time when all the world is split into two vast, increasingly hostile armed camps—a time of a great armaments race.

Today we can almost physically hear the mutterings and rumblings of an invigorated god of war. You can see it, feel it, and hear it all the way from the hills of Indochina, from the shores of Formosa, right over into the very heart of Europe itself.

The one encouraging thing is that the "mad moment" has not yet arrived for the firing of the gun or the exploding of the bomb which will set civilization about the final task of destroying itself. There is still a hope for peace if we finally decide that no longer can we safely blind our eyes and close our ears to those facts which are shaping up more and more clearly. And that is that we are now engaged in a show-down fight—not the usual war between nations for land areas or other material gains, but a war between two diametrically opposed ideologies.

The great difference between our western Christian world and the atheistic Communist world is not political, ladies and gentlemen, it is moral. There are other differences, of course, but those could be reconciled. For instance, the Marxian idea of confiscating the land and factories and running the entire economy as a single enterprise is momentous. Likewise, Lenin's invention of the one-party police state as a way to make Marx's idea work is hardly less momentous.

Stalin's resolute putting across of these two ideas, of course, did much to divide the world. With only those differences, however, the East and the West could most certainly still live in peace.

The real, basic difference, however, lies in the religion of immoralism—invented by Marx, preached feverishly by Lenin, and carried to unimaginable extremes by Stalin. This religion of immoralism, if the Red half of the world wins—and well it may—this religion of immoralism will more deeply wound and damage mankind than any conceivable economic or political system.

Karl Marx dismissed God as a hoax, and Lenin and Stalin have added in clear-cut, unmistakable language their resolve that no nation, no people who believe in a God, can exist side by side with their communistic state.

Karl Marx, for example, expelled people from his Communist Party for mentioning such things as justice, humanity, or morality. He called this soulful ravings and sloppy sentimentality.

Congressional Record, 81st Cong., 2d sess., 96, 1950.

While Lincoln was a relatively young man in his late thirties, Karl Marx boasted that the Communist specter was haunting Europe. Since that time, hundreds of millions of people and vast areas of the world have fallen under Communist domination. Today, less than 100 years after Lincoln's death, Stalin brags that this Communist specter is not only haunting the world, but is about to completely subjugate it.

Today we are engaged in a final, all-out battle between communistic atheism and Christianity. The modern champions of communism have selected this as the time. And, ladies and gentlemen, the chips are down—they are truly down.

Lest there be any doubt that the time has been chosen, let us go directly to the leader of communism today—Joseph Stalin. Here is what he said—not back in 1928, not before the war, not during the war—but 2 years after the last war was ended: "To think that the Communist revolution can be carried out peacefully, within the framework of a Christian democracy, means one has either gone out of one's mind and lost all normal understanding, or has grossly and openly repudiated the Communist revolution."

And this is what was said by Lenin in 1919, which was also quoted with approval by Stalin in 1947:

"We are living," said Lenin, "not merely in a state, but in a system of states, and the existence of the Soviet Republic side by side with Christian states for a long time is unthinkable. One or the other must triumph in the end. And before that end supervenes, a series of frightful collisions between the Soviet Republic and the Bourgeois states will be inevitable."

Ladies and gentlemen, can there be anyone here tonight who is so blind as to say that the war is not on? Can there be anyone who fails to realize that the Communist world has said, "The time is now"—that this is the time for the show-down between the democratic Christian world and the Communist atheistic world?

Unless we face this fact, we shall pay the price that must be paid by those who wait too long.

Six years ago, at the time of the first conference to map out the peace—Dumbarton Oaks[1]—there was within the Soviet orbit 180,000,000 people. Lined up on the antitotalitarian side there were in the world at that time roughly 1,625,000,000 people. Today, only 6 years later, there are 800,000,000 people under the absolute domination of Soviet Russia—an increase of over 400 percent. On our side, the figure has shrunk to around 500,000,000. In other words, in less than 6 years the odds have changed from 9 to 1 in our favor to 8 to 5 against us. This indicates the swiftness of the tempo of Communist victories and American defeats in the cold war. As one of our outstanding historical figures once said, "When a great democracy is destroyed, it will not be because of enemies from without, but rather because of enemies from within."

The truth of this statement is becoming terrifyingly clear as we see this country each day losing on every front.

At war's end we were physically the strongest nation on earth and, at least potentially, the most powerful intellectually and morally. Ours could have been the honor of being a beacon in the desert of destruction, a shining living proof that civilization was not yet ready to destroy itself. Unfortunately, we have failed miserably and tragically to arise to the opportunity.

---

[1]Dumbarton Oaks near Washington, DC, was the site of a conference of the anti-Axis powers in 1944 where plans were made for a United Nations organization after victory—ED.

The reason why we find ourselves in a position of impotency is not because our only powerful potential enemy has sent men to invade our shores, but rather because of the traitorous actions of those who have been treated so well by this Nation. It has not been the less fortunate or members of minority groups who have been selling this Nation out, but rather those who have had all the benefits that the wealthiest nation on earth has had to offer—the finest homes, the finest college education, and the finest jobs in Government we can give.

This is glaringly true in the Statement Department. There the bright young men who are born with silver spoons in their mouths are the ones who have been worst.

Now I know it is very easy for anyone to condemn a particular bureau or department in general terms. Therefore, I would like to cite one rather unusual case—the case of a man who has done much to shape our foreign policy.

When Chiang Kai-shek was fighting our war, the State Department had in China a young man named John S. Service. His task, obviously, was not to work for the communization of China. Strangely, however, he sent official reports back to the Statement Department urging that we torpedo our ally Chiang Kai-shek and stating, in effect, that communism was the best hope of China.

Later, this man—John Service—was picked up by the Federal Bureau of Investigation for turning over to the Communists secret State Department information. Strangely, however, he was never prosecuted. However, Joseph Grew, the Under Secretary of State, who insisted on his prosecution, was forced to resign. Two days after Grew's successor, Dean Acheson, took over as Under Secretary of State, this man—John Service—who had been picked up by the FBI and who had previously urged that communism was the best hope of China, was not only reinstated in the State Department but promoted. And finally, under Acheson, placed in charge of all placements and promotions.

Today, ladies and gentlemen, this man Service is on his way to represent the State Department and Acheson in Calcutta—by far and away the most important listening post in the Far East.

Now, let's see what happens when individuals with Communist connections are forced out of the State Department. Gustave Duran, who was labeled as (I quote) "a notorious international Communist," was made assistant to the Assistant Secretary of State in charge of Latin American affairs. He was taken into the State Department from his job as a lieutenant colonel in the Communist International Brigade. Finally, after intense congressional pressure and criticism, he resigned in 1946 from the State Department—and, ladies and gentlemen, where do you think he is now? He took over a high-salaried job as Chief of Cultural Activities Section in the office of the Assistant Secretary General of the United Nations.

Then there was a Mrs. Mary Jane Kenny, from the Board of Economic Warfare in the State Department, who was named in an FBI report and in a House committee report as a courier for the Communist Party while working for the Government. And where do you think Mrs. Kenny is—she is now an editor in the United Nations Document Bureau.

Another interesting case was that of Julian H. Wadleigh, economist in the Trade Agreements Section of the State Department for 11 years and [sic] was sent to Turkey and Italy and other countries as United States representative. After the statute of limitations had run [out] so he could not be prosecuted for treason, he openly and brazenly not only admitted but proclaimed that he had been a member of the Communist Party . . . that while working for the State Department he stole a vast number of secret documents . . . and furnished these documents to the Russian spy ring of which he was a part.

You will recall last spring there was held in New York what was known as the World Peace Conference—a conference which was labeled by the State Department and Mr. Truman as the sounding board for Communist propaganda and a front for Russia. Dr. Harlow Shapley was the chairman of that conference. Interestingly enough, according to the news release put out by the Department in July, the Secretary of State appointed Shapley on a commission which acts as liaison between UNESCO [United Nations Economic and Social Council] and the State Department.

This, ladies and gentlemen, gives you somewhat of a picture of the type of individuals who have been helping to shape our foreign policy. In my opinion the State Department, which is one of the most important government departments, is thoroughly infested with Communists.

I have in my hand 57 cases of individuals who would appear to be either card carrying members or certainly loyal to the Communist Party, but who nevertheless are still helping to shape our foreign policy.

One thing to remember in discussing the Communists in our Government is that we are not dealing with spies who get 30 pieces of silver to steal the blueprints of a new weapon. We are dealing with a far more sinister type of activity because it permits the enemy to guide and shape our policy. . . .

This brings us down to the case of one Alger Hiss[2] who is important not as an individual any more, but rather because he is so representative of a group in the State Department. It is unnecessary to go over the sordid events showing how he sold out the Nation which had given him so much. Those are rather fresh in all of our minds.

However, it should be remembered that the facts in regard to his connection with this international Communist spy ring were made known to the then Under Secretary of State [Adolf] Berle 3 days after Hitler and Stalin signed the Russo-German alliance pact. At that time one Whittaker Chambers—who was also part of the spy ring—apparently decided that with Russia on Hitler's side, he could no longer betray our Nation to Russia. He gave Under Secretary of State Berle—and this is all a matter of record—practically all, if not more, of the facts upon which Hiss' conviction was based.

Under Secretary Berle promptly contacted Dean Acheson and received word in return that Acheson (and I quote) "could vouch for Hiss absolutely"—at which time the matter was dropped. And this, you understand, was at a time when Russia was an ally of Germany. This condition existed while Russia and Germany were invading and dismembering Poland, and while the Communist groups here were screaming "warmonger" at the United States for their support of the allied nations.

Again in 1943, the FBI had occasion to investigate the facts surrounding Hiss' contacts with the Russian spy ring. But even after that FBI report was submitted, nothing was done.

Then late in 1948—on August 5—when the Un-American Activities Committee called Alger Hiss to give an accounting, President Truman at once issued a Presidential directive ordering all Government agencies to refuse to turn over any information whatsoever in regard to the Communist activities of any Government employee to a congressional committee.

---

[2]Alger Hiss was a former New Deal official accused by Whittaker Chambers, a former editor of *Time*, of being a Soviet spy. Hiss' guilt or innocence became a major political issue between liberals and the left on the one hand, and conservatives on the other—ED.

Incidentally, even after Hiss was convicted—it is interesting to note that the President still labeled the exposé of Hiss as a "red herring."

If time permitted, it might be well to go into detail about the fact that Hiss was Roosevelt's chief adviser at Yalta when Roosevelt was admittedly in ill health and tired physically and mentally . . . and when, according to the Secretary of State, Hiss and Gromyko drafted the report on the conference.

According to the then Secretary of State Edward Stettinius, here are some of the things that Hiss helped to decide at Yalta. (1) The establishment of a European High Commission; (2) the treatment of Germany—this you will recall was the conference at which it was decided that we would occupy Berlin with Russia occupying an area completely circling the city, which, as you know, resulted in the Berlin airlift which cost 31 American lives; (3) the Polish question; (4) the relationship between UNRRA [United Nations Relief and Rehabilitation Administration] and the Soviet Union; (5) the rights of Americans on control commissions of Rumania, Bulgaria, and Hungary; (6) Iran; (7) China—here's where we gave away Manchuria; (8) Turkish Straits question; (9) international trusteeships; (10) Korea.

Of the results of this conference, Arthur Bliss Lane of the State Department had this to say: "As I glanced over the document, I could not believe my eyes. To me, almost every line spoke of a surrender to Stalin."

As you hear this story of high treason, I know that you are saying to yourself, "Well, why doesn't the Congress do something about it?" Actually, ladies and gentlemen, one of the important reasons for the graft, the corruption, the dishonesty, the disloyalty, the treason in high Government positions—one of the most important reasons why this continues is a lack of moral uprising on the part of the 140,000,000 American people. In the light of history, however, this is not hard to explain.

It is the result of an emotional hang-over and a temporary moral lapse which follows every war. It is the apathy to evil which people who have been subjected to the tremendous evils of war feel. As the people of the world see mass murder, the destruction of defenseless and innocent people, and all of the crime and lack of morals which go with war, they become numb and apathetic. It has always been thus after war.

However, the morals of our people have not been destroyed. They still exist. This cloak of numbness and apathy has only needed a spark to rekindle them. Happily, this spark has finally been supplied.

As you know, very recently the Secretary of State[3] proclaimed his loyalty to a man guilty of what has always been considered as the most abominable of all crimes—of being a traitor to the people who gave him a position of great trust.[4] The Secretary of State in attempting to justify his continued devotion to the man who sold out the Christian world to the atheistic world, referred to Christ's Sermon on the Mount as a justification and reason therefor, and the reaction of the American people to this would have made the heart of Abraham Lincoln happy.

When this pompous diplomat in striped pants, with a phony British accent, proclaimed to the American people that Christ on the Mount endorsed communism, high

---

[3]Dean Acheson—ED.

[4]Acheson, without condoning any crime that Hiss might have committed, had stated publicly that he would not "turn his back" on his former colleague.

treason, and betrayal of a sacred trust, the blasphemy was so great that it awakened the dormant indignation of the American people.

He has lighted the spark which is resulting in a moral uprising and will end only when the whole sorry mess of twisted, warped thinkers are swept from the national scene so that we may have a new birth of national honesty and decency in Government.

McCarran Internal Security Act

September 23, 1950

An Act

To protect the United States against certain un-American and subversive activities by requiring registration of Communist organizations, and for other purposes.

SEC. 2. As a result of evidence adduced before various committees of the Senate and House of Representatives, the Congress hereby finds that—

(1) There exists a world Communist movement which, in its origins, its development, and its present practice, is a world-wide revolutionary movement whose purpose it is, by treachery, deceit, infiltration into other groups (governmental and otherwise), espionage, sabotage, terrorism, and any other means deemed necessary, to establish a Communist totalitarian dictatorship in the counties throughout the world through the medium of a world-wide Communist organization. . . .

(4) The direction and control of the world Communist movement is vested in and exercised by the Communist dictatorship of a foreign country.

(15) The Communist movement in the United States is an organization numbering thousands of adherents, rigidly and ruthlessly disciplined. Awaiting and seeking to advance a moment when the United States may be so far extended by foreign engagements, so far divided in counsel, or so far in industrial or financial straits, that overthrow of the Government of the United States by force and violence may seem possible of achievement, it seeks converts far and wide by an extensive system of schooling and indoctrination. Such preparations by Communist organizations in other countries have aided in supplanting existing governments. The Communist organization in the United States, pursuing its stated objective, the recent successes of Communist methods in other countries, and the nature and control of the world Communist movement itself, present a clear and present danger to the security of the United States and to the existence of free American institutions, and make it necessary that Congress, in order to provide for the common defense, to preserve the sovereignty of the United States as an independent nation, and to guarantee to each State a republican form of government, enact appropriate legislation recognizing the existence of such world-wide conspiracy and designed to prevent it from accomplishing its purpose in the United States. . . .

SEC. 4. (a) It shall be unlawful for any person knowingly to combine, conspire, or agree with any other person to perform any act which would substantially contribute to the establishment within the United States of a totalitarian dictatorship, as defined in paragraph (15) of section 3 of this title, the direction and control of which is to be vested in, or exercised by or under the domination or control of, any foreign government, foreign organization, or foreign individual: *Provided, however,* That this subsection shall not apply to the proposal of a constitutional amendment. . . .

(f) Neither the holding of office nor membership in any Communist organization by any person shall constitute per se a violation of subsection (a) or subsection (c) of this section or of any other criminal statute. The fact of the registration of any person under section 7 or section 8 of this title as an officer or member of any Communist organization shall not be received in evidence against such person in any prosecution for any alleged violation of subsection (a) or subsection (c) of this section or for any alleged violation of any other criminal statute. . . .

SEC. 7. (a) Each Communist-action organization (including any organization required, by a final order of the Board, to register as a Communist-action organization) shall, within the time specified in subsection (c) of this section, register with the Attorney General, on a form prescribed by him by regulations, as a Communist-action organization.

(b) Each Communist-front organization . . . shall . . . register with the Attorney General, on a form prescribed by him by regulations, as a Communist-front organization. . . .

(d) Upon the registration of each Communist organization under the provisions of this title, the Attorney General shall publish in the Federal Register the fact that such organization has registered as a Communist-action organization, or as a Communist-front organization, as the case may be, and the publication thereof shall constitute notice to all members of such organization that such organization has so registered. . . .

SEC. 12. (a) There is hereby established a board, to be known as the Subversive Activities Control Board, which shall be composed of five members, who shall be appointed by the President, by and with the advice and consent of the Senate. . . . It shall be the duty of the Board—upon application made by the Attorney General . . . to determine whether any individual is a member of any Communist-action organization registered, or by final order of the Board required to be registered, under Section 7 (a) of this title. . . .

SEC. 22. The Act of October 16, 1918 . . . is hereby amended to read as follows: "That any alien who is a member of any one of the following classes shall be excluded from admission into the United States.

"(1) Aliens who seek to enter the United States whether solely, principally, or incidentally, to engage in activities which would be prejudicial to the public interest, or would endanger the welfare or safety of the United States;

"(2) Aliens who, at any time, shall be or shall have been members of any of the following classes:

"(A) Aliens who are anarchists;

"(B) Aliens who advocate or teach, or who are members of or affiliated with any organization that advocates or teaches, opposition to all organized government;

"(C) Aliens who are members of or affiliated with (i) the Communist Party of the United States, (ii) any other totalitarian party of the United States, (iii) the Communist Political Association, (iv) the Communist or other totalitarian party of any State of the United States, of any foreign state, or of any political or geographical subdivision of any foreign state; (v) any section, subsidiary, branch, affiliate, or subdivision of any such association or party; or (vi) the direct predecessors or successors of any such association or party, regardless of what name such group or organization may have used, may now bear, or may hereafter adopt;

"(D) Aliens not within any of the other provisions of this paragraph (2) who advocate the economic, international, and governmental doctrines of world communism or the economic and governmental doctrines of any other form of totalitarianism, or who are members of or affiliated with any organization that advocates the economic, international, and governmental doctrines of world communism, or the economic and governmental doctrines of any other form of totalitarianism, either through its own utterances or through any written or printed publications issued or published by or with the permission or consent of or under the authority of such organization or paid for by the funds of such organization. . . .

"(F) Aliens who advocate or teach or who are members of or affiliated with any organization that advocates or teaches (i) the overthrow by force or violence or other unconstitutional means of the Government of the United States or of all forms of law; or (ii) the duty, necessity, or propriety of the unlawful assaulting or killing of any officer or officers (either of specific individuals or of officers generally) of the Government of the United States or of any other organized government, because of his or their official character; or (iii) the unlawful damage, injury, or destruction of property; or (iv) sabotage;

"(G) Aliens who write or publish, or cause to be written or published, or who knowingly circulate, distribute, print, or display, or knowingly cause to be circulated, distributed, printed, published, or displayed, or who knowingly have in their possession for the purpose of circulation, publication, or display, any written or printed matter, advocating or teaching opposition to all organized government, or advocating (i) the overthrow by force or violence or other unconstitutional means of the Government of the United States or of all forms of law; or (ii) the duty, necessity, or propriety of the unlawful assaulting or killing of any officer or officers (either of specific individuals or of officers generally) of the Government of the United States or of any other organized government; or (iii) the unlawful damage, injury, or destruction of property; or (iv) sabotage; or (v) the economic, international, and governmental doctrines of world communism or the economic and governmental doctrines of any other form of totalitarianism. . . .

SEC. 102. (a) In the event of any one of the following:

(1) Invasion of the territory of the United States or its possessions,

(2) Declaration of war by Congress, or

(3) Insurrection within the United States in aid of a foreign enemy, and if, upon the occurrence of one or more of the above, the President shall find that the proclamation of an emergency pursuant to this section is essential to the preservation, protection and defense of the Constitution, and to the common defense and safety of the territory and people of the United States, the President is authorized to make public proclamation of the existence of an "Internal Security Emergency."

(b) A state of "Internal Security Emergency" (hereinafter referred to as the "emergency") so declared shall continue in existence until terminated by proclamation of the President or by concurrent resolution of the Congress. . . .

SEC. 103. (a) Whenever there shall be in existence such an emergency, the President, acting through the Attorney General, is hereby authorized to apprehend and by order detain, pursuant to the provisions of this title, each person as to whom there is reasonable ground to believe that such person probably will engage in, or probably will conspire with others to engage in, acts of espionage or of sabotage. . . .

MCCARTHY'S CHARGES ARE FALSE

Millard Tydings Committee

Of the 81 alleged State Department employees,[1] only 40 were found to be employed by the State Department at the time of the review. Seven of the so-called 81 were never employed by the State Department and the remaining 33 are no longer in the Department, having been separated either through resignation, termination, or reduction in force. Specifically, of the 33 former employees, 3 were separated in 1949; 16, in 1948; 12, in 1947; and 2, in 1946. . . .

. . . We have carefully and conscientiously reviewed each and every one of the loyalty files relative to the individuals charged by Senator McCarthy. In no instance was any one of them now employed in the State Department found to be a "card-carrying Communist," a member of the Communist Party, or "loyal to the Communist Party." Furthermore, in no instance have we found in our considered judgment that the decision to grant loyalty and security clearance has been erroneously or improperly made in the light of existing loyalty standards. Otherwise stated, we do not find basis in any instance for reversing the judgment of the State Department officials charged with responsibility for employee loyalty; or concluding that they have not conscientiously discharged their duties. . . .

What the State Department knows concerning an employee's loyalty is to be found in its loyalty and security files. These files contain all information bearing on loyalty, obtained from any and all sources, including, of course, the reports of full field investigations by the FBI. Interestingly, in this regard, no sooner had the President indicated that the files would be available for review by the subcommittee than Senator McCarthy charged they were being "raped," altered, or otherwise subjected to a "housecleaning." This charge was found to be utterly without foundation in fact. The files were reviewed by representatives of the Department of Justice, and the Department has certified that all information bearing on the employee's loyalty as developed by the FBI appears in the files which were reviewed by the subcommittee. . . .

The Facts Behind the Charge of "Whitewash"

Seldom, if ever, in the history of congressional investigations has a committee been subjected to an organized campaign of vilification and abuse comparable to that with which we have been confronted throughout this inquiry. This campaign has been so acute and so obviously designed to confuse and confound the American people that an analysis of the factors responsible therefor is indicated.

The first of these factors was the necessity of creating the impression that our inquiry was not thorough and sincere in order to camouflage the fact that the charges made by Senator McCarthy were groundless and that the Senate and the American people had been deceived. No sooner were hearings started than the cry of "whitewash"

Senate Committee on Foreign Relations, *State Department Loyalty Investigation*, 81st Cong., 2d sess., 20 July 1950, S. Rept. 2108, pt. 1, 9–11, 149–52, 167.

[1]McCarthy had charged that 81 State Department employees were "loyalty risks"—ED.

was raised along with the chant "investigate the charges and not McCarthy." This chant we have heard morning, noon, and night for almost 4 months from certain quarters for readily perceptible motives. Interestingly, had we elected to investigate Senator McCarthy, there would have been ample basis therefor, since we have been reliably informed that at the time he made the charges initially he had no information whatever to support them, and, furthermore, it early appeared that in securing Senate Resolution 231[2] a fraud had been perpetrated upon the Senate of the United States.

From the very outset of our inquiry, Senator McCarthy has sought to leave the impression that the subcommittee has been investigating him and not "disloyalty in the State Department." The reason for the Senator's concern is now apparent. He had no facts to support his wild and baseless charges, and lived in mortal fear that this situation would be exposed.

Few people, cognizant of the truth in even an elementary way, have, in the absence of political partisanship, placed any credence in the hit-and-run tactics of Senator McCarthy. He has stooped to a new low in his cavalier disregard of the facts.

The simple truth is that in making his speech at Wheeling, Senator McCarthy was talking of a subject and circumstances about which he knew nothing. His extreme and irresponsible statements called for emergency measures. As Senator Wherry[3] told Emmanuel S. Larsen, "Oh, Mac has gone out on a limb and kind of made a fool of himself and we have to back him up now." Starting with nothing, Senator McCarthy plunged headlong forward, desperately seeking to develop some information, which colored with distortion and fanned by a blaze of bias, would forestall a day of reckoning.

Certain elements rallied to his support, particularly those who ostensibly fight communism by adopting the vile methods of the Communists themselves and in so doing actually hinder the fight of all right-minded people who detest and abhor communism in all its manifestations. We cannot, however, destroy one evil by the adoption of another. Senator McCarthy and McCarthyism have been exposed for what they are— and the sight is not a pretty one. . . . .

General Observations

In concluding our report, we are constrained to make observations which we regard as fundamental.

It is, of course, clearly apparent that the charges of Communist infiltration of and influence upon the State Department are false. This knowledge is reassuring to all Americans whose faith has been temporarily shaken in the security of their Government by perhaps the most nefarious campaign of untruth in the history of our Republic.

We believe, however, that this knowledge and assurance, while important, will prove ultimately of secondary significance in contemplating the salutary aspects of our investigation. For, we believe that, inherent in the charges that have been made and the sinister campaign to give them ostensible verity, are lessons from which the American people will find inspiration for a rededication to the principles and ideals that have made this Nation great.

---

[2]A resolution authorizing an investigation of disloyalty in the State Department—ED.

[3]Conservative Republican Senator Kenneth Wherry of Nebraska—ED.

We have seen the technique of the "Big Lie," elsewhere employed by the totalitarian dictator with devastating success, utilized here for the first time on a sustained basis in our history. We have seen how, through repetition and shifting untruths, it is possible to delude great numbers of people.

We have seen the character of private citizens and of Government employees virtually destroyed by public condemnation on the basis of gossip, distortion, hearsay, and deliberate untruths. By the mere fact of their associations with a few persons of alleged questionable proclivities an effort has been made to place the stigma of disloyalty upon individuals, some of whom are little people whose only asset is their character and devotion to duty and country. This has been done without the slightest vestige of respect for even the most elementary rules of evidence or fair play or, indeed, common decency. Indeed, we have seen an effort not merely to establish guilt by association but guilt by accusation alone. The spectacle is one we would expect in a totalitarian nation where the rights of the individual are crushed beneath the juggernaut of statism and oppression; it has no place in America where government exists to serve our people, not to destroy them.

We have seen an effort to inflame the American people with a wave of hysteria and fear on an unbelievable scale in this free Nation. Were this campaign founded in truth it would be questionable enough; where it is fraught with falsehood from beginning to end, its reprehensible and contemptible character defies adequate condemnation.

We sincerely believe that charges of the character which have been made in this case seriously impair the efforts of our agencies of Government to combat the problem of subversion. Furthermore, extravagant allegations, which cannot be proved and are not subject to proof, have the inevitable effect of dulling the awareness of all Americans to the true menace of communism. . . .

At a time when American blood is again being shed to preserve our dream of freedom, we are constrained fearlessly and frankly to call the charges, and the methods employed to give them ostensible validity, what they truly are: A fraud and a hoax perpetrated on the Senate of the United States and the American people. They represent perhaps the most nefarious campaign of half-truths and untruth in the history of this Republic. For the first time in our history, we have seen the totalitarian technique of the "big lie" employed on a sustained basis. The result has been to confuse and divide the American people, at a time when they should be strong in their unity, to a degree far beyond the hopes of the Communists themselves whose stock in trade is confusion and division. In such a disillusioning setting, we appreciate as never before our Bill of Rights, a free press, and the heritage of freedom that has made this Nation great.

CHAPTER 12

The Civil Rights Revolution

Black Americans have struggled for respect and equal rights for generations but, except for the brief Reconstruction period, made little headway until after World War II. Well into the 1950s, black citizens virtually everywhere were victims of racial discrimination that denied them equal access to jobs, housing, training, education, and private amenities. In the South, state and local laws imposed a system of segregation (Jim Crow) that confined them to separate, and almost invariably inferior, public services and facilities, while legal sleight of hand, intimidation, and subterfuge also denied them the right to vote.

A victory over a malevolent racist ideology, World War II changed the racial climate. Many white Americans came to recognize the pernicious effects of racism; black soldiers returned from the fighting fronts with new determination to resist bigotry at home. Partially suspended during the war, the movement for racial justice vigorously revived after 1945.

During the late 1940s and early 1950s, the civil rights drive was led by the National Association for the Advancement of Colored People (NAACP), a coalition of white liberals and black activists that had as its ultimate goal an integrated society where race and color would cease to matter. The NAACP's chief weapon was suits in the federal courts to compel enforcement of the equal treatment principles enjoined by the Constitution but long ignored. Its strategy culminated in the 1954 Supreme Court decision *Brown v. Board of Education of Topeka*, declaring segregated schools in violation of the equal protection clause of the Fourteenth Amendment.

By the end of the 1950s, nonviolent civil disobedience, as employed by the Southern Christian Leadership Conference (SCLC) headed by the Baptist minister Martin Luther King, Jr., had begun to eclipse the NAACP's legal action approach. Yet even in this new period the civil rights movement remained committed to a color-blind, integrated society of "black and white together." King inspired millions of both races through his writings and through his highly visible protest tactics of boycotts and marches. The eloquence and bravery of King and his followers deeply moved the liberal public and helped undermine a tottering system of legal discrimination and disfranchisement.

By the mid-1960s, however, the civil rights movement had become more separatist and militant. Although Jim Crow was now virtually dead, blacks still remained poor and relatively powerless. These realities, amplified by the confrontational mood of the decade in general, encouraged black separatism and the willingness to consider aggressive means to force the larger society to confer greater political and economic equality.

In the following selections, you will find a small sampling of the extensive literature of the civil rights movement. The writings include several competing varieties of civil rights thought as well as prosegregation, anti-civil rights documents. Carefully consider them for insight into the minds of participants in the momentous civil rights revolution.

12.1 SCHOOL DESEGREGATION (1954, 1963, 1965)

After years of slow progress, the breakthrough in the legal attack on Jim Crow came in 1954 with the Supreme Court decision Brown v. Board of Education of Topeka. *The conclusion of a suit brought by the NAACP Legal Defense Fund headed by Thurgood Marshall, the Brown decision overthrew the precedent established by* Plessy v. Ferguson (1896) *allowing segregated public facilities for blacks, notwithstanding the Fourteenth Amendment, so long as they were equal to those provided for whites. Separate, by its very nature, said Chief Justice Earl Warren in the Brown decision, must be considered unequal.*

The Court would soon enjoin "all deliberate speed" for the implementation of its school desegregation order. In a few places in the Upper South, school districts quickly complied. But in many Southern communities the Brown decision was met by massive resistance. The Ku Klux Klan revived and soon marshaled its weapons of violence and intimidation against school desegregation. More effective were the White Citizens' Councils, composed of "respectable" middle-class conservatives who deplored the crude methods of the Klan but used moral and economic pressure and legal maneuvering to preserve the Jim Crow system. In several Southern states, conservative administrations countered NAACP legal action with court suits of their own to delay application of the Brown decision.

The two selections that follow represent the poles of opinion on the school desegregation issue. The first is an excerpt from the Brown decision itself, written by Chief Justice Warren. Consider the basis for Warren's rejection of "separate but equal." Is his reasoning convincing? Why did the justices who originally announced the Plessy v. Ferguson *doctrine in the 1890s see matters differently from Warren in 1954?*

The Supreme Court's noble sentiments were insufficient to create significant social change. White America resisted school desegregation efforts for decades. The second selection, a speech by President John F. Kennedy, reveals a key issue of the early 1960s: bringing the federal government into the struggle against the resistance of the Southern local and state governments.

The third selection is part of an article from The Citizen, the official publication of the White Citizens' Councils. It was written for members of the Councils on the occasion of a leadership conference held in Chattanooga, Tennessee, in late 1965. Is the piece militantly racist? How convincing are the author's arguments for segregated schools? Consider the principle of segregation by ability, which is rejected. Is the argument against it convincing? Does the author find any gaps in the integrationists' armor? There is much in this article on the need to preserve religion in the schools. Was there a cultural link between segregationism and some kinds of traditional Christian faith? What seems to be the Citizens' Councils' practical solution to the desegregation dilemma?

BROWN V. BOARD OF EDUCATION OF TOPEKA

WARREN, C. J. (Chief Justice). These cases come to us from the States of Kansas, South Carolina, Virginia, and Delaware. They are premised on different facts and different local conditions, but a common legal question justifies their consideration together in this consolidated opinion.

In each of these cases, minors of the Negro race, through their legal representatives, seek the aid of the courts in obtaining admission to the public schools of their community on a nonsegregated basis. In each instance, they have been denied admission to schools attended by white children under laws requiring or permitting segregation according to race. This segregation was alleged to deprive the plaintiffs of the equal protection of the laws under the Fourteenth Amendment. In each of the cases, other than the Delaware case, a three-judge federal district court denied relief to the plaintiffs on the so-called "separate but equal" doctrine announced by this Court in *Plessy* v. *Ferguson*. . . . Under that doctrine, equality of treatment is accorded when the races are provided substantially equal facilities, even though these facilities be separate. . . .

The plaintiffs contend that segregated public schools are not "equal": and cannot be made "equal," and hence they are deprived of the equal protection of the laws. Because of the obvious importance of the question presented, the Court took jurisdiction. Argument was heard in the 1952 Term, and reargument was heard this Term on certain questions propounded by the Court.

Reargument was largely devoted to the circumstances surrounding the adoption of the Fourteenth Amendment in 1868. It covered exhaustively consideration of the Amendment in Congress, ratification by the states, then existing practices in racial segregation, and the views of proponents and opponents of the Amendment. This discussion and our own investigation convince us that, although these sources cast some light, it is not enough to resolve the problem with which we are faced. At best they are inconclusive. . . .

In the first cases in the Court construing the Fourteenth Amendment, decided shortly after its adoption, the Court interpreted it as proscribing all state-imposed discrimination against the Negro race. The doctrine of "separate but equal" did not make its appearance in this Court until 1896 in the case of *Plessy* v. *Ferguson* . . . , involving not education but transportation. American courts have since labored with the doctrine for over half a century. In this Court, there have been six`cases involving the "separate but equal" doctrine in the field of public education. . . . In none of these cases was it necessary to grant relief to the Negro plaintiff. And in *Sweatt* v. *Painter* . . . , the Court expressly reserved decision on the question whether *Plessy* v. *Ferguson* should be held inapplicable to public education.

In the instant case, that question is directly presented. Here . . . there are findings below that the Negro and white schools involved have been equalized, or are

---

Brown v. Board of Education of Topeka, 347 U.S. 483.

being equalized, with respect to buildings, curricula, qualifications and salaries of teachers, and other "tangible" factors. Our decision, therefore, cannot turn on merely a comparison of these tangible factors in the Negro and white schools involved in each of the cases. We must look instead to the effect of segregation itself on public education.

In approaching this problem, we cannot turn the clock back to 1868 when the Amendment was adopted, or even to 1896 when *Plessy* v. *Ferguson* was written. We must consider public education in the light of its full development and its present place in American life throughout the Nation. Only in this way can it be determined if segregation in public schools deprives these plaintiffs of the equal protection of the laws.

Today, education is perhaps the most important function of state and local governments. Compulsory school attendance and the great expenditures for education both demonstrate our recognition of the importance of education to our democratic society. It is required in the performance of our most basic responsibilities, even service in the armed forces. It is the very foundation of good citizenship. Today it is a principal instrument in awakening the child to cultural values, in preparing him for later professional training, and in helping him to adjust normally to his environment. In these days, it is doubtful that any child may reasonably be expected to succeed in life if he is denied the opportunity of an education. Such an opportunity, where the state has undertaken to provide it, is a right which must be made available to all on equal terms.

We come then to the question presented: Does segregation of children in public schools solely on the basis of race, even though the physical facilities and other "tangible" factors may be equal, deprive the children of the minority group of equal educational opportunities? We believe that it does.

In *Sweatt* v. *Painter,* . . . in finding that a segregated law school for Negroes could not provide them equal educational opportunities, this Court relied in large part on "those qualities which are incapable of objective measurement but which make for greatness in a law school." In *McLaurin* v. *Oklahoma State Regents,* . . . the Court, in requiring that a Negro admitted to a white graduate school be treated like all other students, again resorted to intangible considerations: ". . . his ability to study, to engage in discussion and exchange views with other students and, in general, to learn his profession." Such considerations apply with added force to children in grade and high schools. To separate them from others of similar age and qualifications solely because of their race generates a feeling of inferiority as to their status in the community that may affect their hearts and minds in a way unlikely ever to be undone. . . .

Whatever may have been the extent of psychological knowledge at the time of *Plessy* v. *Ferguson*, this finding is amply supported by modern authority. Any language contrary to this finding is rejected.

We conclude that in the field of public education the doctrine of "separate but equal" has no place. Separate educational facilities are inherently unequal. Therefore, we hold that the plaintiffs and others similarly situated for whom the actions have been brought are, by reason of the segregation complained of, deprived of the equal protection of the laws guaranteed by the Fourteenth Amendment. This disposition makes unnecessary any discussion whether such segregation also violates the Due Process Clause of the Fourteenth Amendment.

A MORAL IMPERATIVE: EQUALITY OF TREATMENT

John F. Kennedy

Delivered over Television and Radio, Washington, D.C., June 11, 1963

Good evening, my fellow citizens. This afternoon, following a series of threats and defiant statements, the presence of Alabama National Guardsmen was required on the University of Alabama to carry out the final and unequivocal order of the United States District Court of the Northern District of Alabama.

That order called for the admission of two clearly qualified young Alabama residents who happened to have been born Negro.

That they were admitted peacefully on the campus is due in good measure to the conduct of the students of the University of Alabama who met their responsibilities in a constructive way.

I hope that every American, regardless of where he lives, will stop and examine his conscience about this and other related incidents.

This nation was founded by men of many nations and backgrounds. It was founded on the principle that all men are created equal, and that the rights of every man are diminished when the rights of one man are threatened.

Today, we are committed to a worldwide struggle to promote and protect the rights of all who wish to be free. And when Americans are sent to Vietnam or West Berlin we do not ask for whites only.

It ought to be possible, therefore, for American students of any color to attend any public institution they select without having to be backed up by troops. It ought to be possible for American consumers of any color to receive equal service in places of public accommodation, such as hotels and restaurants, and theaters and retail stores without being forced to resort to demonstrations in the street.

And it ought to be possible for American citizens of any color to register and to vote in a free election without interference or fear of reprisal.

It ought to be possible, in short, for every American to enjoy the privileges of being American without regard to his race or his color.

In short, every American ought to have the right to be treated as he would wish to be treated, as one would wish his children to be treated. But this is not the case.

The Negro baby born in America today, regardless of the section or the state in which he is born, has about one-half as much chance of completing high school as a white baby, born in the same place, on the same day; one-third as much chance of completing college; one-third as much chance of becoming a professional man; twice as much chance of becoming unemployed; about one-seventh as much chance of earning $10,000 a year; a life expectancy which is seven years shorter and the prospects of earning only half as much.

This is not a sectional issue. Difficulties over segregation and discrimination exist in every city, in every state of the Union, producing in many cities a rising tide of discontent that threatens the public safety.

Nor is this a partisan issue. In a time of domestic crisis, men of goodwill and generosity should be able to unite regardless of party or politics.

This is not even a legal or legislative issue alone. It is better to settle these matters in the courts than on the streets, and new laws are needed at every level. But law alone cannot make men see right.

We are confronted primarily with a moral issue. It is as old as the Scriptures and is as clear as the American Constitution. The heart of the question is whether all Americans are to be afforded equal rights and equal opportunities; whether we are going to treat our fellow Americans as we want to be treated.

If an American, because his skin is dark, cannot eat lunch in a restaurant open to the public; if he cannot send his children to the best public school available; if he cannot vote for the public officials who represent him; if, in short, he cannot enjoy the full and free life which all of us want, then who among us would be content to have the color of his skin changed and stand in his place?

Who among us would then be content with the counsels of patience and delay? One hundred years of delay have passed since President Lincoln freed the slaves, yet their heirs, their grandsons, are not fully free. They are not yet freed from the bonds of injustice; they are not yet freed from social and economic oppression.

And this nation, for all its hopes and all its boasts, will not be fully free until all its citizens are free.

We preach freedom around the world, and we mean it. And we cherish our freedom here at home. But are we to say to the world—and much more importantly to each other—that this is the land of the free, except for the Negroes; that we have no second-class citizens, except Negroes; that we have no class or caste system, no ghettos, no master race, except with respect to Negroes.

Now the time has come for this nation to fulfill its promise. The events in Birmingham and elsewhere have so increased the cries for equality that no city or state or legislative body can prudently choose to ignore them.

The fires of frustration and discord are burning in every city, North and South. Where legal remedies are not at hand, redress is sought in the streets in demonstrations, parades and protests, which create tensions and threaten violence—and threaten lives.

We face, therefore, a moral crisis as a country and a people. It cannot be met by repressive police action. It cannot be left to increased demonstrations in the streets. It cannot be quieted by token moves or talk. It is time to act in the Congress, in your state and local legislative body, and above all, in all of our daily lives.

It is not enough to pin the blame on others, to say this is a problem of one section of the country or another, or deplore the facts that we face. A great change is at hand, and our task, our obligation is to make that revolution, that change, peaceful and constructive for all.

Those who do nothing are inviting shame as well as violence. Those who act boldly are recognizing right as well as reality.

Next week I shall ask Congress of the United States to act, to make a commitment it has not fully made in this century to the proposition that race has no place in American life or law.

The Federal judiciary has upheld that proposition in a series of forthright cases. The Executive Branch has adopted that proposition in the conduct of its affairs, including the employment of federal personnel, and the use of Federal facilities, and the sale of Federally financed housing.

But there are other necessary measures which only the Congress can provide, and they must be provided at this session.

The old code of equity law under which we live commands for every wrong a remedy. But in too many communities, in too many parts of the country wrongs are inflicted on Negro citizens and there are no remedies in law.

Unless the Congress acts their only remedy is the street.

I am, therefore, asking the Congress to enact legislation giving all Americans the right to be served in facilities which are open to the public—hotels, restaurants and theaters, retail stores and similar establishments. This seems to me to be an elementary right.

Its denial is an arbitrary indignity that no American in 1963 should have to endure, but many do.

I have recently met with scores of business leaders, urging them to take voluntary action to end this discrimination. And I've been encouraged by their response. And in the last two weeks over 75 cities have seen progress made in desegregating these kinds of facilities.

But many are unwilling to act alone. And for this reason nationwide legislation is needed, if we are to move this problem from the streets to the courts.

I'm also asking Congress to authorize the Federal Government to participate more fully in lawsuits designed to end segregation in public education. We have succeeded in persuading many districts to desegregate voluntarily. Dozens have admitted Negroes without violence.

Today a Negro is attending a state-supported institution in every one of our 50 states, but the pace is very slow.

Too many Negro children entering segregated grade schools at the time of the Supreme Court's decision nine years ago will enter segregated high schools this fall, having suffered a loss which can never be restored.

The lack of an adequate education denies the Negro a chance to get a decent job. The orderly implementation of the Supreme Court decision, therefore, cannot be left solely to those who may not have the economic resources to carry their legal action or who may be subject to harassment.

Other features will be also requested, including greater protection for the right to vote.

But legislation, I repeat, cannot solve this problem alone. It must be solved in the homes of every American in every community across our country.

In this respect, I want to pay tribute to those citizens, North and south, who've been working in their communities to make life better for all. They are acting not out of a sense of legal duty but out of a sense of human decency. Like our soldiers and sailors in all parts of the world, they are meeting freedom's challenge on the firing line and I salute them for their honor—their courage.

My fellow Americans, this is a problem which faces us all, in every city of the North as well as the South.

Today there are Negroes unemployed—two or three times as many compared to whites—inadequate education; moving into the large cities, unable to find work; young people particularly out of work, without hope, denied equal rights, denied the opportunity to eat at a restaurant or a lunch counter, or go to a movie theater; denied the right to a decent education; denied, almost today, the right to attend a state university even though qualified.

It seems to me that these are matters which concern us all—not merely Presidents, or Congressmen, or Governors, but every citizen of the United States.

This is one country. It has become one country because all of us and all the people who came here had an equal chance to develop their talents.

We cannot say to 10 percent of the population that

"you can't have that right. Your children can't have the chance to develop whatever talents they have, that the only way that they're going to get their rights is to go in the street and demonstrate."

I think we owe them and we owe ourselves a better country than that.

Therefore, I'm asking for your help in making it easier for us to move ahead and provide the kind of equality of treatment which we would want ourselves—to give a chance for every child to be educated to the limit of his talent.

As I've said before, not every child has an equal talent or an equal ability or equal motivation. But they should have the equal right to develop their talent and their ability and their motivation to make something of themselves.

We have a right to expect that the Negro community will be responsible, will uphold the law. But they have a right to expect the law will be fair, that the Constitution will be color blind, as Justice Harlan said at the turn of the century.

This is what we're talking about. This is a matter which concerns this country and what it stands for, and in meeting it I ask the support of all of our citizens.

Thank you very much.

How Can We Educate Our Children?

White Citizens' Councils

Schools are not merely the mark of a civilization. They are the means of maintaining civilization.

Our American school system is at once an inheritance from Europe and an original contribution to the modern world. Ultimately, our system derives from the medieval universities such as Oxford and Cambridge, and from the "grammar" and other schools established to prepare for those universities. . . .

All the universities of the Middle Ages and the earliest universities or colleges in America were established by groups of Christians, whose basic concern was perpetuation of the gospel.

American state universities were frankly imitative of these educational institutions of the Christian church. Early American schools, like their European predecessors, aimed at beginning for children a course of study leading toward college. In this country, however, a new element came to be emphasized—the training of every child, whether he would or would not go to college. This vital feature of our society has now reached the point of undertaking to see that every child goes to college.

White Citizens' Councils, "How Can We Educate Our Children?" *The Citizen*, November 1965, pp. 4–7.

It is this widening of the doors of opportunity which has been the special contribution of America to the world, for to some degree the rest of the world is following us in it.

What needs to be remembered is that there is no point in widening the doors if the treasure within be lost in the process. Our schools and colleges became valuable because they led their student to skill in the arts and knowledge in the sciences, very specifically including the Holy Scripture and the Christian life.

Too often in our time the curriculum has been broadened at the expense of becoming shallower and recently all religious content has been dictatorially excluded from state operated schools. Of course some positive attitude toward religion is inseparable from an educational enterprise. . . .

In the world revolution now being everywhere attempted, the conscious overthrow of the traditional American school system, with its roots in the Christian culture of Western Europe, is a priority item. Many revolutionary techniques have been employed, many massive assaults have been made on the ramparts of the "three R's" and especially of the fourth "R," religion. . . .

No other blow against our educational structure has been quite so violent or damaging as the hysterical attack of the racial integrationists. The results in the District of Columbia are notorious. The school system of the nation's capital was once among the finest in the country. Today it is an educational desert—with one oasis in the far Northwest thanks to a process of *de facto* resegregation.

Central High School in Little Rock was found by a survey in the mid-1950s to be one of the 25 best secondary schools in the United States. Today, even though integration there is hardly more than a token, it is scarcely thought of in terms of overall excellence.

Dr. Henry Garrett and other experts have shown that a sound program of schooling is intrinsically impossible where significant numbers of white and black children are herded together in one classroom. The essential disparity, mentally and temperamentally, is just too great. The mania for homogenization has not yet reached the point where high school boys and girls are integrated in the same gym classes. Yet it would be hardly more absurd than the forced congregation of Negro with white children above the preschool level.

(In the Old South, white children played with Negro children regularly before reaching school age, and even later—outside the school. This fact sometimes caused painful personal readjustments later, which integrationists attribute to the eventual segregation, but which could just as well be attributed to the early integration. More reasonably, one could simply recognize that a full life involves many readjustments.)

Some object to segregationist arguments based on IQ differences by saying: "Well then, group them in class by IQ, or other ability test, without reference to race!" The rejoinder to this is twofold: (1) it is not at all what the militant integrationists want, since it would leave a racially unbalanced situation; and (2) it would create new psychological problems, possibly much more serious than any we now have, and would result in an ever widening gap between the predominantly white group, with its adopted superior Negroes, and the predominantly Negro group with its adopted subnormal whites.

Intelligence is not everything—not enough to justify breaking up groups with other sources of internal cohesion. But a group's average intelligence is important enough to justify separate education for groups with significantly different averages, even if there is some "overlap." By way of analogy, the existence of Amazonian women and effeminate men does not justify drafting women for combat military service (though the Russians have used women for such service).

Not to pursue further the speculative reasons for segregation, a recent analysis of practical school problems which gives the strongest kind of objective support to the segregationist position appeared in, of all places, the *New York Times Magazine* (May 2, 1965) by one Martin Mayer—subjectively, it would appear, an integrationist, but an intelligent observer and skillful writer. Following are excerpts from this revealing article:

> Public confidence in the [New York City] school system is fearfully low and dropping: White children are leaving the city public schools at a rate of 40,000 a year. . . . Of the leaders of the school system itself—the nine-member Board of Education and the 20-odd deputy and associate superintendents— only a handful have children who attend or ever did attend a New York Public school. . . . Of the Negro leaders of the integration drive, . . . not one has or has had a child in a New York public school. . . .

Integration is the main, but not the only threat to the American school system. Indeed, integration itself would not be promoted so fanatically if too many educators had not adopted a philosophy which says that the spirit of man is the result of material processes, and that there is no spirit beyond.

Materialism begins by exalting the schools, for it holds that through them society and the nature of man himself may undergo a revolutionary transformation. Yet materialism ends by destroying the schools, for it reduces them to budgets, buildings and bureaucracy, where blossom at best the beatniks of Berkeley,[1] and from which finer spirits escape altogether. . . .

Because of the integration-at-any-cost policy of both the Federal government and the majority of the nation's educational bureaucrats, the public is daily losing faith in the "serviceability of public education." This is not a condition which the Citizens' Councils have created, but it is one which we recognize. The purpose of the Chattanooga Leadership Conference is to promote the rapidly expanding private school movement as a means of protecting both racial integrity and American education.

12.2   CHRISTIAN LOVE VERSUS RACIAL ANGER (1964, 1967)

The Brown *decision of 1954 unleashed forces that soon dismantled the entire system of legal discrimination. Each step of the way was marked by further court decisions and new federal legislation to enforce job equality and voting rights. But government agencies, whether the courts, Congress, or the Justice Department, would not have moved so fast without the bold challenges to Southern practices by brave civil rights workers willing to face intimidation and physical attack. Inevitably, these challenges created martyrs, but they dramatized the plight of Southern black people and revealed the continuing defiance of the law of the land by conservative whites. The process stirred waves of sympathy among white Americans that impressed Congress and the White House, accelerating the process of federal intervention.*

By the mid-1960s, even these more militant tactics seemed too feeble to some civil rights activists. Driven by an emerging black nationalism and by frustration at the slow pace of

---

[1]1950s social-cultural nonconformists whose dress, attitudes, and lifestyles offended many conventional middle-class people—ED.

economic progress for blacks, the militants lashed out angrily and defiantly at white America, including white liberal sympathizers. In place of the color-blind society, the ideal until this point, they proposed one where distinctive black institutions would function separately from those of the larger society. Infused with such "black power" views, the Student Non-Violent Coordinating Committee[1] (SNCC), along with the Congress of Racial Equality (CORE), expelled their white members and declared themselves separatist organizations. Meanwhile, organizations like the Black Panthers, a menacing paramilitary group from California, adopted Marxist or anticolonialist Third World revolutionary theories to guide their struggles against white America.

By this time outright violence had begun to sweep the inner-city black ghettos. Beginning in Watts in Los Angeles in 1965 and continuing for three years, riots erupted in the ghettos each summer. Often triggered by anger at police brutality, the uprisings expressed the frustrated expectations of the black urban poor. They culminated in April 1968, following the assassination of Martin Luther King, Jr., by a white supremacist, in a spasm of ghetto rage that raised visions of racial apocalypse.

White liberals urged compassion and understanding, but many white Americans resented and feared the new militancy. It soon triggered a surge of antiblack resentment labeled "white backlash." Backlash, King's tragic death, and the discouraging pace of African American economic progress stopped the civil rights movement in its tracks. Advance would eventually resume, but it would be once more primarily through the slow and quiet processes of legislation, legal challenge, bureaucratic ruling, and court review.

The first selection that follows is an SCLC statement of its approach and goals probably composed in 1964. It summarizes the philosophy that guided King and his supporters. What are the intellectual sources of SCLC's philosophy? Do SCLC's tactics place great psychological burdens on its practitioners? What were the SCLC's goals for the American society of the future? Were these goals realistic?

The second selection is a statement made by SNCC after it had been taken over by the black power militants and repudiated SCLC and its tactics. How would you characterize the tone of this selection? Was this late-period SNCC approach practical? Could its plan have been implemented? What do you think of the specific tactics to undermine the system suggested here? One element of this new mood was pan-Africanism. What forces or events help explain this identification of black Americans with Africa in the late 1960s? Have you encountered this view before in this volume? How would you expect most whites to respond to a manifesto such as this one?

This Is SCLC

Southern Christian Leadership Conference

Aims and Purposes of SCLC

The Southern Christian Leadership Conference has the basic aim of achieving full citizenship rights, equality, and the integration of the Negro in all aspects of American life. SCLC is a service agency to facilitate coordinated action of local community groups

---

Southern Christian Leadership Conference, "*This Is SCLC*," rev. ed., 1964.

[1]This group was originally a biracial offshoot of the 1960 student lunch counter sit-in movement of 1960 that helped desegregate restaurants and cafeterias in the South. Composed primarily of students and young men and women, it was affiliated with SCLC, although from the first it often refused to accept SCLC's direction.

within the frame of their indigenous organizations and natural leadership. SCLC activity revolves around two main focal points: the use of nonviolent philosophy as a means of creative protest; and securing the right of the ballot for every citizen.

Philosophy of SCLC

The basic tenets of Hebraic-Christian tradition coupled with the Gandhian concept of *satyagraha*—truth force—is at the heart of SCLC's philosophy. Christian nonviolence actively resists evil in any form. It never seeks to humiliate the opponent, only to win him. Suffering is accepted without retaliation. Internal violence of the spirit is as much to be rejected as external physical violence. At the center of nonviolence is redemptive love. Creatively used, the philosophy of nonviolence can restore the broken community in America. SCLC is convinced that nonviolence is the most potent force available to an oppressed people in their struggle for freedom and dignity.

SCLC and Nonviolent Mass Direct Action

SCLC believes that the American dilemma in race relations can best and most quickly be resolved through the action of thousands of people, committed to the philosophy of nonviolence, who will physically identify themselves in a just and moral struggle. It is not enough to be intellectually dissatisfied with an evil system. The true nonviolent resister presents his physical body as an instrument to defeat the system. Through nonviolent mass direct action, the evil system is creatively dramatized in order that the conscience of the community may grapple with the rightness or wrongness of the issue at hand. . . .

SCLC and Voter-Registration

The right of the ballot is basic to the exercise of full citizenship rights. All across the South, subtle and flagrant obstacles confront the Negro when he seeks to register and vote. Poll taxes, long form questionnaires, harassment, economic reprisal, and sometimes death, meet those who dare to seek this exercise of the ballot. In areas where there is little or no attempt to block the voting attempts of the Negro, apathy generally is deeply etched upon the habits of the community. SCLC, with its specialized staff, works on both fronts: aiding local communities through every means available to secure the right to vote (e.g., filing complaints with the Civil Rights Commission) and arousing interest through voter-registration workshops to point up the importance of the ballot. Periodically, SCLC, upon invitation, conducts a voter-registration drive to enhance a community's opportunity to free itself from economic and political servitude. SCLC believes that the most important step the Negro can take is that short walk to the voting booth.

SCLC and Civil Disobedience

SCLC sees civil disobedience as a natural consequence of nonviolence when the resister is confronted by unjust and immoral laws. This does not imply that SCLC advocates either anarchy or lawlessness. The Conference firmly believes that all people have a moral responsibility to obey laws that are just. It recognizes, however, that there also are unjust laws. From a purely moral point of view, an unjust law is one that is out of harmony with the moral law of the universe, or, as the religionist would say, out of harmony with the Law of God. More concretely, an unjust law is one in which the minority is compelled to observe a code which is not binding on the majority. An unjust law is one in which people are required to obey a code that they had no part in making because they were denied the right to vote. In the face of such obvious inequality, where difference is made legal, the nonviolent resister has no alternative but to disobey the unjust law. In disobeying such a law, he does so peacefully, openly and nonviolently. Most important, he *willingly* accepts the penalty for breaking the law. This distinguishes SCLC's position on civil disobedience from the "uncivil disobedience" of the racist opposition in the South. In the face of laws they consider unjust, they seek to defy, evade, and circumvent the law, BUT they are *unwilling* to accept the penalty for breaking the law. The end result of their defiance is anarchy and disrespect for the law. SCLC, on the other hand, believes that civil disobedience involves the highest respect for the law. He who openly disobeys a law that conscience tells him is unjust and willingly accepts the penalty is giving evidence that he so respects the law that he belongs in jail until it is changed. . . .

SCLC and Segregation

SCLC is firmly opposed to segregation in any form that it takes and pledges itself to work unrelentingly to rid every vestige of its scars from our nation through nonviolent means. Segregation is an evil and its presence in our nation has blighted our larger destiny as a leader in world affairs. Segregation does as much harm to the *segregator* as it does to the *segregated*. The *segregated* develops a false sense of inferiority and the *segregator* develops a false sense of superiority, both contrary to the American ideal of democracy. America must rid herself of segregation not alone because it is politically expedient, but because it is morally right!

SCLC and Constructive Program

SCLC's basic program fosters nonviolent resistance to all forms of racial injustice, including state and local laws and practices, even when this mean going to jail; and imaginative, bold constructive action to end the demoralization caused by the legacy of slavery and segregation—inferior schools, slums, and second-class citizenship. Thus, the Conference works on two fronts. On the one hand, it resists continuously the system of segregation which is the basic cause of lagging standards; on the other hand, it works constructively to improve the standards themselves. There MUST be a balance between attacking the causes and healing the effects of segregation.

SCLC and the Beloved Community

The ultimate aim of SCLC is to foster and create the "beloved community" in America where brotherhood is a reality. It rejects any doctrine of black supremacy for this merely substitutes one kind of tyranny for another. The Conference does not foster moving the Negro from a position of disadvantage to one of advantage for this would thereby subvert justice. SCLC works for integration. Our ultimate goal is genuine intergroup and interpersonal living—*integration*. Only through nonviolence can reconciliation and the creation of the beloved community be effected. The international focus on America and her internal problems against the dread prospect of a hot war, demand our seeking this end.

SONGS OF THE CIVIL RIGHTS MOVEMENTS

Keep Your Eyes on the Prize

Paul and Silas, bound in jail,
Had no money for to go their, bail.

Chorus:

Keep yours eye on the prize,
Hold on, hold on,
Hold on, hold on—
Keep yours eyes on the prize,
Hold on, hold on.
Paul and Silas begin to shout,
The jail door opened and they walked out.
Freedom's name is mighty sweet—
Soon one of these days we're going to meet.
Got my hand on the Gospel plow,
I wouldn't take nothing for my journey now.
The only chain that a man can stand
Is that chain of hand in hand.
The only thing that we did wrong—
Stayed in the Wilderness too long.
But the one thing we did right
Was the day we started to fight.
We're gonna board that big Greyhound,
Carryin' love from town to town.
We're gonna ride for civil rights,
We're gonna ride, both black and white.
We've met jail and violence too,
But God's love has seen us through.
Haven't been to Heaven but I've been told
Streets up there are paved with gold.

Woke Up This Morning with My Mind Stayed on Freedom

Woke up this morning with my mind stayed on freedom,
Woke up this morning with my mind stayed on freedom,
Woke up this morning with my mind stayed on freedom,
Hallelu, hallelu, hallelu, hallelu, hallelujah.
Ain't no harm to keep your mind stayed on freedom, etc.
Walkin' and talkin' with my mind stayed on freedom, etc.
Singin' and prayin' with my mind stayed on freedom, etc.
Doin' the twist with my mind stayed on freedom, etc.

Ain't Gonna Let Nobody Turn Me Round

Ain't gonna let nobody, Lordy, turn me round,
Turn me round, turn me round.
Aint't gonna let nobody, Lordy, turn me round.

Chorus:
I'm gonna keep on a-walkin', Lord,
Keep on a-talkin', Lord,
Marching up to freedom land.
Ain't gonna let Nervous Nelly turn me round, etc.
Ain't gonna let Chief Pritchett turn me round, etc.
Ain't gonna let Mayor Kelly turn me round, etc.
Ain't gonna let segregation turn me round, etc.
Ain't gonna let no jailhouse turn me round, etc.
Ain't gonna let no injunction turn me round, etc.

This Little Light of Mine

This little light of mine, I'm gonna let it shine;
This little light of mine, I'm gonna let it shine;
This little light of mine, I'm gonna let it shine;
Let it shine, let it shine, let it shine.
The light that shines is the light of love,
Lights the darkness from above.
It shines on me and it shines on you,
And shows what the power of love can do.
I'm gonna shine my light both far and near,
I'm gonna shine my light both bright and clear.
Where there's a dark corner in this land,
I'm gonna let my little light shine.
We've got the light of freedom, we're gonna let it shine;
We've got the light of freedom, we're gonna let it shine;
We've got the light of freedom, we're gonna let it shine;
Let it shine, let it shine, let it shine.
Deep down in the South, we're gonna let it shine, etc.
Down in Birmingham, we're gonna let it shine, etc.
All over the nation, we're gonna let it shine, etc.
Everywhere I go, I'm gonna let it shine, etc.
Tell Chief Pritchett, we're gonna let it shine, etc.
All in the jailhouse, we're gonna let it shine, etc.
On Monday he gave me the gift of love;
Tuesday peace came from above;
Wednesday he told me to have more faith;
Thursday he gave me a little more grace;
Friday he told me just to watch and pray;
Saturday he told me just what to say;
Sunday he gave me the power divine—
To let my little light shine.

WE WANT BLACK POWER

Student Non-Violent Coordinating Committee

Black Men of America Are a Captive People

The black man in America is in a perpetual state of slavery no matter what the white man's propaganda tells us.

The black man in America is exploited and oppressed the same as his black brothers are all over the face of the earth by the same white man. We will never be free until we are all free and that means all black oppressed people all over the earth.

We are not alone in this fight, we are a part of the struggle for self-determination of all black men everywhere. We here in America must unite ourselves to be ready to help our brothers elsewhere.

We must first gain BLACK POWER here in America. Living inside the camp of the leaders of the enemy forces, it is our duty to our Brothers to revolt against the system and create our own system so that we can live as MEN.

We must take over the political and economic systems where we are in the majority in the heart of every major city in this country as well as in the rural areas. We must create our own black culture to erase the lies the white man has fed our minds from the day we were born.

The Black Man in the Ghetto Will Lead the Black Power Movement

The black Brother in the ghetto will lead the Black Power Movement and make the changes that are necessary for its success.

The black man in the ghetto has one big advantage that the bourgeois Negro does not have despite his 'superior' education. He is already living outside the value system white society imposes on all black Americans.

He has to look at things from another direction in order to survive. He is ready. He received his training in the streets, in the jails, from the ADC[1] check his mother did not receive in time and the head-beatings he got from the cop on the corner.

Once he makes that first important discovery about the great pride you feel inside as a BLACK MAN and the great heritage of the mother country, Africa, there is no stopping him from dedicating himself to fight the white man's system.

This is why the Black Power Movement is a true revolutionary movement with the power to change men's minds and unmask the tricks the white man has used to keep black men enslaved in modern society.

The Bourgeois Negro Cannot Be a Part of the Black Power Movement

The bourgeois Negro has been force-fed the white man's propaganda and has lived too long in the half-world between white and phony black bourgeois society. He cannot

---

Student Non-Violent Coordinating Committee, Chicago Office, *We Want Black Power*, 1967.

[1]Aid to Dependent Children, a major feature of the federal welfare system—ED.

think for himself because he is a shell of a man full of contradictions he cannot resolve. He is not to be trusted under any circumstances until he has proved himself to be "cured." There are a minute handful of these "cured" bourgeois Negroes in the Black Power Movement and they are most valuable but they must not be allowed to take control. They are aware intellectually but under stress will react emotionally to the pressures of white society in the same way a white 'liberal' will expose an unconscious prejudice that he did not even realize he possessed.

What Brother Malcolm X Taught Us about Ourselves

Malcolm X[2] was the first black man from the ghetto in America to make a real attempt to get the white man's fist off the black man. He recognized the true dignity of man— without the white society prejudices about status, education and background that we all must purge from our minds.

Even today, in the Black Power Movement itself we find Brothers who look down on another Brother because of the conditions that life has imposed upon him. The most beautiful thing that Malcolm X taught us is that once a black man discovers for himself a pride of his blackness, he can throw off the shackles of mental slavery and become a MAN in the truest sense of the word. We must move on from the point our Great Black Prince had reached.

We Must Become Leaders for Ourselves

We must not get hung-up in the bag of having one great leader who we depend upon to make decisions. This makes the Movement too vulnerable to those forces the white man uses to keep us enslaved, such as the draft, murder, prison or character assassination.

We have to all learn to become leaders for ourselves and remove all white values from our minds. When we see a Brother using a white value through error it is our duty to the Movement to point it out to him. We must thank our Brothers who show us our own errors. We must discipline ourselves so that if necessary we can leave family and friends at a moment's notice, maybe forever, and know our Brothers have pledged themselves to protect the family we have left behind.

As a part of our education, we must travel to other cities and make contracts with the Brothers in all the ghettos in America so that when the time is right we can unite as one under the banner of BLACK POWER.

Learning to Think Black and Remove White Things from Our Minds

We have got to begin to say and understand with complete assuredness what black is. Black is an inner pride that the white man's language hampers us from expressing. Black is being a complete fanatic, who white society considers insane.

We have to learn that black is so much better than belonging to the white race with the blood of millions dripping from their hands that it goes far beyond any prejudice or resentment. We must fill ourselves with hate for all white things. This is not vengeance or trying to take the white oppressors' place to become new black oppressors but is a oneness with a worldwide black brotherhood.

---

[2]The former Malcolm Little, a convert to the Nation of Islam, a black separatist group. He was eventually assassinated, apparently by a rival black group—ED.

We must regain respect for the lost religion of our fathers, the spirits of the black earth of Africa. The white man has so poisoned our minds that if a Brother told you he practiced Voodoo you would roll around on the floor laughing at how stupid and superstitious he was.

We have to learn to roll around on the floor laughing at the black man who says he worships the white Jesus. He is truly sick.

We must create our own language for these things that the white man will not understand because a Black Culture exists and it is not the wood-carvings or native dancing, it is the black strength inside of true men.

Ideas on Planning for the Future of Black Power

We must infiltrate all government agencies. This will not be hard because black clerks work in all agencies in poor paying jobs and have a natural resentment of the white men who run these jobs.

People must be assigned to seek out these dissatisfied black men and women and put pressure on them to give us the information we need. Any man in overalls, carrying a tool box, can enter a building if he looks like he knows what he is doing.

Modern America depends on many complex systems such as electricity, water, gas, sewerage and transportation and all are vulnerable. Much of the government is run by computers that must operate in air conditioning. Cut off the air conditioning and they cannot function.

We must begin to investigate and learn all of these things so that we can use them if it becomes necessary. We cannot train an army in the local park but we can be ready for the final confrontation with the white man's system.

Remember your Brothers in South Africa and do not delude yourselves that it could not happen here. We must copy the white man's biggest trick, diversion (Hitler taught them that), and infiltrate all civil rights groups, keep them in confusion so they will be neutralized and cannot be used as a tool of the white power structure.

The civil rights, integrationist movement says to the white man, "If you please, Sir, let us, the 10 percent minority of Americans have our rights. See how nice and nonviolent we are?"

This is why SNCC calls itself a Human Rights Organization. We believe that we belong to the 90 percent majority of the people on earth that the white man oppresses and that we should not beg the white man for anything. We want what belongs to us as human beings and we intend to get it through BLACK POWER.

How to Deal with Black Traitors

Uncle Tom is too kind of a word. What we have are black traitors, quisslings [*sic*], collaborators, sell-outs, white Negroes.

We have to expose these people for once and for all for what they are and place them on the side of the oppressor where they belong. Their black skin is a lie and their guilt the shame of all black men. We must ostracize them and if necessary exterminate them.

We must stop fighting a "fair game." We must do whatever is necessary to win BLACK POWER. We have to hate and disrupt and destroy and blackmail and lie and steal and become blood-brothers like the Mau-Mau.

We must eliminate or render ineffective all traitors. We must make them fear to stand up like puppets for the white men, and we must make the world understand that these so-called men do not represent us or even belong to the same black race because they sold out their birthright for a mess of white society pottage. Let them choke on it.

Pitfalls to Avoid on the Path to Black Power

We must learn how close America and Russia are politically. The biggest lie in the world is the cold-war. Money runs the world and it is controlled completely by the white man.

Russia and America run the two biggest money systems in the world and they intend to keep it under their control under any circumstances. Thus, we cannot accept any help from Communism or any other "ism."

We must seek out poor peoples movements in South America, Africa and Asia and make our alliances with them. We must not be fooled into thinking that there is a ready-made doctrine that will solve all our problems.

There are only white man's doctrines and they will never work for us. We have to work out our own systems and doctrines and culture.

Why Propaganda Is Our Most Important Tool

The one thing that the white man's system cannot stand is the TRUTH because his system is all based on lies.

There is no such thing as "justice" for a black man in America. The white man controls everything that is said in every book, newspaper, magazine, TV and radio broadcast.

Even the textbooks used in the schools and the bible that is read in the churches are designed to maintain the system for the white man. Each and every one of us is forced to listen to the white man's propaganda every day of our lives.

The political system, economic system, military system, educational system, religious system and anything else you name is used to preserve the status quo of white America getting fatter and fatter while the black man gets more and more hungry.

We must spend our time telling our Brothers the truth.

We must tell them that any black woman who wears a diamond on her finger is wearing the blood of her Brothers and Sisters in slavery in South Africa where one out of every three black babies die before the age of one, from starvation, to make the white man rich.

We must stop wearing the symbols of slavery on our fingers.

We must stop going to other countries to exterminate our Brothers and Sisters for the white man's greed.

We must ask our Brothers which side they are on.

Once you know the truth for yourself it is your duty to dedicate your life to recruiting your Brothers and to counteract the white man's propaganda.

We must disrupt the white man's system to create our own. We must publish newspapers and get radio stations. Black Unity is strength—let's use it now to get BLACK POWER.

CHAPTER 13

The Great Society

America's political climate was transformed by the election of John F. Kennedy as president in 1960. JFK was not a flaming liberal, but he was young and bold, and his victory, after eight years of the grandfatherly old soldier, Dwight Eisenhower, in the White House, created a sense of new political possibilities.

In fact, the Kennedy administration's domestic achievements were rather modest. The president aroused the idealism of youth with his Peace Corps program and fed U.S. pride by his program to land a human being on the moon during the decade. But virtually all of his liberal New Frontier legislation stalled in Congress. By the time of his tragic assassination in November 1963, little of it had been enacted into law.

Most of the bold legislative advances of the decade started with Kennedy's successor. Lyndon B. Johnson was a very different person from the young man he succeeded. A physically massive Texan, LBJ lacked the polish, glamour, and personal magnetism of his predecessor, but he made up for them with his extraordinary political skills honed by twenty years in Congress and a decade of Democratic party leadership in the Senate. Johnson was able to break the legislative logjam through persuasion, cajolery, deal-making, and arm-twisting. Between early 1964 and 1968, Congress enacted most of his Great Society program, the most sweeping reform agenda since the New Deal a generation before.

These programs established new systems of health-care benefits for retirees (Medicare) and for the needy (Medicaid). They provided massive aid to public education and scholarships for college students. Clean air, clean water, and highway beautification measures supplemented the environmental legislation of the New Deal era. There were also new federal subsidies for the arts and for academic scholarship. Most innovative and dramatic of all was the War on Poverty, a federal campaign to eliminate want in America through Headstart, the Job Corps, subsidized legal services, a Community Action Program, and many more initiatives, all under an Office of Economic Opportunity.

The Great Society clearly benefited from initial public support. Running in 1964 for president in his own right against conservative Barry Goldwater, Johnson achieved one of the most sweeping electoral victories in this century, carrying every state but Arizona and a few in the South, and leading his party to unprecedented majorities in both houses of Congress.

LBJ interpreted this success as a liberal mandate, and it was. With prices stable and economic growth high, the United States felt flush—and generous—and Congress was quick to approve the costly new social programs.

In the following selections, you will find responses to the Great Society by three groups: defenders, detractors on the right, and detractors on the left. Try to analyze the reasons and reasoning behind each position. Also consider the validity of each viewpoint.

13.1   DEFENDERS (1964)

No one was as eloquent on the goals of the Great Society as Lyndon Johnson. The following extract is from the president's speech at the University of Michigan graduation ceremonies in May 1964, where he laid out his ambitious Great Society plan.

Was Johnson's vision utopian, or was it realistic? Can you detect in it antecedents in the form of similar views held by previous reformers? Although a one-time protégé of Franklin Roosevelt, in his previous career as a representative and senator, Johnson was not considered a liberal. At most he seemed a centrist who reflected the racial views and economic interests of his native Texas. How do you explain the apparent shift, as exemplified by the Great Society, when he became president? Can you think of other political leaders whose perspectives changed when they changed office?

THE GREAT SOCIETY[1]

Lyndon B. Johnson

I have come today from the turmoil of your capital to the tranquility of your campus to speak about the future of your country.

The purpose of protecting the life of our nation and preserving the liberty of our citizens is to pursue the happiness of our people. Our success in that pursuit is the test of our success as a nation.

For a century we labored to settle and to subdue a continent. For half a century we called upon unbounded invention and untiring industry to create an order of plenty for all of our people.

The challenge of the next half century is whether we have the wisdom to use that wealth to enrich and elevate our national life, and to advance the quality of our American civilization.

Your imagination, your initiative, and your indignation will determine whether we build a society where progress is the servant of our needs, or a society where old

---

Public Papers of the Presidents of the United States: Lyndon B. Johnson, 1963–64, vol. 1, (Washington, DC: U.S. Government Printing Office, 1965), pp. 704–7.

[1] Footnotes deleted.

values and new visions are buried under unbridled growth. For in your time we have the opportunity to move not only toward the rich society and the powerful society, but upward to the Great Society.

The Great Society rests on abundance and liberty for all. It demands an end to poverty and racial injustice, to which we are totally committed in our time. But that is just the beginning.

The Great Society is a place where every child can find knowledge to enrich his mind and to enlarge his talents. It is a place where leisure is a welcome chance to build and reflect, not a feared cause of boredom and restlessness. It is a place where the city of man serves not only the needs of the body and the demands of commerce but the desire for beauty and the hunger for community.

It is a place where man can renew contact with nature. It is a place which honors creation for its own sake and for what it adds to the understanding of the race. It is a place where men are more concerned with the quality of their goals than the quantity of their goods.

But most of all, the Great Society is not a safe harbor, a resting place, a final objective, a finished work. It is a challenge constantly renewed, beckoning us toward a destiny where the meaning of our lives matches the marvelous products of our labor.

So I want to talk to you today about three places where we begin to build the Great Society—in our cities, in our countryside, and in our classrooms.

Many of you will live to see the day, perhaps fifty years from now, when there will be 400 million Americans—four-fifths of them in urban areas. In the remainder of this century urban population will double, city land will double, and we will have to build homes, highways, and facilities equal to all those built since this country was first settled. So in the next forty years we must rebuild the entire urban United States.

Aristotle said: "Men come together in cities in order to live, but they remain together in order to live the good life." It is harder and harder to live the good life in American cities today.

The catalogue of ills is long: there is the decay of the centers and the despoiling of the suburbs. There is not enough housing for our people or transportation for our traffic. Open land is vanishing and old landmarks are violated.

Worst of all expansion is eroding the precious and time-honored values of community with neighbors and communion with nature. The loss of these values breeds loneliness and boredom and indifference.

Our society will never be great until our cities are great. Today the frontier of imagination and innovation is inside those cities and not beyond their borders. . . .

A second place where we begin to build the Great Society is in our countryside. We have always prided ourselves on being not only America the strong and America the free, but America the beautiful. Today that beauty is in danger. The water we drink, the food we eat, the very air that we breathe are threatened with pollution. Our parks are overcrowded, our seashores overburdened. Green fields and dense forests are disappearing.

A few years ago we were greatly concerned about the "Ugly American." Today we must act to prevent an ugly America.

For once the battle is lost, once our natural splendor is destroyed, it can never be recaptured. And once man can no longer walk with beauty or wonder at nature his spirit will wither and his sustenance be wasted.

A third place to build the Great Society is in the classrooms of America. There your children's lives will be shaped. Our society will not be great until every young mind is set free to scan the farthest reaches of thought and imagination. We are still far from that goal. . . .

Each year more than 100,000 high school graduates, with proved ability, do not enter college because they cannot afford it. And if we cannot educate today's youth, what will we do in 1970 when elementary school enrollment will be 5 million greater than 1960? And high school enrollment will rise by 5 million. College enrollment will increase by more than 3 million.

In many places, classrooms are overcrowded and curricula are outdated. Most of our qualified teachers are underpaid, and many of our paid teachers are unqualified. So we must give every child a place to sit and a teacher to learn from. Poverty must not be a bar to learning, and learning must offer an escape from poverty.

But more classrooms and more teachers are not enough. We must seek an educational system which grows in excellence as it grows in size. This means better training for our teachers. It means preparing youth to enjoy their hours of leisure as well as their hours of labor. It means exploring new techniques of teaching, to find new ways to stimulate the love of learning and the capacity for creation.

These are three of the central issues of the Great Society. While our government has many programs directed at those issues, I do not pretend that we have the full answer to those problems. . . .

But I do promise this: We are going to assemble the best thought and the broadest knowledge from all over the world to find those answers for America. I intend to establish working groups to prepare a series of White House conferences and meetings—on the cities, on natural beauty, on the quality of education, and on other emerging challenges. And from these meetings and from this inspiration and from these studies we will begin to set our course toward the Great Society.

The solution to these problems does not rest on a massive program in Washington, nor can it rely solely on the strained resources of local authority. They require us to create new concepts of cooperation, a creative federalism, between the national capital and the leaders of local communities.

Within your lifetime powerful forces, already loosed, will take us toward a way of life beyond the realm of our experience, almost beyond the bounds of our imagination.

For better or for worse, your generation has been appointed by history to deal with those problems and to lead America toward a new age. You have the chance never before afforded to any people in any age. You can help build a society where the demands of morality, and the needs of the spirit, can be realized in the life of the nation.

So, will you join in the battle to give every citizen the full equality which God enjoins and the law requires, whatever his belief, or race, or the color of his skin?

Will you join in the battle to give every citizen an escape from the crushing weight of poverty?

Will you join in the battle to make it possible for all nations to live in enduring peace—as neighbors and not as mortal enemies?

Will you join in the battle to build the Great Society, to prove that our material progress is only the foundation on which we will build a richer life of mind and spirit?

There are those timid souls who say this battle cannot be won; that we are condemned to a soulless wealth. I do not agree. We have the power to shape the civilization that we want. But we need your will, your labor, your hearts, if we are to build that kind of society.

Those who came to this land sought to build more than just a new country. They sought a new world. So I have come here today to your campus to say that you can make their vision our reality. So let us from this moment begin our work so that in the future men will look back and say: It was then, after a long and weary way, that man turned the exploits of his genius to the full enrichment of his life.

13.2   THE ATTACK FROM THE RIGHT (1960)

Conservative opponents of the Great Society responded promptly by raising familiar charges of socialist encroachment by government. Not only was the program hopelessly collectivist in nature, they said, it also fostered the inefficient growth of big government, diminished traditional U.S. values such as self-reliance and pride in one's work, and in the long run probably wouldn't accomplish what it hoped to achieve. Barry Goldwater, Johnson's opponent in the 1964 presidential race, raised these objections repeatedly. In the following selection, do you see a connection between Goldwater's way of thinking and the ideas presented by conservatives earlier in the twentieth century? In what ways were Goldwater's ideas similar to those of today's conservatives?

THE CONSCIENCE OF A CONSERVATIVE

Barry Goldwater

For many years it appeared that the principal domestic threat to our freedom was contained in the doctrines of Karl Marx. The collectivists—non-Communists as well as Communists—had adopted the Marxist objective of "socializing the means of production." And so it seemed that if collectivization were imposed, it would take the form of a State owned and operated economy. I doubt whether this is the main threat any longer.

The collectivists have found, both in this country and in other industrialized nations of the West, that free enterprise has removed the economic and social conditions that might have made a class struggle possible. Mammoth productivity, wide distribution of wealth, high standards of living, the trade union movement—these and other factors have eliminated whatever incentive there might have been for the "proletariat" to rise up, peaceably or otherwise, and assume direct ownership of productive property. Significantly, the bankruptcy of doctrinaire Marxism has been expressly acknowledged by the Socialist Party of West Germany, and by the dominant faction of the Socialist Party of Great Britain. In this country the abandonment of the Marxist approach (outside the Communist Party, of course) is attested to by the negligible strength of the Socialist Party, and more tellingly perhaps, by the content of left wing literature and by the programs of left wing political organizations such as the Americans For Democratic Action.

The currently favored instrument of collectivization is the Welfare State. The collectivists have not abandoned their ultimate goal—to subordinate the individual to the State—but their strategy has changed. They have learned that Socialism can be achieved through Welfarism quite as well as through Nationalization. They understand that private property can be confiscated as effectively by taxation as by expropriating it. They understand that the individual can be put at the mercy of the State—not only by making the State his employer—but by divesting him of the means to provide for his personal needs and by giving the State the responsibility of caring for those needs from cradle to grave. Moreover, they have discovered—and here is the critical point—that *Welfarism is much more compatible with the political processes of a democratic society.* Nationalization ran into popular opposition, but the collectivists feel sure the Welfare State can be erected by the simple expedient of buying votes with promises of "free" hospitalization, "free" retirement pay and so on . . . The correctness of this estimate can be seen from the portion of the federal budget that is now allocated to welfare, an amount second only to the cost of national defense.[1]

I do not welcome this shift of strategy. Socialism-through-Welfarism poses a far greater danger to freedom than Socialism-through-Nationalization precisely because it *is* more difficult to combat. The evils of Nationalization are self-evident and immediate. Those of Welfarism are veiled and tend to be postponed. People can understand the consequences of turning over ownership of the steel industry, say, to the State; and they can be counted on to oppose such a proposal. But let the government increase its contribution to the "Public Assistance" program and we will, at most, grumble about excessive government spending. The effect of Welfarism on freedom will be felt later on—after its beneficiaries have become its victims, after dependence on government has turned into bondage and it is too late to unlock the jail.

But a far more important factor is Welfarism's strong emotional appeal to many voters, and the consequent temptations it presents the average politician. It is hard, as we have seen, to make out a case for State ownership. It is very different with the rhetoric of humanitarianism. How easy it is to reach the voters with earnest importunities for helping the needy. And how difficult for Conservatives to resist these demands without appearing to be callous and contemptuous of the plight of less fortunate citizens. Here, perhaps, is the best illustration of the failure of the Conservative demonstration.

I know, for I have heard the questions often. Have you no sense of social obligation? the Liberals ask. Have you no concern for people who are out of work? for sick people who lack medical care? for children in overcrowded schools? Are you unmoved by the problems of the aged and disabled? Are you *against* human welfare?

The answer to all of these questions is, of course, no. But a simple "no" is not enough. I feel certain that Conservatism is through unless Conservatives can demonstrate and communicate the difference between being concerned with these problems and believing that the federal government is the proper agent for their solution.

The long range political consequences of Welfarism are plain enough: as we have seen, the State that is able to deal with its citizens as wards and dependents has gathered unto itself unlimited political and economic power and is thus able to rule as absolutely as any oriental despot.

---

[1] The total figure is substantially higher than the $15,000,000,000 noted earlier if we take into account welfare expenditures outside the Department of Health, Education and Welfare—for federal housing projects, for example.

Let us, however, weigh the consequences of Welfarism on the citizen.

Consider, first, the effect of Welfarism on the donors of government welfare—not only those who pay for it but also the voters and their elected representatives who decide that the benefits shall be conferred. Does some credit redound on them for trying to care for the needs of their fellow citizens? Are they to be commended and rewarded, at some moment in eternity, for their "charity"? I think not. Suppose I should vote for a measure providing for free medical care: I am unaware of any moral virtue that is attached to my decision to confiscate the earnings of X and give them to Y.

Suppose, however, that X approves of the program—that he has voted for welfarist politicians with the idea of helping his fellow man. Surely the wholesomeness of his act is diluted by the fact that he is voting not only to have his own money taken but also that of his fellow citizens who may have different ideas about their social obligations. Why does not such a man, instead, contribute what he regards as his just share of human welfare to a private charity?

Consider the consequences to the recipient of welfarism. For one thing, he mortgages himself to the federal government. In return for benefits—which, in the majority of cases, he pays for—he concedes to the government the ultimate in political power—the power to grant or withhold from him the necessities of life as the government sees fit. Even more important, however, is the effect on him—the elimination of any feeling of responsibility for his own welfare and that of his family and neighbors. A man may not immediately, or ever, comprehend the harm thus done to his character. Indeed, this is one of the great evils of Welfarism—that it transforms the individual from a dignified, industrious, self-reliant *spiritual* being into a dependent animal creature without his knowing it. There is no avoiding this damage to character under the Welfare State. Welfare programs cannot help but promote the idea that the government *owes* the benefits it confers on the individual, and that the individual is entitled, by right, to receive them. Such programs are sold to the country precisely on the argument that government has an *obligation* to care for the needs of its citizens. Is it possible that the message will reach those who vote for the benefits, but not those who receive them? How different it is with private charity where both the giver and the receiver understand that charity is the product of the humanitarian impulses of the giver, not the due of the receiver.

Let us, then, not blunt the noble impulses of mankind by reducing charity to a mechanical operation of the federal government. Let us, by all means, encourage, those who are fortunate and able to care for the needs of those who are unfortunate and disabled. But let us do this in a way that is conducive to the spiritual as well as the material well-being of our citizens—and in a way that will preserve their freedom. Let welfare be a private concern. Let it be promoted by individuals and families, by churches, private hospitals, religious service organizations, community charities and other institutions that have been established for this purpose. If the objection is raised that private institutions lack sufficient funds, let us remember that every penny the federal government does *not* appropriate for welfare is potentially available for private use—and without the overhead charge for processing the money through the federal bureaucracy. Indeed, high taxes, for which government Welfarism is so largely responsible, is the biggest obstacle to fund raising by private charities.

Finally, if we deem public intervention necessary, let the job be done by local and state authorities that are incapable of accumulating the vast political power that is so inimical to our liberties.

The Welfare State is *not* inevitable, as its proponents are so fond of telling us. There is nothing inherent in an industrialized economy, or in democratic processes of government that *must* produce de Tocqueville's "guardian society." Our future, like our past, will be what we make it. And we can shatter the collectivists' designs on individual freedom if we will impress upon the men who conduct our affairs this one truth: that the material and spiritual sides of man are intertwined; that it is impossible for the State to assume responsibility for one without intruding on the essential nature of the other; that if we take from a man the personal responsibility for caring for his material needs, we take from him also the will and the opportunity to be free.

13.3   THE ATTACK FROM THE LEFT (1962)

The years of the Great Society also witnessed a powerful revival of left-wing political activism in the United States. During this period, university students, civil rights militants, and cultural dissenters all came to view white, middle-class, liberal America as repressive, exploitative, and stultifying. To most of the new radicals, the Great Society was at best a feeble response to the country's real problems, and at worst an effort to evade those problems and deflect any fundamental attempt to solve them.

No organization articulated the political aspirations of the emerging New Left more comprehensively and persistently than the Students for a Democratic Society, which by the late 1960s had an active chapter on most college campuses. The following excerpt is taken from the famed "Port Huron Statement," drafted by the group's leaders after lengthy and intense debate in June 1962. Intended to be both a manifesto and a strategic plan, the Statement is probably the most thorough explanation of the philosophy of "the movement" that would soon devote its energy to political protest and civil disobedience. These radicals found the liberalism of Johnson's Great Society to be even more distasteful than conservatism. Running through each sentence lingers a fundamental anger toward the U.S. way of life. Why were they so bitter? How would you compare the New Left to previous radicals? Would you say that they had socialist leanings, or would you consider them anarchistic? Finally, what specifically made them hate liberal programs like the Great Society so much?

The Port Huron Statement

Students for a Democratic Society

We are the people of this generation, bred in at least modest comfort, housed now in universities, looking uncomfortably to the world we inherit.

When we were kids, the United States was the wealthiest and strongest country in the world: the only one with the atom bomb, the least scarred by war, an initiator of the United Nations that we thought would distribute Western influence throughout the world. Freedom and equality for each individual, government of, by, and for the

Students for a Democratic Society, *Statement of the National Convention, June 11–15, 1962,* Port Huron, Michigan.

people—these American values we found good, principles by which we could live as men. Many of us began maturing in complacency.

As we grew, however, our comfort was penetrated by events too troubling to dismiss. First, the permeating and victimizing fact of human degradation, symbolized by the Southern struggle against racial bigotry, compelled most of us from silence to activism. Second, the enclosing fact of the Cold War, symbolized by the presence of the Bomb, brought awareness that we ourselves, and our friends, and millions of abstract "others" . . . might die at any time. We might deliberately ignore, or avoid, or fail to feel all other human problems, but not these two, for these were too immediate and crushing in their impact, too challenging in the demand that we as individuals take responsibility for encounter and resolution. . . .

We witnessed, and continue to witness, other paradoxes. With nuclear energy whole cities can easily be powered, yet the dominant nation-states seem more likely to unleash destruction greater than that incurred in all wars of human history. Although our own technology is destroying old and creating new forms of social organization, men still tolerate meaningless work and idleness. While two-thirds of mankind suffers undernourishment, our own upper classes revel amidst superfluous abundance. Although world population is expected to double in forty years, the nations still tolerate anarchy as a major principle of international conduct and uncontrolled exploitation governs the sapping of the earth's physical resources. Although mankind desperately needs revolutionary leadership, America rests in national stalemate, its goals ambiguous and tradition-bound instead of informed and clear, its democratic system apathetic and manipulated rather than "of, by, and for the people. " . . .

Our work is guided by the sense that we may be the last generation in the experiment of living. But we are a minority—the vast majority of our people regard the temporary equilibriums of our society and the world as eternally functional parts. In this is perhaps the outstanding paradox: We ourselves are imbued with urgency, yet the message of our society is that there is no viable alternative to the present. Beneath the reassuring tones of the politicians, beneath the common opinion that America will "muddle through," beneath the stagnation of those who have closed their minds to the future, is the pervading feeling that there simply are no alternatives, that our times have witnessed the exhaustion not only of Utopias, but of any new departures as well. Feeling the press of complexity upon the emptiness of life, people are fearful of the thought that at any moment things might thrust out of control. They fear change itself, since change might smash whatever invisible framework seems to hold back chaos for them now. For most Americans all crusades are suspect, threatening. . . . Then, too, we are a materially improved society, and by our own improvements we seem to have weakened the case for further change.

Some would have us believe that Americans feel contentment amidst prosperity—but might it not better be called a glaze above deeply felt anxieties about their role in the new world? And if these anxieties produce a developed indifference to human affairs, do they not as well produce a yearning to believe there *is* an alternative to the present, that something *can* be done to change circumstances in the school, the workplace, the bureaucracies, the government? It is to this latter yearning, at once the spark and engine of change, that we direct our present appeal. The search for truly democratic alternatives to the present, and a commitment to social experimentation with them, is a worthy and fulfilling enterprise, one which moves us and, we hope, others today. On such a basis do we offer this document of our convictions and analysis: as an effort in understanding and changing the conditions of humanity in the late twentieth century, an effort rooted in the ancient, still unfinished conception of man attaining and determining influence over his circumstances of life.

Values

Making values explicit . . . is an activity that has been devalued and corrupted. . . . But neither has our experience in the universities brought us moral enlightenment. Our professors and administrators sacrifice controversy to public relations; their curriculums change more slowly than the living events of the world; their skills and silence are purchased by investors in the arms race; passion is called unscholastic. The questions we might want raised—what is really important? can we live in a different and better way? if we wanted to change society, how would we do it?—are not thought to be questions of a "fruitful, empirical nature," and thus are brushed aside.

Unlike youth in other countries, we are used to moral leadership being exercised and moral dimensions being clarified by our elders. But today, for us, not even the liberal and socialist preachments of the past seem adequate to the forms of the present. . . . [A]nd there are few new prophets. It has been said that our liberal and socialist predecessors were plagued by vision without program, while our own generation is plagued by program without vision. All around us there is astute grasp of method, technique, . . . but if pressed critically, such expertise is incompetent to explain its implicit ideals. . . .

Theoretic chaos has replaced the idealistic thinking of old. . . . Doubt has replaced hopefulness—and men act out of a defeatism that is labelled realistic. The decline of utopia and hope is in fact one of the defining features of social life today. . . .

We regard *men* as infinitely precious and possessed of unfulfilled capacities for reason, freedom, and love. In affirming these principles we are aware of countering perhaps the dominant conceptions of man in the twentieth century: that he is a thing to be manipulated, and that he is inherently incapable of directing his own affairs. We oppose the depersonalization that reduces human beings to the status of things. . . . We oppose, too, the doctrine of human incompetence because it rests essentially on the modern fact that men have been "competently" manipulated into incompetence—we see little reason why men cannot meet with increasing skill the complexities and responsibilities of their situation, if society is organized not for minority, but for majority, participation in decision-making.

Men have unrealized potential for self-cultivation, self-direction, self-understanding, and creativity. It is this potential that we regard as crucial and to which we appeal, not to the human potentiality for violence, unreason, and submission to authority. The goal of man and society should be human independence: a concern not with image [or] popularity but with finding a meaning in life that is personally authentic; a quality of mind not compulsively driven by a sense of powerlessness, nor one which unthinkingly adopts status values, nor one which represses all threats to its habits, but one which has full, spontaneous access to present and past experiences, one which easily unites the fragmented parts of personal history, one which openly faces problems which are troublesome and unresolved; one with an intuitive awareness of possibilities, an active sense of curiosity, an ability and willingness to learn. . . .

Loneliness, estrangement, isolation describe the vast distance between man and man today. These dominant tendencies cannot be overcome by better personnel management, nor by improved gadgets, but only when a love of man overcomes the idolatrous worship of things by man. . . .

As a *social system* we seek the establishment of a democracy of individual participation, governed by two central aims: that the individual share in those social decisions determining the quality and direction of his life; that society be organized to encourage independence in men and provide the media for their common participation.

In a participatory democracy, the political life would be based in several root principles:

—that decision-making of basic social consequence be carried out by public groupings;

—that politics be seen positively, as the art of collectively creating an acceptable pattern of social relations;

—that politics has the function of bringing people out of isolation and into community, thus being a necessary, though not sufficient, means of finding meaning in personal life;

—that the political order should serve to clarify problems in a way instrumental to their solution; it should provide outlets for the expression of personal grievance and aspiration; opposing views should be organized so as to illuminate choices and facilitate the attainment of goals. . . .

The economic sphere would have as its basis the principles:

—that work should involve incentives worthier than money or survival. It should be educative, not stultifying; creative, not mechanical; self-direct[ed], not manipulated; encouraging independence, a respect for others, a sense of dignity, and a willingness to accept social responsibility. . . .

—that the economic experience is so personally decisive that the individual must share in its full determination;

—that the economy itself is of such social importance that its major resources should be open to democratic participation and subject to democratic social regulation.

Like the political and economic ones, major social institutions . . . should be generally organized with the well-being and dignity of man as the essential measure of success.

The Students

In the last few years, thousands of American students demonstrated that they at least felt the urgency of the times. They moved actively and directly against racial injustices, the threat of war, violations of individuals rights of conscience and, less frequently, against economic manipulation. They succeeded in restoring a small measure of controversy to the campuses after the stillness of the McCarthy period. They succeeded, too, in gaining some concessions from the people and institutions they opposed, especially in the fight against racial bigotry.

The significance of these scattered movements lies . . . in the fact the students are breaking the crust of apathy and overcoming the inner alienation that remain the defining characteristics of American college life.

If student movements for change are rarities still on the campus scene, what is commonplace there? The real campus . . . is a place of private people engaged in their notorious "inner emigration." It is a place of commitment to business-as-usual, getting ahead, playing it cool. It is a place of mass affirmation of the Twist, but mass reluctance toward the controversial public stance. Rules are accepted as "inevitable," bureaucracy as "just circumstances," irrelevance as "scholarship," selflessness as "martyrdom," . . .

Almost no students value activity as a citizen. . . . Attention is being paid to social status; . . . much too is paid to academic status. . . . But neglected generally is real intellectual status, the personal cultivation of the mind. . . .

Under these conditions university life loses all relevance to some. Four hundred thousand of our classmates leave college every year.

But apathy is not simply an attitude; it is a product of social institutions, and of the structure and organization of higher education itself. The extracurricular life is ordered according to *in loco parentis* theory, which ratifies the Administration as the moral guardian of the young. The accompanying "let's pretend" theory of student extracurricular affairs validates student government as a training center for those who want to spend their lives in political pretense and discourages initiative from more articulate, honest, and sensitive students. . . .

The Society Beyond

Look beyond the campus to America itself. . . . Americans are in withdrawal from public life, from any collective effort at directing their own affairs.

Some regard this national doldrums as a sign of healthy approval of the establishment order—but is it approval by consent or manipulated acquiescence? Others declare that the people are withdrawn because compelling issues are fast disappearing—perhaps there are fewer breadlines in America, but is Jim Crow gone, is there enough work and work more fulfilling, is world war a diminishing threat, and what of the revolutionary new peoples? . . .

There are no convincing apologies for the contemporary malaise. While the world tumbles toward the final war, while men in other nations are trying desperately to alter events, while the very future qua future is uncertain—America is without community, impulse, without the inner momentum necessary for an age when societies cannot successfully perpetuate themselves by their military weapons, when democracy must be viable because of the quality of its life, not the quantity of its rockets.

The apathy here is first *subjective*—the felt powerlessness of ordinary people, the resignation before the enormity of events. But subjective apathy is encouraged by the *objective* American situation—the actual structural separation of people from power, from relevant knowledge, from pinnacles of decision-making. . . .

Politics without Publics

A crucial feature of the political apparatus in America is that greater differences are harbored within each major party than the differences between them. Instead of two parties representing distinctive and significant differences of approach, what dominates the system is a natural interlocking of Democrats from Southern states and the more conservative elements of the Republican party. The arrangement of forces is blessed by the seniority system of Congress which guarantees congressional committee domination by conservatives. . . .

A most alarming fact is that few, if any, politicians are calling for changes in these conditions. . . . In such a setting of status quo politics, where most if not all government activity is rationalized in Cold War anti-communist terms, it is somewhat natural that discontented, super-patriotic groups would emerge . . . and explain their ultra-conservatism as the best means of victory over Communism. They have become a politically influential force within the Republican party, at a national level, through Senator Goldwater. . . .

The Economy

American capitalism today advertises itself as the Welfare State. Many of us comfortably expect pensions, medical care, unemployment compensation, and other social services in our lifetimes. Even with one-fourth of our productive capacity unused, the majority of Americans are living in relative comfort. . . . In many places, unrestrained bosses, uncontrolled machines, and sweatshop conditions have been reformed or abolished and suffering tremendously relieved. But in spite of the benign yet obscuring effects of the New Deal reforms . . . the paradoxes and myths of the economy are sufficient to irritate our complacency and reveal to us some essential causes of the American malaise.

We live amidst a national celebration of economic prosperity while poverty and deprivation remain an unbreakable way of life for millions in the "affluent society," including many of our own generation. . . . Work, too, is often unfilling and victimizing, accepted as a channel to status . . . rarely as a means of understanding and controlling self and events. . . .

The Military-Industrial Complex

The most spectacular and important creation of the authoritarian and oligopolistic structure of economic decision-making in America is the institution called "the military-industrial complex" by former President Eisenhower, the powerful congruence of interest and structure among military and business elites which affects so much of our development and destiny. Not only is ours the first generation to live with the possibility of worldwide cataclysm—it is the first to experience the actual social preparation for cataclysm, the general militarization of American society. . . .

Automation, Abundance, and Challenge

Automation, the process of machines replacing men in performing sensory, motoric, and complex logical tasks, is transforming society in ways that are scarcely comprehensible. . . . Automation is destroying whole categories of work, . . . in blue-collar, service, and even middle management occupations. In addition, it is eliminating employment opportunities for a youth force that numbers one million more than it did in 1950. . . . The consequences of this economic drama . . . are momentous: Five million becomes an acceptable unemployment tabulation, and misery, uprootedness and anxiety become the lot of increasing numbers of Americans. . . . Hard-core poverty exists just beyond the neon lights of affluence, and the "have-nots" may be driven still further from opportunity as the high-technology society demands better education to get into the production mainstream and more capital to get into "business." . . .

The Stance of Labor

Amidst all this, what of organized labor, the historic institutional representative of the exploited, the presumed "countervailing power" against the excesses of Big Business? Today labor remains the most liberal "mainstream" institution, but often its liberalism represents vestigial commitments. . . . In some measure labor has succumbed to institutionalization, its social idealism waning under the tendencies of bureaucracy, materialism, business ethics. . . .

The Individual in the Warfare State

Business and politics, when significantly militarized, affect the whole living condition of each American citizen. Worker and family depend on the Cold War for life. Half of all research and development is concentrated on military ends. . . . To a decisive extent, the means of defense, the military technology itself, determines the political and social character of the state being defended. . . . So it has been with America, as her democratic institutions and habits have shriveled in almost direct proportion to the growth of her armaments. Decisions about military strategy, including the monstrous decision to go to war, are more and more the property of the military and the industrial arms race machine, with the politicians assuming a ratifying role instead of a determining one. . . .

Deterrence Policy

Deterrence advocates, all of them prepared at least to threaten mass extermination, advance arguments of several kinds. At one pole are the minority of open advocates of preventive war. . . . Perhaps more disturbing for their numbers within the Kennedy Administration are the many advocates of the "counterforce" theory of aiming strategic nuclear weapons at military installations. . . . Others would support fighting "limited wars" which use conventional . . . weapons backed by deterrents so mighty that both sides would fear to use them . . . [with] the potential tendency for a "losing side" to push limited protracted fighting on the soil of underdeveloped countries. Still other deterrence artists proposed limited, clearly defensive and retaliatory nuclear capacity, always potent enough to deter an opponent's aggressive designs. . . .

   All the deterrence theories . . . allow insufficient attention to preserving, extending, and enriching democratic values. . . . [T]hey inadequately realize the inherent instabilities of the continuing arms race and balance of fear. They . . . tend to eclipse . . . disarmament by solidifying economic, political, and even moral investments in the continuation of tensions. [T]hey offer a disinterested and even patriotic rationale for the boondoggling, belligerence, and privilege of military and economic elites. . . .

Anti-Communism

An unreasoning anti-communism has become a major social problem for those who want to construct a more democratic America. McCarthyism and other forms of exaggerated and conservative anti-communism seriously weaken democratic institutions and spawn movements contrary to the interests of basic freedoms and peace. In such an atmosphere even the most intelligent of Americans fear to join political organizations, sign petitions, speak out on serious issues. . . . Thus much of American anti-communism takes on the characteristics of paranoia. . . .

Communism and Foreign Policy

As democrats we are in basic opposition to the communist system. The Soviet Union . . . rests on the total suppression of organized opposition, as well as on a vision of the future in the name of which human life has been sacrificed and numerous small and large denials of human dignity rationalized. . . . The communist movement has failed, in every sense, to achieve its stated intentions of leading a worldwide movement for human emancipation.

But present trends in American anti-communism are not sufficient for the creation of appropriate policies with which to relate and counter communist movements in the world. In no instance is this better illustrated than in our basic national policy-making assumption that the Soviet Union is inherently expansionist and aggressive, prepared to dominate the rest of the world by military means. On this assumption rests the monstrous American structure of military "preparedness"; because of it we sacrifice values and social programs to the alleged needs of military power. . . .

Discrimination

Our America is still white. Consider the plight, statistically, of its greatest noncon-formists, the "nonwhites." . . .

[Here follows a page reviewing the inferior circumstances of black Americans in regard to literacy, salaries, skill and professional levels, employment, housing, education, and voting rights.]

Even against this background, some will say progress is being made. The facts belie it, however, unless it is assumed that America has another century to deal with its racial inequalities. . . .

It has been said that the Kennedy administration did more in two years than the Eisenhower administration did in eight. Of this there can be no doubt. But it is analo-gous to comparing whispers to silence when positively stentorian tones are demanded. . . . To avoid conflict with the Dixiecrat-Republican alliance, President Kennedy has developed a civil rights philosophy of "enforcement, not enactment," implying that existing statutory tools are sufficient to change the lot of the Negro. . . .

The Industrialization of the World

The United States' principal goal should be creating a world where hunger, poverty, disease, ignorance, violence, and exploitation are replaced as central features by abun-dance, reason, love, and international cooperation. To many this will seem the product of juvenile hallucination: but we insist it is a more realistic goal than is a world of nuclear stalemate. . . .

We should undertake here and now a fifty-year effort to prepare for all nations the conditions of industrialization. . . . We should not depend significantly on private enter-prise to do the job. . . . We should not lock the development process into the Cold War: We should use it as a way to end that conflict. . . . America should show its commitment to democratic institutions not by withdrawing support from undemocratic regimes, but by making domestic democracy exemplary. . . . Democratic theory must confront the problems inherent in social revolutions. . . .

Towards American Democracy

America must abolish its political party stalemate. Two genuine parties, centered around issue and essential values, demanding allegiance to party principles shall supplant the current system of organized stalemate. . . .

Institutions and practices which stifle dissent should be abolished, and the promotion of peaceful dissent should be actively promoted. . . .

Corporations must be made publicly responsible. It is not possible to believe that true democracy can exist where a minority utterly controls enormous wealth and power. . . .

The allocation of resources must be based on social needs. A truly "public sector" must be established, and its nature debated and planned. . . .

America should concentrate on its genuine social priorities: abolish squalor, terminate neglect, and establish an environment for people to live with dignity and creativeness. . . . A program against poverty . . . must . . . be directed to the abolition of the structural circumstances of poverty. . . . *Medical care* must become recognized as a lifetime human right just as vital as food, shelter, clothing. . . . Existing institutions should be extended so the Welfare State cares for *everyone's* welfare according to need. . . . A full-scale public initiative for civil rights should be undertaken despite the clamor among conservatives (and liberals) about gradualism, property rights, and law and order. . . . We must meet the growing complex of "city" problems. . . . Juvenile delinquency, untended mental illness, crime increase, slums, urban tenantry and uncontrolled housing, the isolation of the individual in the city—are all problems of the city. . . . The *model* city must be projected—more community decision making and participation, true integration of classes, races, vocations—provision for beauty, access to nature and the benefits of the central city as well. . . .

The University and Social Change

[T]he civil rights and peace and student movements are too poor and socially slighted, and the labor movement too quiescent, to be counted with enthusiasm [as agents of change]. From where else can power and vision be summoned? We believe that the universities are an overlooked seat of influence. . . .

1. Any new left in America must be . . . a left with real intellectual skills, committed to the deliberativeness, honesty, [and] reflection as working tools. The university permits the political life to be an adjunct to the academic one, and action to be informed by reason.
2. A new left must be distributed in significant social roles throughout the country. The universities are distributed in such a manner.
3. A new left must consist of younger people who matured in the post-war world, and partially be directed to the recruitment of younger people. The university is the obvious beginning point.
4. A new left must include liberals and socialists. . . . The university is a more sensible place than a political party for these two traditions to begin to discuss their differences and look for political synthesis.
5. A new left must start controversy across the land, if national policies and national apathy are to be reversed. The ideal university is a community of controversy, within itself and in its effects on communities beyond.

6. A new left must transform modern complexity into issues that can be understood and felt close-up by every human being. It must give form to the feelings of helplessness and indifference, so that people may see the political, social, and economic sources of their private troubles and organize to change society. In a time of supposed prosperity, moral complacency and political manipulation, a new left cannot rely on only aching stomachs to be the engine force of social reform. The case for change, for alternatives that will involve uncomfortable personal efforts, must be argued as never before. The university is a relevant place for all these activities.

But we need not indulge in illusions: the university system cannot complete a movement of ordinary people making demands for a better life. From its schools and colleges across the nation, a militant left might awaken its allies, and by beginning the process towards peace, civil rights, and labor struggles, reinsert theory and idealism where too often reign confusion and political barter. The power of students and faculty united is not only potential; it has shown its actuality in the South, and in the reform movements of the North.

The bridge to political power, though, will be built through genuine cooperation, locally, nationally, and internationally, between a new left of young people, and an awakening community of allies. In each community we must look within the university and act with confidence that we can be powerful, but we must look outwards to the less exotic but more lasting struggles for justice.

To turn these possibilities into realities will involve national efforts at university reform by an alliance of students and faculty. They must wrest control of the educational process from the administrative bureaucracy. They must make fraternal and functional contact with allies in labor, civil rights, and other liberal forces outside the campus. They must import major public issues into the curriculum—research and teaching on problems of war and peace is an outstanding example. They must make debate and controversy, not dull pedantic cant, the common style for educational life. They must consciously build a base for their assault upon the loci of power.

As students for a democratic society we are committed to stimulating this kind of social movement, this kind of vision and program in campus and community across the country. If we appear to seek the unattainable, as it has been said, then let it be known that we do so to void the unimaginable.

PAMPHLET OF COLUMBIA UNIVERSITY STUDENTS, NEW YORK CITY, APRIL, 1968

Statement of Columbia Student Strikers

What is the political justification for not disciplining the demonstrators?

There are two basic reasons why the demonstrators should not be punished. First, they took the only actions they could have to successfully win just demands. Second, the authority that promulgated the laws that the demonstrators are accused of violating—the Columbia administration—is totally illegitimate and doesn't have the right to discipline—or pass laws providing for the disciplining of—anyone.

The justice of the demonstrators' goals has been admitted by nearly everyone. Some people object to the tactics we use; they think we should have employed the "legitimate channels" to achieve our demands. We ask these people: Where were you earlier this year when 400 students marched peacefully into Low Library to present Grayson Kirk a letter asking for disaffiliation with IDS? The official response to this letter was, "We cannot answer because there was no return address." Where was the legitimate means for discussion when SDS challenged Kirk to debate on IDA and there was no answer at all? Where were you when peaceful demonstrations were held at gym site and the university pressed charges against a minister for trespassing? And where were you when SDS presented a petition on IDA with 1,700 signatures to the administration and their response was to put the six on disciplinary probation for marching into their building? We ask that you ask yourself if the reason you now care about our demands is because we are using the very tactics we are at this time.

In short, we have used the "legitimate channels." The administration apparently considered them less legitimate than we did, for they never spent a minute paying any attention to them. Lack of administration response to these methods over a long period of time, plus their lack of response to traditional tactics of civil disobedience, convinced us that the tactics we have used over the past two weeks were the *only* way we could achieve our just demands.

Strict civil libertarians argue that those who commit civil disobedience must suffer the legal consequences even if their cause is just. But we say people should not be disciplined for doing what is necessary to achieve what is right.

We also point to the basic illegitimacy of the Columbia administration. As the strikers said in their policy statement of April 28,

> We . . . believe in the right of all people to participate in the decisions that affect their lives. An institution is legitimate only if it is a structure for the exercise of this collective right. The people who are affected by an illegitimate institution have the right to change it.

Columbia University has been governed undemocratically. An administration responsible only to the Trustees has made decisions that deeply affect students, faculty, and the community. It has expropriated a neighborhood park to build a gym. It has participated, through IDA, in the suppression of self-determination throughout the world. It has formulated rules and disciplined students arbitrarily and for the purpose of suppressing justified protest. The actions of the administration in the present crisis have exposed it to students and faculty as the antidemocratic and irresponsible body it has always been.

Our goal is to create a functioning participatory democracy to replace the repressive rule of the administration and Trustees of this university. The acceptance of amnesty by the administration is a fundamental part of this transition because it establishes the illegitimacy of the existing structure. The granting of amnesty is the formal establishment of a new order—the right and power of all people affected by the university not to be judged by illegitimate authority.

For students who took the only actions possible to successfully achieve necessary and just demands to be disciplined for the violation of rules set up by a totally discredited and illegitimate authority would be a travesty.

CHAPTER 14

The New Feminism

The social insurgency of the 1960s extended beyond the civil rights movement. Other Americans besides blacks, feeling denied respect, excluded from power, or kept from economic advancement, also mobilized for collective action against the social and economic status quo. During the 1960s and 1970s, Hispanic Americans, gay Americans, Native Americans, and others formed defense or liberation organizations, often closely modeled on the black civil rights groups.

None of these liberation movements had such pervasive consequences as the New Feminism. Like the others, it owed much to the civil rights crusade, but it had distinctive roots of its own. The new movement was in part a rebound from the 1950s, when most women had acquiesced in the domestic suburban lifestyle and feminism as an ideology virtually disappeared. It also drew sustenance from the frustration of well-educated postwar U.S. women with bright, well-furnished minds and no interesting and rewarding place to go. It differed from the feminism of the past, which emphasized political and civil rights, by its focus on social and economic equality and its sharper challenge to traditional gender roles.

The New Feminism can probably be dated from 1961 with the creation by John F. Kennedy of the President's Commission on the Status of Women. Although it accomplished little directly, the commission helped create a network of activists dedicated to expanding women's rights and improving women's lot. Two years later, a Long Island housewife and magazine writer, Betty Friedan, jolted the New Feminism into full life with a three hundred-page manifesto, *The Feminine Mystique*, that denounced the gilded cage of postwar suburbia and called for a revitalized woman's movement.

In 1966, the activists organized NOW, the National Organization for Women, with Friedan as president. Dedicated to bringing "women into full participation in the mainstream of American society . . . [and] exercising all the privileges and responsibilities thereof in truly equal partnership with men," NOW was middle class in membership and hierarchical in structure. It accepted male members. It lobbied for its goals in Congress and the state legislatures and supported politicians who favored its programs. By the 1970s, one of NOW's chief goals was to secure adoption of the Equal Rights Amendment to the Constitution forbidding both the states and the federal government to deny "equality of rights under the law . . . on account of sex."

Toward the end of the 1960s, still newer groups of feminists who favored more militant tactics and supported more radical goals challenged NOW's positions and leadership. Many of these activists were recruits from the student New Left that had appeared in the early 1960s and caught the public's attention for its attacks on university administrations, racism, and the Vietnam War.

The militants favored more than reforming of "sexist" society by laws expanding and protecting women's rights. Rather, they sought to overthrow the "patriarchal" system they considered fundamental to all oppressive societies and to replace it with one where gender was socially and politically irrelevant. Many demanded the radical transformation of existing male–female relationships and the total reordering of the family. Such militants generally had little faith in electoral politics or legislative lobbying. Some favored inciting socialist revolution to destroy patriarchy. Others believed change would come through the transformation of social sensibility by propaganda, civil disobedience, militant demonstrations, and "consciousness-raising." Most radical feminist groups sought to avoid top-down, hierarchical control of their organizations and often grouped themselves into egalitarian "collectives."

The following selections provide an opportunity to discuss and evaluate the New Feminism, both the middle-of-the-road sort and the more radical kind. You will also find antifeminist viewpoints. Feminism is still a controversial issue today, and it may not be easy to be objective about some of the opinions expressed here. But once again try to use your critical judgment in considering the competing positions.

14.1 THE NATIONAL ORGANIZATION FOR WOMEN'S BILL OF RIGHTS (1967)

At its first annual conference in 1967 NOW adopted the following Bill of Rights. The selection, of course, was intended to parallel the first ten amendments to the federal Constitution, which are the original Bill of Rights. Does the NOW manifesto put forth a program that was bold for its time? Does it still seem bold today? Are any parts of the NOW Bill of Rights still controversial? Which one(s)? Why?

BILL OF RIGHTS

NOW (National Organization for Women)

Adopted at NOW's first national conference, Washington, DC, 1967

I. Equal Rights Constitutional Amendment
II. Enforce Law Banning Sex Discrimination in Employment

"NOW (National Organization for Women) Bill of Rights" from *Sisterhood Is Powerful: An Anthology of Writings from the Women's Liberation Movement*, Robin Morgan, ed. (New York: Vintage Books, 1970), pp. 512–14. Copyright © 1970 by Robin Morgan. Reprinted by permission of Edite Kroll Literary Agency.

   III. Maternity Leave Rights in Employment and in Social Security Benefits
   IV. Tax Deduction for Home and Child Care Expenses for Working Parents
   V. Child Day Care Centers
   VI. Equal and Unsegregated Education
   VII. Equal Job Training Opportunities and Allowances for Women in Poverty
   VIII. The Right of Women to Control Their Reproductive Lives

WE DEMAND:

   I. That the U.S. Congress immediately pass the Equal Rights Amendment to the Constitution to provide that "Equality of rights under the law shall not be denied or abridged by the United States or by any State on account of sex," and that such then be immediately ratified by the several States.

   II. That equal employment opportunity be guaranteed to all women, as well as men, by insisting that the Equal Employment Opportunity Commission enforces the prohibitions against racial discrimination.

   III. That women be protected by law to ensure their rights to return to their jobs within a reasonable time after childbirth without loss of seniority or other accrued benefits, and be paid maternity leave as a form of social security and/or employee benefit.

   VI. Immediate revision of tax laws to permit the deduction of home and child-care expenses for working parents.

   V. That child-care facilities be established by law on the same basis as parks, libraries, and public schools, adequate to the needs of children from the preschool years through adolescence, as a community resource to be used by all citizens from all income levels.

   VI. That the right of women to be educated to their full potential equally with men be secured by Federal and State legislation, eliminating all discrimination and segregation by sex, written and unwritten, at all levels of education, including colleges, graduate and professional schools, loans and fellowships, and Federal and State training programs such as the Job Corps.

   VII. The right of women in poverty to secure job training, housing, and family allowances on equal terms with men, but without prejudice to a parent's right to remain at home to care for his or her children; revision of welfare legislation and poverty programs which deny women dignity, privacy, and self-respect.

   VIII. The right of women to control their own reproductive lives by removing from the penal code laws limiting access to contraceptive information and devices, and by repealing penal laws governing abortion.

14.2 RADICAL FEMINISM (1969, 1968)

Radical feminism came in several varieties. Some radical feminists emphasized the economic roots of women's oppression. Others saw sexism as independent of economic systems. In some ways the second version was more radical than the first, since its partisans often attacked the nuclear family itself as inherently oppressive to women—and children.

Following are two examples of radical feminist views dating from the late 1960s. The first item is a statement adopted by the New York Radical Feminists to express their overall philosophy at their founding meeting in 1969. The second is a manifesto issued by the Radical Feminists' precursors, *Radical Women, shortly before the group held a widely publicized protest demonstration at the 1968 Miss America Beauty Pageant in Atlantic City.*

Is the Radical Feminists' statement antimale, as critics have charged? What forces does it emphasize as crucial for molding women's attitudes and characteristics? Is its grim picture of women as totally oppressed valid?

The Miss America Beauty Pageant protest created a sensation and undoubtedly made a broad public aware of radical feminist views. But it probably did not endear the group or their positions to a majority of Americans. Although none of the protesters at Atlantic City actually burned their brassieres, the media dismissively labeled them "bra-burners," and the tag stuck.

Why would the demonstration at the Miss America Beauty Pageant have offended conventional Americans? How might you defend the radical feminist positions and tactics? Was the pageant a valid target for feminists? What feminist attitudes lay behind their attack on such a public ritual?

POLITICS OF THE EGO: A MANIFESTO FOR NEW YORK RADICAL FEMINISTS[1]

Anne Koedt

Radical feminism recognizes the oppression of women as a fundamental political oppression wherein women are categorized as an inferior class based upon their sex. It is the aim of radical feminism to organize politically to destroy this sex class system.

As radical feminists we recognize that we are engaged in a power struggle with men, and that the agent of our oppression is man insofar as he identifies with and carries out the supremacy privileges of the male role. For while we realize that the liberation of women will ultimately mean the liberation of men from their destructive role as oppressor, we have no illusion that men will welcome this liberation without a struggle.

Radical feminism is political because it recognizes that a group of individuals (men) have organized together for power over women, and that they have set up institutions throughout society to maintain this power.

A political power institution is set up for a purpose. We believe that the purpose of male chauvinism is primarily to obtain psychological ego satisfaction, and that only secondarily does this manifest itself in economic relationships. For this reason we do not believe that capitalism, or any other economic system, is the cause of female oppression, nor do we believe that female oppression will disappear as a result of a purely economic revolution. The political oppression of women has its own class dynamic; and that dynamic must be understood in terms previously called "non-political"—namely the politics of the ego.[2]

Thus the purpose of the male power group is to fulfill a need. That need is psychological, and derives from the supremacist assumptions of the male identity—namely that the male identity be sustained through is ability to have power over the female ego.

[Anne Koedt], "Politics of the Ego: A Manifesto for New York Radical Feminists," in *Notes from the Second Year* (n.p., n.d.).

[1] Footnotes deleted.

[2] Ego: We are using the classical definition rather than the Freudian: that is, the sense of individual self as distinct from others.

Man establishes his "manhood" in direct proportion to his ability to have his ego override woman's, and derives his strength and self-esteem through this process. This male need, though destructive, is in that sense impersonal. It is not out of a desire to hurt the woman that man dominates and destroys her; it is out of a need for a sense of power that he necessarily must destroy her ego and make it subservient to his. Hostility to women is a secondary effect, to the degree that a man is not fulfilling his own assumptions of male power he hates women. Similarly, a man's failure to establish himself supreme among other males (as for example a poor white male) may make him channel his hostility into his relationship with women, since they are one of the few political groups over which he can still exercise power.

As women we are living in a male power structure, and our roles become necessarily a function of men. The services we supply are services to the male ego. We are rewarded according to how well we perform these services. Our skill—our profession—is our ability to be feminine—that is, dainty, sweet, passive, helpless, ever-giving and sexy. In other words, everything to help reassure man that he is primary. If we perform successfully, our skills are rewarded. We "marry well"; we are treated with benevolent paternalism; we are deemed successful women, and may even make the "women's pages."

If we do not choose to perform these ego services, but instead assert ourselves as primary to ourselves, we are denied the necessary access to alternatives to express our self-assertion. Decision-making positions in the various job fields are closed to us; politics (left, right or liberal) are barred in other than auxiliary roles; our creative efforts are *a priori* judged not serious because we are females; our day-to-day lives are judged failures because we have not become "real women."

Rejection is economic in that women's work is underpaid. It is emotional in that we are cut off from human relationships because we choose to reject the submissive female role. We are trapped in an alien system, just as the worker under capitalism is forced to sell his economic services in a system which is set up against his self-interest.

Sexual Institutions

The oppression of women is manifested in particular institutions, constructed and maintained to keep women in their place. Among these are the institutions of marriage, motherhood, love, and sexual intercourse (the family unit is incorporated by the above). Through these institutions the woman is taught to confuse her biological sexual differences with her total human potential. Biology is destiny, she is told. Because she has childbearing capacity, she is told that motherhood and child rearing is her function, not her option. Because she has childbearing capacity she is told that it is her function to marry and have the man economically maintain her and "make the decisions." Because she has the physical capacity for sexual intercourse, she is told that sexual intercourse too is her function, rather than just a voluntary act which she may engage in as an expression of her general humanity.

In each case *her* sexual difference is rationalized to trap her within it, while the male sexual difference is rationalized to imply an access to all areas of human activity.

Love, in the context of an oppressive male-female relationship, becomes an emotional cement to justify the dominant-submissive relationship. The man "loves" the woman who fulfills her submissive ego-boosting role. The woman "loves" the man she is submitting to—that is, after all, why she "lives for him." LOVE, magical and systematically unanalyzed, becomes the emotional rationale for the submission of one ego to the other. And it is deemed every woman's natural function to love.

Radical feminism believes that the popularized version of love has thus been politically to cloud and justify an oppressive relationship between men and women, and that in reality there can be no genuine love until the need to *control* the growth of another is replaced by love *for* the growth of another.

Learning to Become Feminine

The process of training women for their female role begins as far back as birth, when a boy child is preferred over a girl child. In her early years, when the basic patterns of her identity are being established, it is reinforced in her that her female role is not a choice but a fact. Her future will be spent performing the same basic functions as her mother and women before her. Her life is already determined. She is not given the choice of exploring activity toys. Her brothers play astronaut, doctor, scientist, race-car driver. She plays little homemaker, future mother (dolls), and nurse (doctor's helper). Her brothers are given activity toys; the world is their future. She is given service toys. She is already learning that her future will be in the maintenance of others. Her ego is repressed at all times to prepare her for this future submissiveness. She must dress prettily and be clean; speak politely; seek approval; please. Her brothers are allowed to fight, get dirty, be aggressive and be self-assertive.

As she goes through school she learns that subjects which teach mastery and control over the world, such as science and math, are male subjects; while subjects which teach appearance, maintenance, or sentiment, such as home economics or literature, are female subjects. School counselors will recommend nursing for girls, while they will encourage boys to be doctors. Most of the best colleges will accept only a token sprinkling of women (quota system), regardless of academic abilities.

By the time she is of marrying age she has been prepared on two levels. One, she will realize that alternatives to the traditional female role are both prohibitive and prohibited; two, she will herself have accepted on some levels the assumptions about her female role.

Internalization

It is not only through denying women human alternatives that men are able to maintain their positions of power. It is politically necessary for any oppressive group to convince the oppressed that they are in fact inferior, and therefore deserve their situation. For it is precisely through the destruction of women's egos that they are robbed of their ability to resist.

For the sake of our own liberation, we must learn to overcome this damage to ourselves through internalization. We must begin to destroy the notion that we are indeed only servants to the male ego, and must begin to reverse the systematic crushing of women's egos by constructing alternate selves that are healthy, independent and self-assertive. We must, in short, help each other to transfer the ultimate power of judgment about the value of our lives from men to ourselves.

It remains for us as women to fully develop a new dialectic of sex class—an analysis of the way in which sexual identity and institutions reinforce one another.

No More Miss America![1]

Radical Women (Organization)

August 1968

On September 7th in Atlantic City, the Annual Miss America Pageant will again crown "your ideal." But this year, reality will liberate the contest auction-block in the guise of "genyooine" de-plasticized, breathing women. Women's Liberation Groups, black women, high-school and college women, women's peace groups, women's welfare and social-work groups, women's job-equality groups, pro-birth control and pro-abortion groups—women of every political persuasion—all are invited to join us in a day-long boardwalk-theater event, starting at 1:00 p.m. on the Boardwalk in front of Atlantic City's Convention Hall. We will protest the image of Miss America, an image that oppresses women in every area in which it purports to represent us. There will be: Picket Lines; Guerrilla Theater; Leafleting; Lobbying Visits to the contestants urging our sisters to reject the Pageant Farce and join us; a huge Freedom Trash Can (into which we will throw bras, girdles, curlers, false eyelashes, wigs, and representative issues of *Cosmopolitan*, *Ladies' Home Journal*, *Family Circle*, etc.—bring any such woman-garbage you have around the house); we will also announce a Boycott of all those commercial products related to the Pageant, and the day will end with a Women's Liberation rally at midnight when Miss America is crowned on live television. Lots of other surprises are being planned (come and add your own!) but we do not plan heavy disruptive tactics and so do not expect a bad police scene. It should be a groovy day on the Boardwalk in the sun with our sisters. In case of arrests, however, we plan to reject all male authority and demand to be busted by policewomen only. (In Atlantic City, women cops are not permitted to make arrests—dig that!)

Male chauvinist-reactionaries on this issue had best stay away, nor are male liberals welcome in the demonstrations. But sympathetic men can donate money as well as cars and drivers.

Male reporters will be refused interviews. We reject patronizing reportage. *Only newswomen will be recognized.*

The Ten Points

We Protest:

1. *The Degrading Mindless-Boob-Girlie Symbol.* The Pageant contestants epitomize the roles we are all forced to play as women. The parade down the runway blares the metaphor of the 4-H Club county fair, where the nervous animals are judged for teeth, fleece, etc., and where the best "specimen" gets the blue ribbon. So are women in our society forced daily to compete for male approval, enslaved by ludicrous "beauty" standards we ourselves are conditioned to take seriously.

---

[1] Footnotes deleted.

2. *Racism with Roses.* Since its inception in 1921, the Pageant has not had one Black finalist, and this has not been for a lack of test-case contestants. There has never been a Puerto Rican, Alaskan, Hawaiian, or Mexican-American winner. Nor has there ever been a *true* Miss America—an American Indian.

3. *Miss America as Military Death Mascot.* The highlight of her reign each year is a cheerleader-tour of American troops abroad—last year she went to Vietnam to pep-talk our husbands, fathers, sons and boyfriends into dying and killing with a better spirit. She personifies the "unstained patriotic American womanhood our boys are fighting for." The Living Bra and the Dead Soldier. We refuse to be used as Mascots for Murder.

4. *The Consumer Con-Game.* Miss America is a walking commercial for the Pageant's sponsors. Wind her up and she plugs your product on promotion tours and TV—all in an "honest, objective" endorsement. What a shill.

5. *Competition Rigged and Unrigged.* We deplore the encouragement of an American myth that oppresses men as well as women: the win-or-you're-worthless competitive disease. The "beauty contest" creates only one winner to be "used" and forty-nine losers who are "useless."

6. *The Woman as Pop Culture Obsolescent Theme.* Spindle, mutilate, and then discard tomorrow. What is so ignored as least year's Miss America? This only reflects the gospel of our society, according to Saint Male: women must be young, juicy, malleable—hence age discrimination and the cult of youth. And we women are brainwashed into believing this ourselves!

7. *The Unbeatable Madonna-Whore Combination.* Miss America and Playboy's centerfold are sisters over the skin. To win approval, we must be both sexy and wholesome, delicate but able to cope, demure yet tititlatingly bitchy. Deviation of any sort brings, we are told, disaster: "You won't get a man!!"

8. *The Irrelevant Crown on the Throne of Mediocrity.* Miss America represents what women are supposed to be: unoffensive, bland, apolitical. If you are tall, short, over or under what weight The Man prescribes you should be, forget it. Personality, articulateness, intelligence, commitment—unwise. Conformity is the key to the crown—and, by extension, to success in our society.

9. *Miss America as Dream Equivalent To—?* In this reputedly democratic society, where every little boy supposedly can grow up to be President, what can every little girl hope to grow to be? Miss America. That's where it's at. Real power to control our own lives is restricted to men, while women get patronizing pseudopower, an ermine cloak and a bunch of flowers; men are judged by their actions, women by their appearance.

10. *Miss America as Big Sister Watching You.* The Pageant exercises Thought Control, attempts to sear the Image onto our minds, to further make women oppressed and men oppressors; to enslave us all the more in high-heeled, low-status roles; to inculcate false values in young girls; to use women as beasts of buying; to seduce us to prostitute ourselves before our own oppression.

NO MORE MISS AMERICA

14.3 THE COUNTERATTACK (1972)

The opposition of many men to the feminist campaign, especially to its more militant versions, was predictable. But the feminist movement also made enemies among women.

Some of these based their opposition on the conviction that a woman's place was in the home. Others argued in favor of employment gains for women, but maintained a rigorous defense of traditional sexual roles and values. How would you classify Alice Skelsey's speech "Mrs. Homemaker–Mrs. Wonderful"?

MRS. HOMEMAKER–MRS. WONDERFUL: THE NEW MYTHS FROM WOMEN'S LIB

Alice Skelsey

Delivered before the council of Homemaker's Clubs, Montgomery Country, Maryland, November 14, 1972

I'd like first to congratulate you on the theme for your meeting: Mrs. Homemaker–Mrs. Wonderful. As a Working Mother I find it *democratic*—because most working mothers count themselves as homemakers first and jobholders second.

I also think you have been *courageous* in choosing such a theme—because, as I'm sure you are aware, in certain small—but militant groups—the mere words—Mrs. Homemaker, Mrs. Wonderful—could get you stuffed in your oven along with your Sunday roast.

But most of all, your theme seems *practical* to me—because if ever the young women coming along—and for many of us that means our own daughters—if ever these young women needed a reaffirmation of the importance and dignity and common sense that goes along with Mrs. Homemaker, Mrs. Wonderful, that time is now.

Elsie Whitten asked me to talk with you today about a book I wrote a while back entitled the *Working Mother's Guide to Her Home, Her Family and Her Self*. It always seems a bit much for me to be talking on such subjects before groups such as yours because I feel certain that you could tell *me* much more about how to keep the home and family going than I could tell *you*.

But then when I remember why I wrote the book in the first place, I decide all over again that groups such as yours are probably the most appropriate ones I could be talking to. So much has been written and said in the past few years about the job side of a working woman's life, and so very little about the home side, that the book began with no more pretensions than to put down some of the things I had learned—mostly the hard way—on how to juggle two worlds and still keep both of them pasted together.

But a very strange thing happened to me in the course of consigning all of this to paper. As I thought back over all of the things I had done, all of the problems I had, all of these things came welling up from my toes—I hadn't had any idea that I had worked so hard. I couldn't believe it. And by the time the book was finished, I was about

---

Used by permission from *Vital Speeches of the Day* and from the author. Alice Skelsey is the author of *A Working Mother's Guide* (Random House) and a thrice weekly column, "For Women Who Work" (*Chicago Tribune/New York News Syndicate*). Her other books include *Growing Up Green* (Workman) and *Orchids* (Time-Life). As a research fellow at the University of South Carolina, Ms. Skelsey is currently at work on a biography of an eighteenth-century marriage.

convinced that only the most fortunate women are able to manage both—and that we had all better give up and stay home. The effort is just too much.

And yet I know that for a number of very good reasons it would have been impossible for me NOT to have worked. Then, when the book was published and I had the opportunity to go around the country meeting and talking with many, many women, and my newspaper column began, and so many more women began to share their lives with me, the colossal indifference of a philosophy that says a woman should choose: either have a family or have a job—combatting that attitude became almost a crusade with me.

Because I don't think things are getting easier for women in general. I think they're becoming much more difficult. And the options are closing down more rapidly for the woman who might have chosen to stay at home. Financially and socially—it is becoming harder for a one-income family to make it these days.

So it seems to me that it is groups such as yours that are MOST needed today in discussions of how we can meet some of the problems women face on the home front.

So what I would like to do today is take up the three main sections of the book—home, family, and self—and discuss them with you in terms of some of the new myths that are growing up around us these days while we have been busy debunking some of the old ones.

On the latter score, for example, "A woman's place is in the home" has probably been laid to rest permanently. Certainly it is a grossly ignorant statement today when we know that many women are the sole support of their families. More than 2 million working mothers are raising children in homes left fatherless by death, divorce or separation.

Another old saying—"keep her barefoot and pregnant" isn't really all that funny—if it ever was—especially when we know that barefeet and pregnancy can lead to all kinds of problems—from population explosions to fallen arches.

And then there was that grand old saw "If God had wanted women to"—and here you can fit in anything you choose from "wearing pant suits to climbing ladders"—"then He would have made them differently." Well, we have found out that without any alterations at all on our anatomies, pantsuits have become a comfortable, practical and attractive part of our wardrobes. And from that, it follows that climbing ladders present no particular problem for us either.

And yet, while we have been busy presiding over the funeral of the old myths, we have been just as busy creating some new ones to take their place.

For example, let's consider the Home category again. Today we now have the assurance that "A career needn't interfere with a home and family."

I can't imagine who thought this one up. Perhaps it was the successful older woman who reared her children in those by-gone days when "jewels" were still around. A jewel was by definition a housekeeper or nursemaid who was trustworthy, capable and loving, and who, not so incidentally, worked for practically nothing.

Or it might have been the already successful career woman in her 30's who marries Mr. Big Success—either widowed or divorced—and assumes his ready-made family along with the financial resources that can keep the children comfortably ensconced in private boarding schools and summer camps.

Or maybe it's the younger woman in her 20's who believes that careers and families don't interfere with each other. She can afford to. She doesn't have a family yet, and perhaps she hasn't the slightest intention of ever getting into that bag.

But how does the new myth work for a woman with a couple of small children, a regular 9-to-5 job, and a salary something short of fabulous?

Surely she must yearn sometimes for more time to spend at home? Maybe just a few more hours a week to squeeze in the grocery shopping or other errands or to get caught up at home and not feel so pressed.

And isn't she sometimes called at the office to cope with a problem at home: A chipped front tooth on a 10-year-old boy or a burnt-out pilot on a 10-year-old furnace? Sure she is.

And isn't the office in the way sometimes—a field trip she can't make, a Girl Scout leader she can't be, worthwhile meetings such as yours she can't always attend, because she can't get off from work? Of course the office gets in the way.

The fact is that jobs—regular jobs in the structured work world we have today—are NOT basically compatible with family life—and one gets in the way of the other more often than the new myth would have us believe.

So how does the working mother manage? Well, I can tell you that she does it mostly by working harder than nearly anyone else. Certainly, she learns the fine art of doing 2 and 3 things at the same time.

When she cleans out her refrigerator for the week, she is also making out her grocery list and planning her menus for the following week.

She takes a long look ahead so that she can plan her activities rather than fall victim to them. She talks over the various activities her children are involved in and what input they will be counting on from her. She volunteers for a job in Girl Scouts that she knows she can handle rather than waiting to be asked and agreeing to accept a job she knows in her bones she can't really manage.

She could not make it without a long cord on her telephone. (I once wrote a column about that and the response was astounding. You have no idea all the things that can be done and still have one ear attached to a phone with a long cord on it!)

Now if we move on to the Family area, one of the grandest of the new myths can be found. This one says that "it's not the quantity of the time a parent spends with a child that counts, it's the quality."

Somehow this seems to suggest that the less you see your children the more you will love them. Well, certainly there are days when any mother will agree to that.

But if we pick this statement up and turn it around and look at it again, we are left to conclude that having an 8-hour-a-day job along with a home and family will produce left-over time that will automatically be better quality time for spending with your family.

But does the quality of our family time automatically increase as the quantity shrinks? Or does the law of diminishing returns set in here somewhere?

The new myth is built on the idea that if you are going to spend all day with your child, growing irritable, bored, frustrated, lonely and isolated—either suffocating him with over-protective love, or abusing him out of your frustration at spending so much time with him, or lowering the shades and taking to drink—how much BETTER it is, somehow, for you to be up at 6:30 or 7 in the morning, hustling your family along so that you can be off to a stimulating day in the work world. And when you get back at the end of the day, it will be all smiles and hugs and love for the little ones because this is the *quality* time—this is the time that counts.

But does it always work out that way?

Suppose you get home at the end of the day, dead tired; you've had an awful day: you have dinner still to fix; you forgot to thaw the meat loaf; the TV is blaring; the children are fighting; your husband yells down to tell you to hurry he's got a meeting to make; and the dog has thrown up on the living room rug.

Still you are to believe that the quality of this time is going to be better quality time. Well, of course, it isn't so, and most working women quickly find this out for themselves. I can tell you almost the moment it happens. You have decided you are NOT going to scream at your child (just like in the commercial). Instead, anywhere from 15 to 30 minutes later, you wind up bawling—probably while you are leaning over the sink peeling an onion.

And so the working mother discovers before she's been in the game very long that having more to do and less time to do it in, isn't always accompanied with patience and love and understanding.

So her survival techniques here include NEVER forgetting to take the meat loaf out to thaw; NEVER having an onion on the menu that hasn't been peeled the night before; having or training a husband who will NEVER greet you at the front door with a Hurry-up; and a rule that says WHOEVER was unfortunate enough to be closest to the scene when the dog throws up is the one who cleans up. Life is hard for all of us in the working mother's world and the rain sometimes falls on the just and unjust alike.

So much for that myth. Now as for the third one—the one having to do with Self. Here is this one: "Women in this country have been our greatest wasted national resource. What we need is a great united effort to help us break out of our prisons and into a work world where exciting, fulfilling, highly-rewarding jobs are waiting for us to make our contributions to the nation's well being."

This myth is a great deal to ask the older woman to bear. Here she has devoted a good hunk of her life to doing the best job she could with her home and family. And now, suddenly, she discovers that she has been declared a great wasted national resource—something on the order of a wornout coal mine.

This wasted national resource idea also does a disservice to the young women coming along. To suggest to our daughters—as one libber puts it—that "home economics is a cultural ghetto" reveals a great deal of ignorance about how it is in the real world.

The facts of life are these for our daughters:

Most of them will continue to choose marriage in one form or another;

Most will choose to have at least one child;

Most—the Women's Bureau estimates 9 out of every 10—will hold a job at sometime in their lives.

And of these, most will place the welfare of family above job, if and when it comes down to the choices.

It only makes sense, then, it seems to me, that rather than demything the importance of home and family that we set about the business of making the work world more compatible with family life.

How is it that the family unit has become the principal candidate for surgery in remaking society?

Why must family life be mashed up to fit a work world no one is much satisfied with, when the WORK world is just sitting there crying to be reshaped in ways that will make it more compatible with family life?

Suppose we recognized that many, many young parents DO want to spend more time with their children; that they DO want to SHARE work and family roles; that shorter work days could give them more of the flexibility they need—not the 10 hour days we've heard so much about.

Suppose that efforts to help define good parenthood for parents also helped make it possible for parents to be on the scene more of the time to use what they learn.

Suppose that the work world—the managers of business, industry, unions, government, the professions—set about the deliberate identification of those types of jobs that could be done at home just as well as at a specific desk at a specific time and place?

Suppose that jobs could be judged by performance and production not the amount of time punched in on the timecard?

Suppose part-time jobs carried full status in terms of advancement opportunities, retirement, insurance, etc.

Suppose we recognized that the mature woman who wants to enter the work world after raising her family has been using her brains right along, every waking day.

Suppose that her judgment, dependability, maturity were considered important job assets, and she were allowed to advance at least a few steps past "Start" when she does come into the job market.

Suppose we recognized that many women with family responsibilities behind them still have 25 years or more of "steam" to put into a career and we open our educational and job opportunities as widely to them as to any other job entrant.

Suppose we put as much money into pilot programs and research projects on any of the above as we have to parceling out the family's role to other institutions.

The family has been whacked on long enough; I think it's time we started on the work world.

Which is why I was delighted to have the opportunity to be with you today. Because it seems to me that groups such as yours have a great deal to offer the working woman in getting across not only the techniques and know-how in keeping a home and family running, but in helping to focus on the importance of that home and family to the lives of most women, working or not.

It is naive to expect that women who are primarily interested in careers in the work world, as well as those women for whom the Women's Movement has become a source of jobs in itself—it is naive to expect these women to focus much of their attention on the grubby details of daily home and family life. They have their hands full in the equal rights battle on the job front, and aside from the fringies and ego-trippers who gain a lot of the publicity, these women are intelligent, responsible people who are opening up the work world to fair treatment for increasing numbers of women.

But the re-shaping of that work world if it is to be done, is going to be left, I believe, to those who are not so firmly tied to it. From your theme today, Mrs. Homemaker—Mrs. Wonderful, obviously this includes you. It is YOU who can present most clearly the needs of home and family, how they can be met, how the work world can be made more compatible with family life—for both men and women.

The fact is if you don't do it, it's not going to be done, and in my opinion all of us—Mrs. Homemaker and Mrs. Working Mother—will be the poorer for it.

Now just how you go about this: Through themes and club programs and workshops and promotions and representation in legislative considerations and pressures on business and Congress and so on—all these sorts of ideas and questions I hope I will leave running around in your heads to come out in other sessions.

Because I'm now down to the last item—a tool all working mothers learn to use in order to manage their time. (Show kitchen timer) And it's just about to go off!

CHAPTER 15

The Vietnam War

The Vietnam War has been described as America's longest war. It was also America's most demoralizing, divisive, and ultimately most despised war.

The Vietnam conflict was an extension into Southeast Asia of the Cold War between the superpowers and their clients. As viewed by U.S. policy makers in the 1960s, the United States, as prime defender of the free world, had to prevent the conquest of pro-Western South Vietnam by a pro-Soviet regime in North Vietnam led by the Communist leader Ho Chi Minh. If Americans failed in their mission, it would consign much of the region to ultimate Communist domination.

Whatever the rationale, the United States drifted, almost absentmindedly, into a military and political commitment in the region. Vietnam had been part of French Indochina, a dependency of France since the nineteenth century. The Japanese occupied the country during World War II, and when they left in 1945, the French sought to reestablish political control. They were opposed by Indochinese groups determined to oust France and establish independent nations in the former colony.

The most effective of these insurgent forces was the Viet Minh, concentrated around Hanoi in northern Vietnam and led by the Moscow-trained Ho Chi Minh. Ho and his supporters were determined to unite all of Vietnam as a Marxist state under their leadership.

Despite a flood of U.S. money and military supplies, the French failed to subdue the Viet Minh, and after their defeat in battle at Dien Bien Phu in 1954, they agreed to leave their former colony. Their departure left Indochina divided into four small countries: Communist-dominated North Vietnam with its capital at Hanoi; a pro-Western South Vietnam governed from Saigon; and two small states, Laos and Cambodia, which tried to maintain a neutral position.

The Geneva Accords of 1954, confirming French defeat, mandated national elections in two years to decide on the unification of the two Vietnams. But the vote was never held. In the south the pro-Western regime led by Ngo Dinh Diem, fearing defeat, ignored the election provision of the Geneva agreement.

Frustrated by this check to reunification of both Vietnams under its control, Ho's regime in the north supported a guerrilla war by the Communist Vietcong (the National Liberation Front) against the Saigon government.

The U.S. government tried to prop up the Diem regime in South Vietnam with arms, food, and money. In 1961, President Kennedy dispatched the first U.S. military personnel to South Vietnam, although they were advisers to the South Vietnamese armed forces, not combat troops. This aid was not enough. The Diem regime was corrupt, arbitrary, and bigoted and, while failing to win over South Vietnam's peasants, offended the influential Buddhists.

In late 1963, the United States encouraged the overthrow of the Diem regime by pro-American generals. For the next few years confusion reigned in Saigon as various factions and individuals fought for power. By now Lyndon Johnson was president, and the U.S. commitment to preserving the status quo in Vietnam was about to get a major boost.

Soon after LBJ's election in 1964 he escalated the U.S. military investment in Vietnam. In March 1965, he ordered a major bombing campaign ("Rolling Thunder") against North Vietnam to discourage further aid to the Vietcong. Soon after, the first U.S. combat troops arrived in South Vietnam. By the end of the year there would be almost 200,000 U.S. fighting men in the country. Each month thereafter the number grew. At the peak of the Vietnam War in late 1968, some 536,000 U.S. troops would be engaged in a struggle to stop Hanoi from reuniting the two Vietnams under its sole authority.

At home the war proved to be the most divisive in U.S. history. Constrained by fears of Chinese or Soviet intervention, the administration refused to employ nuclear weapons. It also failed to make an effective case to the U.S. people for an all-out war and in fact sought to hide the costs of the U.S. commitment lest they arouse too much domestic opposition. To make matters worse, the U.S. client regime in Saigon never seemed to care as much about saving itself as the United States did; its generals and troops seldom engaged the enemy aggressively.

Significant domestic opposition to the war erupted in early 1965, and thereafter the antiwar movement grew with each new increment of U.S. military investment. Antiwar feelings were amplified by the nightly TV news, which showed the bombings, the firefights, and the daily "body counts" in Vietnam to an appalled U.S. viewership. The president and his advisers kept reassuring the public that there was "light at the end of the tunnel," and that with a few thousand more men and a little more effort, the enemy would collapse. Americans soon greeted each new claim with derision. In late January 1968, after months of optimistic predictions, the prowar "hawks" suffered a devastating setback when a coordinated, multicity Vietcong attack on South Vietnamese and U.S. posts and installations during the Vietnamese Tet new year festival caught the Americans by surprise. The Vietcong captured the provincial capital of Hue and penetrated the U.S. embassy compound in Saigon.

In the end Vietcong losses were appalling, but the Tet Offensive demolished the administration's claim of imminent victory. To the very end a bloc of "hawk" loyalists continued to support the war. But by this time many Americans had lost faith in their government, a mood that fed the political and cultural left and propelled a stream of recruits into such organizations as Students for a Democratic Society, the Resistance, and the Yippies.

In 1968, antiwar Democrats, led by Senators Eugene McCarthy of Minnesota and Robert Kennedy of New York, forced Johnson to drop his reelection bid. The Democratic presidential candidate that year, Hubert Humphrey, was hobbled by his loyalty to Johnson and lost narrowly to Richard Nixon in November. Once in office Nixon began to reduce U.S. combat troops and turn the fighting over to the South Vietnamese, a process he called "Vietnamization." Meanwhile U.S. and North Vietnamese officials conducted frustrating peace negotiations in Paris, out of the public's sight. Yet the fighting continued, and the antiwar activists accused Nixon of hypocrisy.

In January 1973, the United States, North Vietnam, South Vietnam, and the Vietcong finally concluded an agreement to stop the fighting, exchange prisoners, and form a National Council of Reconciliation to determine future relations between Hanoi and Saigon. In March 1973 the last U.S. troops left South Vietnam.

The Nixon administration claimed that the South Vietnamese could protect themselves if the United States continued to provide money and equipment. It was untrue, however, and in any event Congress was unwilling to provide the resources. In April 1975, under powerful attack by North Vietnamese forces, the South Vietnamese government collapsed. As the Communist tanks rumbled into Saigon, the United States hurriedly evacuated the remaining Americans and hundreds of South Vietnamese supporters from the U.S. embassy grounds by helicopter. Over the next few years, as the North Vietnamese imposed a totalitarian regime in the South, hundreds of thousands of South Vietnamese "boat people" fled the Communists, many eventually finding haven in the United States.

America's longest war had ended on a bitter note, leaving behind a legacy of neo-isolationism, internal domestic division, dismay at excessive presidential power, and skepticism of U.S. goals and purposes. It would take years before the wounds healed.

The following selections represent the positions of various groups on the U.S. role in Vietnam. Included are defenders of the administration policies, U.S. peace advocates, and even the Communist North Vietnamese. Needless to say, the disagreements among the parties are striking.

15.1 THE HAWK POSITION (1954, 1964, 1965)

As far back as the 1950s, U.S. leaders saw a victory for the Vietnamese Communists as a grave danger to the other non-Communist regimes in East Asia. Influenced by the containment policy in Europe and the experience of the Korean War, they warned that if the North Vietnamese were not stopped, the Communist virus would soon spread to neutral or pro-Western East Asian nations. This in turn would expand the power of the Soviet Union and the Communist People's Republic of China at the free world's expense.

The most famous expression of this pessimistic view came at a 1954 press conference, reported here, at which President Dwight Eisenhower likened the non-Communist nations of the region to a row of dominoes that would tip over one by one if the Hanoi regime were successful in reuniting Vietnam under its aegis. Yet despite his convictions, Eisenhower proved unwilling to commit U.S. combat forces to Vietnam. Students will want to ask if there were plausible reasons to believe in the "domino effect." Did events prove Eisenhower to be correct?

It took more than a decade before the sort of thinking behind Eisenhower's statement produced a full-scale U.S. military commitment to the defense of South Vietnam. The United States never issued a declaration of war before committing its forces to Vietnam, but the controversial Tonkin Gulf Resolution provided the legal and budgetary basis for U.S. actions. In the height of Cold War enthusiasm, the Resolution passed with near unanimity in 1964, giving the president remarkable powers and discretion in dealing with the emerging crisis in Southeast Asia. Why have some scholars described this law as a "blank check?" How did the Cold War facilitate the accumulation of power by the executive branch of the U.S. government?

The third selection in this section was transmitted secretly but, nevertheless, it came to the attention of the U.S. public as part of the "Pentagon Papers" episode, which stretched several years during the late 1960s and early 1970s. This reading, known as the "White Paper," provided an overview of the "official" rationale for Americanization of the Vietnam War. How does its logic compare to what the government told its people about events in Vietnam? Why did a "credibility gap" emerge as the war dragged on without decisive result?

THE DOMINO THEORY

Dwight D. Eisenhower

Q: ROBERT RICHARDS, COPLEY PRESS: Mr. President, would you mind commenting on the strategic importance of Indochina to the free world? I think there has been, across the country, some lack of understanding on just what it means to us.

THE PRESIDENT: You have, of course, both the specific and the general when you talk about such things.

First of all, you have the specific value of a locality in its production of materials that the world needs.

Then you have the possibility that many human beings pass under a dictatorship that is inimical to the free world.

Finally, you have broader considerations that might follow what you would call the "falling domino" principle. You have a row of dominoes set up, you knock over the first one, and what will happen to the last one is the certainty that it will go over very quickly. So you could have a beginning of a disintegration that would have the most profound influences.

Now, with respect to the first one, two of the items from this particular area that the world uses are tin and tungsten. They are very important. There are others, of course, the rubber plantations and so on.

Public Papers of the Presidents of the United States: Dwight D. Eisenhower, 1954 (Washington, DC: Government Printing Office, 1958), pp. 381–90.

Then with respect to more people passing under this domination, Asia, after all, has already lost some 450 million of its people to the Communist dictatorship, and we simply can't afford greater losses.

But when we come to the possible sequence of events, the loss of Indochina, of Burma, of Thailand, of the Peninsula, and Indonesia following, now you begin to talk about areas that not only multiply the disadvantages that you would suffer through loss of materials, sources of materials, but now you are talking really about millions and millions and millions of people.

Finally, the geographical position achieved thereby does many things. It turns the so-called island defensive chain of Japan, Formosa, of the Philippines and to the southward; it moves in to threaten Australia and New Zealand.

It takes away, in its economic aspects, that region that Japan must have as a trading area or Japan, in turn, will have only one place in the world to go—that is, toward the Communist areas in order to live.

So, the possible consequences of the loss are just incalculable to the free world.

THE GULF OF TONKIN RESOLUTION AUGUST 7, 1964

To Promote the Maintenance of International Peace and Security in Southeast Asia

Whereas naval units of the Communist regime in Vietnam, in violation of the principles of the Charter of the United Nations and of international law, have deliberately and repeatedly attacked United States naval vessels lawfully present in international waters, and have thereby created a serious threat to international peace, and

Whereas these attacks are part of a deliberate and systematic campaign of aggression that the Communist regime in North Vietnam has been waging against its neighbors and the nations joined with them in the collective defense of their freedom; and

Whereas the United States is assisting the peoples of southeast Asia to protect their freedom and has no territorial, military or political ambitions in that area, but desires only that these peoples should be left in peace to work out their own destinies in their own way: Now, therefore, be it

Resolved by the Senate and House of Representatives of the United States of America in Congress assembled.

That the Congress approves and supports the determination of the President as Commander in Chief, to take all necessary measures to repel any armed attack against the forces of the United States and to prevent further aggression.

SEC.2. The United States regards as vital to its national interest and to world peace the maintenance of international peace and security in southeast Asia. Consonant with the Constitution of the United States and the Charter of the United Nations and in

Department of State Bulletin, 51 (August 24, 1964).

accordance with its obligations under the Southeast Asia Collective Defense Treaty, the United States is, therefore, prepared, as the President determines, to take all necessary steps, including the use of armed force, to assist any member or protocol state of the Southeast Asia Collective Defense Treaty requesting assistance in defense of its freedom.

SEC.3. This resolution shall expire when the President shall determine that the peace and security of the area is reasonable assured by international conditions created by action of the United Nations or otherwise, except that it may be terminated earlier by concurrent resolution of the Congress. . . .

3. I should like to receive, within the next several weeks, your views concerning the economic and military effect upon North Vietnam of the patterns of attack contemplated. To put the matter more precisely, assume that attacks 8b, c and d were carried out and that the attacks resulted in the damage levels described in your target studies. In these circumstances, what would be your estimate?

(a) Of the effect upon the capabilities of North Vietnam
    i. to support and assist the PL and VC.
    ii. to escalate through the use of DRV forces against SVN and Laos.
(b) Of the effects upon the economy of North Vietnam (in terms of such factors as internal transportation, imports and exports, industrial production and food production and distribution) within the short run (say three months) and in the long-run (say five years).

4. If the destruction of the 94 targets were not to succeed in its objective of destroying the DRV will and capability, what courses of action would you recommend? Would you recommend further attack on the 94 targets or the addition of more targets? What preparations would be necessary (e.g., target analysis, logistics) in order to carry out such attacks?

THE "WHITE PAPER"

Introduction

South Vietnam is fighting for its life against a brutal campaign of terror and armed attack inspired, directed, supplied, and controlled by the Communist regime in Hanoi. This flagrant aggression has been going on for years, but recently the pace has quickened and the threat has now become active.

The war in Vietnam is a new kind of war, a fact as yet poorly understood in most parts of the world. Much of the confusion that prevails in the thinking of many people, and even many governments, stems from this basic misunderstanding. For in Vietnam a totally new brand of aggression has been loosed against an independent people who want to make their own way in peace and freedom.

Vietnam is *not* another Greece, where indigenous guerrilla forces used friendly neighboring territory as a sanctuary.

U.S. Department of State, *Aggression from the North: The Record of North Vietnam's Campaign to Conquer South Vietnam*. Publication 7839, Far Eastern Series 130 (Washington, DC, February, 1965).

Vietnam is *not* another Malaya, where Communist guerrillas were, for the most part, physically distinguishable from the peaceful majority they sought to control.

Vietnam is *not* another Philippines, where Communist guerrillas were physically separated from the source of their moral and physical support.

Above all, the war in Vietnam is *not* a spontaneous and local rebellion against the established government.

There are elements in the Communist program of conquest directed against South Vietnam common to each of the previous areas of aggression and subversion. But there is one fundamental difference. In Vietnam a Communist government has set out deliberately to conquer a sovereign people in a neighboring state. And to achieve its end, it has used every resource of its own government to carry out its carefully planned program of concealed aggression. North Vietnam's commitment to seize control of the South is no less total than was the commitment of the regime in North Korea in 1950. But knowing the consequences of the latter's undisguised attack, the planners in Hanoi have tried desperately to conceal their hand. They have failed and their aggression is as real as that of an invading army.

This report is a summary of the massive evidence of North Vietnamese aggression obtained by the Government of South Vietnam. This evidence has been jointly analyzed by South Vietnamese and American experts.

The evidence shows that the hard core of the Communist forces attacking South Vietnam were trained in the North and ordered into the South by Hanoi. It shows that the key leadership of the Vietcong (VC), the officers and much of the cadre, many of the technicians, political organizers, and propagandists have come from the North and operate under Hanoi's direction. It shows that the training of essential military personnel and their infiltration into the South is directed by the Military High Command in Hanoi.

The evidence shows that many of the weapons and much of the ammunition and other supplies used by the Vietcong have been sent into South Vietnam from Hanoi. In recent months new types of weapons have been introduced in the VC army, for which all ammunition must come from outside sources. Communist China and other Communist states have been the prime suppliers of these weapons and ammunition, and they have been channeled primarily through North Vietnam.

The directing force behind the effort to conquer South Vietnam is the Communist Party in the North, the Lao Dong (Workers) Party. As in every Communist state, the party is an integral part of the regime itself. North Vietnamese officials have expressed their firm determination to absorb South Vietnam into the Communist World. . . .

I. Hanoi Supplies the Key Personnel for the Armed Aggression Against South Vietnam

The hard core of the Communist forces attacking South Vietnam are men trained in North Vietnam. They are ordered into the South and remain under the military discipline of the Military High Command in Hanoi. Special training camps operated by the North Vietnamese army give political and military training to the infiltrators. Increasingly the forces sent into the South are native North Vietnamese who have never seen South Vietnam. A special infiltration unit, the 70th Transportation Group, is responsible for moving men from North Vietnam into the South via infiltration trails through Laos. Another special unit, the maritime infiltration group, sends weapons and supplies and agents by sea into the South.

The infiltration rate has been increasing. From 1959 to 1960, when Hanoi was establishing its infiltration pipeline, at least 1,800 men, and possibly 2,700 more, moved into South Vietnam from the North. The flow increased to a minimum of 3,700 in 1961 and at least 5,400 in 1962. There was a modest decrease in 1963 to 4,200 confirmed infiltrators, though later evidence is likely to raise this figure.

For 1964 the evidence is still incomplete. However, it already shows that a minimum of 4,400 infiltrators entered the South, and it is estimated more than 3,000 others were sent in.

There is usually a time lag between the entry of infiltrating troops and the discovery of clear evidence they have entered. This fact, plus collateral evidence of increased use of the infiltration routes, suggests strongly that 1964 was probably the year of greatest infiltration so far.

Thus, since 1959, nearly 20,000 VC officers, soldiers, and technicians are known to have entered South Vietnam under orders from Hanoi. Additional information indicates that an estimated 17,000 more infiltrators were dispatched to the South by the regime in Hanoi during the past six years. It can reasonably be assumed that still other infiltration groups have entered the South for which there is no evidence yet available.

To some the level of infiltration from the North may seem modest in comparison with the total size of the armed forces of the Republic of Vietnam. But one-for-one calculations are totally misleading in the kind of warfare going on in Vietnam. First, a high proportion of infiltrators from the North are well-trained officers, cadres, and specialists. Second, it has long been realized that in guerrilla combat the burdens of defense are vastly heavier than those of attack. In Malaya, the Philippines, and elsewhere a ratio of at least 10-to-1 in favor of the forces of order was required to meet successfully the threat of the guerrillas' hit-and-run tactics.

In the calculus of guerrilla warfare the scale of North Vietnamese infiltration into the South takes on a very different meaning. For the infiltration of 5,000 guerrilla fighters in a given year is the equivalent of marching perhaps 50,000 regular troops across the border, in terms of the burden placed on the defenders.

Above all, the number of proved and probable infiltrators from the North should be seen in relation to the size of the VC forces. It is now estimated that the Vietcong number approximately 35,000 so-called hard-core forces, and another 60,000–80,000 local forces. It is thus apparent that infiltrators from the North—allowing for casualties—make up the majority of the so-called hard-core Vietcong. Personnel from the North, in short, are now and have always been the backbone of the entire VC operation.

It is true that many of the lower level elements of the VC forces are recruited within South Vietnam. However, the thousands of reported cases of VC kidnappings and terrorism make it abundantly clear that threats and other pressures by the Vietcong play a major part in such recruitment.

A.   The Infiltration Process

The infiltration routes supply hard-core units with most of their officers and non-commissioned personnel. This source helps fill the gaps left by battle casualties, illness, and defection and insures continued control by Hanoi. Also, as the nature of the conflict has changed, North Vietnam has supplied the Vietcong with technical specialists via the infiltration routes. These have included men trained in armor and ordnance, antiaircraft, and communications as well as medical corpsmen and transport experts.

There is no single infiltration route from the North to South Vietnam. But by far the biggest percentage of infiltrators follow the same general course. The principal training center for North Vietnamese army men assigned to join the Vietcong has been at Xuan Mai near Hanoi. Recently captured Vietcong have also reported an infiltration training camp at Thanh Hoa. After completion of their training course—which involves political and propaganda work as well as military subjects—infiltrating units are moved to Vinh on the east coast. Many have made stopovers at a staging area in Dong Hoi where additional training is conducted. From there they go by truck to the Laos border.

Then usually after several days' rest, infiltrators move southward through Laos. Generally they move along the Laos–South Vietnam border. Responsibility for infiltration from North Vietnam through Laos belongs to the 70th Transportation Group of the North Vietnamese army. After a time the infiltration groups turn eastward, entering South Vietnam in Quang Nam, Quang Tri, Thua Thien, Kontum, or another of the border provinces.

The Communists have established regular lanes for infiltration with way-stations established about one day's march apart. The way-stations are equipped to quarter and feed the Vietcong passing through. Infiltrators who suffer from malaria or other illnesses stay at the stations until they recover sufficiently to join another passing group moving South. . . .

Local guides lead the infiltration groups along the secret trails. Generally they direct their infiltrators from halfway between two stations, through their own base station, and on halfway to the next supply base. Thus the guides are kept in ignorance of all but their own way-stations. Only group leaders are permitted to talk with the guides in order to preserve maximum security. The men are discouraged from asking where they are or where they are going.

The same system of trails and guides used along the Laos infiltration routes is used within South Vietnam itself. Vietcong infiltrators may report directly to a reassignment center in the highlands as soon as they enter South Vietnam. But in the past year or more some groups have moved down trails in South Vietnam to provinces along the Cambodian border and near Saigon before receiving their unit assignment. Within South Vietnam infiltration and supplies are handled by VC units such as the Nam Son Transportation Group.

At the Laos border-crossing point infiltrators are re-equipped. Their North Vietnamese army uniforms must be turned in. They must give up all personal papers, letters, notebooks, and photographs that might be incriminating. Document control over the infiltrators has been tightened considerably over the past two years. A number of Vietnamese infiltrators have told of being fitted out with Lao "neutralist" uniforms for their passage through Laos.

Infiltration groups are usually issued a set of black civilian pajama-like clothes, two unmarked uniforms, rubber sandals, a sweater, a hammock, mosquito netting, and water-proof sheeting. They carry a 3–5 day supply of food. A packet of medicines and bandages is usually provided. . .

II. Hanoi Supplies Weapons, Ammunition, and Other War Material to Its Forces in the South

When Hanoi launched the VC campaign of terror, violence, and subversion in earnest in 1959, the Communist forces relied mainly on stocks of weapons and ammunition left over from the war against the French. Supplies sent from North Vietnam came largely from the same source. As the military campaign progressed, the Vietcong depended heavily on weapons captured from the American Forces in South Vietnam. This remains an important source of weapons and ammunition for the Vietcong. But as the pace of the war has quickened, requirements for up-to-date arms and special types of weapons have risen to a point where the Vietcong cannot rely on captured stocks. Hanoi has undertaken a program to reequip its forces in the South with Communist-produced weapons.

Large and increasing quantities of military supplies are entering South Vietnam from outside the country. The principal supply point is North Vietnam, which provides a convenient channel for material that originates in Communist China and other Communist countries.

An increasing number of weapons from external Communist sources have been seized in the South. These include such weapons as 57-mm. and 75-mm. recoilless rifles, dual-purpose machine guns, rocket launchers, large mortars, and antitank mines.

A new group of Chinese Communist-manufactured weapons has recently appeared in VC hands. These include the 7.62 semiautomatic carbine, 7.62 light machine gun, and the 7.62 assault rifle. These weapons and ammunition for them, manufactured in Communist China in 1962, were first captured in December 1964 in Chuong Thien Province. Similar weapons have since been seized in each of the four Corps areas of South Vietnam. Also captured have been Chinese Communist antitank grenade launchers and ammunition made in China in 1963.

One captured Vietcong told his captors that his entire company had been supplied recently with modern Chinese weapons. The re-equipping of VC units with a type of weapons that require ammunition and parts from outside South Vietnam indicates the growing confidence of the authorities in Hanoi in the effectiveness of their supply lines into the South.

Incontrovertible evidence of Hanoi's elaborate program to supply its forces in the South with weapons, ammunition, and other supplies has accumulated over the years. Dramatic new proof was exposed just as this report was being completed.

On February 16, 1965, an American helicopter pilot flying along the South Vietnamese coast sighted a suspicious vessel. It was a cargo ship of an estimated 100-ton capacity, carefully camouflaged and moored just offshore along the coast of Phu Yen Province. Fighter planes that approached the vessel met machine gun fire from the guns on the deck of the ship and from the shore as well. A Vietnamese Air Force strike was launched against the vessel, and Vietnamese Government troops moved into the area. They seized the ship after a bitter fight with the Vietcong.

The ship, which had been sunk in shallow water, had discharged a huge cargo of arms, ammunition, and other supplies. Documents found on the ship and on the bodies of several Vietcong aboard identified the vessel as having come from North Vietnam. A newspaper in the cabin was from Haiphong and was dated January 23, 1965. The supplies delivered by the ship—thousands of weapons and more than a million rounds of ammunition—were almost all of Communist origin, largely from Communist China and Czechoslovakia, as well as North Vietnam. At least 100 tons of military supplies were discovered near the ship.

A preliminary survey of the cache near the sunken vessel from Hanoi listed the following supplies and weapons:

> approximately 1 million rounds of small-arms ammunition;
>
> more than 1,000 stick grenades;
>
> 500 pounds of TNT in prepared charges;
>
> 2,000 rounds of 82-mm. mortar ammunition;
>
> 500 antitank grenades;
>
> 500 rounds of 57-mm. recoilless rifle ammunition;
>
> more than 1,000 rounds of 75-mm. recoilless rifle ammunition;
>
> 1 57-mm. recoilless rifle;
>
> 2 heavy machine guns;
>
> 2,000 7.92 Mauser rifles;
>
> more than 100 7.62 carbines;
>
> 1,000 submachine guns;
>
> 15 light machine guns;
>
> 500 rifles;
>
> 500 pounds of medical supplies (with labels from North Vietnam, Communist China, Czechoslovakia, East Germany, Soviet Union, and other sources). . . .

III.   North Vietnam: Base for Conquest of the South

The Third Lao Dong Party Congress in Hanoi in September 1960 set forth two tasks for its members: "to carry out the socialist revolution in North Vietnam" and "to liberate South Vietnam."

The resolutions of the congress described the effort to destroy the legal Government in South Vietnam as follows: "The revolution in the South is a protracted, hard, and complex process of struggle, combining many forms of struggle of great activity and flexibility, ranging from lower to higher, and taking as its basis the building, consolidation, and development of the revolutionary power of the masses."

At the September meeting the Communist leaders in the North called for formation of "a broad national united front." Three months later Hanoi announced creation of the "Front for the Liberation of the South." This is the organization that Communist propaganda now credits with guiding the forces of subversion in the South; it is pictured as an organization established and run by the people in the South themselves. At the 1960 Lao Dong Party Congress the tone was different. Then, even before the front existed, the Communist leaders were issuing orders for the group that was being organized behind the scenes in Hanoi. "This front must rally . . . "; "The aims of its struggle . . . "; "The front must carry out . . . "—this is the way Hanoi and the Communist Party addressed the "Liberation Front" even before its founding.

The Liberation Front is Hanoi's creation; it is neither independent nor Southern, and what it seeks is not liberation but subjugation of the South. . . .

IV.   Organization, Direction, Command, and Control of the Attack on South Vietnam Are Centered in Hanoi

The VC military and political apparatus in South Vietnam is an extension of an elaborate military and political structure in North Vietnam which directs and supplies it with the tools for conquest. The Ho Chi Minh regime has shown that it is ready to allocate every resource that can be spared—whether it be personnel, funds, or equipment—to the cause of overthrowing the legitimate Government in South Vietnam and of bringing all Vietnam under Communist rule.

A.   Political Organization

Political direction and control of the Vietcong is supplied by the Lao Dong Party, i.e. the Communist Party, led by Ho Chi Minh. Party agents are responsible for indoctrination, recruitment, political training, propaganda, anti-Government demonstrations, and other activities of a political nature. The considerable intelligence-gathering facilities of the party are also at the disposal of the Vietcong.

Overall direction of the VC movement is the responsibility of the Central Committee of the Lao Dong Party. Within the Central Committee a special Reunification Department has been established. This has replaced the "Committee for Supervision of the South" mentioned in intelligence reports two years ago. It lays down broad strategy for the movement to conquer South Vietnam. . . .

The "Liberation Front." The National Front for the Liberation of South Vietnam is the screen behind which the Communists carry out their program of conquest. It is the creature of the Communist Government in Hanoi. As noted earlier, the Communist Party in the North demanded establishment of such a "front" three months before its formation was actually announced in December 1960. It was designed to create the illusion that the Vietcong campaign of subversion was truly indigenous to South Vietnam rather than an externally directed Communist plan.

The front has won support primarily from the Communist world. Its radio faithfully repeats the propaganda themes of Hanoi and Peking. When its representatives travel abroad, they do so with North Vietnamese passports and sponsorship. The front's program copies that of the Lao Dong Party in North Vietnam.

B.   Military Organization

Military affairs of the Vietcong are the responsibility of High Command of the People's Army of North Vietnam and the Ministry of Defense, under close supervision from the Lao Dong Party. These responsibilities include operational plans, assignments of individuals and regular units, training programs, infiltration of military personnel and supplies, and the like. The six military regions are the same as those of the VC political organization.

The military structure of the Vietcong is an integral part of the political machinery that controls every facet of VC activity in South Vietnam under Hanoi's overall direction. Each political headquarters from the Central Office down to the village has a military component which controls day-to-day military operations. Similarly, each military headquarters has a political element, an individual or a small staff. This meshing of political and military activity is designed to insure the closest cooperation in support of the total Communist mission. It also gives assurance of political control over the military. . . .

The size of the Vietcong regular forces has grown steadily in recent years. For example, the Vietcong have five regimental headquarters compared with two in 1961. And the main VC force is composed of 50 battalions, 50 percent more than before. There are an estimated 139 VC companies. Hard-core VC strength now is estimated at about 35,000, whereas it was less than 20,000 in 1961. . . .

Supporting the main force units of the Vietcong are an estimated 60,000–80,000 part-time guerrillas. They are generally organized at the district level where there are likely to be several companies of fifty or more men each. These troops receive only half pay, which means they must work at least part of the time to eke out a living.

Below the irregular guerrilla forces of the district are the part-time, village-based guerrillas. They are available for assignment by higher headquarters and are used for harassment and sabotage. They are expected to warn nearby VC units of the approach of any force of the legal government. They provide a pool for recruitment into the VC district forces.

The record shows that many of the village guerrillas are dragooned into service with the Vietcong. Some are kidnapped; others are threatened; still others join to prevent their families from being harmed. Once in the Vietcong net, many are reluctant to leave for fear of punishment by the authorities or reprisal by the Communists. . . .

Officials and wealthy people have been kidnapped for ransom. The VC have often stopped buses and taken the money and valuables of all on board. For the most part, the VC have concentrated their attention on individuals, isolated or poorly defended outposts, and small centers of population. They have mercilessly killed or kidnapped thousands of village chiefs and other local officials. But over the past year the VC have moved into larger unit operations. Their ability to operate on a battalion level or larger has substantially increased.

C. Intelligence Organization

A key element in the Vietcong effort is an elaborate organization in Hanoi called the Central Research Agency (C.R.A.) (Cuc Nghien-Cuu Trung-Uong). Though it handles Hanoi's intelligence effort on a worldwide scale, the main focus of its operation is on South Vietnam. This agency is able to draw on the intelligence capabilities of both the Lao Dong Party and the North Vietnamese armed forces for information, personnel and facilities. . . .

Taken as a whole, the North Vietnamese intelligence operation in support of the Vietcong is one of the most extensive of its kind in the world.

V. A Brief History of Hanoi's Campaign of Aggression Against South Vietnam

While negotiating an end to the Indochina War in Geneva in 1954, the Communists were making plans to take over all former French territory in Southeast Asia. When Vietnam was partitioned, thousands of carefully selected party members were ordered to remain in place in the South and keep their secret apparatus intact to help promote Hanoi's cause. Arms and ammunition were stored away for future use. Guerrilla fighters rejoined their families to await the party's call. Others withdrew to remote jungle and mountain hideouts. The majority—an estimated 90,000—were moved to North Vietnam.

Hanoi's original calculation was that all of Vietnam would fall under its control without resort to force. For this purpose, Communist cadres were ordered to penetrate official and non-official agencies, to propagandize and sow confusion, and generally to use all means short of open violence to aggravate war-torn conditions and to weaken South Vietnam's government and social fabric.

South Vietnam's refusal to fall in with Hanoi's scheme for peaceful takeover came as a heavy blow to the Communists. Meantime, the Government had stepped up efforts to blunt Vietcong subversion and to expose Communist agents. Morale in the Communist organization in the South dropped sharply. Defections were numerous.

Among South Vietnamese, hope rose that their nation could have a peaceful and independent future, free of Communist domination. The country went to work. The years after 1955 were a period of steady progress and growing prosperity.

Food production levels of the prewar years were reached and surpassed. While per capita food output was dropping 10 percent in the North from 1956 to 1960, it rose 20 percent in the South. By 1963, it had risen 30 percent—despite the disruption in the countryside caused by intensified Vietcong military attacks and terrorism. The authorities in the North admitted openly to continuing annual failures to achieve food production goals.

Production of textiles increased in the South more than 20 percent in one year (1958). In the same year, South Vietnam's sugar crop increased more than 100 percent. Despite North Vietnam's vastly larger industrial complex, South Vietnam's per capita gross national product in 1960 was estimated at $110 a person while it was only $70 in the North.

More than 900,000 refugees who had fled from Communist rule in the North were successfully settled in South Vietnam. An agrarian reform program was instituted. The elementary school population nearly quadrupled between 1956 and 1960. And so it went—a record of steady improvement in the lives of the people. It was intolerable for the rulers in Hanoi; under peaceful conditions, the South was outstripping the North. They were losing the battle of peaceful competition and decided to use violence and terror to gain their ends.

After 1956, Hanoi rebuilt, reorganized, and expanded its covert political and military machinery in the South. Defectors were replaced by trained personnel from party ranks in the North. Military units and political cells were enlarged and were given new leaders, equipment, and intensified training. Recruitment was pushed. In short, Hanoi and its forces in the South prepared to take by force and violence what they had failed to achieve by other means.

By 1958 the use of terror by the Vietcong increased appreciably. It was used to both win prestige and to back up demands for support from the people, support that political and propaganda appeals had failed to produce. It was also designed to embarrass the Government of Saigon and raise doubts about its ability to maintain internal order and to assure the personal security of its people. From 1959 through 1961, the pace of Vietcong terrorism and armed attacks accelerated substantially.

The situation at the end of 1961 was so grave that the Government of the Republic of Vietnam asked the United States for increased military assistance. That request was met. Meantime, the program of strategic hamlets, designed to improve the peasant's livelihood and give him protection against Vietcong harassment and pressure, was pushed energetically.

But the Vietcong did not stand still. To meet the changing situation, they tightened their organization and adopted new tactics, with increasing emphasis on terrorism, sabotage, and armed attacks by small groups. They also introduced from the North technicians in fields such as armor and antiaircraft. Heavier weapons were sent to the regular guerrilla forces.

The military and insurgency situation was complicated by a quite separate internal political struggle in South Vietnam, which led in November 1963 to the removal of the Diem government and its replacement with a new one. Effective power was placed in the hands of a Military Revolutionary Council. There have been a number of changes in the leadership and composition of the Government in Saigon in the ensuing period.

These internal developments and distractions gave the Vietcong an invaluable opportunity, and they took advantage of it. Vietcong agents did what they could to encourage disaffection and to exploit demonstrations in Saigon and elsewhere. In the countryside the Communists consolidated their hold over some areas and enlarged their military and political apparatus by increased infiltration. Increasingly they struck at remote outposts and the most vulnerable of the new strategic hamlets and expanded their campaign of aggressive attacks, sabotage, and terror.

Any official, worker, or establishment that represents a service to the people by the Government in Saigon is fair game for the Vietcong. Schools have been among their favorite targets. Through harassment, the murder of teachers, and sabotage of buildings, the Vietcong succeeded in closing hundreds of schools and interrupting the education of tens of thousands of youngsters.

Hospitals and medical clinics have often been attacked as part of the anti-Government campaign and also because such attacks provide the Vietcong with needed medical supplies. The Communists have encouraged people in rural areas to oppose the Government's antimalaria teams, and some of the workers have been killed. Village and town officers, police stations, and agricultural research stations are high on the list of preferred targets for the Vietcong.

In 1964, 436 South Vietnamese hamlet chiefs and other Government officials were killed outright by the Vietcong and 1,131 were kidnapped. More than 1,350 civilians were killed in bombings and other acts of sabotage. And at least 8,400 civilians were kidnapped by the Vietcong.

Today the war in Vietnam has reached new levels in intensity. The elaborate effort by the Communist regime in North Vietnam to conquer the South has grown, not diminished. Military men, technicians, political organizers, propagandists, and secret agents have been infiltrating into the Republic of Vietnam from the North in growing numbers. The flow of Communist-supplied weapons, particularly those of large caliber, has increased. Communications links with Hanoi are extensive. Despite the heavy casualties of three years of fighting, the hardcore VC force is considerably larger now than it was at the end of 1961.

The Government in Saigon has undertaken vigorous action to meet the new threat. The United States and other free countries have increased their assistance to the Vietnamese Government and people. Secretary of State Dean Rusk visited Vietnam in 1964, and he promised the Vietnamese: "We shall remain at your side until the aggression from the North has been defeated, until it has been completely rooted out and this land enjoys the peace which it deserves."

President Johnson has repeatedly stressed that the United States' goal is to see peace secured in Southeast Asia. But he has noted that "that will come only when aggressors leave their neighbors in peace."

Though it has been apparent for years that the regime in Hanoi was conducting a campaign of conquest against South Vietnam, the Government in Saigon and the Government of the United States both hoped that the danger could be met within South Vietnam itself. The hope that any widening of the conflict might be avoided was stated frequently.

The leaders in Hanoi chose to respond with greater violence. They apparently interpreted restraint as indicating lack of will. Their efforts were pressed with greater vigor and armed attacks and incidents of terror multiplied.

Clearly the restraint of the past was not providing adequately for the defense of South Vietnam against Hanoi's open aggression. It was mutually agreed between the Governments of the Republic of Vietnam and the United States that further means for providing for South Vietnam's defense were required. Therefore, air strikes have been made against some of the military assembly points and supply bases from which North Vietnam is conducting its aggression against the South. These strikes constitute a limited response fitted to the aggression that produced them.

Until the regime in Hanoi decides to halt its intervention in the South, or until effective steps are taken to maintain peace and security in the area, the Governments of South Vietnam and the United States will continue necessary measures of defense against the Communist armed aggression coming from North Vietnam.

VI. Conclusion

The evidence presented in this report could be multiplied many times with similar examples of the drive of the Hanoi regime to extend its rule over South Vietnam.

The record is conclusive. It establishes beyond question that North Vietnam is carrying out a carefully conceived plan of aggression against the South. It shows that North Vietnam has intensified its efforts in the years since it was condemned by the International Control Commission. It proves that Hanoi continues to press its systematic program of armed aggression into South Vietnam. This aggression violates the United Nations charter. It is directly contrary to the Geneva Accords of 1954 and of 1962 to which North Vietnam is a party. It shatters the peace of Southeast Asia. It is a fundamental threat to the freedom and security of South Vietnam.

The people of South Vietnam have chosen to resist this threat. At their request, the United States has taken its place beside them in their defensive struggle.

The United States seeks no territory, no military bases, no favored position. But we have learned the meaning of aggression elsewhere in the post-war world, and we have met it.

If peace can be restored in South Vietnam, the United States will be ready at once to reduce its military involvement. But it will not abandon friends who want to remain free. It will do what must be done to help them. The choice now between peace and continued and increasingly destructive conflict is one for the authorities in Hanoi to make.

15.2 THE NORTH VIETNAMESE ANALYZE AMERICAN INTERVENTION (1965)

During their decade of conflict with the United States, the North Vietnamese often displayed a more realistic capacity for analysis than the Americans. The following selection is from a July 1965 talk by Le Duan, a high-ranking official in the North Vietnamese Communist Party. His remarks, which were a "pep talk" to a group of Communist leaders, also represent a careful dissection of U.S. options. What factors, according to Le Duan, would influence U.S. choices in Vietnam? Does he emphasize U.S. military weakness or political vulnerability? Was his assessment shrewd or wide of the mark?

THE NORTH VIETNAMESE ANALYZE AMERICAN INTERVENTION

Le Duan

We know that the U.S. sabotaged the Geneva Agreement and encroached on South Vietnam in order to achieve three objectives:

1. To turn the South into a colony of a new type.
2. To turn the South into a military base, in order to prepare to attack the North and the Socialist bloc.
3. To establish a South Vietnam-Cambodia-Laos defensive line in order to prevent the socialist revolution from spreading through Southeast Asia.

At present, we fight the U.S. in order to defeat their first two objectives to prevent them from turning the South into a new-type colony and military base.

We do not yet aim at their third objective, essentially to divide the ranks of the imperialist and to make other imperialists disagree with the U.S. in broadening the war in Vietnam and also to attract the support of other democratic and independent countries for our struggle in the South. Our revolutionary struggle in the South has the character of a conflict between the two camps in fact, but we advocate not making that conflict grow but limiting it in order to concentrate our forces to resolve the contradiction between the people and U.S. imperialism and its lackeys, to complete the national democratic revolution in the whole country. It is for this reason that we put forward the slogan "peace and neutrality" for the South, a flexible slogan to win victory step by step. We are not only determined to defeat the U.S. but must know how to defeat the U.S. in the manner most appropriate to the relation of forces between the enemy and us during each historical phase. Putting forward the slogan peace and neutrality for the South as well as the five points of the National Liberation Front of South Vietnam and the four points in our government's declaration read before the National Assembly as bases for the revolution of the Vietnamese problem means that we know how to fight and defeat the Americans most advantageously.

. . . [T]he U.S. is still strong enough to enter into a limited war in Vietnam, by sending not only 200,00–250,000 but 300,000–400,000 troops to South Vietnam. But if it

Gareth Porter, trans., from *Vietnam: The Definitive Documentation of Human Decisions* (Stanfordville, NY: Earl M. Coleman Enterprises, Inc., Publishers, 1979), vol. 2, pp. 383–85. Reprinted by permission from Gareth Porter.

switches to limited war, the U.S. still will have weaknesses which it cannot overcome. The U.S. rear area is very far away, and U.S. soldiers are "soldiers in chains," who cannot fight like the French, cannot stand the weather conditions, and don't know the battlefield but on the contrary have many weaknesses in their opposition to people's war. If the U.S. puts 300–400,000 [*sic*] troops into the South, it will have stripped away the face of its neocolonial policy and revealed the face of an old style colonial invader, contrary to the whole new-style annexation policy of the U.S. in the world at present. Thus, the U.S. will not be able to maintain its power with regard to influential sectors of the United States. If the U.S. itself directly enters the war in the South it will have to fight for a prolonged period with the people's army of the South,[1] with the full assistance of the North and the Socialist bloc.[2] To fight for a prolonged period is a weakness of U.S. imperialism. The Southern revolution can fight a protracted war, while the U.S. can't, because U.S. military, economic and political resources must be distributed throughout the world. If it is bogged down in one place and can't withdraw, the whole effort will be violently shaken. The U.S. would lose its preeminence in influential sectors at home and create openings for other competing imperialists, and lose the U.S. market. Therefore at present, although the U.S. can immediately send 300,000 to 400,000 troops at once, why must the U.S. do it step by step? Because even if it does send many troops like that, the U.S. would still be hesitant; because that would be a passive policy full of contradictions; because of fear of protracted war, and the even stronger opposition of the U.S. people and the world's people, and even of their allies who would also not support widening the war.

With regard to the North, the U.S. still carries out its war of destruction, primarily by its air force: Besides bombing military targets, bridges and roads to obstruct transport and communications, the U.S. could also indiscriminately bomb economic targets, markets, villages, schools, hospitals, dikes, etc., in order to create confusion and agitation among the people. But the North is determined to fight back at the U.S. invaders in a suitable manner, determined to punish the criminals, day or night, and determined to make them pay the blood debts which they have incurred to our people in both zones. The North will not flinch for a moment before the destructive acts of the U.S., which could grow increasingly mad with every passing day. The North will not count the cost but will use all of its strength to produce and fight, and endeavor to help the South. For a long time, the Americans have boasted of the strength of their air force and navy but during five to six months of directly engaging in combat with the U.S. in the North, we see clearly that the U.S. cannot develop that strength in relation to the South as well as in relation to the North, but revealed more clearly every day its weak-points. We have shot down more than 400 of their airplanes, primarily with rifles, anti-aircraft guns; [but] the high level of their hatred of the aggressors, and the spirit of determination to defeat the U.S. invaders [are strong]. Therefore, if the U.S. sends 300,000–400,000 troops into the South, and turns special war into direct war in the South, escalating the war of destruction in the North, they still can't hope to avert defeat, and the people of both North and South will still be determined to fight and determined to win.

---

[1] The Vietcong—ED.

[2] That is, the other Communist nations of the world, especially China and the Soviet Union—ED.

If the U.S. is still more adventurous and brings U.S. and puppet troops of all their vassal states to attack the North, broadening it into a direct war in the entire country, the situation will then be different. Then it will not be we alone who still fight the U.S. but our entire camp. First the U.S. will not only be doing battle with 17 million people in the North but will also have to battle with hundreds of millions of Chinese people. Attacking the North would mean that the U.S. intends to attack China, because the North and China are two socialist countries linked extremely closely with each other, and the imperialists cannot attack this socialist country without also intending to attack the other. Therefore the two countries would resist together. Could the U.S. imperialists suppress hundreds of millions of people? Certainly they could not. If they reach a stage of desperation, would the U.S. use the atomic bomb? Our camp also has the atomic bomb. The Soviet Union has sufficient atomic strength to oppose any imperialists who wish to use the atomic bomb in order to attack a socialist country, and threaten mankind. If U.S. imperialism uses the atomic bomb in those circumstances they would be committing suicide. The U.S. people themselves would be the ones to stand up and smash the U.S. government when that government used atomic bombs. Would the U.S. dare to provoke war between the two blocks, because of the Vietnam problem; would it provoke a third world war in order to put an early end to the history of U.S. imperialism and of the entire imperialist system in general? Would other imperialist countries, factions in the U.S., and particularly the U.S. people, agree to the U.S. warmongers throwing them into suicide? Certainly, the U.S. could not carry out their intention, because U.S. imperialism is in a weak position and not in a position of strength.

But the possibility of the broadening [of] the direct war to the North is a possibility which we must pay utmost attention, because U.S. imperialism could be adventurous. We must be vigilant and prepared to cope with each worst possibility. The best way to cope, and not to let the U.S. broaden the direct warfare in the South or in the North, is to fight even more strongly and more accurately in the South, and make the puppet military units—the primary mainstay of the U.S.—rapidly fall apart, push military and political struggle forward, and quickly create the opportune moment to advance to complete defeat of U.S. imperialism and its lackeys in the South.

15.3 THE ANTIWAR MOVEMENT STRIKES BACK (1965, 1966, 1968)

As the dreary and painful months and years passed with no resolution of the Vietnam conflict, more and more Americans began to question the wisdom of their country's commitment and demand that it extricate itself from the East Asian morass.

The opposition to the war took many forms. Some Americans opposed the war primarily on pragmatic grounds: The United States had no vital interest in Vietnam and no reason to pay a high price for a dispute not its own. Others considered the war wicked: America was acting as a brutal imperialist nation determined to impose its will on a weaker people.

A majority of the war's opponents confined themselves to petitions, marches, rallies, and protests. For young men of draft age, these measures often did not suffice. Many sought to avoid military service through fraudulent medical exemptions, conscientious objector status, or flight from the country. Organized opposition to Vietnam began with campus "teach-ins" in response to Lyndon Johnson's bombing campaign in the spring of 1965. Thereafter, numerous peace groups— moderates demanding early negotiations, radicals demanding immediate withdrawal—held rallies and demonstrations in major U.S. cities around the country. Professional bodies, religious associations, and circles of intellectuals and artists denounced the war in resolutions and paid advertisements that often depicted Johnson as a coarse and brutal murderer of innocents. Militant black civil rights groups demanded that the United States get out of Vietnam.

The first reading that follows is from a pamphlet distributed by the Vietnam Day Committee (VDC) to army inductees and enlisted men at military bases in northern California. The VDC had been the organizing agency for the Berkeley teach-in in May 1965 following Johnson's "Rolling Thunder" attack. Afterward it became a semipermanent antiwar organization that drew support largely from the student radicals who, some months before, had led the Berkeley Free Speech Movement, the first of the major campus uprisings of the 1960s.

What seems to be the basis for the VDC case against U.S. involvement in Vietnam? Is it ideological? Is it pragmatic? Does it seem to be anti-American? Why do the authors draw an analogy between the U.S. cause in Vietnam and the Nazi rampage in Europe during World War II? Is the analogy valid? Why might the authorities have been particularly dismayed by the circulation of this pamphlet?

The second selection is a statement by the Student Nonviolent Coordinating Committee (SNCC), the militant civil rights group that emerged from the 1960 student lunch-counter sit-ins in the South. By 1966, when SNCC launched this attack, its members were thoroughly disenchanted with U.S. policy in Vietnam. Other groups were also hostile, but SNCC felt that blacks had special reasons to deplore the nation's involvement in Southeast Asia. What were these reasons? Consider the costs of the war. Were blacks paying a disproportionate price? In what ways? What other attitudes common in the civil rights movement after 1965 might have influenced SNCC's views? Do you know if Martin Luther King, Jr., a civil rights leader, ever broke with the Johnson administration over Vietnam?

The last two selections address the draft or Selective Service laws. Why did "draft resisters" not want to go to Vietnam?

ATTENTION ALL MILITARY PERSONNEL

Vietnam Day Committee

You may soon be sent to Vietnam. You have heard about the war in the news; your officers will give you pep talks about it. But you probably feel as confused and uncertain as most Americans do. Many people will tell you to just follow orders and leave the thinking to others. But you have the right to know as much about this war as anyone. After all, it's you—not your Congressman—who might get killed.

Why Are We Fighting in Vietnam?

We are supposed to be fighting to protect democracy in Vietnam, and yet your own government admits that South Vietnam is run by a dictatorship. General Ky,[1] the latest military dictator, is as bad as they come. In a recent interview he said: "People ask me

---

Vietnam Day Committee, "Attention All Military Personnel" (pamphlet, May 1965).

[1] Nguyen Cao Ky, a South Vietnamese air force general who, along with Nguyen Van Thieu, emerged as successor to Ngo Dinh Diem as ruler in Saigon—ED.

who my heroes are. I have only one—Hitler. I admire Hitler because he pulled his country together when it was in a terrible state" (*London Sunday Mirror*, July 4, 1965).

General Ky doesn't mean much to us; we're not even sure how to pronounce his name, but the South Vietnamese have lived under men like him for years. As far as the Vietnamese are concerned, we are fighting on the side of Hitlerism: and they hope we lose.

Who Is the Enemy?

U.S. military spokesmen have often said that their greatest problem is finding the enemy. The enemy, they say, is everywhere. The old woman feeding her chickens may have a stock of hand grenades in her hut. The little boy who trails after the U.S. soldiers during the day slips out to give information to the guerrillas at night. The washerwoman at the U.S. air base brings a bomb to work one day. It is impossible, say the military, to tell which are the Viet Cong and which are the civilians.

And so, because the whole Vietnamese people seem to be the enemy, the military is taking no chances. They use tear gas—a weapon designed for use against civilians. They order U.S. troops to fire at women and children—because women and children, after all, are firing at U.S. troops. U.S. fighter planes destroy civilian villages with napalm; U.S. B-52s are flattening whole regions. That is why the war in Vietnam is so often called a "dirty war."

When the South Vietnamese people see you in your foreign uniform, they will think of you as *their* enemy. You are the ones bombing their towns. They don't know whether you're a draftee or a volunteer, whether you're for the war or against it; but they're not taking any chances either.

Free Elections

The Vietnamese would like to *vote* the foreigners out of their country, but they have been denied the chance. According to the Geneva Agreement of 1954, there were supposed to be elections throughout Vietnam in 1956. But the U.S. government was certain that our man in Vietnam, Premier Diem, would lose. So we decided not to allow any election until we were sure we could win. Diem set up a political police force and put all political opposition—Communist and anti-Communist—in jail. By 1959, it was clear there weren't going to be any elections, and the guerrillas known as the Viet Cong began to fight back. By 1963 our government was fed up with Diem, but still wasn't willing to risk elections. Our CIA helped a group of Vietnamese generals to overthrow Diem and kill him. Since then there have been a series of "better" military dictators. General Ky—the man who admires Hitler—is the latest one.

Fighting for Democracy

Your job as a soldier is supposed to be "to win the people of South Vietnam." Win them to what—democracy? No, we keep military dictators in power. What then? The U.S. way of life? But why should they care any more about our way of life than we care about theirs? We can't speak their language or even pronounce their names. We don't know anything about their religion or even what it is. We never even heard of Vietnam until Washington decided to run it.

You are supposed to be fighting "to save the Vietnamese people from Communism." Certainly Communist influence is very strong in the National Liberation Front [NLF], the rebel government. Yet most of the people support the NLF. Why? Many of the same people who now lead the NLF led the Vietnamese independence movement against the Japanese during World War II, and then went on to fight against French colonial rule. Most Vietnamese think of the NLF leaders as their country's outstanding patriots. In fact, many anti-Communists have joined the guerrilla forces in the belief that the most important thing is to get rid of foreign domination and military dictators. On the other hand, very few Vietnamese support the official government of General Ky. His army has low morale and a high desertion rate.

The Guerrillas

The newspapers and television have told us again and again what a tough fighter the Vietnamese guerrilla is. Short of ammunition and without any air cover, he can beat forces that outnumber him five or ten to one. Why do they have such high morale? They are not draftees; no draftees ever fight like that. They are not high-paid, professional soldiers. Most of them are peasants who work their fields; they can't even spare the ammunition for target practice.

Their secret is that they know why they are fighting. They didn't hear about Vietnam in the newspapers; they've lived there all their lives. While we were in high school, they were living under the Diem regime and hating it. Now U.S. planes are bombing their towns and strafing their fields; U.S. troops have occupied their country; and if they complain out loud, an American-supported dictator sentences them to jail or the firing squad. Is it any wonder that they fight so fiercely?

Crushing the Resistance

The war in Vietnam is not being fought according to the rules. Prisoners are tortured. Our planes drop incendiary bombs on civilian villages. Our soldiers shoot at women and children. Your officers will tell you that it is all necessary, that we couldn't win the war any other way. *And they are right.* Americans are no more cruel than any other people; U.S. soldiers don't enjoy this kind of war. But if you are going to wage war against an entire people, you have to become cruel.

The ordinary German soldier in occupied Europe wasn't especially cruel, either. But as the resistance movements grew, he *became* cruel. He shot at women and children because they were shooting at him; he never asked himself *why* they were shooting at him. When a certain town became a center of resistance activity, he followed his orders and destroyed the whole town. He knew that SS men were torturing captured resistance fighters, but it wasn't his business to interfere.

Following Orders

As a soldier you have been trained to obey orders, but as a human being you must take responsibility for your own acts. International and U.S. law recognize that an individual soldier, even if acting under orders, must bear final legal and moral responsibility for what he does. This principle became a part of law after World War II, when the Allied nations, meeting in London, decided that German war criminals must be punished even if they committed war crimes under orders. This principle was the basis of the Nuremberg trials. We believe that the entire war in Vietnam is criminal and immoral. We believe that the atrocities which are necessary to wage this war against the people of Vietnam are inexcusable.

Oppose the War

We hope that you too find yourself, as a human being, unable to tolerate this nightmare war, and we hope that you will oppose it. We don't know what kind of risks we are taking in giving you this leaflet; you won't know what risk you will be taking in opposing the war. A growing number of GIs have already refused to fight in Vietnam and have been court-martialed. They have shown great courage. We believe that they, together with other courageous men who will join them, will have influence far out of proportion to their numbers.

There may be many other things you can do; since you are in the service, you know better than civilians what sorts of opposition are possible. But whatever you do, keep your eyes open. Draw your own conclusions from the things you see, read, and hear. At orientation sessions, don't be afraid to ask questions, and if you're not satisfied with the answers, keep asking. Take every chance you get to talk to your fellow soldiers about the war.

You may feel the war is wrong, and still decide not to face a court-martial. You may then find yourself in Vietnam under orders. You might be forced to do some fighting—but don't do any more than you have to. Good luck.

THE U.S. GOVERNMENT HAS DECEIVED US

Student Non-violent Coordinating Committee

The Student Nonviolent [sic] Coordinating Committee has a right and a responsibility to dissent with United States foreign policy on any issue when it sees fit. The Student Nonviolent Coordinating Committee now states its opposition to United States' involvement in Vietnam on these grounds:

We believe the United States government has been deceptive in its claims of concern for the freedom of the Vietnamese people, just as the government has been deceptive in claiming concern for the freedom of colored people in such other countries as the Dominican Republic, the Congo, South Africa, Rhodesia, and in the United States itself.

We, the Student Nonviolent Coordinating Committee, have been involved in the black people's struggle for liberation and self-determination in this country for the past five years. Our work, particularly in the South, has taught us that the United States government has never guaranteed the freedom of oppressed citizens, and is not yet truly determined to end the rule of terror and oppression within its own borders.

We ourselves have often been victims of violence and confinement executed by United States governmental officials. We recall the numerous persons who have been murdered in the South because of their efforts to secure their civil and human rights, and whose murderers have been allowed to escape penalty for their crimes.

Student Non-Violent Coordinating Committee, "The U.S. Government Has Deceived Us" (broadside, 1966).

The murder of Samuel Young [a young black man] in Tuskegee, Alabama, is no different than the murder of peasants in Vietnam, for both Young and the Vietnamese sought, and are seeking, to secure the rights guaranteed them by law. In each case, the United States government bears a great part of the responsibility for these deaths.

Samuel Young was murdered because United States law is not being enforced. Vietnamese are murdered because the United States is pursuing an aggressive policy in violation of international law. The United States is no respecter of persons or law when such persons or laws run counter to its needs or desires.

We recall the indifference, suspicion, and outright hostility with which our reports of violence have been met in the past by government officials.

We know that for the most part, elections in this country, in the North as well as the South, are not free. We have seen that the 1965 Voting Rights Act and the 1964 Civil Rights Act have not yet been implemented with full federal power and sincerity.

We question, then, the ability and even the desire of the United States government to guarantee free elections abroad. We maintain that our country's cry of "preserve freedom in the world" is a hypocritical mask behind which it squashes liberation movements which are not bound, and refuse to be bound, by the expediencies of United States Cold War policies.

We are in sympathy with, and support, the men in this country who are unwilling to respond to a military draft which would compel them to contribute their lives to United States aggression in Vietnam in the name of "freedom" we find so false in this country.

We recoil with horror at the inconsistency of a supposedly "free" society where responsibility to freedom is equated with the responsibility to lend oneself to military aggression. We take note of the fact that 16 percent of the draftees from this country are Negroes called on to stifle the liberation of Vietnam, to preserve a "democracy" which does not exist for them at home.

We ask, where is the draft for the freedom fight in the United States?

We therefore encourage those Americans who prefer to use their energy in building democratic forms within this country. We believe that work in the civil rights movement and with other human relations organizations is a valid alternative to the draft. We urge all Americans to seek this alternative, knowing full well that it may cost them their lives—as painfully as in Vietnam.

DECLARATION OF CONSCIENCE AGAINST THE WAR IN VIETNAM

Because the use of the military resources of the United States in Vietnam and elsewhere suppresses the aspirations of the people for political independence and economic freedom;

Because inhuman torture and senseless killing are being carried out by forces armed, uniformed, trained and financed by the United States;

Because we believe that all peoples of the earth, including both Americans and non-Americans, have an inalienable right to life, liberty, and the peaceful pursuit of happiness in their own way; and

Broadside published by the Catholic Worker, Committee for Nonviolent Action, Student Peace Union, and the War Resisters League. (New York, circa 1965.)

Because we think that positive steps must be taken to put an end to the threat of nuclear catastrophe and death by chemical and biological warfare, whether these result from accident or escalation—

We hereby declare our conscientious refusal to cooperate with the United States government in the prosecution of the war in Vietnam.

We encourage those who can conscientiously do so to refuse to serve in the armed forces and to ask for discharge if they are already in.

Those of us who are subject to the draft ourselves declare our own intention to refuse to serve.

We urge others to refuse and refuse ourselves to take part in the manufacture or transportation of military equipment, or to work in the fields of military research and weapons development.

We shall encourage the development of other nonviolent acts, including acts which involve civil disobedience, in order to stop the flow of American soldiers and munitions to Vietnam.

Deserters' Proclamation

We, American Deserters living in Montreal, in opposition to the U.S. imperialist aggression in Vietnam, have banded together to form the American Deserters' Committee.

We Deserters and associates view ourselves as an integral part of the worldwide movement for fundamental social change. We express support and solidarity with the National Liberation Front of South Vietnam and the black liberation struggle at home. We are prepared to fight side by side with anyone who wants to bring fundamental social change to the U.S.

Our aim is to help U.S. Deserters and draft resisters gain a more political outlook toward their own actions—to show them that desertion and draft resistance are in fact political moves. Forced to live our lives as political exiles, we view ourselves as victims of the same oppression as the Vietnamese and the American people, not only minority groups, but also the broad masses of American people who are becoming more aware of the need for change.

We will work to develop the political consciousness of American Deserters and to form a well-educated and determined group which will have a clear understanding of U.S. internal and international policies, especially those which affect Canada and Quebec.

We express solidarity with our fellow servicemen who are still in the military, and as yet are unable to resist actively. We will do all in our power to help all those who resist in the same way—DESERT.

Note: *Signing or distributing this Declaration of Conscience might be construed as a violation of the Universal Military Training and Service Act, which prohibits advising persons facing the draft to refuse service. Penalties of up to 5 years imprisonment, and/or a fine of $5,000 are provided. While prosecutions under this provision of the law almost never occur, persons signing or distributing this declaration should face the possibility of serious consequences.*

American Deserters' Committee pamphlet, 1968.

We recognize U.S. imperialism as the greatest threat to the progress of freedom and self-determination for all people, and view desertion as the most effective way to resist.

American Deserters' Committee
c/o P.O.B. 611
Station H
Montreal 25, Quebec
Canada
December 15, 1968

CHAPTER 16

Crises of the Seventies: Watergate and Energy Shortages

Watergate is the name of a luxury apartment complex on the Potomac River in Washington, DC. It is also the name given to a political scandal that reached the highest levels of the U.S. government and ultimately forced a president to resign. The president was Richard Nixon.

Nixon fought ferociously for every political success he achieved. As Dwight Eisenhower's vice-presidential running mate in 1952, he was almost pushed off the ticket by a scandal over political contributions. In 1960, he lost the presidential race by the narrowest of margins to John Kennedy and, when he ran for governor of California in 1962, he lost again. Six years later he defeated Hubert Humphrey for the presidency, but the result was a squeaker. Running for reelection in 1972, he would leave nothing to chance. This time he intended to win big to make up for all the disappointments and close races of the past.

The collection of crimes and deceptions called Watergate grew out of this win-at-all-costs attitude. Running Nixon's 1972 reelection campaign manager was former attorney general John Mitchell, head of the Committee for the Re-Election of the President (CRP). Under him was a collection of political operators and tricksters. The CRP (called "CREEP" by the Democrats) had large amounts of money, much of it extracted from corporations by promises of government favors or threats of disfavor and laundered to disguise its origins.

If the CRP had stopped at drowning the Democrats in cash, disaster could have been avoided. But Mitchell and other Nixon cronies insisted on using every trick in the book to confuse, distract, unbalance, and obstruct their opponents.

One of these "dirty trick" operations was a break-in on June 18, 1972, at the Democratic National Committee headquarters in the Watergate complex by a group nicknamed the "plumbers," apparently to rifle files for incriminating information on the Democrats and to bug their telephones. The break-in was discovered by the police while underway, and the Watergate burglars were arrested and indicted.

Nixon apparently did not order the break-in, nor, it seems, did he know about it until his aides told him a week later that the men caught at the Watergate worked for either the White House or the CRP. His accusers would claim, however, that he approved the efforts of aides H. R. Haldeman, John Dean, and John D. Ehrlichman to hide the connection between the Watergate "plumbers" and the administration and, still more serious, to offer the arrested men executive clemency and money in exchange for their silence. In the end, it was this cover-up attempt that brought the president down.

During the summer and fall of 1972, George McGovern, the Democratic presidential candidate, sought to make the mysterious Watergate break-in a campaign issue, but the administration was able to hide it until after the Republican election sweep in November. Then the cover-up began to come apart. In January 1973, the "plumbers" were tried before Judge John Sirica, and one of them confessed that he and his fellow defendants had committed perjury in denying their connection to the White House. In February the Senate established a select committee, headed by Sam Ervin of North Carolina, to investigate Watergate and in May the committee began televised hearings that revealed that the break-in had originated with the CRP and that the president may have condoned an attempt to obstruct justice. On July 16, 1973, one of the witnesses before the Ervin committee revealed that since 1971 all confidential discussions in the Oval Office and the Executive Office Building had been taped, which meant that everything that Nixon and his colleagues had said and done about Watergate could be checked. Meanwhile, two *Washington Post* reporters, Carl Bernstein and Robert Woodward, intrigued by the mysterious events at the Watergate, began to follow a trail of proliferating leads. Their sensational revelations soon ignited a race among the media to ferret out details of the complex operations of the CRP and other administration agents. The public watched transfixed as almost daily new details emerged of misdeeds by the White House.

Nixon resisted every effort to make him surrender the tapes to a special prosecutor he had agreed, under pressure, to appoint. When the prosecutor, Archibald Cox, became too aggressive, Nixon fired him in what came to be called the "Saturday Night Massacre." The storm of public outrage that followed forced Nixon to appoint another prosecutor, Leon Jaworski, a conservative Texas lawyer who refused to be intimidated. In late April 1974, under the prodding of Jaworski and Congress, Nixon released 1200 pages of edited tape transcript that revealed the president as a mean-spirited, bigoted, win-at-any-price man, but contained no "smoking gun" directly linking him to an illegal attempt to obstruct justice.

On May 1, the House Judiciary Committee denied that the transcripts submitted represented full compliance with their demands; Nixon had held back crucial sections. In July, with support for the president fast dropping away, the Judiciary Committee began public debate on impeachment, and on July 27 voted three articles of impeachment against Nixon for attempting to "delay, impede, and obstruct the investigation" of the Watergate incident and to "cover-up, conceal, and protect those responsible" for the break-in.

The next step in the constitutional procedure would have been trial by the Senate under the House articles for "high crimes and misdemeanors," with conviction bringing removal from office. This would have been the first impeachment trial of a president since Andrew Johnson's in 1868. It was not to be. On August 5, under order by the Supreme Court, Nixon surrendered the last of the tapes, which included the long-sought "smoking gun": On June 23, 1972, the president had discussed the break-in with Haldeman and had told him that the FBI and CIA must be ordered to desist from any further investigation of the incident on national security grounds.

This second batch of tapes ended the charade. On August 7, 1974, Senators Barry Goldwater of Arizona and Hugh Scott of Pennsylvania, representing both wings of the Republican Party, advised Nixon to resign to spare the country the long agony of an impeachment trial. Goldwater told reporters that he had counted only fifteen senators who would vote against conviction. The next evening Nixon appeared on national television to tell the American people that he had decided to resign the presidency. Shortly after noon the following day, as Nixon and his family flew to California, Gerald Ford took the oath of office as thirty-eighth president of the United States.

Watergate was a devastating blow to U.S. pride and self-confidence. Coming so soon after defeat in Vietnam, it further eroded the legitimacy of the U.S. political process. But did it deserve the response it evoked? In June 1972 White House press secretary Ronald Ziegler had called the break-in a "third-rate burglary," and to this day some people accept this conclusion. To many Nixon loyalists, not to speak of Nixon himself, the president had done nothing seriously wrong, and they see the destruction of his administration as a politically partisan act by liberal enemies. As you read the selections that follow, see if you can objectively evaluate the significance of the acts and the decisions that destroyed the Nixon presidency and shook Americans' faith in "the system."

16.1   THE TAPES (1972)

The Watergate transcripts doomed the Nixon presidency. The House Judiciary Committee, the media, and the American people all concluded from their contents that the president was guilty of obstructing justice and deserved to be impeached. Most Americans were also appalled by the glimpse they afforded of the president's personality and of the slipshod way a great nation was being governed.

The excerpt from the following Watergate tapes is the "smoking-gun" segment of June 23, 1972. Does it prove that Nixon sought to obstruct justice? What does it tell us about his view of the U.S. political process and his opponents? Does it provide any insight into Nixon's personality? What, if anything, does it tell us about the U.S. presidency in those years?

Everyone was appalled by the vulgarity of the president's remarks ("expletive deleted") and his weak syntax and unfocused quality. But remember, this conversation was an unguarded private one between close associates. How many private conversations of people under stress would sound better if reported verbatim? Would your own?

THE SMOKING GUN

Richard Nixon

June 23, 1972

[H. R.] HALDEMAN: Now, on the investigation, you know the Democratic break-in thing, we're back in the problem area because the FBI is not under control, because [Director Patrick] Gray doesn't exactly know how to control it and they have—their investigation is now leading into some productive area. . . . They've been able to trace the money—not through the money itself—but through the bank sources—the banker. And it goes in some directions we don't want it to go. Ah, also there have been some [other] things—like an informant came in off the street to the FBI in Miami who was a photographer or has a friend who is a photographer who developed some films through this guy [Bernard] Barker and the films had pictures of Democratic National Committee letterhead documents and things. So it's things like that are filtering in. . . . [John] Mitchell came up with yesterday, and John Dean analyzed very carefully last night and concludes, concurs now with Mitchell's recommendation that the only way to solve this . . . is for us to have [CIA Assistant Director Vernon] Walters call Pat Gray and just say, "Stay to hell out of this—this is ah, [our] business here. We don't want you to go any further on it." That's not an unusual development, and ah, that would take care of it.

PRESIDENT: What about Pat Gray—you mean Pat Gray doesn't want to?

HALDEMAN: Pat does want to. He doesn't know how to, and he doesn't have any basis for doing it. Given this, he will then have the basis. He'll call [FBI Assistant Director] Mark Felt in, and the two of them—and Mark Felt wants to cooperate because he's ambitious—

PRESIDENT: Yeah.

HALDEMAN: He'll call him in and say, "We've got the signal from across the river[1] to put the hold on this." And that will fit rather well because the FBI agents who are working the case, at this point, feel that's what it is.

PRESIDENT: This is CIA? They've traced the money? Who'd they trace it to?

Hearings before the Committee on the Judiciary, House of Representatives, 93rd Congress, 2d Session (Washington, DC: Government Printing Office, 1974), pp. 512–14.

[1] The CIA headquarters were located in Virginia, across the Potomac from the White House—ED.

HALDEMAN: Well, they've traced it to a name, but they haven't gotten to the guy yet.

PRESIDENT: Would it be somebody here?

HALDEMAN: Ken Dahlberg.

PRESIDENT: Who the hell is Ken Dahlberg?

HALDEMAN: He gave $25,000 in Minnesota and, ah, the check went directly to this guy Barker.

PRESIDENT: It isn't from the Committee though, from [Maurice] Stans?

HALDEMAN: Yeah. It is. It's directly traceable and there's some more through some Texas people that went to the Mexican bank which can also be traced to the Mexican bank—they'll get their names today.

PRESIDENT: Well, I mean, there's no way—I'm just thinking if they don't cooperate, what do they say? That they were approached by the Cubans? That's what Dahlberg has to say, the Texans too.

HALDEMAN: Well, if they will. But then we're relying on more and more people all the time. That's the problem and they'll [the FBI] . . . stop if we could take this other route.

PRESIDENT: All right.

HALDEMAN: [Mitchell and Dean] say the only way to do that is from White House instructions. And it's got to be to [CIA Director Richard] Helms and to—ah, what's his name? . . . Walters.

PRESIDENT: Walters.

HALDEMAN: And the proposal would be that . . . [John] Ehrlichman and I call them in, and say, ah—

PRESIDENT: All right, fine. How do you call him in—I mean you just—well, we protected Helms from one hell of a lot of things.

HALDEMAN: That's what [John] Erhlichman says.

PRESIDENT: Of course; this [Howard] Hunt [business.] That will uncover a lot of things. You open that scab there's a hell of a lot of things and we just feel that it would be very detrimental to have this thing go any further. This involves these Cubans, Hunt, and a lot of hanky-panky that we have nothing to do with ourselves. Well, what the hell, did Mitchell know about this?

HALDEMAN: I think so. I don't think he knew the details, but I think he knew.

PRESIDENT: He didn't know how it was going to be handled though—with Dahlberg and the Texans and so forth? Well who was the asshole that did? Is it [G. Gordon] Liddy? Is that the fellow? He must be a little nuts!

HALDEMAN: He is.

PRESIDENT: I mean he just isn't well screwed on, is he? Is that the problem?

HALDEMAN: No, but he was under pressure, apparently, to get more information, and as he got more pressure, he pushed the people harder.

PRESIDENT: Pressure from Mitchell?

HALDEMAN: Apparently. . . .

PRESIDENT: All right, fine, I understand it all. We won't second-guess Mitchell and the rest. Thank God it wasn't [Special White House Counsel Charles] Colson.

HALDEMAN: The FBI interviewed Colson yesterday. They determined that would be a good thing to do. To have him take an interrogation, which he did, and the FBI guys working the case concluded that there were one or two possibilities—one, that this was a White House (they don't think that there is anything at the Election Committee) they think it was either a White House operation and they have some obscure reasons for it— non-political, or it was a—Cuban [operation] and [involved] the CIA. And after their interrogation of Colson yesterday, they concluded it was not the White House, but are now convinced it is a CIA thing, so the CIA turnoff would—

PRESIDENT: Well, not sure of their analysis, I'm not going to get that involved. I'm (unintelligible).

HALDEMAN: No, sir, we don't want you to.

PRESIDENT: You call them in.

HALDEMAN: Good deal.

PRESIDENT: Play it tough. That's the way they play it and that's the way we are going to play it. . . .

PRESIDENT: O.K. . . . Just say (unintelligible) very bad to have this fellow Hunt, ah, he knows too damned much. . . . If it gets out that this is all involved, the Cuba thing, it would be a fiasco. It would make the CIA look bad, it's going to make Hunt look bad, and it is likely to blow the whole Bay of Pigs thing which we think would be very unfortunate—both for CIA, and for the country, at this time, and for American foreign policy. Just tell him to lay off. Don't you [think] so?

HALDEMAN: Yep. That's the basis to do it on. Just leave it at that. . . .

16.2   NIXON DEFENDS HIMSELF (1973)

As the details of Watergate unfolded, the president sought to staunch the political hemorrhage by appealing to the voters. On April 30, 1973, he went on television to defend himself and to announce the "resignations" of three of his top aides who, he said, had failed to inform him of the "plumbers" operation. The selection that follows is an excerpt from that speech.

What is Nixon's strategy in delivering this speech? Is he throwing Erhlichman, Haldeman, and Dean to the wolves to save his neck, as critics charged? Does he deal with the question of obstruction of justice? Or does he focus purely on the illegality of the break-in and the failure of his aides to admit its authorization by the CRP? Compare Nixon's words here with his private remarks made in the Oval Office on June 23 of the previous year.

I Did Not Know About Watergate

Richard M. Nixon

Good evening: I want to talk to you tonight from my heart on a subject of deep concern to every American.

In recent months, members of my Administration and officials of the Committee for the Re-Election of the President—including some of my closest friends and most trusted aides—have been charged with involvement in what has come to be known as the Watergate affair. These include charges of illegal activity during and preceding the 1972 Presidential election and charges that responsible officials participated in efforts to cover up that illegal activity.

The inevitable result of these charges has been to raise serious questions about the integrity of the White House itself. Tonight I wish to address those questions.

Last June 17, while I was in Florida trying to get a few days rest after my visit to Moscow, I first learned from news reports of the Watergate break-in. I was appalled at this senseless, illegal action, and I was shocked to learn that employees of the Re-election Committee were apparently among those guilty. I immediately ordered an investigation by appropriate Government authorities. On September 15, as you will recall, indictments were brought against seven defendants in the case.

As the investigations went forward, I repeatedly asked those conducting the investigation whether there was any reason to believe that members of my Administration were in any way involved. I received repeated assurances that there were not. Because of these continuing reassurances, because I believed the reports I was getting, because I had faith in the persons from whom I was getting them, I discounted the stories in the press that appeared to implicate members of my Administration or other officials of the campaign committee.

Until March of this year, I remained convinced that the denials were true and that the charges of involvement by members of the White House Staff were false. The comments I made during this period, and the comments made by my Press Secretary in my behalf, were based on the information provided to us at the time we made those comments. However, new information then came to me which persuaded me that there was a real possibility that some of these charges were true, and suggesting further that there had been an effort to conceal the facts both from the public, from you, and from me.

As a result, on March 21, I personally assumed the responsibility for coordinating intensive new inquiries into the matter, and I personally ordered those conducting the investigations to get all the facts and to report them directly to me, right here in this office.

I again ordered that all persons in the Government or at the Re-Election Committee should cooperate fully with the FBI, the prosecutors, and the grand jury. I also ordered that anyone who refused to cooperate in telling the truth would be asked to resign from government service. And, with ground rules adopted that would preserve the basic constitutional separation of powers between the Congress and the Presidency, I directed that members of the White House Staff should appear and testify voluntarily under oath before the Senate committee which was investigating Watergate.

Congressional Quarterly, *Historic Documents, 1973* (Washington, DC: Congressional Quarterly, Inc., 1974), pp. 502–6.

I was determined that we should get to the bottom of the matter, and that the truth should be fully brought out—no matter who was involved.

At the same time, I was determined not to take precipitate action, and to avoid, if at all possible, any action that would appear to reflect on innocent people. I wanted to be fair. But I knew that in the final analysis, the integrity of this office—public faith in the integrity of this office—would have to take priority over all personal considerations.

Announcement of Resignations

Today, in one of the most difficult decisions of my Presidency, I accepted the resignations of two of my closest associates in the White House—Bob Haldeman, John Ehrlichman—two of the finest public servants it has been my privilege to know.

I want to stress that in accepting these resignations, I mean to leave no implication whatever of personal wrongdoing on their part, and I leave no implication tonight of implication on the part of others who have been charged in this matter. But in matters as sensitive as guarding the integrity of our democratic process, it is essential not only that rigorous legal and ethical standards be observed, but also that the public, you, have total confidence that they are both being observed and enforced by those in authority and particularly by the President of the United States. They agreed with me that this move was necessary in order to restore that confidence.

Because Attorney General [Richard] Kleindienst—though a distinguished public servant, my personal friend for 20 years, with no personal involvement whatever in this matter—has been a close personal and professional associate of some of those who are involved in this case, he and I both felt that it was also necessary to name a new Attorney General.

The Counsel to the President, John Dean, has also resigned.

As the new Attorney General, I have today named Elliot Richardson, a man of unimpeachable integrity and rigorously high principle. I have directed him to do everything necessary to ensure that the Department of Justice has the confidence and the trust of every law abiding person in this country.

I have given him absolute authority to make all decisions bearing upon the prosecution of the Watergate case and related matters. I have instructed him that if he should consider it appropriate, he has the authority to name a special supervising prosecutor for matters arising out of the case.

Whatever may appear to have been the case before, whatever improper activities may yet be discovered in connection with this whole sordid affair, I want the American people, I want you to know beyond the shadow of a doubt that during my term as President, justice will be pursued fairly, fully, and impartially, no matter who is involved. This office is a sacred trust and I am determined to be worthy of that trust.

Looking back at the history of this case, two questions arise:

How could it have happened?

Who is to blame?

Political commentators have correctly observed that during my 27 years in politics I have always previously insisted on running my own campaigns for office.

But 1972 presented a very different situation. In both domestic and foreign policy, 1972 was a year of crucially important decisions, of intense negotiations, of vital new directions, particularly in working toward the goal which has been my overriding concern throughout my political career—the goal of bringing peace to America, peace to the world.

That is why I decided, as the 1972 campaign approached, that the Presidency should come first and politics second. To the maximum extent possible, therefore, I sought to delegate campaign operations, to remove the day-to-day campaign decisions from the President's office and from the White House. I also, as you recall, severely limited the number of my own campaign appearances.

Who Is to Blame?

Who, then, is to blame for what happened in this case?

For specific criminal actions by specific individuals, those who committed those actions must, of course, bear the liability and pay the penalty.

For the fact that alleged improper actions took place within the White House or within my campaign organization, the easiest course would be for me to blame those to whom I delegated the responsibility to run the campaign. But that would be a cowardly thing to do.

I will not place the blame on subordinates—on people whose zeal exceeded their judgment, and who may have done wrong in a cause they deeply believed to be right.

In any organization, the man at the top must bear the responsibility. That responsibility, therefore, belongs here, in this office. I accept it. And I pledge to you tonight, from this office, that I will do everything in my power to ensure that the guilty are brought to justice, and that such abuses are purged from our political processes in the years to come, long after I have left this office.

Some people, quite properly appalled at the abuses that occurred, will say that Watergate demonstrates the bankruptcy of the American political system. I believe precisely the opposite is true. Watergate represented a series of illegal acts and bad judgments by a number of individuals. It was the system that has brought the facts to light and that will bring those guilty to justice—a system that in this case has included a determined grand jury, honest prosecutors, a courageous judge, John Sirica, and a vigorous free press.

It is essential now that we place our faith in that system—and especially in the judicial system. It is essential that we let the judicial process go forward, respecting those safeguards that are established to protect the innocent as well as to convict the guilty. It is essential that in reacting to the excesses of others, we not fall into excesses ourselves.

It is also essential that we not be so distracted by events such as this that we neglect the vital work before us, before this Nation, before America, at a time of critical importance to America and the world.

Since March, when I first learned that the Watergate affair might, in fact, be far more serious than I had been led to believe, it has claimed far too much of my time and my attention.

Whatever may now transpire in the case, whatever the actions of the grand jury, whatever the outcome of any eventual trials, I must now turn my full attention—and I shall do so—once again to the larger duties of this office. I owe it to this great office that I hold, and I owe it to you—to my country.

I know that as Attorney General, Elliot Richardson will be both fair and he will be fearless in pursuing this case wherever it leads. I am confident that with him in charge, justice will be done.

There is vital work to be done toward our goal of a lasting structure of peace in the world—work that cannot wait, work that I must do.

Tomorrow, for example, Chancellor Brandt of West Germany will visit the White House for talks that are a vital element of "The Year of Europe," as 1973 has been called. We are already preparing for the next Soviet-American summit meeting later this year.

This is also a year in which we are seeking to negotiate a mutual and balanced reduction of armed forces in Europe, which will reduce our defense budget and allow us to have funds for other purposes at home so desperately needed. It is the year when the United States and Soviet negotiators will seek to work out the second and even more important round of our talks on limiting nuclear arms, and of reducing the danger of a nuclear war that would destroy civilization as we know it. It is a year in which we confront the difficult tasks of maintaining peace in Southeast Asia and in the potentially explosive Middle East.

There is also vital work to be done right here in America: to ensure prosperity, and that means a good job for everyone who wants to work; to control inflation, that I know worries every housewife, everyone who tries to balance a family budget in America; to set in motion new and better ways of ensuring progress toward a better life for all Americans.

When I think of this office—of what it means—I think of all the things that I want to accomplish for this Nation, of all the things I want to accomplish for you.

16.3   THE VOTE FOR IMPEACHMENT (1974)

In July 1974, for the first time in over a century, the Judiciary Committee of the House of Representatives voted articles of impeachment against a president. The following selection is a transcription of these articles. They would have become the basis for Nixon's trial by the Senate had he not resigned first.

Based on the evidence you have seen, were the articles valid? Note that none of the articles were adopted unanimously. Most of the negative votes came from Republicans. Does this support a political interpretation of Watergate? Keep in mind that Nixon himself was a highly partisan politician. He seldom sought or expected consensus, and his partisanship aroused similar responses in his Democratic and liberal opponents. Would a less partisan president have avoided the searching investigation of Watergate that destroyed him? Do you know if other presidents have employed political espionage or "dirty tricks" against their enemies?

IMPEACHMENT ARTICLES

House Judiciary Committee

Article I

In his conduct of the office of President of the United States, Richard M. Nixon, in violation of his constitutional oath faithfully to execute the office of President of the United States and, to the best of his ability, preserve, protect, and defend the Constitution of the

Congressional Quarterly, *Historic Documents, 1974* (Washington, DC: Congressional Quarterly Inc., 1975), pp. 656–60.

United States, and in violation of his constitutional duty to take care that the laws be faithfully executed, had prevented, obstructed, and impeded the administration of justice, in that:

On June 17, 1972, and prior thereto, agents of the Committee for the Re-election of the President committed unlawful entry of the headquarters of the Democratic National Committee in Washington, District of Columbia, for the purpose of securing political intelligence. Subsequent thereto, Richard M. Nixon, using the powers of his high office, engaged personally and through his close subordinates and agents, in a course of conduct or plan designed to delay, impede, and obstruct the investigation of such unlawful entry; to cover up, conceal and protect those responsible; and to conceal the existence and scope of other unlawful covert activities.

The means used to implement this course of conduct or plan included one or more of the following:

1. making false or misleading statements to lawfully authorized investigative officers and employees of the United States;
2. withholding relevant and material evidence or information from lawfully authorized investigative officers and employees of the United States;
3. approving, condoning, acquiescing in, and counseling witnesses with respect to the giving of false or misleading statements to lawfully authorized investigative officers and employees of the United States and false or misleading testimony in duly instituted judicial and congressional proceedings;
4. interfering or endeavoring to interfere with the conduct of investigations by the Department of Justice of the United States, the Federal Bureau of Investigation, the Office of Watergate Special Prosecution Force, and Congressional Committees;
5. approving, condoning, and acquiescing in, the surreptitious payment of substantial sums of money for the purpose of obtaining the silence or influencing the testimony of witnesses, potential witnesses or individuals who participated in such unlawful entry and other illegal activities;
6. endeavoring to misuse the Central Intelligence Agency, an agency of the United States;
7. disseminating information received from officers of the Department of Justice of the United States to subjects of investigations conducted by lawfully authorized investigative officers and employees of the United States, for the purpose of aiding and assisting such subjects in their attempts to avoid criminal liability.
8. making or causing to be made false or misleading public statements for the purpose of deceiving the people of the United States into believing that a thorough and complete investigation had been conducted with respect to allegations of misconduct on the part of personnel of the executive branch of the United States and personnel of the Committee for the Re-election of the President, and that there was no involvement of such personnel in such misconduct; or
9. endeavoring to cause prospective defendants, and individuals duly tried and convicted, to expect favored treatment and consideration in return for their silence or false testimony, or rewarding individuals for their silence or false testimony.

In all of this, Richard M. Nixon has acted in a manner contrary to his trust as President and subversive of constitutional government, to the great prejudice of the cause of law and justice and to the manifest injury of the people of the United States.

Wherefore Richard M. Nixon, by such conduct, warrants impeachment and trial, and removal from office.

—Adopted July 27 by a 27–11 vote

Article II

Using the powers of the office of President of the United States, Richard M. Nixon, in violation of his constitutional oath faithfully to execute the office of President of the United States and, to the best of his ability, preserve, protect, and defend the Constitution of the United States, and in disregard of his constitutional duty to take care that the laws be faithfully executed, has repeatedly engaged in conduct violating the constitutional rights of citizens, impairing the due and proper administration of justice and the conduct of lawful inquiries, or contravening the laws governing agencies of the executive branch and the purposes of these agencies.

This conduct has included one or more of the following:

1. He has, acting personally and through his subordinates and agents, endeavored to obtain from the Internal Revenue Service, in violation of the constitutional rights of citizens, confidential information contained in income tax returns for purposes not authorized by law, and to cause, in violation of the constitutional rights of citizens, income tax audits or other income tax investigations to be initiated or conducted in a discriminatory manner.

2. He misused the Federal Bureau of Investigation, the Secret Service, and other executive personnel, in violation or disregard of the constitutional rights of citizens, by directing or authorizing such agencies or personnel to conduct or continue electronic surveillance or other investigations or purposes unrelated to national security, the enforcement of laws, or any other lawful function of his office; he did direct, authorize, or permit the use of information obtained thereby for purposes unrelated to national security, the enforcement of laws, or any other lawful function of his office; and he did direct the concealment of certain records made by the Federal Bureau of Investigation of electronic surveillance.

3. He has, acting personally and through his subordinates and agents, in violation or disregard of the constitutional rights of citizens, authorized and permitted to be maintained a secret investigative unit within the office of the President, financed in part with money derived from campaign contributions, which unlawfully utilized the resources of the Central Intelligence Agency, engaged in covert and unlawful activities, and attempted to prejudice the constitutional right of an accused to a fair trial.

4. He has failed to take care that the laws were faithfully executed by failing to act when he knew or had reason to know that his close subordinates endeavored to impede and frustrate lawful inquiries by duly constituted executive, judicial, and legislative entities concerning the unlawful entry into the headquarters of the Democratic National Committee, and the cover up thereof, and concerning other unlawful activities including those relating to the confirmation of Richard Kleindienst as Attorney General of the United States, the electronic surveillance of private citizens, the break-in into the offices of Dr. Lewis Fielding and the campaign financing practices of the Committee to Re-elect the President [*sic*].

5. In disregard of the rule of law, he knowingly misused the executive branch, including the Federal Bureau of Investigation, the Criminal Division, and the Office of Watergate Special Prosecution Force, of the Department of Justice, and the Central Intelligence Agency, in violation of his duty to take care that the laws be faithfully executed.

In all of this, Richard M. Nixon has acted in a manner contrary to his trust as President and subversive of constitutional government, to the great prejudice of the cause of law and justice and to the manifest injury of the people of the United States.

Wherefore Richard M. Nixon, by such conduct, warrants impeachment and trial, and removal from office.

—Adopted July 29, by a 28–10 vote

Article III

In his conduct of the office of President of the United States, Richard M. Nixon, contrary to his oath faithfully to execute the office of President of the United States and, to the best of his ability, preserve, protect, and defend the Constitution of the United States, and in violation of his constitutional duty to take care that the laws be faithfully executed, has failed without lawful cause of excuse to produce papers and things as directed by duly authorized subpoenas issued by the Committee on the Judiciary of the House of Representatives on April 11, 1974, May 15, 1974, May 30, 1974, and June 24, 1974, and willfully disobeyed such subpoenas. The subpoenaed papers and things were deemed necessary by the Committee in order to resolve by direct evidence fundamental, factual questions relating to Presidential direction, knowledge, or approval of actions demonstrated by other evidence to be substantial grounds for impeachment of the President. In refusing to produce these papers and things Richard M. Nixon, substituting his judgment as to what materials were necessary for the inquiry, interposed the powers of the Presidency against the lawful subpoenas of the House of Representatives, thereby assuming to himself functions and judgments necessary to the exercise of the sole power of impeachment vested by the Constitution in the House of Representatives.

In all of this, Richard M. Nixon has acted in a manner contrary to his trust as President and subversive of constitutional government, to the great prejudice of the cause of law and justice, and to the manifest injury of the people of the United States.

Wherefore, Richard M. Nixon by such conduct warrants impeachment and trial, and removal from office.

—Adopted July 30 by a 21–17 vote

16.4 ENERGY AND THE "CRISIS OF CONFIDENCE"

The American economy was jolted by an energy crisis in the 1970s that caused both shortages and double digit inflation. President Jimmy Carter came to view this crisis as far more significant than most elected officials in Washington. Near the end of a decade that saw the inglorious end to the Vietnam War, the Watergate Scandal, and the second worse economic downturn in American history, Carter addressed spiraling public gloom in his most famous speech, "Energy and the Crisis of Confidence." The speech called for a new public spirit of sacrifice and a bold departure in national energy policy based upon a new national goal of conservation. Liberal intellectuals warmed to the speech, but Carter's public opinion polls quickly plummeted. The Presidential Campaign of Ronald Reagan and the subsequent twenty-eight years of Conservative politics in many ways can be understood only as a repudiation of this speech and the ideas and policies it attempted to promote. Vice President Dick Cheney's speech of 2001 illustrates this point with dramatic clarity. Nonetheless, Carter's failure to capture the public imagination and embark upon a successful national energy policy continues to haunt us in the twenty-first century. How will we meet our energy needs and what price will we pay in doing so?

"ENERGY AND THE CRISIS OF CONFIDENCE" (1979)

Jimmy Carter

Good evening.

This is a special night for me. Exactly 3 years ago, on July 15, 1976, I accepted the nomination of my party to run for President of the United States. I promised you a President who is not isolated from the people, who feels your pain, and who shares your dreams and who draws his strength and his wisdom from you.

During the past 3 years I've spoken to you on many occasions about national concerns, the energy crisis, reorganizing the Government, our Nation's economy, and issues of war and especially peace. But over those years the subjects of speeches, the talks, and the press conferences have become increasingly narrow, focused more and more on what the isolated world of Washington thinks is important. Gradually, you've heard more and more about what the government thinks or what Government should be doing and less and less about our Nation's hopes, our dreams, and our vision of the future.

Ten days ago I had planned to speak to you again about a very important subject—energy. For the fifth time I would have described the urgency of the problem and laid out a series of legislative recommendations to the Congress. But as I was preparing to speak, I began to ask myself the same question that I now know has been troubling many of you. Why have we not been able to get together as a nation to resolve our serious energy problem?

It's clear that the true problems of our Nation are much deeper—deeper than gasoline lines or energy shortages, deeper even than inflation or recession. And I

Jimmy Carter, "Energy and National Goals," 15 July 1979, *Public Papers of the Presidents of the United States: Jimmy Carter, 1977–81* (Washington, D.C.: Government Printing Office, 1979), 2: 1235–41.

realize more than ever that as President I need your help. So, I decided to reach out and listen to the voices of America.

I invited to Camp David people from almost every segment of our society—business and labor, teachers and preachers, governors, mayors, and private citizens. And then I left Camp David to listen to other Americans, men and women like you. It has been an extraordinary 10 days, and I want to share with you what I've heard.

First of all, I got a lot of personal advice. Let me quote a few of the typical comments that I wrote down.

This from a southern Governor: "Mr. President, you are not leading this Nation—you're just managing the Government."

"You don't see the people enough any more."

"Some of your Cabinet members don't seem loyal. There is not enough discipline among your disciples."

"Don't talk to us about politics or the mechanics of government but about an understanding of our common good."

"Mr. President, we're in trouble. Talk to us about blood and sweat and tears."

"If you lead, Mr. President, we will follow."

Many people talked about themselves and about the condition of our Nation. This from a young woman in Pennsylvania: "I feel so far from government. I feel like ordinary people are excluded from political power."

And this from a young Chicano: "Some of us have suffered from recession all our lives."

"Some people have wasted energy, but others haven't had anything to waste."

And this from a religious leader: "No material shortage can touch the important things like God's love for us or love for one another."

And I like this one particularly from a black woman who happens to be the mayor of a small Mississippi town: "The big-shots are not the only ones who are important. Remember, you can't sell anything on Wall Street unless someone digs it up somewhere else first."

This kind of summarized a lot of other statements: "Mr. President we are confronted with a moral and a spiritual crisis."

Several of our discussions were on energy, and I have a notebook full of comments and advice. I'll read just a few.

"We can't go on consuming 40 percent more energy than we produce. When we import oil we are also importing inflation plus unemployment."

"We've got to use what we have. The Middle East has only 5 percent of the world's energy, but the United States has 24 percent."

And this is one of the most vivid statements: "Our neck is stretched over the fence and OPEC has a knife."

"There will be other cartels and other shortages. American wisdom and courage right now can set a path to follow in the future."

This was a good one: "Be bold, Mr. President We may make mistakes, but we are ready to experiment."

And this one from a labor leader got to the heart of it: "The real issue is freedom. We must deal with the energy problem on a war footing."

And the last that I'll read: "When we enter the moral equivalent of war, Mr. President, don't issue us BB guns."

These 10 days confirmed my belief in the decency and the strength and the wisdom of the American people, but it also bore out some of my long-standing concerns about our Nation's underlying problems.

I know, of course, being President, that government actions and legislation can be very important. That's why I've worked hard to put my campaign promises into law—and I have to admit, with just mixed success. But after listening to the American people I have been reminded again that all the legislation in the world can't fix what's wrong with America. So, I want to speak to you first tonight about a subject even more serious than energy or inflation. I want to talk to you right now about a fundamental threat to American democracy.

I do not mean our political and civil liberties. They will endure. And I do not refer to the outward strength of America, a nation that is at peace tonight everywhere in the world, with unmatched economic power and military might.

The threat is nearly invisible in ordinary ways. It is a crisis of confidence. It is a crisis that strikes at the very heart and soul and sprit of our national will. We can see this crisis in the growing doubt about the meaning of our own lives and in the loss of unity of purpose for our Nation.

The erosion of our confidence in the future is threatening to destroy the social and the political fabric of America.

The confidence that we have always had as a people is not simply some romantic dream or a proverb in a dusty book that we read just on the Fourth of July. It is the idea which founded our Nation and has guided our development as a people. Confidence in the future has supported everything else—public institutions and private enterprises, our own families, and the very Constitution of United States. Confidence has defined our course and has served as a link between generations. We've always believed in something called progress. We've always had a faith that the days of our children would be better than our own.

Our people are losing that faith, not only in government itself but in the ability as citizens to serve as the ultimate rulers and shapers of our democracy. As a people we know our past and we are proud of it. Our progress has been part of the living history of America, even the world. We always believed that we were part of a great movement of humanity itself called democracy, involved in the search for freedom, and that belief has always strengthened us in our purpose. But just as we are losing our confidence in the future, we are also beginning to close the door on our past.

In a nation that was proud of hard work, strong families, close-knit communities, and our faith in God, too many of us now tend to worship self-indulgence and consumption. Human identity is no longer defined by what one does, but by what one owns. But we've discovered that owning thing and consuming thing does not satisfy our longing for meaning. We've learned that piling up material goods cannot fill the emptiness of lives which have no confidence or purpose.

The symptoms of this crisis of the American sprit are all around us. For the first time in the history of our country a majority of our people believe that the next 5 years will be worse than the past 5 years. Two-thirds of our people do not even vote. The productivity of American workers is actually dropping, and the willingness of Americans to save for the future has fallen below that of all other people in the Western world.

As you know, there is a growing disrespect for government and for churches and for schools, the news media, and other institutions. This is not a message of happiness or reassurance, but it is the truth and it is a warning.

These changes did not happen overnight. They've come upon us gradually over the last generation, years that were filled with shocks and tragedy.

We were sure that ours was a nation of the ballot, not the bullet, until the murders of John Kennedy and Robert Kennedy and Martin Luther King, Jr. We were taught that our armies were always invincible and our cause always just, only to suffer the agony of Vietnam. We respected the Presidency as a place of honor until the shock of Watergate.

We remember when the phrase "sound as a dollar" was an expression of absolute dependability, until 10 years of inflation began to shrink our dollar and our savings. We believed that our nation's resources were limitless until 1973, when we had to face a growing dependence on foreign oil.

These wounds are still very deep. They have never been healed.

Looking for a way out of this crisis, our people have turned to the Federal Government and found it isolated from the mainstream of our Nation's life. Washington, D.C., has become an island. The gap between our citizens and our Government has never been so wide. The people are looking for honest answers, not easy answers; clear leadership, not false claims and evasiveness and politics as usual.

What you see too often in Washington and elsewhere around the country is a system of government that seems incapable of action. You see a Congress twisted and pulled in every direction by hundreds of well-financed and powerful special interests. You see every extreme position defended to the last vote, almost to the last breath by one unyielding group or another. You often see a balanced and a fair approach that demands sacrifice, a little sacrifice from everyone, abandoned like an orphan without support and without friends.

Often you see paralysis and stagnation and drift. You don't like it, and neither do I. What can we do?

First of all, we must face the truth, and then we can change our course. We simply must have faith in the future of this Nation. Restoring that faith and that confidence to America is now the most important task we face. It is a true challenge of this generation of Americans.

One of the visitors to Camp David last week put it this way: "We've got to stop crying and start sweating, stop talking and start walking, stop cursing and start praying. The strength we need will not come from the White House, but from every house in America."

We know the strength of America. We are strong. We can regain our unity. We can regain our confidence. We are the heirs of generations who survived threats much more powerful and awesome than those that challenge us now. Our fathers and mothers were strong man and women who shaped a new society during the Great Depression, who fought world wars, and who carved out a new charter of peace for the world.

We ourselves are the same Americans who just 10 years ago put a man on the Moon. We are the generation that dedicated our society to the pursuit of human rights and equality. And we are the generation that will win the war on the energy problem and in that process rebuild the unity and confidence of America.

We are at a turning point in our history. There are two paths to choose. One is a path I've warned about tonight, the path that leads to fragmentation and self-interest. Down that road lies a mistaken idea of freedom, the right to grasp for ourselves some advantage over others. That path would be one of constant conflict between narrow interests ending in chaos and immobility. It is a certain route to failure.

All the traditions of our past, all the lessons of our heritage, all the promises of our future point to another path, the path of common purpose and the restoration of American values. That path leads to true freedom for our Nation and ourselves. We can take the first steps down that path as we begin to solve our energy problem.

Energy will be the immediate test of our ability to unite this Nation, and it can also be the standard around which we rally. On the battlefield of energy we can win for our Nation a new confidence, and we can seize control again of our common destiny.

In little more than two decades we've gone from a position of energy independence to one in which almost half the oil we use comes from foreign countries, at prices that are going through the roof. Our excessive dependence on OPEC has already taken a tremendous toll on our economy and our people. This is the direct cause of the long lines which have made millions of you spend aggravating hours waiting for gasoline. It's a cause of increased inflation and unemployment that we now face. This intolerable dependence on foreign oil threatens our economic independence and the very security of our Nation.

The energy crisis is real. It is worldwide. It is a clear and present danger to our Nation. These are facts and we simply must face them.

What I have to say to you now about energy is simple and vitally important.

Point one: I am tonight setting a clear goal for the energy policy of the United States. Beginning this moment, this Nation will never use more foreign oil than we did in 1977—never. From now on, every new addition to our demand for energy will be met from our own production and our own conservation. The generation-long growth in our dependence on foreign oil will be stopped dead in its tracks right now and then reversed as we move through the 1980s, for I am tonight setting the further goal of cutting our dependence on foreign oil by one-half by the end of the next decade—a saving of over 4½ million barrels of imported oil per day.

Point two: To ensure that we meet these targets, I will use my Presidential authority to set import quotas. I'm announcing tonight that for 1979 and 1980, I will forbid the entry into this country of one drop of foreign oil more than these goals allow. These quotas will ensure a reduction in imports even below the ambitious levels we set at the recent Tokyo summit.

Point three: To give us energy security, I am asking for the most massive peacetime commitment of funds and resources in our Nation's history to develop American's own alternative sources of fuel—from coal, from oil shale, from plant products for gasohol, from unconventional gas, from the Sun.

I propose the creation of an energy security corporation to lead this effort to replace 2½ million barrels of imported oil per day by 1990. The corporation will issue up to $5 billion in energy bonds, and I especially want them to be in small denominations so that average Americans can invest directly in America's energy security.

Just as a similar synthetic rubber corporation helped us win World War II, so will we mobilize American determination and ability to win the energy War. Moreover, I will soon submit legislation to Congress calling for the creation of this Nation's first solar bank, which will help us achieve the crucial goal of 20 percent of our energy coming from power by the year 2000.

These efforts will cost money, a lot of money, and that is why Congress must enact the windfall profits tax without delay. It will be money well spent. Unlike the billions of dollars that we ship to foreign countries to pay for foreign oil, these funds will be paid by Americans to Americans. These funds will go to fight, not to increase, inflation and unemployment.

Point four: I'm asking congress to mandate, to require as a matter of law, that our Nation's utility companies cut their massive use of oil by 50 percent within the next decade and switch to other fuels, especially coal, our most abundant energy source.

Point five: To make absolutely certain that nothing stands in the way of achieving these goals, I will urge Congress to create an energy mobilization board which, like the War Production Board in World War II, will have the responsibility and authority to cut through the red tape, the delays, and the endless roadblocks to completing key energy projects.

We will protect our environment. But when this Nation critically needs a refinery or a pipeline, we will build it.

Point six: I'm proposing a bold conservation program to involve every State, country and city and every average American in our energy battle. This effort will permit you to build conservation into your homes and your lives at a cost you can afford.

I ask Congress to give me authority for mandatory conservation and for standby gasoline rationing. To further conserve energy, I'm proposing tonight an extra $10 billion over the next decade to strengthen our public transportation systems. And I'm asking you for your good and for your Nation's security to take no unnecessary trips, to use carpools or public transportation whenever you can, to park your car one extra day per week, to obey the speed limit, and to set your thermostats to save fuel. Every act of energy conservation like this is more than just common sense—I tell you it is an act of patriotism.

Our Nation must be fair to the poorest among us, so we will increase aid to needy Americans to cope with rising energy prices. We often think of conservation only in terms of sacrifice. In fact, it is the most painless and immediate way of rebuilding our Nation's strength. Every gallon of oil each one of us saves is a new form of production. It gives us more freedom, more confidence, that much more control over our own lives.

So, the solution of our energy crisis can also help us to conquer the crisis of the spirit in our country. It can rekindle our sense of unity, our confidence in the future, and give our Nation and all of us individually a new sense of purpose.

You know we can do it. We have the natural resources. We have more oil in our shale alone than several Saudi Arabias. We have more coal than any nation on Earth. We have the world's highest level of technology. We have the most skilled work force, with innovative genius, and I firmly believe that we have the national will to win this war.

I do not promise you that this struggle for freedom will be easy. I do not promise a quick way out of our Nation's problems, when the truth is that the only way out is an all-out effort. What I do promise you is that I will lead our fight, and I will enforce fairness in our struggle, and I will ensure honesty. And above all, I will act.

We can manage the short-term shortages more effectively and we will, but there are no short-term solutions to our long-range problems. There is simply no way to avoid sacrifice.

Twelve hours from now I will speak again in Kansas City, to expand and to explain further our energy program. Just as the search for solutions to our energy *shortages has now led us to a new awareness of our Nation's deeper problems, so our willingness to work for those solutions in energy can strengthen us to attack those deeper problems.*

I will continue to travel this country, to hear the people of America.

You can help me to develop a national agenda for the 1980s. I will listen and I will act. We will act together. These were the promises I made 3 years ago, and I intend to keep them.

Little by little we can and we must rebuild our confidence. We can spend until we empty our treasuries, and we may summon all the wonders of science. But we can succeed only if we tap our greatest resources—America's people, America's values, and America's confidence.

I have seen the strength of America in the inexhaustible resources of our people. In the days to come, let us renew that strength in the struggle for an energy-secure nation.

In closing, let me say this: I will do my best, but I will not do it alone. Let your voice be heard. Whenever you have a chance, say something good about our country. With God's help and for the sake of our Nation, it is time for us to join hands in America. Let us commit ourselves together to a rebirth of the American spirit. Working together with our common faith we cannot fail.

Thank you and good night.

THE REPUBLICAN PARTY RESPONDS

. . . During our campaign, then-Governor Bush and I spoke of energy as a storm cloud forming over the economy. America's reliance on energy, and fossil fuels in particular, has lately taken on an urgency not felt since the late 1970s. . . .

. . .Throughout the country, we've seen sharp increases in fuel prices, from home heating oil to gasoline. . . Energy costs as a share of household expenses have been rising, and families are really feeling the pinch. . . .

Dick Cheney, Speech, 30 Apr. 2001. http//usinfo.state.gov/topical/global/energy/01043001.htm.

The crisis we face is largely the result of short-sighted domestic policies—or, as in recent years, no policy at all.

As a country, we have demanded more and more energy. But we have not brought online the supplies needed to meet that demand. . .

In January, [President Bush] directed me to form a task force recommend a new nation energy strategy. . . . There will be many recommendations—some obvious, some more complicated. But they will all arise from three basic principles.

Dick Cheney, "We Must Increase Domestic Production from Known Sources of Oil," 2001.

First, our strategy will be comprehensive in approach, and long-term in outlook. By comprehensive, I mean just that—a realistic assessment of where we are, where we need to go, and what it will take. By long term, I mean none of the usual quick fixes, which in the field of energy never fix anything. Price controls, tapping strategic reserves, creating new federal agencies—if these were any solution we'd have resolved the problems a long time ago.

. . .Years down the road, alternative fuels may become a great deal more plentiful. But we are not yet in any position to stake our economy and our own way of life on that possibility. For now we must take the facts as they are. Whatever our hopes for developing alternative sources and for conserving energy, the reality is that fossil fuels supply virtually a hundred percent of our transportation needs, and an overwhelming share of our electricity requirements. For years down the road, this will continue to be true.

We know that in the next two decades, our country's demand for oil will grow by a third. Yet we are producing less oil today—39 percent less—than we were in 1970. We make up the difference with imports, relying ever more on the good graces of foreign suppliers. . . . Think of this: During the Arab oil embargo of '70s, 36 percent of our oil came from abroad. Today it's 56 percent, growing steadily, and under the current trend is set to reach 64 percent less than two decades from now.

Here's what we know about natural gas. By 2020, our demand will rise by two-thirds. This is a plentiful, clean-burning fuel, and we're producing and using more of it than ever. What we have not done is build all of the needed infrastructure to carry it from the source to the user.

Then there is the energy we take most for granted, electricity. We all speak of the new economy and its marvels, sometimes forgetting that it all runs on electricity. And overall demand for electric power is expected to rise by 43 percent over the next 20 years.

So this is where we are with the demand for oil and gas and electricity. The options left to us are limited and they are clear.

For the oil we need, unless we choose to accept our growing dependence on foreign suppliers—and all that goes with that—we must increase domestic production from known sources. . . .

For the natural gas we need, we must lay more pipelines—at least 34,800 miles more—as well as many thousands of miles of added distribution lines to bring natural gas into our homes and workplaces.

For the electricity we need, we must be ambitious. Transmission grids stand in need of repair, upgrading, and expansion. . .

. . . Over the next 20 years, just meeting projected demand will require between 1,300 and 1,900 new power plants. . . .

. . . Coal is still the most plentiful source of affordable energy in this country, and it is by far the primary source of electric power generation. This will be the case for years to come. To try and tell ourselves otherwise is to deny blunt reality.

Coal is not the cleanest source of energy, and we must support efforts to improve clean-coal technology to soften its impact on the environment.

That leads me to the second principle of our energy strategy: Good stewardship.

We will insist on protecting and enhancing the environment, showing consideration for the air and natural lands and watersheds of our country.

This will require overcoming what is for some a cherished myth—that energy production and the environment must always involve competing values. We can explore for energy, we can produce energy and use it, and we can do so with a decent regard for the natural environment.

Alaska is the best case in point. . . .

. . . In Prudhoe Bay, the vast majority of drilling over the past decade has been horizontal, allowing much oil production to go literally unnoticed and habitat undisturbed.

The same sensitivity, and the same methods, would be applied in the event we opened production in the Arctic National Wildlife Reserve. . . . The notion that somehow developing the resources in ANWAR requires a vast despoiling of the environment is provably false. . . .

We can also safeguard the environment by making greater use of the cleanest methods of power generation we know. We have, after all, mastered one form of technology that causes zero emission of green house gases, and that is nuclear power. . . . If we're serious about environmental protection, then we must seriously question the wisdom of backing away from what is, as a matter of record, a safe, clean, and very plentiful energy source. . . .

Another part of our energy future is power from renewable sources. . . . There's been progress in the use of biomass, geothermal, wind and solar energy. Twenty years from now, with continued advances in R&D, we can reasonably expect renewable to meet three times the share of energy needs they meet today. . . .

The third and final principle of our energy strategy is to make better use, through the latest technology, of what we take from the earth. . . .

Here we aim to continue a path of uninterrupted progress in many fields. We have millions of fuel-efficient cars, where silicon chips effectively tune the engine between every firing of a spark plug. . . . Everything from light bulbs to appliances to video equipment is far more energy-efficient than ever before. New technologies are proving that we can save energy without sacrificing our standard of living. And we're going to encourage it in every way possible.

. . . The aim here is efficiency, not austerity. We all remember the energy crisis of the 1970s, when people in positions of responsibility complained that Americans just used too much energy.

Well, it's a good thing to conserve energy in our daily lives, and probably all of us can think of ways to do so. We can certainly think of ways that other people can conserve energy. And therein lies a temptation for policymakers—the impulse to begin telling Americans that we live too well, and—to recall a '70s phrase—that we've got to "do more with less." Already some groups are suggesting that government step in to force Americans to consume less energy, as if we could simply conserve or ration our way out of the situation we're in.

To speak exclusively of conservation is to duck the tough issues. Conservation may be a sign of personal virtue, but it is not a sufficient basis for a sound, comprehensive energy policy. People work very hard to get where they are. And the hardest working are the least likely to go around squandering energy, or anything else that costs them money. Our strategy will recognize that the present crisis does not represent a failing of the Americans people.

American's energy challenges are serious, but they are not perplexing. We know what needs to be done. We've always had the ability. We still have the resources. And, as of one hundred days ago, we once again have the leadership.

CHAPTER **17**

The Reagan Revolution and Conservative Ascendancy

By the late 1970s the public mood in the United States had turned sour. Abroad the United States seemed on the defensive. During these years the Soviet Union expanded its military strength and extended its influence into Central America, West Africa, and Afghanistan. Meanwhile, in the wake of the 1973 Arab-Israeli War, the Organization of Petroleum Exporting Countries (OPEC) raised oil prices to levels that threatened to strangle the U.S. economy. At home, the worst of the 1960s turmoil was past, but crime, drugs, illegitimacy, divorce, sexual permissiveness, pornography, and other social problems lingered and indeed seemed to become worse.

The U.S. economy also seemed sick. A chronic condition called "stagflation"—simultaneous price inflation and stagnant economic growth—had gripped the nation and would not yield. At the same time the United States seemed to be losing its competitive edge in the international economy. Japan, Germany, and other Asian and European nations had captured many of America's foreign customers as well as the U.S. domestic market for cars, steel, clothing, cameras, and electronics goods.

Perceptions of decline and retreat reawakened a dormant conservative movement, which in 1980 triumphed with the presidential election of Ronald Reagan, the former Hollywood actor and recent governor of California.

The Reagan administration that came to power in January 1981 promised to reduce inflation, restore America's international prestige, unleash economic energies, and improve the nation's moral climate. The selections that follow touch on several aspects of this conservative movement that culminated in what has been called the "Reagan Revolution." You will encounter defenders as well as detractors of conservative policies and programs, and as usual you should thoughtfully consider their contending views. The final evaluation, however, as always, is yours to make.

17.1 RONALD REAGAN'S BOUNDLESS OPTIMISM (1988)

Ronald Reagan not only won the election of 1980 by a landslide, he also forged a new conservative coalition that proved to be the most dramatic realignment of American politics in almost half a century. The newly transformed Republican Party addressed the grievances of voting blocs long embittered with decades of liberal politics and, more significantly, took into account major demographic shifts that had been inching along for years. America was now a nation of suburbs, not big cities and small towns. Americans now worked in jobs typical of a postindustrial economy, not in factories or on farms. Most of all, the population center of the country had moved from the liberal Northeast and Midwest to the much more conservative Sunbelt. The ideological base of Reagan's New Conservatism united three formerly disjointed conservative camps: (1) those interested in free-market economic policies desiring smaller government and lower taxes, (2) those preoccupied with the demise of traditional values determined to restore religion and family life to the center of American cultural life, and (3) those eager to assert America's role in international affairs through stronger defense initiatives and a renewed prosecution of the Cold War. As important as any of these factors may have been, it is, nonetheless, impossible to imagine contemporary American Conservatism in its current form without the impact of one individual, Ronald Reagan. Patron saint of conservatives, archenemy of liberals, Reagan, charismatic personality, conveyed boundless optimism about America in all he did. Determined to "get Americans feeling good about themselves again," Reagan was a great communicator who repeatedly tapped into a common heritage of myths, symbols, rhetoric, and shared values to mobilize the public support of his platform. In the following speech given at Moscow State University a year before the collapse of the Soviet Union, he deliberated on the nature of freedom. What age-old American beliefs and values did he invoke? In what ways does the speech reflect confidence and optimism in the American way of life? Why would this speech appeal to most Americans?

RONALD REAGAN'S VISION OF FREEDOM

Standing here before a mural of your revolution, I want to talk about a very different revolution that is taking place right now, quietly sweeping the globe, without bloodshed or conflict. Its effects are peaceful, but they will fundamentally alter our world, shatter old assumptions, and reshape our lives.

It's easy to underestimate because it's not accompanied by banners or fanfare. It has been called the technological or information revolution, and as its emblem, one might take the tiny silicon chip—no bigger than a fingerprint. One of these chips has more computing power than a roomful of old-style computers.

As part of an exchange program, we now have an exhibition touring your country that shows how information technology is transforming our lives—replacing manual labor with robots, forecasting weather for farmers, or mapping the genetic code of DNA for medical researchers. These microcomputers today aid the design of everything from houses to cars to spacecraft—they even design better and faster computers. They can translate English into Russian or enable the blind to read—or help Michael

Public Papers of the Presidents of the United States, Ronald Reagan, 1988, Book I (Washington, DC, 1990), p. 683.

Jackson produce on one synthesizer the sounds of a whole orchestra. Linked by a network of satellites and fiber-optic cables, one individual with a desktop computer and a telephone commands resources unavailable to the largest governments just a few years ago.

Like a chrysalis, we're emerging from the economy of the Industrial Revolution—an economy confined to and limited by the Earth's physical resources—into . . . an era in which there are no bounds on human imagination and the freedom to create is the most precious natural resource.

Think of that little computer chip. Its value isn't in the sand from which it is made, but in the microscopic architecture designed into by ingenious human minds. Or take the example of the satellite relaying this broadcast around the world, which replaces thousands of tons of copper mined from the Earth and molded into wire. In the new economy, human invention increasingly makes physical resources obsolete. We're breaking through the material conditions of existence to a world where man creates his own destiny. Even as we explore the most advanced reaches of science, we're returning to the age-old wisdom of our culture, a wisdom contained in the book of Genesis in the Bible: In the beginning was the spirit, and it was from this spirit that the material abundance of creation issued forth.

But progress is not foreordained. The key is freedom—freedom of thought, freedom of information, freedom of communication. The renowned scientist, scholar, and founding father of this University, Mikhail Lomonosov, knew that. "It is common knowledge," he said, "that the achievements of science are considerable and rapid, particularly once the yoke of slavery is cast off and replaced by the freedom of philosophy." . . .

The explorers of the modern era are the entrepreneurs, men with vision, with the courage to take risks and faith enough to brave the unknown. These entrepreneurs and their small enterprises are responsible for almost all the economic growth in the United States. They are the prime movers of the technological revolution. In fact, one of the largest personal computer firms in the United States was started by two college students, no older than you, in the garage behind their home.

Some people, even in my own country, look at the riot of experiment that is the free market and see only waste. What of all the entrepreneurs that fail? Well, many do, particularly the successful ones. Often several times. And if you ask them the secret of their success, they'll tell you, it's all that they learned in their struggles along the way—yes, it's what they learned from failing. Like an athlete in competition, or a scholar in pursuit of the truth, experience is the greatest teacher.

And that's why it's so hard for government planners, no matter how sophisticated, to ever substitute for millions of individuals working night and day to make their dreams come true. . . .

We Americans make no secret of our belief in freedom. In fact, it's something of a national pastime. Every four years the American people choose a new president, and 1988 is one of those years. At one point there were 13 major candidates running in the two major parties, not to mention all the others, including the Socialist and Libertarian candidates—all trying to get my job.

About 1,000 local television stations, 8,500 radio stations, and 1,700 daily newspapers, each one an independent, private enterprise, fiercely independent of the government, report on the candidates, grill them in interviews, and bring them together for debates. In the end, the people vote—they decide who will be the next president.

But freedom doesn't begin or end with elections. Go to any American town, to take just an example, and you'll see dozens of churches, representing many different beliefs—in many places synagogues and mosques—and you'll see families of every conceivable nationality, worshipping together.

Go into any schoolroom, and there you will see children being taught the Declaration of Independence, that they are endowed by their Creator with certain inalienable rights—among them life, liberty, and the pursuit of happiness—that no government can justly deny—the guarantees in their Constitution for freedom of speech, freedom of assembly, and freedom of religion. . . .

Go to any university campus, and there you'll find an open, sometimes heated discussion of the problems in American society and what can be done to correct them. Turn on the television, and you'll see the legislature conducting the business of government right there before the camera, debating and voting on the legislation that will become the law of the land. March in any demonstration, and there are many of them—the people's right of assembly is guaranteed in the Constitution and protected by the police. . . .

But freedom is even more than this: Freedom is the right to question, and change the established way of doing things. It is the continuing revolution of the marketplace. It is the understanding that allows us to recognize shortcomings and seek solutions. It is the right to put forth an idea, scoffed at by the experts, and watch it catch fire among the people. It is the right to follow your dream, to stick to your conscience, even if you're the only one in a sea of doubters.

Freedom is the recognition that no single person, no single authority or government has a monopoly on the truth, but that every individual life is infinitely precious, that every one of us put on this earth has been put here for a reason and has something to offer. . . .

Democracy is less a system of government than it is a system to keep government limited, unintrusive: A system of constraints on power to keep politics and government secondary to the important things in life, the true sources of value found only in family and faith.

But I hope you know I go on about these things not simply to extol the virtues of my own country, but to speak to the true greatness of the heart and soul of your land. Who, after all, needs to tell the land of Dostoevsky about the quest for truth, the home of Kandinsky and Scriabin about imagination, the rich and noble culture of the Uzbek man of letters, Alisher Navio, about beauty and heart?

The great culture of your diverse land speaks with a glowing passion to all humanity. Let me cite one of the most eloquent contemporary passages on human freedom. It comes, not from the literature of America, but from this country, from one of the greatest writers of the twentieth century, Boris Pasternak, in the novel *Dr. Zhivago*. He writes, "I think that if the beast who sleeps in man could be held down by threats—any kind of threat, whether of jail or retribution after death—then the highest emblem of humanity would be the lion tamer in the circus with his whip, not the prophet who sacrificed himself. But this is just the point—what has for centuries raised man above the beast is not the cudgel, but an inward music—the irresistible power of unarmed truth."

The irresistible power of unarmed truth. Today the world looks expectantly to signs of change, steps toward greater freedom in the Soviet Union. . . .

Your generation is living in one of the most exciting, hopeful times in Soviet history. It is a time when the first breath of freedom stirs the air and the heart beats to the accelerated rhythm of hope, when the accumulated spiritual energies of a long silence yearn to break free.

I am reminded of the famous passage near the end of Gogol's *Dead Souls*. Comparing his nation to a speeding troika, Gogol asks what will be its destination. But he writes, "There was no answer save the bell pouring forth marvelous sound."

We do not know what the conclusion of this journey will be, but we're hopeful that the promise of reform will be fulfilled. In this Moscow spring, this May 1988, we may be allowed that hope—that freedom, like the fresh green sapling planted over Tolstoi's grave, will blossom forth at last in the rich fertile soil of your people and culture. We may be allowed to hope that the marvelous sound of a new openness will keep rising through, ringing through, leading to a new world of reconciliation, friendship, and peace. . . .

17.2   THE NEW RIGHT (1980, 1978)

The political right of the late 1970s and 1980s was a composite movement. One strand derived from the individualistic conservatism that had coalesced around Barry Goldwater in 1964. Inspired by the frontier tradition, this brand was sustained and financed by self-made entrepreneurs from California, Texas, the mountain states, and the newly prosperous South.

The first selection, "Why the New Right Is Winning" by Richard Viguerie, focuses on what the author sees as wrong with liberalism. Can you sense a backlash in this article against that which had been conventional? Which specific complaints about liberalism reflect traditional U.S. conservative values? Which complaints are tied specifically to political issues of the Carter years? Did the right win, or the liberals lose, the election of 1980?

The second selection incorporates still another theme of the new right revival of the 1980s: "supply-side" economics. A creation of Arthur Laffer, Robert Mundell, and other conservative economists, the new theory sought to explain, and proposed a remedy for, stagflation. The economy's poor performance, supply-siders claimed, was the result of high taxes, government deficit spending, and the excessive emphasis on consumption (demand), all of which discouraged enterprise and investment. Rather than worrying about insufficient demand, they argued, the government should encourage a greater supply of goods and services by stimulating economic effort and increased investment through tax cuts. Higher investment and production would put money in the pockets of the public in the form of wages and dividends and indirectly increase demand as well. Not only would the economy rebound in the short run, but America would be better prepared for sustained long-term growth as well.

One of the most eloquent supply-side publicists was Jude Wanniski, a conservative journalist who wrote for the Wall Street Journal. The article excerpted here represents Arthur Laffer's ideas as interpreted by Wanniski. In what way is supply-side economic theory consistent with other conservative views? How were the supply-siders able to test their theories in practice during the Reagan administration? Did events confirm the value of the theories? Who gained and who lost by the application of supply-side economics to federal policies?

THE NEW RIGHT: WE'RE READY TO LEAD

Richard Viguerie

The election of 1980 came as a great shock to Americans who depended on the establishment media for their forecasts.

Not only did Ronald Reagan win the Presidency in an electoral landslide of historic proportions, for the first time in nearly a generation, Republicans took over the Senate.

Nationally known liberal Democrats—George McGovern, Frank Church, John Culver, Warren Magnuson, Gaylord Nelson, Birch Bayh—went down to defeat. The nation's leading liberal Republican senator (one of the few remaining after the 1978 elections) went down too: Jacob Javits lost to Alfonse D'Amato.

Americans learned early on the evening of November 4 that the election the media had called a "cliffhanger" was going to be, instead, a rout.

It was not until the next morning, when they woke to find the Senate in Republican hands, that they began to sense the full dimensions of the conservative revolution.

Suddenly it was the most cautious forecasters who looked most foolish. It was the people who had played it "safe" who had proved wildly wrong.

A few of us were not surprised. We in the New Right had been working for this moment for many years. We saw that our labors were bearing fruit, and we said so.

In the first edition of this book, written in the summer of 1980 and published six weeks *before* the election, I wrote:

"I firmly believe that we are on the brink of capturing one of those Houses, the U.S. Senate, perhaps this year and almost surely by 1982."

At the same time it must have sounded as if I hadn't been reading the papers!

On the night of November 4, history walked in on the liberals uninvited.

- Ronald Reagan, the country's foremost conservative politician since 1966, won the Presidency of the United States.
- His popular vote total topped that of the incumbent President, the highly-publicized third-party candidate John Anderson, and all the splinter-party standard-bearers *combined*.
- His electoral college margin—489 to 49—was among the greatest in history. And among challengers facing incumbents, only Franklin Roosevelt in 1932—with a three-year Depression on his side—did better.

Meanwhile, in the Senate races, the results were just as astonishing.

Backed by the support and organization of the New Right, conservatives like Steve Symms of Idaho, Don Nickles of Oklahoma, Bob Kasten of Wisconsin, Jeremiah Denton of Alabama, John East of North Carolina, Charles Grassley of Iowa, James Abdnor of South Dakota, Dan Quayle of Indiana, and the only woman to win, Paula Hawkins of Florida, stepped forth to offer the nation a new generation of conservative congressional leadership.

Richard Viguerie, *The New Right: We're Ready to Lead* (Falls Church, VA: Viguerie Company, 1980), pp. 1–7.

It has been obvious for a long time that conservatism is rising and liberalism is declining. Despite all the talk in the media about "trends," "cliffhangers," and "last-minute shifts," the plain truth is that more and more Americans are sick of liberalism—and aren't afraid to say so.

The election of 1980 was the first modern conservative landslide. But it wasn't the first anit-liberal landslide.

In 1968 two anti-liberal candidates, Richard Nixon and George Wallace, won a combined 57 percent of the popular vote against the well-liked—but liberal—incumbent Vice President, Hubert Humphrey.

In 1972 Nixon, never very popular, won more than 60% of the total vote against the flamingly liberal George McGovern, who carried only one state (not even his home state of South Dakota).

Jimmy Carter didn't win election as a liberal. In the 1976 primaries he presented himself as the most conservative candidate in the field, and it was not until after he was safely in office that it became clear he intended to be a liberal President.

Even in 1980, when Democrats were sick of Carter, he won primaries—when his opponent was the even further left Edward Kennedy. Meanwhile, Ronald Reagan piled up victories against conservative, moderate and liberal candidates in his own party.

After the televised debate a week before the election, an ABC phone-in poll gave Reagan a 2 to 1 edge over Carter. Many others in media denounced the poll as "unscientific."

Maybe it was. But the election on November 4 wasn't conducted in a laboratory either. The ABC poll was just one more sign of the times—for anyone who was interested.

All the signs pointed one way. They've been pointing that way for years, and years, and years. They still do.

America is basically a conservative country. The potential for conservative revolt has always been there, under the most favorable conditions. But those conditions have to be made.

That's where the New Right comes in.

For many years, conservatives were frustrated. We had no way to translate our vision into reality.

Most importantly, we lacked a vehicle to carry our message to the voters without going through the filter of the liberal-leaning news media.

During the 1950s, 1960s, and most of the 1970s liberal politicians were able to make speeches that sounded as if they were written by Barry Goldwater. The liberals could come home on weekends and make speeches calling for a strong America, attacking waste in Washington, and complaining about big government. Then, on Monday, they could go back to Washington and vote to block new weapons systems, to give away the Panama Canal, to increase taxes, to create new government agencies, and to weaken the CIA and FBI.

Occasionally, liberal politicians would visit Communist leaders like Fidel Castro and return to the U.S. with wonderful words of praise for the Cuban dictator, praise that most voters in South Dakota or Idaho never heard.

Why did the voters in South Dakota, Idaho, Iowa, Indiana, and Wisconsin not know about their congressmen's and senators' double lives—conservative-sounding at home, actively liberal in Washington or abroad?

Because most of the national (and some of the local) media didn't report the double life the politicians were leading.

Thanks to the New Right, the "people's right to know"—which the establishment media pay loud lip-service to, when it serves their own purposes—finally became a reality.

"You can't turn back the clock."

How often we hear this line from liberals. What they really mean is that we shouldn't try to correct their mistakes.

Well, the New Right has news for them. We aren't in the business of turning back clocks.

It's the Left that has tried to stop the clock and even bring back evils civilization has left behind.

- It's the Left that has re-introduced guild privileges based on compulsory unionism, government-imposed racial and sexual discrimination, and oppressive taxes.
- It's the Left that favors a society based on state regulation, supervision, and coercion.
- It's the Left that has defended and even promoted pornography and abortion. (The clock has stopped forever for eight million unborn American children.)
- It's the Left that focuses its compassion on the criminal rather than his victims.
- It's the Left that attacks our allies rather than our enemies.
- It's the Left that favors the non-producers over the people who work.
- It's the Left that encourages American women to feel that they are failures if they want to be wives and mothers.
- It's the Left that tears apart families and neighbors by the forced busing of children.
- It's the Left that has failed to protest Communist slavery and religious persecution— evils afflicting 1.8 *billion* human beings.
- It's the Left that's fought to keep prayer out of the schools.
- It's the Left that allowed ruthless Communist take-overs in Vietnam, Laos, Cambodia and Afghanistan.
- It's the Left that allowed the takeover of Iran, one of America's strongest allies, by a group of terrorists and extremists.
- It's the Left who crippled the CIA and FBI.
- It's the Left who sold the Russians computers and other sophisticated equipment used to oppress their people.

Liberalism has pitted itself against the best instincts of the American people. Journalist Tom Bethell says the abortion issue alone has destroyed the liberals' "moral monopoly."

Put simply, most Americans no longer look up to liberals. They look down on them.

Liberals have long sensed this. They have tried to make their mistakes irreversible and election-proof. As far as possible, they have sought to turn the powers of government over to the courts and administrative agencies—that is, to unelected and unaccountable public officials.

They have found other ways to impose their will. One of the most sophisticated has been deficit spending—producing an inflation that reduces blue-collar workers' real pay by pushing them into what used to be executive tax brackets. By such means liberals have increased government's grip on our wealth without openly raising tax rates.

Somebody had to call a halt to this devious elitism. What used to be liberalism has turned into socialism on the installment plan.

With the New Right, America has found a new voice. In 1980, that voice rang out—loud and clear.

The voters of Idaho and South Dakota finally got to know the *real* Frank Church and the *real* George McGovern—the ones Fidel Castro knows.

Because conservatives have mastered the new technology, we've been able to bypass the Left's near-monopoly of the national news media.

The New Right has also had its own ready-made network: the thousands of conservative Christian ministers whose daily broadcasts on local and national radio and TV reach an audience of 27 million. Every week, approximately 20 million people view just three such ministers—Jerry Falwell, Pat Robertson, and James Robison.

Until now this whole culture has been a dark continent to the Northeast, coastal-based national media. But these ministers are attacking issues the national media hardly mention: issues like worldwide Communist aggression, school prayer, sex on TV, the failures of the public schools. The conservative ministers are in touch with the people, and now they are in touch with each other.

The conservatism was always there. It took the New Right to give it leadership, organization, and direction.

The key word is *leadership*. Conservatives have had no lack of brilliant thinkers, brilliant writers, brilliant debaters, brilliant spokesmen. But none of these is the same thing as a leader.

George Gallup has found that 49% of registered voters in the U.S. now place themselves "right of center"—as against only 29% who say they are "left of center" and only 10% who call themselves "middle of the road."

And yet, with this tremendous potential support, the Republican Party has proved itself incapable of even mounting a consistent and effective opposition, much less rallying that 49% behind an agenda of its own. If it can't find its base with both hands, how is it going to lead the whole nation?

The New Right has proved it can lead. We're doing it. Leadership doesn't just show up on the first Tuesday in November. It has to be out there ahead of time—organizing, mailing, phoning, advertising, informing, getting names on the ballot.

The simple truth is that there is a new majority in America—and it's being led by the New Right.

TAXES, REVENUES, AND THE "LAFFER CURVE"

Jude Wanniski

As Arthur Laffer has noted, "There are always two tax rates that yield the same revenues." When an aide to President Gerald Ford asked him once to elaborate, Laffer (who is Professor of Business Economics at the University of Southern California) drew a simple curve to illustrate his point. The point, too, is simple enough—though, like so many simple points, it is also powerful in its implications.

Jude Wanniski, "Taxes, Revenues, and the 'Laffer Curve.' " Reprinted from *The Public Interest*, No. 50 (Winter 1978), pp. 3–16. © 1978 by National Affairs, Inc.

When the tax rate is 100 percent, all production ceases in the money economy (as distinct from the barter economy, which exists largely to escape taxation). People will not work in the money economy if all the fruits of their labors are confiscated by the government. And because production ceases, there is nothing for the 100-percent rate to confiscate, so government revenues are zero.

On the other hand, if the tax rate is zero, people can keep 100 percent of what they produce in the money economy. There is no governmental "wedge" between earnings and after-tax income, and thus no governmental barrier to production. Production is therefore maximized, and the output of the money economy is limited only by the desire of workers for leisure. But because the tax rate is zero, government revenues are again zero, and there can be no government. So at a 0-percent tax rate the economy is in a state of anarchy, and at a 100-percent tax rate the economy is functioning entirely through barter.

In between lies the curve. If the government reduces its rate to something less than 100 percent, say to point A, some segment of the barter economy will be able to gain so many efficiencies by being in the money economy that, even with near-confiscatory tax rates, after-tax production would still exceed that of the barter economy. Production will start up, and revenues will flow into the government treasury. By lowering the tax rate, we find an increase in revenues.

On the bottom end of the curve, the same thing is happening. If people feel that they need a minimal government and thus institute a low tax rate, some segment of the economy, finding that the marginal loss of income exceeds the efficiencies gained in the money economy, is shifted into either barter or leisure. But with that tax rate, revenues do flow into the government treasury. This is the situation at point B. Point A represents a very high tax rate and very low production. Point B represents a very low tax rate and very high production. Yet they both yield the same revenue to the government.

The same is true of points C and D. The government finds that by a further lowering of the tax rate, say from point A to point C, revenues increase with the further expansion of output. And by raising the tax rate, say from point B to point D, revenues also increase, by the same amount.

Revenues and production are maximized at point E. If, at point E, the government lowers the tax rate again, output will increase, but revenues will fall. And if, at point E, the tax rate is raised, both output and revenue will decline. The shaded area is *the prohibitive range for government*, where rates are unnecessarily high and can be reduced with gains in *both* output and revenue.

Tax Rates and Tax Revenues

The next important thing to observe is that, except for the 0-percent and 100-percent rates, there are no numbers along the "Laffer curve." Point E is not 50 percent, although it may be, but rather a variable number: *It is the point at which the electorate desires to be taxed.* At points B and D, the electorate desires more government goods and services and is willing—without reducing its productivity—to pay the higher rates consistent with the revenues at point E. And at points A and C, the electorate desires more private goods and services in the money economy, and wishes to pay the lower rates consistent with the revenues at point E. It is the task of the statesman to determine the location of point E, and follow its variations as closely as possible. . . .

Work vs. Productivity

The idea behind the "Laffer curve" is no doubt as old as civilization, but unfortunately politicians have always had trouble grasping it. In his essay, *Of Taxes*, written in 1756, David Hume pondered the problem:

> Exorbitant taxes, like extreme necessity, destroy industry by producing despair; and even before they reach this pitch, they raise the wages of the labourer and manufacturer, and heighten the price of all commodities. An attentive disinterested legislature will observe the point when the emolument ceases, and the prejudice begins. But as the contrary character is much more common, 'tis to be feared that taxes all over Europe are multiplying to such a degree as will entirely crush all art and industry; tho' perhaps, their first increase, together with other circumstances, might have contributed to the growth of these advantages.

The chief reason politicians and economists throughout history have failed to grasp the idea behind the "Laffer curve" is their confusion of work and productivity. Through both introspection and observation, the politician understands that when tax rates are raised, there is a tendency to work harder and longer to maintain after-tax income. What is not so apparent, because it requires analysis *at the margin*, is this: As taxes are raised, individuals in the system may indeed work harder, but their productivity declines. . . .

Imagine that there are three men who are skilled at building houses. If they work together, one works on the foundation, one on the frame, and the third on the roof. Together they can build three houses in three months. If they work separately, each building his own home, they need six months to build the three houses. If the tax rate on homebuilding is 49 percent, they will work together, since the government leaves them a small gain from their division of labor. But if the tax rate goes to 51 percent, they suffer a net loss because of their teamwork, and so they will work separately. When they were pooling their efforts, since they could produce six houses in the same time it would take them to build three houses working alone, the government was collecting revenues almost equivalent to the value of three completed homes. At the 51-percent tax rate, however, the government loses all the revenue, and the economy loses the production of the three extra homes that could have been built by their joint effort. . . .

The Politics of the "Laffer Curve"

The "Laffer curve" is a simple but exceedingly powerful analytical tool. In one way or another, all transactions, even the simplest, take place along it. The homely adage, "You can catch more flies with molasses than with vinegar," expresses the essence of the curve. But empires are built on the bottom of this simple curve and crushed against the top of it. The Caesars understood this, and so did Napoleon (up to a point) and the greatest of the Chinese emperors. The Founding Fathers of the United States knew it well; the arguments for union (in *The Federalist Papers*) made by [Alexander] Hamilton, [James] Madison, and [John] Jay reveal an understanding of the notion. Until War I— when progressive taxation was sharply increased to help finance it—the United States successfully remained out of the "prohibitive range."

In the 20th century, especially since World War I, there has been a constant struggle by all the nations of the world to get down the curve. The United States managed to do so in the 1920's, because Andrew Mellon understood the lessons of the "Laffer curve" for the domestic economy. . . .

The stock market crash of 1929 and the subsequent global depression occurred because Herbert Hoover unwittingly contracted the world economy with his high-tariff policies, which pushed the West, as an economic unit, up the "Laffer curve." Hoover compounded the problem in 1934 by raising personal tax rates almost up to the levels of 1920. . . .

The British empire was built on the lower end of the "Laffer curve" and dismantled on the upper end. The high wartime rates imposed to finance the Napoleonic wars were cut back sharply in 1816, despite warnings from "fiscal experts" that the high rates were needed to reduce the enormous public debt of £900 million. For the following 60 years, the British economy grew at an unprecedented pace, as a series of finance ministers used ever-expanding revenues to lower steadily the tax rates and tariffs.

In Britain, though, unlike the United States, there was no Mellon to risk lowering the extremely high tax rates imposed to finance World War I. As a result, the British economy struggled through the 1920's and 1930's. After World War II, the British government again made the mistake of not sufficiently lowering tax rates to spur individual initiative. Instead, the postwar Labour government concentrated on using tax policy for Keynesian objectives—i.e., increasing consumer demand to expand output. On October 23, 1945, tax rates were cut on lower-income brackets and surtaxes were added to the already high rates on the upper-income brackets. Taxes on higher incomes were increased, according to Chancellor of the Exchequer Hugh Dalton, in order to "continue that steady advance toward economic and social equality which we have made during the war and which the Government firmly intends to continue in peace."

From that day in 1945, there has been no concerted political voice in Britain arguing for the reduction of the high tax rates. Conservatives have supported and won tax reductions for business, especially investment-tax income credits. But while arguing for a reduction of the 83-percent rate on incomes above £20,000 (roughly $35,000 at current exchange rates) of earned income and the 98-percent rate on "unearned income" from investments, they have insisted that government *first* lower its spending, in order to permit the rate reductions. Somehow, the spending levels never can be cut. Only in the last several months of 1977 has Margaret Thatcher, the leader of the opposition Conservative Party, spoken of reducing the high tax rates as a way of expanding revenues.

In the United States, in September 1977, the Republic National Committee unanimously endorsed the plan of Representative Jack Kemp of New York for cutting tax rates as a way of expanding revenues through increased business activity. This was the first time since 1953 that the GOP had embraced the concept of tax cuts! In contrast, the Democrats under President Kennedy sharply cut tax rates in 1962–64 (though making their case in Keynesian terms). The reductions successfully moved the United States economy down the "Laffer curve," expanding the economy and revenues.

It is crucial to Western economic expansion, peace, and prosperity that "conservative" parties move in this direction. They are, after all, traditionally in favor of income growth, with "liberals" providing the necessary political push for income redistribution. A welfare state is perfectly consistent with the "Laffer curve," and can function successfully along its lower range. But there must be income before there can be income redistribution. Most of the economic failures of this century can rightly be charged to the failure of conservatives to press for tax rates along the lower range of the "Laffer curve." Presidents Eisenhower, Nixon and Ford were timid in this crucial area of public policy. The Goldwater Republicans of 1963–64, in fact, emphatically opposed the Kennedy tax-rate cuts!

If, during the remainder of this decade, the United States and Great Britain demonstrate the power of the "Laffer curve" as an analytical tool, its use will spread, in the developing countries as well as the developed world. Politicians who understand the curve will find that they can defeat politicians who do not, other things being equal. Electorates all over the world always know when they are unnecessarily perched along the upper edge of the "Laffer curve," and will support political leaders who can bring them back down.

17.3 THE LIBERALS HIT BACK (1982)

Needless to say, many Americans never accepted the views of the revived political right. Liberal and left-of-center publications and critics disliked virtually everything about the New Right and denounced the Reagan administration and its policies. The first selection is an attack from the political left by economist Robert L. Heilbroner on Reaganite economic policy that goes beyond objections to supply-side tax policies. What is Heilbroner really indicting? Are his characterizations of the prevailing socioeconomic system well taken? Is it fair to hold the Reagan administration, or conservatives generally, responsible for the failings that Heilbroner sees in U.S. society in the 1980s?

The religious right also encountered opposition. Religious liberals objected to the theology as well as the social philosophy of the Moral Majority and of the Protestant fundamentalists who formed its core. In the second selection, Robert McAfee Brown, a prominent Presbyterian minister and professor of religion at New York's liberal Union Theological Seminary, takes issue with Falwell and his colleagues. What is the stated religious basis for Brown's disagreements with the Moral Majority? Do you think Brown is solely concerned with what the Bible teaches? In what way do his politics disagree with Falwell's? Why do the two clergymen reach such different social and political conclusions?

THE DEMAND FOR THE SUPPLY-SIDE

Robert L. Heilbroner

Supply-side economics has taken Washington by storm. Both a diagnosis and a prescription, supply-side economics comprises ideas about what is wrong with the economy and remedies to put it right. As its name would indicate, both diagnosis and prescription emphasize the actual production of goods and services rather than the buying of them.

Robert L. Heilbroner, "The Demand for the Supply-Side," in Robert Fink, ed., *Supply-Side Economics: A Critical Appraisal* (Frederick, MD: University Publications of America, 1982), pp. 80–91. An imprint of Greenwood Publishing Group, Inc., Westport, CT. Reprinted with permission.

From this vantage point, supply-siders see our fundamental difficulties as constraints, mainly caused by taxes that deter productive effort, rather than as problems deriving from a lack of purchasing power. We catch a vision of the economy as a coiled spring held down by the weight of government. Remove the weight, and the spring will reveal its inherent force.

Most of the heated discussions about supply-side economics are concerned with how much tension the spring really has and how vigorously it will respond to the removal of various tax disincentives. I shall come back to these matters later. But it seems foolish to begin an appraisal of supply-side economics with debates about how far we must cut income taxes to achieve renewed growth, or how quickly inflation will be overcome by increased output. At the root of all supply-side remedies lie profoundly held if sometimes implicit convictions about the nature of the capitalist system itself. Since I am convinced that these views are wrong, I cannot get much exercised about the particular prescription on supply-side medicines. . . .

To turn to . . . strictly economic matters: supply-side economics puts forward two policy prescriptions. First, it advocates a substantial reduction in marginal tax rates, in order to create a burst of response. A response of what? The supply-siders are convinced that more hours will be worked, that less effort will be diverted into the underground economy, that more risks will be taken. In a word, we will produce more, giving rise to more employment, and ultimately to a diminution of inflationary pressure.

Here everything hinges on the crucial matter of how individuals or firms respond to tax cuts. The fact of the matter is that we do not know very much about this problem. Worse, it is possible to construct two quite opposing, but equally convincing predictions. The supply-siders[1] see individuals using their tax bonanzas, such as the Kemp-Roth proposed reduction of taxes by 10 percent a year for three years, to add to their savings, or as a spur to more effort because more income will be kept. Skeptics see an entirely different picture. They see families reacting to a tax bonanza the way they react to all income increases: they will spend about 95 percent of it. They also see an increase in their after-tax incomes permitting a lot of people to give up moonlighting, overtime, or other distasteful tasks to which high taxes have driven them. Thus the skeptics see the impact of supply-side policies as boosting inflation far more than production. I number myself among the skeptics.

And what about the stimulus to production that firms will experience, as taxes are rolled back and onerous regulations repealed? In all likelihood there will be some response: the crucial question is how much. Again two views are plausible. One of them, exemplified by George Gilder's[2] stress on the creative efforts of individual entrepreneurs, sees a great burst of small business formation, not only creating jobs but providing the innovative zest needed to restore economic vitality. The other, more skeptical view looks to the great corporations that dominate so much of economic life and asks whether tax reductions or milder regulation will suffice to turn the automobile industry around, to reinvigorate the steel industry, to strengthen the transportation system, to solve the energy problem, and the like. Once again, I number myself among the skeptics.

---

[1] A supply-side measure introduced in Congress by Representative Jack Kemp of New York and Senator William Roth of Delaware to federal income taxes—ED.

[2] A conservative writer on social and economic themes—ED.

Second, supply-siders want to roll back government, not merely to get it off our backs, but also because government is perceived as essentially a wasteful, not a productive, use of resources. This last is a very interesting contention. I would be the last to deny the presence of government waste: the MX missile system, the space shuttle, the tax subsidies to various upper-income groups, not to mention the petty cadging and occasional grand larceny among welfare clients. However, I want to call attention to a curious aspect of the question of waste. It is that there is no waste in the private sector. This is the case because all "wasteful" activities are eliminated by the market, like the famous Edsel. On the other hand, whatever survives the test of the market is not waste. The five giant buildings that will be erected between 53rd and 57th Streets along Madison Avenue are not waste, whatever chaos they create, unless they cannot be rented. The $100,000 Rolls Royce is not waste, assuming that it sells. There is not waste in the production of *anything* that sells, because the very act of purchase provides the justification for whatever resources have been used.

Clearly there are entirely different criteria for waste in the public and private domains. Suppose that the scrutiny usually directed at government were brought to bear on private output, and that each act of private production had to justify itself by the *noneconomic* criteria we apply to public output. Would we not find a great deal of waste in the private sphere? And suppose that the government limited its production to those things it could sell—pocket-sized missiles and salable services of all kinds. Would not all waste disappear from the public sphere? This leads one to think about the meaning of the "waste" perceived from the supply side.

It leads one also to reflect on the ideological element within supply-side thinking. To be sure, all social orders have ideologies, and none could exist without them. Therefore societies never think of their prevailing views as being "ideological," but rather as expressing self-evident or natural truths. As [historian] Immanuel Wallerstein has acutely remarked, during most periods of history there is effectively only one class that is conscious of itself, and this dominant class sincerely expresses its own views as representing those of the entire society. Thus the senators of Rome, the lords of the manor, the monarchs of France and England, and the members of the Soviet elite all speak with unself-conscious assurance in the name of their societies. None feels itself to be a "privileged" class or thinks its views to be other than universal. . . .

The question to be pondered is why supply-side economics has attracted the worst ideology, and why it has dulled the sensibilities of the best ideologists. I am ashamed to say the one convincing reason that occurs to me: supply-side economics has as its immediate objective the improvement of the conditions of the rich. What bonanzas will result from the lowering of the high marginal rate on property income and on the reduction of the capital gains tax! I too rub my hands at the prospect. To be sure, like all policies, the *ultimate* objective of supply-side economics is the improvement of the condition of everyone. Just the same, I do not think supply-side economics would adduce quite the same fervor, or quite the same dulling of critical sensibilities, if its *immediate* aim were the improvement of the poor and its ultimate aim the bettering of the rich. Self-interest has extraordinary powers of persuasion. . . .

What is likely to happen over the next decade? Nothing. I say so from a profound skepticism about the efficacy of supply-side stimuli. But from a more history-laden point of view, I mean something different by "nothing." I mean that the slow, almost invisible trends of the past will continue to have their way, not because these trends have a life of their own but because they express the inner motions, the self-created dynamic of the system. I will mention only two of these trends:

1. *State-owned or state-dependent organizations will emerge as the leading agents of accumulation.* We are all familiar with the slow drift in the texture of the representative firm, from a single-product, single-plant, single-family enterprise to a multi-product, multi-plant, multi-national managerial bureaucracy. This has been the consequence of the continuing division of labor and of technologies of control which have brought concentration and centralization in virtually every field of human endeavor.

   This trend now seems likely to move to a new level of organizational size and strength by combining the capital-mobilizing and competition-buffering abilities of the state with the independence and drive of private management. Most capitalist nations today have public-private firms in airlines or airframes, in steel, automobiles, chemicals, and the like.

   Many of these public-private firms have been formed to prevent private bankruptcies. That in no way weakens my argument. But the Japanese present a more interesting case. Japan is evidently now preparing to enter the semiconductor industry on a public-private basis with one or two huge firms. That industry today is still dominated by the United States, where numerous businesses compete vigorously for market shares. The result, as Lester Thurow[3] has written, is that in the U.S. the market is likely to eliminate the losers, and the Japanese will thereafter eliminate the winners.

   Whether or not the Japanese "model" of public-private coordination can be exported, I would think that statist enterprise of some sort is very likely to be the form in which the accumulation of capital is carried on in the coming years.

2. As part of this statist movement, I would also expect to see the emergence of an even more explicit reliance on national planning. This will assume two forms. One will be macroplanning for adequate employment, probably through government work programs, for acceptable price behavior through a network of controls and mandatory incomes policies, and for international buffers through protectionism. The other form of planning will be microplanning aimed at channeling labor and capital into socially advantageous uses and at coping with disruptive problems such as energy, urban decay, etc.

   It may be objected that planning does not "work," that we are now in retreat from it—a retreat led by supply-side economics. That depends on what one means by "work." As I see it, *no organizational system can smoothly combine the explosive technology, restless polity, and deadening work experience of contemporary industrial society.* This is as true for self-styled socialist societies as for capitalist ones. Hence I do not expect state capitalism to "work" particularly well, but I expect it to survive and to continue the function that is the driving force of capitalism—the accumulation of capital by means of wage labor.

   It is possible, of course, that ideological opposition may reverse this two-century-long trend toward centralization. Social orders sometimes refuse to adopt changes which, to outsiders, would preserve their regimes: one thinks of the

---

[3] Thurow is a liberal economist—ED.

refusal of the Roman senators to undertake land reform, or of the opposition of the French aristocracy to tax reform. To identify historical trends is not to deny social orders the right to commit suicide.

These considerations lead inescapably to the question of how long capitalism is likely to survive. I would think for quite a long while. No one can project an "indefinite" life span for capitalism. It is by its nature dynamic, and is constantly changing. Today it is pressing against the absorptive limits of the environment and thereby threatening the pace and scope of accumulation. Its moral cement, as I have remarked, is dissolving in its commercial ethic. It faces the contradictions of its antagonistic policy and economy, and the Laocoön-like struggles of its accumulation mechanics. Its broad movement today seems toward a bureaucratic statist regime. After that, who can tell?

Nonetheless, I do not see any immediate "end" of capitalism. Much of the world remains to be penetrated by its formidable mode of labor organization, its seductive technology, its intellectual brilliance. However decadent at its center, capitalism is today without a serious rival as an economic system, dangerous though the Soviet Union may be as a military rival.

This expectation of continued life seems all the more likely because, as I have just said, there is really nothing yet visible beyond capitalism. As an imaginable institutional arrangement, socialism has become a word almost without content. If it means the nationalization of industry or private-public planning, it can be seen—at least, so I suggest—as the extension of capitalism. As a deindustrialization of society it holds forth the specter of a catastrophic decline in living standards. As a vast extension of worker participation, it suffers from a complete lack of any economic and political institutions—or conception of such institutions—within which workers' autonomy could be expressed. In the underdeveloped world it is all too likely that socialist revolutions will usher in narrow, inefficient, and xenophobic regimes.

Hence there is little enthusiasm for socialism today, always excepting the burning desire of oppressed peoples or abused workers to throw off cruel or simply sclerotic regimes. After that, the realities of the industrial process, the impatient expectations of the masses, the contagion of Western ideas and goods must somehow be accommodated. The next stage of economic history, whatever its label, will not be a pleasant one. That supply-side economics, the darling and fad of conservative thought, imagines itself to be the vehicle of this next stage strikes me as an extraordinary fantasy. It is to confuse a small eddy, located in a few board rooms and academic centers, with the Gulf Stream of history.

THE NEED FOR A MORAL MINORITY

Robert McAfee Brown

Some of you may have misread the title "The Need for a Moral Minority," and assumed that I was going to address the Moral Majority. I am going to make some references to the Moral Majority in the course of these remarks, but I do not want to concentrate exclusively on that movement. I particularly do not want to have the Moral Majority

---

Robert McAfee Brown, "The Need for a Moral Minority," in Herbert Vetter, ed., *Speak Out Against the New Right* (Boston: Beacon Press, 1982), pp. 118–26.

setting my agenda, or our agendas, for the eighties. I think that agenda is somewhat politically naive and theologically un-Biblical; I will try to footnote that in a little while.

My overall concern is much more how we can relate religion and politics positively. If along the way we can learn some things from the Moral Majority, about how not to do it, I am willing to call that a gain.

This whole problem of a religious presence on the political scene which has been highlighted for us in this rather recent emergence of the theological right wing, the problem of religion of the political scene is illustrated for me by a comment from an anonymous 17th century writer, one of my favorite anonymous comments. This writer wrote: "I had rather see coming toward me a whole regiment with drawn swords, than one lone Calvinist convinced that he is doing the will of God." Now that statement illustrates both the glory and demonry of Calvinism, and by a not very difficult extension, the potential glory and potential demonry of all political involvement on the part of religiously minded persons. On the one hand, there is something immensely freeing and energizing about the feeling that one is doing God's will, and that the outcome of one's activity is therefore safe in God's hands. Such an attitude can liberate one to new kinds of courage, to immense risk taking, even to the point of death. . . .

But there can be a demonry as well in the invoking of God's support which we find exhibited when individuals or groups decide what they want to impose on others, and then claim divine sanction for it. This gives them carte blanche to do whatever they feel is necessary to stop their opponents since their opponents, being opposed to them, are clearly opposed to God as well, and do not finally deserve the right to speak or act or persuade, and Christians have often been guilty of this. The Crusades were an example, Christian anti-Semitism is another, and sometimes the Christian willingness to kill, whether in support of a Nazi ideology, or extreme nationalism, whether of the Russian or American variety, these are other instances that come to mind. And as I look at the current American religious scene, it is this tendency that seems to me in danger of characterizing this recently emerged religious right of which [the] Moral Majority is at least one very clear-cut example.

Mr. Falwell, Jerry Falwell, the leader of that movement, states that he knows just what is wrong with our country, and tells us: "God has called me to action. I have a divine mandate to go into the halls of Congress and fight for laws that will save America." As this position develops, it turns out that those who disagree with him are really by definition disagreeing with God, since he, and not they, have access to God's will. Liberals, for example, who Mr. Falwell abominates, are not just political liberals or theological liberals, they are godless liberals. They are the ones who must be removed from public office, since they are not only wrong, but evil. What we must have in office are God-fearing, Bible-believing Christians, which is bad news to Jews and secularists.

I do not for a moment challenge Mr. Falwell's right or anybody's right to get into the American political process, to work for change, to support candidates, urge people to vote and all the rest. That is the way the American system works, and the more people that are doing that, the better for the health of the system. And it would be a very perverse logic to claim that only people with whom I agree ought to be engaging in political activity and I want no part of such an argument. I have taken my own political stands in the past; I intend to keep doing so in the present and in the future, so can and should everyone, whether named Billy Graham or Bill Coffin, whether named Jerry Falwell or Robert Drinan.[1]

---

[1] Billy Graham, a conservative Protestant revivalist; William Sloane Coffin, a liberal Protestant minister; Robert Drinan, a liberal Catholic priest—ED.

Furthermore, this emergence of the Radical Right on the political scene means that there is one ancient battle we are not going to have to fight for a while. For the most of my adult life, at any rate, people on the theological right have been saying religion and politics do not mix. The rest of us have been saying, "They do too mix." And now, for better or for worse, that message has been heard.

The question is no longer, "Do religion and politics mix?" The question is simply, "What is the nature of the mix?" And it is the nature of the mix, as far as groups like [the] Moral Majority are concerned, that is increasingly concerning me, and even on some levels beginning to frighten me. Now let me say just enough about that kind of mix so that I can then set the stage in the latter part of these comments, for what seems to me a more appropriate alternative.

In Christian terms, and I think in terms with which all Jews could also agree, my real complaint about the Moral Majority's intrusion of the Bible into American politics is that they are not biblical enough. I do not for a moment concede that they have the Bible on their side and that the rest of us are nothing but godless liberals or secular humanists which, in Mr. Falwell's lexicon, is very close to being either a Socialist or a Communist.

So let me illustrate that in two ways. First of all, it seems to me that the Moral Majority's biblically inspired political agenda involves a very selective, very partial, and therefore very distorted use of the Bible. They have isolated a set of concerns that they say get to the heart of what is wrong with America—homosexuality, abortion, and pornography. These are the things that are wrong and that are destroying our nation. What we need to do, what we need to be for, basically for prayer in public schools, and for more bombs. Jesus wants our kids to pray and he wants the Pentagon to be able to kill more people if necessary. I know that sounds a little crude, but I believe it is. I am not denying that there are moral dimensions involved in all those issues and that people can take different moral positions in response to them, but the notion that they represent what the Hebrew and Christian scriptures offer us as the key for understanding what is wrong with the world today is one that strikes me as grotesque.

Take the issue of homosexuality. If one turns to the scriptures as a whole, to try to come up with their central concerns, homosexuality is going to be very low on such a list even if indeed it makes the list at all. There are perhaps seven very ambiguous verses in the whole biblical canon that even allude to it and I will any day subordinate the minuscule import of those seven verses, isolated verses, to hundreds and hundreds of places where the scriptures are dealing over and over again with questions of social justice, the tendency of the rich to exploit the poor, the need for all of us to have a commitment to the hungry, the need for nations not to put their major trust in armaments, the concern for the sick, the recognition that all people are children of God, even if they are Russians or Cubans or Salvadoreans. The Moral Majority creates an agenda and then proceeds to impose that agenda on scripture by developing little strings of unrelated verses to give divine sanction to the position. As those who work with the Bible know, one can prove absolutely anything that way. You can make a biblical case for militarism or pacifism, nationalism or internationalism, for male dominance or for women's rights, though it is a bit more difficult with women's rights. One can make a case for capital punishment or for letting the prisoners go free. One can make a case for socialism or for capitalism, simply by selecting a few verses very carefully and ignoring all the others.

It seems clear to me that there are great and central overriding themes and concerns in the scriptures. You and I might have slightly different lists of what these themes would be, but there would be certain ones that simply could not be ignored if we were going to respond honestly to the text. There are huge sections, for example, on the dangers of national idolatry, that is to say, making the nation into God, accepting uncritically whatever we have to do as a nation against other nations.

Those major emphases stand in very sharp contrast to Mr. Falwell's assessment that we should have done whatever we needed to win in Vietnam because our national honor was at stake. That was the criterion and I submit that national honor is a criterion that the Bible unremittingly attacks. There are long sections in scripture dealing with the need to be concerned about the poor and the destitute. There are treatments of the "virus" of racism. There are many recognitions that those with wealth will always be tempted to act repressively against the poor and so on and so on. It is breathtaking that when one looks over the agendas of the Moral Majority there is absolutely no mention of such things, there is a total silence. We seem to be living in two different worlds, reading two different books. . . .

So let me now, to conclude, suggest very briefly five characteristics that I think would be appropriate to the moral minority. . . .

First . . . the Bible does not talk about minorities as much as about remnants. Since the demise of . . . Constantinian Christianity[2] where Christians were running the show . . . this remnant posture has become both appropriate and descriptive for Christians. We are a small percentage, a remnant, of the whole human family, particularly when we look at ourselves globally. . . .

[One remnant within the remnant might be to dissent from the prevailing views of local church establishments. Our model for this might be the circumstances of Latin America.] For centuries . . . the Catholic Church in Latin America was at the beck and call of the little group of the wealthy who had all the power, who had all the money, all the prestige. . . . But in recent years the churches have been getting away from that uncritical alliance with those in power [and speaking up and working for social justice]. . . .

Secondly . . . if we could break out of the kind of "culturally conditioned" ways we have read the Bible, we could find it an explosive arsenal of material for creative change. . . . When the Bible talks about good news for the poor we immediately interpret that to mean the spiritually poor. . . . Now, I am sure that is part of what was meant, but it seems to me very clear what is also meant [is] that when Jesus is talking about the poor, he also meant the materially poor, the really impoverished, who do not have enough to eat, . . . who do not have enough power. . . .

The third thing the moral minority could stress, perhaps the most important thing in the time in which we live, would be the necessity of a global perspective. This world is now just too small to allow for anything else. And to look at the world simply in terms of what is good for the United States is ultimately going to be self-defeating. To put the main stress and priority on more weapons, as the national debate is now suggesting, is truly likely to increase the likelihood that we will use them. . . .

That suggests a fourth thing the moral minority might become; it could become that group in our society which is genuinely committed to the powerless and voiceless.

---

[2] The emperor Constantine the Great in the fourth century A.D. made Christianity the supreme religion of the Roman world—ED.

. . . [T]he church . . . must be that place where the voiceless are empowered to speak on their own behalf, and are guaranteed a hearing. . . .

Fifth, and finally, a moral minority must . . . set its own agendas. . . . Our agendas must not be set by the Moral Majority movement. We must not fall into the trap of single-issue politics. . . . I find it kind of morally oppressive to be told, again and again, some kind of obsession about other people's sex life [*sic*] is the burning issue of the day, when the majority of the human family went to bed hungry every night or to be told to rally around getting prayers back into schools when millions of people are unable to find jobs, or get minimal help if they are unemployed and disadvantaged. . . . [T]he whole human family is hurting from the mad escalation of the arms race, the need for more equitable distribution of food, coming to terms with denials, both abroad and home, of basic human rights, such as education and medical care and jobs and all the rest.

I think we need to rally around these problems in a context which provides a forum for seeking the good of all, not just small segments of the population. We must try to present issues without demagoguery cheating. We must acknowledge that problems are complex and that simplistic solutions will be misleading and wrong, and acknowledge also that ambiguities abound not only within the positions of those with whom we disagree, but within our own positions as well. With some such way of engaging in political life, we might be able to create a moral minority that could propose convictions without arrogance but insight without absolutism, with commitment but without coercion and with democracy but without demagoguery.

CHAPTER 18

The War on Terror

On September 11, 2001, terrorist attacks shattered assumptions of national security that Americans had taken for granted for centuries. Across the United States and around the world, billions watched in shock and disbelief as thousands of lives and billions of dollars worth of property were lost. While most of the human community viewed the events with a genuine sense of horror, in certain places militant leaders urged on jubilant mobs, proclaiming that not only had American power and the forces of modernization been dealt a serious blow, but that many more such attacks would follow altering the world's balance of power. In the days following the attacks, Americans tried to sort out seemingly incomprehensible facts and complex emotions in a new world that seemed permanently changed. The then president George W. Bush quickly declared "War on Terror," and Congress promptly passed legislation authorizing him to deploy American military forces into combat. The president charged that an "axis of evil" consisting of governments hostile to the United States was determined to challenge national security. Americans were introduced to a new generation of international adversaries led by leaders like Osama bin-Laden, Saddam Hussein, and militant regimes like the Taliban in Afghanistan and multinational paramilitary groups like al Qaeda and Hezbollah. Increased security measures transformed domestic life, with transportation systems and big cities, particularly New York, being most dramatically affected. Despite spending billions of dollars to reorganize the federal government and create the new Department of Homeland Security, Americans continued to feel nervous as anthrax attacks and "the DC Sniper" kept tensions high. Month after month, Tom Ridge, the new Secretary of Homeland Security, issued new "terror alerts" and developed a security risk warning system that announced daily levels of danger. Although the system was designed to communicate intelligence to local law enforcement authorities, media coverage reminded Americans of their vulnerabilities on a regular basis. In the months that followed, the United States engaged in two major military operations, one in Afghanistan and one in Iraq. In both instances President Bush asserted that regimes hostile to the United States and its allies had to be overthrown. American armed forces quickly accomplished these goals, but in both countries, reconstructing stable governments, functional economies, and democratic cultures proved far more difficult to achieve. America would continue to act as a superpower and assert its role in world leadership, but the road would be long and the cost would be great. The mobilization of resources to prosecute the War on Terror would cost billions of dollars, create massive deficits, and compound historic levels of public debt to be borne by generations of Americans to come. Furthermore, the plan proved to create more problems than it solved: Deposing militant Sunnite Regimes in Iraq and Afghanistan destabilized the regional balance of power and ended local encirclement of a far more formidable opponent: Shi'ite Iran. Years later, as the decade ended, Americans found themselves hopelessly mired in increasingly unpopular conflicts in Iraq and Afghanistan and ever more threatened by a militant regime in Iran determined to deploy nuclear weapons, attack Israel, and provide direct and covert assistance to radical Islamist parties throughout the world. As early as 2004, the bipartisan and authorized report of the 9/11 Commission admitted and outlined deep flaws in the American response to the attacks. In analyzing this chapter, try to assess what do you think were the most important concerns of American key policy makers at the time.

18.1 AMERICA'S RESPONSE TO TERROR (2001)

In this group of selections, America's leaders respond to the September 11 attacks. First the president makes a brief statement on September 11 after the attacks. The next selection is Congress's succinct action in response to the president's request to address the crisis. What powers did Congress grant the President? How did Americans come to understand the causes and consequences of these tragic events? What courses of action were available to them in responding to the crisis? The War in Iraq emerged as a major component of the President's efforts to take the fight against terrorists to them on their own ground, but the early optimism over combat operations in Iraq as expressed by President Bush in the next selection quickly gave way to pessimism. Next, Secretary of Defense Rumsfeld outlines the vast scope and spectacular anticipated cost of the American War in Iraq, and, finally, the official 911 Commission reports on numerous aspects of the complexity of the War on Terror. To what extent has the War on Terror consumed American resources? Has the effort been worthwhile? Were military objectives clearly outlined? What unforeseen consequences emerged from the complexity of issues involved?

ADDRESS BY GEORGE W. BUSH, PRESIDENT OF THE UNITED STATES

Delivered to the Nation, Washington, DC, September 11, 2001

Good evening. Today, our fellow citizens, our way of life, our very freedom came under attack in a series of deliberate and deadly terrorist acts. The victims were in airplanes, or in their offices; secretaries, businessmen and women, military and federal workers; moms and dads, friends and neighbors. Thousands of lives were suddenly ended by evil, despicable acts of terror. The pictures of airplanes flying into buildings,

---

Address by George W. Bush, President of the United States, Delivered to the Nation, Washington, DC, September 11, 2001, cited from *Vital Speeches of the Day*, Vol. LXVII, October 1, 2001.

fires burning, huge structures collapsing have filled us with disbelief, terrible sadness, and a quiet, unyielding anger. These acts of mass murder were intended to frighten our nation into chaos and retreat. But they have failed; our country is strong.

A great people has been moved to defend a great nation. Terrorist attacks can shake the foundations of our biggest buildings, but they cannot touch the foundation of America. These acts shattered steel, but they cannot dent the steel of American resolve. America was targeted for attack because we're the brightest beacon for freedom and opportunity in the world. And no one will keep that light from shining.

Today, our nation saw evil, the very worst of human nature. And we responded with the best of America—with the daring of our rescue workers, with the caring for strangers and neighbors who came to give blood and help in any way they could.

Immediately following the first attack, I implemented our government's emergency response plans. Our military is powerful, and it's prepared. Our emergency teams are working in New York City and Washington, D.C. to help with local rescue efforts.

Our first priority is to get help to those who have been injured, and to take every precaution to protect our citizens at home and around the world from further attacks.

The functions of our government continue without interruption. Federal agencies in Washington, which had to be evacuated today, are reopening for essential personnel tonight, and will be open for business tomorrow. Our financial institutions remain strong, and the American economy will be open for business, as well.

The search is underway for those who are behind these evil acts. I've directed the full resources of our intelligence and law enforcement communities to find those responsible and to bring them to justice. We will make no distinction between the terrorists who committed these acts and those who harbor them.

I appreciate so very much the members of Congress who have joined me in strongly condemning these attacks. And on behalf of the American people, I thank the many world leaders who have called to offer their condolences and assistance.

America and our friends and allies join with all those who want peace and security in the world, and we stand together to win the war against terrorism. Tonight, I ask for your prayers for all those who grieve, for the children whose worlds have been shattered, for all whose sense of safety and security has been threatened. And I pray they will be comforted by a power greater than any of us, spoken through the ages in Psalm 23: "Even though I walk through the valley of the shadow of death, I fear no evil, for You are with me."

This is a day when all Americans from every walk of life unite in our resolve for justice and peace. America has stood down enemies before, and we will do so this time. None of us will ever forget this day. Yet, we go forward to defend freedom and all that is good and just in our world. Thank you. Good night, and God bless America.

Senate Joint Resolution 23
Authorization for Use of Military Force

September 14, 2001

Public Law No. 107-40

Joint Resolution

To authorize the use of United States Armed Forces against those responsible for the recent attacks launched against the United States.

Whereas, on September 11, 2001, acts of treacherous violence were committed against the United States and its citizens; and

Whereas, such acts render it both necessary and appropriate that the United States exercise its rights to self-defense and to protect United States citizens both at home and abroad; and

Whereas, in light of the threat to the national security and foreign policy of the United States posed by these grave acts of violence; and

Whereas, such acts continue to pose an unusual and extraordinary threat to the national security and foreign policy of the United States; and

Whereas, the President has authority under the Constitution to take action to deter and prevent acts of international terrorism against the United States: Now, therefore be it

Resolved by the Senate and House of Representatives of the United States of America in Congress assembled,

Section 1.   Short Title.

This joint resolution may be cited as the "Authorization for Use of Military Force."

Sec. 2. Authorization for Use of United States Armed Forces.

(a) IN GENERAL—That the President is authorized to use all necessary and appropriate force against those nations, organizations, or persons he determines planned, authorized, committed, or aided the terrorist attacks that occurred on September 11, 2001, or harbored such organizations or persons, in order to prevent any future acts of international terrorism against the United States by such nations, organizations or persons.

(b) War Powers Resolutions Requirements—

(1) SPECIFIC STATUTORY AUTHORIZATION—Consistent with section 8(a)(1) of the War Powers Resolution, the Congress declares that this section is intended to constitute specific statutory authorization within the meaning of section 5(b) of the War Powers Resolution.

(2) APPLICABILITY OF OTHER REQUIREMENTS—Nothing in this resolution supercedes [sic] any requirement of the War Powers Resolution.

COMBAT OPERATIONS IN IRAQ HAVE ENDED: THOSE IN DARKNESS MAY BE FREE

President George W. Bush

Delivered to the Nation from the USS Abraham Lincoln, At Sea Off the Coast of San Diego, California, May 1, 2003

Thank you all very much. Admiral Kelly, Captain Card, officers and sailors of the USS Abraham Lincoln, my fellow Americans: Major combat operations in Iraq have ended.

"Combat Operations in Iraq Have Ended: Those in Darkness May Be Free," President George W. Bush speech delivered to the Nation from the USS *Abraham Lincoln*, at sea off the coast of San Diego, California, May 1, 2003. Cited from *Vital Speeches of the Day*, Vol. 69, May 15, 2003.

In the battle of Iraq, the United States and our allies have prevailed. And now our coalition is engaged in securing and reconstructing that country.

In this battle, we have fought for the cause of liberty, and for the peace of the world. Our nation and our coalition are proud of this accomplishment—yet, it is you, the members of the United States military, who achieved it. Your courage, your willingness to face danger for your country and for each other, made this day possible. Because of you, our nation is more secure. Because of you, the tyrant has fallen, and Iraq is free.

Operation Iraqi Freedom was carried out with a combination of precision and speed and boldness the enemy did not expect, and the world had not seen before. From distant bases or ships at sea, we sent planes and missiles that could destroy an enemy division, or strike a single bunker. Marines and soldiers charged to Baghdad across 350 miles of hostile ground, in one of the swiftest advances of heavy arms in history. You have shown the world the skill and the might of the American Armed Forces.

This nation thanks all the members of our coalition who joined in a noble cause. We thank the Armed Forces of the United Kingdom, Australia, and Poland, who shared in the hardships of war. We thank all the citizens of Iraq who welcomed our troops and joined the liberation of their own country. And tonight, I have a special word for Secretary Rumsfeld, for General Franks, and for all the men and women who wear the uniform of the United States: America is grateful for a job well done.

The character of our military through history—the daring of Normandy, the fierce courage of Iwo Jima, the decency and idealism that turned enemies into allies—is fully present in this generation. When Iraqi civilians looked into the faces of our servicemen and women, they saw strength and kindness and goodwill. When I look at the members of the United States military, I see the best of our country, and I'm honored to be your Commander-in-Chief.

In the images of falling statues, we have witnessed the arrival of a new era. For a hundred of years of war, culminating in the nuclear age, military technology was designed and deployed to inflict casualties on an ever-growing scale. In defeating Nazi Germany and Imperial Japan, Allied forces destroyed entire cities, while enemy leaders who started the conflict were safe until the final days. Military power was used to end a regime by breaking a nation.

Today, we have the greater power to free a nation by breaking a dangerous and aggressive regime. With new tactics and precision weapons, we can achieve military objectives without directing violence against civilians. No device of man can remove the tragedy from war; yet it is a great moral advance when the guilty have far more to fear from war than the innocent.

In the images of celebrating Iraqis, we have also seen the ageless appeal of human freedom. Decades of lies and intimidation could not make the Iraqi people love their oppressors or desire their own enslavement. Men and women in every culture need liberty like they need food and water and air. Everywhere that freedom arrives, humanity rejoices; and everywhere that freedom stirs, let tyrants fear.

We have difficult work to do in Iraq. We're bringing order to parts of that country that remain dangerous. We're pursuing and finding leaders of the old regime, who will be held to account for their crimes. We've begun the search for hidden chemical and biological weapons and already know of hundreds of sites that will be investigated. We're helping to rebuild Iraq, where the dictator built palaces for himself, instead of hospitals and schools. And we will stand with the new leaders of Iraq as they establish a government of, by, and for the Iraqi people.

The transition from dictatorship to democracy will take time, but it is worth every effort. Our coalition will stay until our work is done. Then we will leave, and we will leave behind a free Iraq.

The battle of Iraq is one victory in a war on terror that began on September the 11, 2001—and still goes on. That terrible morning, 19 evil men—the shock troops of a hateful ideology—gave America and the civilized world a glimpse of their ambitions. They imagined, in the words of one terrorist, that September the 11th would be the "beginning of the end of America." By seeking to turn our cities into killing fields, terrorists and their allies believed that they could destroy this nation's resolve, and force our retreat from the world. They have failed.

In the battle of Afghanistan, we destroyed the Taliban, many terrorists, and the camps where they trained. We continue to help the Afghan people lay roads, restore hospitals, and educate all of their children. Yet we also have dangerous work to complete. As I speak, a Special Operations task force, led by the 82nd Airborne, is on the trail of the terrorists and those who seek to undermine the free government of Afghanistan. America and our coalition will finish what we have begun.

From Pakistan to the Philippines to the Horn of Africa, we are hunting down al Qaeda killers. Nineteen months ago, I pledged that the terrorists would not escape the patient justice of the United States. And as of tonight, nearly one-half of al Qaeda's senior operatives have been captured or killed.

The liberation of Iraq is a crucial advance in the campaign against terror. We've removed an ally of al Qaeda, and cut off a source of terrorist funding. And this much is certain: No terrorist network will gain weapons of mass destruction from the Iraqi regime, because the regime is no more.

In these 19 months that changed the world, our actions have been focused and deliberate and proportionate to the offense. We have not forgotten the victims of September the 11th—the last phone calls, the cold murder of children, the searches in the rubble. With those attacks, the terrorists and their supporters declared war on the United States. And war is what they got.

Our war against terror is proceeding according to principles that I have made clear to all: Any person involved in committing or planning terrorist attacks against the American people becomes an enemy of this country, and a target of American justice.

Any person, organization, or government that supports, protects, or harbors terrorists is complicit in the murder of the innocent, and equally guilty of terrorist crimes.

Any outlaw regime that has ties to terrorist groups and seeks or possesses weapons of mass destruction is a grave danger to the civilized world—and will be confronted.

And anyone in the world, including the Arab world, who works and sacrifices for freedom has a loyal friend in the United States of America.

Our commitment to liberty is America's tradition—declared at our founding; affirmed in Franklin Roosevelt's Four Freedoms; asserted in the Truman Doctrine and in Ronald Reagan's challenge to an evil empire. We are committed to freedom in Afghanistan, in Iraq, and in a peaceful Palestine. The advance of freedom is the surest strategy to undermine the appeal of terror in the world. Where freedom takes hold, hatred gives way to hope. When freedom takes hold, men and women turn to the peaceful pursuit of a better life. American values and American interests lead in the same direction: We stand for human liberty.

The United States upholds these principles of security and freedom in many ways—with all the tools of diplomacy, law enforcement, intelligence, and finance. We're working with a broad coalition of nations that understand the threat and our shared responsibility to meet it. The use of force has been—and remains—our last resort. Yet all can know, friend and foe alike, that our nation has a mission: We will answer threats to our security, and we will defend the peace.

Our mission continues. Al Qaeda is wounded, not destroyed. The scattered cells of the terrorist network still operate in many nations, and we know from daily intelligence that they continue to plot against free people. The proliferation of deadly weapons remains a serious danger. The enemies of freedom are not idle, and neither are we. Our government has taken unprecedented measures to defend the homeland. And we will continue to hunt down the enemy before he can strike.

The war on terror is not over; yet it is not endless. We do not know the day of final victory, but we have seen the turning of the tide. No act of the terrorists will change our purpose, or weaken our resolve, or alter their fate. Their cause is lost. Free nations will press on to victory.

Other nations in history have fought in foreign lands and remained to occupy and exploit. Americans, following a battle, want nothing more than to return home. And that is your direction tonight. After service in the Afghan—and Iraqi theaters of war—after 100,000 miles, on the longest carrier deployment in recent history, you are homeward bound. Some of you will see new family members for the first time—150 babies were born while their fathers were on the Lincoln. Your families are proud of you, and your nation will welcome you.

We are mindful, as well, that some good men and women are not making the journey home. One of those who fell, Corporal Jason Mileo, spoke to his parents five days before his death. Jason's father said, "He called us from the center of Baghdad, not to brag, but to tell us he loved us. Our son was a soldier."

Every name, every life is a loss to our military, to our nation, and to the loved ones who grieve. There's no homecoming for these families. Yet we pray, in God's time, their reunion will come.

Those we lost were last seen on duty. Their final act on this Earth was to fight a great evil and bring liberty to others. All of you—all in this generation of our military—have taken up the highest calling of history. You're defending your country, and protecting the innocent from harm. And wherever you go, you carry a message of hope—a message that is ancient and ever new. In the words of the prophet Isaiah, "To the captives, 'come out,'—and to those in darkness, 'be free.' "

Thank you for serving our country and our cause. May God bless you all, and may God continue to bless America.

WHAT WE LEARNED FROM THE WAR: TRANSFORMATION TAKES MONEY

Donald Rumsfeld, Secretary of Defense

Statement for the Senate Appropriations Defense Subcommittee: 2004 Defense Budget Request, Washington, D.C., May 14, 2003

Mr. Chairman and Members of the Committee, thank you for this opportunity to update the Committee on our progress in strengthening the Department of Defense for the 21st century challenges, and to discuss the President's budget request for FY 2004–2009.

I also want to thank you and the members for your action on the President's emergency supplemental request for the global war on terror. Your prompt passage of that legislation will help to provide for our fighting men and women as they prosecute the global war on terror in the weeks and months ahead.

Our troops are doing a superb job and deserve our thanks for their courage and dedication to duty.

What coalition forces have accomplished in Operation Iraqi Freedom is remarkable. They crossed hundreds of miles in Iraq—facing death squads and dust storms—to liberate Baghdad in less than a month.

Today, because of coalition forces' tenacity and skill, the regime of Saddam Hussein is no longer—and the Iraqi people are free to determine their own destiny.

Visiting with the troops, I told them that what they accomplished will go down in the history books. And it will. But at the Department, we cannot afford to wait for history to be written. The threats we face in this dangerous new century are emerging, often without warning. We need to apply the lessons from the experience in Iraq to transform how the Department and the Services organize, train and equip for the 21st century.

The "lessons learned" process for Operation Iraqi Freedom is well underway. It will likely impact budgets and procedures, training and doctrine, and the security of our country for some years to come. But even now, while that process is still in its early stages, we can already see that the experience in Iraq has validated a number of the strategic decisions that were made in our defense reviews over the past two years—decisions that drove the development of this 2004 budget.

Consider a few of those lessons:

One lesson is that speed matters. Coalition forces pressed through Southern Iraq in a matter of weeks, racing towards Baghdad. The enemy was unable to mount a coherent defense, use WMD, attack neighboring countries with SCUD missiles, destroy oil wells, or blow up dams, bridges and infrastructure—in part, we believe—because the coalition advance was so fast. This experience highlights the value of capabilities that can move quickly into theater and reach targets with speed and agility.

Another is the importance of intelligence—and the ability to act on that intelligence rapidly. In Iraq, using "Time Sensitive Targeting Cells," the coalition was able to

---

"Transformation Takes Money," statement by Donald Rumsfeld, Secretary of Defense, to the Senate Appropriations Defense Subcommittee: 2004 Defense Budget Request, Washington, DC, May 14, 2003. Cited from *Vital Speeches of the Day*, Vol. 69, June 1, 2003.

launch attacks on enemy targets, in some cases within 20 minutes of receiving the intelligence information. Planes taking off for bombing runs on occasion did not receive their targeting information until they were in the air and well on their way. Ground forces were able to stay "in contact" with the enemy forces, and attack them with great effect, even as those forces made every effort to avoid contact. The success of these efforts in Operation Iraqi Freedom validates the recommendation in this budget for increased investments in command, control, communications, intelligence, and persistent surveillance.

Another is the importance of precision. The capabilities employed in Iraq were discreet. One new weapon used for the first time in Iraq—a "thermobaric" Hellfire missile—can take out the first floor of a building without damaging the floors above, and is capable of reaching around corners, into niches and behind walls to strike enemy forces hiding in caves, bunkers and hardened multi-room complexes. It went from development to deployment in less than a year. Coalition military planners also used a sophisticated computer model to determine the precise direction, angle of attack and type of weapon needed to destroy a desired target, while sparing nearby civilian facilities.

This unprecedented precision allowed the coalition to fight this war with unprecedented care—protecting innocent lives while delivering devastating damage to the Iraqi regime. There was no refugee crisis because Iraqis felt safe to stay in the cities as long as they stayed clear of military targets. As a result, the Iraqi people saw that this war was being waged not against a country, or a people or a religion, but against a regime—and that we were coming not as conquerors but as liberators. We believe these experiences support the decision to request increases in the 2004 budget for research, development, testing and evaluation, and for procurement, as well as the decision to change how we develop those new capabilities—by employing "spiral development" to allow us to bring new weapons to the field in months or years instead of decades.

Another lesson in Iraq was the importance of joint operations. U.S. forces did not fight as individual deconflicted services. Instead, they fought as a truly joint force. One example is the rescue of Pfc. Jessica Lynch—it was made possible by a joint team of Navy SEALs, Army Rangers, Marines, and Air Force Special operators—with the help of an Iraqi citizen. The joint war fighting experience in Iraq supports the request in the 2004 budget to make new investments in joint training and in joint war fighting capabilities.

Another lesson was the critical importance of special operations forces. In Iraq, special operators were the first coalition forces to hit the ground—some of them before the war formally began—with hundreds more pouring into Western Iraq and other regions just before the ground invasion—securing airfields, attacking terrorist facilities and regime targets, and taking out the regime's capability to launch attacks against neighboring countries. These experiences—as well as the remarkable performance of special operators in Afghanistan—support the decisions to transform the Special Operations Command and to request needed new investments in Special Operations in the 2004 budget.

There will be other important lessons as we study Operation Iraqi Freedom. But the point is this: the 2004 budget was developed with warfare of this kind in mind—and the experiences in fighting this war have confirmed the decisions made in the defense review which are reflected in the budget before the Committee today.

Mr. Chairman, over the past two years, the senior civilian and military leaders of the Department have been working to determine how DoD can best transform to meet the changing threats of a new century. Together we have:

- Fashioned a new defense strategy.
- Replaced the decade-old two Major Theater War approach to sizing our forces with an approach more appropriate for the 21st century.
- Developed a new approach to balancing risks that takes into account the risks in contingency plans and also the risks to the force, to modernization and to transformation.
- Reorganized the Department to better focus our space activities.
- Adopted a new Unified Command Plan, which establishes the new Northern Command to better defend the homeland; a Joint Forces Command that focuses on transformation; and a new Strategic Command responsible for early warning of, and defense against, missile attack and the conduct of long-range attacks.
- Expanded the mission of the Special Operations Command, so that it can not only support missions directed by the regional combatant commanders, but also plan and execute its own missions in the global war on terror.
- Worked with Allies to develop a new NATO command structure and begin the development of a NATO Response Force that must be able to deploy in days and weeks, instead of months.
- Taken steps to attract and retain needed skills in the Armed Forces, with targeted pay raises and quality of life improvements.
- Reorganized and revitalized the missile defense research, development and testing program, freed from the constraints of the ABM Treaty.
- Completed the Nuclear Posture Review, with a new approach to deterrence that will enhance our security, while permitting historic deep reductions in offensive nuclear weapons.
- Moved from a "threat-based" to a "capabilities-based" approach to defense planning, focusing not only on who might threaten us, or where, or when—but also on how we might be threatened, and what portfolio of capabilities we will need to deter and defend against those new asymmetric threats.

These are significant changes. Last year's budget—the 2003 request—was finalized just as this defense review process was nearing completion. So while it included a top-line increase, and made important and long-delayed investments in readiness, people, maintenance, and replacement of aging systems and facilities, we were only able to begin funding some transforming initiatives as the new defense strategy came into focus.

But this year's budget—the 2004 request before you today—is the first to fully reflect the new defense strategies and policies and the lessons of the global war on terror.

Our defense review identified six goals that drive our transformation efforts:

- First, we must be able to defend the U.S. homeland and bases of operation overseas;
- Second, we must be able to project and sustain forces in distant theaters;
- Third, we must be able to deny enemies sanctuary;
- Fourth, we must improve our space capabilities and maintain unhindered access to space;

- Fifth, we must harness our substantial advantages in information technology to link up different kinds of U.S. forces, so they can fight jointly; and
- Sixth, we must be able to protect U.S. information networks from attack—and to disable the information networks of our adversaries.

The President's 2004 budget requests funds for investments that will support these transformational goals. For example:

- For programs to help defend the U.S. homeland and bases of operation overseas—such as missile defense—we are requesting $7.9 billion in the 2004 budget, and $55 billion over the Future Years Defense Program (FYDP).
- For programs to project and sustain forces in distant theaters—such as the new unmanned underwater vehicle program and the Future Combat Systems—we are requesting $8 billion in 2004, and $96 billion over the FYDP.
- For programs to deny enemies sanctuary—such as unmanned combat aerial vehicles, and the conversion of SSBN to SSGN submarines—we are requesting $5.2 billion in 2004 and $49 billion over the FYDP.
- For programs to enhance U.S. space capabilities—such as Space Control Systems—we are requesting $300 million in 2004 and $5 billion over the FYDP.
- For programs to harness our advantages in information technology—such as laser satellite communications, Joint Tactical Radio, and the Deployable Joint Command and Control System—we are requesting $2.7 billion in 2004 and $28 billion over the FYDP.
- For programs to protect U.S. information networks and attack those of our adversaries—such as the Air and Space Operations Center—we are requesting $200 million in 2004 and $6 billion over the FYDP.

Over the next six years, we have proposed a 30% increase in procurement funding and a 65% increase in funding for research, development, testing and evaluation (RDT&E) above the 2002 baseline budget—an investment of roughly $150 billion annually.

In addition to these increases, RDT&E spending will rise from 36% to 42% of the overall investment budget. This shift reflects a decision to accept some near-term risk in order to accelerate the development of needed next generation systems.

Among the more important transformational investments we propose is a request for funds to establish a new Joint National Training Capability. As we saw in Iraq, wars in the 21st century will be fought jointly. Yet too often our forces still train and prepare for war as individual services. That needs to change.

To ensure that U.S. forces train like they fight and fight like they train, we have budgeted $1.8 billion over the next six years to fund range improvement and permit more of both live and virtual joint training—an annual investment of $300 million.

The total investment in transforming military capabilities in the 2004 request is $24.3 billion, and about $240 billion over the FYDP.

We propose not only transforming the capabilities at our disposal, but also the way we develop new capabilities. The old way was to develop a picture of the perfect system, and then build the system to meet that vision of perfection, however long it took or cost. The result was that, as technology advanced, and with it dreams of what a perfect system could do, capabilities were taking longer and longer to develop and the cost of systems increased again and again: Time is money.

A different approach is to start with the basics, simpler items, and roll out early models faster—and then add capabilities to the basic system as they become available. This is what the private sector does—companies bring a new car or aircraft on line, for example, and then update it over a period of years with new designs and technologies. We need to do the same.

Take, for example, the approach to ballistic missile defense. Instead of taking a decade or more to develop someone's vision of a "perfect" shield, we have instead decided to develop and put in place a rudimentary system by 2004—one which should make us somewhat safer than we are now—and then build on that foundation with increasingly effective capabilities as the technologies mature.

We intend to apply this "spiral development" approach to a number of systems, restructured programs and new starts alike over the course of the FYDP. The result should be that new capabilities will be available faster, so we can better respond to fast moving adversaries and newly emerging threats.

Balancing Risk

Even as we accept some increased near-term risk so we can prepare for the future, this budget also recognizes that new and unexpected dangers will likely be waiting just over the horizon—and that we must be flexible to face them.

That is why the 2004 budget requests increased investments in critical areas such as readiness, quality of life improvements for the men and women in uniform, and to make certain existing capabilities are properly maintained and replenished.

Over the next six years, the President has requested a 15% increase for Military Personnel accounts, above the 2002 baseline budget, and an increase in funding for family housing by 10% over the same period. The 2004 budget includes $1 billion for targeted military pay raises, ranging from 2% to 6.25%. Out of pocket expenses for those living in private housing drop from 7.5% to 3.5% in 2004, and are on a path to total elimination by 2005.

Over the next six years, we have requested a 20% increase for Operations and Maintenance accounts above the 2002 baseline budget. We have proposed $40 billion for readiness of all the services and $6 billion for facilities sustainment over the same period.

These investments should stabilize funding for training, spares and OPTEMPO, and put a stop to the past practice of raiding the investment accounts to pay for the immediate operations and maintenance needs, so we stop robbing the future to pay today's urgent bills.

In our 2004 request:

- We increased the shipbuilding budget by $2.7 billion, making good on our hope last year that we could increase shipbuilding from five to seven ships.
- We increased the Special Operations budget by $1.5 billion, to pay for equipment lost in the global war on terror and for an additional 1,890 personnel.
- We increased military and civilian pay by $3.7 billion.
- We increased missile defense by $1.5 billion, including increased funds for research and development of promising new technologies, and to deploy a small number of interceptors beginning in 2004.

The President has asked Congress for a total of $379.9 billion for fiscal year 2004—a $15.3 billion increase over last year's budget. That is a large amount of the taxpayers' hard-earned money. But even that increase only moves us part of the way.

Our challenge is to do three difficult things at once:

- Win the global war on terror;
- Prepare for the threats we will face later this decade; and
- Continue transforming for the threats we will face in 2010 and beyond.

Any one of those challenges is difficult—and expensive. Taking on all three, as we must, required us to make tough choices between competing demands—which meant that, inevitably, some desirable capabilities do not get funded. For example:

- Despite the significant increase in shipbuilding, we did not get the shipbuilding rate up to the desired steady state of 10 ships per year. Because of planned retirements of other ships, we will drop below a 300-ship fleet during the course of the FYDP. The Navy is in the process of transforming, and has two studies underway for amphibious ships and for submarines. We have increased shipbuilding in 2004, but we do not want to lock ourselves into a shipbuilding program now until we know precisely which ships we will want to build in the out-years.
- We have not been able to modernize our tactical air forces fast enough to reduce the average age of our aircraft fleet.
- We have had to delay elimination of all inadequate family housing by 2007—though we got close!
- We have not fully resolved our so-called "high-demand/low density" problems—systems like JSTARS, which, because they have been chronically under funded in the past, will still be in short supply in this budget.
- We opted not to modernize a number of legacy programs—taking on some near-term risks to fund transforming capabilities we will need in this fast moving world.
- We did not achieve the level of growth in the Science and Technology (S&T) accounts we had hoped for. Our request is $10.2 billion, or 2.69% of the 2004 budget.
- We have delayed investments to completely fix the recapitalization rate for DoD infrastructure. We still intend to get the rate down from 148 years to 67 years by 2008, and we expect to accelerate facilities investments in 2006 after we have made the needed decisions with respect to the appropriate base structure, at home and abroad. We are reviewing our worldwide base structure, and starting the steps to prepare for the 2005 BRAC. We want to think carefully about how best to match our base structure and force structure.

That's the bad news. But there is good news as well. In making those difficult decisions, we believe we made better choices this year because we followed the new approach to balancing risks that we developed in last year's defense review—an approach that takes into account not just the risks in operations and contingency plans, but also the risks to our force—the people, and risks to modernization and to the future risks that, in the past, often had been crowded out by more immediate pressing demands. The result, we believe, is a more balanced approach and a more coherent program.

To help free resources, the services have stepped up, and will be canceling, slowing or restructuring a number of programs so they can invest those savings in transforming capabilities. For example:

- The Army came up with savings of some $22 billion over the six-year FYDP, by terminating 24 systems, including Crusader, the Bradley A3 and Abrams upgrades and reducing or restructuring another 24, including Medium Tactical Vehicles. The Army used these savings to help pay for new transformational capabilities, such as the Future Combat Systems.
- The Navy reallocated nearly $39 billion over the FYDP, by retiring 26 ships and 259 aircraft, and merging the Navy and Marine air forces. They invested these savings in new ship designs and aircraft.
- The Air Force shifted funds and changed its business practices to account for nearly $21 billion over the FYDP. It will tire 114 fighter and 115 mobility/tanker aircraft. The savings will be invested in readiness, people, modernization and new system starts and cutting edge systems like unmanned aerial vehicles (UAVs) and unmanned combat aerial vehicles (UCAVs).

In all, by retiring or restructuring less urgent programs, we believe we can achieve savings of some $80 billion over the FYDP—money that will be reinvested by the services in capabilities for the 21st century.

We feel a deep obligation to not waste the taxpayers' dollars. We need to show the taxpayers that we are willing to stop doing things that we don't need to be doing, and take that money and put it into investments we do need.

As you consider this budget, I am sure you will hear pleading for a number of programs—and plausible arguments for why this or that program should be saved or funded at a higher rate. I suspect some may disagree with decisions that have been made, and may want to make changes in this budget proposal. As a former Member of Congress, I recognize that the Congress is Article 1 of the Constitution—the President proposes and Congress disposes. But it is also important that, as the Committee considers potential changes, it recognizes that this budget has been crafted to balance a number of risks. And with every change, that balance of risks is affected.

This is not to suggest that the budget before you is perfect—no one has a monopoly on wisdom. And there are numerous examples of instances when Congress pressed the executive branch to invest in programs—such as JSTARS and UAVs—that later proved critical. What I am suggesting is that if changes are made, they be made in a coherent way—that we talk them through, and that the decisions be made with a full understanding of the effects they may have—not only on the program in question, but the costs in terms of the investments in other areas that will be put off as a result.

We have done our best to develop this budget with what we believe has been unprecedented transparency—providing detailed briefings to those interested in defense here on Capital Hill. Congress was not simply presented with the President's budget—it was kept in the loop as decisions were being made. I am told that the extent of consultation from the Defense Department to the Congress this year has been unprecedented. We hope that this spirit of openness and cooperation will continue as Congress deliberates— so that the final budget is crafted in a way that preserves the balance of risks.

Our hope is that, with this budget, we can further transform not only our military capabilities, but also the relationship between the Defense Department and the Congress—by establishing a new spirit of trust and cooperation.

Results

As a result of these strategic investments and decisions, we can now see the effects of transforming begin to unfold. Consider just some of the changes that are taking place:

- Today, the missile defense research, development and testing program has been revitalized and we are on track for limited land/sea deployment in 2004–5.
- Today, the Space Based Radar, which will help provide near-persistent 24/7/365 coverage of the globe, is scheduled to be ready in 2012.
- In this budget, we believe SBIRS-High is properly funded.
- Today, we are converting 4 Trident SSBN subs into conventional SSGNs, capable of delivering special forces and cruise missiles to denied areas.
- Today, we are proposing to build the CVN-21 aircraft carder in 2007, which will include many new capabilities that were previously scheduled to be introduced only in 2011.
- Today, instead of 1 UCAV program in development, the X45, which was designed for a limited mission of suppression of enemy air defense, we have set up competition among a number of programs that should produce UCAVs able to conduct a broad range of missions.
- Today, we are revitalizing the B-1 fleet by reducing its size and using savings to modernize remaining aircraft with precision weapons, self-protection systems, and reliability upgrades—and thanks to these efforts, we are told the B-1 now has the highest mission capable rates in the history of the program.
- Today, in place of the Crusader, the Army is building a new family of precision artillery—including precision munitions and Non-Line-of-Sight Cannon for the Future Combat Systems.
- Today, we have seen targeted pay raises and other reforms help retain mid-career officers and NCOs, so that fewer of them leave the service while still in their prime, so the country can continue to benefit from their talent and experience.

These are positive changes that will ensure that our country will have the capabilities needed to defend our people, as well as a menu of choices from which we can select to shape the direction of the Department, as the 21st century security environment continues to change and evolve.

Defense Transformation Act

Finally, Mr. Chairman, we can't truly transform, unless we have the ability to better manage this Department. To win the global war on terror, our forces need to be flexible, light and agile—so they can respond quickly to sudden changes. The same is true of the men and women who support them in the Department of Defense. They also need flexibility—so they can move money, shift people, and design and buy new weapons more rapidly, and respond to the continuing changes in our security environment.

Today, we do not have that kind of agility. In an age when terrorists move information at the speed of an email, money at the speed of a wire transfer, and people at the speed of a commercial jetliner, the Defense Department is bogged down in the bureaucratic processes of the industrial age—not the information age.

Some of our difficulties are self-imposed by the Department, to be sure. Others, however, are the result of law and regulation. Together they have created a culture that too often stifles innovation. Consider just a few of the obstacles we face each day:

- This department spends an average of $42 million an hour, and yet we are not allowed to move $15 million from one account to another without getting permission from four to six committees, a process that sometimes takes months.
- Instead of being streamlined for the fast-paced 21st century, the defense authorization bill has grown with each passing year. Just consider the changes over my brief career:
- When I was first elected to Congress in 1962, the defense authorization bill was one page.
- The last time I was Secretary of Defense, a quarter of a century ago, the 1977 authorization bill had grown to 16 pages.
- When I came back to the Pentagon for this second tour, the 2001 authorization bill had grown to 534 pages.
- I can't even imagine what it will look like in another 25 years.
- Today we have some 320,000 uniformed people doing what are essentially non-military jobs. And yet we are calling up Reserves to help deal with the global war on terror. The inability to put civilians in hundreds of thousands of jobs that do not need to be performed by men and women in uniform puts unnecessary strain on our uniformed personnel and added cost to the taxpayers. This has to be fixed.
- The department is required to prepare and submit some 26,000 pages of justification, and over 800 required reports to Congress each year—many of marginal value, I am sure many not read, consuming hundreds of thousands of man-hours to develop, and untold number of trees destroyed.
- Despite 128 acquisition reform studies, we have a system in the Defense Department that since 1975 has doubled the time it takes to produce a new weapons system, in an era when new technologies are arriving in years and months, not decades.

The point is this: we are fighting the first wars of the 21st century with a Defense Department that was fashioned to meet the challenges of the mid-20th century. We have an industrial age organization, yet we are living in an information age world, where new threats emerge suddenly, often without warning, to surprise us. We cannot afford not to change and rapidly, if we hope to live successfully in this new world.

The Department is already engaged in substantial transformation. We have reduced management and headquarters staffs by 11 percent. We have streamlined the acquisition process by eliminating hundreds of pages of unnecessary rules and self-imposed red tape. And we have begun implementing a new business management structure. These internal changes are important—but they are not enough. We also need legislative relief.

Our legislative proposal, the Defense Transformation Act for the 21st Century, would give the Department some of the needed flexibility, and ability to more rapidly move resources, shift people and bring new weapons systems on line more quickly, so we can adapt to changing events.

Among the provisions in this legislation:

- We have proposed more flexible rules for the flow of money through the Department to give us the ability to respond to urgent needs as they emerge.
- We have proposed elimination of some of the more onerous regulations that make it difficult or virtually impossible for many small businesses to do business with the Department of Defense.
- We have proposed expanded authority for competitive outsourcing so that we can get military personnel out of non-military tasks and back into the field.
- We have proposed measures that would protect our military training ranges so that our men and women will be able to continue to train as they fight while honoring our steadfast commitment to protecting the environment.
- We have proposed measures for transforming our system of personnel management, so that we can gain more flexibility and agility in how we manage the more than 700,000 civilians who provide the Department such vital support. We need a performance-based promotion system for our civilian workforce that rewards excellence just like the one Congress insisted on for our men and women in uniform.

In other U.S. Government agencies, major portions of the national workforce have already been freed from archaic rules and regulations. We need similar relief. If the Department of Defense is to prepare for the security challenges of 21st century, we must transform not just our defense strategies, our military capabilities, and the way we deter and defend, but also the way we conduct our daily business.

Transformation is not an event—it is a process. There is no point at which the Defense Department will move from being "untransformed" to "transformed." Our goal is to set in motion a process and a culture that will keep the United States several steps ahead of potential adversaries.

To do that we need not only resources, but equally, we need the flexibility to use them with speed and agility, so we can respond quickly to the new threats we will face as this century unfolds. Thank you Mr. Chairman.

FINAL REPORT OF THE NATIONAL COMMISSION ON TERRORIST ATTACKS UPON THE UNITED STATES

Authorized Edition Ny: www.norton Company, 2004, page 330–33.

10.2 Planning for War

. . . By late in the evening of September 11, the President had addressed the nation on the terrible events of the day. Vice President Cheney described the President's mood as somber. The long day was not yet over. When the larger meeting that included his domestic department heads broke up, President Bush chaired a smaller meeting of top advisers, a group he would later call his "war council." This group usually included Vice President Cheney, Secretary of State Powell, Secretary of Defense Donald Rumsfeld, General Hugh Shelton, Vice Chairman of the Joint Chiefs (later to become chairman) General Myers, DCI Tenet, Attorney General Ashcroft, and FBI Director Robert Mueller. From the White House staff, National Security Advisor Condoleezza

Rice and Chief of Staff Card were part of the core group, often joined by their deputies, Stephen Hadley and Joshua Bolten.

In this restricted National Security Council meeting, the President said it was a time for self-defense. The United States would punish not just the perpetrators of the attacks, but also those who harbored them. Secretary Powell said the United States had to make it clear to Pakistan, Afghanistan, and the Arab states that the time to act was now. He said we would need to build a coalition. The President noted that the attacks provided a great opportunity to engage Russia and China. Secretary Rumsfeld urged the President and the principals to think broadly about who might have harbored the attackers, including Iraq, Afghanistan, Libya, Sudan, and Iran. He wondered aloud how much evidence the United States would need in order to deal with these countries, pointing out that major strikes could take up to 60 days to assemble.

President Bush chaired two more meetings of the NSC on September 12. In the first meeting, he stressed that the United States was at war with a new and different kind of enemy. The President tasked principals to go beyond their pre-9/11 work and develop a strategy to eliminate terrorists and punish those who support them. As they worked on defining the goals and objectives of the upcoming campaign, they considered a paper that went beyond al Qaeda to propose the "elimination of terrorism as a threat to our way of life," an aim that would include pursuing other international terrorist organizations in the Middle East.

Rice chaired a Principals Committee meeting on September 13 in the Situation Room to refine how the fight against al Qaeda would be conducted. The principals agreed that the overall message should be that anyone supporting al Qaeda would risk harm. The United States would need to integrate diplomacy, financial measures, intelligence, and military actions into an overarching strategy. The principals also focused on Pakistan and what it could do to turn the Taliban against al Qaeda. They concluded that if Pakistan decided not to help the United States, it too would be at risk.

The same day, Deputy Secretary of State Richard Armitage met with the Pakistani ambassador to the United States, Maleeha Lodhi, and the visiting head of Pakistan's military intelligence service, Mahmud Ahmed. Armitage said that the United States wanted Pakistan to take seven steps:

- to stop al Qaeda operatives at its border and end all logistical support for Bin Ladin;
- to give the United States blanket overflight and landing rights for all necessary military and intelligence operations;
- to provide territorial access to U.S. and allied military intelligence and other personnel to conduct operations against al Qaeda;
- to provide the United States with intelligence information;
- to continue to publicly condemn the terrorist acts;
- to cut off all shipments of fuel to the Taliban and stop recruits from going to Afghanistan; and,
- If the evidence implicated bin Ladin and al Qaeda and the Taliban continued to harbor them, to break relations with the Taliban government.

Pakistan made its decision swiftly. That afternoon, Secretary of State Powell announced at the beginning of an NSC meeting that Pakistani President Musharraf had agreed to every U.S. request for support in the war on terrorism. The next day, the U.S.

embassy in Islamabad confirmed that Musharraf and his top military commanders had agreed to all seven demands. "Pakistan will need full US support as it proceeds with us," the embassy noted, "Musharraf said the GOP [government of Pakistan] was making substantial concessions in allowing use of its territory and that he would pay a domestic price. His standing in Pakistan was certain to suffer. To counterbalance that he needed to show that Pakistan was benefiting from his decisions."

At the September 13 NSC meeting, when Secretary Powell described Pakistan's reply, President Bush led a discussion of an appropriate ultimatum to the Taliban. He also ordered Secretary Rumsfeld to develop a military plan against the Taliban. The President wanted the United States to strike the Taliban, step back, wait to see if they got the message, and hit them hard if they did not. He made clear that the military should focus on targets that would influence the Taliban's behavior.

President Bush also tasked the State Department, which on the following day delivered to the White House a paper titled "Game Plan for a Political-Military Strategy for Pakistan and Afghanistan." The paper took it as a given that Bin Ladin would continue to act against the United States even while under Taliban control. It therefore detailed specific U.S. demands for the Taliban: surrender Bin Ladin and his chief lieutenants, including Ayman al Zawahiri; tell the United States what the Taliban knew about al Qaeda and its operations; close all terrorist camps; free all imprisoned foreigners; and comply with all UN Security Council resolutions.

The State Department proposed delivering an ultimatum to the Taliban:

produce Bin Ladin and his deputies and shut down al Qaeda camps within 24 to 48 hours, or the United States will use all necessary means to destroy the terrorist infrastructure. The State Department did not expect the Taliban to comply. Therefore, State and Defense would plan to build an international coalition to go into Afghanistan. Both departments would consult with NATO and other allies and request intelligence, basing, and other support from countries, according to their capabilities and resources. Finally, the plan detailed a public U.S. stance: America would use all its resources to eliminate terrorism as a threat, punish those responsible for the 9/11 attacks, hold states and other actors responsible for providing sanctuary to terrorists, work with a coalition to eliminate terrorist groups and networks, and avoid malice toward any people, religion, or culture.

President Bush recalled that he quickly realized that the administration would have to invade Afghanistan with ground troops. But the early briefings to the President and Secretary Rumsfeld on military options were disappointing. Tommy Franks, the commanding general of Central Command (CENTCOM), told us that the President was dissatisfied. The U.S. military, Franks said, did not have an off-the-shelf plan to eliminate the al Qaeda threat in Afghanistan. The existing Infinite Resolve options did not, in his view, amount to such a plan.

All these diplomatic and military plans were reviewed over the weekend of September 15–16, as President Bush convened his war council at Camp David. Present were Vice President Cheney, Rice, Hadley, Powell, Armitage, Rumsfeld, Ashcroft, Mueller, Tenet, Deputy Secretary of Defense Paul Wolfowitz, and Cofer Black, chief of the DCI's Counterterrorist Center.

Tenet described a plan for collecting intelligence and mounting covert operations. He proposed inserting CIA teams into Afghanistan to work with Afghan warlords who would join the fight against al Qaeda. These CIA teams would act jointly with the military's Special Operations units. President Bush later praised this proposal, saying it had been a turning point in his thinking.

General Shelton briefed the principals on the preliminary plan for Afghanistan that the military had put together. It drew on the Infinite Resolve "phased campaign" plan the Pentagon had begun developing in November 2000 as an addition to the strike options it had been refining since 1998. But Shelton added a new element—the possible significant use of ground forces—and that is where President Bush reportedly focused his attention.

After hearing from his senior advisers, President Bush discussed with Rice the contents of the directives he would issue to set all the plans into motion. Rice prepared a paper that President Bush then considered with principals on Monday morning, September 17. "The purpose of this meeting," he recalled saying, "is to assign tasks for the first wave of the war against terrorism. It starts today."

In a written set of instructions slightly refined during the morning meeting, President Bush charged Ashcroft, Mueller, and Tenet to develop a plan for homeland defense. President Bush directed Secretary of State Powell to deliver an ultimatum to the Taliban along the lines that his department had originally proposed. The State Department was also tasked to develop a plan to stabilize Pakistan and to be prepared to notify Russia and countries near Afghanistan when hostilities were imminent.

In addition, Bush and his advisers discussed new legal authorities for covert action in Afghanistan, including the administration's first Memorandum of Notification on Bin Ladin. Shortly thereafter, President Bush authorized broad new authorities for the CIA.

President Bush instructed Rumsfeld and Shelton to develop further the Camp David military plan to attack the Taliban and al Qaeda if the Taliban rejected the ultimatum. The President also tasked Rumsfeld to ensure that robust measures to protect American military forces against terrorist attack were implemented worldwide. Finally, he directed Treasury Secretary Paul O'Neill to craft a plan to target al Qaeda's funding and seize its assets. NSC staff members had begun leading meetings on terrorist fund-raising by September 18.

Also by September 18, Powell had contacted 58 of his foreign counterparts and received offers of general aid, search-and-rescue equipment and personal, and medical assistance teams. On the same day, Deputy Secretary of State Armitage was called by Mahmud Ahmed regarding a two-day visit to Afghanistan during which the Pakistani intelligence chief had met with Mullah Omar and conveyed the U.S. demands. Omar's response was "not negative on all these points." But the administration knew that the Taliban was unlikely to turn over Bin Ladin.

The pre-9/11 draft presidential directive on al Qaeda evolved into a new directive, National Security Presidential Directive 9, now titled "Defeating the Terrorist Threat to the United States." The directive would now extend to a global war on terrorism, not just on al Qaeda. It also incorporated the President's determination not to distinguish between terrorists and those who harbor them. It included a determination to use military force if necessary to end al Qaeda's sanctuary in Afghanistan. The new directive—formally signed on October 25, after the fighting in Afghanistan had already begun—included new material followed by annexes discussing each targeted terrorist group. The old draft directive on al Qaeda became, in effect, the first annex. The United States would strive to eliminate all terrorist networks, dry up their financial support, and prevent them from acquiring weapons of mass destruction. The goal was the "elimination of terrorism as a threat to our way of life."

10.3 "Phase Two" and the Question of Iraq

President Bush had wondered immediately after the attack whether Saddam Hussein's regime might have had a hand in it. Iraq had been an enemy of the United States for 11 years, and was the only place in the world where the United States was engaged in ongoing combat operations. As a former pilot, the President was struck by the apparent sophistication of the operation and some of the piloting, especially Hanjour's high-speed dive into the Pentagon. He told us he recalled Iraqi support for Palestinian suicide terrorists as well. Speculating about other possible states that could be involved, the President told us he also thought about Iran.

Clarke has written that on the evening of September 12, President Bush told him and some of his staff to explore possible Iraqi links to 9/11. "See if Saddam did this," Clarke recalls the President telling them. "See if he's linked in any way." While he believed the details of Clarke's account to be incorrect, President Bush acknowledged that he might well have spoken to Clarke at some point, asking him about Iraq.

Responding to a presidential tasking, Clarke's office sent a memo to Rice on September 18, titled "Survey of Intelligence Information on Any Iraq Involvement in the September 11 Attacks." Rice's chief staffer on Afghanistan, Zalmay Khalilzad, concurred in its conclusion that only some anecdotal evidence linked Iraq to al Qaeda. The memo found no "compelling case" that Iraq had either planned or perpetrated the attacks. It passed along a few foreign intelligence reports, including the Czech report alleging an April 2001 Prague meeting between Atta and an Iraqi intelligence officer and a Polish report that personnel at the headquarters of Iraqi intelligence in Baghdad were told before September 11 to go on the streets to gauge crowd reaction to an unspecified event. Arguing that the case for links between Iraq and al Qaeda was weak, the memo pointed out that Bin Ladin resented the secularism of Saddam Hussein's regime. Finally, the memo said, there was no confirmed reporting on Saddam cooperating with Bin Ladin on unconventional weapons.

On the afternoon of 9/11, according to contemporaneous notes, Secretary Rumsfeld instructed General Myers to obtain quickly as much information as possible. The notes indicate that he also told Myers that he was not simply interested in striking empty training sites. He thought the U.S. response should consider a wide range of options and possibilities. The secretary said his instinct was to hit Saddam Hussein at the same time—not only Bin Ladin. Secretary Rumsfeld later explained that at the time, he had been considering either one of them, or perhaps someone else, as the responsible party.

According to Rice, the issue of what, if anything, to do about Iraq was really engaged at Camp David. Briefing papers on Iraq, along with many others, were in briefing materials for the participants. Rice told us the administration was concerned that Iraq would take advantage of the 9/11 attacks. She recalled that in the first Camp David session chaired by the President, Rumsfeld asked what the administration should do about Iraq. Deputy Secretary Wolfowitz made the case for striking Iraq during "this round" of the war on terrorism.

A Defense Department paper for the Camp David briefing book on the strategic concept for the war on terrorism specified three priority targets for initial action: al Qaeda, the Taliban, and Iraq. It argued that of the three, al Qaeda and Iraq posed a strategic threat to the United States. Iraq's long-standing involvement in terrorism was cited, along with its interest in weapons of mass destruction.

Secretary Powell recalled that Wolfowitz—not Rumsfeld—argued that Iraq was ultimately the source of the terrorist problem and should therefore be attacked. Powell said that Wolfowitz was not able to justify his belief that Iraq was behind 9/11. "Paul was always of the view that Iraq was a problem that had to be dealt with," Powell told us. "And he saw this as one way of using this event as a way to deal with the Iraq problem." Powell said that President Bush did not give Wolfowitz's argument "much weight."[67] Though continuing to worry about Iraq in the following week, Powell said, President Bush saw Afghanistan as the priority.

President Bush told Bob Woodward that the decision not to invade Iraq was made at the morning session on September 15. Iraq was not even on the table during the September 15 afternoon session, which dealt solely with Afghanistan. Rice said that when President Bush called her on Sunday, September 16, he said the focus would be on Afghanistan, although he still wanted plans for Iraq should the country take some action or the administration eventually determine that it had been involved in the 9/11 attacks.

At the September 17 NSC meeting, there was some further discussion of "phase two" of the war on terrorism. President Bush ordered the Defense Department to be ready to deal with Iraq if Baghdad acted against U.S. interests, with plans to include possibly occupying Iraqi oil fields.

Within the Pentagon, Deputy Secretary Wolfowitz continued to press the case for dealing with Iraq. Writing to Rumsfeld on September 17 in a memo headlined "Preventing More Events," he argued that if there was even a 10 percent chance that Saddam Hussein was behind the 9/11 attack, maximum priority should be placed on eliminating that threat. Wolfowitz contended that the odds were "far more" than 1 in 10, citing Saddam's praise for the attack, his long record of involvement in terrorism, and theories that Ramzi Yousef was an Iraqi agent and Iraq was behind the 1993 attack on the World Trade Center. The next day, Wolfowitz renewed the argument, writing to Rumsfeld about the interest of Yousef's co-conspirator in the 1995 Manila air plot in crashing an explosives-laden plane into CIA headquarters, and about information from a foreign government regarding Iraqis' involvement in the attempted hijacking of a Gulf Air flight. Given this background, he wondered why so little thought had been devoted to the danger of suicide pilots, seeing a "failure of imagination" and a mind-set that dismissed possibilities.

On September 19, Rumsfeld offered several thoughts for his commanders as they worked on their contingency plans. Though he emphasized the worldwide nature of the conflict, the references to specific enemies or regions named only the Taliban, al Qaeda, and Afghanistan. Shelton told us the administration reviewed all the Pentagon's war plans and challenged certain assumptions underlying them, as any prudent organization or leader should do.

General Tommy Franks, the commanding general of Central Command, recalled receiving Rumsfeld's guidance that each regional commander should assess what these plans meant for his area of responsibility. He knew he would soon be striking the Taliban and al Qaeda in Afghanistan. But, he told us, he now wondered how that action was connected to what might need to be done in Sornalia, Yemen, or Iraq.

On September 20, President Bush met with British Prime Minister Tony Blair, and the two leaders discussed the global conflict ahead. When Blair asked about Iraq, the President replied that Iraq was not the immediate problem. Some members of his administration, he commented, had expressed a different view, but he was the one responsible for making the decisions.

Franks told us that he was pushing independently to do more robust planning on military responses in Iraq during the summer before 9/11—a request President Bush denied, arguing that the time was not right. (CENTCOM also began dusting off plans for a full invasion of Iraq during this period, Franks said.) The CENTCOM commander told us he renewed his appeal for further military planning to respond to Iraqi moves shortly after 9/11, both because he personally felt that Iraq and al Qaeda might be engaged in some form of collusion and because he worried that Saddam might take advantage of the attacks to move against his internal enemies in the northern or southern parts of Iraq, where the United States was flying regular missions to enforce Iraqi no-fly zones. Franks said that President Bush again turned down the request.

• • •

Having issued directives to guide his administration's preparations for war, on Thursday, September 20, President Bush addressed the nation before a joint session of Congress. "Tonight," he said, "we are a country awakened to danger." The President blamed al Qaeda for 9/11 and the 1998 embassy bombings and, for the first time, declared that al Qaeda was "responsible for bombing the USS *Cole*." He reiterated the ultimatum that had already been conveyed privately. "The Taliban must act, and act immediately," he said. "They will hand over the terrorists, or they will share in their fate." The President added that America's quarrel was not with Islam: "The enemy of America is not our many Muslim friends; it is not our many Arab friends. Our enemy is a radical network of terrorists, and every government that supports them." Other regimes faced hard choices, he pointed out: "Every nation, in every region, now has a decision to make: Either you are with us, or you are with the terrorists."

President Bush argued that the new war went beyond Bin Ladin. "Our war on terror begins with al Qaeda, but it does not end there," he said. "It will not end until every terrorist group of global reach has been found, stopped, and defeated." The President had a message for the Pentagon: "The hour is coming when America will act, and you will make us proud." He also had a message for those outside the United States. "This is civilization's fight," he said. "We ask every nation to join us."

President Bush approved military plans to attack Afghanistan in meetings with Central Command's General Franks and other advisers on September 21 and October 2. Originally titled "Infinite Justice," the operation's code word was changed—to avoid the sensibilities of Muslims who associate the power of infinite justice with God alone—to the operational name still used for operations in Afghanistan: "Enduring Freedom."

The plan had four phases.

- In *Phase One*, the United States and its allies would move forces into the region and arrange to operate from or over neighboring countries such as Uzbekistan and Pakistan. This occurred in the weeks following 9/11, aided by overwhelming international sympathy for the United States.

- In *Phase Two*, air strikes and Special Operations attacks would hit key al Qaeda and Taliban targets. In an innovative joint effort, CIA and Special Operations forces would be deployed to work together with each major Afghan faction opposed to the Taliban. The Phase Two strikes and raids began on October 7. The basing arrangements contemplated for Phase One were substantially secured—after arduous effort—by the end of that month.

- In *Phase Three*, the United States would carry out "decisive operations" using all elements of national power, including ground troops, to topple the Taliban regime and eliminate al Qaeda's sanctuary in Afghanistan. Mazar-e-Sharif, in northern Afghanistan, fell to a coalition assault by Afghan and U.S. forces on November 9. Four days later the Taliban had fled from Kabul. By early December, all major cities had fallen to the coalition. On December 22, Hamid Karzai, a Pashtun leader from Kandahar, was installed as the chairman of Afghanistan's interim administration. Afghanistan had been liberated from the rule of the Taliban.

  In December 2001, Afghan forces, with limited U.S. support, engaged al Qaeda elements in a cave complex called Tora Bora. In March 2002, the largest engagement of the war was fought, in the mountainous Shah-i-Kot area south of Gardez, against a large force of al Qaeda jihadists. The three-week battle was substantially successful and almost all remaining al Qaeda forces took refuge in Pakistan's equally mountainous and lightly governed frontier provinces. As of July 2004, Bin Ladin and Zawahiri are still believed to be at large.

- In *Phase Four*, civilian and military operations turned to the indefinite task of what the armed forces call "security and stability operations."

  Within about two months of the start of combat operations, several hundred CIA operatives and Special Forces soldiers, backed by the striking power of U.S. aircraft and a much larger infrastructure of intelligence and support efforts, had combined with Afghan militias and a small number of other coalition soldiers to destroy the Taliban regime and disrupt al Qaeda. They had killed or captured about a quarter of the enemy's known leaders. Mohammed Atef, al Qaeda's military commander and a principal figure in the 9/11 plot, had been killed by a U.S. air strike. According to a senior CIA officer who helped devise the overall strategy, the CIA provided intelligence, experience, cash, covert action capabilities, and entrée to tribal allies. In turn, the U.S. military offered combat expertise, firepower, logistics, and communications. With these initial victories won by the middle of 2002, the global conflict against Islamist terrorism became a different kind of struggle.

18.2 THE TORTURE OF PRISONERS

Not long after the fall of Saddam Hussein's regime in Iraq, reports began to appear in some Western media markets that American forces were torturing prisoners to obtain information relevant to the War on Terror. In 2002, international attention turned to Iraq's most notorious prison, Abu Graib, and the role and techniques employed by American interrogators in questioning prisoners. Our final two selections speak for themselves and should be read carefully before joining the emotionally inflamed debate which remains alive almost a decade later.

GENERAL PROTECTION OF PRISONERS OF WAR

Article 12

Enter into force 21 October 1950

Prisoners of war are in the hands of the enemy Power, but not of the individuals or military units who have captured them. Irrespective of the individual responsibilities that may exist, the Detaining Power is responsible for the treatment given them.

Prisoners of war may only be transferred by the Detaining Power to a Power which is a party to the Convention and after the Detaining Power has satisfied itself of the willingness and ability of such transferee Power to apply the Convention. When prisoners of war are transferred under such circumstances, responsibility for the application of the Convention rests on the Power accepting them while they are in its custody.

5 Nevertheless if that Power fails to carry out the provisions of the Convention in any important respect, the Power by whom the prisoners of war were transferred shall, upon being notified by the Protecting Power, take effective measures to correct the situation or shall request the return of the prisoners of war such requests must be complied with.

Article 13

Prisoners of war must at all times be humanely treated. Any unlawful act or omission by the Detaining Power causing death or seriously endangering the health of a prisoner of war in its custody is prohibited, and will be regarded as a serious breach of the present Convention. In particular, no prisoner of war may be subjected to physical mutilation or to medical or scientific experiments of any kind which are not justified by the medical, dental or hospital treatment of the prisoner concerned and carried out in his interest.

Likewise, prisoners of war must at all times be protected, particularly against acts of violence or intimidation and against insults and public curiosity.

Measures of reprisal against prisoners of war are prohibited.

Article 14

Prisoners of war are entitled in all circumstances to respect for their persons and their honour. Women shall be treated with all the regard due to their sex and shall in all cases benefit by treatment as favourable as that granted to men. Prisoners of war shall retain the full civil capacity which they enjoyed at the time of their capture. The Detaining Power may not restrict the exercise, either within or without its own territory, of the rights such capacity confers except in so far as the captivity requires.

Adopted on 12 August 1949 by the Diplomatic Conference for the Establishment of International Conventions for the Protection of Victims of War, held in Geneva from 21 April to 12 August 1949.

Article 15

The Power detaining prisoners of war shall be bound to provide
Free of charge for their maintenance and for the medical attention required by their state of health.

Article 16

Taking into consideration the provisions of the present Convention relating to rank and sex, and subject to any privileged treatment which may be accorded to them by reason of their state of health, age or professional qualifications, all prisoners of war shall be treated alike by the Detaining Powers without any adverse distinction based on race, nationality, religious belief or political opinions, or any other distinction founded on similar criteria.

Part III   CAPTIVITY

Section I   Beginning of Captivity

Article 17

Every prisoner of war, when questioned on the subject, is bound to give only his surname, first names and rank, date of birth, and army, regimental, personal or serial number, or failing this, equivalent information. If he willfully infringes this rule, he may render himself liable to a restriction of the privileges accorded to his rank or status.

Each Party to a conflict is required to furnish the persons under its jurisdiction who are liable to become prisoners of war, with an identity card showing the owner's surname, first names, rank, army, regimental, personal or serial number or equivalent information, and date of birth. The identity card may, furthermore, bear the signature or the fingerprints, or both, of the owner, and may bear, as well, any other information the Party to the conflict may wish to add concerning persons belonging to its armed forces. As far as possible the card shall measure 6.5 × 10 cm. and shall be issued in duplicate. The identity card shall be shown by the prisoner of war upon demand, but may in no case be taken away from him.

No physical or mental torture, nor any other form of coercion, may be inflicted on prisoners of war to secure from them information of any kind whatever. Prisoners of war who refuse to answer may not be threatened, insulted, or exposed to any unpleasant or disadvantageous treatment of any kind.

Prisoners of war who, owing to their physical or mental condition, are unable to state their identity shall be handed over to the medical service. The identity of such prisoners shall be established by all possible means, subject to the provisions of the preceding paragraph. The questioning of prisoners of war shall be carried out in a language which they understand.

MEMORANDUM TO PRESIDENT BUSH ON TREATMENT OF PRISONERS (2002)

SUBJECT: DECISION RE APPLICATION OF THE GENEVA
CONVENTION ON PRISONERS OF WAR TO THE
CONFLICT WITH AL QUEDA AND THE TALIBAN

Purpose

On January 18, I advised you that the Department of Justice had issued a formal legal
opinion concluding that the Geneva Convention III on the Treatment of Prisoners of
War (GPW) does not apply to the conflict with al Queda. I also advised you that DOJ's
opinion concludes that there are reasonable grounds for you to conclude that GPW does
not apply with respect to the conflict with the Taliban. I understand that you decided
that GPW does not apply and, accordingly, that al Queda and Taliban detainees are not
prisoners of war under the GPW.

The Secretary of State has requested that you reconsider that decision. Specifically,
he has asked that you conclude that GPW does apply to both al Queda and the Taliban.
I understand, however, that he would agree that al Queda and Taliban fighters could be
determined not to be prisoners of war (POWs) but only on a case-by- case basis following
individual hearings before a military board.

This memorandum outlines the ramifications of your decision and the Secretary's
request for reconsideration.

Legal Background

As an initial matter, I note that you have the constitutional authority to make the determination you made on January 18 that the GPW does not apply to al Queda and the
Taliban. (Of course, you nevertheless, as a matter of policy, decide to apply the principles of GPW to the conflict with al Queda and the Taliban.) The Office of Legal Counsel
of the Department of Justice has opined that, as a matter of international and domestic
law, GPW does not apply to the conflict with al Queda. OLC has further opined that
you have the authority to determine that GPW does not apply to the Taliban. As I
discussed with you, the grounds for such a determination may include:

- A determination that Afghanistan was a failed state because the Taliban did
  not exercise full control over the territory and people, was not recognized by
  the international community, and was not capable of fulfilling its international
  obligations (e.g., was in widespread material breach of its international
  obligations).
- A determination that the Taliban and its forces were, in fact, not a government, but
  a militant, terrorist-like group.

Alberto Gonzales, Counsel to the President, Memorandum written January 25, 2002. Released to
9/11 Commission Hearings.

OLC's interpretation of this legal issue is definitive. The Attorney General is charged by statute with interpreting the law for the Executive Branch. This interpretive authority extends to both domestic and international law. He has, in turn, delegated this role to OLC. Nevertheless, you should be aware that the Legal Adviser to the Secretary of State has expressed a different view.

Ramifications of Determination That GPW Does Not Apply

The consequences of a decision to adhere to what I understand to be your earlier determination that the GPW does not apply to the Taliban include the following:

POSITIVE:

Preserves flexibility:

- As you have said, the war against terrorism is a new kind of war. It is not the traditional clash between nations adhering to the laws of war that formed the backdrop for GPW. The nature of the new war places a high premium on other factors, such as the ability to quickly obtain information from captured terrorists and their sponsors in order to avoid further atrocities against American civilians, and the need to try terrorists for war crimes such as wantonly killing civilians. In my judgment, this new paradigm renders obsolete Geneva's strict limitations on questioning of enemy prisoners and renders quaint some of its provisions requiring that captured enemy be afforded such things as commissary privileges, scrip (i.e., advances of monthly pay), athletic uniforms, and scientific instruments.
- Although some of these provisions do not apply to detainees who are not POWs, a determination that GPW does not apply to al Queda and the Taliban eliminates any argument regarding the need for case-by-case determinations of POW status. It also holds open options for the future conflicts in which it may be more difficult to determine whether an enemy force as a whole meets the standard for POW status.
- By concluding that GPW does not apply to al Queda and the Taliban, we avoid foreclosing options for the future, particularly against nonstate actors.

    Substantially reduces the threat of domestic criminal prosecution under the War Crimes Act (18 U.S.C. 2441).

- That stature, enacted in 1996, prohibits the commission of a "war crime" by or against a U.S. person, including U.S. officials. "War crime" for these purposes is defined to include any grave breach of GPW or any violation of common Article 3 thereof (such as "outrages against personal dignity"). Some of these provisions apply (if the GPW applies) regardless of whether the individual being detained qualifies as a POW. Punishments for violations of Section 2441 include the death penalty. A determination that the GPW is not applicable to the Taliban would mean that Section 2441 would not apply to actions taken with respect to the Taliban.
- Adhering to your determination that GPW does not apply would guard effectively against misconstruction or misapplication of Section 2441 for several reasons.
- First, some of the language of the GPW is undefined (it prohibits, for example, "outrages upon personal dignity" and "inhuman treatment"), and it is difficult to predict with confidence what actions might be deemed to constitute violations of the relevant provisions of GPW.

- Second, it is difficult to predict the needs and circumstances that could arise in the course of the war on terrorism.
- Third, it is difficult to predict the motives of prosecutors and independent counsels who may in the future decide to pursue unwarranted charges based on Section 2441. Your determination would create a reasonable basis in law that Section 2441 does not apply, which would provide a solid defense to any future prosecution.

NEGATIVE:

On the other hand, the following arguments would support reconsideration and reversal of your decision that the GPW does not apply to either al Qaeda or the Taliban:

- Since the Geneva Conventions were concluded in 1949, the United States has never denied their applicability to either U.S. or opposing forces engaged in armed conflict, despite several opportunities to do so. During the last Bush Administration, the United States stated that it "has a policy of applying the Geneva Conventions of 1949 whenever armed hostilities occur with regular foreign armed forces, even if arguments could be made that the threshold standards for the applicability of the Conventions . . . are not met."
- The United States could not invoke the GPW if enemy forces threatened to mistreat or mistreated U.S. coalition forces captured during operations in Afghanistan, or if they denied Red Cross access or other POW privileges.
- The War Crimes Act could not be used against the enemy, although other criminal statutes and the customary law of war would still be available.
- Our position would likely provoke widespread condemnation among our allies and in some domestic quarters, even if we make clear that we will comply with the core humanitarian principles of the treaty as a matter of policy.
- Concluding that the Geneva Convention does not apply may encourage other countries to look for technical "loopholes" in future conflicts to conclude that they are not bound by GPW either.
- Other countries may be less inclined to turn over terrorists or provide legal assistance to us if we do not recognize a legal obligation to comply with the GPW.
- A determination that GPW does not apply to al Qaeda and the Taliban could undermine U.S. military culture which emphasizes maintaining the highest standards of conduct in combat, and could introduce an element of uncertainty in the status of adversaries.

Response to Arguments for Applying GPW to the [*sic*] at Qaeda and the Taliban

On balance, I believe that the arguments for reconsideration and reversal are unpersuasive.

- The argument that the U.S. has never determined that GPW did not apply is incorrect. In at least one case (Panama in 1989) the U.S. determined that GPW did not apply even though it determined for policy reasons to adhere to the convention. More importantly, as noted above, this is a new type of warfare—one not contemplated in 1949 when the GPW was framed—and requires a new approach in our actions toward captured terrorists. Indeed, as the statement quoted from the administration of President George Bush makes clear, the US. will apply GPW "whenever hostilities occur *with regular armed forces.*" By its terms, therefore the policy does not apply to a conflict with terrorists, or with irregular forces, like the Taliban, who are armed militants that oppressed and terrorized the people of Afghanistan.

• In response to the argument that we should decide to apply GPW to the Taliban in order to encourage other countries to treat captured U.S. military personnel in accordance with the GPW, it should be noted that your policy of providing humane treatment to enemy detainees gives us the credibility to insist on like treatment for our soldiers. Moreover, even if GPW is not applicable, we can still bring war crimes charges against anyone who mistreats U.S. personnel. Finally, I note that our adversaries in several recent conflicts have not been deterred by GPW in their mistreatment of captured U.S. personnel, and terrorists will not follow GPW rules in any event.

• The statement that other nations would criticize the U.S. because we have determined that GPW does not apply is undoubtedly true. It is even possible that some nations would point to that determination as a basis for failing to cooperate with us on specific matters in the war against terrorism. On the other hand, some international and domestic criticism is already likely to flow from your previous decision not to treat the detainees as POWs. And we can facilitate cooperation with other nations by reassuring them that we fully support GPW where it is applicable and by acknowledging that in this conflict the U.S. continues to respect other recognized standards.

• In the treatment of detainees, the U.S. will continue to be constrained by, (i) its commitment to treat the detainees humanely and, to the extent appropriate and consistent with military necessity, in a manner consistent with the principles of GPW, (ii) its applicable treaty obligations, (iii) minimum standards of treatment universally recognized by the nations of the world, and (iv) applicable military regulations regarding the treatment of detainees.

• Similarly, the argument based on military culture fails to recognize that our military remain bound to apply the principles of GPW because that is what you have directed them to do.